Data Structures & Algorithms Using C++

Theory, Design and Object-Oriented Implementation

"We want that education by which character is formed, strength of mind is increased, the intellect is expanded, and by which one can stand on one's own feet..."

... Swami Vivekananda

"The meaning of education is to encourage in people a sense of self-introspection, the ability to grasp and to develop the capacity for constructive works..."

... Dr. S. Radhakrishnan

"Dream, Dream, Dream,
Dream translates into thoughts, and
Thoughts result into actions"

... Dr. A. P. J. Kalam

"Always surround yourself with the kind of people who can make you believe that you can do it..."

... R. S. Salaria

"Treat others the way you wish to be treated..."

... R. S. Salaria

Data Structures & Algorithms Using C++

THIRD EDITION

Theory, Design and Object-Oriented Implementation

Prof. R. S. Salaria

Alumnus of IIT, Delhi.
Certified Software Quality Professional, Govt. of India.
SUN Certified Programmer, SUN Microsystems, USA.
SUN Certified Trainer, SUN Microsystems, USA.

Former Head

Department of Computer Science & Engineering
Thapar University, PATIALA-147004.

Assisted by

Anita Salaria

KHANNA BOOK PUBLISHING CO. (P) LTD.

Publisher of Engineering and Computer Books

4C/4344, Ansari Road, Darya Ganj, New Delhi-110002

Phone : 011-23244447-48 **Mobile:** +91-9910909320

E-mail : contact@khannabooks.com

Website : www.khannabooks.com

Dear Readers,

To prevent the piracy, this book is secured with HIGH SECURITY HOLOGRAM on the front title cover. In case you don't find the hologram on the front cover title, please write us to at contact@khannabooks.com or whatsapp us at +91-99109 09320 and avail special gift voucher for yourself.

Specimen of Hologram on front Cover title:

Moreover, there is a SPECIAL DISCOUNT COUPON for you with EVERY HOLOGRAM.

How to avail this SPECIAL DISCOUNT:

Step 1: Scratch the hologram
Step 2: Under the scratch area, your "coupon code" is available
Step 3: Logon to www.khannabooks.com
Step 4: Use your "coupon code" in the shopping cart and get your copy at a special discount
Step 5: Enjoy your reading!

Price: ₹ 575.00

ISBN: 978-93-81068-59-5

Data Structures & Algorithms using C++
by R.S. Salaria

First Edition: 1998
Third Edition: 2016
Reprint Edition: 2024, **2026**

To view complete list of books, Please scan the QR Code:

Published by:
Khanna Book Publishing Co. (P) Ltd.
CIN: U22110DL1998PTC095547

Visit us at: **www.khannabooks.com**
Write us at: **contact@khannabooks.com**

Printed in India.

Dedication

Our Dearest Parents,
Daughters Surbhi & Mehak,
Beloved Readers,

AND

Our Country Men/Women at Large.

My Slogan for My Fellow Citizens

India . . .

. . . is a Great Country

AND

Indians . . .

. . . are Outstanding.

Preface to the Third Edition

Continuing with the tradition of earlier editions of providing the rich content on the subject of *"Data Structures & Algorithms"*, which can make Computer Science and Information Technology students' competent professionals, the present edition lays more emphasis on the overall layout of the subject matter so as to make it more appealing and attractive. I am certain that the present edition will help the students in inculcating the habit of reading and self-learning.

Most of the topics are thoroughly revised, presented in a kind of manner with visuals where ever possible so that the students can grasp them with quite each.

More number of illustrative programming problems has been added so as to enable the students to learn the technique of problem solving and then writing efficient programs for those problems.

Plenty of programming exercises are added to provide an intellectual challenge to the students, and the students are advised to convert this challenge to an opportunity and at the end of the day, you will be a very satisfied person.

I am hopeful that this edition will go beyond your expectations. Do keep on writing, as your valuable feedback and suggestions will help me in tuning the book to your expectations.

. . . R. S. Salaria

Preface to the First Edition

The study of *"Data Structures & Algorithms"* is very important subject for the students of Computer Science and Information Technology. The subject of "Data Structures & Algorithms" is an essential part of course curricula in various undergraduate and graduate programmes in Computer Science and Information Technology

The present text lays emphasis on theory and design of data structures, and their object-oriented implementation using C++ language. The organization chosen is different from most other books on this subject. Most of the present books either deal with the theoretical concepts in data structures, but ignore their design and implementation aspects or lays very little stress on theoretical concepts and shows their implementation straight away. In that situation, the readers have to consult number of books. The present text fills this gap. The reader will be able to get each and every thing required for the study of data structures under one shelf.

Another important feature of the present text is in the context of complete working programs that have been tested on personal computer using *Borland's Turbo C++ Compiler version 3.0.*

The bulk of the text is devoted to data structures. Programming style and development methodology are introduced as the applications are presented. This has the advantage of allowing the reader to concentrate on data structures, while showing how good practices can make programming easier.

For implementation, I preferred C++ language because it is more efficient and better standardized. Further, since C++ is becoming the natural choice at almost all levels, and a text combining both C++ and data structures provide an easy way of gaining proficiency in both.

During the preparation of this text it is assumed that the reader has a sufficient knowledge object-oriented concepts and programming experience in C++ language, especially regarding classes, structures and pointers.

I hope that this book will go beyond your expectations. Do keep on writing, as your valuable feedback and suggestions will help me in tuning the book to your expectations.

. . . R. S. Salaria

Word of Advice for Students

My beloved students, we would like to remind you that we can categorize people as:

People who watch the things happening,
People who look into how things are happening, and
People who make the things happen.

Now you are to find out where you fit-in and where you want to be.

We firmly believe that youth of our country is second to none, and this fact is recognized world wide.

Our honorable former president Dr. APJ Kalam (first and may be the last president known as *people's president*) has been saying at all the platform that in India there is no dearth of resources and talent, only thing we need to change is *the mindset* (we have to shed *chalta hai* attitude). He has set a vision for us to see India a developed country by 2020, and the basis for his vision is the talent of our youth.

Take some time to discover yourself and try to assess how much talent you possess. Utilize your period of study to harness that talent. I can assure you that you will have a great future.

We want to share a popular game with you which all of us used to play in our childhood. The game is of burning a peace of paper using a lens under the sun. When the lens and the paper are held stationery, it starts burning in a few seconds. However, if you keep moving either the paper or the lens, the paper will never burn. *Why it happens so?* The answer is simple – the light energy emitted by the sun is not focused. The same is with us. We have enough energy in ourselves, but we don't focus it, rather we waste it in meaningless acts. The next question arises is – *where to focus our energy?* The natural answer of this question should be – what you want to become in your life (that basically defines your goal). So you need to focus your entire energy on your goal, and surely you will achieve your goal.

We would also like to share with you a scene from the popular epic – *Mahabharta*. When Dronacharya, Guru of Pandvas, asked his disciples to aim at the eye of the sparrow placed on a tree. All his disciples, except Arjuna, replied in a same manner – *Guru ji, we see a sparrow*. However, when the turn of Arjuna came, his reply was – *Guru ji, I see only the eye*. That is the kind of the focus you also need to develop in your life.

The next point is that when you have identified your goal, you need to identify the steps that you need to follow in order to accomplish your goal. Once the goal and the steps to accomplish your goal are identified, write them nicely on a piece of a paper and paste that paper at a place which you visit regularly. Whenever you will visit that place, the writing on the paper will remind you about your goal and what you have to do to achieve your goal.

The final word, you may set any goal for yourself and that may be of becoming a successful doctor, an engineer, an administrator or a businessman, but you must also try to be a *nice human being*. You know a nice human being is like a fruit of all seasons, and is welcome every where, anytime. We believe, the basic mantra to become a nice human being is too simple and can be stated as

"Treat the others the way you want to be treated, in other words, don't do anything with others which you wish others shouldn't do with you."

Enjoy your student life and make best use of it . . .

Wish you good luck and a nice time ahead.

. . . R. S. Salaria

List of Programs

1. Program to illustrate the implementation of unsorted linear linked list.
2. Program to illustrate the implementation of unsorted doubly linked list.
3. Program to add two polynomials.
4. Program to multiply two polynomials.
5. Program to multiply two sparse matrices, where sparse matrices are represented by linked lists.
6. Program to demonstrate the various operations on array based stack.
7. Program to demonstrate the various operations on linked stack.
8. Program to demonstrate the use of stack in checking whether the arithmetic expression is properly parenthesized.
9. Program to demonstrate the use of stack in converting arithmetic expression from infix notation to postfix notation.
10. Program to demonstrate the use of stack in evaluating arithmetic expression in postfix notation.
11. Program to demonstrate the use of stack in implementing quicksort algorithm to sort an array of integers in ascending order.
12. Program to demonstration the implementation of various operations on a linear queue represented using a linear array.
13. Program to demonstration the implementation of various operations on a circular queue represented using a linear array.
14. Program to demonstration the implementation of various operations on a queue represented using a linear linked list (linked queue).
15. Program to illustrate the implementation of different operations on a binary search tree.
16. Program to illustrate the implementation of different operations on a AVL tree
17. Program to illustrate the implementation of different operations on a threaded binary search tree
18. Program to illustrate the input and output of a graph.
19. Program to illustrate traversal of a graph using breadth-first search.

Brief Table of Contents

Detailed Table of Contents

Chapter 1

Review of OOP Concepts

1.1 INTRODUCTION

When Thermos Flask was invented, it was labeled as one of the greatest inventions in the sense that how it remembers to keep hot things hot and cold things cold. The same analogy holds true for object-oriented programming (OOP). OOP is the most dramatic innovation in software development and some of its features draw parallels to that of Thermos Flask.

The primary objective of OOP is to provide clearer, reliable, and easily maintainable approach to program design. OOP involves concepts that are new to programmers of traditional programming languages, also known as *procedural languages, imperative languages* or *problem oriented languages*, such as Pascal, C, FORTRAN, etc. These concepts, such as *data abstraction*, *encapsulation, data hiding*, *inheritance*, *overloading* and *polymorphism*, lie at the heart of object-oriented programming. It is very important to understand that object-oriented programming is not primarily concerned with the details of the program operation; instead it deals with the overall organization of the program.

Object-oriented programming is not just another way of programming; it is a new way of organizing programs.

In this chapter, before covering the concepts of object-oriented programming, let us have a look at procedural programming and object-oriented programming and their relative merits and demerits.

1.2 A LOOK AT PROCEDURAL PROGRAMMING

In *procedural programming*, also known by other names as *structured programming*, *functional programming* or *traditional programming*, the problem in hand is viewed as a sequence of things to be done such as reading, calculating and printing. Separate functions are written to accomplish these tasks. Thus, the primary focus is on functions.

In other words, we can say that a given problem is divided into small sized sub problems; each sub problem represents a specific task that can be handled efficiently and effectively. Then to solve each sub problem, a function/procedure is written.

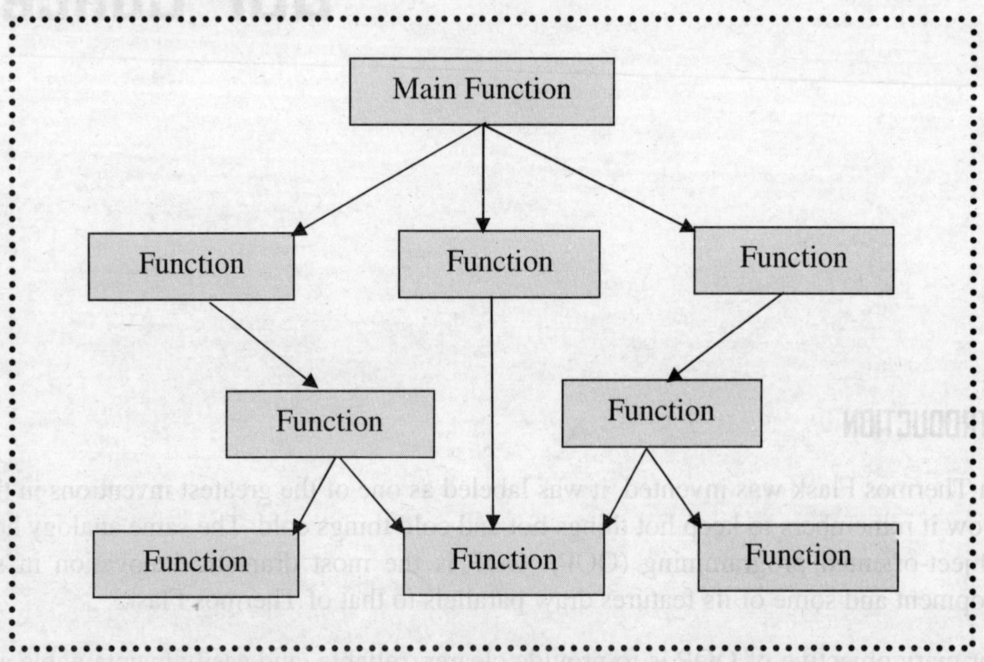

Figure 1.1: Typical Structure of a procedural program

The technique of hierarchical decomposition has been used to specify the tasks to be completed to find the solution of a problem.

Note here that there is no mention of data. These functions are written to manipulate the data to accomplish a specific task. Thus, the data that is key to the existence of functions and hence a program gets a raw treatment.

Further, the data in a procedural program is spread across entire software in the form of local and global data structures. The global data is more vulnerable to an inadvertent change by a function. Functions communicate with each other either by passing arguments or by accessing and modifying data structures. In a very large program it is very difficult to identify what data is used by which function.

Key characteristics of procedural programming are:

- Emphasis is on doing things (algorithms).
- Large programs are divided into smaller independent subprograms known as functions or procedures (algorithmic decomposition).
- Majority the functions share global data.
- Data is scattered around the program in the form of local and shared data.
- Functions transform data from one form to another.
- Employs *top-down* approach to program design.

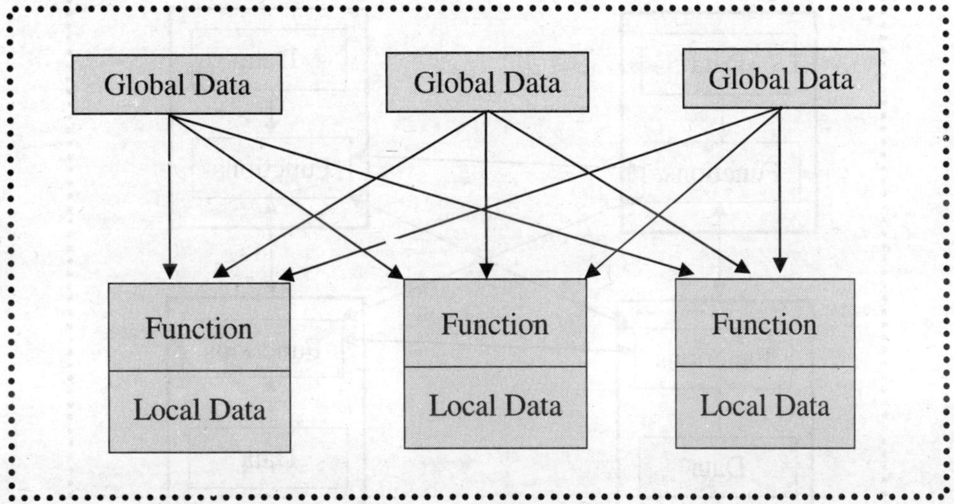

Figure 1.2: Relationship of data and functions in a procedural program

The organisation of programs using procedural programming approach suffers from following problems:

- The procedural programming approach does not model the real world problems very well.
- The program logic is dependent on the organisation of the data and the vice a versa. You cannot change one without change to another.
- The parts of the program are heavily dependent on each other, *i.e.*, tightly coupled to each other. Therefore, it is very difficult to make a change in one part of the program without affecting the other part.

These problems magnify further as the size and the complexity of the problem under consideration increases, and almost become unmanageable for very large and complex systems.

As change is inevitable, we want that our program design should be capable of handling a change without or with minimal effort and without introducing any anomalies.

The need of change can be because of the following reasons:

- There is problem in some part of the program and it needs to be fixed.
- There is need to extend the functionality of the program by including new features.
- There is a need to replace the existing algorithm by a better one.

1.3 A LOOK AT OBJECT-ORIENTED PROGRAMMING

The major motivation for the invention of new programming approach, object-oriented programming, was to remove the flaws of procedural programming approach. Object- oriented programming treats the data as a most critical element in the program design and does not allow it be scattered around the program. It ties the data and the functions that operate on it and protects it from the other functions.

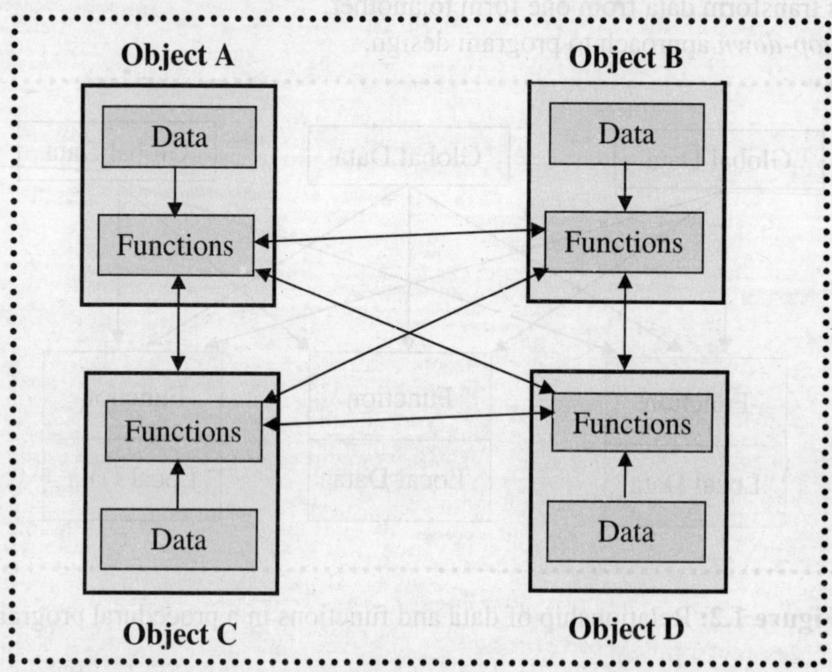

Figure 1.3: Typical Structure of an object-oriented program

Object-oriented programming allows decomposition of a problem into a number of entities called *objects* and then builds data and functions around these objects.

The typical structure of an object-oriented program and the relationship between the data and functions is shown in Figure 1.3.

The data of an object can only be accessed by functions associated with it. However, function of one object can access the function of another object. The communications among functions of different objects is called *messaging*.

Key characteristics of object-oriented programming are:

- Emphasis is on data rather than functions.
- Programs are divided into set of related objects.

- Data structures are designed in such way so as to characterize the objects.
- Functions that operate on the data of an object are tied together with the data structure.
- Data of an object is hidden and cannot be accessed by external functions.
- Objects communicate with each other through functions.
- Employs *bottom-up* approach to program design.

The organisation of programs using object-oriented programming approach overcomes all the problems of procedural programming.

1.4 BASIC CONCEPTS OF OBJECT-ORIENTED PROGRAMMING

Object-oriented programming is built upon a sound engineering foundation whose elements we collectively called as the *object model*. The object model encompasses the principles of *abstraction*, *encapsulation*, *data hiding*, *inheritance*, *overloading*, and *polymorphism*. Nothing is new about these principles. The important feature of the object model is that these elements are brought together in a synergistic way.

The object-oriented programming can formally be defined as *a method of implementation in which programs are organized as cooperative collection of objects, each of which represent an instance of some class, and whose classes are all members of a hierarchy of classes united via inheritance relationship*.

The object-oriented programming use objects as basic building blocks, where each object is an instance of some class, and classes are related to each other through inheritance.

Before we move on, it is necessary to understand some concepts that are used extensively in object-oriented programming. These include:

- Objects
- Classes
- Abstraction
- Encapsulation
- Data Hiding
- Inheritance
- Overloading
- Polymorphism
- Dynamic binding
- Message passing

1.4.1 Concept of an Object

An *object* is an entity that has *state, behavior* and *identity*. The structure and behavior of similar objects are defined in their common class. The term *instance* and *object* are interchangeable.

Each object has following characteristics:

- ***State*** – The *state* of an object encompasses all of the (usually static) property of the object plus the current (usually dynamic) values of each of these properties.
- ***Behavior*** – The *behavior* of an object tells how it acts and reacts to the outside world in terms of its state changes and message passing.
  With this, the state of the object can now be defined as - *the state of an object represents the cumulative results of its behaviour*.
- ***Identity*** – The *identity* of an object is that property which distinguishes it from all other objects.

1.4.1.1 Operations on Objects

The kind of operations that are performed on objects comprises:

- ***Modifier*** – An operation that alters the state of an object.
- ***Selector*** – An operation that access the state of the object but does not alter it.
- ***Iterator*** – An operation that permits all parts of an object to be accessed in some well-defined order.
- ***Constructor*** – An operation that creates an object and/or initializes its state.
- ***Destructor*** – An operation that frees the state of an object and/or destroys the object itself.

1.4.1.2 Relationship Among Objects

Objects contribute to the behaviour of a system by collaborating with one another. The relationship between any two objects encompasses the assumptions that each make about the other, including what operations can be performed and what behaviour results.

Objects communicate with each other through links, where a link defined as a physical or a conceptual connection between objects.

As a participant in a link, an object may play one of the following roles:

- ***Client/Actor*** – that operate on other objects, but is never operated upon by other objects.
- ***Server*** – that never operates upon other objects, it is only operated upon by other objects.
- ***Agent*** – that can operate on other objects and be operated upon by other objects; an agent is usually created to do some work on behalf of an actor or another agent.

1.4.2 Concept of a Class

The concepts of class and object are tightly interwoven, for example, we cannot talk about an object without regard for its class. However, there are important differences between these two terms. An object is a concrete entity that exists in time and space. A class represents only an abstraction, the *essence* of an object, as it were. Thus, we may speak of the class mammal, which represents characteristics common to all mammals. To identify a particular mammal in this class, we must speak of *this mammal* or *that mammal*. In the context of object-oriented programming, we define class as a set of objects that share a common structure and a common behaviour. A single object is simply an instance of a class.

1.4.2.1 Interface of a Class

The interface of a class provides outside view of a class and encompasses the abstraction while hiding its structure and the secrets of its behaviour. This interface primarily consists of the declarations of all the operations applicable to instances of this class, but it may include the declarations of other classes, constants, variables, and exceptions that are needed to complete the abstraction.

1.4.2.2 Implementation of a Class

Implementation of a class is its inside view that encompasses the secrets of its behaviour. It primarily consists of implementation of all the operations defined in the interface of the class. Interface of a class is divided into following parts:

- ***Public*** – A part that is accessible to all clients.
- ***Protected*** – A part that is accessible to the class and its subclasses.
- ***Private*** – A part that is accessible to the class only.

Different object-oriented programming languages provide different mixtures of *public*, *protected*, and *private* parts, which developers can choose among to establish specific access rights for each part of the class's interface, and thereby exercise control over what clients can see and what they cannot see.

1.4.3 Abstraction and Encapsulation

The notion of abstraction and encapsulation are commonly used in human-machine interaction and are widely prevalent in the technology-oriented world in which we are living. Consider, far example, the videocassette recorder (VCR), which is an integral part of every household today.

We make two observations about how VCRs are packaged and used.

- All our interactions with a VCR are made through buttons on the control panel such as PLAY, FF (forward), REW (rewind), REC (record), STOP, EJECT, etc.

- The VCR is packaged in such a way that we cannot interact directly with the internal circuitry. So, the *internal representation* of the VCR is *hidden* from the user. This is the principle of *encapsulation*.
- The instruction manual that accompanies the VCR tells us what the VCR is supposed to do if we press a particular button. It does not tell us how it is implemented inside the VCR. For example, it does not explain the sequence of electronic and mechanical events that result when the REW button is pressed. So, the instruction manual makes a clear distinction between what the VCR does and how it does. This distinction is the principle of *abstraction*.

1.4.3.1 Abstraction

Dictionary meaning of word *abstraction* refers to the act of emphasizing and representing essential features and ignoring the irrelevant features. In the context of object-oriented programming, word *abstraction* refers to the separation between the specification of data and its implementation. It results in better quality programs and more efficient programming techniques. These, in turn, reduce the number of man-hours required to develop a software system, and hence reduce the total cost of the final software product.

Since classes use the concept of data abstraction, they are also known as *abstract data types* (ADTs).

1.4.3.2 Encapsulation

Encapsulation is the concealing of the implementation details of a data object from the outside world. The data and functions are wrapped into a single unit, called class. Encapsulation is the most striking feature of a class.

1.4.4 Data Hiding

Data hiding deals with visibility of the members. The level of visibility determines which parts of the code can access the member. All most all the object-oriented programming languages provide three levels of visibility – *private*, *protected*, and *public*. Private members are accessible to members of the class only. Protected members are accessible to members of the class and members of the derived class. Public members are accessible from everywhere.

1.4.5 Inheritance

It means exactly what it says - *getting something from something that already exists*. For example, we inherit property, skills, features etc., from our parents.

Inheritance is a relationship among classes wherein one class inherits the structure and/or behavior defined in one (single inheritance) or more (multiple inheritance) classes. We call the class from which another class inherits its *super class, parent class* or *father class* and a class that inherits from one or more classes is a *subclass, derived class* or *child class*.

The concept of inheritance provides reusability. This means that we can add new features to an existing class without modifying it. The new class will have the combined features of both the classes.

1.4.6 Overloading

Overloading is the way of giving several meanings to an operator or a function. The meaning selected depends on the types of the arguments used by an operator or a function. The concept of overloading provides extensibility. This means that we can extend the existing features to meet new requirements. For example, by overloading operators, we make a new data type to behave like a built-in data type.

1.4.7 Polymorphism

Polymorphism is another important feature of object-oriented programming. Polymorphism is a combination of two words *poly* and *morphism*. The word *poly* means *many* and the word *morphism* means *forms*. Thus, *polymorphism* means *many forms*. More formally, polymorphism can be defined as a technique that allow to define various forms of a single function or operator that can be shared by various objects to perform the operations.

The polymorphism is achieved using the following:

- Overloading
- Dynamic binding

1.4.8 Dynamic Binding

Binding is the linking of a function call to the function definition that will be executed on the call during program execution. Normally the function call is tied to the function definition during the linking process. This process is known as *early binding*. However, the OOP permits dynamic binding, also called *late binding*, where the tie-up of function call to the address code is delayed until the run-time.

1.4.9 Message Passing

An object-oriented program consists of set of objects that communicate with each other in order to solve a particular problem. Objects communicate with one another by sending and receiving information much the same way as people pass messages to one another. A message for an object is a request for execution of a function, and therefore will invoke a function in the receiving object that generates the desired results. Message passing involves specifying the name of the object, the name of the function and the information to be sent.

Every object has a life cycle – they are created and destroyed. Communication with an object is feasible as long as it is alive.

REVIEW EXERCISES

1. What is procedural programming? What are its key characteristics?
2. What are the disadvantages of procedural programming?
3. What is object-oriented programming? What are its key characteristics?
4. What are the advantages of object-oriented programming?
5. Distinguish between the following:
   (*a*) Objects and classes
   (*b*) Abstraction and encapsulation
6. Explain the following terms:
   (*a*) Inheritance
   (*b*) Polymorphism
   (*c*) Dynamic binding
   (*d*) Message passing
   (*e*) Overloading
7. What is meant by the interface of a class?
8. What is meant by the implementation of a class?
9. What are the types of operations that can be performed on objects?
10. What are the relationships among objects?

❑ ❑ ❑

Chapter 2

Essential of C++ Language

2.1 INTRODUCTION

The C++ programming language is a very powerful general-purpose programming language that supports procedural programming as well as object-oriented programming. It incorporates all the ingredients required for building software for large and complex problems. Since its inception in the early 1980's, the language underwent a number of changes and improvements.

The C++ language is treated as super set of C language because the developer of C++ language have retained all features of C, enhanced some of the existing features, and incorporated new features to support for object-oriented programming.

It is important to note that for implementing the data structures effectively and efficiently using C++ language, the in-depth knowledge of C++ language is essential. In particular, the deep understanding of the pointers and their usage is essential.

This chapter gives an overview of the features of C++ language that are essential for the study of data structures.

2.2 KEY FEATURES OF C++ LANGUAGE

Let us briefly examine a few key features of C++ as an object-oriented language.

- **C++ supports data abstraction and data encapsulation.**

  Data abstraction is the separation between the specification of data and its implementation whereas *data encapsulation* or *information hiding* is the concealing of the implementation details of a data object from the outside world. These features ultimately lead to better quality programs and more efficient programming techniques, which in turn, reduce the number of man-hours required to develop a software system, and hence reduce the total cost of the final software product. C++ support both of these features.

- **C++ supports reusability.**

  Once a class has been developed, it can be distributed to other programmers for use in their own programs. This is called *reusability*. It is similar to library functions in a procedural language that can be incorporated into different programs. However, the concept of inheritance provides an important extension to the idea of reusability. A programmer can take an existing class and can add additional features and capabilities to it, without modifying the original class. This is done by deriving a new class from the existing class where the new class inherits the capabilities of the existing class and adds new features of its own. This ease with which existing software can be reused is an important benefit of object-oriented programming, and C++ supports it.

- **C++ supports extensibility.**

  Another benefit of object-oriented programming is that it allows the user to create new data types that behave similar to built-in data types, *i.e.*, not only in terms of values, in terms of operations too. These operations include input/output, arithmetic operations, comparisons and assignment. *Operator overloading* is one of the exciting features of object-oriented languages that make a new data type behave much like built-in data types.

  Thus, operator-overloading feature of object-oriented programming allows the programmer to extend the exiting capabilities, and C++ supports it.

- **C++ supports generic programming.**

  Generic programming is the concept of developing programs to solve identical problem on data of different type. For example, in the absence of generic programming, we have to write separate functions to sort an array of *int*, *float*, *double*, etc. The feature of generic programming makes its possible to have only once instance of sort function capable of handling data of variety of types. C++ makes its possible through templates. Templates are one of the C++'s most powerful features for software reuse. Templates enable programmer to specify, with a single code segment, an entire range of related (overloaded) functions — called *template functions*; or an entire range of related classes — called *template classes*.

We can write a single *function template* to sort an array and then C++ compiler will generate separate functions that will sort an array of *int*, sort an array of *float*, sort an array of *double*, etc.

Likewise, we can write a single *class template* for a stack class and then C++ compiler will generate separate classes such as stack of *int* class, stack of float class, stack of string class, etc.

- **C++ supports exception handling.**

  Exceptions are basically runtime anomalies or unusual conditions that the program may encounter during execution. Examples include division by zero, attempting to access an array element outside array index bound, running out of memory, etc. When program encounters such a situation, the program may terminate abnormally in the absence of error handling mechanism. Exception handling is another powerful feature of object-oriented languages that enable a programmer to write clearer, robust, and fault-tolerant programs. C++ also supports this feature.

2.3 DATA TYPES

The ability to divide the data into different types is one of the most important features of the programming languages. It enables us to work with relatively complex data objects instead of elementary data objects that a computer can understand and manipulate. We can deal with integer number, real numbers, and characters; all of which are familiar entities. At the bit level, the computer may not understand these concepts. Therefore, it is up to the compiler to make sure that the computer handles bits and bytes in a way consistent with their data type. A *data type* is just an interpretation applied to a string of bits. A data type is also defined as a finite set of values together with set of rules for permissible operations.

Data in C++ belongs to one of following types:

1. Basic Data Types
   - Integer (*short int, int, long int*)
   - Real/Floating-point (*float, double, long double*)
   - Character (*char*)
2. Derived Data Types
   - Array
   - String
   - Structure
   - Union
   - Class
   - Enumeration
   - Pointer
3. The *void* Data Type

Latest ANSI standard of C++ also supports following data types:

- Unicode Character (*wchar_t*)
- Boolean (*bool*)

These data types are not supported by old C++ Compilers such as Turbo C++ Ver 3.0, Microsoft Visual C++ Ver 6.0.

2.4 CONSTANTS AND VARIABLES

A program must be able to store its input somewhere so that it can work with the data and process it into a form that is meaningful to the user. All the data processed by a program is stored either as a *variable* or a *literal constant*.

When a value, such as 250, occurs in a program, it is referred to as a *literal constant*:

- Literal because we can speak of it only in terms of its value, and
- Constant because its value cannot be changed.

Every literal constant has an associated data type. For example, 12 is of type *int*, 3.14142 is of type *double*, 'a' is of type *char*, etc.

We refer to a literal constant as *non-addressable* though its value is stored somewhere in computer's memory; we have no means of accessing its address.

A variable provides us with named storage that we can write to, retrieve, and manipulate throughout the course of the program. In other words, variables are memory locations in the computer's memory that holds data. Contents of a variable may vary — hence the name *variable*. Variables hold different kind of data and the same variable might hold different values during the execution of a program. Each variable in C++ language has some characteristics associated with it, called its *storage class*. The different storage classes supported by C++ language are *auto*, *static*, *register*, and *extern*. Further, each variable in C++ language is associated with a specific type, which determines the size and layout its associated memory, the range of values that can be stored within that memory, and the set of operations that can be applied to it.

Unlike a literal constant, a variable is *addressable* and its address can be accessed using *address of* (&) operator.

There are two values associated with a variable:

1. Its data value that is stored at some memory address. This sometimes referred to as variable's *rvalue* (pronounced as "are-value"). We may think *rvalue* as meaning *read value*. Both a literal constant and a variable can serve as *rvalue*.
2. Its address value that is its address in memory within which its data value is stored. This sometimes referred to as variable's *lvalue* (pronounced as "ell-value"). We may think *lvalue* as meaning *location value*. Only a variable can serve as *lvalue*.

Different units of a C++ program are identified by names, where a name, also called *identifier* or *word*, may denote a variable, an array, a structure, a union, a class, a function in a program, whether defined by the programmer or by the system. A name consists of a sequence of alphanumeric characters. The names that have pre-defined meaning are known as *reserved words* or *key words*, and can't be used by the programmer for other purpose. A valid name can begin with a letter or underscore and the subsequent letters can be an alphabet, a digit, or an underscore.

Variables in C++ are classified as follows:

- ***Value Variable*** — variable that holds some value of a given type.
- ***Pointer Variable*** — variable that holds an address of some value variable.
- ***Reference Variable*** — variable that acts as an alias for another variable.

Variables in C++ can be declared anywhere in the program. By declaring the variables nearer to its first usage and by limiting the scope of the variable to the block where it is to be used, the programmer can economize the memory usage by the program.

2.4.1 Declaring Value Variables

The value variables are declared using following syntax

```
type vname-1, vname-2, ... ;
```

where *type* is *pre-defined* or *user-defined* data types, *vname*–1, *vname*–2, ... etc. are the names of variables.

The value variables can also be initialized during their declaration itself. For example, the following statement declares variable *sum* of type integer and initializes it to a value 0.

```
int sum = 0;
```

Un-initialized value variables take initial value depending on their storage class. If the storage class is not specified, their storage class, by default, is *auto* and their initial value is undefined (garbage).

2.4.2 Declaring Pointer Variables

The pointer variables are declared using following syntax

```
type *ptrName;
```

where *type* is a *pre-defined* or *user-defined* data types and indicates that the pointer will point to the variables of that specific data type, and character '*' indicates that variable is a pointer variable.

The pointer variable declaration can also be combined with the declaration of other variables, provided they are of same type. For example, the statement

```
int x, *ptrX;
```

declares an integer variable *x* and a pointer variable *ptrX*.

Once a pointer has been declared, it must be initialized prior to its use. It is important to note here that like other variables, a pointer variable will take a garbage value, which can be an address of any storage location. Therefore, if not properly initialized, a pointer may point to any location in memory including those locations where operating system is running, and your system may hang-up, *i.e.*, stop responding. Such un-initialized pointers are sometimes referred to as *dangling/wild pointers*.

2.4.3 Declaring Reference Variables – *Aliases*

A reference variable acts as an alias (alternative name) for other variable. Reference variables enjoy the simplicity of value variables and power of pointer variables. A reference variable is bound to a value/pointer variable only at the point of its declarations using following syntax

```
type &ReferenceVariable = Variable;
```

The following examples illustrate the binding of reference variables.

```
char &ch1 = ch;      // ch1 is an alias of ch
int &x = y[100];     // x is an alias of y[100]
int n = 20;
int *p = &n;
int &m = *p;         // m an alias of *p and refers to n
```

The reference variable declaration can also be combined with the declaration of other variables, provided they are of same type.

Reference variables enjoy the simplicity of value variables and power of pointer variables. They are mainly used for passing arguments to a function.

2.5 OPERATORS

Operators are the verbs of a language that let the user perform computations on values. You can think of operators as verbs and of operands as the subjects and object of those verbs.

Operators in C++ fall in following categories:

- Arithmetic Operators (+, -, /, *, %)
- Relational Operators (<,<=, >, >=, ==, !=)
- Logical Operators (&&, ||, !)
- Bit-wise Operators (~, ^, &, |, >>, <<)
- Special Operators
  - Increment & Decrement Operators (++, --)
  - The *sizeof* Operator
  - The *addressof* Operator (&)
  - Indirection Operator (*)
  - Ternary Operator (?:)
  - Scope Resolution Operator (::)
  - Comma Operator (,)

2.6 INPUT/OUTPUT

The C++ I/O subsystem is designed to work with a wide variety of devices that includes keyboard, monitor, disks, tape drives, etc. The working principle (characteristics) of each of these devices is quite different. The C++ I/O subsystem is designed in such a way that it provides a uniform interface that is independent of the actual device being used.

Thus, the programmer can write a C++ program that can receive input from, and send output to any device without bothering about the characteristics of device being used. This interface is called a *stream*.

A stream basically is a sequence of bytes. It can either act as a *source* from which the program can take (extract) input data or as a *destination* to which the program can send (insert) output data. The source stream that supplies data to the program is called *input stream* and the destination stream that receives data from the program is called *output stream*. These streams collectively are called *data streams*.

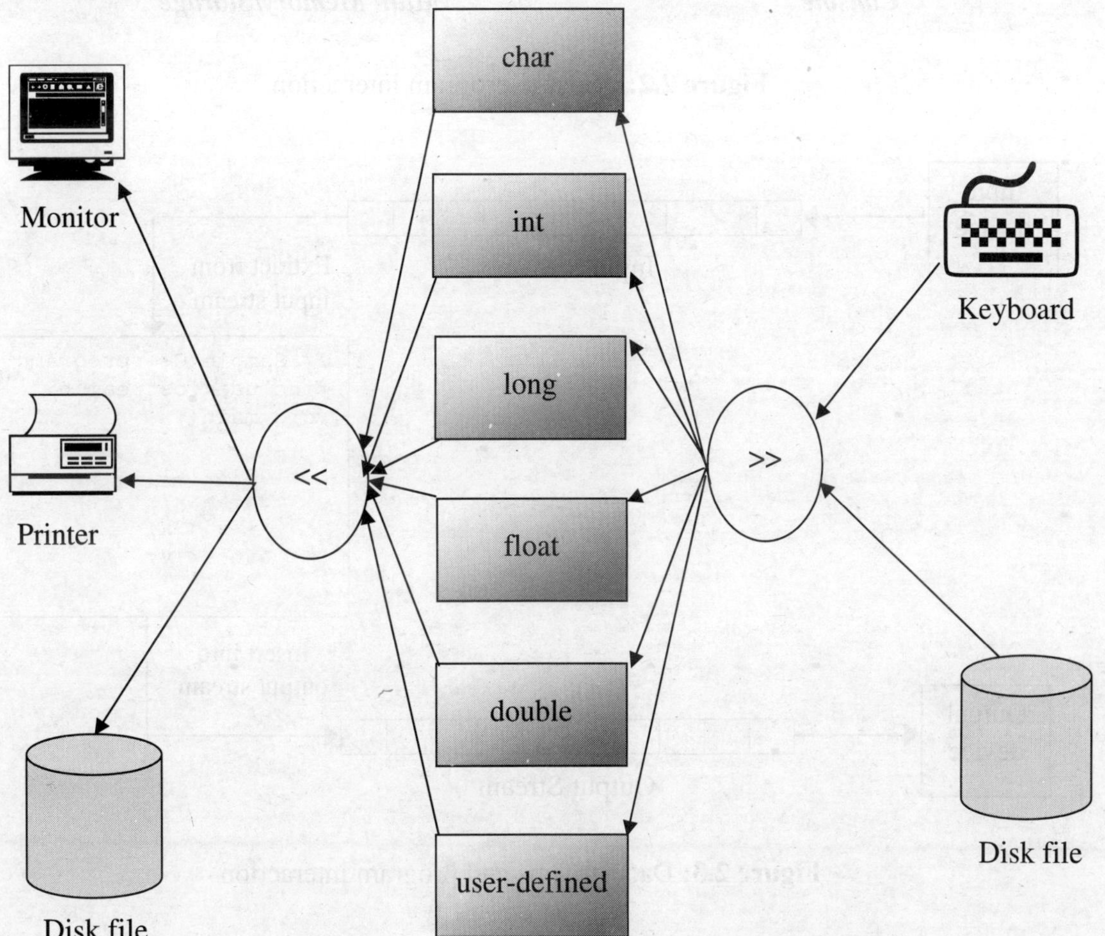

Figure 2.1: Consistent stream interface with I/O devices

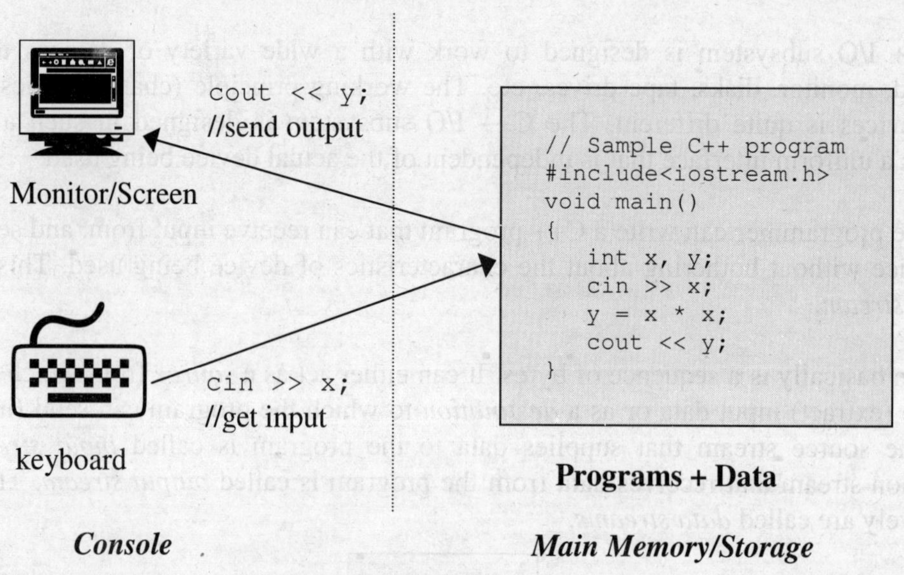

Figure 2.2: Console-program interaction

Input device

Input Stream

Extract from input stream

```
// Sample C++ program
#include<iostream.h>
void main()
{
    int x, y;
    cin >> x;
    y = x * x;
    cout << y;
}
```

Insert into output stream

Output device

Output Stream

Figure 2.3: Data streams and program interaction

2.7 CONROL STATEMENTS

A computer program is a set of instructions for a computer. These instructions, also known as *statements*, are executed sequentially, i.e., one after the other as they appear in a program. This order of executing the statement works well for simple problems where no decision-making process is involved. However, in practice, it is often desired to change the order of execution of statements or repeat a group of statements for known number of times or until certain specified conditions are met. In such cases, the order in which these statements will be executed is to be controlled.

Changing the order of execution of the statements, i.e., changing the flow of control, might involve one of the following situations.

- *Jumping* - transferring control from one point to another point in the same program unit.
- *Branching* - executing one group of instructions depending on the outcome of a decision.
- *Looping* - executing a group of instructions repetitively either for a given number of times or until the required conditions are met.

The C++ Language provides facilities for controlling the order of execution of the statements, which are referred to as *flow control statements*. The various flow control statements are clubbed in the following categories:

- *Decision Making Statements* — In this category, C++ language provides the following statements:
  - *if* statement
  - *if – else* statement
  - *else if* construct
  - *switch* statement
- *Looping/Iterative Statements* — In this category, C++ language provides the following statements:
  - *for* statement
  - *while* statement
  - *do – while* statement
- *Jumping Statements* — In this category, C++ language provides the following statements:
  - *break* statement
  - *continue* statement
  - *goto* statement

2.7.1 Decision Making Statements

2.7.1.1 The *if* Statement

The syntax of *if* statement is

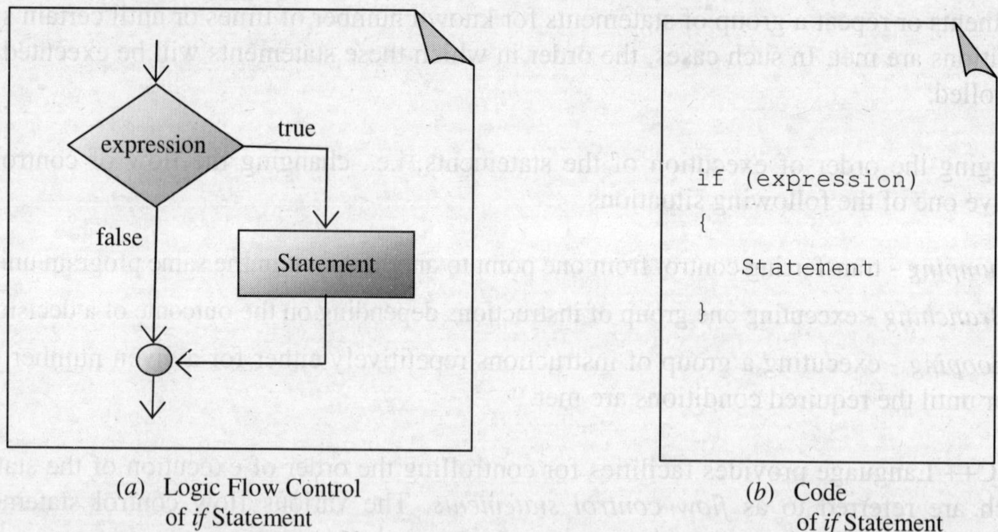

(*a*) Logic Flow Control of *if* Statement

(*b*) Code of *if* Statement

Figure 2.4: Logic flow control and code of *if* statement

The *expression* may represent a relation expression, a logical expression, a numeric variable or a numeric constant. The specified expression may be a simple expression or compound expression.

The expression in C++ language evaluates to a *zero* or *non-zero* value. If expression evaluates to a *non-zero* value, then the statements in the statement-block are executed; otherwise they are bypassed.

2.7.1.2 The *if– else* Statement

The *if* statement executes a single statement (simple or compound), when the specified expression evaluates to a *non-zero* value. It does nothing when it evaluates to a *zero* value. *Is there any way whereby a one statement is executed if the expression evaluates to a non-zero value and another statement if the expression evaluates to a zero value*? The answer is yes.

This objective is achieved by using *if – else* statement whose syntax is

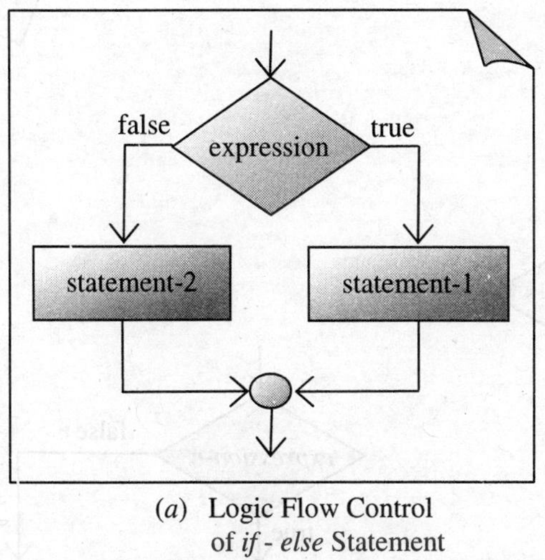

(*a*) Logic Flow Control of *if - else* Statement

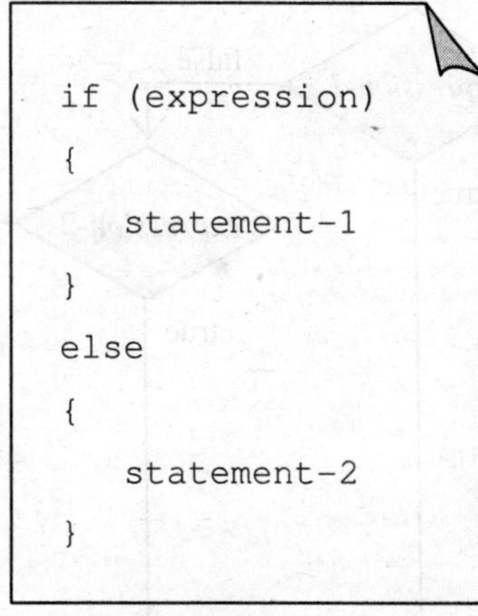

```
if (expression)
{
    statement-1
}
else
{
    statement-2
}
```

(*b*) Code of *if - else* Statement

Figure 2.5: Logic flow control and code of *if-else* statement

If expression evaluates to a non-zero value, the *statement-1* is executed and the *statement-2* is bypassed. However, if the expression evaluates to a zero value, the *statement-1* is bypassed and the *statement-2* is executed.

2.7.1.3 The else – *if* Construct

If the nesting of *if* or *if-else* statements gets deep and deep, the program becomes more and more difficult to read. In that case *else-if* construct is handier. But it cannot be used as standalone statement, *i.e.*, it can only be used in conjunction with opening *if* statement.

The syntax of *else-if* construct is given in Figure 2.6.

The expressions are evaluated in order, and if any expression is true then the statement block associated with it is executed, and this terminates the whole chain. The last *else* part handles *none of the above* or default case where none of the specified expressions are satisfied. This sequence of *if* statements is the most general way of writing a multi-way decision.

```
if ( expression-1 )
    statement-1
else if ( expression-2 )
    statement-2
else if ( expression-3 )
    statement-3
    :
    :
else if ( expression-n )
    statement-n
else
    statement-s
```

Figure 2.6: Code of *else if* Construct

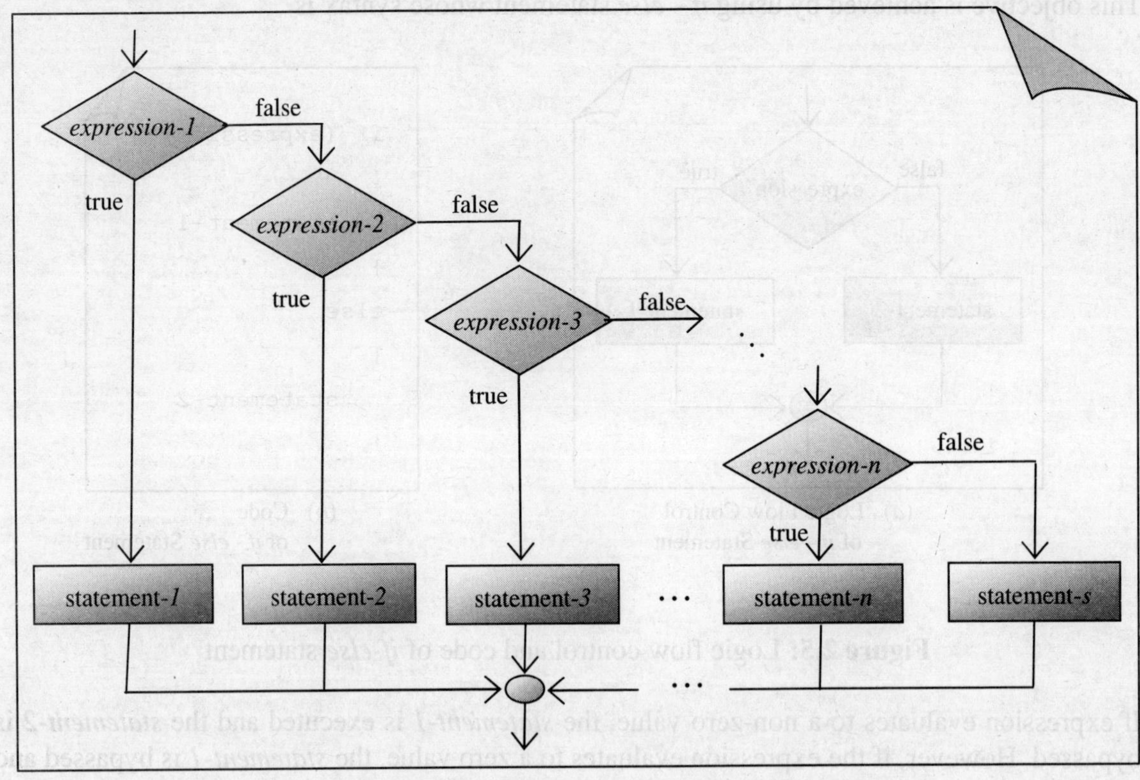

Figure 2.7: Logic Flow Control of *else if* Construct

2.7.1.4 The *switch* Statement

The *switch* statement provides an alternative to *else if* construct. The *switch* statement has more flexibility and a clearer format than *else if* construct. The syntax of *switch* statement is

```
switch ( expression )
{
   case val-1 : statement-1
                break;
   case val-2 : statement-2
                break;
   case val-3 : statement-3
                break;
   :
   case val-n : tatement-n
               break;
   default    : statement-d
}
```

Figure 2.8: Code of *switch* Statement

If *expression* takes any value from *val-1*, *val-2*, *val-3*, ..., *val-n*, the control is transferred to that appropriate case. In each case, the statements are executed and then the *break* statement transfers the control out of *switch* statement. If no *break* statement is used following a case, except the last one in the absence of *default* keyword, the control will fall through to the next case.

If the value of the *expression* does not match any of the case values, control goes to the *default* keyword, which is usually at the end of the *switch* statement.

The use of the *default* keyword can be of a great convenience. If there is no *default* keyword, the whole *switch* statement simply terminates when there is no match.

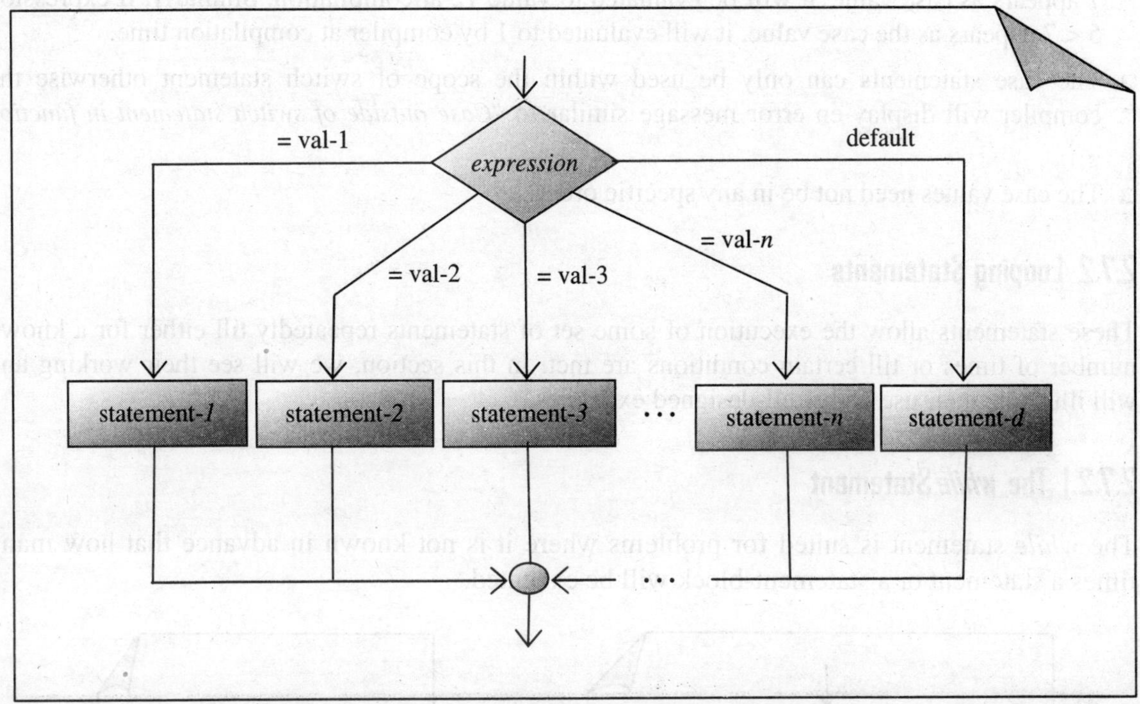

Figure 2.9: Logic Flow Control of *switch* Statement

However, if you want that a same statement is to executed for more than one value of the *expression*, then we have to code these *cases* one after the other, and then the specified statement as shown below:

```
switch ( expression )
{
        :
   case val-4 :
   case val-5 :
   case val-6 : statement-block
                break;
        :
}
```

The *statement-block* will be executed whenever the value of the *expression* is *val-4*, *val-5*, or *val-6*.

The following are some more points about switch statement:

- The *expression* of switch statement must be of type integer or character type.
- The *default* case need not be used as the last case. It can be placed at any place.

- The case values must be integer constants or character constants. These values can also be constant expressions as these are evaluated at compilation time. For example, if expression 5 + 7 appears as case value, it will be evaluated to value 12 at compilation. Similarly, if expression 5 < 7 appears as the case value, it will evaluated to 1 by compiler at compilation time.
- The case statements can only be used within the scope of switch statement otherwise the compiler will display en error message similar to *"Case outside of switch statement in function ..."*.
- The case values need not be in any specific order.

2.7.2 Looping Statements

These statements allow the execution of some set of statements repeatedly till either for a known number of times or till certain conditions are met. In this section, we will see their working and will illustrate their use with well-designed examples.

2.7.2.1 The *while* Statement

The *while* statement is suited for problems where it is not known in advance that how many times a statement or a statement-block will be executed.

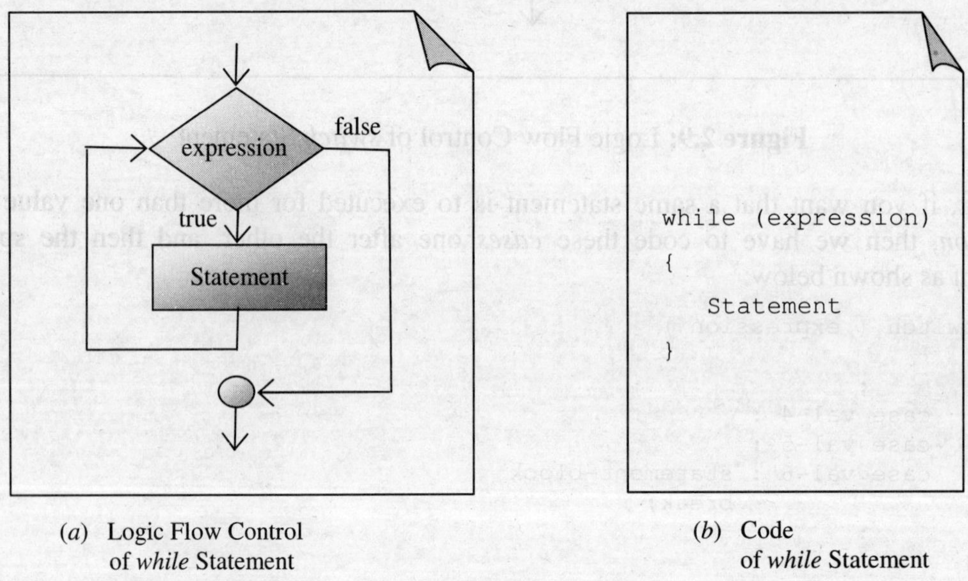

(*a*) Logic Flow Control of *while* Statement

(*b*) Code of *while* Statement

Figure 2.10: Logic flow control and code of *while* statement

where *expression* is a constant, a variable or an expression. The *statement* is executed repeatedly till the *exp* evaluates to a *non-zero* value. Whenever *exp* evaluates to a *zero* value, the execution of *while* statement will terminate and control will pass to a statement immediately following it.

Though in C++ language there are certain exceptions, but in general, the following points must be kept in mind while using the *while* statement:

- There must be a statement prior to *while* statement that initializes the *exp*.
- In the statement-block, there must be a statement that modifies the expression.

2.7.2.2 The *for* Statement

The *for* statement is suited for problems where the number of times a statement or statement-block will be executed is known in advance.

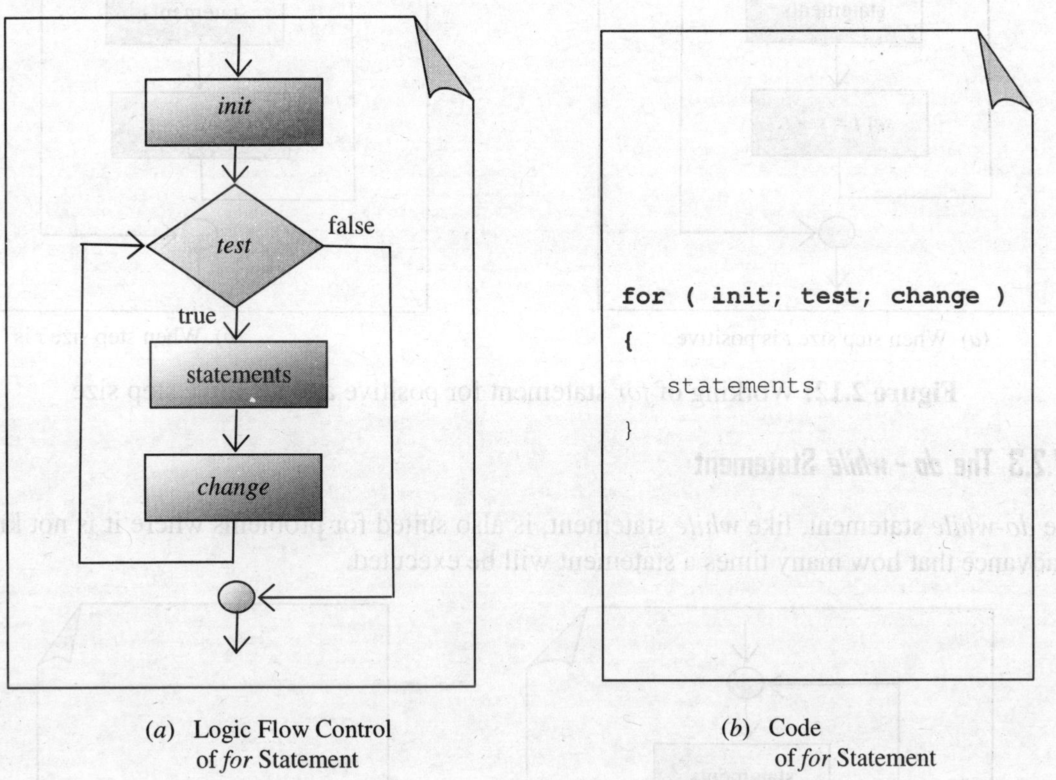

(*a*) Logic Flow Control of *for* Statement

(*b*) Code of *for* Statement

Figure 2.11: Logic flow control and code of *for* statement

where *init* is an expression to initialize the counter, the *test* is an expression to see when to stop iterating, and *change* is an expression to change the counter for each pass of the loop. The *init* and *change* parts can have more than one statement separated by a comma.

The change for the counter can be positive as well as negative, as illustrated below:

```
        :
for ( k = r; k <= s; k += t )
{
        // statements
}
        :
```

```
        :
for ( k = r; k >= s; k -= t )
{
        // statements
}
        :
```

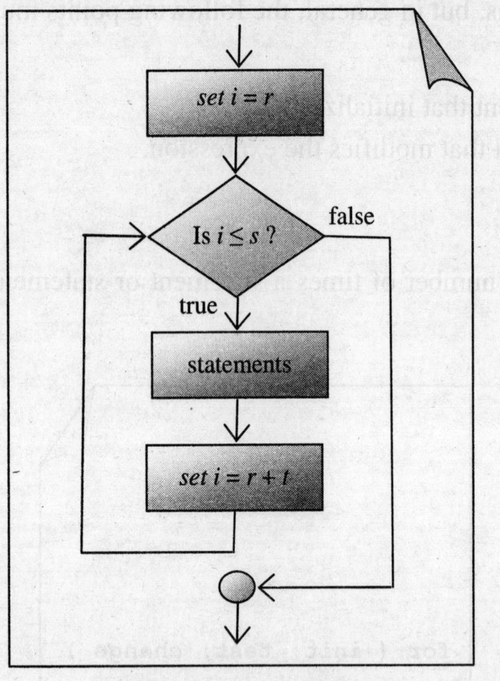

(*a*) When step size *t* is positive

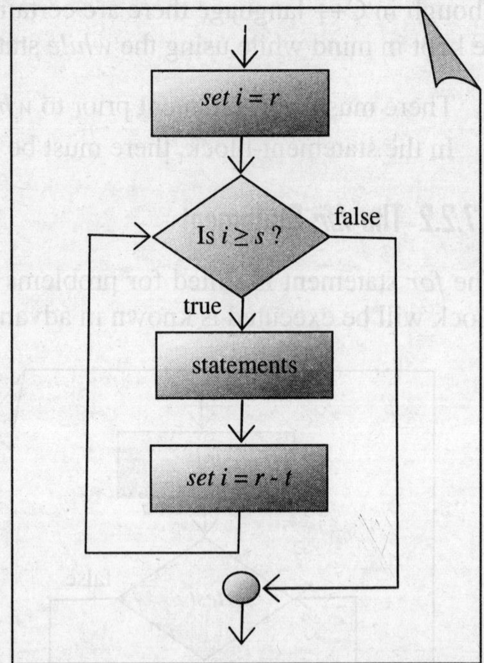

(*b*) When step size *t* is

Figure 2.12: Working of *for* statement for positive and negative step size

2.7.2.3 The *do - while* Statement

The *do-while* statement, like *while* statement, is also suited for problems where it is not known in advance that how many times a statement will be executed.

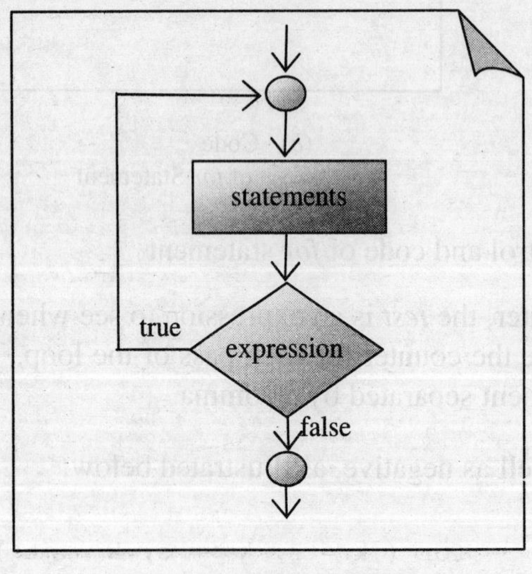

(*a*) Logic Flow Control of *do-while* Statement

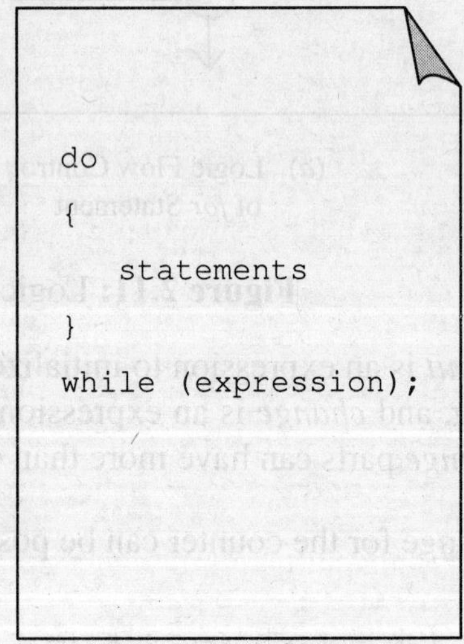

```
do
{
    statements
}
while (expression);
```

(*b*) Code of *do-while* Statement

Figure 2.13: Logic flow control and code of *do-while* statement

where *exp* is a constant, a variable or an expression. The *statement-block* is executed repeatedly till the *exp* evaluates to a *non-zero* value.

2.7.2.4 Nested *while, for* and *do-while* Statements

Just as *if* statements can be nested, these statements can also be nested. The inner loop is executed from the beginning for each iteration of the outer loop. The following sections of code show the nesting of looping statements within their own types.

```
for(i=0;i<m;i++)
{
    :
    for(j=0;j<n;j++)
    {
        :
    }
}
```

```
i=0;
while(i<m)
{
    :
    j=0;
    while(j<n)
    {
        :
        j++;
    }
    i++;
}
```

```
i=0;
do
{
    :
    j=0;
    do
    {
        :
        j++;
    } while(j<n);
    i++;
} while(i<m);
```

In general, it is possible to nest while and do-while statements inside *for* statement, *for* statement inside the *while* and *do-while* statements, *i.e.*, all sort of nesting combinations are permitted.

2.7.3 Jumping Statements

These statements transfer the control from one part of the program to another part. In this section, we will see their working.

2.7.3.1 The *break* Statement

The *break* statement is always used inside the body of the switch statement, and looping statements.

In *switch* statement, it is used as the last statement of the statement block of every case except the last one. When executed, it transfers the control out of *switch* statement and the execution of the program continues from the statement following *switch* statement.

```
switch ( expression )
{
    case val-1 : statement-block-1
                 break;
    case val-2 : statement-block-2
                 break;
    case val-3 : statement-block-3
                 break;
        :
        :
    case val-n : statement-block-n
                 break;
    default    :
                statement-block-default
}
```

In *for*, *while* and *do-while* statements, it is always used in conjunction with *if* statement. Note that it is never used with *if* statement if it is not part of the body of the looping statement. When executed, it transfers the control out of looping statement and the execution of the program continues from the statement following looping statement.

```
for(i=0;i<m;i++)
{
   :
   if (condition)
      break;
   :
}
```

```
i=0;
while(i<m)
{
   :
   if (condition)
      break;
   :
}
```

```
i=0;
do
{
   :
   if (condition)
      break;
   :
} while(i<m);
```

In simple terms, we can say that the *break* when executed terminates the execution of the loop.

Consider the following code segment

```
i = 0;
  while ( i <= 100 ) {
  . . . . . .
  scanf("%d", &k);
  if ( k == 0 )
     break;
  m = i / k;
  . . . . . .
}
```

The execution of the *while* loop will be terminated as soon as the user enters value 0 for variable *k* as input or the value of variable *i* exceeds 100, which ever happens earlier.

2.7.3.2 The *continue* Statement

The *continue* statement is always used inside the body of the looping statements. In looping statements, sometimes a situation may arise where we want that from a given statement onward, the rest of the statement up to the last statement of the loop are to be bypassed. This task is accomplished by using *continue* statement.

The *continue* statement transfers the control to the beginning of the next iteration of the loop thus bypassing the statements which are not yet executed. But note that the *continue* statement is always used in conjunction with the *if* statement.

```
for(i=0;i<m;i++)
{
   :
   if (condition)
      continue;
   :
}
```

```
while(i<m)
{
   :
   if (condition)
      continue;
   :
}
```

```
do
{
   :
   if (condition)
      continue;
   :
} while(i<m);
```

In simple terms, we can say that the continue statement when executed terminates the current iteration of the loop.

Consider the following segment

```
i = 0;
    while ( i <= 100 )
{
   . . . . . .
   if ( i  % 10 == 0 )
      continue;
   . . . . . .
}
```

The use of *continue* statement in conjunction with *if* statement skips the rest of the statements of the *while* loop for values of *i* divisible by 10.

2.7.3.3 The *goto* Statement

Though in C++ language, every program can be written without the use of *goto* statement, still a situation may arise where we are forced to use *goto* statement. For example, to transfer a control from deeply nested statements, such as jumping out of two or more loops at once. Please note a *break* statement can not be used directly since it exits only from the innermost loop.

The *goto* statement can transfer the control to any part of the program. The target destination of the *goto* statement is marked by a label. The syntax for using *goto* statement is

```
  // some statements
  goto label;
  // some more statements
label:
  // still more statements
```

```
  // some statements
label:
  // some more statements
  goto label;
  // still more statements
```

Though in C++, every program can be written without the use of *goto* statement, still a situation may arise where we are forced to use *goto* statement. For example, to transfer a control from deeply nested statements, such as jumping out of two or more loops at once. Please note a *break* statement cannot be used directly since it exits only from the innermost loop.

2.8 FUNCTIONS

The best way to handle complex problems is to split the problem into small problems, called *subproblems* that can be handled easily. This we are used to do in our day-to-day working. Once all these subproblems are solved separately, solutions of these subproblems can be synthesized to generate the solution of the given complex problem.

In a similar way, if program to be developed is very large and complex, it is always recommended to split into two or more functions (subprograms) that can be developed separately, tested separately and then integrated.

2.8.1 Defining a Function

The syntax for defining a function is

```
type functionName( type1 arg1, type2 arg2, type3 arg2)
{
    //  declaration of local variable
    //  statements that define the task to be performed
    //  by the function
}
```

The first line of the function definition specifies the return type of the function, its name followed by list of arguments, called *formal* or *dummy* arguments, enclosed in parentheses. The *return type* is either one of the built-in data types or user-defined data type. The return type tells the type of value to be sent back via the return statement to the calling function. If there are no formal arguments, i.e., formal argument list is empty, then the keyword *void* is written in the parentheses. If the function is not supposed to return a value, its return type is also specified as *void*. The body of the function is enclosed in braces. If the function is supposed to return a value, then there must be at least one *return* statement to send back the value to the calling function. However, if the return type is *void*, then the return statement is not mandatory.

Following are some points to remember while defining functions in C++:

- The first statement of the function must be the function defining statement specifying the return type, name and formal arguments.
- If the type of the function is omitted, then it is assumed of type integer (*int*). But it is recommended that the return type must be explicitly specified.
- Rules for naming a function are same as for variable names.
- The formal arguments should neither be constants nor expressions.
- If a formal argument is an array name, it must be declared as an array in a type declaration statement before the body of the function starts and its maximum size must be equal to the actual size in the calling function.

2.8.2 Accessing a Function

Like library functions, the user-defined functions are accessed from a function simply by its name, including the actual arguments, if any, enclosed within parentheses. However, parentheses must follow the function name even if there is no actual argument to be passed to the function. The actual arguments, if any, must correspond in *number*, *type*, and *order* with formal arguments.

When the name of the function is encountered, the control is transferred to the called function. The formal arguments are replaced by the actual arguments and the execution of the function is carried out. When the *return* statement is executed or last statement has finished its execution, the control is transferred back to the calling function.

2.8.3 Passing Arguments to a Function

The mechanism used to pass data to a function is via argument list, where individual arguments are called *actual arguments*. These arguments are enclosed in parentheses after the function name. The actual arguments must correspond in *number*, *type*, and *order* with formal arguments specified in the function definition. The actual arguments can be *constants*, *variables*, *array names*, or *expressions*. There are three approaches to passing arguments to a function:

- Pass by value
- Pass by address
- Pass by reference

2.8.3.1 Parameter Passing by Value

In this approach, the names of the actual arguments are used in the function call. In this way the values of the actual arguments are passed to the function. When control is transferred to the called function, the values of the actual arguments are substituted to the corresponding formal arguments and the body of the function is executed. If the called function is supposed to return a value, it is returned via *return* statement.

Following code segment illustrates the mechanism of passing parameters by value.

```
void swap( int a, int b )
{
      int temp;
      temp  = a;
      a = b;
      b = temp;
}
```

The above function will be accessed as

```
swap(x, y);
```

where *x* and *y* are actual arguments in the calling function.

2.8.3.2 Parameter Passing by Address

In this approach, the addresses of the actual arguments are used in the function call. In this way the addresses of the actual arguments are passed to the function. When control is transferred to the called function, the addresses of the actual arguments are substituted to corresponding formal arguments and the body of the function is executed. The formal arguments are declared as pointers to *types* that match the data types of the actual arguments. This approach is of practical importance while passing arrays and structures among function, and also for passing back more than one value to the calling functions.

Following code segment illustrates the mechanism of passing parameters by address.

```
void swap( int *a, int *b )
{
    int temp;
    temp  = *a;
    *a = *b;
    *b = temp;
}
```

The above function will be accessed as

```
swap(&x, &y);
```

where *x* and *y* are actual arguments in the calling function.

2.8.3.3 Parameter Passing by Reference

The parameter passed by reference has the functionality of pass-by-address and the syntax of pass-by-value. Any modification made through the formal reference parameter is also reflected in the actual parameter.

Following code segment illustrates the mechanism of passing parameters by reference.

```
void swap( int &a, int &b )
{
    int temp;
    temp  = a;
    a = b;
    b = temp;
}
```

The above function will be accessed as

```
swap(x, y);
```

where *x* and *y* are actual arguments in the calling function.

2.8.4 Inline Functions

During program execution, a function call involves transfer of control to a specified address (address of first executable statement of the function), and returning to the instruction following the function call. Before transferring the control, CPU stores the contents of its registers and the address of the instruction following the function call, pushes actual arguments onto the system stack. After the transfer of control, the CPU pops the actual arguments from the system stack and copies into formal arguments that acts as local variables in the called function. Then it executes the function code, and stores the return value, if any, in a predefined memory location or register and returns control to the calling function. On return, the CPU retrieves the value returned by the function, if any, from the specified memory location or register, and resumes the execution from the instruction following the function calls. The time taken during this whole process is called *context switch time*, and constitutes an overhead in the execution of the program.

This overhead is relatively large if the time required to execute a function is small than the context switch time. In that case, we would like to repeat the code in multiple places in a function rather than creating a separate function for it. C++ provides an alternative to above problem in the form of *inline functions*.

Inline functions are those functions whose body is inserted in place of the function call during the compilation process. Therefore, with inline functions, the program will not incur any context-switching overhead.

Hence, the inline functions enjoy both the flexibility and power of normal functions and macro functions. The inline functions are best used for small and frequently used functions.

An *inline* function definition is similar to an ordinary function except the keyword *inline* precedes the function definition.

2.8.5 Default Arguments

In a C++ function call, one or more arguments can be omitted with the condition that function is defined to take default values for the arguments that can be omitted by providing the default values in the function prototype or declarator.

In the function prototype or declarator, parameters without default arguments are placed first and those with default values are placed later. The arguments specified in the function call explicitly override the default values.

The following example illustrates the definition of a function with default arguments:

```
void println ( char ch = '-', int count = 80)
{
    cout << endl;
    for ( int i = 0; i < count; i++ )
        cout << ch;
    cout << endl;
}
```

The above function can be used in following ways

```
printline();            //use both default arguments
printline('*');         //use second argument as default
printline('+', 45);     //use explicit arguments
```

The prototype of a function with default arguments can be specified as

```
void println ( char ch = '-', int count = 80);
```

The following prototype statement is also acceptable

```
void println ( char = '-', int = 80 );
```

If you are using prototype for a function with default arguments, then the default values need to be specified only in the prototype. Specifying default values in the declarator too will lead to error indicating the default argument(s) is/are re-declared.

2.8.6 Function Templates

The C++ language allow to define a single function capable of processing elements of different data types. Such a function is known as *function template* or *generic function*.

The syntax of function template is

```
template <class T1, class T2, . . .>
DataType FunctionName (arguments of type T1, T2, . . . ) {
      // local variables of type T1, T2, or any other type
      // function body, operating on variable of type T1, T2
      // any other variables
}
```

where *template* is the keyword for declaring function template
Following is the function template for swapping the values of two variables that are passed by reference.

```
template <class T>
void swap ( T &a, T &b ) {
     T temp; //temporary variable
     temp = a; a = b;  b = temp;
}
```

The formal arguments of a template definition are used in the same way as built-in types or user-defined types. They can be used to specify formal argument(s) for the function, to declare variables within the function, to specify the return type of the function. The function definition follows and is defined like any other function.

The *swap()* function template declares a single formal type parameter *T* (*T* can be any valid identifier) for the type of the variables to be swapped by the function. Here *T* is referred to as a *type parameter*.

When the compiler detects a *swap()* function call in the source code, the type of the actual arguments is substituted for T throughout the template definition and the it creates a complete function for swapping two variables of specified data type. Then, the newly created function is compiled.

For example, if the function call statement appears as

```
swap( first, second );
```

where actual argument *first* and *second* are of type *float*.

The C++ Compiler first creates the following function definition

```
void swap( float &a, float &b ) {
     float temp;
     temp = a; a = b; b = temp;
}
```

by replacing *T* by *float* throughout the template definition, and then compiles it to create an object code.

2.8.7 Function Overloading

Suppose in our program we require the functionality to swap two values of *int* type, *float* type, *double* type, *char* type. Normally, this situation is dealt with by writing four different functions with different names as shown below:

```
// function to swap two int values
void swapInt ( int &first, int &second ) {
    int temp;
    temp = first; first = second; second = temp;
}
// function to swap two float values
void swapFloat ( float &first, float &second ) {
    float temp;
    temp = first; first = second; second = temp;
}
// function to swap two double values
void swapDouble ( double &first, double &second ) {
    double temp;
    temp = first; first = second; second = temp;

}
// function to swap two char values
void swapChar ( char &first, char &second ) {
    char temp;
    temp = first; first = second; second = temp;
}
```

Thus we have four different functions with different names for identical functionality. It would have been nice if we can use single name instead of four different names.

In C++, it is possible to use the same function name to perform identical operation. Such functions are called *overloaded functions* and the process of defining such functions is called *function overloading*.

The overloaded functions must differ in argument list in either of the following ways:

- They may differ in number of arguments.
- They may differ in data types of arguments.
- They may differ both in number and type of arguments.

Therefore, in the above example case, we can use one name, say *swap*, for all four versions of the swap function to swap different values and depending on the type of actual arguments in the function call, the compiler will resolve the function call.

Note that the return type does not play any role in function overloading. The reason is that it is not necessary to collect the returned value even if the called function returns a value.

2.8.7.1 Name Mangling

If there have been no overloading, then functions are always called by their name as given by the programmer. But, in case the compiler permits overloading, then to handle overloading, the compiler changes the names of all functions during compilations. This is known as *name mangling*.

Name mangling, also known as *name decoration*, is the process where the compiler changes the names of the functions to facilitate overloading.

2.9 STRUCTURES

Structures are generally used as a mechanism to group data elements that may be of different data types in one unit that belong to the same family. For example, if we want to create a user-defined data type to represent an employee in an organization, the structure definition may look like

```
struct employee
{
    int empCode;
    char empName[20];
    float empSalary;
};
```

Here, for simplicity, we have considered only three elements viz. employee's code (*empCode*), employee's name (*empName*) and employee's salary (*empSalary*) while leaving out other elements such as date of birth, date of joining, educational and professional qualification, etc.

In order to process a variable (that represents an employee, an instance of family *employees*), either it must declared as global variable so that it is accessible to all functions or must be passed as an argument to an appropriate set of functions in order to process it.

However, structures further permit the inclusion of functions in addition to data members, and thus provide a true mechanism of handling data abstraction.

The general syntax of such a structure is

```
struct structureName {
    public:
            // data and functions
    protected:
            // data and functions
    private:
            // data and functions
};
```

The structure has two types of members: *data member* and *function members*. Function defined in a structure can access any data member. The keywords *public*, *protected* and *private* are called *access specifiers*, and will be discussed in detail when we will discuss about classes in the next section. If none of the above specifier appears in the structure definition, all the members have default access.

The private and protected members of a structure can only be accessed by the member function where as public members are accessible by members functions as well its instances (structure variables). Therefore, with appropriate use of these access specifiers, we can control the access to data members as desired in the application.

When we define a structure, member functions can be defined within the structure definition or outside the structure definition. When they are defined outside the structure definition, they are just declared (prototyped) in the structure definition and are bound to an appropriate structure definition by using scope resolution operator. Both of the ways are illustrated below:

When the member functions are defined inside the structure definition:

```
struct employee
{
    private:
        int empCode;                // private data members
        char empName[20];
        float empSalary;
    public:
        // public member function defined inside the class
        void readData()
        {
            cout << "Enter code : ";
            cin >> empCode;
            cout << "Enter name : ";
            cin >> empName;
            cout << "Enter salary : ";
            cin >> empSalary;
        }
        void showData()
        {
            cout << endl << "Employee information" << endl;
            cout << "Code   : " << empCode << endl;
            cout << "Name   : " << empName << endl;
            cout << "Salary : " << setprecision(2);
            cout << empSalary << endl;
        }
};
```

When the member functions are defined outside the structure definition:

```
struct employee
{
    private:
        int empCode;                // private data members
        char empName[20];
        float empSalary;
    public:
         // public member function declared inside the
         // class and defined outside the class
        void readData ();
        void showData ();
};
```

```
void employee :: readData()
{
    cout << "Enter code : ";
    cin >> empCode;
    cout << "Enter name : ";
    cin >> empName;
    cout << "Enter salary : ";
    cin >> empSalary;
}
void employee :: showData()
{
    cout << endl << "Employee information" << endl;
    cout << "Code    : " << empCode << endl;
    cout << "Name    : " << empName << endl;
    cout << "Salary  : " << setprecision(2);
    cout << empSalary << endl;
}
```

The following points about structures are important to remember:

1. When we compute the size of a structure, the member functions are not included in its size. This fact you can verify using *sizeof* operator. For example, for employee structure defines above, the *sizeof* operator will return value 26, *i.e.*, size of structure employee is 26 bytes (2 bytes for *empCode*, 20 bytes for *empName* and 4 bytes for *empSalary*).

2. The data member can be *private*, *protected* or *public*, but the member functions must be *public* otherwise it will not be possible to call member functions on a structure variable and thus serves no purpose.

3. If the access specifier for the data members is *private*, then a structure variable initialization cannot be combined with declaration. Therefore, we have to write a member functions to initialize a structure variable.

   Consider the following structure definition

```
struct date
{
        int day;          //data members with default access
        int month;        //(public)
        int year;
        // member functions
};

  or

struct date
{
     public:
        int day;          //public data members
        int month;
        int year;
        // member functions
};
```

Then compiler permits the following

```
date dd = { 10, 12, 2003 };
```

However, if the structure definition is

```
struct date {
   private:
      int day;      //private data members
      int month;
      int year;
     // member functions
};
```

Then compiler will not permits the following

```
date dd = { 10, 5, 2003 };
```

Therefore, in this case the only way is to use a member function as illustrated below:

```
struct date {
   private:
      int day;      //private data members
      int month;
      int year;
      void initialize(int dd, int mm, int yy) {
          day = dd;
          month = mm;
          year = yy;
      }
     // more member functions
};
```

Now, we can declare a structure variable and then call member function *initialize()* to form the initialization.

```
date d;
d.initialize(10,5, 2003);
```

You may think that these two statements can be combined as we do in normal case, but it is not permitted. You first have to create a variable (instance), and only then you can call member function. Therefore, following statement is not permitted:

```
date d.initialize(10,5, 2003);
```

2.10 CLASSES

A class and an object are tightly interwoven, for example, we cannot talk about an object without regard for its class. However, there are important differences between these two terms. An object is a concrete entity that exists in time and space and has an identity, whereas a class represents only an abstraction, the *essence* of an object. Thus, we may speak of the class *student*, which represents characteristics common to all students. To identify a particular student in this class, we must speak of *this student* or *that student*.

In the context of object-oriented programming, we define class as a set of objects that share a common structure and a common behaviour. An object is simply an instance of a class.

2.10.1 Specifying a Class

The syntax for specifying a class is much like specifying a structure as shown below:

```
class ClassName
{
     AccessSpecifier:
          // data members
          // function members
};
```

The *AccessSpecifier* (*private*, *protected* or *public*) determines which parts of a software system can access these members of a class. By default, access specifier for a class is *private*, and an access specifier remain in effect till overridden by another access specifier.

The data members describe the structure of the objects and at particular instant the values of these data members represents the state of an object. The function members describe the behavior of the objects, *i.e.,* how object responds to external events.

Each of these members can be declared as *private*, *protected* or *public*. The private members can only be accessed from within the class. Members of the class and members of its subclass can access a protected member. The public members can also be accessed by non-members of the class, *i.e.*, from outside the class.

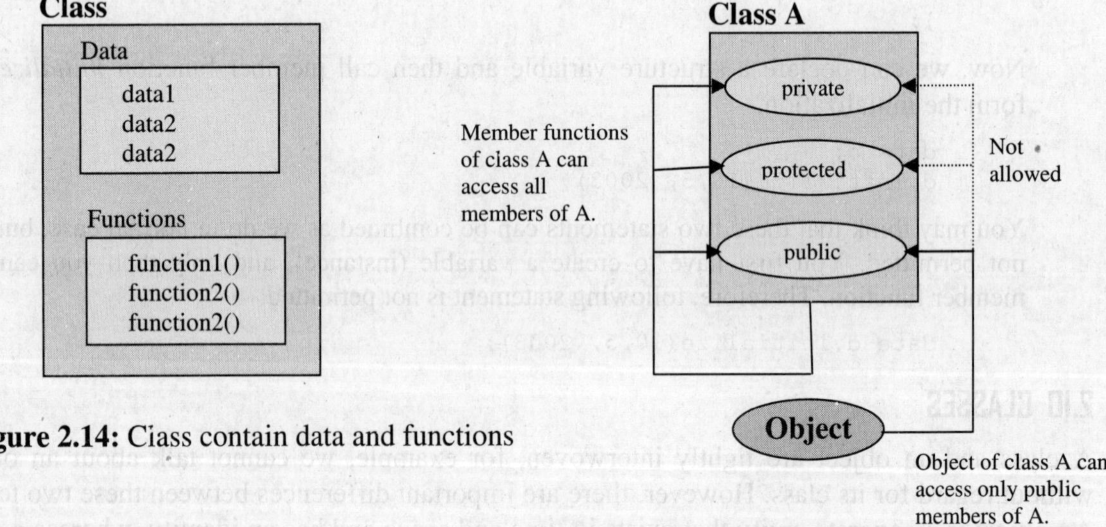

Figure 2.14: Class contain data and functions

Figure 2.15: Access limits within a class

The following declaration illustrates the specification of a class called *StudentType* having *studentRollNo* and *studentName* as its data members; *setData()* and *printData()* as its member functions.

```
class StudentType
{
      private:               // data members
          int  studentRollNo;
          char studentName[20];
      public:                // function members
          void setData( int rollNo, char *name )
          {
             studentRollNo = rollNo;
             strcpy ( studentName, name );
          }
          void printData()
          {
             cout << endl;
             cout << "Roll No of Student : ";
             cout << studentRollNo << endl;
             cout << "Name of Student    : ";
             cout << studentName << endl;
          }
};
```

In the above class definition, even if we omit the use of keyword private, the data members will be declared as private since private is the default access, and remain in effect till new access specifier is encountered in the class definition.

The class should be given some meaningful name reflecting the kind of information it holds. The class name *StudentType* becomes a new data type identifier, and can be used to define instances of class *StudentType* type. The class *StudentType* contains two data members and two member functions. The data members are private while both the member functions are public. The member function *setData()* is used to assign values to data members. The member function *printData()* is used to output the values of data members. The data members of the class *StudentType* cannot be accessed from any other part of the program.

2.10.2 Creating Class Objects

A class specification only declares the structure and behaviour of objects. Before using objects and services provided by them, we need to define them. The process of defining the objects is known as *instantiation*. It is the definition of an object that creates object in a program and sets aside memory for its storage *i.e.*, necessary resources are allocated only when a class is instantiated.

The syntax for defining objects of a class as shown below:

```
ClassName objectName;
```

The declaration of an object is similar to that of a value variable of any basic data type.

```
StudentType student;
```

The class specification and object definition can also be combined by placing the name of objects after the closing brace of the class specification as shown below:

```
class StudentType
{
     private:                  // data members
          int  studentRollNo;
          char studentName[20];
     public:                   // function members
          void setData( int rollNo, char *name )
          {
               studentRollNo = rollNo;
               strcpy ( studentName, name );
          }
          void printData()
          {
               cout << endl;
               cout << "Roll No of Student : ";
               cout << studentRollNo << endl;
               cout << "Name of Student    : ";
               cout << studentName << endl;
          }
} student;
```

But this practice is seldom used because the developer would always prefer to declare the objects close to the place where they will be used and not at the time of the class definition.

2.10.3 Accessing Class Members

The syntax for accessing a class member is similar to that of accessing a member of a structure, *i.e.*, using dot operator as shown below:

```
ObjectName.publicDataMemberName;
ObjectName.publicFunctionMemberName(actualArguments);
```

Note that only public members can be accessed outside the class specification. The private and protected class members can only be accessed by member functions that can be private or public. Similarly, the function members that are declared as public are accessible from outside the class specification. These public functions can access private data members as well as private functions of the class.

For example, the statement

```
student.setData( 100, "Ravi Kiran" );
```

will invoke member function *setData()* which assign value 100 to data member *studentRollNo* and string "Ravi Kiran" to data member *studentName.*

The data declaration of an object is similar to that of a value variable of any basic data type.

Similarly, the statement

```
student.printData();
```

will output the values of the data members.

A member function can only be called (invoked) by using an object. Thus, the statement

```
getData();
```

is illegal.

The following statements are also illegal:

```
student.studentRollNo = 10;
strcpy( student.studentName, "Ravi Kiran" );
```

These data members being private can only be accessed from within the class. Thus, to assign values to them, to process them or to output their values, a class specification must incorporate a set of appropriate member functions.

2.10.4 Constructors & Destructors

These are special types of member functions. These are special in the sense that they are invoked automatically and have the same name as that of a class. The constructor is invoked when the object is created whereas the destructor is invoked when the object goes out of scope or deleted with the *delete* operator if the object is created dynamically using *new* operator. Like, other member functions, they can also be defined inside or outside the class template. Consider the following class declaration

```
class Test
{
    private:
        // . . . data member declared here
    public:
        Test()              // constructor
        {
            // code for initializing data members
        }
        ~Test()    // destructor
        {
            // code for releasing the resources held by the object
        }
        // . . . other member functions
};
```

Here *Test()* is a constructor while *~Test()* is a destructor.

In general, every class must have these member functions. However, if no constructor is defined in the class, the compiler automatically inserts a constructor of following type

```
ClasName() { }  // default constructor, that does nothing
```

Therefore, when an object is created using following statement

```
ClasName objectName;
```

The default constructor is invoked. As default constructor does nothing, the initial values of the data members will be undefined, and thus the object will have undefined state.

In practice, we want the object should have a well-defined initial state whenever it is created. In order to achieve this, we have to write our own constructor that initializes the object to a specified state.

On the other side, we have to write destructor in the class, especially when an object claims resources dynamically. Remember that compiler does not provide any default destructor.

2.10.5 Defining Member Functions

The data members of a class can only de declared within the body of the class, whereas the member functions of the class can be defined in following ways:

- Inside class definition
- Outside class definition

The syntax for defining a member function depends on whether it is defined inside or outside the class definition. However, irrespective of the location of the definition, the member function must perform the same operation. Therefore, the code inside the function body will be identical in both the cases. The compiler treats these definitions in a different manner.

2.10.5.1 Member Functions Inside the Class Definition

The syntax for defining a member function is same as of a normal function except that it is enclosed within the body of a class. All the member functions defined inside the class definition are treated as inline by default except those members having looping statements. If the member functions are defined inside the class definition, then there is no need for function prototype (declaration).

The following example illustrates the definition of member function inside class definition.

```
class StockItem
{
    private:                        // data members
        int   itemCode;
        char  itemDescription[20];
        int   itemQuantity;
        float itemUnitPrice;
    public:                         // function members
      void readData()
      {
         cout << "\n\nEnter particulars of a Stock item\n\n";
         cout << "Enter item code              : ";
         cin  >> itemCode;
         cout << "Enter item description : ";
         cin  >> itemDescription;
         cout << "Enter item quantity     : ";
         cin  >> itemQuantity;
```

```
            cout << "Enter item unit price  : ";
            cin  >> itemUnitPrice;
        }
        void displayData()
        {
            cout << "\n\nParticulars of a Stock item are\n\n";
            cout << "Enter item code          : ";
            cout << itemCode << endl;
            cout << "Enter item description : ";
            cout << itemDescription << endl;
            cout << "Enter item quantity    : ";
            cout << itemQuantity << endl;
            cout << "Enter item unit price  : ";
            cout << itemUnitPrice << endl;
        }
};
```

2.10.5.2 Member Functions Outside the Class Definition

When the member functions are to be defined outside the class definition, then following tasks are need:

- Declare the prototypes of the member functions inside the class definition.
- Bind the member function definition to a class to whom it belongs. This is done using the *scope resolution operator* "::".

The syntax for defining a member function outside the class definition is

```
ReturnType ClassName :: memberFunctionName(formalArguments)
{
    // body of the function
}
```

The class *StockItem* is rewritten here to demonstrate the writing of member functions outside the class definition.

```
class StockItem
{
    private:              // data members
        int   itemCode;
        char  itemDescription[20];
        int   itemQuantity;
        float itemUnitPrice;
    public:
         void readData();     // prototypes of member functions
         void displayData();
};

 void StockItem :: readData()
 {
     cout << "\n\nEnter particulars of a Stock item\n\n";
     cout << "Enter item code          : ";
     cin >> itemCode;
     cout << "Enter item description : ";
```

```
        cin  >> itemDescription;
        cout << "Enter item quantity     : ";
        cin  >> itemQuantity;
        cout << "Enter item unit price   : ";
        cin  >> itemUnitPrice;
    }

    void StockItem :: displayData()
    {
        cout << "\n\nParticulars of a Stock item are\n\n";
        cout << "Enter item code         : ";
        cout << itemCode << endl;
        cout << "Enter item description : ";
        cout << itemDescription << endl;
        cout << "Enter item quantity     : ";
        cout << itemQuantity << endl;
        cout << "Enter item unit price   : ";
        cout << itemUnitPrice << endl;
    }
```

A member function defined inside the class is by default inline function except those functions involving loops. However, when a member function is defined outside the class definition it is treated as a normal function. If the developer wants a member function to be inline, then one has to make it inline explicitly.

2.10.6 Making Member Function Defined Outside Class Inline

C++ provides features where member functions can be defined outside the class definition, and still they can be made inline. The syntax for doing so is

```
inline ReturnType
ClassName::memberFunctionName(formalArguments)
{
    // body of the function
}
```

The class *StockItem* is rewritten once again here to demonstrate the writing of member functions outside the class definition.

```
class StockItem {
   private:                    // data members
      int   itemCode;
      char itemDescription[20];
      int   itemQuantity;
      float itemUnitPrice;
   public:
      void readData();    // prototypes of member functions
      void displayData();
};
inline void StockItem :: readData() {
    cout << "\n\nEnter particulars of a Stock item\n\n";
    cout << "Enter item code         : ";
```

```
        cin  >> itemCode;
        cout << "Enter item description : ";
        cin  >> itemDescription;
        cout << "Enter item quantity    : ";
        cin  >> itemQuantity;
        cout << "Enter item unit price  : ";
        cin  >> itemUnitPrice;
    }
    inline void StockItem :: displayData() {
        cout << "\n\nParticulars of a Stock item are\n\n";
        cout << "Enter item code        : ";
        cout << itemCode << endl;
        cout << "Enter item description : ";
        cout << itemDescription << endl;
        cout << "Enter item quantity    : ";
        cout << itemQuantity << endl;
        cout << "Enter item unit price  : ";
        cout << itemUnitPrice << endl;
}
```

2.10.7 Classes, Objects and Memory

You may be having this impression that each object created from a class contains separate copies of that class's data and member functions. This may seem to be a good approximation in the beginning as it emphasizes that objects are complete, self-contained entities, created using the class definition.

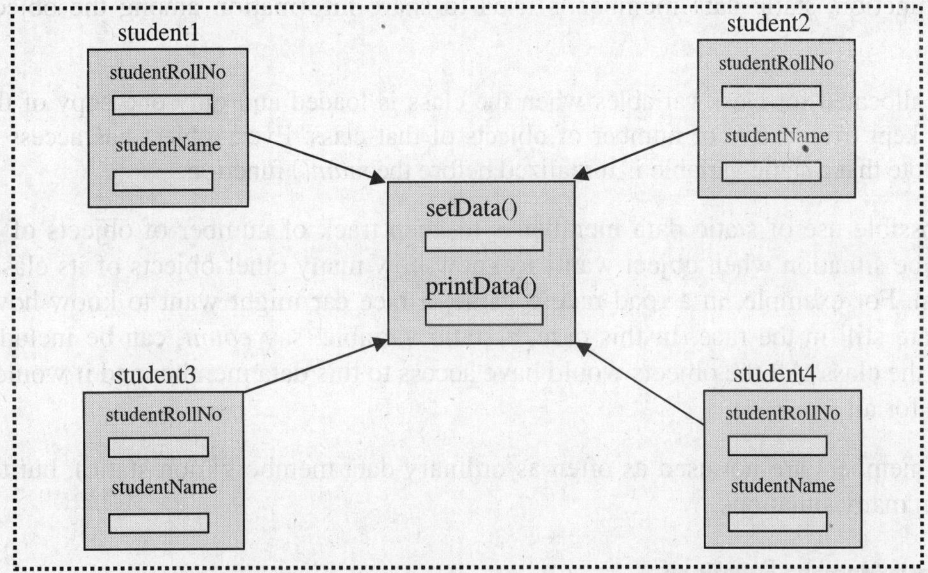

Figure 2.16: Representation of objects in memory

However, the things are not that simple. In fact, each object has its own copy of data and on contrary; all the objects use the same member functions. The member functions are placed in the memory only once and it happens when the class definition is loaded. This makes sense since there is no point in duplicating all the member functions in a class every time a new object is created, since functions for each object are identical. The data members, however, will hold different values, so there must be separate instance of each data member for each object.

Therefore, data is placed in memory when each object is created, so there is a separate set of data for each object.

Suppose we have created four objects of class *StudentType* using following statement

```
StudentType student1, studen2, student3, student4;
```

The memory view of these objects will look like as shown in Figure 2.16.

2.10.8 Static Members

2.10.8.1 Static Data Members

There can be data members that are common to all objects, whereas there can be data members that belong to an individual object. The data members common to all objects are known as *class variables* and are declared with *static* modifier. The static data member is useful when all the objects of the same class must share a common piece of information. A member variable defined as static has characteristics similar to a normal static variable. It is visible only within a class, but its lifetime is the entire program. It continues to exist even there are no objects of the class. However, while a normal static variable is used to retain information between function calls to a function, static data member is used to share information among the objects of a class.

Memory is allocated for class variables when the class is loaded and only one copy of the class variables is kept irrespective of number of objects of that class. Every object has access to class variables. Note that a static variable is initialized before the *main()* function.

The one possible use of static data member is to keep track of number of objects of a class. There may be situation when object wants to know how many other objects of its class are in the program. For example, in a road-racing game, a race car might want to know how many other cars are still in the race. In this case, a static variable, say *count*, can be included as a member of the class. All the objects would have access to this data member and it would be the same count for all.

Static data members are not used as often as ordinary data members (non-static), but they are important in many situations.

2.10.8.2 Static Member Functions

Like, data members that are common to all objects, the member function can also be declared as *static*. Since static members (data members as well as member functions) are associated with the class, static member functions can access static data members only. In contrast non-static member functions can access non-static data members as well as static data members. The static member functions can be invoked using class name or object name.

A static member function is declared and defined by prefixing keyword *static* before the return type of the function.

2.10.9 The *const* Keyword and Classes

We know that the keyword *const* can be used as modifier with normal variables in order to prevent them from being modified. Likewise, *const* can be used with function arguments to prevent the function from modifying a variable passed to it by reference. In this section, we will see some uses of *const* in respect of class – *const on member functions, const on member function arguments* and *const on objects*. These concepts work together to provide some surprising benefits.

2.10.9.1 The *const* Member Functions

If a function that does not alter any data in the class or we want in the class design that a function should not be allowed to alter any data in the class, then it is more efficient to declare it as a *const* member function as follows:

The following statement declares a *const* function

```
ReturnType functionName(argList) const;
```

The following statement defines a *const* function

```
ReturnType functionName(argList) const
{
    // . . .
}
```

Note that the *const* qualifier is appended after the function header in both declaration and definition. The compiler will flag an error if the function attempts to alter the data member.

The following code segment shows how this works.

```
class Test
{
    private:
        int x;
        int y;
    public:
        void func1()        // non-const member function
        {
            x += 5;         // OK
            y -= 10;        // OK
        }
        void func2() const // const member function
        {
            x -= 5;         // ERROR: can't modify a data member
            y += 10;        // ERROR: can't modify a data member
        }
};
```

2.10.9.2 The *const* Member Function Arguments

For normal variables, we know that if an argument is passed by reference to a function and you don't want the function to modify, the argument should be made *const* in the function declaration (and definition). The same is true for member functions of a class.

The following code segment shows how this works.

```
class ComplexNumber
{
    private:
        float realPart;
        float imaginaryPart;
    public:
        //. . . other member functions
        void add(const ComplexNumber& n1,const ComplexNumber& n2) {
            realPart = n1.realPart;
            imaginaryPart = n1.imaginaryPart;
            realPart += n2.realPart;
            imaginaryPart += n2.imaginaryPart;
        }
};
```

2.10.9.3 Mutable Data Members

To allow a class data member to be modified even though it is the data member of a *const* object, we can declare the data member as *mutable*. A mutable data member is a member that is never *const*, even when it is a data member of a *const* object. A mutable member can always be updated, even in a *const* member function. To declare a data member as a mutable data member, the keyword mutable must precede the declaration.

2.10.10 Friends of a Class

The concepts of encapsulation and data hiding demands that non-member function should not be able to access an object's private or protected data. The policy is simple — if you are not a member, you cannot get it. However, there may be some situations when such rigid discrimination leads to considerable inconvenience. Such inconvenience can be overcome to some extent by allowing non-members of a class to gain access to its data members. This is possible by making non-members as friends of a class.

Consider a situation, where you want a function to operate on objects of two or more classes in order to manipulate their private data. One possible solution is to make this function member function of every class. The other alternative, and better in design, is to define the function as global function and make it friend of the class so that it can gain access to class's private data.

For making friends, the following situation can arise:

- Global function (a function that is not member of any class) as friend of a class.
- Member function of a class as friend of another class
- Class as a friend of another class.

2.10.10.1 Global Function as Friend of a Class

The syntax for declaring a global function as friend of another class is

```
class TestClass1 {
        private:
                //. . .
        public:
                // . . .
        friend ReturnType functionName( argList );
}
```

A friend function has following characteristics:

- It can be declared in public or private section of the class without affecting its meaning.
- It is not in the scope of the class to which it has been declared as friend.
- It cannot access the members directly. To access members, it uses *object* and *dot* operator.
- It takes objects of classes as arguments.

2.10.10.2 Member Function of a Class as Friend of another Class

The syntax for declaring member function of a class as a friend of another class is

```
class TestClass2 {
        private
                //. . .
        public:
                // . . .
        friend ReturnType className::funtionName(argList);
}
```

The member function, which you want to make a friend of another class, can only be defined after the definitions of both the classes.

2.10.10.3 Class as Friend of another Class

The syntax for declaring a class as a friend of another class is

```
class TestClass3 {
        private:
                //. . .
        public:
                // . . .
        friend class className;
}
```

2.10.11 Nested Classes

A class can be defined within another class. Such a class is called *nested class*. A nested class is a member of its enclosing class. The definition of a nested class can occur within a public, protected, or private section of its enclosing class. The name of a nested class is visible only in its enclosing class scope.

The following points must be taken into considerations while defining and using local classes:

- Nested classes can use member of its enclosing class.
- Nested classes cannot have static data members.
- Member functions can only be defined inside the local class.
- The enclosing class cannot access the private members of a nested class. However, by making the enclosing function as friend function makes it possible.

The following code gives an example of nested classes, where the *StudentType* class is enhanced to include date of birth of a student:

```
class StudentType
{
    private:
        int  studentRollNo;
        char studentName[20];
    public:
        class Date   // nested class
        {
            private:
                int day;
                int month;
                int year;
            public:
                // . . . member functions of Date class
        } dateOfBirth;
        // . . . member functions of StudentType class
};
```

2.10.12 Abstract Classes

These are the classes, which are not complete and cannot be used to create objects. These classes contain at least one pure virtual function. These classes are used as framework upon which new classes can be built to provide new functionality.

2.10.13 Container Classes

These are the classes, also known as *container types*, which are used to hold other objects. These classes are very helpful in managing resources required by the application. There is a rich collection of container classes supported by most of the modern C++ compilers in the form of Standard Template Library (STL). The STL not only contains container classes but also set of functions that can manipulate these container classes.

As mentioned earlier that the only difference between a structure and a class is that by default members of the structure are public where as the members of the class are private.

2.11 ARRAYS

Array is a collection of homogeneous data elements described by a single name, and each individual element of an array is referenced by a *subscripted* variable, formed by affixing to the array name a *subscript* or *index* enclosed in brackets. Array provides elegant and convenient way of processing collections of homogeneous data. The syntax for array declarations is

```
type arrayName[dim1][dim2] ...;
```

where *type* is the data type (built-in or user-defined), *arrayName* is the name of the array, and *dim1*, *dim2*, . . ., are dimension specifiers and they prescribe the size for the corresponding dimension.

When the array is declared, the individual elements of the array will get values according the storage class of the array. However, it is possible to initialize the elements of the array at the compilation time, by specifying the values of the individual elements in the array declaration itself. For example, the following declaration statement

```
int b[10] = { 12, 0, 14, -4, 7, 8, 10, 11, 9, 15 };
```

initialize element *b*[0] to 12, *b*[1] to 0, *b*[2] to 14, *b*[3] to –4, *b*[4] to 7, *b*[5] to 8, *b*[6] to 10, *b*[7] to 11, *b*[8] to 9, *b*[9] to 15.

What you can expect from the following declaration statement?

```
int b[10] = { 12, 0, 14, -4, 7 };
```

The first five elements gets values 12, 0, 14, –5, and 7 respectively; the rest gets value 0 as the elements of the partially initialized array initialized to 0, by default.

What you can expect from the following declaration statement?

```
int b[] = { 12, 0, 14, -4, 7 };
```

In this declaration statement, no number is supplied for the size of the array. In this case, the compiler counts the number of elements in the initialization list and fixes that as the array size.

What you can expect from the following declaration statement?

```
int a[6] = { 12, 0, 14, -4, 7, 15, -20, 22, 25, 100 };
```

The compiler will flag an error message as the initialization list contains more elements than the declared size.

The following segment shows the way two-dimensional arrays are initialized.

```
int a[5][5] = { { 0, 0, 0, 0, 0 },
                { 1, 1, 1, 1, 1 },
                { 2, 2, 2, 2, 2 },
                { 3, 3, 3, 3, 3 },
                { 4, 4, 4, 4, 4 } };
```

There is one outer set of braces, and five inner sets of braces separated from each other by a comma. In each inner set contains five values. The first set of inner braces consists of values for the first row (indexed as 0), the second set of inner braces consists of values for the second row (indexed as 1), and so on.

The following example shows the way an array of objects is initialized.

```
class ComplexNumber {
    private:
        float realPart;
        float imaginaryPart;
     public:
        ComplexNumber() {     //  zero argument constructor
           realPart = 0.0;
           imaginaryPart = 0.0;
        }
        // parametrized constructor
        ComplexNumber( float real, float imaginary ) {
           realPart = real;
           imaginaryPart = imaginary;
        }
        // member function to output complex number
        void displayComplexNumber() {
           cout << setiosflags ( ios::showpoint )
                << setprecision ( 2 ) << endl
                << realPart << " + j" << imaginaryPart << endl;
        }
};
ComplexNumber numbers[5] = { ComplexNumber(0,0),
                             ComplexNumber(1,1),
                             ComplexNumber(2,2),
                             ComplexNumber(3,3),
                             ComplexNumber(4,4)
                           };
```

As shown above, the initialization list contains appropriate set of constructors.

Since array represents a collection of values, so to input data into the individual elements and output individual elements of the array, we make use of looping statements.
When an array is to be passed as argument to a function, then in the function prototype as well as in the function definition, the corresponding formal argument must be specified as an array with empty pair of brackets.

However, in the function call, as actual argument only name of the array is specified along with size of the array as other actual arguments. This is illustrated in the following segment:

```
#include <iostream.h>
#define SIZE 10
void main()
{
    int a[SIZE] = {0,1,2,3,4,5,6,7,8,9};
    void display(int x[], int n);    // function prototype
```

```
    // . . .
    display(a,SIZE);
}
void display(int x[], int n)  // function definition
{
    cout << "\n";
    for(int i=0; i<n; ++i)
        cout << x[i] << "  ";
    cout << "\n";
}
```

2.12 INHERITANCE

Reusability and extensibility is among the most important features of object-oriented programming paradigm. It is always nice if we can reuse something that already exists instead of creating it afresh. The reusability offers following advantages:

- It saves time and effort.
- It reduces development cost of new software product.
- Increases reliability because the class is already tested and used many times.

Inheritance allows new class, *called derived class*, to be built from the existing and generalized class, called *base class*, instead of building from the scratch. New classes can be build by inheriting the general features of some given class and then adding specific features.
The derived class inherits all of the capabilities of the base class and can add refinements and extensions of its own.

2.12.1 Defining Derived Classes

The syntax for defining a derived class is

```
class DerivedClassName : AccessSpecifier BaseClassName
{
    . . . . .   // members of the derived class
    . . . . .
};
```

The *AccessSpecifier* is optional and can be *public*, *private* or *protected.* The default access specifier is *private*. The role of the access specifier is described below:

- **When *public* access specifier is used, the public members of the base class remain public members of the derived class. Similarly, the protected members of the base class remain protected members of the derived class.**
- **When *private* access specifier is used, the public and protected members of the base class become private members of the derived class.**
- **When *protected* access specifier is used, the public members of the base class become protected members of the derived class and protected members of the base class remain protected members of the derived class.**

2.12.2 Forms of Inheritance

The derived class inherits all of the features of the base class. Level of inheritance refers to length of its (derived class) path from the root (top base class).

Inheritance is classified into the following forms based on the levels of inheritance and interrelation among the classes involved in the inheritance process:

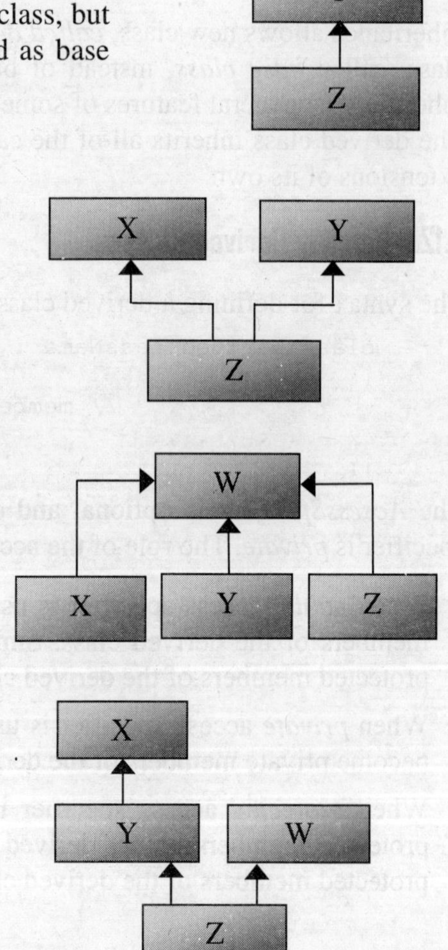

- ***Single Inheritance***

Derivation of a single class from only one base class. The class *X* is the base class and *Y* is the derived class. Further no class is derived from *Y*.

- ***Multilevel Inheritance***

Derivation of a class from another derived class. The class *X* is the top base class and *Y* is the derived class of *X*. Further class *Z* is derived from class *Y*. Here, class *Y* is not just derived class, but also base class for class *Z*. Further, class *Z* can be used as base class for further derivation.

- ***Multiple Inheritance***

Derivation of a class from two or more base classes. The class *X* and class *Y* are base classes and class *Z* is the derived class. Class *Z* inherits properties of both class *X* and class *Y*. Further, no class is derived from class *Z*.

- ***Hierarchical Inheritance***

Derivation of two or more classes from a single base class. Class *W* is the only base class and classes *X*, *Y* and *Z* are derived classes. Further, none of the class *X*, *Y* and *Z* is used as base class.

- ***Hybrid Inheritance***

Derivation of a class involving two or more forms of inheritance. In this case, multilevel and multiple inheritances are involved. Class *Y* is derived from class *X*. It is a single type of inheritance. Further, derived class *Y* acts as a base class. The class *Z* is derived from classes *Y* and *W*. This type of inheritance that uses more than one base class is called multiple inheritance.

- ***Multipath Inheritance***

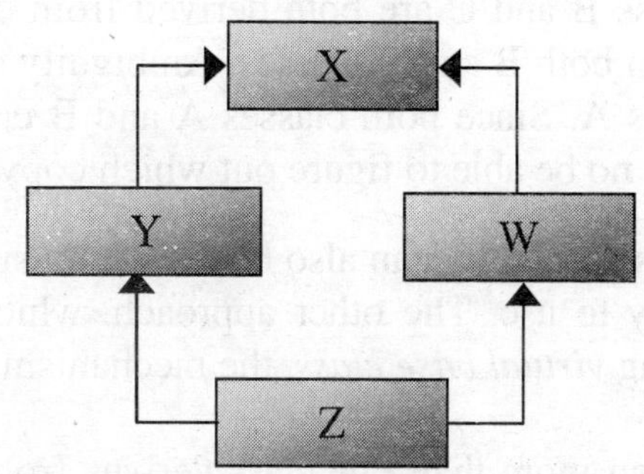

Derivation of a class from two or more classes that are derived from the same base class. Class *X* is the base class. Classes *Y* and *W* are derived from base class *X*. Further, class *Z* is derived from classes *Y* and *W*. Since, classes *Y* and *W* have inherited same members of *X*. In this case, an ambiguity is generated which in turn is resolved using virtual keyword. The virtual mechanism is explained later.

As for as possible, in the class design should restrict the inheritance to multilevel inheritance or at most multiple inheritance.

2.12.3 Possible Ambiguities in Inheritance

2.12.3.1 Ambiguity in Multiple Inheritance

When the base classes have members with same name, while the classes derived from these classes have no member with that name, then accessing that common member causes ambiguity. When an object of the derived class access the member of the base class, the compiler will not be able to figure out which of these members should be used.

This ambiguity can be resolved using scope-resolution operator to specify the class in which the member lies. Thus

```
className::Member
```

2.12.3.2 Ambiguity in Multipath Inheritance

When a class is derived from two or more base classes, and these base classes are derived from the same class. This creates a diamond shaped inheritance tree as shown figure 2.7.

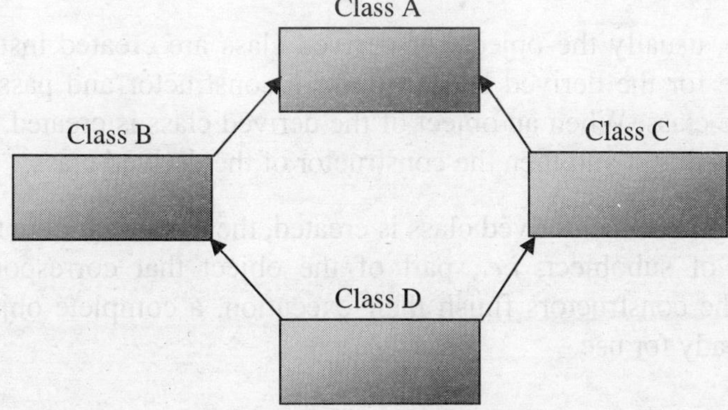

Figure 2.17: Diamond shaped inheritance tree

Class B and C are both derived from class A, and class D is derived by multiple inheritance from both B and C classes. Ambiguity occurs when an object of class D accesses a member of class A. Since both classes A and B contain a copy of the members of class A, the compiler will no be able to figure out which copy of the member, inherited from class A, to use.

This ambiguity can also be resolved using scope-resolution operator to specify the class whose copy to use. The other approach, which is more professional, is to handle this ambiguity is using *virtual base class,* the mechanism also called *virtual inheritance*.

When more than one class derives from the same class, and these derived classes are further used in the derivation, prefix the keyword *virtual* before the access specifier in the class derivation. With virtual derivation, only single shared copy of the base class subobject is inherited regardless of how many times the base class occurs within the derivation hierarchy. The shared base class subobject is called *virtual base class*.

Using virtual inheritance, the duplication of base class subobjects and the ambiguity to which the duplication gives rise are removed.

2.12.4 Overriding Member Functions

The derived class can have a member functions with same *name*, same *return type* and same *list of arguments*, as defined in the base class. In such a case, the member function of the derived class overrides the member function of the base class. The overriding function can make refinements or enhancements suited to the derived class. With overriding functions, the calls in the program work the same way for objects of both base and derived classes.

2.12.5 Order of Execution of Constructors

Constructors play an important role in initializing an object's data members and allocating required resources such a memory. The derived class need not have a constructor as long as the base class has a no-argument (default) constructor. However, if the base class has one or more constructors with arguments then it is mandatory for the derived class to have a constructor with arguments and pass the arguments to the base class constructor.

In case of inheritance, usually the objects of derived class are created instead of base class. Hence, it makes sense for the derived class to have a constructor and pass arguments to the constructor of the base class. When an object of the derived class is created, the constructor of the base class is executed first and then the constructor of the derived class.

Basically, when the object of the derived class is created, the constructors in the class hierarchy build their own part of subobject, *i.e.*, part of the object that corresponds to that class. Ultimately when all the constructors finish their execution, a complete object of the derived class is in place and ready for use.

The order of execution of constructors is always as following:

1. *Base class constructor*. If there is more than base class, the constructors are executed in the order the base classes appear in the class derivation list, not in the order in which they are listed in the member initialization list. However, if there is a virtual base class in the class derivation list, its constructor will be executed first irrespective of its position the derivation list.
2. *Member class object constructor*. If there is more than one member class object, the constructors are executed in the order the objects are declared in the class, not in the order in which they are listed in the member initialization list.
3. *Derived class constructor*.

As a general rule, the derived class constructor should never assign a value to the base class data member directly, but rather pass the value to the appropriate base class constructor. Otherwise, the implementation of two classes becomes *tightly coupled*, and it can be more difficult to modify or extend the base class implementation correctly. It is our responsibility, as the base class designed, to provide appropriate set of base class constructors.

The following points must be kept in mind about constructors in relation to inheritance.

- If no constructor is defined in a class, the compiler inserts no-argument constructor with empty body, *i.e.*, constructor of type

```
className() { }
```

- If a class contains parameterized constructor(s), the compiler will not insert no-argument constructor even if it is not defined in the class. In this case, if you want to use no-argument constructor, you have to define yourself.
- In case of multiple inheritance, the constructors are invoked in the order of derivation. However, if a class is virtually derived, its constructor will be invoked first irrespective of its position the derivation.
- If a base class has a parameterized constructor, then the derived class must make an explicit call to the base class constructor and pass the required parameter.

2.12.6 Order of Execution of Destructors

Unlike constructors, destructors in the class hierarchy are invoked in the reverse order of constructor invocation. The destructor of that class, whose constructor was executed last, while building the object of derived class, will be executed first whenever the object of the derived class goes out of scope.

Basically, when the object of the derived class goes out of scope, the destructors in the class hierarchy destroy their own part of sub object, *i.e.*, part of the object that corresponds to that class. Ultimately when all the destructors finish their execution, complete object of the derived class is destroyed.

If the destructors are missing in any class in the class hierarchy, then nothing is done to subobject that corresponds to that class.

However, if the object of the derived class is created dynamically using the *new* operator, then it must be destroyed explicitly using the *delete* operator.

2.13 OPERATOR OVERLOADING

Operator overloading is one of the exciting features of C++ and it aims to make user-defined data types behave much like built-in data types. Like built-in data types, operator overloading facilitates the use of most of the operations permissible on user-defined data types. These operations include input/output, arithmetic operations, comparisons and assignment. This means that C++ has the facility to provide the operators new meanings as per user-defined data type. This mechanism of giving new meanings to an operator is known as *operator overloading*.

It is important to note that the semantics of an operator can be extended but its syntax can't be changed. This precisely means that the rules that govern its use such as number of operands, precedence and associatively cannot be changed.

2.13.1 Defining Operator Overloading

To give an additional meaning to an operator, we must specify what it means in relation to the class to which the operator is applied. This is done with the help of a special function, called *operator function*, which describes the task.

The general syntax for overloading an operator is

```
[friend] ReturnType ClassName :: operator op ( argList )
{
    . . . . .
    // function body defining the task
    . . . . .
}
```

where *op* is the operator being overloaded and *argList* is the list of arguments for the operator that may be empty.

Operator function is either non-static member function or friend function. The basic difference between them is that a friend function will have only one argument for unary operators and two for binary operators while a member function has no argument for unary operators and only one for binary operators. This is because that an object that is used to invoke a member function is passed explicitly and therefore is available for the member function. This is not the case for friend function. Arguments can be passed either by value or by reference.

The process of overloading involves the following steps:

- Create a class that defines a data type that is to be used for overloading an operator.
- Declare the *operator function op(argList)* in the public part of the class. It can be a member function or friend function.
- Define the operator function to implement the required operation.

Overloaded operator functions can be invoked in following ways:

Member Functions	Friend Functions
For unary operators	*For unary operators*
`op operand` or `operand op`	`operator op(operand)`
For binary operators	*For binary operators*
`operand1 op operand2`	operator op (operand1, operand2)
and will be interpreted as	
`operand1.operator op(operand2)`	

When both the member functions and friend functions are used then standard argument matching is applied to resolve the ambiguity.

2.13.2 Rules for Overloading Operators

The following are some restrictions that must be observed while overloading operators:

- Only existing operators can be overloaded. New operators cannot be created.
- The overloaded operator must have at least one operand of user-defined data type.
- We cannot change the meaning of the operator for their behaviour for the built in data types. This precisely means that, for example, we cannot make the plus '+' to subtract one value from the other.
- The overloaded operators follow the syntax rules of the original operators. They cannot be overridden.
- The following operators cannot be overloaded.

Table 2.1: Operators that cannot be overloaded

Operator	Description
sizeof	Size of operator
.	Membership operator
.*	Pointer-to-member operator
::	Scope resolution operator
:?	Conditional operator

- Friend function cannot be used to overload the following operators, however, the member functions can be used.

Table 2.2: Operators where a friend function cannot be used

Operator	Description
=	Assignment operator
()	Function call operator
[]	Subscripting operator
–>	Class member access operator

- Unary operators overloaded by means of a member function takes no parameter and return no value, but overloaded by means of friend function take one parameter of its class and return a value.
- Binary operators overloaded by means of a member function take single parameter and return a value, but overloaded by means of friend function take two parameters of its class and return a value.

2.14 POLYMORPHISM

Polymorphism is another important feature of object-oriented programming. Polymorphism is a combination of two words *poly* and *morphism*. The word *poly* means *many* and the word *morphism* means *forms*. Thus, *polymorphism* means *many forms*. More formally, polymorphism can be defined as a technique that allows defining various forms of a single function that can be shared by various objects to perform the operations.

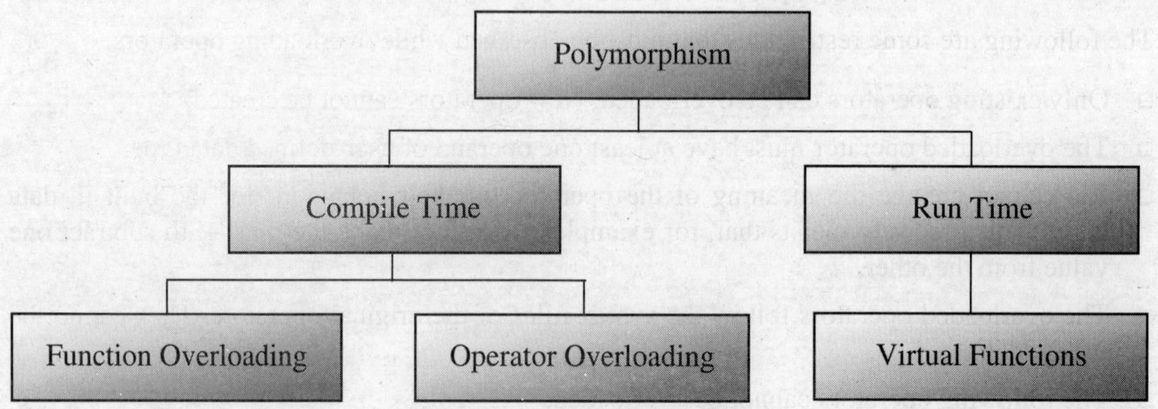

Figure 2.18: Polymorphism in C++

We have already seen how concept of polymorphism is implemented using overloaded operators and functions. The overloaded functions are selected for call by matching the arguments, both in number and type, also called as *signature* of a function. Note that the compiler knows the information about the number and type of arguments at the time of compilation, therefore, the compiler is able to select the appropriate function for a particular call at the compile time itself. This is called *early binding* or *static binding*. It is *early* in the sense that a function definition is bound to its call at the compile time and *static* in the sense that this binding cannot be changed at execution time.

There have been situations, where it is more appropriate that member function could be selected while the program is executing. At execution time, when it is known what objects are under consideration, the appropriate version of member is invoked. This is known as *run time polymorphism*. Since, the function is linked with a particular object after the compilation, *i.e.*, during program execution, the process is called *late binding* or *dynamic binding*. It is *late* in the sense that a function definition is bound to its call at the execution time and *dynamic* in the sense that this binding can be changed at execution time.

2.14.1 Concept of Binding

Binding is the process of resolving the function call, *i.e.*, linking the function call to its definition. The binding can take place at either of the following stages:

- Binding at compilation time and is known as *early binding* or *static binding*.
- Binding at execution time and is known as *late binding* or *dynamic binding*.

Each of these types of bindings is further explained in the following sections.

2.14.1.1 Early (Static) Binding

The information about the number and type of arguments is available the compiler at the time of compilation. Therefore, the compiler is able to select the appropriate function for particular call at the compile time itself. This is called *early binding* or *static binding*. It is *early* in the sense that a function definition is bound to its call at the compile time and *static* in the sense that this binding cannot be changed at execution time.

2.14.1.2 Late (Dynamic) Binding

There have been situations, where it is more appropriate that member function could be selected while the program is running. At run time, when it is known what objects are under consideration, the appropriate version of member is invoked. This is known as *run time polymorphism*. Since, the function is linked with a particular class after the compilation, *i.e.*, during program execution, the process is called *late binding* or *dynamic binding*. It is *late* in the sense that a function definition is bound to its call at execution time and *dynamic* in the sense that this binding can be changed at execution time.

Run time polymorphism is achieved using following steps:

- Preceding the member function with keyword *virtual* in the base class.
- Accessing the member function through a pointer of a base class.

2.14.2 Virtual Functions

A member function whose function declaration is preceded by *virtual* keyword is known as a virtual function. These functions are defined in a base class in public section and they provide a mechanism by which derived classes can override it. These functions are bound dynamically.

The syntax for defining a member function as a virtual function is

```
virtual ReturnType FunctionName( agruments )
{
    . . . . .
    . . . . . // body of the virtual function
    . . . . .
}
```

At run time, it allows to decide which overridden form of the function to used based on the type of object pointed by the base pointer rather than the type of pointer.

2.14.3 Pure Virtual Functions

Virtual functions normally serves as a framework for the future design of the class hierarchy as they can be overridden in the derived classes. In many cases, these virtual functions are declared without any body, *i.e.*, they don't have any definition. Such virtual functions are called *pure virtual functions*. These functions are also called *do-nothing* functions. The syntax for defining a pure virtual function is

```
virtual ReturnType FunctionName ( agruments ) = 0;
```

Any derived class of a base class containing pure virtual functions must either define these functions or re-declare them as pure virtual functions.

It is not possible to define body of a pure virtual function in class template, however, it can be defined outside the class template.

2.14.4 Virtual Destructors & Polymorphism

A problem can occur when using polymorphism to process dynamically allocated objects of a class of hierarchy. If an object with a non-virtual destructor is destroyed explicitly by applying a *delete* operator to a base class pointer to the object, the base class destructor, matching the pointer type, is called on the object. This occurs regardless of the type of fact that each class's destructor has a different name.

The simple solution to this problem is that you declare the base-class destructor as *virtual*. This makes all derived class destructors virtual even they do not have the same name as the base class destructor. Now, if an object in the hierarchy is destroyed explicitly by applying a *delete* operator to a base class pointer to the derived class object, the destructor for the appropriate class is invoked. Remember that when a derived class object is destroyed, the base class part of the derived class object is also destroyed — the base class destructor automatically executed after the derived class destructor.

- If a class has *virtual* functions, provide a *virtual* destructor, even if one is not required for the class. Classes derived from this class may contain destructors that must be called properly.

- When a destructor in a base class is declared as *virtual*, the destructors of all the derived classes, down the line, in the class hierarchy automatically become *virtual*.
- Constructors cannot be *virtual*. Declaring a constructor as a virtual is a syntax error. The reason why constructors cannot be virtual is that virtual mechanism works on objects, and an object exists only after the successful execution of the constructor.

2.15 TEMPLATES

Templates are one of the C++'s most powerful features for software reuse. Templates enable us to specify, with a single code segment, an entire range of related (overloaded) functions — called *template functions*; or an entire range of related classes — called *template classes*.

We can write a single *function template* to sort an array and then C++ compiler will generate separate functions that will sort an array of *int*, sort an array of float, sort an array of double, etc.

Likewise, we can write a single *class template* for a stack class and then C++ compiler will generate separate classes such as stack of *int* class, stack of float class, stack of string class, etc.

2.15.1 Function Templates

Note that overloaded functions are normally used to perform similar kind of operations on different types of data. However, if the operations are same, they can be performed in more compact and convenient way using function templates.

The programmer writes a single function template definition. Based on the argument types in the function call, the compiler generates separate object code to handle each call appropriately. The syntax of function template is

```
template < class T1, class T2, ...>
DataType FunctionName(arguments of type T1, T2, ... )
{
   //local variables of type T1, T2, or any other type
   //function body, operating on variable of type T1, T2
   //any other variables
}
```

All function templates begin with the keyword *template* followed by a list of formal arguments to the function template enclosed in angle brackets where each formal argument must be preceded by the keyword *class*.

The following examples illustrate this concept:

```
1.template <class T>

2.template <class T1, class T2>

3.template <class T, int intArg>

4.template <class T1, class T2, float floatArg>
```

The formal arguments of a template definition are used in the same way as built-in types or user-defined types. They can be used to specify formal argument(s) for the function, to declare variables within the function, to specify the return type of the function. The function definition follows and is defined like any other function.

2.15.2 Overloading Template Functions

A template function can be overloaded either by another template function or normal function. In such case the compiler uses overloading resolution to call the proper function.

The compiler performs a matching process to determine what function to call when a function call is encountered in the source code. This is done in the following order:

1. At first step, the compiler tries to find a match where the function name and argument types match perfectly with those of the function call, i.e. call the normal function that has an exact match.

2. If first step fails, then in the second step, the compiler checks if any function template is available that can be used to generate a template function with a precise match of function name and argument types. If such a function template is found, the compiler generates and uses the appropriate template function.

3. And, if the second step also fails, then the compiler flags an error message.

2.15.3 Class Templates

We know that stack is a data structure that works on the principle of Last-In-First-Out (LIFO) principle. The items in the stack are inserted (pushed) and removed (poped) in a manner that is independent of the type of the items. But when it comes to actually implementing a stack, the data type of the items must be specified. Therefore, if we want to have a stack class that could handle all the data types, then we would have to define a stack class generically and then instantiating classes that are type-specific. The class templates in C++ provide this capability. The syntax of class template is

```
template < class T1, class T2, ... >
class className
{
    //class member specification with type T1, T2
    //wherever appropriate
}
```

All class templates begin with the keyword template followed by a list of formal parameters to the class template enclosed in angle brackets where each formal parameter must be preceded by the keyword *class* or type name.

If the member functions are defined outside the class body, then we have to mention the template header before each member function.

2.16 EXCEPTION HANDLING

Exception handling is another powerful feature of C++ that enables the programmer to write clearer, robust, and fault-tolerant programs.

Recall that it is very rare that the program works correctly first time. It may have *errors* (*bugs*) in it. These bugs can be classified as either *syntax errors* or *logical errors*. The cause of syntax errors is incorrect use of language constructs, whereas the cause of logical errors is the poor understanding of the solution procedure. The syntax errors are caught by the compiler where as the logical errors can be tracked and fixed (corrected) by carefully debugging the program.

There is another kind of problem that can cause your program to fail. This problem is known as *exception.* Exceptions are basically runtime anomalies or unusual conditions that the program may encounter during execution. Examples include division by zero, attempting to access an array element outside array index bound, running out of memory, etc. When program encounters such a situation, the program may terminate abnormally in the absence of error handling mechanism.

Exception handling is designed for dealing with synchronous errors such as an attempt to divide by zero (that occurs as the program executes the divide instruction). With exception handling, before the program executes the divide instruction, it checks the denominator and throws (issues) an exception if the denominator is zero.

Exception handling is not designed to deal with asynchronous errors such as disk I/O completions, network message arrivals, mouse clicks, and the like; these are best handled through other means, such as interrupt processing.

Exception handling is used in situations in which the system can recover from the error causing the exception. The recovery procedure is called an *exception handler*. Exception handling is typically used when the error will be dealt with by a different part of the program (i.e., a different scope) from that which detected the error. The program that carries on interactive dialog with a user should not use exceptions to process input errors.

Exception handling is especially appropriate for situations in which the program will not be able to recover, but needs to provide orderly cleanup and then terminates gracefully.

Exception handling helps improve a program's fault tolerance. It becomes more pleasant to write error-processing code, so programmers are more likely to provide it. It also becomes possible to catch exceptions in a variety of ways such as by the type or even by specifying that exceptions of any type are to be caught.

The mechanism of exception handling involves the following steps:

1. Find the problem (*Hit the exception*).
2. Inform that an error has occurred (*Throw the exception*).
3. Receive the error information (*Catch the exception*).
4. Take corrective actions (*Handle the exception*).

The style of exception handling varies in nature and amount depending on the language and the application. Commercial software products tend to contain for more error-handling code that casual software product.

The C++ language exception handling mechanism is built upon three keywords: *try*, *throw* and *catch*. The keyword *try* is used to preface the block of statement that may generate exception(s). This block of statements is known as *try block*. When an exception is detected, it is thrown using keyword *throw* in the try block. A *catch block* that is defined by prefacing a block of statement with *catch* keyword, catches the exception thrown by the throw statement in the try block, and handles it appropriately.

Following program skeleton shows a program structure with exceptional handling features.

```
void main()
{
   . . . . .
   try {
        . . . . .                   // statements which can cause,
        . . . . .                   // detect and throw an exception
        throw exception;
        . . . . .
   } catch (DataType argument) {
        . . . . .                   // statements that handles
        . . . . .                   // the exception
   }
   . . . . .
}
```

As soon as the *try block* throws an exception, the program control leaves the try block and enters the catch block. Note that exceptions are objects used to transmit information about a problem. If the type of the object thrown matches the data type of the *argument* in the catch statement, then catch block is executed for handling the exception. If they do not match, the program is aborted with the help of *abort()* function which is invoked by default. When no exception is detected, the control goes to the statement immediately after the catch block, *i.e.*, catch block is skipped.

There are many situations when the functions called from within try block throw exceptions. The point at which exception is thrown is called *throw* point. Once an exception is thrown to catch block, control cannot return to the throw point.

```
DataType functionName( formal argument list ) {
     . . . . .          // statements which can cause,
     . . . . .          // detect and throw an exception
     throw exception;
     . . . . .
}
void main()
{
     . . . . .
     try {
         . . . . .
         functionName(actual argument list);
         . . . . .
     } catch (DataType argument) {
         . . . . .                // statements that handles
         . . . . .                // the exception
     }
     . . . . .
}
```

The *catch block* immediately follows *try block*, irrespective of the location of the throw point.

There may situations where it may not be possible to anticipate the possible type of exceptions. In such situations it will not be possible to write separate catch handlers to catch them. What we can do is that we can write a catch handler that can catch all exception instead of catching an exception of particular type.

This is achieved by defining the *catch* statement using three ellipses as follows:

```
catch (...)
{
      . . . . .
      // statements for handling all exception
      . . . . .
}
```

It may be good idea to use the *catch(. . .)* as a default statement along other catch handlers that it can catch all those exceptions which are not handled explicitly.

The *catch(. . .)* handler must be placed last in the list of handlers. Placing it before other catch handlers would prevent those blocks from catching exceptions.

It is also possible to restrict a function to throw only certain specified exceptions. This is achieved by adding a throw list clause to the function prototype/definition. The general form of using an exception specification is:

```
DataType functionName(arg-list) throw (exceptions-list)
{
    . . . . .              // function body
    . . . . .
}
```

Throwing any other type of exception will cause abnormal program termination. If we wish to prevent a function from throwing any exception, we may do so by making the exception-list empty as shown below:

```
DataType functionName(arg-list) throw ()
{
    . . . . .              // function body
}
```

2.17 STANDARD TEMPLATE LIBRARY

Besides maintainability and understandability, another great promise of object orientation is reuse, reuse, and reuse. As mentioned earlier, using templates we can write generic functions, or generic classes that support all data types. In addition, C++ language includes a Standard Template Library (STL) of many reusable components. **Alexander Stepanov** and **Meng Lee** at Hewlett-Packard developed the STL library. It is based on their research in the field of generic programming, with significant contribution from **David Musser**. STL contains several functions and operators that help the programmer develop complex programs rapidly. The programmers only need to include appropriate header file in their program file.

The STL is now widely used and has been accepted as part of the C++ standard. All famous compiler vendors provide support for STL in their C++ compilers.

2.17.1 Programming Model of STL

It is very easy to use STL once you understand how it is constructed and what elements it employs. Therefore, in this section we will have an overview of STL.

At the heart of the programming model of STL are three foundational items: *containers*, *algorithms*, and *iterators*. These items work in tandem to provide off-the-shelf solutions to a variety of programming problems.

2.17.1.1 Containers

Containers are the objects that hold other objects. STL has number of container classes that allow programmers to perform common tasks. These container classes support generic programming and can be used for handling data of different data types. Each container class defines a set of functions that may be applied to the container. For example, a *list* container includes functions that *insert*, *delete*, and *merge* elements; a *stack* container includes functions to *push* and *pop* values.

Containers are further classified as *sequence containers* and *associative containers*. In sequence containers, the elements are stored in a sequence and only can be retrieved in that sequence where as in associative containers the elements can be retrieved according to keys. In addition, STL provides three containers that are derived from sequence containers, and are known as *derived containers* or *container adapters*.

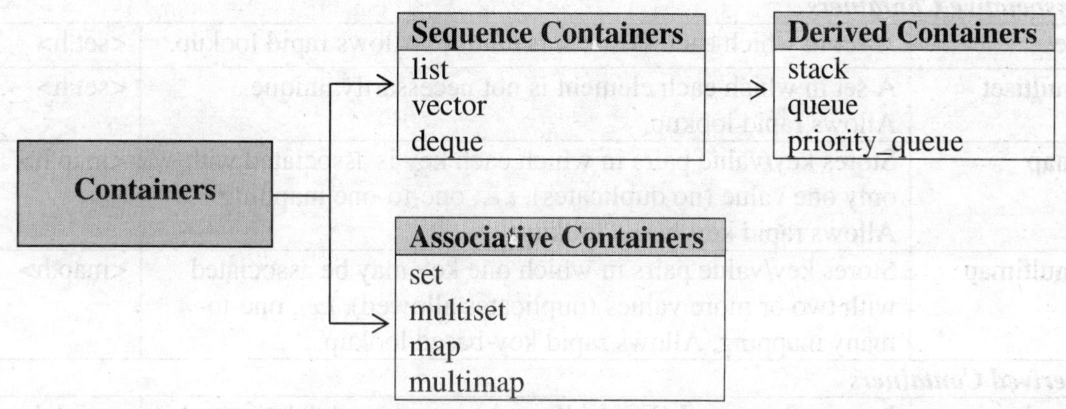

Figure 2.19: Classification of Containers

2.17.1.2 Algorithms

Algorithms act on containers. They provide the means by which you will manipulate the contents of the containers. Their capabilities include *initializing*, *sorting*, *searching*, and *transforming* the contents of containers. Many algorithms operate on a range of elements within a container. It is important to note that these algorithms are neither member functions nor friends of containers. These are standalone template functions. To use these algorithms, we must include header file *algorithm.h* in the program.

These algorithms, depending on the nature of operations they perform, can be categorized as follows:

- *Non-mutating algorithms* – algorithms that do not modify the container.
- *Mutating algorithms* – algorithms that modify the container.

Table 2.3: List of Containers, their description, and required header files

Container	Description	Header file
Sequence Containers		
list	A doubly linear list. Allows rapid insertions and deletion anywhere.	<list.h>
vector	A dynamic array. Allows rapid insertions and deletion at back. Allows direct access to any element.	<vector.h>
deque	A double-ended queue. Allows rapid insertions and deletion at front and back.	<deque.h>
Associative Containers		
set	A set in which each element is unique. Allows rapid lookup.	<set.h>
multiset	A set in which each element is not necessarily unique. Allows rapid lookup.	<set.h>
map	Stores key/value pairs in which each key is associated with only one value (no duplicates), *i.e.*, one-to-one mapping. Allows rapid key-based lookup.	<map.h>
multimap	Stores key/value pairs in which one key may be associated with two or more values (duplicates allowed), *i.e.*, one-to-many mapping. Allows rapid key-based lookup.	<map.h>
Derived Containers		
stack	Last-in-first-out (LIFO). Allows insertions and deletion only at one end, called *top*.	<stack.h>
queue	First-in-first-out (FIFO). Allows insertions at back and deletion from front.	<queue.h>
Priority_queue	A priority queue. Always keeps highest priority element as the first element of the queue.	<queue.h>

2.17.1.3 Iterators

Iterators are objects that allow to cycle through the contents of a container in much the same way that you would use a pointer to cycle through a linked list. Iterators are of five types — *random access*, *bidirectional*, *forward*, *input*, and *output*.

Table 2.4: Types of Iterators

Iterator	Access Allowed
Random Access	Stores and retrieve values. Elements can be accessed randomly.
Bidirectional	Stores and retrieve values. Elements can be accessed in forward and backward order.
Forward	Stores and retrieve values. Elements can be accessed only in forward direction.
Input	Retrieve, but not store, values. Forward moving only.
Output	Store, but not retrieve, values. Forward moving only.

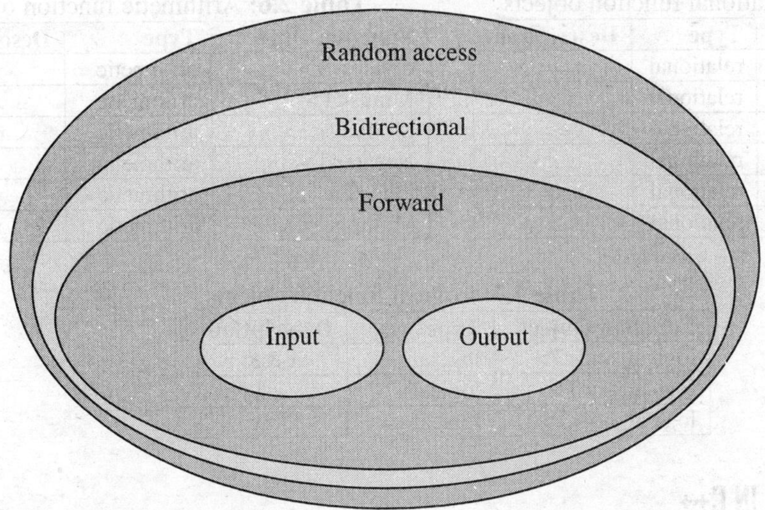

Figure 2.20: Functionality Venn diagram of Iterators

In general, an iterator that has greater access capabilities can be used in place of one that has lesser capabilities. For example, a forward iterator can be used in place of an input iterator.

Iterators are handled just like pointers. You can increment and decrement them. You can apply '*' operator to them. Iterators are declared using the *iterator* type defined by various containers.

The STL also supports *reverse iterators*. Reverse iterators are either bidirectional or random access iterators but move through a sequence in the reverse direction. Thus, if a reverse iterator points to the end of a sequence, incrementing that iterator will cause it to point one element before the end.

2.17.2 Function Objects

A function object is basically a function that has been wrapped in a class so that it looks like an object. This class has only one member function, the overloaded operator '()' and contains no data member. The class is created as template class so that it can be used with variety of data types.

These function objects are often used as arguments to certain containers and algorithms. For example, in the following statement

```
sort( a, a +10, greater<int>() );
```

the function object *greater<int>* is used as an argument in *sort()* algorithm to sort the first eleven elements contained in array named *a* in descending order.

The STL provides many predefined function objects for performing arithmetic and logical operations. To use these predefined function objects, include header file *functional.h* in your program file.

Table 2.5: Relational function objects

Function Object	Type	Description
equal_to<T>	relational	$x == y$
greater<T>	relational	$x > y$
greater_equal<T>	relational	$x >= y$
less<T>	relational	$x < y$
less_equal<T>	relational	$x <= y$
not_equal_to<T>	relational	$x != y$

Table 2.6: Arithmetic function objects

Function Object	Type	Description
divides<T>	arithmetic	x / y
Minus<T>	arithmetic	$x - y$
Modulus<T>	arithmetic	$x \% y$
Negate<T>	arithmetic	$-x$
Plus<T>	arithmetic	$x + y$
Multiplies<T>	arithmetic	$x * y$

Table 2.7: Logical function objects

Function Object	Type	Description
logical_and<T>	logical	$x \&\& y$
logical_or<T>	logical	$x \| y$
logical_not<T>	logical	$!x$

2.18 MEMORY USE IN C++

Let us understand what is going on in computer's main memory when running a C program. When a C++ program runs, the allocated memory to the program by the operating system is divided into several different sections/areas.

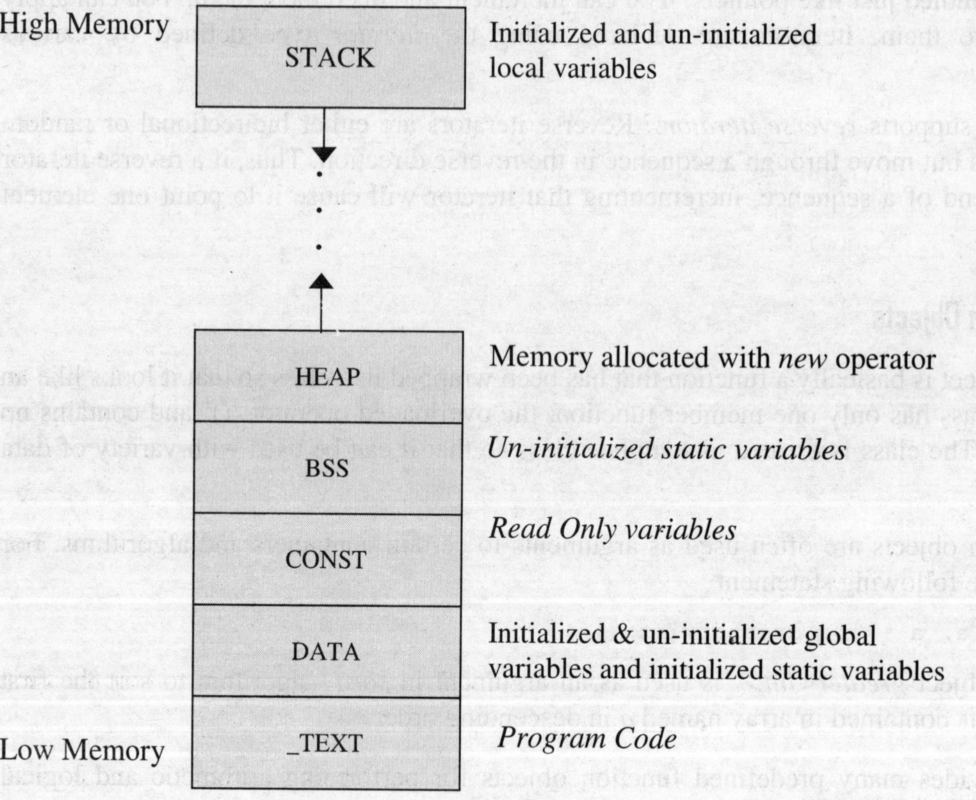

Figure 2.21: Use of Memory in a C++ Program

These sections/areas are — *code area*, *data area*, *stack area*, and *heap*.

Code Area — This is the first area, named *_TEXT*, where the program resides. This area, usually, is never changed when a program runs.

Data Area — This area is the second one and is further divided into three sections —

- First is named *DATA* that contains un-initialized global data, initialized global data, and initialized static data.
- Second is named *CONST* that contains read only data, *i.e.*, constants stored in variables.
- Third is named Block Started Segment (*BSS*) that contains un-initialized static data.

Stack Area — This is the area that is set up at the top of available memory and grows towards lower memory as it is filled.

Heap/Free Store — This area is located on the top of code and data area. It grows just like stack except it grows towards high memory rather than towards lower memory.

The C++ language runtime system automatically maintains stack for us, but the allocation of memory from heap and its use is programmer's responsibility. To allocate memory from heap, the *new* operator is used. Once the memory allocated to the program from heap is not required further in the program, it is returned to the heap using the *delete* operator.

2.19 POINTERS AND DYNAMIC MEMORY MANAGEMENT

2.19.1 World of Pointers

Pointers are one of the most important features of C++ language. Pointers, by most people, are regarded as one of the most difficult topics in C++. Let me tell you frankly, it is more a myth rather a fact. I would prefer to say that pointers are one of the most delicate aspects of C++ language, and you know delicate things need very careful handling. Therefore, pointers need very careful handling.

There are many reasons for using pointers; some of them are enumerated below:

- A pointer allows a function or a program to access a variable (better we say memory location) outside the preview of function or a program. In fact, using a pointer, your program can access any memory location in the computer's memory.
- Since using *return* statement, a function can only pass back a single value to the calling function, pointers allows a function to pass back more than one value by writing them into memory locations that are accessible to the calling function.
- Use of pointer increases makes the program execution faster.
- Using pointers, arrays and structures can be handled in more efficient way.

- Without pointers, it will be impossible to create complex data structures, such as *linked lists*, *trees* and *graphs*.
- To communicate with operating system about memory. For example, the operator *new* returns the location of free memory block by using a pointer and the operator *delete* returns the memory block pointed to by a pointer to the operating system.

In totality, we can say that the real power of C++ language lies in the judicious use of pointers. Therefore, every reader of C++ must learn and master the art of using pointers.

Computer's memory is organized as a linear collection of bytes or words. For Intel processors, memory is byte-organized whereas for most of the non-Intel processors, memory is word-organized. In byte-organized memory, each memory location is of one byte, whereas in word-organized, each memory location is of one word. Each memory location is assigned a unique number called *location number* or *address*.

We know that one byte is equal to 8 bits, whereas one word may be made up of two or more bytes. A word is a measure of the capacity of processor in terms of the size of operands that it can process (i.e. add, subtract, multiply, divide, compare, etc.) in single operation. When we say that a processor is a 16-bit processor, it means that its word size is 16-bits (2 bytes) and it can process 16-bit operands in single operations. For large size operands, it needs more operations.

A *memory cell* is either of one byte/word or more contiguous bytes/words. Each cell can store one value at a given time. The address of a cell is always the address of the first byte/word.

When you give a command to run a program, the operating system first finds a free block of requisite size from computer (main) memory, and then loads the program into that block. Even in that block, usually, the program's code is loaded in one part and the program's data in another part of the block. Each of the data operand is stored in a cell and the system associates each of the variables with these addresses.

In order to access the data operand either we use either variable name or we can use address of the memory cell. Since these addresses are simply positive integer numbers, they can also be assigned to some variables and stored in memory, like any other variable. Such a variable that holds an address is known as a *pointer*. A pointer is, therefore, nothing but a variable that contains address of another variable in memory. Since pointer is a variable, its value is also stored in memory in another address.

The actual address of a variable is a system dependent. During compilation and linking, addresses are assumed to be relative to some base address, usually 0. When the operating system loads the program in a free block, all the address are transformed with relative to address of the first memory location of the free block. Hence, we do not know the address of a variable. Therefore, a question arises — *how can we determine the address of a variable*? This is done with the help of *address of* operator (&).

Consider the following statement

```
ptr = &code;
```

It will assign the number address of variable *code* to the variable *ptr*.

The following restrictions must be observed carefully:

1. The address of operator can only be used with variables or an array element. The following are illegal use of *address of* operator:

   (*a*) `&1200` (pointing at constant expression)
   (*b*) `&(a/b)` (pointing at expression)

2. Pointer variable can be initialized only with the use of *address of* operator or by assigning the value of another compatible pointer variable. The following way of initializing a pointer variable *ptr* is illegal:

   ```
   ptr  = 1500;
   ```

   Though, the number 1500 happen to be the address of variable code.

2.19.1.1 Declaring and Initializing Pointers

Like other variables, the pointer variables are to be declared first in the declaration block to tell the compiler that to which kind of values these variables will be pointing. The syntax for declaring pointer variable is

```
type *ptrName;
```

where *type* is a *pre-defined* or *user-defined* data types and indicates that the pointer will point to the variables of that specific data type, and character '*' indicates that variable is a pointer variable. For example, the statement

```
int *ptr1;
```

declares a pointer variable *ptr1* that can point to an integer type variable.

The pointer variable(s) declaration can also be combined with the declaration of other variables, provided they are of same type. For example, the statement

```
int x, *ptrX;
```

declares an integer variable *x* and a pointer variable *ptrX*.

Once a pointer has been declared, it must be initialized prior to its use. It is important to note here that like other variables, a pointer variable will take a garbage value, which can be an address of any storage location. Therefore, if not properly initialized, a pointer may point to any location in memory including those locations where operating system is running, and your system may hang-up, *i.e.,* stop responding. Such un-initialized pointers are sometimes referred to as *dangling/wild pointers.*

2.19.1.2 Accessing a Variable Through Its Pointer

Once a pointer has been assigned the address of a variable, the question remains as how to access the value of the variable using the pointer. This is done by using operator * (asterisk), usually known as the *indirection* operator.

Consider the following statements

```
int *ptrX, x = 10, y;
    :
ptr_x = &x;
    :
y = *ptrX;
```

The declaration statement tells the compiler that *ptrX* is pointer variable that will point to an integer value, *x* is an integer variable and it also initializes the variable *x* with value 10, and y is another integer variable.

Note that writing the statements

```
ptrX = &x;
y = *ptrX
```

is equivalent to writing

```
y = *&x;
```

or for more clarity as

```
y = *(&x);
```

which in turn is equivalent to writing

```
y = x;
```

It is important to note that assignment of pointers and addresses is always done symbolically, by means of symbolic names. You cannot access the value stored at address 1098 by writing *1098. It will not work.

2.19.1.3 Type of Pointers

Based on the fact that whether a pointer variable holds the address of an integer, a float, or a character variable, the pointers are classified as *integer pointers*, *real pointers*, *character pointers*, and so on.

2.19.1.4 Pointer Arithmetic

The C++ language is very consistent in its approach to pointer arithmetic. The integration of pointers, arrays, and pointer arithmetic is one of the strengths of the C++ language. In this section, we will briefly describe the various operations permissible on pointers.

The following operations are permitted on pointers.

1. **Addition of a number to a pointer variable.**

   Suppose *p* is a pointer variable pointing to an element of integer type, then the statement

   ```
   p++;        or    ++p;
   ```

   increment the value of *p* by a factor of 2, so that it points to the next location that holds another value of integer type. This increment factor will be 1 for *character*, 4 for *long integer* and *float*, and 8 for *long float*. The statement

   ```
   p += i;
   ```

   where *i* is either a positive integer constant or an integer variable having positive value, increments *p* such that it points to the *i*th location beyond the location to which it is currently pointing.

2. **Subtraction of a number from a pointer variable.**

   Suppose *p* is a pointer variable pointing to an element of integer type, then the statement

   ```
   p--;        or    --p;
   ```

   decrement the value of *p* by a factor of 2, so that it now points to the location preceding the current location. The statement

   ```
   p -= i;
   ```

   where *i* is either a positive integer constant or an integer variable having positive value, decrements *p* such that it points to the *i*th location before the location to which it is currently pointing.

3. **Subtraction of one pointer variable from another.**

   One pointer variable can be subtracted from another provided both point to the same data type. The difference of the two indicates the number of bytes separating the corresponding elements.

In addition to these arithmetic operations, the pointer variables can be compared with one another, provided they are compatible i.e. point to the variables of same data type.

The following arithmetic operations on pointers are not permitted.

- Addition of two pointer variables.
- Multiplication of a pointer variable by a number.
- Division of a pointer variable by a number.

2.19.1.5 Pointer to a Pointer

As mentioned, a pointer is variable that holds the address of another variable. This concept can be further extended. We can have a variable that hold an address of a variable that in turn holds an address of another variable. This type of variable is known as a *pointer to a pointer*. The underlying concept is known as *double indirection*. This concept can be further extended to triple level, fourth level, and so on.

A pointer to a pointer will be declared as

```
int **ptr;
```

The value pointed to by a pointer to another pointer will be accessed as

```
**ptr;
```

A practical example of using pointers to pointers is when pointers are passed by address to a calling function.

The following skeleton of code demonstrates this:

```
void main()
{
    int *ptr1;
    // . . .
    func1( &ptr1, . . . );
}
void func1( int **ptr2, . . . ) {
    // . . .
    func2( &ptr2 );
}
void func2( int ***ptr3, . . .) {
    // . . .
}
```

and so on.

In the rest of the sections, we will extensively demonstrate the of use pointers. This is the area that is given a secondary treatment in most of the textbooks on C++ language. It is important to remember that pointers are the backbone of C++ language. Therefore every reader of C++ language must master them.

2.19.2 Memory Allocation

It is important to note that anything that needs to be executed (programs) or processed (data) must be loaded into memory before it can be executed or processed. Therefore, for every program to be executed or data to be processed, some memory must be allocated for them. The memory allocation can be done in two ways – *statically* and *dynamically*. Let us look at both the ways.

2.19.2.1 Static Memory Allocation

When you give a command to run your program, the operating system allocates a block of memory for your program, loads it from the secondary storage (Floppy disk, hard disk, CD or DVD, etc.) into that block and then initiates its execution. When the program finishes its execution, the memory occupied by the program is automatically released. It means that the memory requirements are determined prior to execution of your program, and thereafter your program neither can acquire more memory nor can release the free memory, if not required.

The above situations depicts a situation where the amount of memory required is known before hand, and the compiler then can determine the memory requirements for the data as well as the instructions. In such a situation, memory allocation is known as *static memory allocation.*

2.19.2.2 Dynamic Memory Allocation

Further, it is important to note that the memory requirements for the instructions are always fixed. However, there may be situation when the exact memory requirements for the data may not be known in advance or the data requirements may vary from one program execution to another program execution, *i.e.*, memory requirements for the data are dynamic.

Therefore, when the amount of memory is not known before hand for a particular data item(s), then it is allocated at the execution time, *i.e.*, when the program is running. In such a situation, memory allocation is known as *dynamic memory allocation.*

2.19.2.3 Heap/Free Store

As mentioned earlier, every program is provided with a pool of unallocated memory that it can utilize during execution. This pool of unallocated memory is known as *heap* or *free store.* Therefore, whenever the memory of requisite size (amount) is required by the program, it is taken from the free store, and when the previously allocated memory is not required further, it is returned back to the free store.

The memory requirements for the instructions (program code) are always fixed.

2.19.3 Dynamic Memory Management Operators

The C++ language provides following operators to perform dynamic memory management:

- ***new* operator** – for dynamic memory allocation.
- ***delete* operator** – for dynamic memory deallocation.

2.19.3.1 The *new* Operator

The *new* operator allocates the memory from the heap (free pool of memory) and returns a pointer to an appropriate type. The *new* operator is defined as

```
DataType * new  DataType [ size in integer ];
```

The use of *new* operator is illustrated in the following examples:

```
int * intPtr;
intPtr = new int[100];
```

It allocates a memory block of 200 bytes for 100 integers.

Similar statements will be used for other primitive data types.

```
struct date {
    int day;
    int month;
    int year;
};
date *ptrToDate;
ptrToDate = new date;
```

It allocates memory for one structure item of type *date*, *i.e.*, 6 bytes.

The *new* operator also permits the initialization of memory locations during allocation. The syntax for doing so is

```
DataType *ptrVar = new DataType ( InitialValue );
```

This is illustrated in following examples:

```
int *intPtr = new int(100);
```

This statement allocates memory for an integer number and initializes it with value 100. The address of the memory allocated memory is assigned to pointer variable *intPtr*.

```
float *floatPtr = new float(125.75);
```

This statement allocates memory for a float number (single precision real number) and initializes it with value 125.75. The address of the memory allocated memory is assigned to pointer variable *floatPtr*.

2.19.3.2 The *delete* Operator

The *delete* operator is a counterpart of *new* operator and it deallocates (releases) memory allocated by the new operator back to the heap (free poll of memory).

The syntax of *delete* operator is defined as

```
delete pointerVariable;
```

However, if the memory is allocated for an array holding objects, then delete operators must be used in either of the following forms:

```
delete arrayName[];      or      delete [] arrayName;
```

The reason is that if the empty pair of subscripts is not used, then destructor will be invoked only on the first object.

2.19.4 Possible Problems with Pointers

Pointers can be the source of mysterious and catastrophic program bugs. Common bugs related to pointers and memory management is *dangling/wild pointers*, *memory leaks*, and *allocation failures*. Each of these problems is discussed below. Every student must understand these carefully.

2.19.4.1 Problem of Dangling/Wild Pointers

The most common problem with pointers is that the programmer fails to initialize a pointer with a valid address. Such an initialized pointer, referred to as *dangling/wild pointer*, can end up pointing anywhere in memory that may include the program code itself or to the code of the operating system. If the programmer assign a value to such pointer, the value will overwrite the program or operating system instructions, and the computer program may show undesirable behaviour or may even crash, *i.e.*, stop responding. When the system stop responding, we say the system has hanged up and the only option left is to reboot the system. Therefore, care must be taken to initialize pointers with valid address.

2.19.4.2 Problem of Null Pointer Assignment

One particular situation that happens is when the pointer points to address 0, which is called NULL. For example, this may happen that if the pointer variable is declared as global since global variables are initialized to 0. Likewise, this can also happen for a local un-initialized pointer variable, particularly for local static variables, they are also initialized to 0.

When it happens, and no catastrophic situations had occurred, then the system will display a message "*Null pointer assignment*" on termination of the program. Try the following mini program.

```
// Program to illustrate the cause of NULL pointer assignment
#include<iostream.h>
int *intPtr;    // global pointer variable, initialized to 0
void main()
{
   *intPtr = 200;         //  write value on 0 address
   cout << "\nValue stored as address 0 = %d\n" << *intPtr;
}
```

2.19.4.3 Problem of Memory Leak

Another very serious problem with pointers is that of *memory leak*. Memory leak is a situation where the programmer fails to release the memory allocated at run time in a module. Note that when memory is allocated, a pointer variable is used to hold the address of the allocated block, however, when the module completes its execution, the pointer variable goes out of scope and there will be no way to reach that memory block. Therefore, care must be taken to release the allocated memory block in a module where memory was allocated. Look at the following program code.

```
//  Program skeleton to illustrate the cause of memory leak
#include <iostream.h>
void main() {
   void fun(void);          // function prototype
   fun();                   // function call
}
void fun() {                // function definition
   int *intPtr;
```

```
    //  allocate memory for 'n' integer numbers
    intPtr = new int[n];
    //   work on the allocated block
}
```

2.19.4.4 Problem of Allocation Failures

Allocation failure is a situation when the program through *new* operator request for a block of memory, and the operating system could not fulfill the request of the program because the sufficient memory may not be available in the free pool of memory. In that case, the *new* operator returns a NULL pointer indicating the allocation failure. Therefore, the programmer should take care of allocation failures and provide a safe exit in their programs on such failures. Look at the following program code.

```
// Program to illustrate the allocation failure, and
// the way it should be handled
#include<iostream.h>
void main()
{
    int *intPtr;
    //  allocate memory for 'n' integer numbers
    intPtr = new int[20];
    if ( intPtr == NULL )
    {
        cout << "\nUnable to allocate memory . . .\n";
        return;
    }
    //   work on the allocated block
    delete intPtr;    // release the memory
}
```

It is recommended that when you declare a pointer variable, initialize all un-initialized pointer variables to NULL. The reason is that assigning a value to such pointer is always safe, the only thing the system will generate a message *"NULL pointer assignment."*

2.20 DATA FILES

A data file is a collection of related records. For example, file containing records of all students in class; a file containing records of all employees of an organization; a file containing records of all items in a stock, etc. A record is a collection of related data-items, where a data item refers to a single unit of values. Examples of data items are *roll number*, *name*, *date of birth*, *sex*, and *class*, etc. The collection of *roll number*, *name*, *date of birth*, *sex*, and *class* data items of a particular student such as *1234*, *Surbhi*, *12/03/1993*, *F*, *9* constitutes a record. File organization refers to the way records are physically arranged on a storage device.

2.20.1 File Streams

The C++ I/O subsystem is designed to work with a wide variety of devices that includes keyboard, monitor, disks, tape drives, etc. The working principle (characteristics) of each of these devices is quite different. The C++ I/O subsystem is designed in such a way that it provides a uniform interface that is independent of the actual device being used. Thus, the programmer can write a C++ program that can receive input from, and send output to any device without bothering about the characteristics of device being used. This interface is called a *stream*.

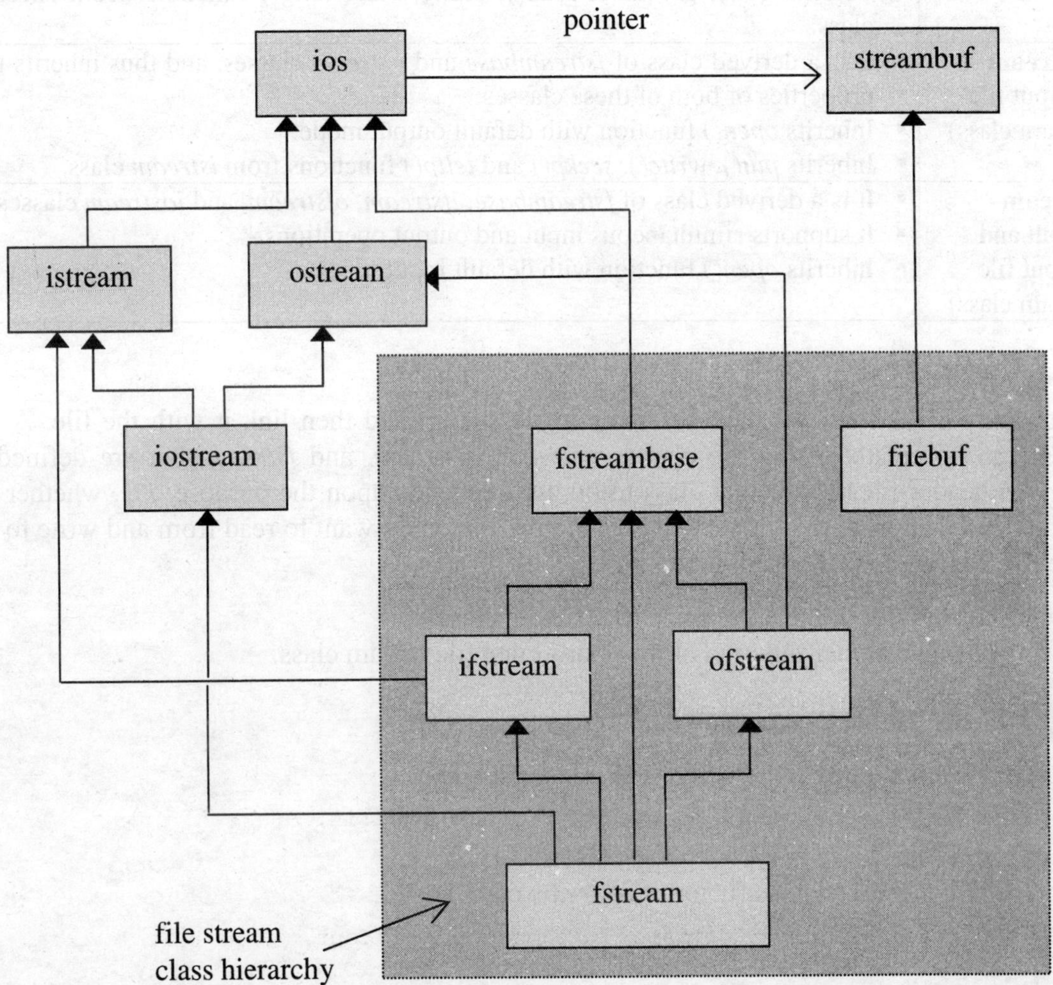

Figure 2.22: Hierarchy of file stream classes

Table 2.8: Description of File Stream Classes

Class Name	Brief Description
fstreambase (Base class for file streams)	▪ It is a base class for all file stream classes. Thus, supports operations common to file streams. ▪ Contains *open()* and *close()* function in addition to other member functions.
ifstream (input file stream class)	▪ It is a derived class of *fstreambase* and *istream* classes, and thus inherits the properties of both of these classes. ▪ Inherits *open()* function with default input mode. ▪ Inherits *get()*, *getline()*, *read()*, *seekg()* and *tellg()* functions from *istream* class.
ofstream (output file stream class)	▪ It is a derived class of *fstreambase* and *ostream* classes, and thus inherits the properties of both of these classes. ▪ Inherits *open()* function with default output mode. ▪ Inherits *put()*, *write()*, *seekp()* and *tellp()* functions from *istream* class.
fstream (input and output file stream class)	▪ It is a derived class of *fstreambase*, *ifstream*, *ofstream*, and *iostream* classes. ▪ It supports simultaneous input and output operations. ▪ Inherits *open()* function with default input mode.

2.20.2 Opening a File

For opening a file, first we have to create a file stream and then link it with the file. A file stream can be created using the classes *ifstream*, *ofstream*, and *fstream* that are defined in *fstream.h* header file. The actual class to be used depends upon the purpose, *i.e.*, whether we want to read data from the file or write data to the file or we want to read from and write to the same file. A file can be opened in two ways:

- Using constructor of the appropriate file stream class.
- Using *open()* member function of the appropriate file stream class.

2.20.2.1 Opening a File Using Constructor

Prototype of generalized constructor of *ifstream* class is

```
ifstream( const char *path, int mode = ios::in,
          int prot = filebuf::openprot );
```

Prototype of generalized constructor of *ofstream* class is

```
ofstream( const char *path, int mode = ios::out,
          int prot = filebuf::openprot );
```

Prototype of generalized constructor of *fstream* class is

```
fstream( const char *path, int mode = ios::in | ios::out,
         int prot = filebuf::openprot );
```

where *path* is filename with path information, however, if path information is omitted, file is considered to be in the working directory; *mode* is file opening mode; *prot* is access specifier with default value 'openprot' for read and write access permissions.

Table 2.9: File *mode* parameters

Parameter	Purpose
binary	Open file in binary mode. Default mode is text..
in	Open file for read only.
out	Open file for write only.
trunc	Delete the contents of the file if it exists.
app	Append to the end of file.
ate	Move the file pointer to the end-of-file on opening.
nocreate	Open fails if the file does not exist.
noreplace	Open file if file already exists.

Table 2.10: File *prot* parameters

Parameter	Access Permission
S_IREAD	Read permission.
S_IWRITE	Write permission.
S_IEXEC	Execute permission.

These parameters can be combined using bit-wise OR operator ('|').

2.20.2.2 Opening a File Using *open()* Member Function

The prototype of *open()* function is

```
void open( const char *path, int mode, int prot = filebuf::openprot );
```

where *path* is filename with path information, however, if path information is omitted, file is considered to be in the working directory; *mode* is file opening mode; *prot* is access specifier, default argument with default value 'openprot' for read and write access permissions.

2.20.3 Closing a File

When a program has finished with reading/writing of a file, it must be closed. This task is carried out by using *close()* member function of *fstreambase* class.

2.20.4 Reading/Writing of Files

In C++ I/O file subsystem, files can be of type text and binary. In text format, numbers are stored as sequence of characters, whereas in binary files numbers are stored in the similar fashion as they are stored in the main memory.

2.20.4.1 Reading/Writing of Text Files

2.20.4.1.1 Reading and Writing of Character Data

Character data is read and written using character input/output member function of *ifstream* and *ofstream* classes.

Character output function *put()* of *ofstream* class is used to write one character at a time to a file where as character input function *get()* of *ifstream* class is used to read one character at a time from a file.

2.20.4.1.2 Reading and Writing of String Data

String data is read and written using string input/output member function of *ifstream* and *ofstream* classes.

String output function *write()* of *ofstream* class is used to write a string at a time to a file where as string input function *getline()* of *ifstream* class is used to read a string at a time from a file.

2.20.4.1.3 Reading and Writing of Formatted Data

It is important to note that in formatted I/O, numbers are stored as a series of characters. Thus, number 6.352 which may be of type *float* or *double*, will be stored as character '6', '.', '3', '5', and '2' rather that being stored as 4-byte type *float* or 8-byte type *double*. This type of storage of numbers is inefficient particularly with numbers having large number of digits, but may be appropriate in many situations and is easy to implement. Characters and strings are stored in this fashion only. The overloaded insertion (>>) and extraction (<<) operators are used to write and read format data.

2.20.4.1.4 Reading and Writing of Objects

The objects can be read and written in a text format using overloaded >> and << operators, respectively.

2.20.4.2 Reading/Writing of Binary Files

When we want to write few numbers to a disk file, it is possible with formatted I/O, though not efficient. But when we want to store a large amount of numerical data, the more efficient way of doing the same is using binary I/O, *also known as block I/O*, in which numbers are stored as they are stored in the computer's main memory, rather than as strings of characters. Likewise, objects can be stored in a file more efficiently using binary I/O.

2.20.4.2.1 Reading and Writing of Structures

A structure or an entire array can be read and written in a single read and write operation. These are written using *write()* function of *ofstream* class while they are read using *read()* function of *ifstream* class.

A structure is written to a file using *write()* function as

```
outFile.write((char *)&structname, sizeof(structname));
```

An array is written to a file using *write()* function as

```
outFile.write((char *)arrayname, sizeof(arrayname));
```

A structure is read from a file using *read()* function as

```
inFile.read((char *)&structname, sizeof(structname));
```

An array is read from a file using *read()* function as

```
inFile.read((char *)arrayname, sizeof(arrayname));
```

The first argument is the address of the structure or array, and the second argument is the size of the structure or array in bytes. The address of the structure or array must be cast of type *char* * (pointer to *char* type).

2.20.4.2.2 Reading and Writing of Objects

Object is written to a file using *write()* function as

```
outFile.write((char *)&object, sizeof(object));
```

Object can be read from a file using *read()* function as

```
inFile.read((char *)&object, sizeof(object));
```

2.20.5 Accessing Records Randomly

In previous cases, the reading and writing has been sequential. While writing to a file, data items are placed one after the other in a sequence. Similarly, while reading from a file, the data items are read from the beginning of the file in sequence until the end of the file is reached.

It is also possible to access a particular data item that may be in the middle of the file. This way of accessing a file is called *direct accessing* or *random accessing*. The only restriction for direct/random addressing is that all the data items must be of same size.

2.20.5.1 File Pointers and their Manipulations

A *file pointer* is a pointer to a particular byte in a file. Every time, when we write to a file, the file pointer moves to the end of the data item written so that writing can continue from that point. When a file is closed, and subsequently opened for reading, the file pointer is set to the beginning of the file. So we can read the file from beginning. After reading a data item, the file pointer moves to the beginning of the next data item, which can subsequently be read. However, if the file is opened in append mode, then the file pointer will be positioned at the end of the exiting file, so that new data items can be written from there onwards.

C++ I/O system associates *file pointers* with files. These pointers are called *get pointer* (input pointer) and *put pointer* (output pointer). It associates get pointer with a file that is opened for reading, put pointer with a file that is opened for writing, and both of these pointers with a file that is opened for reading and writing. On successful completion of a read or write operation, the appropriate pointer is advanced automatically.

There may be situations where these file pointers are to be set at desired position in a file so the read or write operation can take place. The file stream classes contain member functions that allow moving these file pointers within a file. In addition, stream classes also contain member functions that return the current position of a file pointer in a file.

Table 2.11: File pointer control functions

Function	Class in which defined	Action Performed
`seekg()`	`ifstream` class	Moves get file pointer to specified position.
`seekp()`	`ofstream` class	Moves put file pointer to specified position.
`tellg()`	`ifstream` class	Returns the position of the get pointer.
`tellp()`	`ofstream` class	Returns the position of the put pointer.

The *seek()* functions have the following prototypes:

```
ifstream & seekg ( long offset, seek_dir origin = ios::beg );
ofstream & seekp ( long offset, seek_dir origin = ios::beg );
```

where *offset* specifies number of bytes by which file pointer is to be moved; *origin* specifies the reference point from where the offset is to measured, default argument with default value is beginning of the file as reference point. These functions return a reference to the respective streams.

An enumeration named *seek_dir* defined in the *ios* class, specifies the reference point.

```
enum seek_dir { beg, cur, end };
```

Table 2.12: Description of file seek origins

Origin value	Offset is measured from
`Beg`	Reference point is the beginning of the file.
`Cur`	Reference point is the current position of the file pointer in the file.
`End`	Reference point is the end of the file.

The *tell()* functions have the following prototypes:

`long tellg();` and `long tellp();`

These functions return the current position as number of bytes from the beginning of the respective files.

REVIEW EXERCISES

1. What are the key features of the C++ language?
2. Give an account of the various data types supported by C++.
3. Give an account of the various operators available in C++.
4. Give an account of the various control statements operators available in C++.
5. What are the different types of variable supported by C++?
6. How do pointer variables compare with reference variables?
7. What are different ways of passing arguments to a function?
8. What are inline functions?
9. How can we specify default arguments for a function?
10. What is a function template? How can it be useful?
11. What is function overloading? What are the necessary conditions for overloading a function? How can it be useful?
12. Give the general syntax for defining a member function outside the class template.
13. What is special about special member functions – *constructors* and *destructors*?
14. What is role of friendship? What can be the possible situations for making friends?
15. What is an abstract class?
16. What is a container class?
17. How an array of objects can be initialized?
18. What are the advantages of inheritance?

19. What can be the possible ambiguities in multiple and multipath inheritance? How can they be resolved?
20. How function overriding is different from function overloading?
21. What is the order of execution of constructors and destructors?
22. Name the operators that can't be overloaded.
23. How polymorphism is implemented in C++?
24. How dynamic binding is different from static binding? Which of these is more flexible? Which of these involves more overhead?
25. Compare and contrast between traditional error handling and exceptional handling?
26. What are the various steps in exception handling?
27. What is STL? Describe the programming model of STL.

❑ ❑ ❑

Chapter 3

Overview of Data Structures

3.1 INTRODUCTION

We know that the main memory is *volatile*, *i.e.*, it looses its contents when the system is turned off, whereas the secondary memory is *non-volatile*, *i.e.*, retains its contents unless overwritten with new ones. We also know that the processor can only process the data that is available in main memory. Therefore, if the data to be processed is not available in the main memory, then it has to be transferred from secondary memory to the main memory. Similarly, if the new data entered in the main memory under program control or intermediate and/or final results produced by the program are to be preserved for the future use, they are transferred from main memory to the secondary memory.

In order to represent and store data in main memory and/or secondary memory, we need an appropriate model. The different models used to organize data in the main memory are collectively referred to as *data structures*, whereas the different models used to organize data in the secondary memory are collectively referred to as *file structures*.

This chapter provides an overview of data structures and other related issues.

3.2 BASIC TERMINOLOGY OF DATA ORGANIZATION

This section introduces the basic terminology related to data organization. Every student must understand these terms.

Data – The term *data* simply refers to a value or set of values. These values may represent some observations from an experiment, some figures collected during some survey (such as *census*, *exit polls*, etc.), marks obtained by a student in an examination, etc.

Data item – A *data item* refers to a single unit of values. For example, *roll number*, *name*, *date of birth*, *age*, *address* and *marks in each subject* are data items. Data items that can be divided into sub items are called *group items* whereas those who can not be divided into sub items are called *elementry items*. For example, an address is a group item as it is usually divided into sub items such as *house number*, *street number*, *locality*, *city*, *pin code*, etc. Likewise, a *date* can be divided into *day*, *month* and *year*; a *name* can be divided into *first name* and *surname*. On the other hand, *roll number*, *marks*, *city*, *pin code*, etc. are normally treated as elementry items.

Entity – An *entity* is something that has certain *attributes* or *properties* which may be assigned values. The values assigned may be either numeric or non-numeric. For example, a student is an entity. The possible attributes for a student can be *roll number*, *name*, *date of birth*, *sex* and *class*. The possible values for these attributes can be *1234*, *Surbhi*, *12/03/1993*, *F*, *9*.

Each attribute of an entity has a defined set of values, called *domain*. For example, the domain for *sex* attribute consists of only *M* (for males) and *F* (for females) value.

Entity set – An *entity set* is a collection of similar *entities.* For example, students of a class, employees of an organization, products manufactured by a manufacturing unit, etc. forms an entity set.

Record – A *record* is a collection of related data items. For example, *roll number*, *name*, *date of birth*, *sex*, and *class* of a particular student such as *1234*, *Surbhi*, *12/03/1993*, *F*, *9*. In fact, a record represents an entity.

File – A *file* is a collection of related records. For example, a file containing records of all students in class, a file containing records of all employees of an organization. In fact, a file represents an entity set.

Key – A *key* is a data item in a record that takes unique values and can be used to distinguish a record from other records. It may happen that more than one data item has unique values. In that case, there exist multiple keys. But at a time, we may be using only one data item as a key, called *primary key*, that too depending on the problem in hand. The other key(s) are then known as *alternate key(s)*.

In some cases, there is no field that has unique values. Then a combination of some fields can be used to form a key. Such a key is known as *composite key*.

In worst case, if there is no possibility of forming a key from within the record, then an extra data item can be added to the record that can be used as a key.

Information – The terms *data* and *information* have been used to mean same thing. But actually information is more than just data. In simple terms, information is a processed data. Data is just a collection of values (raw data), from which no conclusions can be drawn. Thus data as such is not useful for decision making. When the data is processed, by applying certain rules, new generated data becomes information. This new generated data (information) conveys some meaning and hence can be used for decision-making. For more clarity, consider the following example.

Example 3.1:

An agricultural scientist wants to study the effect of a particular pesticide on a new variety of wheat. He uses a different amount of pesticide for different fields of wheat and notes down the yield of wheat in each field. Here, the amount of pesticide used and yield of wheat in each field represents data.

As such these values do not convey anything regarding the effect of pesticide on the yield. Next he applies the technique of correlation analysis to determine the correlation coefficient whose value lies in the range –1 to +1. This coefficient, which is also a value, conveys valuable information about the effect of pesticide on yield of wheat. If correlation coefficient is greater than 0, it means increased amount of pesticide has positive effect on the yield. If correlation coefficient is less than 0, it means increased amount of pesticide has negative effect on the yield. If correlation coefficient is equal to 0, it means increased amount of pesticide has no effect on the yield.

3.3 CONCEPT OF A DATA TYPE

A *data type* is a collection of values and a set of operations that act on those values. Whether our program is dealing with pre-defined data types or user-defined types, following two aspects must be considered:

- Set of values
- Set of operations

For example, consider an integer data type which consists of values {MININT, . . ., –3, –2, –1, 0, 1, 2, 3, . . ., MAXINT}, where MININT and MAXINT are the smallest and largest integers that can be represented by an integer type on a particular computer. The operations on integers include the arithmetic operations of addition (+), subtraction (–), multiplication (*), and division (/). There are also operations that test for equality/inequality and the operation that assign an integer value to a variable.

3.3.1 Primitive Data Type

A *primitive data type* is a data type that is *predefined.* The predefined data type is also known as *built-in data type.* These primitive data types may be different for different programming languages. For example, C & C++ programming languages provide *built-in* support for integers (*int, long*), reals (*float, double*) and characters (*char*).

3.3.2 User-Defined Data Type

A *user-defined data type* is one that user defines as per his/her own requirement. The programming languages provide support for creating user-defined data types. For various C and C++ languages support user-defined data types by means of structures (*struct*), unions (*union*), and enumerations (*enum*).

3.3.3 Abstract Data Type

An *abstract data type* is a data type that is organized in such a way that the specification of the values and the specification of the operations on those values are separated from the representation of the values and the implementation of the operations. For example, consider *list* abstract data type. A *list* is basically a collection of elements which can be ordered or unordered. The primitive operations on a list may include adding new elements, deleting elements, determining number of elements in the list, and applying a particular process to each element in the list. Here, we are not concerned with how a list is represented and how the above mentioned operations are implemented. We only need to know that it is a list whose elements are of given type, and what can we do with the list.

3.4 DATA STRUCTURE DEFINED

A *data structure* is a logical model of a particular organization of data. The choice of a particular data structure depends on the following consideration:

- It must be able to represent the inherent relationship of the data in the real world.
- It must be simple enough so that it can process efficiently as and when necessary.

The study of data structures includes:

- Logical description of the data structure.
- Implementation of the data structure.
- Quantitative analysis of the data structure. This analysis includes determining the amount of memory needed to store the data structure and the time required processing it.

3.5 DESCRIPTION OF VARIOUS DATA STRUCTURES

This section introduces various data structures, which will be discussed in detail later in the book.

The various data structures are divided into following categories:

- ***Linear data structures*** – a data structure whose elements form a sequence, and every element in the structure has a unique predecessor and unique successor. Examples of linear data structures are *arrays*, *linked lists*, *stacks* and *queues*.
- ***Non-linear data structures*** – a data structure whose elements do not form a sequence, there is no unique predecessor or unique successor.. Examples of non-linear data structures are *trees* and *graphs*.

In the subsequent sections, we will have a look on these data structures.

3.5.1 Arrays

An *array* is a list of finite number of elements of same data type, *i.e.*, integers, reals or strings etc. The individual elements of an array are accessed using an index or indices to the array. Depending on the number of indices required to access an individual element of an array, arrays can be classified as:

- *One-dimensional array* or *linear array* that requires only one index to access an individual element of the array.
- *Two-dimensional arrays* that requires two indices to access an individual element of the array. In Mathematics, equivalent to two-dimensional array, we have a *matrix* and in business terminology we have a *table*.
- The arrays for which we need two or more indices are generally known as *multi-dimensional arrays*.

3.5.1.1 Linear Arrays

A *linear array* is a list of a finite number, say *n*, of homogeneous data elements such that

- The elements of the array are referenced by an index set consisting of *n* consecutive integer numbers.
- The elements of the array are stored in consecutive memory locations.

The number *n* of the elements is called the *size* of the linear array. In general, if *lb* is the smallest index, called the *lower bound*, and *ub* is the largest index, called *upper bound*, then size of the linear array is given by

```
size = ub - lb + 1
```

Note that the size of the array = *ub* if *lb* = 1. If not explicitly stated, generally we will consider the index set consists of 1, 2, 3, . . ., *n* or *ub*.

Suppose *a* is the name of the linear array with *n* elements, then its elements can be denoted as

$a_1, a_2, a_3, \ldots, a_n$	in mathematical notation
$a(1), a(2), a(3), \ldots, a(n)$	in BASIC and FORTRAN languages
$a[1], a[2], a[3], \ldots, a[n]$	in PASCAL language
$a[0], a[1], a[2], \ldots, a[n-1]$	in C/C++ and Java languages

The number *k* in $a(k)$ or $a[k]$ is called a *subscript* and $a(k)$ or $a[k]$ itself is called a *subscripted variable*.

To be consistent with the C language notation, if an array has *n* elements for a given dimension, its index set will be considered as 0, 1, 2, . . ., *n*–1.

Example 3.2:

Consider a linear array *rn* consisting of roll numbers of 5 students of a particular class. This array can be pictured as shown in Figure 3.1.

	rn
0	1200
1	1201
2	1202
3	1203
4	1204

Figure 3.1: One-dimensional array *rn* storing roll numbers

Here *rn*[0] denotes 1200, *rn*[1] denotes 1201 and so on.

3.5.1.2 Two-dimensional Array

A two-dimensional array is a list of a finite number, say *m*n*, of homogeneous data elements such that

- The elements of the array are referenced by two index sets consisting of *m* and *n* consecutive integer numbers.
- The elements of the array are stored in consecutive memory locations.

The *size* of the two-dimensional array is denoted by $m \times n$ and pronounced as *m* by *n*.

Suppose b is the name of the two-dimensional array, then its element in *ith* row and *jth* column can be denoted as

b_{ij}	in mathematical notation
$b(i, j)$	in BASIC and FORTRAN languages
$b[i, j]$	in PASCAL language
$b[i][j]$	in C/C++ and Java languages

Example 3.3:

Suppose a manufacturing company has a chain of five stores and five departments in each store. The weekly sales for the company can be stored using two-dimensional array named *sale*. This array can be pictured as shown in the Figure 3.2.

sale

	0	1	2	3	4
0	2000	1200	1500	1000	1005
1	1500	1450	2010	1550	1250
2	1000	1250	1400	2000	3000
3	1250	1275	1575	3500	1750
4	5200	4000	1000	1200	1575

Figure 3.2: Two-dimensional array *sale* to storing sales

Here *sale*[0][0] denotes 2000, *sale*[0][1] denotes 1200, . . ., *sale*[4][4] denotes 1575.

In business terminology, a two-dimensional array is better known as a table, where as in mathematical terminology, it is known as a matrix.

Arrays and matrices are discussed in detail in *Chapter 4*.

3.5.2 Linked Lists

A *linked list* is a linear collection of data elements, called *nodes*. The linear order is maintained by pointers. Each node is divided into two or more parts. A linked list can be linear linked list (one-way list) or doubly linked list (two-way list).

3.5.2.1 Linear Linked List

In linear linked list, each node is divided in two parts:

- first part contains the information of the element.
- second part, called the *link field* or *nextpointer field*, contains the address of the next node in the list.

Example 3.4:

The following figure shows a linear linked list with 4 nodes.

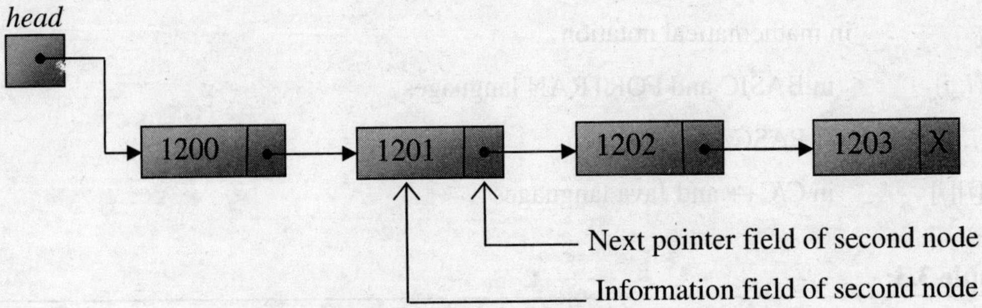

Figure 3.3: Linear linked list with 4 nodes

In addition, another pointer variable, say *head*, is used that contains the address of the first element of the list. The last element of the linear linked list has *NULL* value, pictured as *X*, in the *nextpointer* field to mark the end of the list. A Linear linked list can be traversed only in one direction.

3.5.2.2 Doubly Linked List

In the doubly linked list, each node is divided into three parts:

- first part contains the information of the element,
- second part, called *previouspointer field*, contains the address of the preceding element in the list, and
- third part, called *nextpointer field*, contains the address of the succeeding element in the in the list.

Example 3.5:

The following figure shows a doubly linked list with 3 nodes.

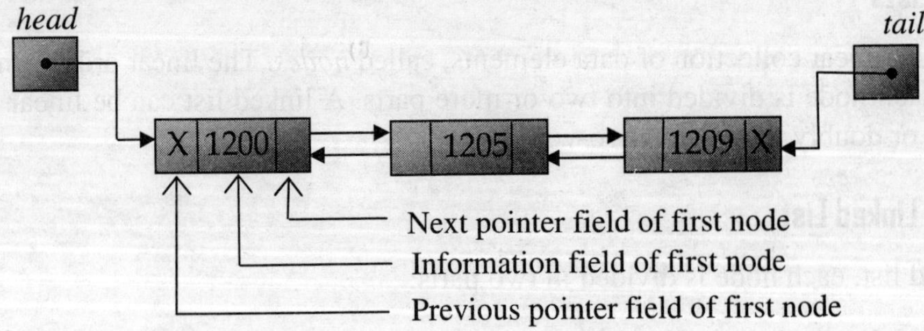

Figure 3.4: Doubly linked list with 3 nodes

In addition, two pointer variables, say *head* and *tail*, are used that contains the address of the first element and the last element of the doubly linked list, respectively. The first element contains *NULL* value in the *previouspointer* to indicate there is no element preceding it, and the last element of the linked list have *NULL* value in the *nextpointer* field to indicate that there is no element succeeding it. Doubly linked lists can be traversed in both directions.

3.5.2.3 Circular List

A circular list is a linear linked list, except that the last element points to the first element.

Example 3.6:

The following figure shows a circular list with 4 nodes.

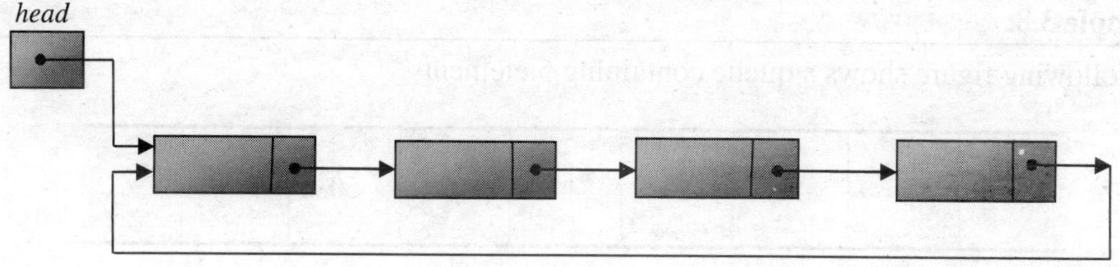

Figure 3.5: Circular list with 4 nodes

Linked lists are discussed in detail in *Chapter 6*.

3.5.3 Stacks

A *stack*, also called a Last-In-First-Out (LIFO) system, is a linear list in which insertions and deletions can take place only at one end, called the *top*.

Example 3.7:

The following figure shows a stack with 6 elements.

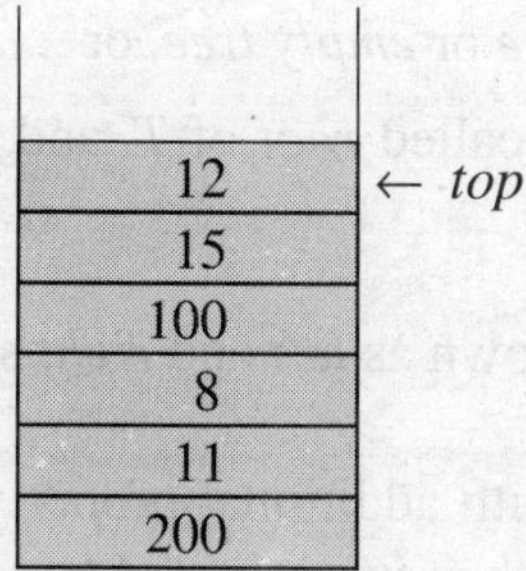

Figure 3.6: Stack with 6 elements

This structure operates in much the same way as stack of trays. If we want to place another tray, it can be placed only at the top. Likewise, if we want to remove a tray.from stack of trays, it can only be removed from the top.

Stacks are discussed in detail in *Chapter 7*.

3.5.4 Queues

A *queue*, also called a First-In-First-Out (FIFO) or First-Come-First-Serve (FCFS) system, is a linear list in which insertions can take place at one end of the list, called the *rear* of the list, and deletions can take place only at other end, called the *front* of the list. This structure operates in much the same way a line of people waiting at a bus stop or at a cinema hall for their turn.

Example 3.8:

The following figure shows a queue containing 5 elements.

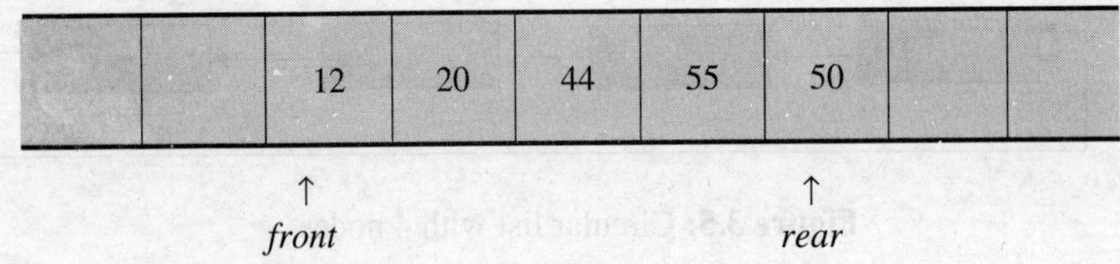

Figure 3.7: Queue with 5 elements

Queues are discussed in detail in *Chapter 8*.

3.5.5 Trees

A *tree* is a data structure that represents a hierarchical relationship between various elements. A *binary tree* is a tree that can have utmost two children. Formerly, a binary tree T is defined as finite set of elements, called *nodes*, such that:

- Either T is empty, called the *null tree* or *empty tree*, or
- T contains a distinguished node R, called *root* of T, and remaining nodes form an ordered pair of binary trees T_1 and T_2.

Where the binary trees T_1 and T_2 are known as *left* and *right* subtrees respectively.

A *binary search tree* is a binary tree with additional property — *the key value of any node N is larger than its left child and smaller than its right child.*

Example 3.9:

The following figure shows a binary tree and a binary search tree.

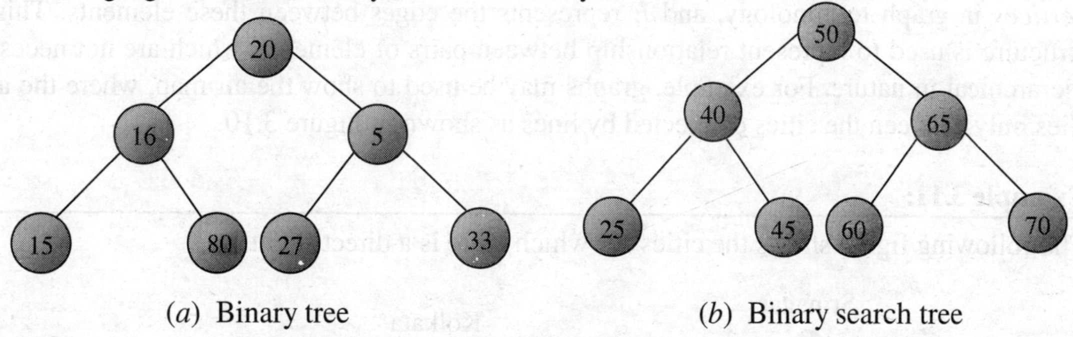

(*a*) Binary tree (*b*) Binary search tree

Figure 3.8: Binary and binary search trees

Trees are discussed in detail in *Chapter 9*.

3.5.6 Heaps

A *heap* is a binary tree that satisfies the following properties:

- Shape property
- Order property

The shape property states that heap is a *complete* or *nearly complete* binary tree. And the order property states that

- Either the element at any node is smallest of all of its children, called *min heap*, or
- Element at any node is largest of all of its children, called *max heap*.

A heap is represented in memory by sequential representation i.e. using linear arrays. The most important application of a heap structure is to implement priority queues in addition to being used for sorting an array, a technique popularly known as *heapsort*.

Example 3.10:

The following figure shows a *min heap* and a *max heap*.

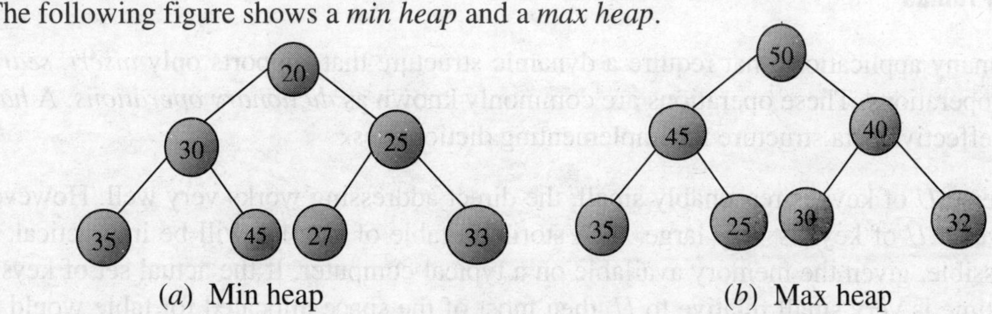

(*a*) Min heap (*b*) Max heap

Figure 3.9: Min and Max heaps

Heaps are discussed in detail in *Chapter 10*.

3.5.7 Graphs

A *graph G* is a ordered set (*V*, *E*), where *V* represent the set of elements, called *nodes* or *vertices* in graph terminology, and *E* represents the edges between these elements. This data structure is used to represent relationship between pairs of elements, which are not necessarily hierarchical in nature. For example, graphs may be used to show the air map, where the airline flies only between the cities connected by lines as shown in Figure 3.10.

Example 3.11:

The following figure shows the cities for which there is a direct flight.

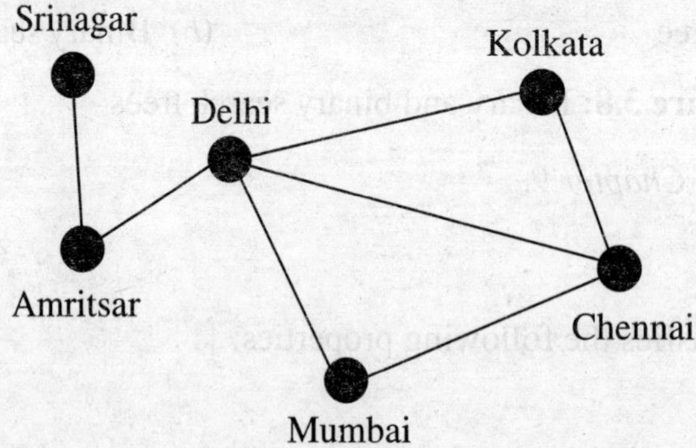

Figure 3.10: Airline Flights

In the above graph

V = { Srinagar, Amritsar, Delhi, Mumbai, Chennai, Kolkata }

E = { (Srinagar, Amritsar), (Amritsar, Delhi), (Delhi, Mumbai), (Delhi, Chennai), (Delhi, Kolkata), (Chennai, Kolkata), (Mumbai , Chennai) }

Graphs are discussed in detail in *Chapter 11*.

3.5.8 Hash Tables

There are many applications that require a dynamic structure that supports only *insert*, *search* and *delete* operations. These operations are commonly known as *dictionary operations*. A *hash table* is an effective data structure for implementing dictionaries.

If the universe *U* of keys is reasonably small, the direct addressing works very well. However, if this universe *U* of keys is very large, then storing a table of size |*U*| will be impractical, or even impossible, given the memory available on a typical computer. If the actual set of keys *K* at a given time is very small relative to *U*, then most of the space allocated for table would be wasted.

A hash table requires much less storage than direct address table. Specifically, the storage requirement can be reduced to O(|*K*|), even though searching for an element in the hash table requires constant time.

Hash tables and hashing is discussed in detail in *Chapter 12*.

3.6 COMMON OPERATIONS ON DATA STRUCTURES

The various operations that can be performed on different data structures are described below:

- ***Traversal*** – Accessing each element exactly once in order to process it. This operation is called *visiting* the element.
- ***Searching*** – Finding the location of a given element.
- ***Insertion*** – Adding a new element to the structure.
- ***Deletion*** – Removing a existing element from the structure.
- ***Sorting*** – Arranging the elements in some logical order. This logical order may be ascending or descending in case of numeric key. In case of alphanumeric key, it can be dictionary order.
- ***Merging*** – Combining the elements of two similar sorted structures into a single structure.

Not all the data structures support all of the above-mentioned operations.

A QUICK REVIEW

In this chapter, we have learnt

- About the basic terms related to data organization.
- About the concept of data type.
- About the primitive, abstract and polymorphic data types.
- About the definition of data structure.
- About the different factors that influence the choice of a particular data structure for a given problem.
- About the different data structures with suitable examples.
- About the different operations that can be performed on these data structures.

In the next chapter, we will discuss the various technical issued related to program design.

REVIEW EXERCISES

1. Explain the terms: *data*, *elementary item*, *entity*, *primary key*, *domain*, *attribute* and *information*. Also give example in support of your answer.
2. What is difference between *data* and *information*?
3. What is a *data type*? Differentiate between *primitive data type*, *abstract data type* and *polymorphic data type*.
4. What is a *data structure*? What are the factors that influence the choice of a particular data structure?
5. What are the areas of study under the domain of data structures?
6. Describe, in brief, the various data structures.
7. Describe the various operations that, in general, can be performed on different data structures.

❑ ❑ ❑

Chapter 4

Program Design and Development

4.1 INTRODUCTION

In the early day of computer era, there were no well-defined procedures for managing the software development process. The use of computers was limited to scientific and engineering applications. The programs were written for well-defined problems, such as calculating missile trajectories. If the program did not work, the programmer will correct it. People started calling this approach of program development as *code-and-fix*.

When the use of computers for solving complex problems started, the problems begin to appear with this approach. In many cases, it was found that the programmer could not really understand what the user wanted the program to do, and correcting problems often turned into an expensive, time-consuming nightmare. The programmers did not document their programs and even some programmers developed their own cryptic style so that they can secure their continued employment as no one else can figure out what the program is doing. Because of these practices, these early programs were almost impossible to debug and maintain, especially if the original programmer had left the company.

To address these problems, the Program Development Life Cycle (PDLC) was introduced in the 70s, and is still in widespread use. The PDLC provides an organized plan for breaking down the task of program development into manageable chunks, each of which must be successfully completed before moving on to the next phase.

This chapter describes the various activities carried in a program development life cycle to produce a piece of quality software. In addition, it describes algorithms, notations to be used in this book for expressing algorithms. It also describes various control structures that are building blocks for structured programming. Finally, it describes the algorithmic complexity, and big oh (O) notation to express algorithmic complexity.

4.2 PROGRAM DEVELOPMENT LIFE CYCLE

Program development life cycle is a systematic way of developing quality software. It provides an organized plan for breaking down the task of program development into manageable chunks, each of which must be successfully completed before moving on to the next phase.

The program development process is divided into following phases:

- Defining the problem.
- Designing the program.
- Coding the program.
- Testing and debugging the program.
- Documenting the program.
- Deploying and maintaining the program.

4.2.1 Defining the Problem

The first step in developing a program is to define the problem. In major software projects, this is a job for system analyst, who provides the results of their work to programmers in the form of a *program specification*. The program specification precisely defines the input data, the processing that should take place, the format of the output reports and the user interface. Depending on the size of the job, the program development might be handled by an individual or a team.

4.2.2 Designing the Program

An architect doesn't design a home just by going to the site with a bunch of boards and bricks. After determining the needs of the house's owner, the next step in designing a house is an architectural drawing – a plan drawn up on the paper that can be discussed and reviewed until everything is right. Likewise, programmers create program designs. Like an architect's drawing, the program design specifies the components that make the program work.

Program design begins by focusing on the main goal that the program is trying to achieve and then breaking the program into manageable components, each of which contributes to this goal. This approach of program design is called *top-down program design* or *modular programming*. The first step involves identifying the *main routine*, which is the program's major activity. From there, programmers try to break down the various components of the main routine into smaller units called *modules*, until each module is highly focused. Experience shows that this is the best way to ensure program quality. If an error appears in a program designed this way, it is relatively easy to identify the module that must be causing the error.

For each module, the programmer draws a conceptual plan using an appropriate program design tool to visualize how the module will do its assigned job.

4.2.2.1 Program Design Tools

The various program design tools are described below.

- ***Structure charts*** – A *structure chart*, also called *hierarchy chart*, show the top-down design of a program. Each box in the chart indicates a task that the program must accomplish. The top module, called the *main module* or *control module*, oversees the transfer of control to other modules.

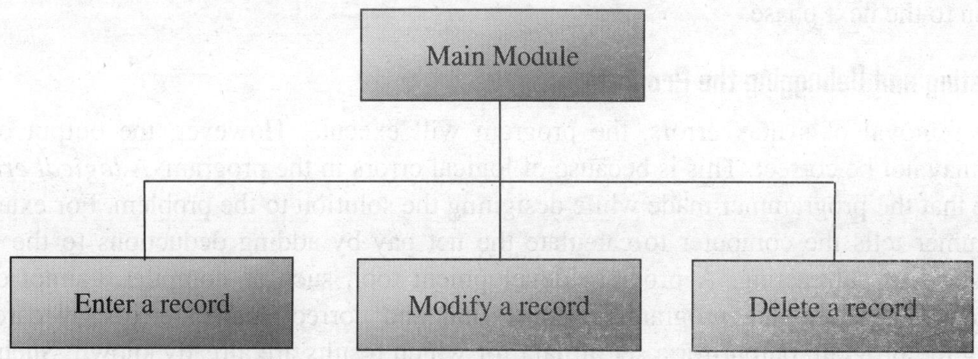

Figure 4.1: Structure Chart for a Data Entry Program

- ***Algorithms*** – An *algorithm* is a step-by-step description of how to arrive at a solution. Algorithms are not restricted to computers. In fact, we use them every day.
- ***Flowcharts*** – A *flowchart* is a diagram that shows the logic of the program. Programmers create flowcharts either by hand using a flowchart template or on the computer. Each flowcharting symbol has a meaning. For example, parallelogram indicates an input or output, rectangle indicates a process, and diamond indicates a condition.
- ***Decision tables*** – A *decision table* is a special kind of table, which is divided into four parts by a pair of horizontal and vertical lines. The left top part, called *condition stub*, contains the different questions being asked for decision making. The right top part, called *condition entries*, contains the answers to these questions. The left bottom part, called *action stub*, contains the actions to be carried out. The right bottom part, called *action entries*, contains either 'X' entry or '–'. The 'X' entry represents an action while '–' represents no action. The decision tables are usually used as supplementary to flowcharts.

- ***Pseudocodes*** – A *pseudocode* is another tool to describe the way to arrive at a solution. In some sense, it is considered as a form of an algorithm. The only difference is that instead of expressing the action to be carried in form of steps, they are expressed in program language like constructs. In the present text, we will follow this approach.

4.2.3 Coding the Program

Coding the program involves translating the algorithm into specific program language instructions. While writing the code, prefer to use only well defined control structures. This technique of programming using only well defined control structures is known as *structured programming*.

The programmer must choose an appropriate programming language and then create the program by typing the code. The programmer must carefully follow the language's rules, which precisely specify how to express certain operations. Violation of language rules results in grammatical errors, more precisely known as *syntax errors*. Program development tools; such as a compiler, can check these syntax errors. These syntax errors must be eliminated before moving on to the next phase.

4.2.4 Testing and Debugging the Program

After the removal of syntax errors, the program will execute. However, the output of the program may not be correct. This is because of logical errors in the program. A *logical error* is a mistake that the programmer made while designing the solution to the problem. For example, a programmer tells the computer to calculate the net pay by adding deductions to the gross salary instead of subtracting. A program development tool, such as compiler, cannot detect these errors. Therefore, the programmer must find and correct logical errors by carefully examining the program output for a set of data for which results are already known. Such type of data is known as *test data*.

If the software developed is a complex one and consists of a large number of modules, then testing must be performed on these modules separately. This is known as *unit testing*. Once each module is thoroughly tested, they are integrated together to form a software package. Finally, testing is performed on the software package to uncover any sort of error that may creep in as a result of integration of different modules. This is known as *system testing*.

Remember that it is not always possible to examine every output for each program condition, *i.e.*, exhaustive testing is not always possible. Inevitably, some errors will surface only when the system is put into use.

Syntax errors and logical error are collectively known as *bugs*. The process of identifying and eliminating these errors is known as *debugging*.

4.2.5 Documenting the Program

After testing, the software project is almost complete. The *structure charts*, *pseudocodes*, *flowcharts* and *decision tables* developed during the design phase become documentation for others who are associated with the software project. In addition, more documentation needs to be done as the programs are being coded such as list of variable names and definitions, description of files that the program need to work with, and format of output that the program produces. All of this documentation needs to be saved and placed together for future reference.

This phase ends by writing a manual that provides an overview of the program's functionality, tutorials for the beginner, in-depth explanations of major program features, reference documentation of all program commands and a thorough description of the error messages generated by the program. This manual is given to the user when the program is installed.

4.2.6 Deploying and Maintaining the Program

In the final phase, the program is deployed (installed) at the user's site. Here also, the program is kept under watch till the user gives green signal to it. Users may discover errors that were not caught in the testing phase, no matter how exhaustively the program was tested.

Even after the software project is complete, it needs to be maintained and evaluated regularly. In program maintenance, the programming team fixes program errors that users discover during its day-to-day use. In periodic evaluations, the team asks whether the program is fulfilling its objectives. This evaluation may lead to modifications to update the program or to add more features for the user. It may even lead to a decision to abandon the current system and develop a new one, and so the program development life cycle begins afresh.

It is important to note that best-written software may fail if either it does not meet the user's requirements or the user interface is poorly designed. Note that the user is not concerned with the technicalities of the program logic, his/her prime concern is that whether the software solves his/her problem and the ease with which he/she can use the software.

4.3 INTRODUCTION TO ALGORITHMS

An *algorithm* is a finite set of steps defining the solution of a particular problem. An algorithm can be expressed in English like language, called *pseudocode*, in a programming language, or in the form of a flowchart. In this book, we will describe the algorithms in pseudocode that very much like Pascal and C language. The coding of algorithms expressed in pseudocode is very simple and straightforward. If you are familiar with these languages, you can understand the algorithms developed in the book very easily.

Every algorithm must satisfy the following criteria:

- ❑ ***Input*** : There are zero or more values which are externally supplied.
- ❑ ***Output*** : At least one value is produced.
- ❑ ***Definiteness*** : Each step must be clear and unambiguous.
- ❑ ***Finiteness*** : If we trace the steps of an algorithm, then for all cases, the algorithm must terminate after a finite number of steps.
- ❑ ***Effectiveness*** : Each step must be sufficiently basic that it can in principle be carried out by a person using only paper and pencil. In addition, not only each step be definite, it must also be feasible.

4.3.1 A Typical Example

Given an one-dimensional array *a*[0:*n*−1] of real values, and we want to find the location of its largest element.

Suppose that the location of the largest element is stored in variable *loc* and the variable *max* is used to keep track of the largest element. The problem can be solved as follows:

We begin with *loc* = 0 and *max* = a_0. We then compare *max* with each successive element a_k. If a_k is greater that *max*, we then update *loc* and *max* as *loc* = *k* and *max* = a_k respectively. The final value of *loc* gives the location of the largest element. The formal presentation of the algorithm is given below.

Algorithm 4.1:

Let *a*[0:*n*−1] be one-dimensional array with *n* real values. This algorithm finds the location *loc* of its largest element. The variable *i* is used as index variable, and *max* as temporary variable to store the current largest element.

```
Begin
  read: n                       // enter value of n
  for i = 0 to (n-1) by 1 do
     read: a_i                  // enter elements of array
  endfor
  Set max = a_0                    // take first element as the largest
  Set loc = 0                   // set location of the element to 0
  for i = 1 to (n-1) by 1 do
     if (a_i > max ) then          // compare the next element with max
        Set max = a_i           // take this element as the current largest
        Set loc = i             // update location of the largest element
     endif
  endfor
  write: "Location of the largest element = ", loc
End.
```

4.3.2 Algorithm Description

The development of algorithms for various operations on data structures is a key feature of this book. Developing an efficient algorithm requires lot of practice and skill. It must be noted that an efficient algorithm is one that is capable of giving the solution of the problem using minimum resources of the system such as memory used and processor's time. In this section, we will describe the format to be used for presentation of the algorithms. This format is language free, well structured and detailed. It will enable the readers to translate it into a computer program using any high-level language such as FORTRAN, Pascal or C/C++.

The format for the formal presentation of the algorithm consists of two parts:

- The first part describes the input data, the purpose of the algorithm and identifies the variables used in the algorithms.
- The second part is composed of sequence of instructions that lead to the solution of the problem.

The following description summarizes certain conventions used in presenting the above algorithm.

Comments

Each instruction may be followed by a comment. The comments begin with a double slash, and the explain the purpose of the instruction, such as

```
// this is a sample comment
```

Appropriate use of comments enhances the readability of the algorithm, which in turn helps in maintaining the algorithm.

Variable Names

For variable names, we will use italicized lowercase letters such as a *max*, *loc*, etc., whereas for defined constants, if any, we will use uppercase letters.

Assignment Statement

The assignment statement will use the notation as

Set $max = a_i$

to assign the value of a_i to *max*. The right hand side of the assignment statement can have a *value*, *a variable* or *an expression*.

However, if several assignment statements appear in the same line, such as

Set $k = 1$, $loc = 1$, $max = a_i$

then they are executed from left to right.

Input/Output

Data may be input and assigned to variables by means of a *read* statement with the following format

```
read: variable list
```

where the *variable list* consists one or more variables separated by comma.

Similarly, the data held by the variables and the messages, if any, enclosed in double quotes can be output by means of a *write* statement with the following format

```
write: message and/or variable list
                  or
print: message and/or variable list
```

where the *message* and the variables in the *variable list* are separated by comma.

Execution of Instructions

The instructions in the algorithm are usually executed one after the other as they appear in the algorithm. However, there may be instances when some instructions are skipped or some instructions may be repeated as a result of certain conditions.

Completion of the Algorithm

The algorithm is completed with the execution of the last instruction. However, the algorithm can be terminated at any intermediate state using the *exit* instruction.

4.3.3 Sub-Algorithms

The algorithm 3.1 has its own input statements as well as output statements. That type algorithm, when implemented, can run on its own. But in most of the cases, when the problem is too complex, we do divide the given problem into small manageable independent sub problem, which can be designed separately. Finally, we can integrate all those sub problems as a solution to the overall problem. So we can develop algorithms for these sub problems, called *sub algorithms,* which when implemented can't run on its own. They have to be called either by a main algorithm or by another sub algorithm. So for the calling purpose, we can assign them name and given a parameter lists through which they will communicate with the calling algorithms.

In the last example, if we assume that the array is in memory, and we want to develop sub algorithm that finds and returns the location *loc* of the largest element to the main algorithm, then formal presentation of this sub algorithm may look as shown on next page.

Algorithm 4.2:

FindLocation(*a*, *n*, *loc*)

Here *a*[0:*n*–1] is an one-dimensional array with *n* values in memory. This algorithm finds the location *loc* of its largest element. The variable *i* is used as index variable, and *max* as temporary variable to store the current largest element.

```
Begin
   Set loc = 0
   Set max = a0
   for i = 1 to (n-1) by 1 do
      if ( ai > max )  then
         Set max = ai
         Set loc = i
      endif
   endfor
End.
```

Then, the problem of finding the largest element of the given array can be solved as shown below.

Algorithm 4.3:

Let *a*[0:*n*–1] be one-dimensional array with *n* real values. This algorithm finds the location *loc* of its largest element.

```
Begin
   read: n
   for i = 0 to (n-1) by 1 do
      read: ai
   endfor
   Call FindLocation( a, n, loc )
   write: "Location of the largest element = ", loc
End.
```

4.4 PROGRAMMING CONSTRUCTS

Algorithms and their equivalent programs can be easily understood if they mainly use following type of programming constructs:

- Sequential programming construct
- Selection programming construct
- Iterative programming constructs

These programming constructs are discussed below, and in each case the equivalent flowchart is also given.

4.4.1 Sequential Programming Construct

In sequential programming construct, the steps are executed one after the other. Most processing, even of complex problems, will generally follow this elementary sequential flow of control.

Sequential programming construct has the following form:

```
        :
        :
        :
   statement-1
   statement-2
   statement-3
        :
        :
        :
```

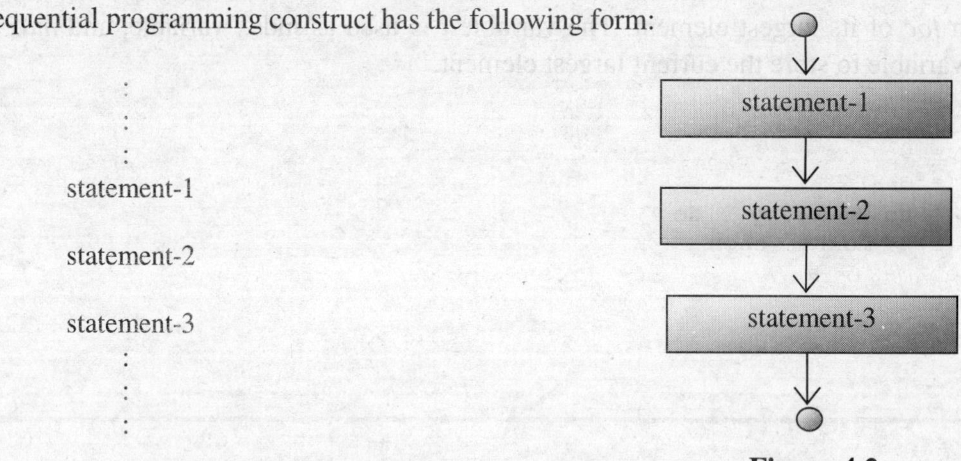

Figure 4.2

4.4.2 Selection Programming Construct

The selection programming construct employ conditions and depending on the outcome of the conditions may select one of the alternatives. The structure which implement this type of logic is called *if structure* or *conditional structure*.

These *if structure* fall into following categories:

- Single alternative
- Double alternative
- Multiple alternatives

4.4.2.1 Single Alternative

This structure has the following form:

```
        :
        :
if ( expression ) then
        statement
endif
        :
        :
```

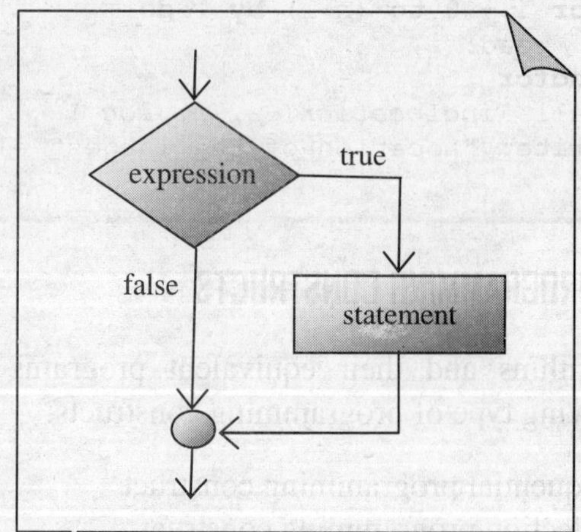

Figure 4.3

If the expression is met, then the instruction(s) between the words *then* and *endif* is/are executed; otherwise the control transfers to the next statement after the word *endif*.

4.4.2.2 Double Alternative

This structure has the following form:

```
    :
    :
if ( expression ) then
    statement-1
else
    statement-2
endif
    :
    :
```

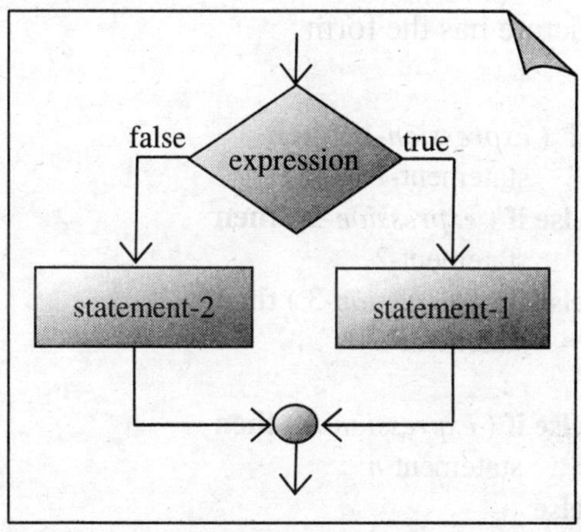

Figure 4.4

If the expression is met, then the instruction(s)-1 is/are executed and block instruction(s)-2 is/are skipped; otherwise the instruction(s)-1 is/are skipped and instruction(s)-2 is/are executed.

4.4.2.3 Multiple Alternatives

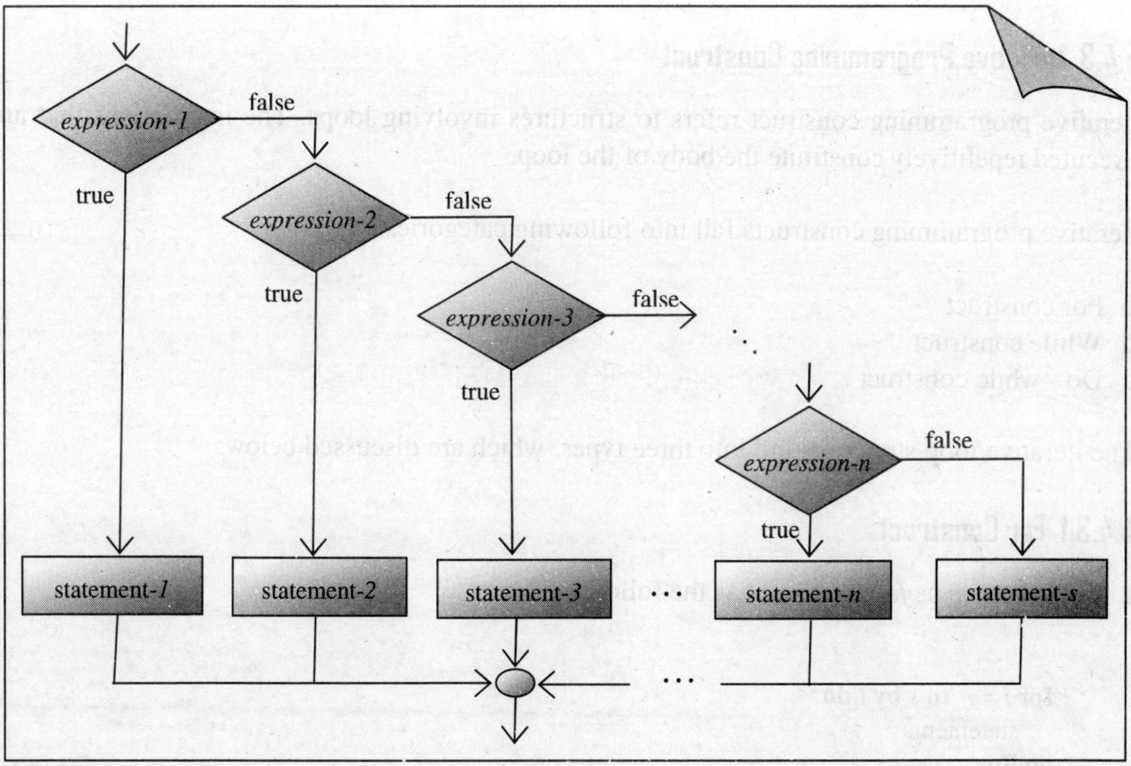

Figure 4.5

This structure has the form

```
:
if ( expression-1 ) then
    statement-1
else if ( expression-2 ) then
    statement-2
else if ( expression-3 ) then
    statement-3
    :
else if ( expression-n ) then
    statement-n
else
    statement-s
endif
    :
```

If the *expression*-1 is satisfied, then *instruction(s)-1* is/are executed; if the *expression*-2 is satisfied, then *instruction(s)-2* is/are executed; if the *expression*-3 is satisfied, then *instruction(s)-3* is/are executed; and so on. If none of the expression is satisfied, then *instruction(s)-e* is/are executed.

4.4.3 Iterative Programming Construct

Iterative programming construct refers to structures involving loops. The instructions that are executed repetitively constitute the body of the loop.

Iterative programming constructs fall into following categories:

- For construct
- While construct
- Do - while construct

The iterative/loop structures fall into three types, which are discussed below:

4.4.3.1 For Construct

It is also known as *for loop* and has the following form:

```
:
for i = r  to s by t do
    statements
endfor
:
```

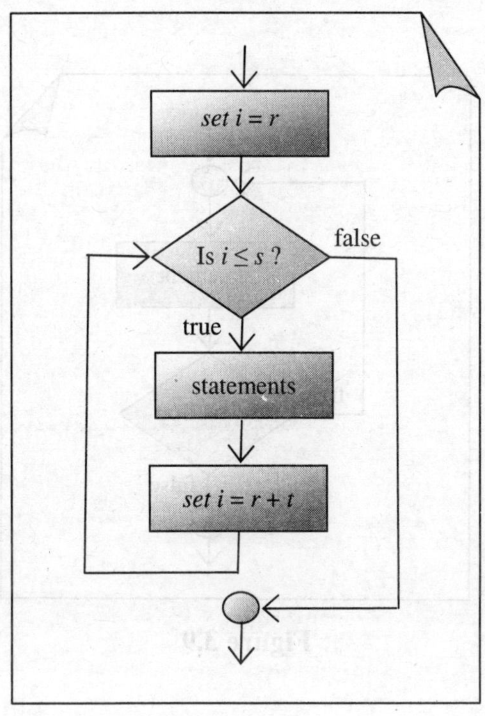

Figure 4.6

Figure 4.7

It uses an index variable *k* to control the loop. Here *r* is called the initial value, *s* is called the final value and *t* is called the step size. (increment) or negative (decrement).

4.4.3.2 While Construct

It is also known as *while loop* and has the following form:

:

while (*expression*) **do**
  statement
endwhile

:

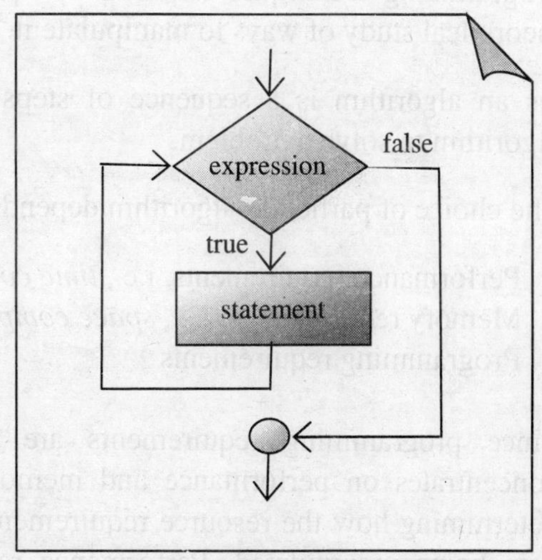

Figure 3.8

It uses a expression to control the loop. The loop is executed until the expression remains true. But before the control enters into the while loop, there must be instruction that initializes this expression, and in order that the loop must terminate, there must be an instruction in the loop that changes the expression.

4.4.3.3 Do – while Construct

It is also known as *do – while loop* and has the following form:

```
    :
do
    statement
while ( expression )
    :
```

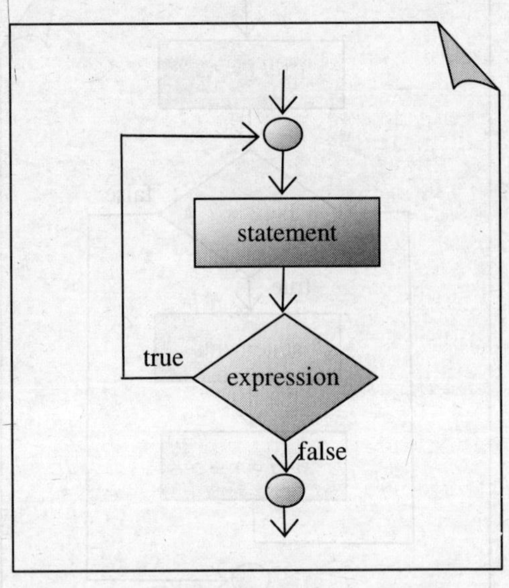

Figure 3.9

This structure also uses a expression to control the loop like while structure, with the difference that the expression is tested after the body of the loop. The body of the loop is executed repetitively until the expression remains true. In this structure the body of the loop is always executed once.

4.5 ALGORITHM COMPLEXITY

There are basically two aspects of computer programming. One is the data organization i.e. the data structures to represent the data of the problem in hand, and is the subject of the present text. The other one involves choosing the appropriate algorithm to solve the problem in hand. Data structures and algorithms are inseparably linked. Once one has developed a firm base in programming techniques required to represent information, it is logical to proceed to more theoretical study of ways to manipulate it.

As an algorithm is a sequence of steps to solve a problem, there may be more than one algorithm to solve a problem.

The choice of particular algorithm depends on following considerations:

- Performance requirements, i.e., *time complexity*
- Memory requirements, *i.e.*, *space complexity*
- Programming requirements

Since programming requirements are difficult to analyze precisely, complexity theory concentrates on performance and memory requirements. Specifically, it is used to help in determining how the resource requirements of an algorithm grow in relation to the size of the data being manipulated. Performance requirements are usually more critical than memory requirements; hence, in general, it is not necessary to worry about memory unless they grow faster than performance requirements. Therefore, in general, the algorithms are analyzed only on the basis of performance requirements, *i.e.*, running-time efficiency.

Based on an algorithm written in a pseudocode, it is impossible to measure the exact resource requirements of real implementations. This is because certain variable factors such as the language and hardware being used are unknown. Although this may seem to imply that it is better to specify an algorithm in a high-level language and perform actual measurements, but it is rather incorrect. If a specific implementation of the algorithm is studied, general conclusions about the algorithm may be invalid. Hence, algorithms should be compared at the pseudocode stage.

4.5.1 Space Complexity

The space complexity of an algorithm, hence program, is the amount of memory it needs to run to completion. Some of the reasons for studying space complexity are:

- If the program is to run on multi-user system, it may be required to specify the amount of memory to be allocated to the program.
- We may be interested to know in advance that whether sufficient memory is available to run the program.
- There may be several possible solutions with different space requirements.
- Can be used to estimate the size of the largest problem that a program can solve.

The space needed by a program consists of following components:

- ***Instruction space*** – space needed to store the executable version of the program and is fixed.
- ***Data space*** – space needed to store all constants, variable values and has further two components:
  - Space needed by constants and simple variables. This space is fixed.
  - Space needed by fixed sized structured variables, such as arrays and structures.
  - Dynamically allocated space. This space usually varies.
- ***Environment stack space*** – space needed to store the information needed to resume the suspended (partially completed) functions. Each time a function is invoked, the following data is saved on the environment stack:
  - Return address i.e. from where it has to resume after completion of the called function.
  - Values of all local variables and the values of formal parameters in the function being invoked.

The amount of space needed by recursive functions is called the *recursion stack space*. For each recursive function, this space depends on the space needed by the local variables and the formal parameters. In addition, this space depends on the maximum depth of the recursion i.e. maximum number of nested recursive calls.

In general, the total space needed by a program can be divided in two parts:

- A fixed part that is independent of particular problem, and includes instruction space, space for constants, simple variables and fixed size structured variables.
- A variable part that includes structured variables whose size depends on the particular problem being solved dynamically allocated space and the recursion stack space.

4.5.2 Time Complexity

The time complexity of an algorithm is the amount of time it needs to run to completion. Some of the reasons for studying time complexity are:

- We may be interested to know in advance that whether the program will provide a satisfactory real-time response. For example, an interactive program, such as an editor, must provide such a response. If it takes even a few seconds to move the cursor one page up or down, it will not be acceptable to the user.
- There may be several possible solutions with different time requirements.

The time complexity of a program depends on all factors that the space complexity depends on.

To measure the time complexity accurately, we can count the all sort of operations performed in an algorithm. If we know the time for each one of the primitive operations performed on a given computer, we can easily compute the time taken by an algorithm to complete its execution. This time will vary from system to system.

Our intention is to estimate the execution time of an algorithm irrespective of the computer on which it will be used. Hence, the more reasonable approach is to identify the key operation and count such operations performed till the program completes its execution. A key operation in our algorithm is an operation that takes maximum time among all possible operations in the algorithm. The time complexity can now be expressed as a function of number of key operations performed.

4.5.3 Time-space Trade-off

The best algorithm, hence best program, to solve a given problem is one that requires less space in memory and takes less time to complete its execution. But in practice, it is not always possible to achieve both of these objectives. As said earlier, there may be more than one approach to solve a same problem. One such approach may require more space but takes less time to complete its execution while the other approach requires less space but takes more time to complete its execution. Thus, we may have to sacrifice one at the cost of the other. That is what we can say that there exits a *time-space* trade among algorithms.

Therefore, if space is our constraint, then we have to choose a program that requires less space at the cost of more execution time. On the other hand, if time is our constraint such as in real time systems, we have to choose a program that takes less time to complete it execution at the cost of more space.

In the analysis of algorithms, we are interested in the *average case*, the amount of time a program might be expected to take on typical input data, and in the *worst case*, the amount of time a program would take on the worst possible input configuration.

4.5.4 Expressing Space and Time Complexity

The space and/or time complexity is usually expressed in the form of a function $f(n)$, where n is the input size for a given instance of the problem being solved. Expressing space and/or time complexity as a function $f(n)$ is important because of following reasons:

- We may be interested to predict the rate of growth of complexity as the size of the problem increases.
- To compare the complexities of two or more algorithms solving the same problem in order to find which is more efficient.

The most important notation used to express this function $f(n)$ is *Big Oh* notation, which provides the upper bound for the complexity, and is described in the next section.

Since in modern computers, the memory is not a severe constraint, therefore, our analysis of algorithms will be on the basis of time complexity.

4.6 BIG Oh NOTATION

Big Oh is a characterization scheme that allows measuring the properties of algorithms such as performance and/or memory requirements in a general fashion. The algorithm complexity can be determined ignoring the implementation dependent factors. Eliminating constant factors in the analysis of the algorithms does this. Basically, these are the constant factors that differ from computer to computer. Clearly, the complexity function $f(n)$ of an algorithm increases as n increases. It is the rate of increase of $f(n)$ that we want to examine.

Suppose, $f(n)$ and $g(n)$ are functions defined on positive integer number n, then function $f(n) = O(g(n))$, read as "*f* of *n* is big oh of *g* of *n*", or as "$f(n)$ is of the order of $g(n)$", if there exists positive constants c and n_0, such that $f(n) \leq c \times g(n)$ for all values of $n \geq n_0$. That is, for all sufficiently large amount of input data ($n > n_0$), $f(n)$ will grow no more than a constant factor than $g(n)$. Thus g is an upper bound, except for a constant factor c on the value of f for all suitably large n i.e. $n \geq n_0$. While providing an upper bound function g for f, we will use only simple functional forms. These typically contain a single term in n with a multiplicative constant of one.

Theorem 4.1:

There is an important theorem in literature, which states that if

$$f(n) = a_m n^m + a_{m-1} n^{m-1} + \ldots + a_2 n^2 + a_1 n + a_0 \text{ and } a_m > 0$$

then $f(n) = O(n^m)$

Proof : $f(n) \le \sum_{i=0}^{m} |a_i| n^i$

$$= n^m \sum_{i=0}^{m} |a_i| n^{i-m}$$

$$\le n^m \sum_{i=0}^{m} |a_i| \quad \text{for } n \ge 1$$

Hence $f(n) = O(n^m)$

Table 4.1: Some examples

$g(n)$	$f(n) = O(g(n))$
20	O(1) i.e. Constant
$1/2\, n^2 + 3$	$O(n^2)$
$500\, n^2 - 25$	$O(n^2)$
$n^3 + n^2 - 1$	$O(n^3)$
$5n^3 + 3n + 6$	$O(n^3)$

Note that the exact constant values do not matter and that the relationship $f(n) \le c \times g(n)$ may not hold for small input sizes. Since the purpose of *Big Oh* notation is to compare the algorithms in a general fashion, the anomalies that appear for small input sizes are ignored.

4.6.1 Categories of Algorithms

Based on *Big Oh* notation, the algorithms can be categorized as follows:

- Constant time (O(1)) algorithms
- Logarithmic time (O(log*n*)) algorithms
- Linear time (O(*n*)) algorithms
- Polynomial time ($O(n^k)$, for $k > 1$) algorithms
- Exponential time ($O(k^n)$, for $k > 1$) algorithms

Many algorithms are O(*n*log*n*).

Table 4.2: Rate of growth of some standard functions

n \ *f(n)*	$\log_2 n$	n	n^2	n^3	2^n	$n\log_2 n$
5	3	5	25	125	32	15
10	4	10	100	10^3	10^3	40
100	7	100	10^4	10^6	10^{30}	700
1000	10	10^3	10^6	10^9	10^{300}	10^4

Observe that the logarithmic function log*n* grows most slowly, whereas the exponential function 2^n grows most rapidly, and the polynomial function n^k grows according to the exponent *k*.

4.6.2 Limitations of Big Oh Notation

Big Oh notation has two basic limitations:

- It contains no consideration of programming effort.
- It masks (hides) potentially important constants.

As an example of later limitation, imagine two algorithms, one using $500000n^2$ time, and the other n^3 time. The first algorithm is $O(n^2)$, which implies that it will take less time than the other algorithm which is $O(n^3)$. However, the second algorithm will be faster for $n < 500000$, and this would be faster for many applications.

With these factors in mind, the Big Oh notation will be applied to determine algorithm complexity in this book.

4.7 CONCEPT OF RECURSION

A powerful concept in the development of programs is the ability for a function to refer to itself to solve a problem. This control technique, called *recursion* is an important concept in computer science and is convenient for a variety of problems that would be difficult to solve using iterative constructs such as *for, while* and *do –while* loops. Recursion is used extensively in many of the data structures and algorithms in the present text. Recursive functions can be directly implemented in C language. This section introduces recursion, and illustrates the implementation of recursion through various illustrative examples using C language.

4.7.1 Recursion Defined

In mathematics and computer science, recursion means self -reference. A recursive function, therefore, is a function whose definition is based upon itself. In other words, a function containing either a call statement to itself or a call statement to another function that may eventually may result in a call statement back to the original function, then that function is called a recursive function.

In order that the program should not continue indefinitely, a recursive function must have the following properties:

1. There must be certain criteria, called *base criteria*, for which the function does not call itself.
2. Each time the function does call itself (directly or indirectly), it must be closer to the base criteria, *i.e.*, it uses an argument(s) closer than the one it was given.

A recursive function with these two properties is said be well-defined.

4.7.2 Depth of Recursion

Suppose P is a recursive function. During the execution of a program, which contains P, we associate *level number* with each execution of P as follows. The original execution of P is assigned level 1; and each time P is executed because of recursive call, its level is one more than the level of execution that had made the recursive call.

The *depth* of a recursive function P with given set of arguments refers to the maximum level number of P during its execution.

4.7.3 Examples of Some Recursive Functions

Let us take some examples of recursive functions and their implementation in C language.

4.7.3.1 Factorial Function

The factorial of a positive number n, written as $n!$, is the product of the positive integers from 1 to n:

$$n! = 1.2.3...(n\text{-}2).(n\text{-}1).n$$

where as

$$0! = 1$$

Thus the definition of the iterative version of the factorial function can be written as

$$n! = \begin{cases} 1 & \text{if } n = 0 \\ \prod_{i=1}^{n} i & \text{if } n > 0 \end{cases}$$

From this definition, we have

$0! = 1$ $\quad$ $1! = 1$

$2! = 1.2 = 2$ $\quad$ $3! = 1.2.3 = 6$

$4! = 1.2.3.4 = 24$ $\quad$ $5! = 1.2.3.4.5 = 120$

and so on.

Observe that

$4! = 4.3! = 4.6 = 24$ and $5! = 5.4! = 5.24 = 120$

And this is true for every positive integer n; that is

$$n! = n.(n\text{-}1)!$$

Thus, the factorial function can be defined recursively as

$$n! = \begin{cases} 1 & \text{if } n = 0 \\ n.(n-1)! & \text{if } n > 0 \end{cases}$$

This definition of $n!$ is recursive, since it refers to itself when it uses $(n-1)!$. However,

1. The value of $n!$ is explicitly given when $n = 0$. Thus 0 is the base value for n, and
2. The value of $n!$ is defined in terms of a smaller value of n which is closer the base value.

Thus the factorial function is well defined.

Example 4.1:

Let us compute 4! using recursive definition. This computation requires following steps

1) 4! = 4.3!
2) 3! = 3.2!
3) 2! = 2.1!
4) 1! = 1.0!
5) 0! = 1
6) 1! = 1.1 = 1
7) 2! = 2.1 = 2
8) 3! = 3.2 = 6
9) 4! = 4.6 = 24

In other words, the above computations can be described in the following steps:

1. This step defines 4! in terms of 3!, so to compute 4!, we need to compute first 3!. Thus we have to postpone the computation of 4! until we compute 3!. This postponement is shown by indenting the next step.
2. This step defines 3! in terms of 2!, so we postpone computing 3!, until we compute 2!.
3. This step defines 2! in terms of 1!, so we postpone computing 2!, until we compute 1!.
4. This step defines 1! in terms of 0!, so we postpone computing 1!, until we compute 0!.
5. This step explicitly compute 0!, since 0 is the base value, and it equals 1.
6. Backtrack and compute 1! using the value of 0!.
7. Backtrack and compute 2! using the value of 1!.
8. Backtrack and compute 3! using the value of 2!.
9. Backtrack further and compute 4! using the value of 3!.

Observe that we backtrack in the reverse order of the original postponed computations. This type of postponed processing lends itself to the use of *stacks*. A stack data structure is described in *Chapter 7*.

In the above example, step 1 belongs to level 1, because it is original call to compute 4!. Hence step 2 belongs to level 2, step 3 belongs to level 3, step 4 to level 4, step 5 to level 5. On the other hand, step 6 belongs to level 4, since it is the result of a return from level 5. In other words, step 6 and step 4 belongs to same level of execution. Similarly, step 7 and step 3 belongs to same level, step 8 and step 2 to same level, and step 9 and step 1 to same level number i.e. level number 1.

The factorial function can be implemented using iterative procedure as shown below.

Listing 4.1:

```
int factorial( int n )
{
   if ( n == 0 )
       return 1;
   else
   {
       int i, fact = 1;
       for ( i = 2, i <= n; i++ )
           fact *= i;
       return fact;
   }
}
```

The factorial function can also be implemented using recursion as shown below.

Listing 4.2:

```
int factorial( int n )
{
   if ( n == 0 )
       return 1;
   else
       return ( n * factorial ( n - 1 ) );
}
```

Table 4.3: Trace of recursive function *factorial()* for $n = 3$

Function call	first	second	third	fourth				
Origin of call	calling program	first level	second level	third level				
Return					first	second	third	fourth
Place of return					fourth level	third level	second level	calling program
factorial	?	?	?	?	?	?	?	6
n_1	3	3	3	3	3	3	3	
$factorial_1$	?	?	?	?	?	?	6	
n_2		2	2	2	2	2		
$factorial_2$		?	?	?	?	2		
n_3			1	1	1			
$factorial_3$			?	?	1			
n_4				0				
$factorial_4$				1				

In the trace, the *subscripts* are attached to the variables to indicate the corresponding level. For example, n_3 denotes the third level of the parameter.

The recursive factorial function uses *tail recursion* i.e. the last statement contains a single recursive call. Because of this structure, tail recursive functions always have direct iterative equivalents.

If you compare the two codes, you will find that the recursive version is more natural and appealing. However, in this particular case, iteration is more efficient, but the choice of a tail recursion or iteration is largely a question of style, and depends on how the problem is viewed.

4.7.3.1.1 Recursive Function and Run Time Stack

A function is a sequence of instructions that are executed in response to a function call. The flow of control during this function call from a calling function and exit from the called function is shown in Figure 4.11.

The execution process begins by having the calling function set up an *activation record* that includes the list of actual parameters and the location of the next instruction to execute after returning to the calling function.

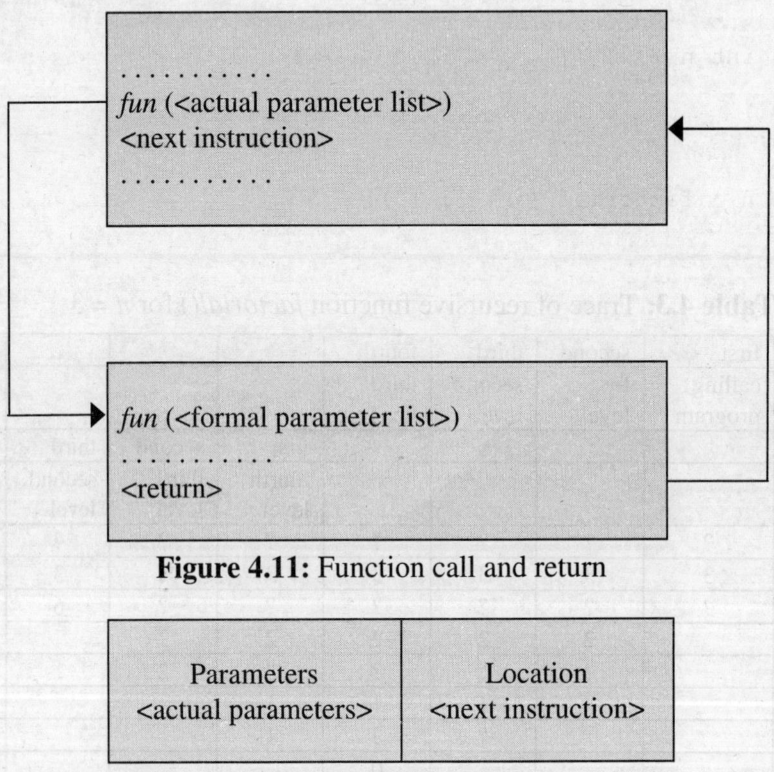

Figure 4.11: Function call and return

Figure 4.12: Structure of activation record

When the function is called, data from activation record is pushed on a system-supplied stack, known as *runtime stack*. This data along with local variables is used to define an activation frame that is made available to the function.

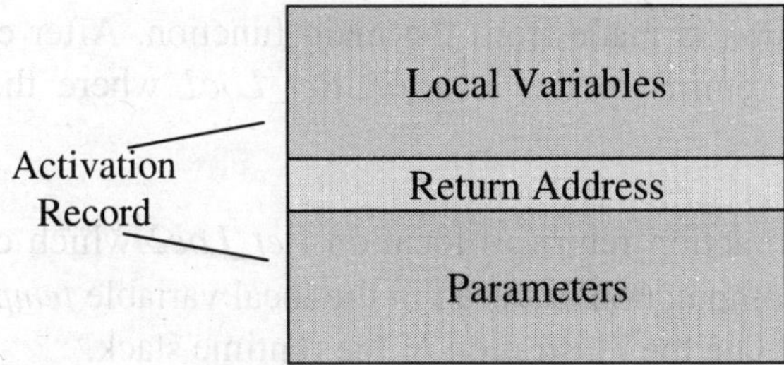

Figure 4.13: Structure of activation frame

The process of exiting the function code identifies the location of the next instruction and then destroys the data on the stack that corresponds to the activation record. A recursive function makes repeated calls to itself using a modified parameter list for each call. The process pushes a series of activation records on the stack until the stopping condition is reached. The subsequent popping of the activation records gives the recursive solution.

To understand the runtime stack and the activation records setup during evaluations, consider the following *main()* function and the modified version of recursive factorial function:

Listing 4.3:

```
void main()
{
   int n;
   . . . . . . . .
   /*push activation record with call factorial(3)*/
   n = factorial(3);
                    / *Ret_Loc1is the address of assignment */
      . . . . . . . /*   n = factorial(3)   */
   . . . . . . . .
}
Ret_Loc1

int factorial( int n )
{
   int temp;
   if ( n == 0 )
      return 1;     /*  pop activation record    */
   else
   {
      /*push activation record with call    */
      temp = n*factorial(n-1);
                              /* factorial(n-1), Ret_Loc2 is the */
          return temp;  /*  address of computation */
                          /*    n*factorial(n-1)   */
      }
}
Ret_Loc2
```

The initial call to the factorial function is made from the main function. After executing the factorial function, program control returns to the location *Ret_Loc1* where the value 6 is assigned to *n*.

The recursive calls in the factorial function return to location *Ret_Loc2* which computes the product $n \times (n-1)!$. The result of the computation is stored in the local variable *temp* to assist the reader in tracing the code and to facilitate the illustration of the runtime stack.

Calling Function	Parameter	Return
Itself as factorial (1)	Parameter 0	Return : Ret_Loc2
Itself as factorial (2)	Parameter 1	Return : Ret_Loc2
Itself as factorial (3)	Parameter 2	Return : Ret_Loc2
main	Parameter 3	Return : Ret_Loc1

Figure 4.14: Activation Stack

For the factorial function, the activation record has following structure

Parameters int *n*	Location <next instruction>

Figure 4.15: Activation record for factorial function

The function call *factorial(3)* initiates a sequence of four function calls. Figure 4.16 describes the activation record for each call. The stopping condition occurs in the function call *factorial(0)* and the sequence of return statements begins to execute. The activation record at the top of the stack is popped and the program control passes to the return location. The following operations describe the clearing of the activation records from the stack.

Parameter	Return Location	Instruction Upon Return
0	Ret_Loc2	Ret_Loc2 temp = 1 * 1 /* 1 form call factorial(0) */ return temp; /* temp = 1 */
1	Ret_Loc2	Ret_Loc2 temp = 2 * 1 /* 1 form call factorial(1) */ return temp; /* temp = 2 */
2	Ret_Loc2	Ret_Loc2 temp = 3 * 2 /* 2 form call factorial(2) */ return temp; /* temp = 6 */
3	Ret_Loc1	Ret_Loc1 n = factorial(3) /* back to main function */

Figure 4.16: Activation record for each recursive call to *factorial()* function

4.7.3.2 Positive Exponential Power Function

Like factorial function, similar iterative and recursive definitions exist for computing the positive exponential power of a number.

Its iterative version is

$$x^n = \begin{cases} 1 & \text{if } n = 0 \\ \prod_{i=1}^{n} x & \text{if } n > 0 \end{cases}$$

where as its recursive version is

$$x^n = \begin{cases} 1 & \text{if } n = 0 \\ x.x^{n-1} & \text{if } n > 0 \end{cases}$$

The iterative implementation of power function is shown below.

Listing 4.4:

```
float power( float x, int n )
{
   if ( n == 0 )
       return 1;
   else
   {
       int i, prod = x;
       for ( i = 2, i <= n; i++ )
           prod *= x;
       return prod;
   }
}
```

The recursive implementation of the power function is shown below.

Listing 4.5:

```
float power( float x, int n )
{
   if ( n == 0 )
      return 1;
   else
      return ( x * power( x, n - 1 ) );
}
```

Table 4.4: Trace of recursive function *power()* for $x = 3.0$ and $n = 3$

Function call Origin of call	first calling program	second first level	third second level	fourth third level				
Return Place of return					first fourth level	second third level	third second level	fourth calling program
Power	?	?	?	?	?	?	?	27.0
x_1	3.0	3.0	3.0	3.0	3.0	3.0	3.0	
n_1	3	3	3	3	3	3	3	
power$_1$	?	?	?	?	?	?	27.0	
x_2		3.0	3.0	3.0	3.0	3.0		
n_2		2	2	2	2	2		
power$_2$		?	?	?	?	9.0		
x_3			3.0	3.0	3.0			
n_3			1	1	1			
power$_3$			?	?	3.0			
x_4				3.0				
n_4				0				
power$_4$				1.0				

4.7.3.3 Fibonacci Numbers

A very important sequence, *Fibonacci sequence,* usually denoted by F_0, F_1, . . ., F_n, is as follows:

0, 1, 1, 2, 3, 5, 8, 13, . . .

That is, $F_0 = 0$ and $F_1 = 1$ and the subsequent terms are the sum of the two preceding terms. For example, the next term in the above sequence is

8 + 13 = 21

A formal definition for Fibonacci number F_n is:

$$fib(n) = \begin{cases} n & \text{if } n \le 1 \\ fib(n-1) + fib(n-2) & \text{if } n > 1 \end{cases}$$

Figure 4.17 shows how *fib(5)* will be computed using recursive definition.

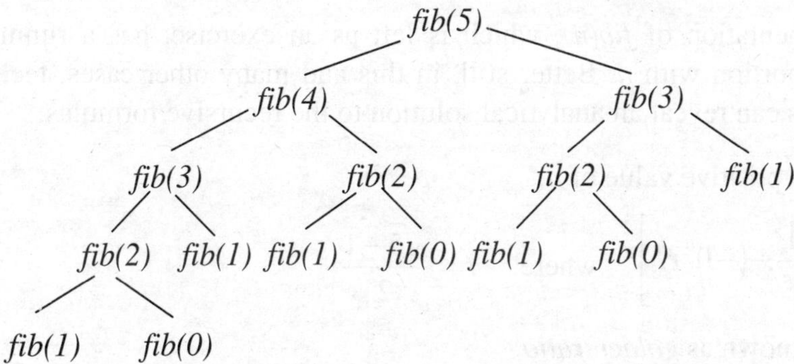

Figure 4.17: Recursive computation of *fib(5)*

Notice that the recursive definition of the Fibonacci numbers differs from the recursive definitions of the factorial function and positive exponential power function in the sense that it refers to itself twice.

As you must have observed, the problem with the above recursive definition is that the recursive sub problems overlap, causing many redundant computations. The time required to compute *fib(n)* thus grows exponentially.

This is demonstrated in Table 4.5. It shows that a large number of function calls are required to compute *n*th Fibonacci number even for moderate value of *n*.

Table 4.5: Illustration of Function call for *fib(n)*

Value of *n*	Value of *fib(n)*	Number of function calls required recursively to compute *fib(n)*
0	0	1
1	1	1
2	1	3
...	...	...
23	28657	92735
24	46368	150049
...	...	...
42	267914296	866988873
43	433494437	14028817465

The recursive function *fib(n)* can be implemented as

Listing 4.6:

```
int fib( int n )
{
   if ( n <= 1 )
      return n;
   else
      return ( fib ( n - 1 ) + fib ( n - 2 ) );
}
```

An iterative implementation of *fib(n)*, which is left as an exercise, has a running time that grows in linear proportion with *n*. Better still, in this and many other cases, techniques from discrete mathematics can reveal an analytical solution to the recursive formulas.

For example, for any positive value of *n;*

$$F_n = \frac{1}{\sqrt{5}}\left[\frac{1}{r^n} - (-1)^n r^n\right] \quad \text{where} \quad r = \frac{\sqrt{5}-1}{2}$$

The factor *r* is also known as *golden ratio*.

Thus, three methods for solving a problem may exist. These are

1. A recursive solution
2. An iterative solution
3. An analytical solution

4.7.3.4 Towers of Hanoi

Another famous recursive problem is the *Towers of Hanoi*. This is actually a game consisting of three pins and a set of disks of different sizes. The game starts with the disks stacked in the decreasing size on the first pin.

The aim of this game is to move the disks to another pin with the following constraints:

- Only one disk can be moved at a time, and that too the top disk.
- No disk can be placed on the top of smaller disk.

All the three pins can be used, and a disk can be moved directly from any pin to other one. Assume that disks are numbered in the increasing order of their size. In order to design a general algorithm for solving this problem with *n* disks from pin A to pin C using third pin B, let us look at some examples using few disks.

Case 1: *Given one disk only*

In this case, which is the *base case*, the disk can be directly moved from pin A to pin C as shown in Figure 4.18.

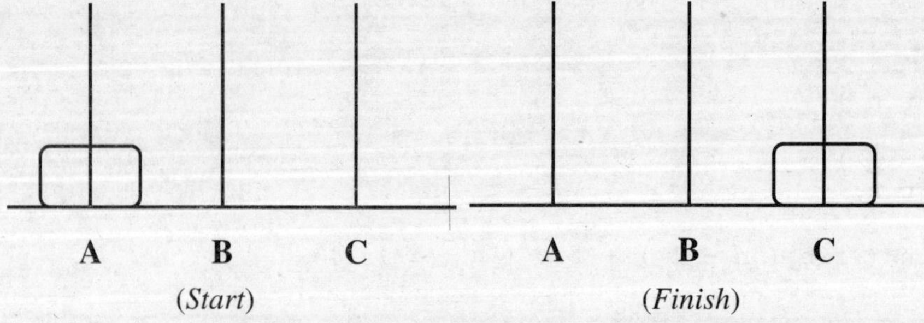

Figure 4.18: Tower of Hanoi for one disk

Case 2: *Given two disks*

In this case, first move disk 1 to pin B, then move disk 2 to pin C. The last step places the disk 1 on the top of disk 2 in pin C.

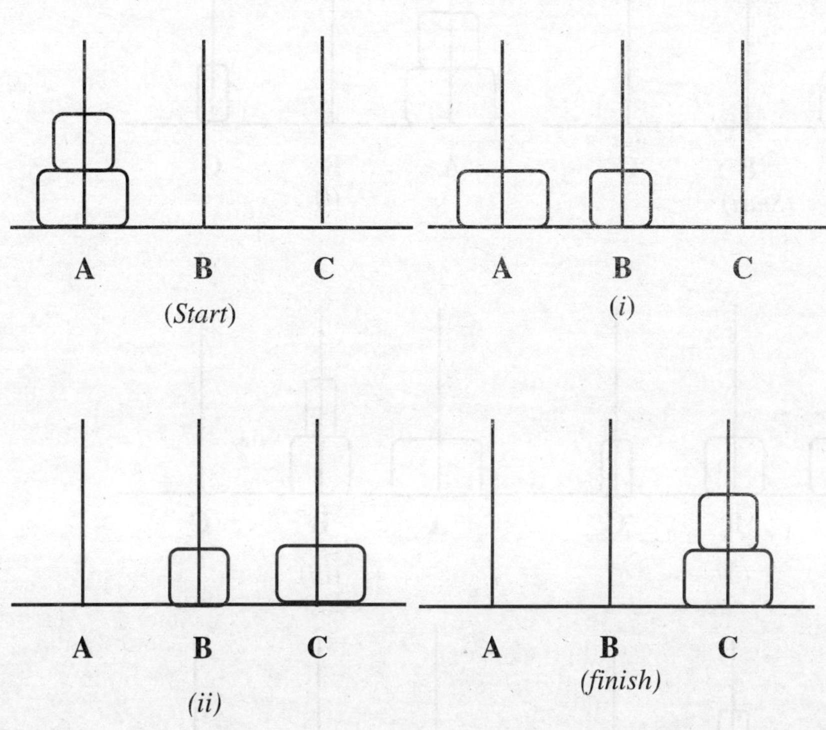

Figure 4.19: Tower of Hanoi for two disks

Case 3: *Given three disks*

In this case, the problem becomes little complex. Proceed as follows:

- move disk 1 from pin A to pin C
- move disk 2 from pin A to pin B
- move disk 1 from pin C to pin B
- move disk 3 from pin A to pin C
- move disk 1 from pin B to pin A
- move disk 2 from pin B to pin C
- finally move disk 1 from pin A to pin C

So we need total seven steps, and these number of steps increases with the increase of number of disks.

These steps are illustrated below.

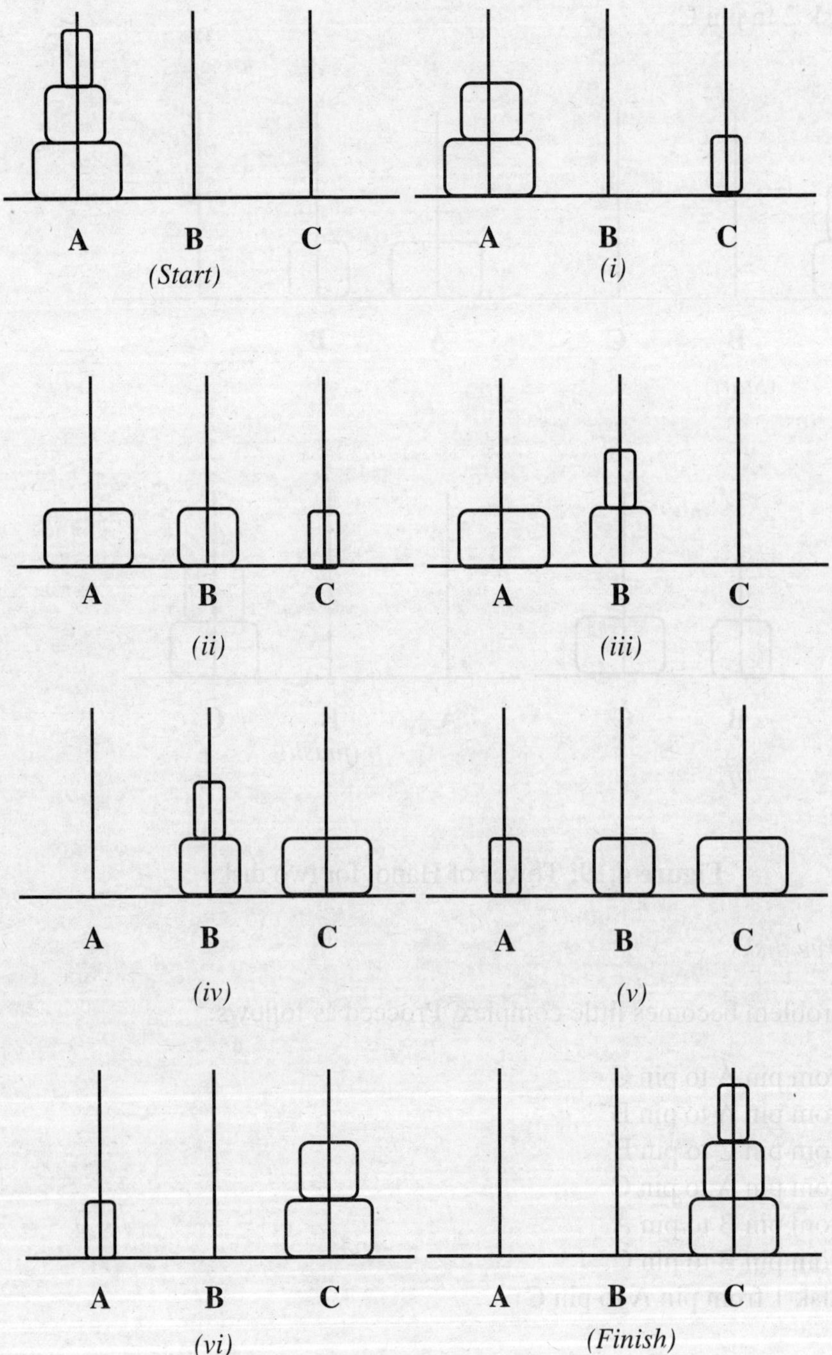

Figure 4.20: Tower of Hanoi for three disks

Having examined the above cases with two or three disks, the following observations can be made:

- In order to move the largest disk from pin A to pin C, we must move the smaller disks that are on the top to pin B.
- Then move the largest disk from pin A to pin C.

Once the largest disk has been moved, we must move, in the similar manner, all the smaller disks to pin C.

We can now describe recursively the required steps needed to move *n* disks from pin A to pin C using pin B as given below:

```
if ( N = 1 ) then
    Move the disk from pin A to pin C
else
    Move the (N-1) smaller disks from pin A to pin B
    Move the largest disks from pin A to pin C
    Move the (N-1) smaller disks from pin B to pin C
endif
```

The implementation of the above algorithm is as given below.

Listing 4.7:

```
/*  Recursive function for towers of Hanoi game */
void towerOfHanoi( char from, char to, char other, int n )
{
   if ( n == 1 ) {
      printf( "Move disk from %c to %c \n", from, to );
   } else {
      towerOfHanoi( from, other, to, n-1 );
      towerOfHanoi( from, to, other, 1 );
      towerOfHanoi( other, to, from, n-1 );
   }
}
```

This recursive function is used in the following program.

Listing 4.8:

```
/*  Program to play towers of Hanoi game  */
#include <stdio.h>
#include <stdlib.h>
void main()
{
   int n;
   /*   function prototype   */
   void towerOfHanoi( char, char, char, int );
   printf( "\nEnter number of disks: " );
   scanf( "%d", &n );
   printf( "\n" );
   if ( n < 1 ) {
```

```
        printf ( "\nIllegal input ...\n" );
        exit(1);
    }
    else
        towerOfHanoi( 'A', 'C', 'B', n );
}
```

4.7.3.5 Counting Problem

As an example of counting problem, consider an alphabet of *m* letters, and our aim is to find the number of strings of length *n* that can be formed using above alphabet.

In order to design a general algorithm for solving this problem, let us look at some examples using an alphabet consisting of letters 'a' and 'b' only ($m = 2$).

Case 1: *String of length one*

In this case, which is the *base case*, the number of strings is equal to number of letters in the alphabet i.e.

```
a, b    (2 (m) only)
```

Case 2: *Strings of length two*

In this case, the possible strings (4) are

```
aa, ab, ba, bb    (2 * number of strings of length 1)
```

Case 3: *Strings of length three*

First form the strings of length two as in case 2 to obtain

```
aa, ab, ba, bb
```

and then prefix the above strings with each of the letters of the given alphabet. First prefixing with letter 'a', we get

```
aaa, aab, aba, abb
```

then prefixing with letter 'b', we get

```
baa, bab, bba, bbb
```

So, we get the possible strings as

```
aaa, aab, aba, abb, baa, bab, bba, bbb
                    (2 * number strings of length 2)
```

The recursive idea for this problem is that we can produce all strings of length *n* using *m* letters of an alphabet by first producing all strings of length ($n-1$) and then prefixing each of them with each of the *m* letters.

Suppose we use the notation *strings_nm(n, m)* to denote the number of strings of length *n* using *m* letters, then the recursive formula becomes

$$strings\_nm(n, m) = \begin{cases} m & \text{if } n = 1 \\ m \times strings\_nm(n-1, m) & \text{if } n > 1 \end{cases}$$

From this definition, the recursive function *strings_nm(n, m)* can be written as:

Listing 4.9:

```
int strings_nm( int n, int m )
{
   if ( n == 1 )
      return m;
   else
      return ( m * strings_nm(n - 1,  m )  );
}
```

4.7.3.6 Minmax Problem

Recursive algorithms, in general, are based on the principle of solving problems by decomposing them into discrete sub problems of smaller sizes. Tail recursion generates the solution for the *n*th case from the (n −1)th case. More generally, recursive functions may recombine several sub problems i.e. making several recursive calls, before generating the solution. This technique is called *divide and conquer*, often leads to more efficient solution than a naive iterative approach.

To demonstrate this, let us consider the problem of finding the minimum and the maximum, also known as *minmax problem*, of an array of integers.

Consider the following naive iterative procedure to solve *minmax* problem;

Listing 4.10:

```
void minmax( int *a, int n, int *p_max, int *p_min )
{
   int i;
   *p_max = *p_min = a[0];
   for ( i = 1; i < n; i++ ) {
      if ( a[i] < *p_min )
         *p_min = a[i];
      if ( a[i] > *p_max )
         *p_max = a[i];
   }
}
```

This procedure makes 2*(n−1) comparisons, because at each of the (n−1) iterations of *for* loop, two comparison are made. Now consider the following recursive algorithm;

Algorithm 4.5:

Here *a*[0:*n*−1] is an one-dimensional array with *n* values in memory. This algorithm finds the minimum *min* and maximum *max* element of the above array using divide and conquer strategy.

```
Begin
  if (n = 1 )  then
     Set min = max = a[0]
```

```
    else if ( n = 2 ) then
        Compare a[0] & a[1] and assign smaller to min and larger to max
    else
        Divide the array into two subarrays, and recursively find min & max
        of each half
        Assign the smaller of two min's to min and larger of two max's to max
    endif
End.
```

It can be shown that this algorithm makes only (1.5*n–2) comparisons. Although these two algorithms differ only by a constant, there are algorithms where the technique of divide and conquer can be used to realize more significant improvements. The implementation of the above algorithm is given below.

Listing 4.11:

```
void minmax( int *a , int n, int *p_max, int *p_min )
{
  if ( n == 1 )
     *p_max = *p_min = a[0];
  else if ( n == 2 ) {
     if ( a[0] < a[1] ) {
        *p_min = a[0];
        *p_max = a[1];
     } else {
        *p_min = a[1];
        *p_max = a[0];
     }
  } else {
     int nby2, min2, max2;
     nby2 = n/2;
     minmax( a, nby2, p_max, p_min );
     minmax( a + nby2,   n - nby2, &min2, &max2 );
     if ( min2 < *p_min )
        *p_min = min2;
     if ( max2 > *p_max )
        *p_max = max2;
  }
}
```

4.7.4 Recursion, Iteration or . . .?

When there are number of ways of solving a problem, the obvious question that arises is *"Which one should be selected?"*. There is no set of pre-defined rules to select a particular way; however, we must consider the following issues:

1. Processing time taken.
2. Computer memory used.
3. Time taken to develop the program.
4. Time taken to debug the program.
5. Time to maintain the program.

As a generalization, recursive solutions tend to do well in categories 3, 4, and 5. Because recursive solutions tend to be simple and small, the time and to modify the programs later on is less than the time needed for non-recursive solution of the same problem, if it does exists.

On the other hand, in general, recursive solutions do not tend to do well in their use of computer processing time and the amount of computer memory they require. When we are writing and running programs on our own computer, we often don't care about the time that a program takes to run as long as it gets finished in a reasonable amount of time. We usually don't care about the memory utilization if the program doesn't require more than the amount of memory that is available in our own computer. However, when we are programming for an environment that allows several programs to execute concurrently (multitasking) or that allows several users to work concurrently (multi-user), we should be very careful about the use of shared processor time and the computer memory resources.

There is no simple formula for obtaining the answer to the question of which one of several solutions for a problem is best. Even, if we have accurate statistics for each of the above categories, it isn't obvious how to compare the sets of numbers. Factors such as predicted life span of the program, frequency of usage, relative importance of the program, and cost of programming and processing must enter into the decision procedure. The field of *Software Engineering*, which beyond the scope of present text, attempts to address categories 3, 4, and 5. The field of *Algorithm Design and Analysis* attempts to address the theoretical aspects of categories 1 and 2. This part is taken is taken care of in next chapters.

A QUICK REVIEW

In this chapter, we have learnt

- About the basics of program development life cycle.
- About the different program design tools.
- About the structured programming constructs.
- About the algorithmic notations.
- About the algorithm complexity, its objectives and various factors contributing to it.
- About the Big Oh notation.
- About the recursion.

In the next chapter, we will discuss arrays and matrices.

REVIEW EXERCISES

1. Describe the program development life cycle.
2. What are the various activities carried out in the *testing and debugging* phase of program development life cycle?
3. What are the various activities carried out in the *implementation and maintenance* phase of program development life cycle?

4. What is a *bug*?
5. What is debugging?
6. How a *syntax error* is different from a *logical error*? Which one is more difficult to handle?
7. What are *structure charts* and *flowcharts*?
8. What do you mean by *documentation*?
9. What is the role of *testing* in a program development life cycle?
10. Describe the *top-down program design* approach.
11. Differentiate between *modular programming* and *structured programming*.
12. Describe the different structured programming constructs.
13. How a *while* construct differs from a *do – while* construct?
14. What is an *algorithm*? What is the criterion that every algorithm must satisfy?
15. What is a *sub-algorithm*? How is it helpful?
16. What is *algorithm complexity*? What is the need of measuring the complexity of an algorithm?
17. What are the components of *space complexity*?
18. What are the components of *time complexity*?
19. What do you mean by *time-space trade-off* among algorithms?
20. Which notation is popularly used to express the complexity of an algorithm?
21. Describe the *Big Oh* notation.
22. Name the different categories of algorithms based on *Big Oh* notation.
23. What are the limitations of *Big Oh* notation?
24. What is recursion?
25. What is meant by depth of recursion?
26. How recursion compares with iteration?

PROGRAMMING EXERCISES

1. Give recursive definition of a function to compute the greatest common divisor of the two positive integer numbers. Also show its implementation in C language.
2. Give the recursive definition and implementation of combination function *C*(*n, r*).
3. The *Ackerman* function is defined, for all non-negative values of *m* and *n* as follows:

$$A(m,n) = \begin{cases} n+1 & \text{if } m = 0 \\ A(m-1,1) & \text{if } m \neq 0 \text{ but } n = 0 \\ A(m-1, A(m, n-1)) & \text{if } m \neq 0 \text{ and } n \neq 0 \end{cases}$$

   Write a recursive C function to compute *A*(*m, n*). Also find *A*(1,3) manually.
4. Give the recursive definition of the function to convert a positive decimal integer to its equivalent binary number.
5. Give the recursive definition and implementation of Towers of Hanoi problem.

❑ ❑ ❑

Chapter 5

Arrays and Matrices

5.1 INTRODUCTION

An *array* is a collection of homogeneous data elements (i.e. elements of same type) described by a single name. Each element of an array is referenced by a subscripted variable formed by affixing to the array name a subscript or index enclosed in parentheses. The term subscript has the same meaning as in the mathematical notations. If single subscript is required to reference an element of an array, the array is known as *one-dimensional array* or *linear array*, and if two subscripts are required to reference an element, the array is known as *two-dimensional array*, and so on. Analogously, the arrays whose elements are referenced by two or more subscripts are called *multi-dimensional arrays*.

This chapter describes the different types of arrays and various operations that can be performed on arrays.

5.2 LINEAR ARRAYS

A linear array *a* is a list of a finite number *n* of homogeneous data elements such that

- The elements of the array are referenced by an index set consisting of *n* consecutive integer numbers.
- The elements of the array are stored in consecutive memory locations.

The number *n* of the elements is called the *size* of the array. In general, if *lb* is the smallest index called the *lower bound*, and *ub* is the largest index called *upper bound*, then size of the array is given by

```
size = ub - lb + 1
```

Note that the size of the array = *ub* if *lb* = 1.

Suppose *a* is the name of the linear array of size *n*, then its *k*th elements is denoted as

a_k	in subscript/mathematical notation
$a(k)$	in BASIC and FORTRAN languages, called parentheses notation
$a[k]$	in Pascal, C/ C++ and Java languages, called bracket notation

The number *k* in *a*(*k*) or *a*[*k*] is called a *subscript* and *a*(*k*) or *a*[*k*] is itself called a *subscripted variable.*

In the present text, we will be using the bracket notation as it is also used in C/C++ languages, the languages of your implementation. Further, if an array is declared with size *n*, then its lower bound *lb* will be taken as 0 and upper bound *ub* as (*n*−1).

The index set is dependent on the language being used to implement arrays. For example

- In BASIC or FORTRAN, if arrays size is *n*, the index set consists of 1, 2, 3, . . ., *n*.
- In Pascal, we have to specify the lower bound and upper bound for the array.
- In C/ C++ and Java, if array size is *n*, the index set consists of 0, 1, 2, . . ., *n*–1.

5.2.1 Representing Linear Arrays in Memory

Recall that the memory of the microcomputer is simply a sequence of addressed locations as pictured in Figure 5.1.

Let *a* be a linear array with *n* elements. As arrays are stored in consecutive memory location, the system need not keep track of the address of every element of *a*, but needs to keep track of the address of first element only. The address of the first element is also known as the *base address* of the array, and is denoted by *base*(*a*).

Using this base address, the computer computes the address of the *k*th element, *loc*(*a*[*k*]), using the following formula:

$$loc(a[k]) = base(a) + w\,(k - lb) \qquad \text{in general}$$

$$loc(a[k]) = base(a) + w * k \qquad \text{in C/C++ languages}$$

where *w* is the number of bytes per storage location for one element of the array. Observe that the time taken to compute *loc*(*a*[*k*]) is essentially the same for any value of *k*. Hence, computer takes same time to access any element of the array. Furthermore, by giving any value to *k*, one can access any element of the array without scanning other elements of array *a*.

Example 5.1:

Consider that array *a* is declared as array of integers with size 10, and its first element is stored at memory address 1197, *i.e.*, its base address is 1197, as pictured in Figure 5.2. We know that an integer number requires two bytes of memory, therefore, address of the element for $k = 3$, where k can take values from 0 to 9, is given by

$loc(a[3]) = 1197 + 2 * 3 = 1201$ [Example of C/C++ implementation]

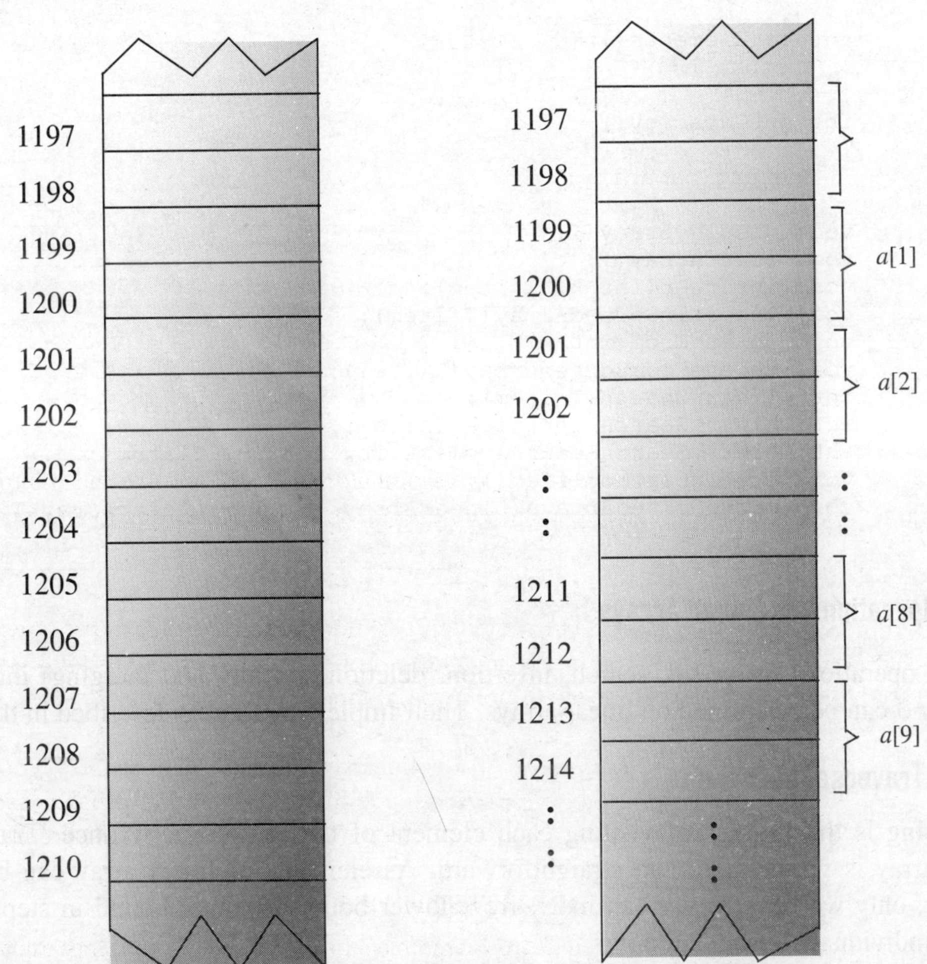

Figure 5.1: Computer Memory Map   **Figure 5.2:** Storage of array *a* of integers

The ADT to represent a linear array

```
template <class T>
class LinearArray
{
   private:
      T *a;
      int n;          // number of elements
      int capacity; // capacity of array
```

```
    public:
        LinearArray(int size)
        {
            n = 0;
            capacity = size;
            a = new T[capacity];
        }
        ~LinearArray()
        {
            delete a; // delete dynamic array
        }
        int getElements() {
            return n;
        }
        int getCapacity()
        {
            return capacity;
        }
        void displayArray();
        void inputArray();
        void insertAt(int k, T item);
        void insertInSortedArray(T item);
        void deleteFrom(int k);
        void deleteFromSortedArray(T item);
        int  linearSearch(T item);
        int  binarySearchIterative(T item);
        int  binarySearchRecursive(int lb, int ub, T item);
        void bubbleSortModified();
        void mergeSortedArrays(LinearArray<T> &la, LinearArray<T> &lb);
};
```

5.2.2 Operations on Linear Arrays

All the operations (traversal, search, insertion, deletion, sorting, and merging) introduced in *Chapter 3* can be performed on linear arrays. Their implementation is described in this section.

5.2.2.1 Traversal Operation

Traversing is the process of visiting each element of the array exactly once. Traversal of a linear array is very simple and straightforward. As elements of linear array can be accessed directly, only we have to vary an index from lower bound to upper bound in steps of one to access individual elements in order.

The following algorithm summarizes the various steps.

Algorithm 5.1:

TraverseLinearArray(*a*, *n*)

Here *a* is a linear array of size *n*. This algorithm traverses the array and applies the operation *process* to each element of the array.

```
Begin
  for i = 0 to (n-1) by 1 do
     Apply process ( a[i] )
  endfor
End.
```

The following code illustrates the traversal of the linear array by modifying above algorithm in order to compute the average of the elements of the array. Therefore, the process here will be to add the individual elements.

Listing 5.1:

```
template <class T>
void LinearArray<T>::displayArray()
{
   int i;
   cout << endl;
   for ( i = 0; i < n; i++ )
      cout << a[i] << "   ";
   cout << endl;
}
```

Analysis of Traversal Operation

As you must have observed in the above code that to access the elements the index is varied from lower bound to upper bound. Also we know that the time to access individual element is same irrespective of its position in the array. Therefore, for an array of size *n*, *for* loop executes *n* times. Thus, the traversal operation on linear arrays is O(*n*) operation.

5.2.2.2 Search Operation

Searching is the process of finding the location of given element in the linear array. The search is said to be successful if the given element is found i.e. the element does exists in the array; otherwise unsuccessful. There are two approaches to search operation:

- Linear search
- Binary search

The algorithm that one chooses generally depends on organization of the array elements. If the elements are in random order, then one have to use linear search technique, and if the array elements are sorted, then it is preferable to use binary search technique. These two search techniques are described in the next sections.

5.2.2.2.1 Linear Search

Given no information about the array *a*, the only way to search for given element *item* is to compare *item* with each element of *a* one by one. This method, which traverses *a* sequentially to locate *item* is called *linear search* or *sequential search*.

Algorithm 5.2:

LinearSearch(***a, n, item, loc*** **)**

Here a is a linear array of size n. This algorithms finds the location of the element *item* in linear array a. If search ends in success it sets *loc* to the index of the element; otherwise it sets *loc* to -1.

```
Begin
  for i = 0 to (n-1) by 1 do
     if ( a[i] = item ) then
        Set loc = i
        Exit
     endif
  endfor
  Set loc = -1
End.
```

The following code shows the implementation of above algorithm.

Listing 5.2:

```
template <class T>
int LinearArray<T>::linearSearch(T item )
{
   int i;
   for ( i = 0; i < n; i++ ) {
      if ( a[i] == item )
            return i;
   }
   return -1;
}
```

Analysis of Linear Search

In the best possible case, the *item* may occur at first position. In this case, the search operation terminates in success with just one comparison. However, the worst case occurs when either the item is present at last position or missing from the array. In the former case, the search terminates in success with n comparisons. In the later case, the search terminates in failure with n comparisons. Thus, we find that in worst case the linear search is $O(n)$ operations.

5.2.2.2.2 Binary Search

Suppose the elements of the array A are sorted in ascending order (if the elements are numbers) or dictionary order (if the elements are strings). The best searching algorithm, called *binary search,* is used to find the location of the given element. We do use this approach in our daily life. For example, suppose we want to find the meaning of the term *modem* in a computer dictionary. Obviously, we don't search page by page. We open the dictionary in the middle (roughly) to determine which half contains the term being sought. Then for the subsequent search one half is discarded, and we search in the other half. This process is continued till either we have located the required term or that term is missing from the dictionary, which will be indicated by the fact that at the end we will be left with only one page.

Example 5.2:

To illustrate the working of the binary search technique, consider the following sorted array *A* with 7 elements

3, 10, 15, 20, 35, 40, 60

and we want to search element 15.

Solution:

	$a[0]$	$a[1]$	$a[2]$	$a[3]$	$a[4]$	$a[5]$	$a[6]$
Given Array *a*	3	10	15	20	35	40	60

To start with, we take $beg = 0$, $end = 6$, and compute location of the middle element as

$$mid = (beg + end) / 2 = (0 + 6) / 2 = 3$$

Since $a[mid]$, *i.e.*, $a[3] \neq 15$, and $beg < end$. We start next iteration.

As $a[mid] = 20 > 15$, therefore, we take $end = mid - 1 = 3 - 1 = 2$, where as *beg* remains unchanged. Thus

$$mid = (beg + end) / 2 = (0 + 2) / 2 = 1$$

Since $a[mid]$, *i.e.*, $a[1] \neq 15$, and $beg < end$. We start next iteration.

As $a[mid] = 10 < 15$, therefore, we take $beg = mid + 1 = 1 + 1 = 2$, where as *end* remains unchanged.

Since $beg = end$, again compute location of the middle element as

$$mid = (beg + end) / 2 = (2 + 2) / 2 = 2$$

Since $a[mid]$, *i.e.*, $a[2] = 15$, the search terminates on success.

The element 15 is found at index 2.

Algorithm 5.3:

BinarySearch(*a*, *n*, *item*, *loc*)

Here *a* is a sorted (ascending) linear array of size *n*. This algorithms finds the location of the element *item* in linear array *a*. If search ends in success it sets *loc* to the index of the element; otherwise it sets loc to −1. Here variables *beg* and *end* to keep track of the first element and last element of the array to be searched, and variable *mid* is used as index of the middle element of the array under consideration.

```
Begin
   Set beg = 0
   Set end = n-1
   Set mid = ( beg + end ) / 2
   while ( ( beg ≤ end ) and ( a[mid] ≠ item ) ) do
      if ( item < a[mid] ) then
         Set end = mid-1
      else
         Set beg = mid+1
      endif
      Set mid = ( beg + end ) / 2
   endwhile
   if ( beg > end ) then
      Set loc = -1
   else
      Set loc = mid
   endif
End.
```

The following code shows the implementation of above algorithm.

Listing 5.3*a*:

```
template <class T>
int LinearArray<T>::binarySearchIterative(T item )
{
   int beg, end, mid;
   beg = 0;   end = n - 1;
   mid  = ( beg + end ) / 2;
   while ( ( beg <= end ) && ( a[mid] != item ) ) {
      if ( element < a[mid] )
         end = mid - 1;
      else
         beg = mid  + 1;
      mid  = ( beg + end ) / 2;
   }
   return ( ( beg > end ) ? -1 : mid );
}
```

You must have observed that binary search is recursive procedure, with the base criteria that search will terminate either the element is located or *beg* becomes greater than *end*.

The implementation of the recursive algorithm is given below.

Listing 5.3*b*:

```
template <class T>
int LinearArray<T>::binarySearchRecursive(int lb, int ub, T item)  {
```

```
    int mid;
    if ( lb > ub )
       return -1;
    else {
        mid  = ( lb + ub ) / 2;
        if ( item == a[mid] )
           return mid;
        else if  ( item < a[mid] )
           return binarySearchRecursive(lb, mid-1, item );
        else
           return binarySearchRecursive(mid+1, ub, item );
    }
}
```

Analysis of Binary Search

In each iteration, or in each recursive call, the search is reduced to one half of the array. Therefore, for n elements in the array, there will be $\log_2 n$ iterations or recursive calls. Thus, the complexity of binary search is $O(\log_2 n)$. This complexity will be same irrespective of the position of the element, even if it is not present in the array.

5.2.2.3 Insert Operation

Insertion refers to the operation of adding an element to existing list of elements. After insertion the size of the linear array is increased by factor of one. Insertion is possible only if the memory space allocated is large enough to accommodate the additional element. Inserting an element at the end of the linear array can be done very easily. However, to insert an element at any other location, the elements are to be moved downward to new locations to accommodate the new element and keep the order of other elements. The term *downward* refers to locations with larger subscripts.

5.2.2.3.1 Inserting at Given Position

Suppose we want to insert an element at position *k*. In this case, first we have to move elements starting from *k*th position down by one position in order to accommodate the element at *k*th position. The steps required are shown in the following code.

Listing 5.4:

```
template <class T>
void LinearArray<T>::insertAt(int k, T item)
{
    int j;
    if ( n == capacity ) {
        cout << "\nArray is full...\n";
        return;
    }
    j = n - 1;
```

```
    while ( j >=  k ) {
        a[j+1] = a[j];
        j--;
    }
    a[k] = item;
    n++;
}
```

5.2.2.3.2 Inserting in a Sorted Array

Let us assume that array under consideration is sorted on ascending order. In this case, the best possible approach is to move the elements of the array down one by one till the first element of the array less than the element to be inserted is encountered. Then the new element is inserted to the right of this element. For example, if the element at the *k*th index is less than the element to be inserted, then the new element is inserted at index (*k*+1)th index. The following code shows implementation of these steps.

Listing 5.5:

```
template <class T>
void LinearArray<T>::insertInSortedArray(T item)
{
    int k;
    if ( n == capacity ) {
        cout << "\nArray is full...\n";
        return;
    }
    k = n - 1;
    while ( ( item < a[k] ) && (  k >= 0 ) ) {
        a[k+1] = a[k]; k--;
    }
    a[k+1] = item;
    n++;
}
```

In the test condition of *while* loop, an additional condition ($k \geq 0$), is added to avoid the index falling to a negative value. When k becomes equal to -1, it means that the new element is smaller that all the elements in the array, therefore, it must be inserted at the first position.

Analysis of Insert Operation

The best possible case occurs when the *item* is inserted at the last position. In this case, no element is moved down. The worst case occurs when the element is to be inserted at the first position. In this case, all the elements (n in number) are moved down. Therefore, the while loop executes n time, each time moving one element down. Thus, the complexity of insertion operation is $O(n)$, *i.e.*, linear time.

5.2.2.4 Delete Operation

Deletion refers to the operation of removing an element from existing list of elements. After deletion the size of the linear array is decreased by factor of one. Like insertion operation, deleting an element from the end of the linear array can be done very easily. However, to delete an element from any other location, the elements are to be moved upward in order to fill up the location vacated by the removed element. The term *upward* refers to locations with smaller subscripts.

5.2.2.4.1 Deleting from Given Position

Suppose we want to delete an element from position *k* In this case, we have to move elements starting from (*k*+1)th position up by one position to fill the hole created by deleted element from *k*th position. The steps required are shown in the following code.

Listing 5.6:

```
template <class T>
void LinearArray<T>::deleteFrom(int k) {
    int j;
    if ( n == 0 ) {
        cout << "\nArray is empty...\n";
        return;
    }
    j = k + 1;
    while ( j <= n ) {
        a[j-1] = a[j]; j++;
    }
    n--;
}
```

5.2.2.4.2 Deleting from a Sorted Array

In this case, first we have to find the position, say *k*, from where the given element is to be deleted and then starting from (*k*+1)th position, the elements are moved up by one position in order to fill the hole created at *k*th position.

The steps required are shown in listing 5.7.

Listing 5.7:

```
template <class T>
void LinearArray<T>::deleteFromSortedArray(T item) {
    int j, k;
    if ( n == 0 ) {
        cout << "\nArray is empty...\n";
        return;
    }
```

```
    k = binarySearchRecursive(0, n-1, item);
    if ( k == -1 ) {
        cout << "\nElement " << item << "is not in the array\n";
        return;
    }
    j = k + 1
    while ( j < n ) {
        a[j -1] = a[j]; j++;
    }
    n--;
}
```

We have used function *binarySearchRecursive()* to find the location of the element in the given sorted array.

Analysis of Delete Operation

The best possible case occurs when the *item* is deleted from the last position. In this case, no element is moved up. The worst case occurs when the element is deleted from the first position. In this case, almost all the elements ($n-1$ in number) are moved up. Therefore, the while loop executes $n-1$ times, each time moving one element down. Thus, the complexity of deletion operation is also $O(n)$ i.e. linear time.

5.2.2.5 Sort Operation

Sorting is the process of arranging the elements of the array in some logical order. This logical order may be ascending or descending in case of numeric values or dictionary order in case of alphanumeric values. We do, almost, use this process daily in our routine activities. For example, we do arrange our class notes in increasing order of date in order to refer them quickly later on. Like this there are many situations, which you can enumerate.

In this section, we will discuss one very popular technique, *Bubble sort*, to sort an array *a* with *n* elements in ascending order.

5.2.2.5.1 Bubble Sort Method

The Bubble sort method requires ($n-1$) pass to sort an array. In each pass every element $a[i]$ is compared with $a[i+1]$, for $i = 0$ to ($n-k$), where k is the pass number and if they are out of order, *i.e.*, if $a[i] > a[i+1]$, they are swapped. This will cause the largest element move or bubble up. Thus after the end of first pass the largest element in the array will be placed in nth position, and on each successive pass, the next largest element is placed at position ($n-1$), ($n-2$), ($n-2$), ..., 4, 3, 2, respectively.

For more clarity, carefully examine the following steps.

Pass 1.

Step 1. If $a[0] > a[1]$ then swap $a[0]$ and $a[1]$.
Step 2. If $a[1] > a[2]$ then swap $a[1]$ and $a[2]$.

:

Step n–1. If $a[n-2] > a[n-1]$ then swap $a[n-2]$ and $a[n-1]$.

Pass 2.

Step 1. If $a[0] > a[1]$ then swap $a[0]$ and $a[1]$.
Step 2. If $a[1] > a[2]$ then swap $a[1]$ and $a[2]$.

:

Step n–2. If $a[n-3] > a[n-2]$ then swap $a[n-3]$ and $a[n-2]$.

:

Pass *k*.

Step 1. If $a[0] > a[1]$ then swap $a[0]$ and $a[1]$.
Step 2. If $a[1] > a[2]$ then swap $a[1]$ and $a[2]$.

:

Step n–k. If $a[n-k+1] > a[n-k]$ then swap $a[n-k+1]$ and $a[n-k]$.

:

Pass *n*–1.

Step 1. If $a[0] > a[1]$ then swap $a[0]$ and $a[1]$.

Example 5.3:

To illustrate the working of bubble sort method, consider the sorting of the following array in ascending order.

12 40 3 2 15

Note that, the output of a given pass becomes the input for the next pass.

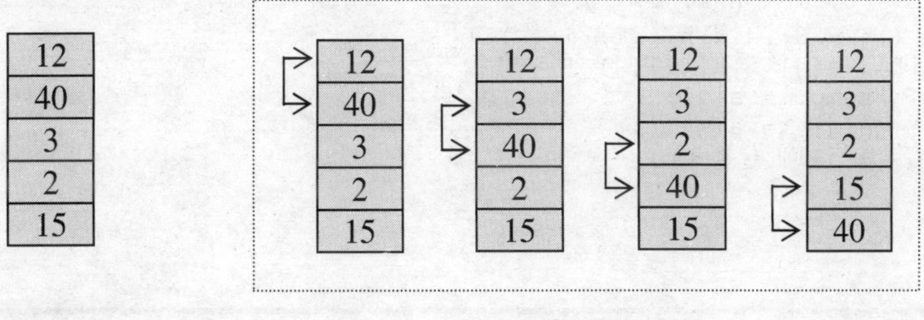

(*a*) Given Array (*b*) Pass 1

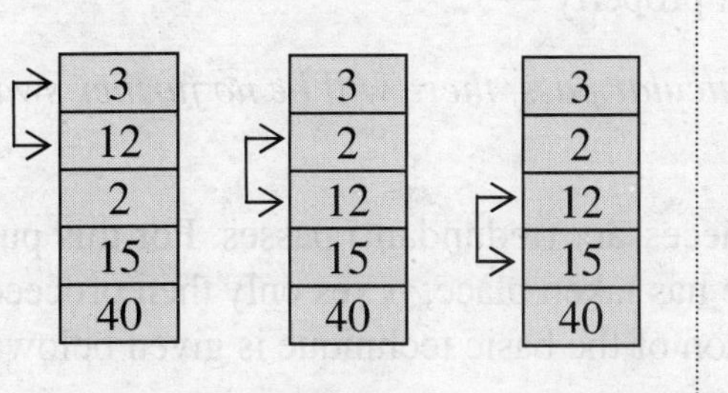

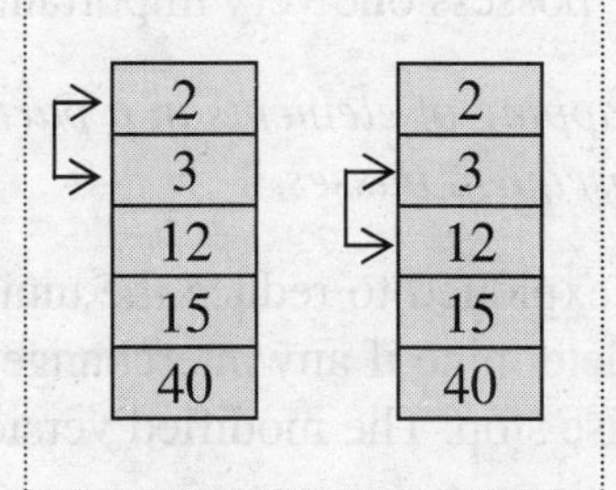

2 3 12 15 40

(*c*) Pass 2 (*d*) Pass 3 (*e*) Pass 4

Figure 5.3: Illustration of Bubble sort method

Algorithm 5.4:

bubbleSortBasic(*a*, *n*)

Here *a* is a linear array with *n* elements in memory. This algorithm sorts the elements in the ascending order. It uses a temporary variable *temp* to facilitate the exchange of two values and variable *i* to is used as loop control variable.

```
Begin
    for k = 1 to (n–1) by 1 do
        for j = 0 to (n–k–1) by 1 do
            if ( a[j] > a[j+1] ) then
                Set temp = a[j]
                Set a[j] = a[j+1]
                Set a[j+1] = temp
            endif
        endfor
    endfor
End.
```

The following code shows the implementation of the above algorithm.

Listing 5.8:

```
template <class T>
void LinearArray<T>::bubbleSortBasic()
{
    int j, i, temp;
    for ( i = 0; i < n-1; i++ ) {
        for ( j = 0; j < n-i-1; j++ ) {
            if ( a[j] > a[j+1] ) {
                temp   = a[j];
                a[j]   = a[j+1];
                a[j+1] = temp;
            }
        }
    }
}
```

Bubble sort technique possess one very important property —

"*Once there is no swapping of elements in a particular pass, there will be no further swapping of elements in the subsequent passes.*"

This property can be exploited to reduce the unnecessary (redundant) passes. For this purpose, we can use a flag to determine if any interchange has taken place, if yes only then proceed with the next pass; otherwise stop. The modified version of the basic technique is given below.

Listing 5.9:

```
template <class T>
void LinearArray<T>::bubbleSortModified()
{
   int j, i, temp, exchange_flag = 1;
   i = 0;
   while ( ( i < n-1 )  && ( exchange_flag ) ) {
      exchange_flag = 0;
      for ( j = 0; j < n-i-1; j++ ) {
         if ( a[j] > a[j+1] ) {
            exchange_flag = 1;
            temp = a[j];
            a[j] = a[j+1];
            a[j+1] = temp;
         }
      }
      i++;
   }
}
```

Analysis of Bubble Sort Method

As explained above, after (n–1) passes, the array will be sorted in ascending order. As you must have noticed, the first pass requires (n–1) comparisons, the second pass requires (n–2), ..., kth pass requires (n–k), and the last pass requires only one comparison. Therefore, total comparisons are

$$f(n) = (n-1) + (n-2) + (n-3) + \ldots + (n-k) + \ldots + 3 + 2 + 1$$

$$= n(n-1)/2$$

$$f(n) = O(n^2)$$

5.2.2.6 Merge Operation

Merging is the process of combining the elements of two similar structures (linear arrays) into a single structure. Suppose that two arrays are unsorted, we can combine them end to end i.e. we can first put elements of array a into third array c, and then the elements of the second array b are placed after it in array c as pictured in Figure 5.4.

Array									
Array *a*	12	40	–3	2					
Array *b*	15	5	7	10	60				
Array *c*	12	40	–3	2	15	5	7	10	60

Figure 5.4: Merging end-to-end

In many cases, we may have sorted arrays and our aim is to combine them in such a way that the combined array is also in the sorted order. One straightforward approach is to join them end to end and then sort the combined array, but this approach in not efficient and economical. Therefore the best approach is to compare the elements of the given array, and based on this comparison; decide which element should go first to the third array.

This process is illustrated in Figure 5.5, for arrays sorted in the ascending order.

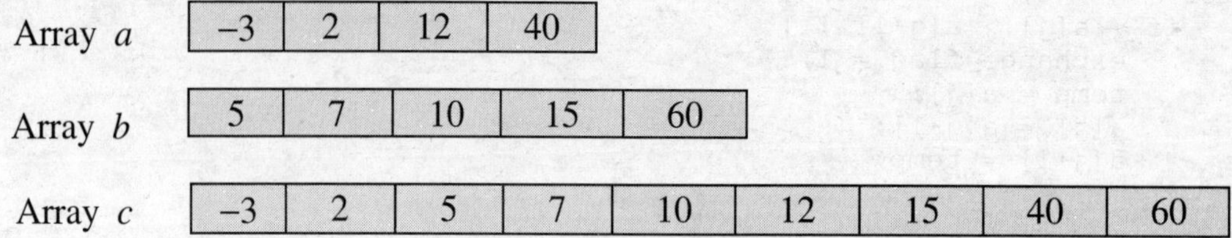

Figure 5.5: Merging of sorted arrays

In case of sorted arrays, to start with, compare first element of array *a* (element -3) with the first element of array *b* (element 5), and put the smallest of these (−3) into array *c*. Since first element of array *a* is put in array *c*, next we compare second element of array *a* (element 2) with the first element of array *b* (element 5), since 2 is the smallest, put it into *c*. Next compare third element of *a* (element 12) with first element of *b* (element 5), since 5 is the smallest, put it into *c*. Next compare third element of *a* (element 12) with second element of *b* (element 7), since 7 is the smallest, put it into *c*, and so on., and when one array is exhausted, the elements of the other array are copied one by one to *c*. To accomplish the above task, we use counters to keep track of the current element which is a candidate to go in *c*, and the position in *c* where it will be stored. The various steps required for its implementation are shown in algorithm 5.5.

Algorithm 5.5:

MergingSortedArrays(*a, m, b, n, c, r*)

Here *a* and *b* are sorted (ascending) linear arrays of size *m* and *n*, respectively. This algorithm merges these arrays, by comparing their elements, into array c, which will be of size *m+n*. It uses variables *na* and *nb* to keep track of the respective elements of arrays *a* and *b*, and a variable *nc* to keep track of index in array *c* where the incoming element (either from array *a* or *b*) will be stored.

```
Begin
  Set na = 0
  Set nb = 0
  Set nc = 0
  while ( ( na < m ) and ( nb < n ) ) do
     if ( a[na] < b[nb] ) then
        Set c[nc] = a[na]
        Set na = na+1
     else
        Set c[nc] = b[nb]
        Set nb = nb+1
     endif
```

```
        Set nc = nc+1
    Endwhile
    if ( na = m ) then              // array 'a' is exhausted
        while ( nb < n ) do
            Set c[nc] = b[nb]
            Set nb = nb+1
            Set nc = nc+1
        endwhile
    else                            // array 'b' is exhausted
        while ( na < m ) do
            Set c[nc] = a[na]
            Set na = na+1
            Set nc = nc+1
        endwhile
    endif
End.
```

The following code shows the implementation of the above algorithm.

Listing 5.10:

```
template <class T>
void LinearArray<T>::mergeSortedArrays(LinearArray<T> &la,
                                       LinearArray<T> &lb) {
   int na=0, nb=0, nc=0;
   int r, s;
   r = la.getElements();
   s = lb.getElements();
   n = r + s;
   while ( (na < r) && (nb < s) ) {
     if ( la.a[na] < lb.a[nb] )
        a[nc] = la.a[na++];
     else
        a[nc] = lb.a[nb++];
     nc++;
   }
  if (na == r) {              // first array is exhausted
     while ( nb < s )
     a[nc++] = lb.a[nb++];
  }
  else if (nb == s) {         // second array is exhausted
     while ( na < r )
     a[nc++] = la.a[na++];
  }
}
```

Analysis of Merge Operation

The input to this algorithm consists of the total number r (= $m + n$) of elements of a and b. each comparison assigns an element to array c, which eventually has r elements. According the number $f(r)$ of comparison cannot exceed r:

$$f(r) \leq r = O(r)$$

which means, the merging algorithm can be run in linear time.

Listing 5.11:

```
// Program to demonstrate the implementation of linear array
#include <iostream.h>
#include <iomanip.h>
template <class T>
class LinearArray
{
   private:
      T *a;
      int n;            // number of elements
      int capacity;     // capacity of array
   public:
      LinearArray(int size)
      {
        n = 0;
        capacity = size;
        a = new T[capacity];
      }
      ~LinearArray()
      {
        delete a;       // delete dynamic array
      }
      int getElements()
      {
        return n;
      }
      int getCapacity()
      {
        return capacity;
      }
      void displayArray();
      void inputArray();
      void insertAt(int k, T item);
      void insertInSortedArray(T item);
      void deleteFrom(int k);
      void deleteFromSortedArray(T item);
      int  linearSearch(T item);
      int  binarySearchIterative(T item);
      int  binarySearchRecursive(int lb, int ub, T item);
      void bubbleSortModified();
      void mergeSortedArrays(LinearArray<T> &la, LinearArray<T> &lb);
};
template <class T>
void LinearArray<T>::displayArray() {
   for ( int i = 0; i < n; i++ )
      cout << a[i] << " ";
   cout << endl;
}
template <class T>
void LinearArray<T>::inputArray() {
   char choice;
   while(1)
   {
      cout << "Enter element a[" << (n+1) << "] : ";
```

```
      cin >> a[n++];
      cout << "More element Y/N? : ";
      cin >> choice;
      if ( choice == 'Y' || choice == 'y' )
      continue;
      else
      break;
   }
}
template <class T>
void LinearArray<T>::insertAt(int k, T item)
{
   int j;
   if ( n == capacity ) {
      cout << "\nArray is full...\n";
      return;
   }
   j = n - 1;
   while ( j >=  k ) {
      a[j+1] = a[j];
      j--;
   }
   a[k] = item;
   n++;
}
template <class T>
void LinearArray<T>::insertInSortedArray(T item)
{
   int k;
   if ( n == capacity ) {
      cout << "\nArray is full...\n";
      return;
   }
   k = n - 1;
   while ( ( item < a[k] ) && (  k >= 0 ) )
   {
      a[k+1] = a[k];
      k--;
   }
   a[k+1] = item;
   n++;
}
template <class T>
void LinearArray<T>::deleteFrom(int k)
{
   int j;
   if ( n == 0 ) {
      cout << "\nArray is empty...\n";
      return;
   }
   j = k + 1;
   while ( j <= n ) {
      a[j-1] = a[j];
      j++;
   }
   n--;
}
```

```
template <class T>
void LinearArray<T>::deleteFromSortedArray(T item)
{
   int j, k;
   if ( n == 0 ) {
      cout << "\nArray is empty...\n";
      return;
   }
   k = binarySearchRecursive(0, n-1, item );
   if ( k == -1 ) {
       cout << "\nElement " << item << " is not in the array\n";
       return;
   }
   j = k + 1;
   while ( j <= n ) {
      a[j-1] = a[j];
      j++;
   }
   n--;
}
template <class T>
int LinearArray<T>::linearSearch(T item)
{
   int i;
   for(i=0; i<n; ++i) {
      if ( a[i] == item )
      return i;
   }
   return -1;
}
template <class T>
int LinearArray<T>::binarySearchRecursive(int lb, int ub, T item) {
   int mid;
   if ( lb > ub )
      return -1;
   else {
      mid  = ( lb + ub ) / 2;
      if ( item == a[mid] )
      return mid;
      else if  ( item < a[mid] )
      return binarySearchRecursive(lb, mid-1, item );
      else
      return binarySearchRecursive(mid+1, ub, item );
   }
}
template <class T>
void LinearArray<T>::bubbleSortModified()
{
   int j, i, temp, exchange_flag = 1;
   i = 0;
   while ( ( i < n-1 )  && ( exchange_flag ) ) {
      exchange_flag = 0;
      for ( j = 0; j < n-i-1; j++ ) {
      if ( a[j] > a[j+1] ) {
         exchange_flag = 1;
         temp = a[j];
         a[j] = a[j+1];
         a[j+1] = temp;
```

```
        }
      }
      i++;
   }
}
template <class T>
void LinearArray<T>::mergeSortedArrays(LinearArray<T> &la,
                                       LinearArray<T> &lb)
{
   int na=0, nb=0, nc=0;
   int r, s;
   r = la.getElements();
   s = lb.getElements();
   n = r + s;
   while ( (na < r) && (nb < s) ) {
     if ( la.a[na] < lb.a[nb] )
     a[nc] = la.a[na++];
     else
     a[nc] = lb.a[nb++];
     nc++;
   }
  if (na == r) {              // first array is exhausted
     while ( nb < s )
       a[nc++] = lb.a[nb++];
  }
  else if (nb == s) {         // second array is exhausted
     while ( na < r )
       a[nc++] = la.a[na++];
  }
}
//  main function
void main()
{
    LinearArray<int> la(10);
    LinearArray<int> lb(15);
    LinearArray<int> lc(40);
    int element, pos;
    cout << "\nEnter elements for array LB\n";
    la.inputArray();
    cout << "\nElements of array LA : ";
    la.displayArray();
    cout << "\nEnter new element to insert : ";
    cin >> element;
    cout << "\nEnter position where to insert : ";
    cin >> pos;
    la.insertAt(pos-1, element);
    cout << "\nElements of array LA after insertion : ";
    la.displayArray();
    cout << "\nEnter position from where to delete element : ";
    cin >> pos;
    la.deleteFrom(pos-1);
    cout << "\nElements of LA after deletion : ";
    la.displayArray();
    cout << "\nEnter the element to search : ";
    cin >> element;
    pos = la.linearSearch(element);
```

```
    if ( pos < 0 )
        cout << "\nElement not found!\n";
    else
        cout << "\nElement found at index " << pos << "\n";
    la.bubbleSortModified();
    cout << "\nElements of array LA ater sorting : ";
    la.displayArray();
    cout << "\nEnter the element to search : ";
    cin >> element;
    pos = la.binarySearchRecursive(0, la.getElements(),element);
    if ( pos < 0 )
        cout << "\nElement not found!\n";
    else
        cout << "\nElement found at index " << pos << "\n";
    cout << "\nEnter new element to insert : ";
    cin >> element;
    la.insertInSortedArray(element);
    cout << "\nElements of array LA after insertion : ";
    la.displayArray();
    cout << "\nEnter element to delete : ";
    cin >> element;
    la.deleteFromSortedArray(element);
    cout << "\nElements of LA after deletionn : ";
    la.displayArray();
    cout << "\nEnter elements for array LB\n";
    lb.inputArray();
    cout << "\nElements of array LB : ";
    lb.displayArray();
    lb.bubbleSortModified();
    cout << "\nElements of array LB after sorting : ";
    lb.displayArray();
    lc.mergeSortedArrays(la, lb);
    cout << "\nElements of array LC after merging sorted arrays "
         << "LA & LB\n\n";
    lc.displayArray();
}
```

5.2.3 Applications of Linear Arrays

Linear arrays are one of the primitive data structures. These are used represent all sorts of lists. In addition, these are used implement other data structures such as *stacks*, *queues, heaps*, etc.

5.2.4 Limitations of Linear Arrays

The main limitations of linear arrays are

1. The prior knowledge of number of elements in the linear array is necessary.
2. These are static structures. Static in the sense that whether memory is allocated at compilation time or runtime, the memory used by them cannot be reduced or extended.
3. Since the elements of these arrays are stored in consecutive locations, the insertions and deletions in these arrays are time consuming. This is because of moving elements down to create a space for new element or moving elements up to occupy the space vacated by the deleted element.

5.3 TWO-DIMENSIONAL ARRAYS

A two-dimensional array is a list of a finite number $m*n$ of homogeneous data elements such that

- The elements of the array are referenced by two index sets consisting of m and n consecutive integer numbers.
- The elements of the array are stored in consecutive memory locations.

The *size* of the two-dimensional array is denoted by $m \times n$ and pronounced as m by n.

Suppose b is the name of the two-dimensional array, then its element in the ith row and jth column is denoted as

b_{ij}	in mathematical notation
$b(i, j)$	in BASIC and FORTRAN languages
$b[i, j]$	in Pascal language
$b[i][j]$	in C/C++ and Java languages

Two-dimensional arrays are called *matrices* in mathematics and *tables* in business applications.

A two-dimensional $m \times n$ array a is pictured as a rectangular pattern of m row and n columns, where the element a_{ij} appears in row i and column j. Figure 5.6 pictures two-dimensional array a of size 3×5.

	Col #0	Col #1	Col #2
Row #0	a_{00}	a_{01}	a_{02}
Row #1	a_{10}	a_{11}	a_{12}
Row #2	a_{20}	a_{21}	a_{22}

Figure 5.6: Picturing a two-dimensional array *a*

5.3.1 Representing Two-dimensional Array in Memory

Let a be a two-dimensional $m \times n$ array. Though a is pictured as a rectangular pattern with m row and n columns, it is represented in memory by a block of $m*n$ sequential memory locations. However, the elements can be stored in two different ways —

- ***Column major order*** – the elements are stored column by column i.e. m elements of the first column and stored in first m locations, elements of the second column are stored in next m locations, and so on.
- ***Row major order*** – the elements are stored row by row i.e. n elements of the first row and stored in first n locations, elements of the second row are stored in next n locations, and so on.

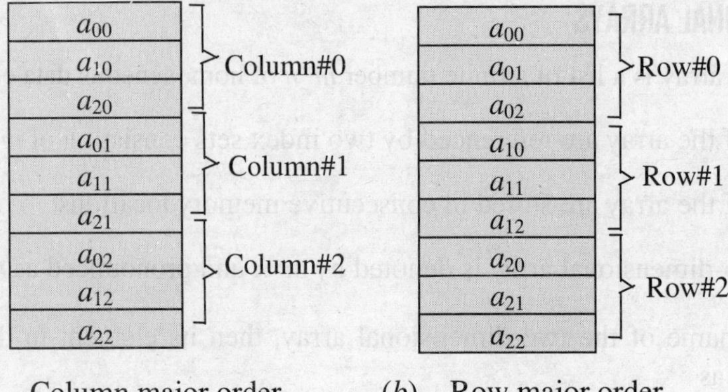

Figure 5.7: Representation of two-dimensional array *a* of size 3×3 in memory

In Pascal and C/C++ the storage order is row-major order, where as in FORTRAN the storage order is column-major order

Let us consider a two-dimensional array *a* of size *m*×*n*. Further consider that the lower bound for the row index is *lbr* and for column index is *lbc*.
Like linear array, system keeps track of the address of first element only i.e. the *base address* of the array.

Using this base address, the computer computes the address of the element in the *i*th row and *j*th column, *i.e.*, *loc*(*a*[*i*][*j*]), using the following formulae:

Column Major Order

$loc(a[i][j]) = base(a) + w\,[m\,(j - lbc) + (i - lbr)]$ in general

$loc(a[i][j]) = base(a) + w\,(m \times j + i)$ in C/C++ languages

Row Major Order

$loc(a[i][j]) = base(a) + w\,[n\,(i - lbr) + (j - lbc)]$ in general

$loc(a[i][j]) = base(a) + w\,(n \times i + j)$ in C/C++ languages

where *w* is the number of bytes per storage location for one element of the array.

5.4 MATRICES

An *m*×*n* (pronounced as *m* by *n*) matrix is a two-dimensional array whose *m.n* elements are arranged in *m* rows and *n* columns. A matrix is denoted by capital letters such as *A*, *B*, *C*, . . ., and its elements are denoted by corresponding lower letters suffixed with row index and column index such as a_{ij}, b_{ij}, c_{ij}, . . ., respectively.

$$\begin{pmatrix} 2 & 6 & 2 & 0 \\ 3 & 5 & 0 & 9 \\ 8 & 6 & 7 & 1 \\ 4 & 1 & 4 & 9 \end{pmatrix}$$

Figure 5.7: A 4×4 matrix

Matrices are often used to organize data for business and scientific applications. It has been proved that many scientific and engineering problems can be solved efficiently if they are expressed using matrices.

5.4.1 Representation of Matrices

The following declarations will be used to represent a matrix in computer's memory.

```
class Matrix
{
    private:
        int rows;
        int cols;
        int **ptr;
    public:
        Matrix(int, int);
        Matrix(Matrix &);
        ~Matrix ();
        friend istream & operator >> ( istream &, Matrix & );
        friend ostream & operator << ( ostream &, Matrix & );
        Matrix operator + ( Matrix & );
        Matrix operator - ( Matrix & );
        Matrix operator * ( Matrix & );
        Matrix operator = ( Matrix & );
        void transpose( Matrix & );
};      // end of class definition
```

5.4.2 Common Operations on Matrices

The operations most commonly performed on matrices are — transpose of a matrix, addition of matrices, difference of matrices, product of matrices, and inverse of a matrix.

5.4.2.1 Transpose of a Matrix

The transpose of a $m \times n$ matrix A is an $n \times m$ matrix B (denoted as A^T) with the property

$$b_{ij} = a_{ji} \qquad \text{for } 0 \le i \le n-1 \text{ and } 0 \le j \le m-1$$

Listing 5.12:

```
// member function to find the transpose of a matrix
void Matrix::transpose( Matrix &m )
{
    int i, j;
```

```
    for ( i = 0; i < rows; i++ )
    {
        for ( j = 0; j < cols; j++ ) {
         ptr[j][i] = m.ptr[i][j];
        }
    }
}
```

5.4.2.2 Addition of Matrices

The addition of two matrices is defined only when the two matrices are compatible i.e. have the same number of rows and columns. The sum of two $m \times n$ matrices A and B is a third $m \times n$ matrix C such that

$$c_{ij} = a_{ij} + b_{ij} \qquad \text{for } 0 \le i \le m-1 \text{ and } 0 \le j \le n-1$$

Listing 5.13:

```
// member function to add two matrices
Matrix Matrix::operator + ( Matrix &mat )
{
    Matrix temp(rows, cols);
    for ( int i = 0; i < rows; i++ ) {
        for ( int j = 0; j < cols; j++ ) {
         temp.ptr[i][j] = ptr[i][j] + mat.ptr[i][j];
        }
    }
    return temp;
}
```

5.4.2.3 Difference of Matrices

Like addition, the difference of two matrices is also defined only when the two matrices are compatible. The difference of $m \times n$ matrix B from an $m \times n$ matrix A is a third $m \times n$ matrix C such that

$$c_{ij} = a_{ij} - b_{ij} \qquad \text{for } 0 \le i \le m-1 \text{ and } 0 \le j \le n-1$$

Listing 5.14:

```
// member function to subtract one matrix from another
Matrix Matrix::operator - ( Matrix &mat )
{
    Matrix temp(rows, cols);
    for ( int i = 0; i < rows; i++ ) {
        for ( int j = 0; j < cols; j++ ) {
         temp.ptr[i][j] = ptr[i][j] - mat.ptr[i][j];
        }
    }
    return temp;
}
```

5.4.2.4 Product of Matrices

The product, $A*B$, of a $m \times n$ matrix A and a $q \times p$ matrix B is defined only when the number of columns in A equals the number of rows in B, i.e. $n = q$. When $n = q$, the product is a $m \times p$ matrix C with the property

$$c_{ij} = \sum_{k=1}^{n-1} a_{ik} b_{jk} \qquad \text{for } 0 \le i \le m-1 \text{ and } 1 \le j \le p-1 \text{ or } n-1$$

Listing 5.15:

```
// member function to multiply two matrices
Matrix Matrix::operator * ( Matrix &mat )
{
   Matrix temp(rows, cols);
   int i, j, k, tt;
   for ( i = 0; i < rows; i++ ) {
      for ( j = 0; j < cols; j++ ) {
       tt = 0;
       for ( k = 0; k < rows; k++ ) {
           tt += ptr[i][k] * mat.ptr[k][j];
       }
       temp.ptr[i][j] = tt;
      }
   }
   return temp;
}
```

Listing 5.16

```
//
// Program to demonstrate the operations on matrices
//
#include <iostream.h>
#include <iomanip.h>
#include <string.h>
class Matrix {
   private:
      int rows;
      int cols;
      int **ptr;
   public:
      Matrix ( int, int );
      Matrix(Matrix &);
      ~Matrix ();
      friend istream & operator >> ( istream &, Matrix & );
      friend ostream & operator << ( ostream &, Matrix & );
      Matrix operator + ( Matrix & );
      Matrix operator - ( Matrix & );
      Matrix operator * ( Matrix & );
      Matrix operator = ( Matrix & );
      void transpose( Matrix & );
};     // end of class definition
```

```
// definition of parameterized constructor
Matrix::Matrix ( int m, int n )
{
   rows = m;
   cols = n;
   ptr = new int* [m] ;
   for ( int i = 0; i < m; i++ ) {
       ptr[i] = new int[n];
   }
}
// definition of the copy constructor
Matrix::Matrix(Matrix &m)
{
   rows = m.rows;
   cols = m.cols;
   ptr = new int* [rows] ;
   for ( int i = 0; i < rows; i++ )
       ptr[i] = new int[cols];
   for ( i = 0; i < rows; i++ )
       for ( int j = 0; j < cols; j++ )
             ptr[i][j]=m.ptr[i][j];
}
// definition of friend function to overload >> operator
istream & operator >> ( istream &din, Matrix &mat )
{
   for ( int i = 0; i < mat.rows; i++ ) {
      for ( int j = 0; j < mat.cols; j++ ) {
        din >> mat.ptr[i][j];
      }
   }
   return din;
}
// definition of friend function to overload << operator
ostream & operator << ( ostream &dout, Matrix &mat )
{
   for ( int i = 0; i < mat.rows; i++ ) {
      for ( int j = 0; j < mat.cols; j++ ) {
        dout << setw(5)
             << mat.ptr[i][j];
      }
      dout << endl;
   }
   return dout;
}
// member function to add two matrices
Matrix  Matrix::operator + ( Matrix &mat )
{
   Matrix temp(rows, cols);
   for ( int i = 0; i < rows; i++ ) {
      for ( int j = 0; j < cols; j++ ) {
       temp.ptr[i][j] = ptr[i][j] + mat.ptr[i][j];
      }
   }
   return temp;
}
// member function to subtract one matrix from another
Matrix Matrix::operator - ( Matrix &mat )
{
```

```
   Matrix temp(rows, cols);
   for ( int i = 0; i < rows; i++ ) {
      for ( int j = 0; j < cols; j++ ) {
       temp.ptr[i][j] = ptr[i][j] - mat.ptr[i][j];
      }
   }
   return temp;
}
// member function to multiply two matrices
Matrix Matrix::operator * ( Matrix &mat )
{
   Matrix temp(rows, cols);
   int i, j, k, tt;
   for ( i = 0; i < rows; i++ ) {
      for ( j = 0; j < cols; j++ ) {
       tt = 0;
       for ( k = 0; k < rows; k++ ) {
           tt += ptr[i][k] * mat.ptr[k][j];
       }
       temp.ptr[i][j] = tt;
      }
   }
   return temp;
}
Matrix Matrix::operator = ( Matrix &m )
{
   for ( int i = 0; i < rows; i++ ) {
      for ( int j = 0; j < cols; j++ ) {
       ptr[i][j] =  m.ptr[i][j];
      }
   }
   return *this;
}
// member function to find the transpose of a matrix
void Matrix::transpose ( Matrix &m )
{
   int i, j;
   for ( i = 0; i < rows; i++ ) {
      for ( j = 0; j < cols; j++ ) {
       ptr[j][i] = m.ptr[i][j];
      }
   }
}
// definition of destructor
Matrix::~Matrix()
{
   for ( int i = 0; i < rows; i++ ) {
     delete ptr[i];
   }
   delete ptr;
}
void main()     // main program
{
   int m, n, p, q;
   cout << "Enter size of matrix A as m n : ";
   cin >> m >> n;
   cout << "Enter size of matrix B as p q : ";
   cin >> p >> q;
```

```
    Matrix A(m,n), B(p,q), C(n,m);
    cout << "Enter " << m*n << " elements of matrix A row-wise" << endl;
    cin >> A;
    cout << "Enter " << p*q << " elements of matrix B row-wise" << endl;
    cin >> B;
    C.transpose(A);
    cout << "Transpose(A)" << endl;
    cout << C;
    if ( m == p && n == q ) {
       C = A + B;
       cout << endl << "A + B" << endl << endl;
       cout << C;
       C = A - B;
       cout << endl << "A - B" << endl << endl;
       cout << C;
    } else {
       cout << endl << "Addition & Difference is not feasible"
         << endl << endl;
    }
    if ( n == p ) {
       Matrix D(m,q);
       D = A * B;
       cout << endl << "A * B" << endl << endl;
       cout << D;
    } else {
       cout << endl << "Product AxB is not feasible"
         << endl << endl;
    }
}
```

5.4.3 Special Matrices

A *square* matrix has the same number of rows and columns. Some special forms of square matrices that arise frequently are:

- **Diagonal matrix** – A matrix B is diagonal iff $B(i, j) = 0$ for $i \neq j$; see Figure 5.8(*a*).
- **Tridiagonal matrix** – A matrix B is tridiagonal iff $B(i, j) = 0$ for $|i - j| > 1$; see Figure 5.8(*b*).
- **Lower triangular matrix** – A matrix B is lower triangular iff $B(i, j) = 0$ for $i < j$; see Figure 5.8(*c*).
- **Upper triangular matrix** – A matrix B is upper triangular iff $B(i, j) = 0$ for $i > j$; see Figure 5.8(*d*).

$$\begin{pmatrix} 2 & & & \\ & 5 & & \\ & & 7 & \\ & & & 9 \end{pmatrix} \quad \begin{pmatrix} 2 & 1 & & \\ 3 & 5 & 8 & \\ & 6 & 7 & 2 \\ & & 4 & 9 \end{pmatrix} \quad \begin{pmatrix} 2 & & & \\ 3 & 5 & & \\ 8 & 6 & 7 & \\ 4 & 1 & 4 & 9 \end{pmatrix} \quad \begin{pmatrix} 2 & 1 & 8 & 6 \\ & 5 & 3 & 4 \\ & & 7 & 2 \\ & & & 9 \end{pmatrix}$$

(*a*) Diagonal (*b*) Tridiagonal (*c*) Lower triangular (*d*) Upper triangular

Figure 5.8: 4×4 Special matrices

5.4.3.1 Representing Special Matrices in Memory

If a general square matrix of order $n \times n$ is to be stored, the memory requirements for its storage will be n^2*sizeof(T) bytes, where T is the data type of its elements. However for special matrices, the memory requirements can be reduced to considerable extent. This section illustrates how this can be done.

```
template <class T>
class DiagonalMatrix
{
    private:
        int n;
        T *d;
    public:
        DiagonalMatrix(int m)
        {
            n = m;
            d = new T[n];
        }
        ~DiagonalMatrix()
        {
            delete d;
        }

        void storeElement(int i, int j, T element);
        T retrieveElement(int i, int j);
        // . . .
};        // end of class definition
```

Diagonal Matrix

One way to represent an $n \times n$ diagonal matrix D with elements of type T is to use a two-dimensional array created as

```
T d[n][n]
```

This representation requires n^2*sizeof(T) bytes of memory. However, since a diagonal matrix contains at most n nonzero elements, we can use one-dimensional array created as

```
T d[n]
```

and use array element $d[i]$ to represent matrix element $D[i][i]$. The elements of the matrix D that are not represented in the array are all zero. This representation will use n*sizeof(T) bytes of memory.

However, with this representation, we need functions that map matrix element of diagonal matrix D to one-dimensional array element, and retrieves matrix element from the array. The implementation of these functions is trivial and is left as an exercise for the readers.

Tridiagonal Matrix

In a $n{\times}n$ tridiagonal matrix A, the nonzero elements lie on one of the three diagonals:

1. Main diagonal, for which $i = j$. It has n elements.
2. Diagonal below main diagonal, for which $i = j + 1$. It has $n - 1$ elements.
3. Diagonal above main diagonal, for which $i = j - 1$. It also has $n - 1$ elements.

Therefore, an $n{\times}n$ tridiagonal matrix A has $3n - 2$ nonzero elements on these three diagonals. We can use one-dimensional array a of size $(3n - 2)$ to represent tridiagonal matrix A. The element can be mapped in following ways:

1. Row-wise,
2. Column-wise, and
3. Diagonal-wise, beginning with the lowest.

Consider the 4×4-tridiagonal matrix of Figure 5.8(b).

If the elements are mapped row-wise, then $a[0:9]$ = [2, 1, 3, 5, 8, 6, 7, 2, 4, 9].

If the elements are mapped column-wise, then $a[0:9]$ = [2, 3, 1, 5, 6, 8, 7, 4, 2, 9].

If the elements are mapped diagonal-wise, starting with the lowest, then $a[0:9]$ = [3, 6, 4, 2, 5, 7, 9, 1, 8, 2].

Following are declarations for mapping elements row-wise.

```
template <class T>
class TriDiagonalMatrix {
   private:
      int n;
      T *a;
   public:
      TriDiagonalMatrix(int m) {
         n = m;
         a = new T[3*n-2];
      }
      ~TriDiagonalMatrix() {
         delete a;
      }
      void storeElement(int i, int j, T element);
      T retrieveElement(int i, int j);
      //
};      // end of class definition
```

Each of the above mapping requires different code for *storeElement()* and *retrieveElement()* functions.

The following codes shows the implementation of *storeElement()* function in which the mapping is done by diagonals.

Listing 5.17:

```
void TriDiagonalmatrix<T>::storeElement(int i, int j, T element)
{
    switch(i-j)
    {
        case 1  : a[i-2] = element;      // lower diagonal
                  break;
        case 0  : a[n+i-2] = element;         // main diagonal
                  break;
        case -1 : a[2*n+i-2] = element;  // lower diagonal
                  break;
        default : cout << "\nElement must be zero\n";
    }
}
```

The following codes shows the implementation of *retrieveElement()* function in which the mapping is done by diagonals.

Listing 5.18:

```
T TriDiagonalmatrix<T>::retrieveElement(int i, int j)
{
    switch (i-j)
    {
        case 1  : return a[i-2];       // lower diagonal
        case 0  : return a[n+i-2];     // main diagonal
        case -1 : return a[2*n+i-2];   // lower diagonal
        default : return 0;
    }
}
```

The implementation of *storeElement()* and *retrieveElement()* functions for other mappings is left as an exercise for the readers.

Triangular Matrices

In an $n \times n$ lower triangular matrix A, row 1 has one nonzero element, row 2 has 2, . . ., and row n has n. Whereas, in an $n \times n$ upper triangular matrix A, row 1 has n nonzero elements, row 2 has $n - 1$, . . ., and row n has 1. In both the cases, the total number of nonzero elements is $n(n+1)/2$.

Both of these matrices can be represented using an one-dimensional array *la* of size $n(n+1)/2$.

First consider lower triangular matrix *L*. The elements can be mapped by rows or by columns.

If the lower triangular matrix of Figure 5.8(c) is mapped by rows then *la*[0:9] = [2, 3, 5, 8, 6, 7, 4, 1, 4, 9].

The column-wise mapping results in *la*[0:9] = [2, 3, 8, 4, 5, 6, 1, 7, 4, 9].

In a row-wise mapping, the element $L[i, j]$, $i \geq j$, is preceded by $\sum_{k=1}^{i-1} k$ elements that are in rows 1 through $i - 1$, and $j - 1$ such elements from row i. The total number of elements that precede it in a row-wise mapping is $i(i - 1)/2 + j - 1$. This expression also gives the position of $L[i, j]$ in *la*.

```
template <class T>
class LowerTriangularMatrix
{
   private:
      int n;
      T *la;
   public:
      TriDiagonalMatrix(int m)
      {
         n = m;
         la = new T[(n*(n+1))/2];
      }
      ~TriDiagonalMatrix()
      {
         delete la;
      }
      void storeElement(int i, int j, T element);
      T retrieveElement(int i, int j);
      //. . .
};     // end of class definition
```

Listing 5.19 shows the implementation of *storeElement()* function.

Listing 5.19:

```
template <class T>
void LowerTriangularMatrix::storeElement(int i, int j, T element)
{
   if  ( i >= j )
      la[((i-1)*(i-2))/2+j-2] = element;
   else
      cout << "\nElement must be zero\n";
}
```

Listing 5.20 shows the implementation of *retrieveElement()* function.

Listing 5.20:

```
template <class T>
T LowerTriangularMatrix<T>::retrieveElement(int i, int j)
{
  if  ( i >= j )
     return la[((i-1)*(i-2))/2+j-2];
  else
     return 0;
}
```

The implementation of *store* and *retrieve* functions for column-wise mappings for the lower triangular matrix is left as an exercise for the readers. Similarly, the implementation of *store* and *retrieve* functions for upper triangular matrix is left as an exercise for the readers.

5.4.4 Sparse Matrices

An $m \times n$ matrix A is said to be *sparse* if many of its elements are zero. A matrix that is not sparse is called *dense* matrix. It is not possible to define an exact boundary between dense and sparse matrices. The diagonal and tridiagonal matrices fit into the category of sparse matrices. However, these matrices have sufficient structure in their zero and nonzero regions that helps us in devising a simple representation schemes whose space requirements equals the number of elements in the nonzero region. In this section, we will consider sparse matrices with an irregular or unstructured nonzero region.

Figure 5.9 shows a 5×6 sparse matrix with five nonzero elements.

$$\begin{pmatrix} 0 & 0 & 0 & 2 & 0 & 0 \\ 0 & 0 & 1 & 0 & 0 & 5 \\ 0 & 4 & 0 & 0 & 0 & 0 \\ 0 & 0 & 0 & 0 & 0 & 0 \\ 0 & 0 & 0 & 0 & 7 & 0 \end{pmatrix}$$

Figure 5.9: A 5×6 Sparse matrix

5.4.4.1 Representation of Sparse Matrices

The schemes used to represent sparse matrices are described below.

5.4.4.1.1 Array Representation

In array representation, an array of triplets of type

```
< row, col, element >
```

is used to store non-zero elements, where first field of the triplet is used to record row position, second to record column position, and the third one to record the nonzero element of the sparse matrix.

In addition, we need to record the size of the matrix (*i.e.*, number of rows and number of columns) and nonzero elements. For this purpose, the first element of array of triplets is used for this purpose, where first fields stores number of rows, the second field stores number of column, and third field stores number of nonzero elements. The remaining elements of the array store nonzero elements of the sparse matrix on row-major order.

The array representation will use [2*(*n*+1)**sizeof*(*int*) + *n***sizeof*(*T*)] bytes of memory, where *n* is the number of nonzero elements and *T* is the data type of elements.

The matrix of Figure 5.9 will be stored in array representation as

$$\begin{pmatrix} 5 & 6 & 5 \\ 1 & 4 & 2 \\ 2 & 3 & 1 \\ 2 & 6 & 5 \\ 3 & 2 & 4 \\ 5 & 5 & 7 \end{pmatrix}$$

Figure 5.10: Array representation of sparse matrix of Figure 5.9

The array representation very rarely used for practical purposes. The major limitation of array representation of a sparse matrix is that we need to know the number of nonzero terms in each of the sparse matrices we plan to use when the array is created. Although, this number is known for array being input, the number of nonzero terms in the matrix that results from the addition, subtraction, and multiplication of two matrices cannot be accurately computed without actually performing the operation. Without this information, we cannot estimate the number of nonzero terms in each matrix and hence cannot declare each array to have this estimated size.

An alternate approach is to use a pointer-based representation.

5.4.4.1.2 Linked Representation

The linked representation overcomes the limitations of the array representation with a little space overhead to store pointers and other information not stored in the array representation. The prior knowledge of nonzero items in a sparse matrix is not necessary here. This representation is described in *Chapter 6* on linked lists.

REVIEW EXERCISES

1. What is an array? What are different types of arrays?
2. Give an example to show the usefulness of arrays.
3. How a linear array is represented in memory?
4. How a two-dimensional array is represented in memory?
5. Name some areas of application of two-dimensional arrays.

6. What is a symmetric matrix? Design a data structure to store a symmetric matrix of order $n \times n$ efficiently.
7. What is a sparse matrix?
8. How sparse matrices can be represented efficiently in memory?
9. What are the limitations of arrays?

PROGRAMMING EXERCISES

1. Write a function that removes all duplicate elements from a linear array.
2. Write a function that interchanges the first element with the last element, second element with the second last element, and so on.
3. Write a function that returns the sum of squares of the reciprocal of each row of a matrix X of size $m \times n$.
4. Write a function that returns the sum of squares of the reciprocal of each column of a matrix X of size $m \times n$.
5. Write a function, say *void transpose(float a[][], int n)*, that computes the transpose of a square matrix A of size $n \times n$. Note that the transpose of the matrix is to be stored in the original matrix itself not in a separate matrix.
6. Given a matrix A of size $m \times n$, write a function that returns the sum of elements above the main diagonal; i.e. those elements a_{ii} for which $i < j$.
7. Given a matrix A of size $m \times n$, write a function that returns the sum of elements below the main diagonal; i.e. those elements a_{ii} for which $i > j$.
8. A square matrix A of size $n \times n$ is said to be upper triangular if element $a_{ij} = 0$ for $i > j$. Write a function, say *int isUpperTriangular(int **a, int n)* that returns value 1 if the input matrix is upper triangular else returns value 0.
9. A square matrix A of size $n \times n$ is said to be lower triangular if element $a_{ij} = 0$ for $i < j$. Write a function, say *int isLowerTriangular(int a[][], int n)* that returns value 1 if the input matrix is lower triangular else returns value 0.
10. A square matrix A of size nxn is said to be symmetric if element $a_{ij} = a_{ji}$ for all values of i and j. Write a function, say *int isSymmetric(int a[][], int n)* that returns value 1 if the input matrix is symmetric else returns value 0.
11. A $m \times n$ matrix is said to have a *saddle point* if some entry $a[i][j]$ is the smallest value in row i and the largest value in column j. Write a C program that determines the saddle point if one exists.

12. A *magic square* is an $n \times n$ matrix of integer from 1 to n^2, where n is odd, such that the sum of every row, column, and diagonal is the same. The rule is

    Start with 1 in the middle of the first row; then go up and left, assigning numbers in increasing order to empty squares; if you fall off the square i.e. if it is the first column, move to last column in the same row and similarly handle the first row; if the square is occupied, move down instead and continue.

$$\begin{pmatrix} 15 & 8 & 1 & 24 & 17 \\ 16 & 14 & 7 & 5 & 23 \\ 22 & 20 & 13 & 6 & 4 \\ 3 & 21 & 19 & 12 & 10 \\ 9 & 2 & 25 & 18 & 11 \end{pmatrix}$$

    One such example of a magic square of size 5×5 is shown.

    Write a function to generate such a magic square of size $n \times n$ matrix, where n is odd.

❑ ❑ ❑

Chapter 6

Linked Lists

6.1 INTRODUCTION

Intuitively all of us know what a list is? Almost everyday, we use lists of all kinds, such as list of items to be purchased from market, list of addresses, list of references, etc. Lists are very useful and are common data structures. Formerly, a list can be described as a homogeneous collection of elements, with a linear relationship between the elements. The lists can be *unordered* – their elements be placed without a particular order, or *ordered* – their elements are placed in a particular order.

Stacks and *queues* are lists whose elements are ordered according to the time when they are added to them. The lists can also be ordered by the value. For example, a list of names of students can be ordered alphabetically, and a list of grades of student's can ordered numerically (in ascending or descending order). The *value-ordered* lists are frequently referred to as *sorted lists*.

When the elements in a value-ordered list are records rather than scalar data, their logical order is determined by one of the fields in the record, the *record key*. For example, a list of students in a class can be ordered alphabetically by name or numerically by roll number. In the first case, the name field of the record is the key; in the second case, the roll number field is the key. Such value-ordered lists are also called *key-ordered-lists*.

In this chapter, we will learn about the lists that are maintained in memory by means of linked lists.

6.2 LINKED LIST DEFINED

A *linked list* is a linear collection of data elements, called *nodes*. The linear order is given by pointers. Each node is divided into two or more parts.

A linked list can be of the following types:

- Linear linked list or one-way list
- Doubly linked list or two-way list
- Circular linked list
- Header linked list

In this chapter, we will describe the representation of these lists and implementation of some operations on them. We will also cover some applications of linked lists.

6.3 LINEAR LINKED LIST

In a *linear linked list*, also called *singly linked list* or *one-way list*, each node is divided in two parts:

- first part contains the information of the element, and
- second part, called the *link field* or *nextpointer field*, contains the address of the next node in the list.

In addition, another pointer variable, for example *head*, is used that contains the address of the first element of the list. The last element of the linked list have *NULL* value in the *nextpointer* field (usually pictured as *X*) to mark the end of the list. Figure 6.1 shows a linear linked list with 4 nodes.

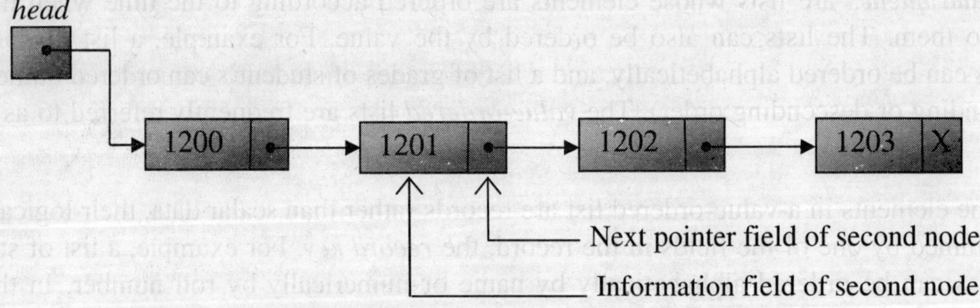

Figure 6.1: Linear linked list with 4 nodes

6.3.1 Representation of Linear Linked List

Suppose that the elements of the linear linked list can be of any primitive type or pointer type, the following is the required ADT to represent a linear linked list:

```
//   structure of the node
template <class T>
class node {
   public:
     T info;
     node *next;
};

//   class that models a linear linked list
template <class T>
class Llist
{
   private:
     node<T> *head;
   public:
     // zero argument constructor that initializes the head
     // to value NULL
     LList()
     {
     head = NULL;
     }
     // destructor that removes the list from memory
     ~LList();

     //-------  member function prototypes  --------

     //  member function that return value 1 if list is empty
     //  else returns value 0
    int isEmpty();
     //  member function that traverses the list from beginning
     //  to end and prints its elements
     void traverseInOrder();
     //  member function that invokes recursive function
     //  traverseReverse() that prints the elements from end to
     //  beginning
     void traverseReverseOrder();
     //  recursive member function that prints the elements from
     //  end to beginning
     static void traverseReverseRecursive(node<T> *);
     //  member function that insert an element in the
     //  beginning of the list
     void insertAtBeginning(T item);
     //  member function that insert an element in the end
     //  of the list
     void insertAtEnd(T item);
     //  member function that insert an element after a given
     //  element
     void insertAfterElement(T item, T after);
     //  member function that delete an element from the beginning
     //  of the list
     void deleteFromBeginning();
```

```
        //  member function that delete an element from the end
        //  of the list
        void deleteFromEnd();
        //  member function that delete a given element from the list
        void deleteElement(T element);
        //  member function that delete an element after a given
        //  element of the list
        void deleteAfterElement(T after);
        //  member function that reverses the element of the list
        void reverseList();
    };  //---------- end of class definition ---------
```

The implementation of the member functions is given in the subsequent sections.

6.3.2 Operations on Linear Linked Lists

In this section, we will describe some operations on linear linked lists.

6.3.2.1 Creating an Empty List

The data member *head* is declared as pointer to a *node<T>* data type. The variable *head* is not yet given a value. This variable is used to point to the first element of the list. Since the list will be empty in the beginning, the variable *head* is assigned a sentinel value to indicate that list is empty. This sentinel value is *NULL* defined in header file named *stdio.h*.

This simple task is accomplished using following zero argument constructor that initializes the *head* to NULL value.

Listing 6.1:

```
// zero argument constructor that initializes head to value NULL
LList()
{
   head = NULL;
}
```

6.3.2.2 Traversing a List

Linear linked list can be traversed in two ways. These are

- In-order traversal
- Reverse-order traversal

6.3.2.2.1 In-Order Traversal

To traverse the linear linked list, we move along the pointer, and process each element till we reach the last element. The following listing shows the various steps required.

Listing 6.2:

```
template <class T>
void LList<T>::traverseInOrder()
{
    node<T> *ptr;
    ptr = head;
    while ( ptr != NULL ) {
       cout << "   " << ptr->info;
       ptr = ptr->next;
    }
}
```

6.3.2.2.2 Reverse-Order Traversal

To traverse the linear linked list in reverse order, we move along the pointer till we reach the last element. The last element is processed first, then the second last, and so on, and finally the first element of the list. Since there is no way to reach the second last element from the last element, third last element from the second last element, and so on. So to accomplish this task, one possible way is to use a stack to store pointer to these individual elements of the list, and the then print the contents of the memory locations to which these pointers are pointing. Since stack is a Last-In-First-Out (LIFO) structure, the element that is printed first is the last element, then the second last element, and so on.

However, the elegant way to accomplish the same task is to use recursion. The following listing shows the various steps required.

Listing 6.4:

```
//  member function that invokes recursive function
//  traverseReverse() that prints the elements from end to
//  beginning
template <class T>
void LList<T>::traverseReverseOrder()
{
    traverseReverse(head);
}

//  recursive member function that prints the elements from
//  end to beginning
template <class T>
static void LList<T>::traverseReverseRecursive(node<T> *ptr)
{
    if ( ptr->next != NULL )
       traverseReverse(ptr->next);
    cout << "   " << ptr->info;
}
```

6.3.2.3 Searching an Element

In linear linked lists, only linear searching is possible. This is one of the limitations of linked lists as there is no way to find the location of the middle element of the list. Further, the list may be sorted or unsorted.

6.3.2.3.1 List is Unsorted

We traverse the list from the beginning, and compare each element of the list with the given element, say *item*, to be searched. If the match occurs, the location of the element is returned. If we reach the end of the list, and no match is found, then NULL value is returned to indicate the element is not in the list. The following listing shows the various steps required searching an element in the unsorted list.

Listing 6.6:

```
//  member function to search an element in the unsorted list
template <class T>
node LList<T>::*searchInUnsortedList(T item)
{
   node<T> *ptr;
   ptr = head;
   while ( ( ptr != NULL ) && (ptr->info != item ) )
       ptr = ptr->next;
   return ptr;
}
```

6.3.2.3.2 List is Sorted

If the list is sorted (say in ascending order), then we traverse the list from the beginning, and compare each element of the list with element, say *item*, to be searched. If the match occurs, the location of the element is returned. If we reach the element that is greater than *item* or end of the list, then NULL value is returned to indicate the element is not in the list. The following listing shows the various steps required searching an element in the sorted list.

Listing 6.7:

```
//  member function to search an element in the unsorted list
template <class T>
node LList<T>::*searchInSortedList(T item)
{
   node<T> *ptr;
   ptr = head;
   while ( ptr != NULL ) {
      if ( ptr->info == item )
         return ptr;
      else if ( item < ptr->info )
         return NULL;
      else
```

```
        ptr = ptr->next;
    }
    return NULL;
}
```

6.3.2.4 Inserting an Element

To insert an element in the list, the first task is to get a free node, assign the element to be inserted to the *info* field of the node, and then new node is placed at the appropriate position by adjusting the appropriate pointer. The insertion in the list can take place at the following positions:

- at the beginning of the list
- at the end of the list
- after a given element

6.3.2.4.1 Inserting at the Beginning of the List

To insert an element at the beginning of the list, first we test whether the linked list is initially empty. If yes, then the element is inserted as the first and only element of the list by performing the following steps:

- Assign NULL value to the next pointer field of the new node.
- Assign address of the new node to *head*.

However, if the list is initially not empty, then the element is inserted as the first element of the list by performing the following steps:

- Assign value of the *head* variable (the address of the first element of the existing list) to the next pointer field of the new node.
- Assign address of the new node to *head*.

Listing 6.8 shows the various steps required to accomplish this task.

Listing 6.8:

```
//  member function that insert an element in the
//  beginning of the list
template <class T>
void LList<T>::insertAtBeginning(T item)
{
    node<T> *ptr;
    ptr = new node<T>;
    ptr->info = item;
    if ( head == NULL )   // list initially empty
        ptr->next = NULL;
    else
        ptr->next = head;
    head = ptr;
}
```

6.3.2.4.2 Inserting at the End of the List

To insert the element at the end of the list, first we test whether the linked list is initially empty. If yes, then the element is inserted as the first and only element of the list by performing the following steps:

- Assign NULL value to the next pointer field of the new node.
- Assign address of the new node to *head.*

However, if the list is initially not empty, then the list is traversed to reach the last element, and then the element is inserted as the last element of the list by performing the following steps:

- Assign NULL value to the next pointer field of the new node.
- Assign address of the new node to next pointer field of the last node.

Listing 6.9 shows the implementation of the various steps.

Listing 6.9:

```
//  member function that insert an element in the end
//  of the list
template <class T>
void LList<T>::insertAtEnd(T item)
{
    node<T> *ptr, *loc;
    ptr = new node<T>;
    ptr->info = item;
    ptr->next = NULL;
    if ( head == NULL )   // list initially empty
        head =  ptr;
    else {
        loc = head;
        while ( loc->next != NULL )
            loc = loc->next;
        loc->next = ptr;
    }
}
```

6.3.2.4.3 Inserting after the Given Element of the List

To insert the new element after the given element, first we find the location, say *loc*, of the given element in the list, and then the element is inserted in the list by performing the following steps:

- Assign the next pointer field of the node pointed by *loc* to the next pointer field of the new node.
- Assign address of the new node to the next pointer field of the node pointed by *loc*.

Listing 6.10 shows the implementation of the various steps.

Listing 6.10:

```
//  member function that insert an element after a given element
template <class T>
void LList<T>::insertAfterElement(T item, T after)
{
   node<T> *ptr1, *ptr2;
   ptr1 = head;
   while ( ptr1 != NULL ) {
      if ( ptr1->info == after )
         break;
      ptr1 = ptr1->next;
   }
   if ( ptr1 == NULL ) {       //  element 'after' not found
      cout << "\n\nelement " << after << " not found\n\n";
      return;
   }
   ptr2 = new node<T>;
   ptr2->info = item;
   ptr2->next = ptr1->next;
   ptr1->next = ptr2;
}
```

6.3.2.5 Deleting an Element

To delete an element from the list, first the pointers are set properly and then the memory occupied by the node to be deleted is deallocated (released).

The deletion in the list can take place at the following positions:

- at the beginning of the list.
- at the end of the list.
- after a given element.
- given element.

6.3.2.5.1 Deleting from the Beginning of the List

An element from the beginning of the lists can be deleted by performing following steps:

- Assign the value of *head* (address of the first element of the list) to a temporary variable (say *ptr*),
- Assign the value of the next pointer field of the first node to *head.*
- Deallocate the memory occupied by the node pointed to by *ptr*.

Listing 6.11 shows the implementation of the various steps.

Listing 6.11:

```
//  member function that delete an element from the beginning
//  of the list
template <class T>
```

```
void LList<T>::deleteFromBeginning()
{
    node<T> *ptr;
    if ( head == NULL )  // list initially empty
        return;
    else
    {
        ptr = head;
        head = head->next;
        delete ptr;
    }
}
```

6.3.2.5.2 Deleting from the End of the List

To delete an element from the end of the list, we first traverse to the second last element of the list. Then the last element can be deleted by performing following steps:

- Assign the next pointer field of the second last node to a temporary variable (say *ptr*),
- Assign value NULL to the next pointer field of the second last node of the list.
- Deallocate the memory occupied by the node pointed to by *ptr*.

Listing 6.12 shows the implementation of the various steps.

Listing 6.12:

```
//  member function that delete an element from the end
//  of the list
template <class T>
void LList<T>::deleteFromEnd()
{
    node<T> *ptr, *loc;
    if ( head == NULL )  // list initially empty
        return;
    else if ( head->next == NULL )
    {
        ptr = head;
        head = NULL;
        delete ptr;
    }
    else
    {
        loc = head;
        ptr =  head->next;
        while ( ptr->next != NULL )
        {
            loc = ptr;
            ptr = ptr->next;
        }
        loc->next = NULL;
        delete ptr;
    }
}
```

6.3.2.5.3 Deleting after a Given Element of the List

To delete an element after a given element, first we find the location (say *loc*) of the element after which the element to be deleted comes. After that the element can be deleted by performing the following steps:

- Assign next pointer field of the node pointed by *loc* to temporary variable (say *ptr*),
- Assign the next pointer field of the node to be deleted to the node pointed to by *loc*
- Deallocate the memory occupied by the node pointed to by *ptr*.

Listing 6.13 shows the implementation of the various steps.

Listing 6.13:

```
//  member function that delete an element after a given
//  element of the list
template <class T>
void LList<T>::deleteAfterElement(T after)
{
   node<T> *ptr1, *ptr2;
   ptr1 = head;
   while ( ptr1 != NULL ) {
      if ( ptr1->info == after )
         break;
      ptr1 = ptr1->next;
   }
   if ( ptr1 == NULL ) {       //  element 'after' not found
      cout << "\n\nelement " << after << " not found\n\n";
      return;
   }
   ptr2 = ptr1->next;
   ptr1->next = ptr2->next;
   delete ptr2;
}
```

6.3.2.5.4 Deleting a Given Element of the List

To delete an element after a given element, first we find the location (say *loc*) of the element after which the element to be deleted comes. After that the element can be deleted by performing the following steps:

- Assign next pointer field of the node pointed by *loc* to temporary variable (say *ptr*),
- Assign the next pointer field of the node to be deleted to the node pointed to by *loc*
- Deallocate the memory occupied by the node pointed to by *ptr*.

Listing 6.14 shows the implementation of the various steps.

Listing 6.14:

```
//  member function that delete a given element from the list
template <class T>
void LList<T>::deleteElement(T item)
```

```
{
   node<T> *loc, *ploc = NULL;
   loc = head;
   while ( ( loc->info != item ) && ( loc != NULL ) )
   {
      ploc = loc; loc = loc->next;
   }
   if ( loc->info == item )
   {
      ploc->next = loc->next;
      delete loc;
   }
}
```

6.3.2.6 Reversing a List

To reverse a linear linked lists, three pointer filed are used. These are *previousNode*, *currentNode* and *nextNode*, which hold the address of previous node, current node and next node in the linear linked lists. To begin with, the address of the first node, which is held in pointer variable *head*, is assigned to variable *currentNode*, the address of the second node is assigned to *nextNode*, and the *previousNode* variable is assigned value NULL as there is no element preceding the first element. In addition the next pointer filed of the first node is set to NULL as it going to become the last node in the reversed list. Then in each iteration, following steps are performed:

1. Assign *currentNode* to *previousNode*
2. Assign *nextNode* to *currentNode*
3. Assign *currentNode–>next* to *nextNode*
4. Assign *previousNode* to *currentNode–>next*

These steps are repeated, till the last element becomes the current element. At this point, assign the address of the last element, held in variable *currentNode*, to *head* variable.

Listing 6.15:

```
//  member function that reverses the element of the list
template <class T>
void LList<T>::reverseList()
{
   node<T> *previousNode, *currentNode, *nextNode;
   currentNode = head;
   nextNode = currentNode->next;
   previousNode = currentNode->next = NULL;
   while ( nextNode != NULL )
   {
      previousNode = currentNode;
      currentNode = nextNode;
      nextNode = currentNode->next;
      currentNode->next = previousNode;
   }
   head = currentNode;
}
```

6.3.2.7 Deleting Entire List

Before the program terminates, the entire list must be deleted so that the memory occupied by the nodes of list can be used for other purposes. This task can be accomplished by performing the following steps:

- Assign the *head* pointer to a temporary variable, say *ptr*,
- Advance the *head* pointer to the next node,
- Deallocate the memory occupied by the node pointed to by *ptr*.

The above steps are repeated till the entire list is deleted.

Listing 6.16 shows the implementation of the various steps.

Listing 6.16:

```
// destructor that removes the list from memory
template <class T>
LList<T>::~LList()
{
   node<T> *ptr;
   while ( head != NULL ) {
      ptr = head;
      head = head->next;
      delete ptr;
   }
}
```

Listing 6.17:

```
//  Program to illustrate the implementation of linear linked list
#include <iostream.h>
#include <stdlib.h>
#include <iomanip.h>
#include <conio.h>
template <class T>
class node {
   public:
      T info;
      node *next;
};
template <class T>
class LList {
   private:
      node<T> *head;
   public:
      LList() {              // zero argument constructor
         head = NULL;
      }
      ~LList();              // destructor
     //-------  member function prototypes ---------
     int isEmpty();
     void traverseInOrder();
```

```
      void traverseReverseOrder();
      static void traverseReverse(node<T> *);
      void insertAtBeginning(T item);
      void insertAfterElement(T item, T after);
      void insertAtEnd(T item);
      void deleteFromBeginning();
      void deleteFromEnd();
      void deleteElement(T item);
      void deleteAfterElement(T after);
      void reverseList();
};    //---------- end of class definition ---------
template <class T>
int LList<T>::isEmpty()
{
   if ( head == NULL )
      return 1;
   else
      return 0;
}
template <class T>
void LList<T>::traverseInOrder()
{
   node<T> *ptr;
   ptr = head;
   while ( ptr != NULL ) {
      cout << "  " << ptr->info;
      ptr = ptr->next;
   }
}
template <class T>
void LList<T>::traverseReverseOrder()
{
   traverseReverse(head);
}
template <class T>
void LList<T>::traverseReverseRecursive(node<T> *ptr)
{
   if ( ptr->next != NULL )
      traverseReverse(ptr->next);
   cout << "  " << ptr->info;
}
template <class T>
void LList<T>::insertAtBeginning(T item)
{
   node<T> *ptr;
   ptr = new node<T>;
   ptr->info = item;
   if ( head == NULL )  // list initially empty
      ptr->next = NULL;
   else
      ptr->next = head;
   head = ptr;
}
template <class T>
void LList<T>::insertAfterElement(T item, T after)
{
   node<T> *ptr1, *ptr2;
   ptr1 = head;
```

```
   while ( ptr1 != NULL ) {
      if ( ptr1->info == after )
         break;
      ptr1 = ptr1->next;
   }
   if ( ptr1 == NULL ) {       //  element 'after' not found
      cout << "\n\nelement " << after << " not found\n\n";
      return;
   }
   ptr2 = new node<T>;
   ptr2->info = item;
   ptr2->next = ptr1->next;
   ptr1->next = ptr2;
}
template <class T>
void LList<T>::insertAtEnd(int item)
{
   node<T> *ptr, *loc;
   ptr = new node<T>;
   ptr->info = item;
   ptr->next = NULL;
   if ( head == NULL )  // list initially empty
      head =  ptr;
   else {
      loc = head;
      while ( loc->next != NULL )
         loc = loc->next;
      loc->next = ptr;
   }
}
template <class T>
void LList<T>::deleteFromBeginning()
{
   node<T> *ptr;
   if ( head == NULL )  // list initially empty
      return;
   else {
      ptr = head;
      head = head->next;
      delete ptr;
   }
}
template <class T>
void LList<T>::deleteFromEnd()
{
   node<T> *ptr, *loc;
   if ( head == NULL )  // list initially empty
      return;
   else if ( head->next == NULL ) {
      ptr = head;
      head = NULL;
      delete ptr;
   } else {
      loc = head;
      ptr =  head->next;
      while ( ptr->next != NULL ) {
         loc = ptr;
         ptr = ptr->next;
```

```
        }
        loc->next = NULL;
        delete ptr;
    }
}
template <class T>
void LList<T>::deleteElement(T item)
{
    node<T> *loc, *ploc;
    ploc = NULL;
    loc = head;
    while ( ( loc->info != item ) && ( loc != NULL ) ) {
        ploc = loc;
        loc = loc->next;
    }
    if ( loc->info == item ) {
        ploc->next = loc->next;
        delete loc;
    }
}
template <class T>
void LList<T>::deleteAfterElement(T after)
{
    node<T> *ptr1, *ptr2;
    ptr1 = head;
    while ( ptr1 != NULL ) {
        if ( ptr1->info == after )
            break;
        ptr1 = ptr1->next;
    }
    if ( ptr1 == NULL ) {        //  element 'after' not found
        cout << "\n\nelement " << after << " not found\n\n";
        return;
    }
    ptr2 = ptr1->next;
    ptr1->next = ptr2->next;
    delete ptr2;
}
template <class T>
void LList<T>::reverseList()
{
    node<T> *previousNode, *currentNode, *nextNode;
    currentNode = head;
    nextNode = currentNode->next;
    previousNode = NULL;
    currentNode->next = NULL;
    while ( nextNode != NULL ) {
        previousNode = currentNode;
        currentNode = nextNode;
        nextNode = currentNode->next;
        currentNode->next = previousNode;
    }
    head = currentNode;
}
template <class T>
LList<T>::~LList()
{
    node<T> *ptr;
```

```
    while ( head != NULL ) {
       ptr = head;
       head = head->next;
       delete ptr;
    }
}
//  ---------- main function ------------
void main()
{
   LList<int> list;
   int choice, element, after;
   while ( 1 )
   {
      cout << "\n\n           Options available \n" ;
      cout << "++++++++++++++++++++++++++++++++++ \n\n";
      cout << "    1.  Insert at beginning\n";
      cout << "    2.  Insert at end\n";
      cout << "    3.  Insert after a given element\n";
      cout << "    4.  Traverse in order\n";
      cout << "    5.  Traverse in reverse order\n";
      cout << "    6.  Delete from beginning\n";
      cout << "    7.  Delete from end\n";
      cout << "    8.  Delete given element\n";
      cout << "    9.  Delete after a given element\n";
      cout << "   10.  Reverse linked list\n";
      cout << "   11.  Exit\n\n";
      cout << "Enter your choice ( 1-11 ) : ";
      cin >> choice;
      switch ( choice )
      {
        case 1 : cout << "\nEnter element : ";
                 cin >> element;
                 list.insertAtBeginning(element);
                 break;
        case 2 : cout << "\nEnter element : ";
                 cin >> element;
                 list.insertAtEnd(element);
                 break;
        case 3 : cout << "\nEnter element : ";
                 cin >> element;
                 cout << "\nEnter element after which to insert : ";
                 cin >> after;
                 list.insertAfterElement(element, after);
                 break;
        case 4 : if ( list.isEmpty() )
                    cout << "\nList is empty ... ";
                 else
                    list.traverseInOrder();
                 cout << "\n\nPress any key to continue ... ";
                 getch();
                 break;
        case 5 : if ( list.isEmpty() )
                    cout << "\nList is empty ... ";
                 else
                    list.traverseReverseOrder();
                 cout << "\n\nPress any key to continue ... ";
                 getch();
                 break;
```

```
            case 6 : list.deleteFromBeginning();
                     break;
            case 7 : list.deleteFromEnd();
                     break;
            case 8 : cout << "\nEnter element to be deleteted : ";
                     cin >> element;
                     list.deleteElement(element);
                     break;
            case 9 : cout << "\nEnter element after which to delete : ";
                     cin >> after;
                     list.deleteAfterElement(after);
                     break;
           case 10 : list.reverseList();
                     break;
           case 11 : return;
        }
    }
}           //****** end of main function ******
```

6.4 DOUBLY LINKED LIST

In a *doubly linked list*, also called *two-way list*, each node is divided into three parts:

- the first part, called *previouspointer field*, contains the address of the preceding element in the list,
- the second part contains the information of the element, and
- the third part, called *nextpointer field*, contains the address of the succeeding element in the in the list.

In addition, two pointer variables, for example *head* and *tail*, are used that contains the address of the first element and the address of the last element of the list, respectively. The first element contains NULL value in the *previouspointer* to indicate there is no element preceding it in the list, and the last element have NULL value in the *nextpointer* field to indicate that there is no element succeeding it in the list. Doubly linked lists can be traversed in both directions. Figure 6.2 shows a doubly linked list with 3 nodes.

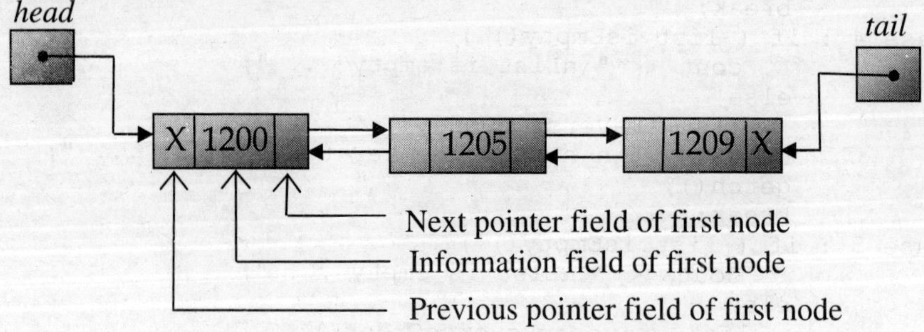

Figure 6.2: Doubly linked list with 3 nodes

6.4.1 Representation of Doubly Linked Lists

Suppose that the elements of the linear linked list can be of any primitive type or pointer type, the following is the required ADT to represent a linear linked list:

```
//   structure of the node
template <class T>
class node {
   public:
      T info;
      node *prev;
      node *next;
};
//   class that models a doubly linked list
template <class T>
class DList {
   private:
      node<T> *head;
      node<T> *tail;
   public:
      // zero argument constructor that initializes the
      // head and tail to value NULL
      DList() {
         head = tail = NULL;
      }
      // destructor that removes the list from memory
      ~DList();
      //-------  member function prototypes   -------

     //  member function that return value 1 if list is empty
     //  else returns value 0
     boolean isEmpty();
     //  member function that traverses the list from beginning
     //  to end and prints its elements
     void traverseForward();
     //  member function that traverses the list from end to
     //  beginning
     void traverseBackward();
     //  member function that insert an element in the
     //  beginning of the list
     void insertAtBeginning(T item);
     //  member function that insert an element in the end
     //  of the list
     void insertAtEnd(T item);
     //  member function that insert an element after a given
     //  element
     void insertAfterElement(T item, T after);
     //  member function that insert an element before a given
     //  element
     void insertBeforeElement(T item, T before);
     //  member function that delete an element from the beginning
     //  of the list
     void deleteFromBeginning();
     //  member function that delete an element from the end
     //  of the list
     void deleteFromEnd();
```

```
        //  member function that delete an element before a given
        //  element of the list
        void deleteBeforeElement(T before);
        //  member function that delete an element after a given
        //  element of the list
        void deleteAfterElement(T after);
    };      //---------- end of class definition ---------
```

The implementation of the member functions is given in the subsequent sections.

6.4.2 Implementation of Operations on Doubly Linked Lists

In this section, we will describe some operations on doubly linked lists.

6.4.2.1 Creating an Empty List

In the above declarations, the variable *head* and *tail* are declared as pointers to a *node* data type. These variables are not yet given any value. Since the list will be empty in the beginning, the variable *head* and *tail* are assigned a sentinel value to indicate that list is empty.

Listing 6.18 shows the implementation of this function.

Listing 6.18:

```
// zero argument constructor that initializes head to value NULL
DList<T>::DList()
{
   head = tail = NULL;
}
```

6.4.2.2 Traversing a List

The doubly linked list can be traversed in both way and that too very conveniently.

6.4.2.2.1 In-Order Traversal

The following listing shows the various steps required for traversing a doubly linked list in the forward direction.

Listing 6.19:

```
//  member function that traverses the list from beginning
//  to end and prints its elements
template <class T>
void DList<T>::traverseForward()
{
   node<T> *ptr = head;
   while ( ptr != NULL ) {
      cout << "  " << ptr->info;
      ptr = ptr->next;
   }
}
```

6.4.2.2.2 Reverse-Order Traversal

The following listing shows the various steps required for traversing a doubly linked list in the backward direction.

Listing 6.20:

```
// member function that traverses the list from end to beginning
template <class T>
void DList<T>::traverseBackward()
{
    node<T> *ptr = tail;
    while ( ptr != NULL ) {
        cout << "  " << ptr->info;
        ptr = ptr->prev;
    }
}
```

6.4.2.3 Searching an Element

The doubly linked lists can be traversed in any order to search the given element. The following listing shows the various steps required for searching an element from the beginning.

Listing 6.21:

```
//  member function that searches a given element in the list
template <class T>
node DList<T>::*search(T item )
{
    node<T> *ptr;
    ptr = head;
    while ( ptr != NULL )
    {
        if ( ptr->info == item )
            return ptr;
        ptr = ptr->next;
    }
    return NULL;
}
```

The element can also be searched from the other end also. The implementation of this operation is left as an exercise for the readers.

6.4.2.4 Inserting an Element

To insert an element in the list, the first task is to get a free node, assign the element to be inserted to the *info* field of the node, and then new node is placed at the appropriate position by adjusting the appropriate pointer. The insertion in the list can take place at the following positions:

- at the beginning of the list
- at the end of the list

- after a given element
- before a given element

6.4.2.4.1 Inserting at the Beginning of the List

To insert an element at the beginning of the list, first we test whether the linked list is initially empty. If yes, then the element is inserted as the first and only element of the list by performing the following steps:

- Assign NULL value to the next pointer and previous pointer fields of the new node.
- Assign address of the new node to *head* and *tail* pointer variables.

However, if the list is initially not empty, then the element is inserted as the first element of the list by performing the following steps:

- Assign NULL value to the previous pointer field of the new node.
- Assign value of the *head* variable (the address of the first element of the existing list) to the next pointer field of the new node.
- Assign address of the new node to previous pointer field of the node currently pointed by *head* variable, i.e., first element of the existing list.
- Finally, assign the address of the new to node to *head* variable.

The following listing shows the various steps required accomplishing this task.

Listing 6.22:

```
//  member function that insert an element in the
//  beginning of the list
template <class T>
void DList<T>::insertAtBeginning(T item)
{
   node<T> *ptr;
   ptr = new node<T>;
   ptr->info = item;
   if ( head == NULL ) {        // list initially empty
      ptr->next = ptr->prev = NULL;
      head = tail = ptr;
   } else {
      ptr->prev = NULL;
      ptr->next = head;
      head->prev = ptr;
      head = ptr;
   }
}
```

6.4.2.4.2 Inserting at the End of the List

To insert the element at the end of the list, first we test whether the linked list is initially empty. If yes, then the element is inserted as the first and only element of the list by performing the following steps:

- Assign NULL value to the next pointer and previous pointer fields of the new node.
- Assign address of the new node to *head* and *tail* pointer variables.

However, if the list is initially not empty, then the element is inserted as the last element of the list by performing the following steps:

- Assign NULL value to the next pointer field of the new node.
- Assign value of the *tail* variable (the address of the last element of the existing list) to the previous pointer field of the new node.
- Assign address of the new node to next pointer field of the node currently pointed by *tail* variable, i.e., last element of the existing list.
- Finally, assign the address of the new to node to *tail* variable.

Listing 6.23 shows the implementation of the various steps.

Listing 6.23:

```
//  member function that insert an element in the end
//  of the list
template <class T>
void DList<T>::insertAtEnd(T item)
{
   node<T> *ptr;
   ptr = new node<T>;
   ptr->info = item;
   if ( head == NULL ) {          // list initially empty
      ptr->next = ptr->prev = NULL;
      head = tail = ptr;
   } else {
      ptr->next = NULL;
      ptr->prev = tail;
      tail->next = ptr;
      tail = ptr;
   }
}
```

6.4.2.4.3 Inserting after a Given Element

The following listing shows the various steps required accomplishing this task.

Listing 6.24:

```
//  member function that insert an element after a given element
template <class T>
void DList<T>::insertAfterElement(T item, T after)
{
   node<T> *ptr1, *ptr2;
   ptr1 = head;
   while ( ptr1 != NULL ) {      // list initially empty
      if ( ptr1->info == item )
          break;
      ptr1 = ptr1->next;
   }
```

```
   if ( ptr1 == NULL ) {
      cout << "\nElement " << after << " not present\n\n";
      return;
   }
   ptr2 = new node<T>;
   ptr2->info = item;
   if ( ptr1->next == NULL ) {
      ptr2->next = NULL;
      ptr1->next = ptr2;
      ptr2->prev = tail;
      tail = ptr2;
   } else {
      ptr2->prev = ptr1;
      ptr2->next = ptr1->next;
      (ptr1->next)->prev = ptr2;
      ptr1->next = ptr2;
   }
}
```

6.4.2.4.4 Inserting before a Given Element

The following listing shows the various steps required accomplishing this task.

Listing 6.25:

```
//  member function that insert an element before a given element
template <class T>
void DList<T>::insertBeforeElement(T item, T before)
{
   node<T> *ptr1, *ptr2;
   ptr1 = head;
   while ( ptr1 != NULL ) {
      if ( ptr1->info == item )
         break;
      ptr1 = ptr1->next;
   }
   if ( ptr1 == NULL ) {
      cout << "\nElement " << before << " not present\n\n";
      return;
   }
   ptr2 = new node<T>;
   ptr2->info = item;
   if ( ptr1->prev == NULL ) {
      ptr2->prev = NULL;
      ptr1->prev = ptr2;
      ptr2->next = head;
      head = ptr2;
   } else {
      ptr2->prev = ptr1->prev;
      ptr2->next = ptr1;
      (ptr1->prev)->next = ptr2;
      ptr1->prev = ptr2;
   }
}
```

6.4.2.5 Deleting an Element

To delete an element from the list, first the pointers are set properly and then the memory occupied by the node to be deleted is deallocated (freed).

The deletion in the list can take place at the following positions:

- at the beginning of the list.
- at the end of the list.
- after a given element.
- before a given element.

6.4.2.5.1 Deleting from the Beginning of the List

An element from the beginning of the lists can be deleted by performing following steps:

- Assign the value of *head* (address of the first element of the list) to a temporary variable (say *ptr*),
- Further, there are two cases:
  - o If there is only one element in the existing list, both *head* and *tail* variable are set to NULL.
  - o If there are more than one element in the list, then following steps given below:
    - ◊ Assign NULL value to the previous pointer field of the second node.
    - ◊ Assign address of the second node to *head.*
- Deallocate the memory occupied by the node pointed to by *ptr*.

Listing 6.26 shows the implementation of the various steps.

Listing 6.26:

```
//  member function that delete an element from the beginning
//  of the list
template <class T>
void DList<T>::deleteFromBeginning()
{
    node<T> *ptr;
    if ( head == NULL )
        return;
    ptr = head;
    if ( head == tail )            // one element only
        head = tail = NULL;
    else
    {
        (ptr->next)->prev = NULL;
        head = ptr->next;
    }
    delete ptr;
}
```

6.4.2.5.2 Deleting from the End of the List

An element from the end of the lists can be deleted by performing following steps:

- Assign the value of *tail* (address of the last element of the list) to a temporary variable (say *ptr*),
- Further, there are two cases:
  - o If there is only one element in the existing list, both *head* and *tail* variable are set to NULL.
  - o If there are more than one element in the list, then following steps given below:
    - ◊ Assign NULL value to the next pointer field of the second last node.
    - ◊ Assign address of the second last node to *tail*.
- Deallocate the memory occupied by the node pointed to by *ptr*.

Listing 6.27 shows the implementation of the various steps.

Listing 6.27:

```
//  member function that delete an element from the end of list
template <class T>
void DList<T>::deleteFromEnd()
{
    node<T> *ptr;
    if ( head == NULL )   // list initially empty
        return;
    ptr = tail;
    if ( head == tail )    // one element only
        head = tail = NULL;
    else {
        (ptr->prev)->next = NULL;
        tail = ptr->prev;
    }
    delete ptr;
}
```

6.4.2.5.3 Deleting after a Given Element

An element after a given element can be deleted by performing following steps:

- Assign the value of *tail* (address of the last element of the list) to a temporary variable (say *ptr*),
- Further, there are two cases:
  - o If there is only one element in the existing list, both *head* and *tail* variable are set to NULL.
  - o If there are more than one element in the list, then following steps given below:
    - ◊ Assign NULL value to the next pointer field of the second last node.
    - ◊ Assign address of the second last node to *tail*.
- Deallocate the memory occupied by the node pointed to by *ptr*.

Listing 6.28 shows the various steps required to accomplish this task in an unsorted list.

Listing 6.28:

```
//  member function that delete an element after a given
//  element of the list
template <class T>
void DList<T>::deleteAfterElement(T after)
{
   node<T> *ptr1, *ptr2;
   ptr1 = head;
   while ( ptr1 != NULL ) {
      if ( ptr1->info == after )
         break;
      ptr1 = ptr1->next;
   }
   if ( ptr1 == NULL ) {
      cout << "\nElement " << after << " not present\n\n";
      return;
   }
   else if ( (ptr1->next)->next == NULL ) {
      ptr2 = ptr1->next;
      ptr1->next = NULL;
      tail = ptr1;
      delete ptr2;
   } else {
      ptr2 = ptr1->next;
      ptr1->next = ptr2->next;
      (ptr2->next)->prev = ptr1;
      delete ptr2;
   }
}
```

6.4.2.5.4 Deleting before a given Element

Listing 6.29 shows the various steps required accomplishing this task in an unsorted list.

Listing 6.29:

```
//  member function that delete an element before a given
//  element of the list
template <class T>
void DList<T>::deleteBeforeElement(T before)
{
   node<T> *ptr1, *ptr2;
   ptr1 = head;
   while ( ptr1 != NULL ) {
      if ( ptr1->info == before )
         break;
      ptr1 = ptr1->next;
   }
   if ( ptr1 == NULL ) {
      cout << "\nElement " << before << " not present\n\n";
      return;
   }
   else if ( (ptr1->prev)->prev == NULL ) {
```

```
        ptr2 = ptr1->prev;
        ptr1->prev = NULL;
        head = ptr1;
        delete ptr2;
    } else {
        ptr2 = ptr1->prev;
        ptr1->prev = ptr2->prev;
        (ptr2->prev)->next = ptr1;
        delete ptr2;
    }
}
```

6.4.2.6 Deleting Entire List

The doubly linked list can be deleted either by heading from the beginning or from the end. The list can be deleted from the beginning by performing following steps:

- Assign the *head* pointer to a temporary variable, say *ptr*,
- Advance the *head* pointer to the next node,
- Deallocate the memory occupied by the node pointed to by *ptr*.

The above steps are repeated till the entire list is deleted. Finally the *tail* pointer is set to NULL value.

Listing 6.30 shows the implementation of the various steps.

Listing 6.30:

```
// destructor that removes the list from memory
template <class T>
DList<T>::~DList()
{
    node<T> *ptr;
    while ( head != NULL ) {
      ptr = head;
      head = head->next;
      delete ptr;
    }
    tail = NULL;
}
```

Listing 6.31:

```
//
//  Program to illustrate the implementation doubly linked list
//
#include <iostream.h>
#include <stdlib.h>
#include <iomanip.h>
#include <conio.h>
//------ defining a node  -------
template <class T>
```

```
class node {
   public:
      T info;
      node *prev;
      node *next;
};
template <class T>
class DList {
   private:
      node<T> *head;
      node<T> *tail;
   public:
      DList() {
         head = tail = NULL;
      }
      ~DList();
      //-------  member function prototypes   -------
      boolean isEmpty();
      void traverseForward();
      void traverseBackward();
      void insertAtBeginning(int item);
      void insertAtEnd(int item);
      void insertAfterElement(int item, int after);
      void insertBeforeElement(int item, int before);
      void deleteFromBeginning();
      void deleteFromEnd();
      void deleteBeforeElement(int before);
      void deleteAfterElement(int after);
};    //---------- end of class definition ---------
template <class T>
DList<T>::~DList()
{
   node<T> *ptr;
   while ( head != NULL ) {
      ptr = head;
      head = head->next;
      delete ptr;
   }
   tail = NULL;
}
template <class T>
boolean DList<T>::isEmpty()
{
   return ( ( head == NULL ) ? 1 : 0 );
}
template <class T>
void DList<T>::traverseForward()
{
   node<T> *ptr = head;
   while ( ptr != NULL ) {
      cout << "  " << ptr->info;
      ptr = ptr->next;
   }
}
template <class T>
void DList<T>::traverseBackward()
{
   node<T> *ptr = tail;
```

```
   while ( ptr != NULL ) {
      cout << "  " << ptr->info;
      ptr = ptr->prev;
   }
}
template <class T>
void DList<T>::insertAtBeginning(T item)
{
   node<T> *ptr;
   ptr = new node<T>;
   ptr->info = item;
   if ( head == NULL ) {           // list initially empty
      ptr->next = ptr->prev = NULL;
      head = tail = ptr;
   } else {
      ptr->prev = NULL;
      ptr->next = head;
      head->prev = ptr;
      head = ptr;
  }
}
template <class T>
void DList<T>::insertAtEnd(T item)
{
   node<T> *ptr;
   ptr = new node<T>;
   ptr->info = item;
   if ( head == NULL ) {           // list initially empty
      ptr->next = ptr->prev = NULL;
      head = tail = ptr;
   } else {
      ptr->next = NULL;
      ptr->prev = tail;
      tail->next = ptr;
      tail = ptr;
   }
}
template <class T>
void DList<T>::insertAfterElement(T item, T after)
{
   node<T> *ptr1, *ptr2;
   ptr1 = head;
   while ( ptr1 != NULL ) {       // list initially empty
      if ( ptr1->info == item )
          break;
      ptr1 = ptr1->next;
   }
   if ( ptr1 == NULL ) {
      cout << "\nElement " << after << " not present\n\n";
      return;
   }
   ptr2 = new node<T>;
   ptr2->info = item;
   if ( ptr1->next == NULL ) {
      ptr2->next = NULL;
      ptr1->next = ptr2;
```

```
        ptr2->prev = tail;
        tail = ptr2;
    } else {
        ptr2->prev = ptr1;
        ptr2->next = ptr1->next;
        (ptr1->next)->prev = ptr2;
        ptr1->next = ptr2;
    }
}
template <class T>
void DList<T>::insertBeforeElement(T item, T before)
{
    node<T> *ptr1, *ptr2;
    ptr1 = head;
    while ( ptr1 != NULL ) {
        if ( ptr1->info == item )
            break;
        ptr1 = ptr1->next;
    }
    if ( ptr1 == NULL ) {
        cout << "\nElement " << before << " not present\n\n";
        return;
    }
    ptr2 = new node<T>;
    ptr2->info = item;
    if ( ptr1->prev == NULL ) {
        ptr2->prev = NULL;
        ptr1->prev = ptr2;
        ptr2->next = head;
        head = ptr2;
    } else {
        ptr2->prev = ptr1->prev;
        ptr2->next = ptr1;
        (ptr1->prev)->next = ptr2;
        ptr1->prev = ptr2;
    }
}
template <class T>
void DList<T>::deleteFromBeginning()
{
    node<T> *ptr;
    if ( head == NULL )
        return;
    ptr = head;
    if ( head == tail )            // one element only
        head = tail = NULL;
    else {
        (ptr->next)->prev = NULL;
        head = ptr->next;
    }
    delete ptr;
}
template <class T>
void DList<T>::deleteFromEnd()
{
    node<T> *ptr;
    if ( head == NULL )  // list initially empty
        return;
```

```
   ptr = tail;
   if ( head == tail )   // one element only
      head = tail = NULL;
   else {
      (ptr->prev)->next = NULL;
      tail = ptr->prev;
   }
   delete ptr;
}
template <class T>
void DList<T>::deleteAfterElement(T after)
{
   node<T> *ptr1, *ptr2;
   ptr1 = head;
   while ( ptr1 != NULL ) {
      if ( ptr1->info == after )
         break;
      ptr1 = ptr1->next;
   }
   if ( ptr1 == NULL ) {
      cout << "\nElement " << after << " not present\n\n";
      return;
   }
   else if ( (ptr1->next)->next == NULL ) {
      ptr2 = ptr1->next;
      ptr1->next = NULL;
      tail = ptr1;
      delete ptr2;
   } else {
      ptr2 = ptr1->next;
      ptr1->next = ptr2->next;
      (ptr2->next)->prev = ptr1;
      delete ptr2;
   }
}
template <class T>
void DList<T>::deleteBeforeElement(T before)
{
   node<T> *ptr1, *ptr2;
   ptr1 = head;
   while ( ptr1 != NULL ) {
      if ( ptr1->info == before )
         break;
      ptr1 = ptr1->next;
   }
   if ( ptr1 == NULL ) {
      cout << "\nElement " << before << " not present\n\n";
      return;
   }
   else if ( (ptr1->prev)->prev == NULL ) {
      ptr2 = ptr1->prev;
      ptr1->prev = NULL;
      head = ptr1;
      delete ptr2;
   } else {
      ptr2 = ptr1->prev;
```

```
    ptr1->prev = ptr2->prev;
    (ptr2->prev)->next = ptr1;
    delete ptr2;
  }
}
//---- main function starts -----
void main()
{
   DList<int> list;
   int choice, element, after, before;
   while ( 1 )
   {
      cout <<  "\n\n        Options available \n" ;
      cout << "++++++++++++++++++++++++++++++++ \n\n";
      cout << "   1.  Insert at beginning\n";
      cout << "   2.  Insert at end\n";
      cout << "   3.  Insert after a given element\n";
      cout << "   4.  Insert before a given element\n";
      cout << "   5.  Traverse in Forward directrion\n";
      cout << "   6.  Traverse in backward direction\n";
      cout << "   7.  Delete from beginning\n";
      cout << "   8.  Delete from end\n";
      cout << "   9.  Delete after a given element\n";
      cout << "  10.  Delete before a given element\n";
      cout << "  11.  Exit\n\n";
      cout << "Enter your choice ( 1-11 ) : ";
      cin >> choice;
      switch ( choice ) {
         case 1 : cout << "\nEnter element : ";
                  cin >> element;
                  list.insertAtBeginning(element);
                  break;
         case 2 : cout << "\nEnter element : ";
                  cin >> element;
                  list.insertAtEnd(element);
                  break;
         case 3 : cout << "\nEnter element : ";
                  cin >> element;
                  cout << "\nEnter element after which to insert : ";
                  cin >> after;
                  list.insertAfterElement(element, after);
                  break;
         case 4 : cout << "\nEnter element : ";
                  cin >> element;
                  cout << "\nEnter element before which to insert : ";
                  cin >> before;
                  list.insertBeforeElement(element, before);
                  break;
         case 5 : if ( list.isEmpty() )
                     cout << "\nList is empty ... ";
                  else
                     list.traverseForward();
                  cout <<  "\n\nPress any key to continue ... ";
                  getch();
                  break;
         case 6 : if ( list.isEmpty() )
                     cout << "\nList is empty ... ";
```

```
                    else
                        list.traverseBackward();
                    cout <<  "\n\nPress any key to continue ... ";
                    getch();
                    break;
            case 7 : list.deleteFromBeginning();
                    break;
            case 8 : list.deleteFromEnd();
                    break;
            case 9 : cout << "\nEnter element after which to delete : ";
                    cin >> after;
                    list.deleteAfterElement(after);
                    break;
            case 10: cout << "\nEnter element before which to delete : ";
                    cin >> before;
                    list.deleteBeforeElement(before);
                    break;
            case 11: return;
        }
    }
}        //  ****** end of main function ******
```

6.5 MORE TYPES OF LISTS

This section introduces some more types of linked lists, which often occur in literature.

6.5.1 Circular Linked List

A circular list is a linear linked list, except that the last element points to the first element. Figure 6.3 shows a circular linked list with 3 nodes. For non-empty circular linked lists, there are no NULL pointers. The memory declarations for representing circular linked lists are the same as for linear linked lists.

All operations performed on linear linked lists can be easily extended for circular linked lists with following exceptions:

1. While inserting new node at the end of the lists, its next pointer field is made to point to the first node.
2. While testing for end of the lists, we compare the next pointer field with the address of the first node.

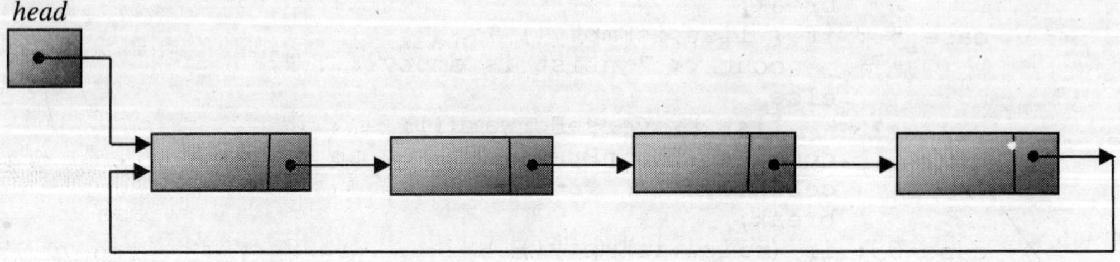

Figure 6.3: Circular linked list with 4 nodes

6.5.2 Header Linked Lists

A header list is linked list, which always contains a special node, called *header node*, at the beginning of the linked list. This header node usually contains vital information about the linked list such as the number of nodes in the lists, whether the list is sorted or not.

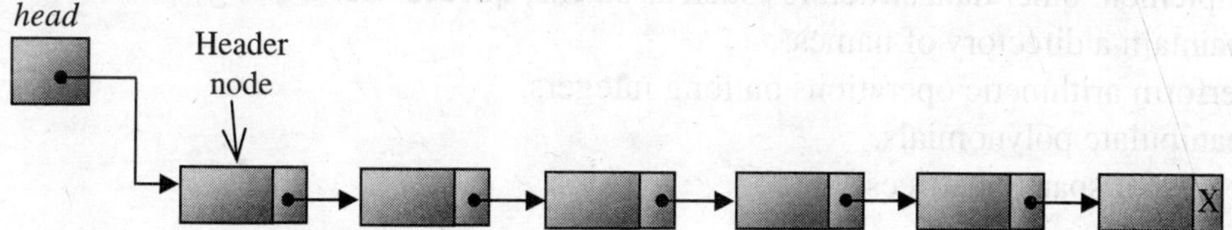

Figure 6.4: Header linear linked list, also known as grounded header list

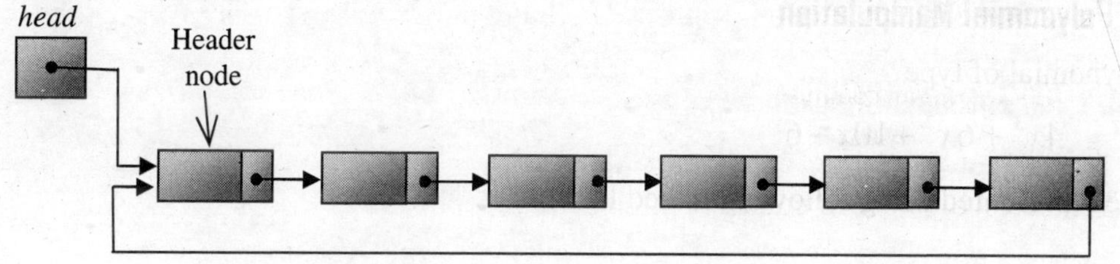

Figure 6.5: Circular header list

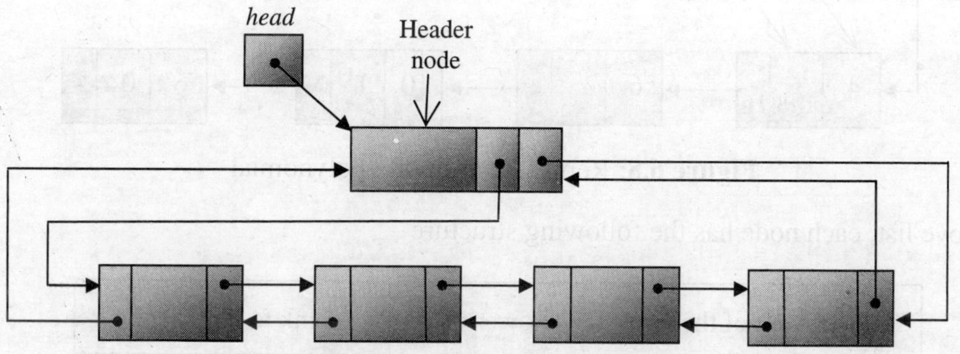

Figure 6.6: Two-way header list

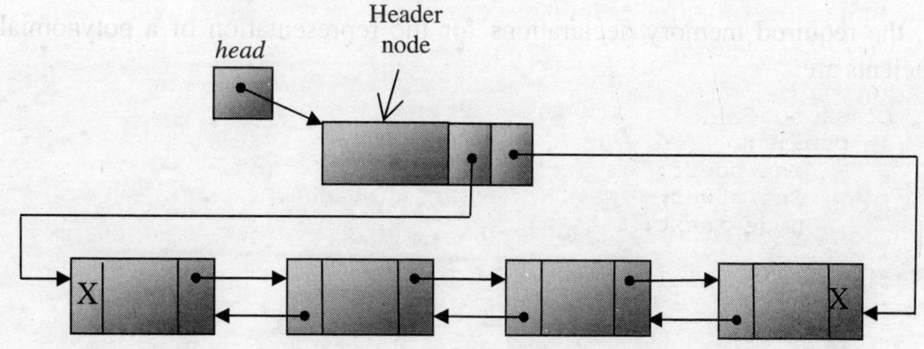

Figure 6.7: Two-way circular header list

6.6 APPLICATIONS OF LINKED LISTS

Like arrays, linked list is a primitive data structure. Linked lists are used in a wide variety of applications. Some of the applications of the linked lists are:

- To implement other data structures such as stacks, queues, trees, and graphs.
- To maintain a directory of names.
- To perform arithmetic operations on long integers.
- To manipulate polynomials.
- To represent sparse matrices.

The last two applications are described in this section.

6.6.1 Polynomial Manipulation

A polynomial of type

$$4x^3 + 6x^2 + 10x + 6$$

can be represented using following linked list

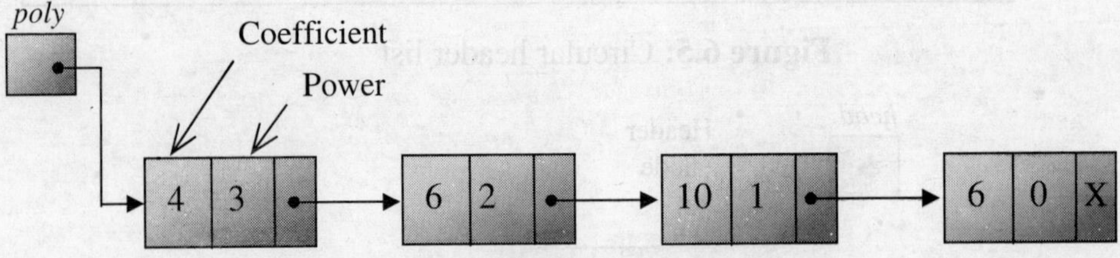

Figure 6.8: Representation of a polynomial

In the above list, each node has the following structure

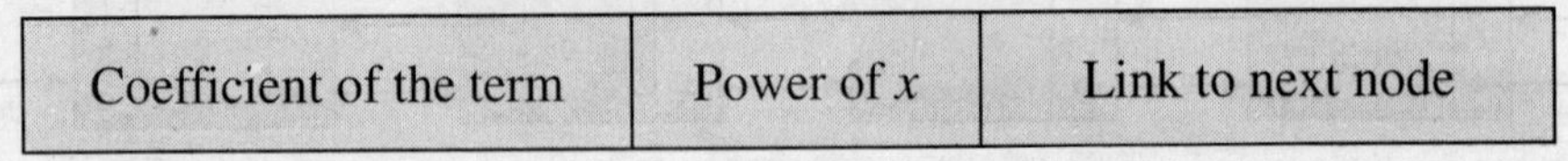

Figure 6.9: Structure of a node to represent a polynomial term

Thus, the required memory declarations for the representation of a polynomial with integer coefficients are

```
class node {
    public:
        int coeff;
        int power;
        node *next;
};
class Polynomial
{
    private:
        node *head;
    public:
        Polynomial() {       // constructor
```

```
        head = NULL;
      }
      ~Polynomial();          // destructor
      void read();            // input polynomial
      void display();         // output polynomial

      //  other member function

  }; // ---- end of class template ---
```

With these declarations let us develop the logic to add and multiply two polynomials.

6.6.1.1 Addition of Polynomials

Recall how we have done the addition of two polynomials in algebra at school level. We write the polynomial terms with same power under each other and then we add the coefficients. This is illustrated for addition of polynomials $5x^4 + 6x^2 + 10x - 6$ and $7x^3 + 3x^2 + 2x + 7$ as

$$
\begin{array}{rrrrr}
 & 5x^4 & & +6x^2 & +10x - 6 \\
+ & & 7x^3 & +3x^2 & +\ 2x + 7 \\
\hline
 & 5x^4 & +7x^3 & +9x^2 & +12x + 1 \\
\hline
\end{array}
$$

To produce the sum following steps are to be performed:

1. The terms of the polynomials are scanned from left to right.
2. The terms with powers that occur only in one polynomial are simply copied into the resulting polynomial.
3. The coefficients of terms with same powers are added and then the new term is copied into the resulting polynomial.

The following code shows the complete program to add the two polynomials. You can enter it in your computer and see its working.

Listing 6.32:

```
// Program to add two polynomials with integer coefficients.
#include<iostream.h>
#include<iomanip.h>
#include<ctype.h>
class node {
   public:
      int coeff;
      int power;
      node *next;
};
class Polynomial
{
   private:
      node *head;
   public:
      Polynomial() {      // constructor
        head = NULL;
```

```
    }
    ~Polynomial();      // destructor
    void read();        // input polynomial
    void display();       // output polynomial
    void add(Polynomial &p1, Polynomial &p2);  // add polynomials
    void addNodeAtEnd(int coef, int powe);       // add node
};  // ---- end of class template ---
void Polynomial::add(Polynomial &p1, Polynomial &p2)
{
   node *ptr1, *ptr2;
   int powe;
   int coef;
   ptr1 = p1.head;
   ptr2 = p2.head;
   while ( ( ptr1 != NULL) && ( ptr2 != NULL) ) {
      if ( ptr1->power > ptr2->power ) {
        coef = ptr1->coeff;
        powe = ptr1->power;
        ptr1 = ptr1->next;
      } else if ( ptr1->power < ptr2->power ) {
        coef = ptr2->coeff;
        powe = ptr2->power;
        ptr2 = ptr2->next;
      } else {
        coef = ptr1->coeff + ptr2->coeff;
        powe = ptr1->power;
        ptr1 = ptr1->next;
        ptr2 = ptr2->next;
      }
      if ( coef != 0 )
        addNodeAtEnd(coef, powe);
     }
     if ( ptr1 == NULL ) {
        for ( ; ptr2 != NULL; ptr2 = ptr2->next)
          addNodeAtEnd(ptr2->coeff, ptr2->power );
     } else if ( ptr2 == NULL ) {
       for ( ; ptr1 != NULL; ptr1 = ptr1->next)
          addNodeAtEnd(ptr1->coeff, ptr1->power);
     }
}
// Function to add term to the end of the list
void Polynomial::addNodeAtEnd(int coef, int powe)
{
   node *ptr1, *ptr2;
   ptr1 = new node;
   ptr1->coeff = coef;
   ptr1->power = powe;
   ptr1->next = NULL;
   if ( head == NULL ) {
     head = ptr1;
   } else {
     ptr2 = head;
     while ( ptr2->next != NULL ) {
       ptr2 = ptr2->next;
     }
     ptr2->next = ptr1;
   }
}
```

```
// Function to read a polynomial
void Polynomial::read()
{
    char ch;
    int coef, powe;
    cout << "\nEnter the terms in descending order of power";
    while ( 1 ) {
        cout << "\nEnter the degree of x : ";
        cin >> powe;
        cout << "Enter its coefficient : ";
        cin >> coef;
        addNodeAtEnd(coef, powe);
        cout << "\nAny More term (Y/N) ? : ";
        cin >> ch;
        if ( toupper(ch) == 'Y' )
           continue;
        else
           break;
    }
}
//  Function to print a polynomial
void Polynomial::display()
{
    if ( head != NULL )
       cout << head->coeff << "x^" << head->power;
    node *ptr = head;
    for (ptr = ptr->next; ptr != NULL; ptr = ptr->next )
    {
       if ( ptr->coeff != 0 ) {
          if ( ptr->coeff > 0 )
              cout << " + ";
          if ( ptr->coeff < 0 ) {
              cout << " - ";
              ptr->coeff = -ptr->coeff;
          }
          if ( ptr->power == 0 )
              cout << ptr->coeff;
          else if ( ptr->power == 1 )
              cout << ptr->coeff << "x";
          else
              cout << ptr->coeff << "x^" << ptr->power;
       }
    }
}
//  destructor to remove a polynomial from memory
Polynomial::~Polynomial()
{
   node *temp, *ptr =  head;
   while ( ptr != 0 ) {
     temp = ptr;
     ptr = ptr->next;
     delete temp;
   }
}
// ------  main function ------
void main()
```

```
{
    Polynomial poly1, poly2, poly3;
    cout << "\nProgram to add two polynomials";
    cout << "\n+++++++++++++++++++++++++++++++\n\n";
    cout << "Enter first polynomial\n";
    poly1.read();
    cout << ( "\n\nEnter second polynomial\n" );
    poly2.read();
    poly3.add(poly1,poly2);
    cout << "\nSum of polynomials\n\n";
    poly1.display();
    cout << "\n\nand\n\n";
    poly2.display();
    cout << "\n\nis\n\n";
    poly3.display();
}
```

6.6.1.2 Multiplication of Polynomials

Recall how we have done the multiplication of two polynomials in algebra at school level. We multiply the first polynomial with each term of the second polynomial and write the partial product in such a way that terms with same power comes in one column. This is illustrated for multiplication of polynomials $5x^4 + 6x^2 + 10x - 6$ and $3x^2 + 2x + 7$ as

$$
\begin{array}{ccccccc}
 & & & 5x^4 & +6x^2 & +10x & -6 \\
 & & & \times & 3x^2 & +2x & +7 \\
\hline
15x^6 & & +18x^4 & +30x^3 & -18x^2 & & \\
 & 10x^5 & & +12x^3 & +20x^2 & -12x & \\
 & & 35x^4 & & +42x^2 & +70x & -42 \\
\hline
15x^6 & +10x^5 & +53x^4 & +42x^3 & +44x^2 & +58x & -42 \\
\hline
\end{array}
$$

To produce the product following steps are performed:

1. The second polynomial is scanned from left to right.
2. For each term of the second polynomial, the first polynomial is scanned from left to right and its each term is multiplied by the term of the second polynomial.
3. If the product term already exists in the resulting polynomial, then its coefficients are added; otherwise a new node is inserted to represent this product term.

The following code shows the complete program to add the two polynomials. You can enter it in your computer and see its working.

Listing 6.34:

```
//  Program to multiply two polynomials with integer coefficients.
#include<iostream.h>
#include<iomanip.h>
```

```
#include<ctype.h>
class node {
   public:
      int coeff;
      int power;
      node *next;
};

class Polynomial
{
   private:
      node *head;
   public:
      Polynomial() {
       head = NULL;
      }
      ~Polynomial();
      void read();
      void display();
      void multiply(Polynomial &p1, Polynomial &p2);
      void addNodeAtEnd(int coef, int powe);
      void insertNode(int coef, int powe );
      node *search( node *ptr, int powe );
};
// Function to insert new term at its place in the polynomial
void Polynomial::insertNode(int coef, int powe )
{
   node *temp, *loc, *ploc;
   temp = new node;
   temp->coeff = coef;
   temp->power = powe;
   if ( head == NULL ) {
      temp->next = NULL;
      head = temp;
   } else {
      ploc = NULL;
      loc = head;
      while ( ( loc != NULL && powe < loc->power ) ) {
         ploc = loc;
         loc = loc->next;
      }
      temp->next = ploc->next;
      ploc->next = temp;
   }
}
// Function to multiply two polynomials    */
void Polynomial :: multiply(Polynomial &p1, Polynomial &p2)
{
   int powe, coef;
   node *loc, *ptr1, *ptr2;
   ptr1 = p1.head;
   while ( ptr1 != NULL ) {
      ptr2 = p2.head;
      while ( ptr2 != NULL ) {
        coef = ptr1->coeff * ptr2->coeff;
        powe = ptr1->power + ptr2->power;
        loc = search(head,powe);
```

```
        if ( loc == NULL )
            insertNode( coef, powe );
        else
            loc->coeff += coef;   // add coeffients
        ptr2 = ptr2->next;
      }
      ptr1 = ptr1->next;
   }
}
// Function that returns location of node with given power
node* Polynomial::search( node *ptr, int degree )
{
   node *ptr1;
   ptr1 = ptr;
   while ( ptr1 != NULL ) {
      if ( ptr1->power == degree )
         break;
      ptr1 = ptr1->next;
   }
   return ptr1;
}
// Function to add term to the end of the list
void Polynomial::addNodeAtEnd(int coef, int powe)
{
    node *ptr1, *ptr2;
    ptr1 = new node;
    ptr1->coeff = coef;
    ptr1->power = powe;
    ptr1->next = NULL;
    if ( head == NULL ) {
        head = ptr1;
    } else {
        ptr2 = head;
        while ( ptr2->next != NULL ) {
          ptr2 = ptr2->next;
        }
        ptr2->next = ptr1;
    }
}
// Function to read a polynomial
void Polynomial::read()
{
   char ch;
   int coef, powe;
   cout << "\nEnter the terms in descending order of power";
   while ( 1 ) {
      cout << "\nEnter the degree of x : ";
      cin >> powe;
      cout << "Enter its coefficient : ";
      cin >> coef;
      addNodeAtEnd(coef, powe);
      cout << "\nAny More term (Y/N) ? : ";
      cin >> ch;
      if ( toupper(ch) == 'Y' )
        continue;
      else
        break;
   }
```

```
}
// Function to print a polynomial
void Polynomial::display()
{
   if ( head != NULL )
      cout << head->coeff << "x^" << head->power;
   node *ptr = head;
   for (ptr = ptr->next; ptr != NULL; ptr = ptr->next )
   {
      if ( ptr->coeff != 0 )
      {
         if ( ptr->coeff > 0 )
            cout << " + ";
         if ( ptr->coeff < 0 ) {
            cout << " - ";
            ptr->coeff = -ptr->coeff;
         }
         if ( ptr->power == 0 )
            cout << ptr->coeff;
         else if ( ptr->power == 1 )
            cout << ptr->coeff<< "x";
         else
            cout << ptr->coeff << "x^" << ptr->power;
      }
   }
}
// destructor to remove a polynomial from memory
Polynomial::~Polynomial()
{
   node *temp, *ptr =  head;
   while ( ptr != 0 )
   {
      temp = ptr;
      ptr = ptr->next;
      delete temp;
   }
}

// ------- main function ----------
void main()
{
   Polynomial poly1, poly2, poly3;
   cout << "\nProgram to add two polynomials";
   cout << "\n+++++++++++++++++++++++++++++++\n\n";
   cout << "Enter first polynomial\n";
   poly1.read();
   cout << ( "\n\nEnter second polynomial\n" );
   poly2.read();
   poly3.multiply(poly1,poly2);
   cout << "\nSum of polynomials\n\n";
   poly1.display();
   cout << "\n\nand\n\n";
   poly2.display();
   cout << "\n\nis\n\n";
   poly3.display();
}
```

6.6.2 Representing Sparse Matrices

Many schemes of representing sparse matrices using linked lists have been proposed. Each one has its own advantages and disadvantages. I find the representation shown in Figure 6.9 simple to understand and implement.

The description of this representation is as

- It contains one *header node* that has four fields — *nrow* (number of rows), *ncol* (number of columns), *num* (number of nonzero elements), and *head* (a pointer to the first row containing at least one nonzero element).
- A linked list of rows containing at least one nonzero term, in the ascending order of their row values. Each node of this lists has three fields — *row* (row number for corresponding row list), *next* (a pointer to next node in the row list), and *first* (a pointer to the first column in a row having nonzero item).

$$\begin{pmatrix} 0 & 0 & 0 & 2 & 0 & 0 \\ 0 & 0 & 1 & 0 & 0 & 5 \\ 0 & 4 & 0 & 0 & 0 & 0 \\ 0 & 0 & 0 & 0 & 0 & 0 \\ 0 & 0 & 0 & 0 & 7 & 0 \end{pmatrix}$$

Figure 6.8: A 5×6 Sparse matrix

- A linked list of columns containing nonzero terms, in the ascending order of their column values. Each node of this lists has three fields — *col* (column number for corresponding row list), *term* (a nonzero value in column *col*), and *link* (a pointer to the next column having nonzero element).

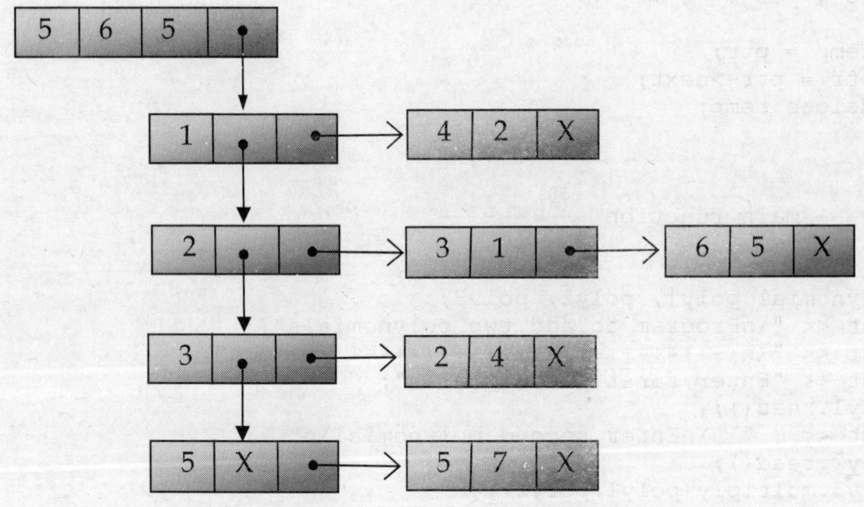

Figure 6.9: Linked representation of sparse matrix of Figure 6.8

Required memory declarations for the linked representation will look like

```
struct columnNode {     // structure of column node
    int col;
    int element;
```

```
        columnNode *link;
    };
    struct rowNode {            // structure of row node
        int row;
        rowNode *next;
        columnNode *first;
    };
    struct headerNode {         // structure of header node
        int nrow;
        int ncol;
        int num;
        rowNode *head;
    };
    class SparseMatrix {
        private:
            headerNode matrix;
        public:
            SparseMatrix(int rows, int cols) {
                matrix.nrow = rows;
                matrix.ncol = cols;
                matrix.num = 0;
                matrix.head = NULL;
            }
            ~SparseMatrix();
            void storeElement( int i, int j, int element );
            int  retrieveElement( int i, int j );
            void read();
            void display();
    };
```

With these declarations, we need functions that stores matrix element of a sparse matrix in linked representation, and retrieves matrix element from the linked representation.

The following codes shows the implementation of *storeElement()* member function.

Listing 6.36:

```
void SparseMatrix::storeElement( int i, int j, int element )
{
    rowNode *rptr, *pptr1, *ptr1;
    columnNode *cptr, *pptr2, *ptr2;
    matrix.num++;
    cptr = new columnNode;
    cptr->col = j;
    cptr->element = element;
    if ( matrix.head == NULL ) {      // sparse matrix is empty
        matrix.head = rptr = new rowNode;
        rptr->next = NULL;
        rptr->row = i;
        rptr->first = cptr;
        cptr->link = NULL;
        return;
    }
    pptr1 = NULL;
    ptr1 = matrix.head;
    while ( ( ptr1 != NULL ) && ( ptr1->row < i ) )  {
        pptr1 = ptr1;
```

```
      ptr1 = ptr1->next;
   }
   if ( ptr1->row == i ) { //  if row already exists
      pptr2 = NULL;
      ptr2 = ptr1->first;
      while ( ( ptr2 != NULL ) && ( ptr2->col < j) ) ) {
         pptr2 = ptr2;
         ptr2 = ptr2->link;
      }
      // insert as first column node
      if ( pptr2 == NULL ) {
         cptr->link = ptr1->first;
         ptr1->first = cptr;
      } else {
         cptr->link = ptr2;
         pptr2->link = cptr;
      }
      return;
   } else if ( ptr1 == NULL ) { // insert new row at end
      rptr = new rowNode;
      pptr1->next = rptr;
      rptr->next = NULL;
      rptr->row = i;
      rptr->first = cptr;
      cptr->link = NULL;
      return;
   } else {
      rptr = new rowNode;
      rptr->row = i;
      rptr->next = ptr1;
      pptr1->next = rptr;
      rptr->first = cptr;
      cptr->link = NULL;
   }
}
```

The following codes shows the implementation of *retrieveElement()* member function.

Listing 6.37:

```
int SparseMatrix::retrieveElement( int i, int j )
{
   int value;
   rowNode *rptr;
   columnNode *cptr;
   rptr = matrix.head;
   while ( ( rptr != NULL ) && ( rptr->row < i ) )
      rptr = rptr->next;
   if ( rptr == NULL )  // row not found
      value = 0;
   else if ( rptr->row > i )   //  row 'i' does not exist
      value = 0;
   else if ( rptr->row == i )    //  row 'i' if found
   {
      cptr = rptr->first;  // search for column
      while ( ( cptr != NULL ) && ( cptr->col < j ) )
         cptr = cptr->link;
```

```
      if ( cptr == NULL )  // column not found
         value = 0;
      else if ( cptr->col > j )    //  column 'j' does not exist
         value = 0;
      else if ( cptr->col == j )    //  column 'j' if found
         value = cptr->element;
   }
   return value;
}
```

The following listing shows the complete code of the program to multiply two sparse matrices represented using linked lists.

Listing 6.38:

```
//
//  Program to multiply two sparse matrices that are
//  represented using linked list
//
#include <iostream.h>
#include <iomanip.h>
#include <ctype.h>
struct columnNode {  // structure of column node
   int col;
   int element;
   columnNode *link;
};
struct rowNode { // structure of row node
   int row;
   rowNode *next;
   columnNode *first;
};
struct headerNode {  // structure of header node
   int nrow;
   int ncol;
   int num;
   rowNode *head;
};

class SparseMatrix {
   private:
      headerNode matrix;
   public:
      SparseMatrix(int rows, int cols) {
         matrix.nrow = rows;
         matrix.ncol = cols;
         matrix.num = 0;
         matrix.head = NULL;
      }
      ~SparseMatrix();
      void storeElement( int i, int j, int element );
      int retrieveElement( int i, int j );
      void read();
      void display();
};
```

```
SparseMatrix::~SparseMatrix() {
   rowNode *rptr, *temp1;
   columnNode *cptr, *temp2;
   rptr = matrix.head;

   // first remove column nodes
   while ( rptr != NULL ) {
      cptr = rptr->first;
      while ( cptr != NULL ) {
         temp2 = cptr;
         cptr = cptr->link;
         delete temp2;
      }
      rptr = rptr->next;
   }
   // remove row nodes
   rptr = matrix.head;
   while ( rptr != NULL ) {
      temp1 = rptr;
      rptr = rptr->next;
      delete temp1;
   }
}
void SparseMatrix::storeElement( int i, int j, int element )
{
   rowNode *rptr, *pptr1, *ptr1;
   columnNode *cptr, *pptr2, *ptr2;
   matrix.num++;
   cptr = new columnNode;
   cptr->col = j;
   cptr->element = element;
   if ( matrix.head == NULL ) {      // sparse matrix is empty
      matrix.head = rptr = new rowNode;
      rptr->next = NULL;
      rptr->row = i;
      rptr->first = cptr;
      cptr->link = NULL;
      return;
   }
   pptr1 = NULL;
   ptr1 = matrix.head;
   while ( ( ptr1 != NULL ) && ( ptr1->row < i ) )  {
      pptr1 = ptr1;
      ptr1 = ptr1->next;
   }
   if ( ptr1->row == i ) { //  if row already exists
      pptr2 = NULL;
      ptr2 = ptr1->first;
      while ( ( ptr2 != NULL ) && ( ptr2->col < j ) ) {
         pptr2 = ptr2;
         ptr2 = ptr2->link;
      }
      // insert as first column node
      if ( pptr2 == NULL ) {
         cptr->link = ptr1->first;
```

```
            ptr1->first = cptr;
        } else {
            cptr->link = ptr2;
            pptr2->link = cptr;
        }
        return;
    } else if ( ptr1 == NULL ) { // insert new row at end
        rptr = new rowNode;
        pptr1->next = rptr;
        rptr->next = NULL;
        rptr->row = i;
        rptr->first = cptr;
        cptr->link = NULL;
        return;
    } else {
        rptr = new rowNode;
        rptr->row = i;
        rptr->next = ptr1;
        pptr1->next = rptr;
        rptr->first = cptr;
        cptr->link = NULL;
    }
}
int SparseMatrix::retrieveElement( int i, int j )
{
    int value;
    rowNode *rptr;
    columnNode *cptr;
    rptr = matrix.head;
    while ( ( rptr != NULL ) && ( rptr->row < i ) )
        rptr = rptr->next;
    if ( rptr == NULL )  // row not found
        value = 0;
    else if ( rptr->row > i )    // row 'i' does not exist
        value = 0;
    else if ( rptr->row == i )   // row 'i' if found
    {
        cptr = rptr->first;   // search for column
        while ( ( cptr != NULL ) && ( cptr->col < j ) )
            cptr = cptr->link;
        if ( cptr == NULL )  // column not found
            value = 0;
        else if ( cptr->col > j )    //  column 'j' does not exist
            value = 0;
        else if ( cptr->col == j )    //  column 'j' if found
            value = cptr->element;
    }
    return value;
}
void SparseMatrix::read()
{
    int i, j, element;
    char yes_no;
    while ( 1 ) {
        cout << "\n\nEnter row number : ";
        cin >> i;
        cout << "Enter column number : ";
        cin >> j;
```

```
      cout << "Enter element : ";
      cin >> element;
      storeElement( i, j, element );
      cout << "\n\nAny more element Y/N ? : ";
      cin >> yes_no;
      if ( toupper(yes_no) == 'Y' )
        continue;
      else
        break;
    }
}
void SparseMatrix::display()
{
   int i, j;
   for ( i = 1; i <= matrix.nrow; i++ ) {
      for ( j = 1; j <= matrix.ncol; j++ ) {
         cout << setw(4) << retrieveElement(i,j);
      }
      cout << endl;
   }
}
void main()
{
   int i, j, k, m, n, p, q, temp;
   cout << "\nEnter size of first matrix as m n : ";
   cin >> m >> n;
   cout << "Enter size of second matrix as p q  : ";
   cin >> p >> q;
   if ( n != p ) {
      cout << "\n\nProduct is not feasible\n";
      return;
   }
   SparseMatrix mat1(m,n), mat2(p,q), mat3(m,q);
   cout << "\nENTER NONZERO ELEMENTS OF FIRST SPARSE MATRIX\n";
   mat1.read();
   cout << "\nENTER NONZERO ELEMENTS OF SECOND SPARSE MATRIX\n";
   mat2.read();
   //  compute product
   for ( i = 1; i <= m; i++ ) {
      for ( j = 1; j <= q; j++ ) {
         temp = 0;
         for ( k = 1; k <= n; k++ ) {
            temp += mat1.retrieveElement(i,k) *
            mat2.retrieveElement(k,j);
         }
         if ( temp != 0 )
            mat3.storeElement(i,j,temp);
      }
   }
   // output the result
   cout << "\n\nProduct of sparse matrix\n\n";
   mat1.display();
   cout << "\n\nand\n\n";
   mat2.display();
   cout << "\n\nequals\n\n";
   mat3.display();
}
```

REVIEW EXERCISES

1. How does a linear linked list compare with a linear array?
2. Is it possible in C++ language to implement a heterogeneous list? If, yes how?
3. What advantages does a doubly linked list have over linear linked lists?
4. How a linked list can be used to represent a polynomial of following type

   $9x^3y^2 - 8x^2y^2 + 10xy + 3y^2$

5. What is the advantage of a header node in a linked list?
6. What will be the complexity of the operation to remove an element from the end of the linear linked list?
7. What will be the complexity of the operation to add an element in the beginning of the linear linked list?
8. You are given a linear linked list sorted on ascending order. Can we apply binary search technique to search an element? Argue.
9. While implementing a linked list, do the programmers needs to implement a list of free nodes? Comment.
10. In a circular linked lists, how the end-of-list condition will be tested?
11. How many pointers need to be modified in the following operations?
    (*a*) Insert an element in the beginning of a linear linked list
    (*b*) Insert an element in the beginning of a doubly linked list
    (*c*) Insert an element in the middle of a doubly linked list
    (*d*) Delete an element from the end of a doubly linked list
    (*e*) Delete an element from the middle of a doubly linked list
    (*f*) Delete an element from the middle of a linear linked list

PROGRAMMING EXERCISES

1. Write a function that removes all duplicate elements from a linear linked list.
2. Write a function to traverse a circular linked list.
3. Write a function that returns value 1 if the linear linked list is sorted in the ascending order otherwise it returns value 0.
4. Write a function that makes copies of the given linear linked list.
5. Write a function that returns the number of elements in a linear linked list.
6. Write a function that merges two sorted linear linked lists.
7. Write a function that creates a new linear linked list by selecting alternate elements of a given linear linked list.
8. Write a function that sorts a linear linked list of integer values in the descending order.

9. Given a linear linked list whose elements are of type integer. Write function that copies the even integer numbers in one list and the odd integer numbers in another list.
10. For a given a linear linked, write the following functions that:
    (*a*) returns the location of the successor of a given element.
    (*b*) returns the location of the predecessor of a given element
    (*c*) returns the locations of the first element
    (*d*) returns the location of the last element
    (*e*) deletes the alternate elements from the list
11. Write a function to concatenate two linear linked lists.
12. Write a function to remove all occurrences of a given element from a linear linked list.
13. Write a function to remove last occurrence of a given element from a linear linked list.
14. Write a function to remove first occurrence of a given element from a linear linked list.
15. Write a recursive function to reverse a linear linked list.
16. Repeat all of the above programming exercises for doubly linked list.
17. **Josephus Problem** - It consists of a group of soldiers surrounded by a heavy enemy force and there is only one horse to escape and hence only one soldier can escape. In order to determine which soldier will escape, they form a circle and pick up a number *n* from a hat. A name is also picked up from the hat. They start counting clockwise around the circle from a soldier whose name is picked up from the hat. And the soldier on which count reaches *n* is removed from the circle. And the count again starts from the soldier who was next to the soldier who is removed from the circle. This process goes on till only one soldier is left. This soldier will take the horse and escapes. Write a program to solve this problem. Input to your program is list of names of soldiers and number *n* and the output should be the name of soldier left.

❑ ❑ ❑

Chapter 7

Stack

7.1 INTRODUCTION

A *stack* is one of the most commonly used data structures. A *stack*, also called a Last-In-First-Out (LIFO) system, is a linear list in which insertions and deletions can take place only at one end, called the *top*. This structure operates in much the same way as stack of trays. If we want to place another tray, it can be placed only at the top. Similarly, if we want to remove a tray from stack of trays, it can only be removed from the top. The insertion and deletion operations in stack terminology are known as *push* and *pop* operations.

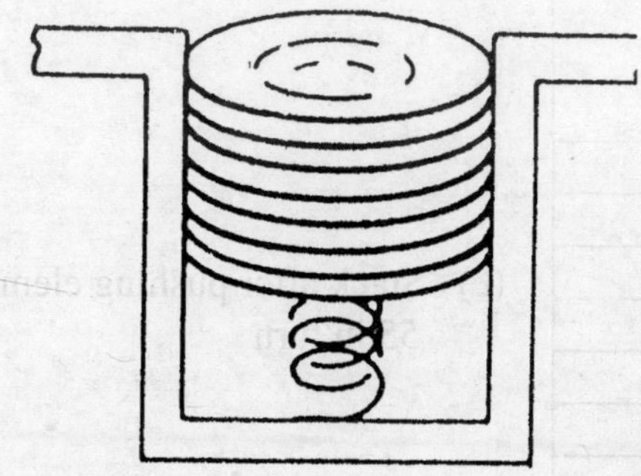

Figure 7.1: Stack of trays

Example 7.1:

The following figure illustrates a stack, which can accommodate maximum of 10 elements.

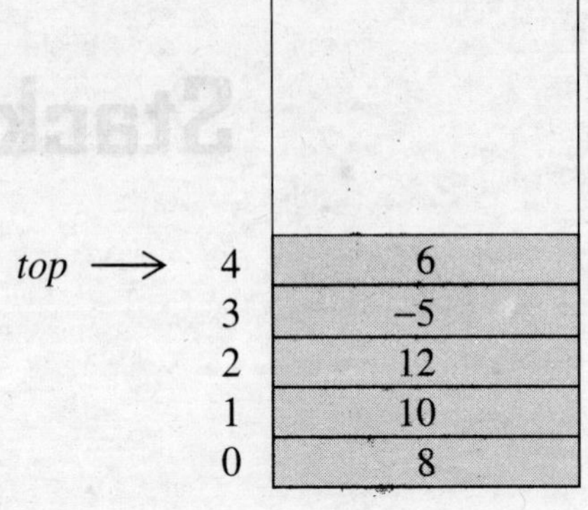

(*a*) Stack after pushing elements 8, 10, 12, –5, 6 in turn

(*b*) Stack after poping top two elements, *i.e.*, 6, and –5 in turn

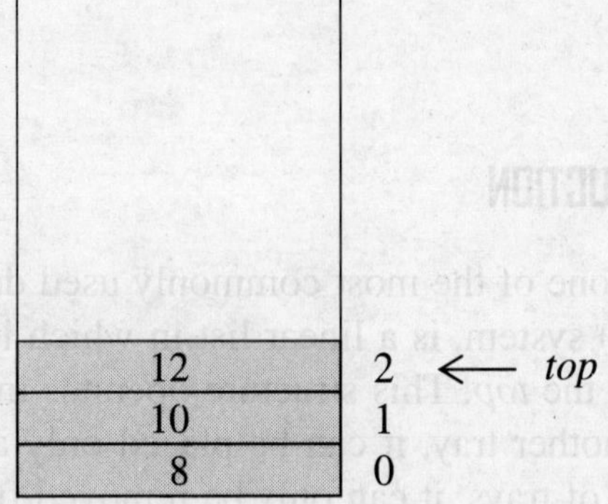

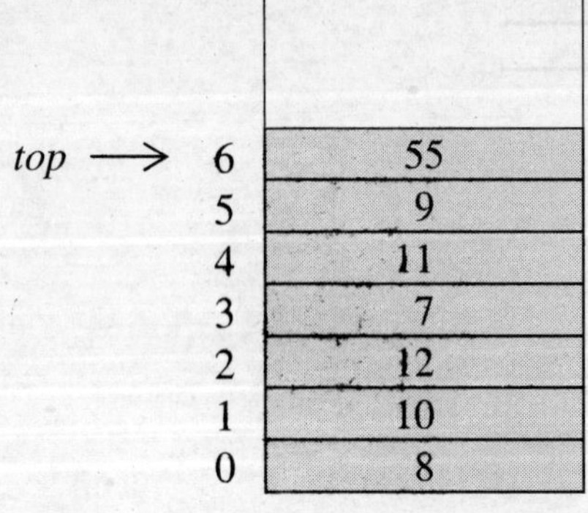

(*c*) Stack after pushing elements 7, 11, 9, 55 in turn

Figure 7.2: Illustration of a stack whose elements are integer values

7.2 OPERATIONS ON STACKS

The following operations are performed on stacks.

Table 6.1: Various operations performed on queues

Operation	Description
create	To create an initial stack. This task will be accomplished using a constructor.
destroy	To remove (delete) stack from memory. This task will be accomplished using a destructor.
push	Insert (push) an element at the top of stack.
pop	Access and remove the top element of the stack.
peek	Access the top element of the stack without removing it from the stack.
isFull	Check whether the stack is full.
isEmpty	Check whether the stack is empty.

All of these operation runs in O(1) time.

Note that if the stack *s* is empty then it is not possible to pop the stack *s*. Similarly, as there is no element in the stack, the *Peek(s)* operations is also valid. Therefore, we must ensure that the stack is not empty before attempting to perform these operations.

Likewise, if the stack *s* is full then it is not possible to push a new element on the stack *s*. Therefore, we must ensure that the stack is not full before attempting to perform push operation.

7.3 REPRESENTATION OF A STACK IN MEMORY

A stack can be represented in memory using a linear array or a linear linked list. Let us first discuss array representation of stacks.

7.3.1 Representing a Stack using an Array

To implement a stack we need a variable, called *top*, that holds the index of the top element of the stack and an array, named *elements*, to hold the elements of the stack.

Suppose that the elements of the stack can be any primitive type or pointer type, the following is the required ADT to represent a generic stack:

```
template <class T>
class ArrayStack
{
   protected:              // data members
      int top;
      int size;
      T *elements;
   public:                 // member functions
      // zero argument constructor,
      // it constructs a stack with default size = 10
```

```
        ArrayStack();
        // parametrized constructor that constructs,
        // a stack with size = n
        ArrayStack(int n);
        // destructor that removes the stack from memory
        ~ArrayStack();
        // Check whether the stack is empty
        int isEmpty();
        // Check whether the stack is full
        int isFull();
        // Insert (push) an element at the top of stack
        void push(T value);
        // Access and remove the top element of the stack
        T pop();
        // Access the top element of the stack
        // without removing it from the stack
        T peek();
    }; // -------- End of ArrayStack class --------
```

We have defined our own data type named *ArrayStack*, which is class and whose first data member *top* will be used as an index to the top element, second data member *size* will be used to hold the size of the stack, and third data member *elements*, a dynamic array whose elements can be any primitive type or pointer type.

The implementation of the member functions is given in the subsequent sections.

With these declarations, assuming a stack whose elements are of type *int* and size is 10, a stack of Figure 7.2 will be represented in computer memory as

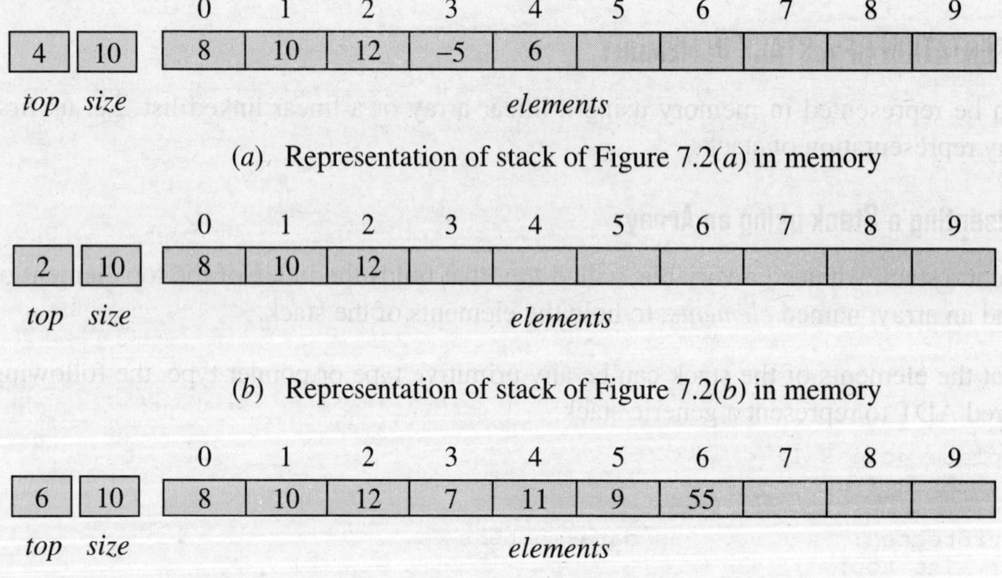

(*a*) Representation of stack of Figure 7.2(*a*) in memory

(*b*) Representation of stack of Figure 7.2(*b*) in memory

(*c*) Representation of stack of Figure 7.2(*c*) in memory

Figure 7.3: Array representation of stack of Figure 7.2

7.3.1.1 Creating an Empty Stack

Before we can use a stack, it is to be initialized. As the index of array elements can take any value in the range 0 to *size*–1, the purpose of initializing the stack is served by assigning value –1 (sentinel value) to the *top* variable. This simple task is accomplished using following constructors, where the zero argument constructors create a stack with default size 10 while the parameterised constructor creates a stack of use-defined size (*n*).

Listing 7.1:

```
// zero argument constructor,
// it constructs a stack with default size = 10
template <class T>
ArrayStack<T>::ArrayStack()
{
   elements = new T[10];
   size = 10;
   top = -1;
}
// parametrized constructor that constructs,
// a stack with size = n
template <class T>
ArrayStack<T>::ArrayStack(int n)
{
   elements = new T[n];
   size = n;
   top = -1;
}
```

7.3.1.2 Testing Stack for Underflow

Before we remove an item from a stack, it is necessary to test whether stack still have some elements, *i.e.*, to test that whether the stack is empty or not. If it is not empty then the pop operation can be performed to remove the top element. This test is performed by comparing the value of *top* with sentinel value –1, as shown in the following function.

Listing 7.2:

```
// Check whether the stack is empty
template <class T>
int ArrayStack<T>::isEmpty()
{
   if ( top == -1 )
      return 1;
   else
      return 0;
}
```

The above function returns value 1, indicating that stack is empty, if the test condition is satisfied; otherwise it returns value 0, indicating that stack is not empty.

The *isEmpty()* function can also be written using conditional operator (?:) as

Listing 7.3:

```
// Check whether the stack is empty
template <class T>
int ArrayStack<T>::isEmpty()
{
    return ( top == -1 ? 1 : 0 );
}
```

7.3.1.3 Testing Stack for Overflow

Before we insert new item onto the stack, it is necessary to test whether stack still have some space to accommodate the incoming element i.e. to test that whether the stack is full or not. If it is not full then the *push* operation can be performed to insert the element at top of the stack. This test is performed by comparing the value of the *top* with value *size*−1, the largest index value that the *top* can take, as shown in the following function.

Listing 7.4:

```
// Check whether the stack is empty
template <class T>
int ArrayStack<T>::isFull()
{
    if ( top == size-1 )
        return 1;
    else
        return 0;
}
```

The above function returns value 1, indicating that stack is full, if the test condition is satisfied; otherwise it returns value 0, indicating that stack is not full.

The *isFull()* function can also be written using conditional operator (?:) as

Listing 7.5:

```
// Check whether the stack is full
template <class T>
int ArrayStack<T>::isFull()
{
    return ( top == size-1 ? 1 : 0 );
}
```

7.3.1.4 Push Operation

Before the push operation, if the stack is empty, then the value of the *top* will be −1 (sentinel value) and if the stack is not empty then the value of the *top* will be the index of the element currently on the top. Therefore, before we place value onto the stack, the value of the *top* is incremented so that it points to the new top of stack, where incoming element is placed. This task is accomplished as shown in the following function.

Listing 7.6:

```
// Insert (push) an element at the top of stack
template <class T>
void ArrayStack<T>::push(T value)
{
    top++;
    elements[top] = value;
}
```

The above function can also be written as

Listing 7.7:

```
// Insert (push) an element at the top of stack
template <class T>
void ArrayStack<T>::push(T value)
{
    elements[++top] = value;
}
```

7.3.1.5 Pop Operation

The element on the top of stack is assigned to a local variable, which later on will be returned via the *return* statement. After assigning the top element to a local variable, the variable *top* is decremented so that it points to the new top.

This task is accomplished as shown in the following function.

Listing 7.8:

```
// Access and remove the top element of the stack
template <class T>
T ArrayStack<T>::pop()
{
   T temp;
   temp = elements[top];
   top--;
   return temp;
}
```

The above function can also be written as

Listing 7.9:

```
// Access and remove the top element of the stack
template <class T>
```

```
T ArrayStack<T>::pop()
{
        return elements[top--];
}
```

In the above two versions of the *pop()* function, the top element is returned via the *return* statement.

7.3.1.6 Accessing Top Element

There may be instances where we want to access the top element of the stack without removing it from the stack, *i.e.*, without popping it. This task is accomplished as shown in the following function:

Listing 7.10:

```
// Access the top element without removing it from the stack
template <class T>
T ArrayStack<T>::peek()
{
   return elements[top];
}
```

7.3.1.7 Removing Stack from Memory

As soon as the *ArrayStack* goes out of scope, it needs to be removed from computer memory. This is done using following destructor:

Listing 7.11:

```
// destructor that removes the stack from memory
template <class T>
T ArrayStack<T>::~ArrayStack()
{
   delete elements;
   top = -1;
   size = 0;
}
```

Following is the complete listing of the source code of the menu driven program to demonstrate the implementation of *ArrayStack*.

Listing 7.12:

```
//   Program to demonstrate the various operations on array based stack
#include<iostream.h>
#include<iomanip.h>

template <class T>
class ArrayStack
{
   protected:            // data members
```

```
      int top;
      int size;
      T *elements;
   public:             // member functions
      // zero argument constructor,
      // it constructs a stack with default size = 10
      ArrayStack();
      // parametrized constructor that constructs,
      // a stack with size = n
      ArrayStack(int n);
      // destructor that removes the stack from memory
      ~ArrayStack();
      // Check whether the stack is empty
      int isEmpty();
      // Check whether the stack is full
      int isFull();
      // Insert (push) an element at the top of stack
      void push(T value);
      // Access and remove the top element of the stack
      T pop();
      // Access the top element of the stack
      // without removing it from the stack
      T peek();
}; // -------- End of ArrayStack class --------

// zero argument constructor,
// it constructs a stack with default size = 10
template <class T>
ArrayStack<T>::ArrayStack() {
   elements = new T[10];
   size = 10;
   top = -1;
}
// parametrized constructor that constructs,
// a stack with size = n
template <class T>
ArrayStack<T>::ArrayStack(int n) {
   elements = new T[n];
   size = n;
   top = -1;
}
// destructor that removes the stack from memory
template <class T>
ArrayStack<T>::~ArrayStack() {
   delete elements;
   top = -1;
   size = 0;
}
// Check whether the stack is empty
template <class T>
int ArrayStack<T>::isEmpty() {
   return ( top == -1 ? 1 : 0 );
}
// Check whether the stack is full
template <class T>
int ArrayStack<T>::isFull() {
   return ( top == size-1 ? 1 : 0 );
```

```
}
// Insert (push) an element at the top of stack
template <class T>
void ArrayStack<T>::push(T value) {
   top++;
   elements[top] = value;
}
// Access and remove the top element of the stack
template <class T>
T ArrayStack<T>::pop() {
   T temp;
   temp = elements[top];
   top--;
   return temp;
}
// Access the top element of the stack
// without removing it from the stack
template <class T>
T ArrayStack<T>::peek() {
   return elements[top];
}
// -------- main function ---------
void main()
{
   int choice, element, m;
   cout << "\nSize of stack you want to use : ";
   cin >> m;
   ArrayStack<int> intStack(m);
   do
   {
      cout << "\n     Options available \n";
      cout << "     ++++++++++++++++++ \n\n";
      cout << "        1. Push  \n";
      cout << "        2. Pop \n";
      cout << "        3. Peek \n";
      cout << "        4. Exit\n\n";
      cout << "Enter your choice ( 1-4 ) : ";
      cin >> choice;
      switch ( choice )
      {
         case 1 : if ( intStack.isFull() ) {
                     cout << "Stack full, press any key to continue";
                  } else {
                     cout  << "Enter value : ";
                     cin >> element;
                     intStack.push(element);
                  }
                  break;
         case 2 : if ( intStack.isEmpty() ) {
                     cout << "Stack empty, press any key to continue";
                  }
                  else
                     cout << "Value poped is " << intStack.pop();
                  break;
         case 3 : if ( intStack.isEmpty() ) {
                     cout << "Stack empty, press any key to continue";
                  }
```

```
                    else
                        cout << "Value at top is " << intStack.peek();
        }
    }
    while ( choice != 4 );
} // ----  end of main function ----
```

7.3.2 Representing a Stack using a Linked List

A stack represented using a linked list is also known as *linked stack*. The array-based representation of stacks suffers from following limitations

- Size of the stack must be known in advance.
- We may come across situations when an attempt to push an element causes overflow. However, stack, as an abstract data structure can not be full. Hence, abstractly, it is always possible to push an element onto stack. Therefore, representing stack as an array prohibits the growth of stack beyond the finite number of elements.

The linked list representation allows a stack to grow to a limit of the computer's memory.

```
template <class T>
class node
{
   public:
      T info;
      node *next;
};
template <class T>
class LinkStack
{
   protected:              // data member
      node<T> *top;
   public:                 // member functions
      // zero argument constructor,
      // it constructs a empty stack
      LinkStack();
      // destructor
      ~LinkStack();
      // Check whether the stack is empty
      int isEmpty();
      // Insert (push) an element at the top of stack
      void push(T value);
      // Access and remove the top element of the stack
      T pop();
      // Access the top element of the stack
      // without removing it from the stack
      T peek();
}; // ************ End of Stack class ****************
```

We have defined our own data type named *LinkStack*, which has a pointer to a self-referential class and whose first data member *info* hold the element of the stack and the second data member *next* holds the address of the element under it in the stack.

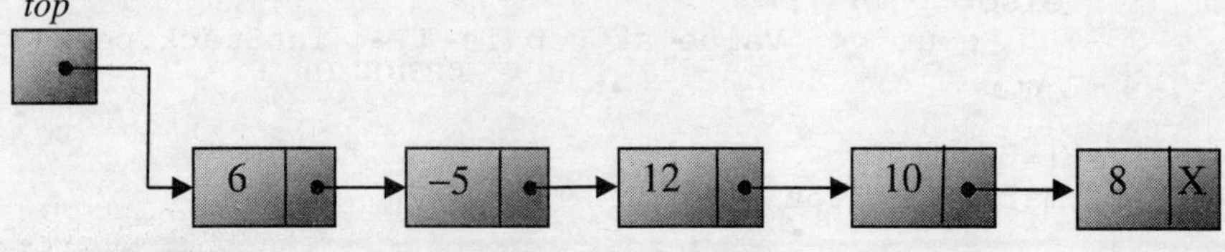

(*a*) Representation of stack of Figure 7.2(*a*) in memory

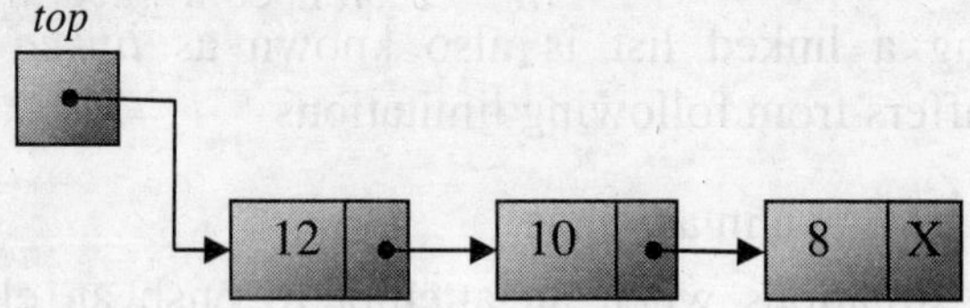

(*b*) Representation of stack of Figure 7.2(*b*) in memory

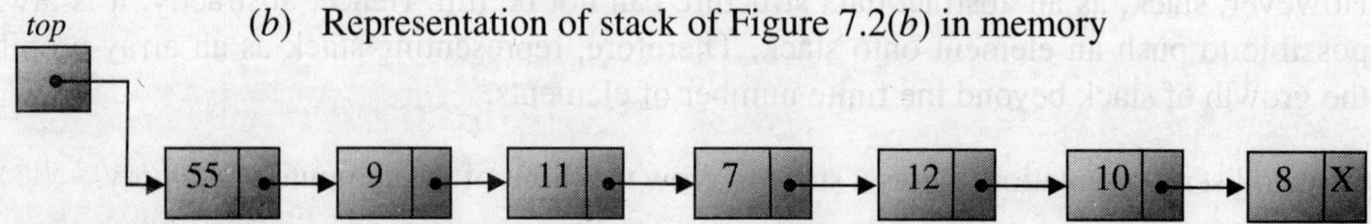

(*c*) Representation of stack of Figure 7.2(*c*) in memory

Figure 7.4: Linked representation of stack of Figure 7.2

With these declarations, we will write functions for various operations to be performed on a stack represented using linked list.

7.3.2.1 Creating an Empty Stack

Before we can use a stack, it is to be initialized. To initialize a stack, we will create an empty linked list. The empty linked list is created by setting pointer variable *top* to value NULL.

This simple task can be accomplished by the following function.

Listing 7.13:

```
// zero argument constructor,
// it constructs a empty stack
template <class T>
LinkStack<T>::LinkStack()
{
   top = NULL;
}
```

7.3.2.2 Testing Stack for Underflow

The stack is tested for underflow condition by checking whether the linked list is empty. The empty status of the linked lists will be indicated by the NULL value of pointer variable *top*. This is shown in the following function.

Listing 7.14:

```
// Check whether the stack is empty
template <class T>
int LinkStack<T>::isEmpty()
{
   return ( top == NULL ? 1 : 0 );
}
```

The above function returns value 1, indicating that stack is empty, if the test condition is satisfied; otherwise it returns value 0, indicating that stack is not empty.

7.3.2.3 Testing Stack for Overflow

Since a stack represented using a linked list can grow to a limit of a computer's memory, there overflow condition never occurs. Hence, this operation is not implemented for linked stacks.

7.3.2.4 Push Operation

To push a new element onto the stack, the element is inserted in the beginning of the linked list. This task is accomplished as shown in the next function.

Listing 7.16:

```
// Insert (push) an element at the top of stack
template <class T>
void LinkStack<T>::push(T value)
{
   node<T> *ptr;
   ptr = new node<T>;
   ptr->info = value;
   ptr->next = top;
   top = ptr;
}
```

7.3.2.5 Pop Operation

To pop an element from the stack, the element is removed from the beginning of the linked list. This task is accomplished as shown in the following function.

Listing 7.17:

```
//Access and remove the top element of the stack
template <class T>
T LinkStack<T>::pop()
{
   T temp;
   node<T> *ptr;
   temp = head->info;
   ptr = top;
   top = head->next;
```

```
    delete ptr;
    return temp;
}
```

The element in the beginning of the linked list is assigned to a local variable *temp*, which later on will be returned via the *return* statement. And the first node from the linked list is removed.

7.3.2.6 Accessing Top Element

The top element is accessed as shown in the following function.

Listing 7.18:

```
// Access the top element of the stack
// without removing it from the stack
template <class T>
T LinkStack<T>::peek()
{
    return ( top->info );
}
```

7.3.2.7 Dispose a Stack

Because stack is implemented using linked lists, therefore it is programmer's job to write the code to release the memory occupied by the stack. The following listing shows the different steps to be performed.

Listing 7.19:

```
// remove stack from memory
template <class T>
LinkStack<T>::~LinkStack()
{
    node<T> *ptr;
    while ( head != 0 ) {
        ptr = head;
        head = head->next;
        delete ptr;
    }
}
```

This dispose operations is O(*n*) time.

Following is the complete listing of the source code of the menu driven program to demonstrate the implementation of *LinkStack*.

Listing 7.20:

```
//   Program to demonstrate the various operations on linked stack
#include<iostream.h>
#include<iomanip.h>
```

```
template <class T>
class node
{
   public:
      T info;
      node *next;
};
template <class T>
class LinkStack
{
   protected:           // data member
      node<T> *top;
   public:              // member functions
      // zero argument constructor,
      // it constructs a empty stack
      LinkStack();
      // destructor
      ~LinkStack();
      // Check whether the stack is empty
      int isEmpty();
      // Insert (push) an element at the top of stack
      void push(T value);
      // Access and remove the top element of the stack
      T pop();
      // Access the top element of the stack
      // without removing it from the stack
      T peek();
}; // ************ End of Stack class ****************
// zero argument constructor,
// it constructs a empty stack
template <class T>
LinkStack<T>::LinkStack()
{
   top = NULL;
}
// Check whether the stack is empty
template <class T>
int LinkStack<T>::isEmpty()
{
   return ( top == NULL ? 1 : 0 );
}
// Insert (push) an element at the top of stack
template <class T>
void LinkStack<T>::push(T value)
{
   node<T> *ptr;
   ptr = new node<T>;
   ptr->info = value;
   ptr->next = top;
   top = ptr;
}
// Access and remove the top element of the stack
template <class T>
T LinkStack<T>::pop()
{
   T temp;
   node<T> *ptr;
   temp = head->info;
```

```
   ptr = top;
   top = head->next;
   delete ptr;
   return temp;
}
// Access the top element of the stack without removing it from the stack
template <class T>
T LinkStack<T>::peek()
{
   return ( top->info );
}
// remove stack from memory
template <class T>
LinkStack<T>::~LinkStack()
{
   node<T> *ptr;
   while ( head != 0 ) {
      ptr = head;
      head = head->next;
      delete ptr;
   }
}
// ------ main function -------
void main()
{
   int choice, element;
   LinkStack<int> intStack;
   do
   {
      cout << "\n     Options available \n";
      cout << "    ++++++++++++++++++ \n\n";
      cout << "      1. Push   \n";
      cout << "      2. Pop \n";
      cout << "      3. Peek \n";
      cout << "      4. Exit\n\n";
      cout << "Enter your choice ( 1-4 ) : ";
      cin >> choice;
      switch ( choice )
      {
        case 1 : cout  << "Enter value : ";
                 cin >> element;
                 intStack.push(element);
                 break;
        case 2 : if ( intStack.isEmpty() )
                    cout << "Stack empty, press any key to continue";
                 else
                    cout << "Value poped is " << intStack.pop();
                 break;
        case 3 : if ( intStack.isEmpty() )
                    cout << "Stack empty, press any key to continue";
                 else
                    cout << "Value at top is " << intStack.peek();
      }
   }
   while ( choice != 4 );
} /*----  end of main function ----*/
```

7.4 MULTIPLE STACKS

We have seen that if we represent a stack using an array, we have to allocate sufficient space for the stack. If the space allocated to an array is less, it may result in frequent overflows and we may have to modify the code and reallocate more space for array. On other side, if we attempt to reduce the number of overflows by allocating large space for array, it may result in sheer wastage of space if the typical size of the stack is very small as compared to actual size of the array. In this case, we may say that there exists a trade-off between the number of overflows and the space.

One possibility to reduce this trade-off is to represent more than one stack in the same array of sufficient size. How this can be done is illustrated below.

7.4.1 Representing Two Stacks

Figure 7.5 shows the scheme to represent two stacks in a same array *stack*[0..*n*–1] of size *n*. Here our basic assumption is that the combined size of these two stacks will not exceed *n*.

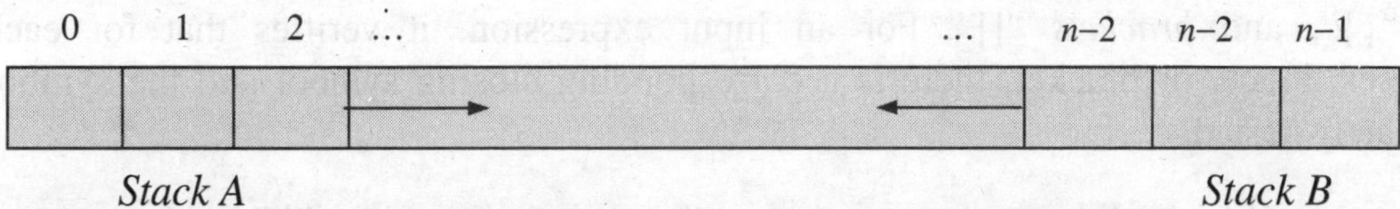

Figure 7.5: Representation of two stacks by an array of size *n*

Stack A grows from left to right whereas Stack B grows from right-to-left. The implementation of different operations on these stacks is left as an exercise for the readers.

7.4.2 Representing More than two Stacks

Figure 7.6 shows the scheme to represent six stacks in a same array *stack*[0..*n*–1] of size *n*. Each stack *i* is allocated an equal amount of space bounded by array indices *b*[*i*] and *t*[*i*].

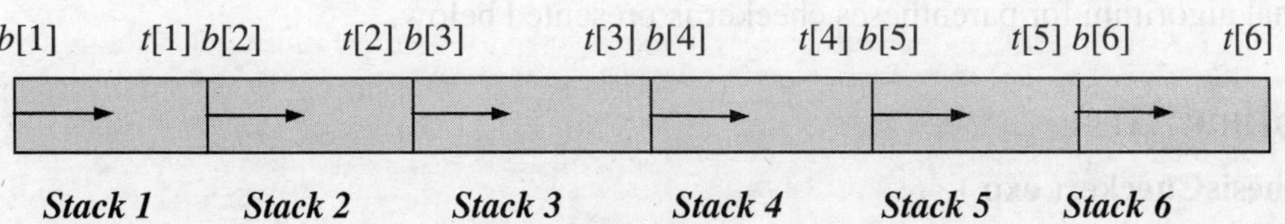

Figure 7.6: Representation of six stacks by an array of size *n*

The implementation of different operations on these stacks is left as an exercise for the students.

7.5 APPLICATIONS OF STACKS

As mentioned earlier, stack is one of the most commonly used data structures. Some of its applications are

1. Stacks are used to pass parameters between functions. On a call to a function, the parameters and local variables are stored on a stack.
2. High-level programming languages, such as Pascal, C, etc., that provides support for recursion use stack for bookkeeping. Remember, in each recursive call, there is need to save the current values of parameters, local variables and the return address (the address where the control has to return from the call).

In addition, stacks are used in solving enormous number of problems. Some of the problems are discussed in this section. In the later chapters, we will also see the use of stack.

7.5.1 Parenthesis Checker

Parenthesis Checker is a program that checks whether a mathematical expression is properly parenthesised. We will consider three sets of grouping symbols: *the standard parentheses* "()", *braces* "{}", and *brackets* "[]". For an input expression, it verifies that for each left parentheses, brace, or bracket, there is a corresponding closing symbol and the symbols are appropriately nested.

Some examples of valid inputs are

Valid Input
( )
({ } [ ])
({ [ ] [ ] })
[{ { { } ( ) } [ ] } [ ] ( ) { }]

Some examples of invalid inputs are

Invalid Input
([ ] { }
{ } [ ])
({ [ ]] })
[{ { { } ( ) [ ] } [ ] ( ) { }]

Inside parentheses (braces or brackets), there can be any valid arithmetic expression. The actual arithmetic expression is of no concern in this problem.

The formal algorithm for parentheses checker is presented below.

Algorithm 7.1:

PranethesisChecker(exp)

Here *exp* is character string representing an arithmetic expression comprising all types of bracketing symbols.

```
Begin
  read: exp
  Create empty stack
  for each character c in exp
      if ( current character is a left symbol) then
```

```
        Push the character onto stack
    else if ( current character is a right symbol) then
        if ( stack is empty ) then
            Print: "Error: No matching open symbol"
            Exit
        else
            Pop a symbol s from the stack
            if ( s doesn't correspond to c ) then
                Print: "Error: Incorrect nesting of symbols"
                Exit
            endif
        endif
    endif
  endfor
  if ( stack is not empty ) then
     Print: "Error: Missing closing symbol(s)"
  else
     Print: "Input expression is OK"
  endif
End.
```

The following is the implementation of parentheses checker.

Listing 7.21:

```
void pranethesisChecker( char *exp )
{
   char ch;
   LinkStack<char> charStack;
   while ( *exp )
   {
      if ( *exp == '('|| *exp == '{' || *exp == '[' )
         charStack.push(*exp);
      else if ( *exp == ')' || *exp == '}' || *exp == ']' ) {
         if ( charStack.isEmpty() ) {
            cout << "\nError: No matching open symbol" ;
            return;
         } else {
            ch = charStack.pop();
            if ( ch != getMatchingSymbol( *exp ) ) {
               cout << "\nError: Incorrect nesting of symbols";
               return;
            }
         }
      }
      exp++;
   }
   if ( !charStack.isEmpty() ) {
      cout << "\nError: Missing closing symbol(s)";
      return;
   } else {
      cout << "\nInput Expression is OK";
   }
}
```

The *pranethesisChecker()* function uses *getMatchingSymbol()* function whose listing is given below.

Listing 7.22:

```
char getMatchingSymbol( char ch )
{
   char matchingChar;
   switch ( ch )
   {
      case '(' : matchingChar = ')';
                 break;
      case ')' : matchingChar = '(';
                 break;
      case '{' : matchingChar = '}';
                 break;
      case '}' : matchingChar = '{';
                 break;
      case '[' : matchingChar = ']';
                 break;
      case ']' : matchingChar = '[';
   }
   return matchingChar;
}
```

Listing 7.23:

```
// Program to demonstrate the use of stack in checking whether the
// the arithmetic expression is properly parenthesised

#include <iostream.h>
#include <iomanip.h>

// header file containing code for generic stack implemented
// using linear linked list
#include "stlnk.h"

void pranethesisChecker(char *);
char getMatchingSymbol(char);
void main()
{
   char *charExpression = "";
   cout << "\nEnter any expression\n\n" ;
   cin.getline(charExpression,80);
   pranethesisChecker( charExpression );
} /*---- end of main function ----*/
void pranethesisChecker( char *exp )
{
   char ch;
   LinkStack<char> charStack;
   while ( *exp )
   {
      if ( *exp == '('|| *exp == '{' || *exp == '[' )
        charStack.push(*exp);
```

```
      else if ( *exp == ')' || *exp == '}' || *exp == ']' ) {
        if ( charStack.isEmpty() ) {
           cout << "\nError: No matching open symbol" ;
           return;
        } else {
           ch = charStack.pop();
           if ( ch != getMatchingSymbol( *exp ) ) {
             cout << "\nError: Incorrect nesting of symbols";
             return;
           }
        }
      }
      exp++;
   }
   if ( !charStack.isEmpty() ) {
      cout << "\nError: Missing closing symbol(s)";
      return;
   }else {
      cout << "\nInput Expression is OK";
   }
}
char getMatchingSymbol( char ch )
{
   char matchingChar;
   switch ( ch )
   {
      case '(' : matchingChar = ')'; break;
      case ')' : matchingChar = '('; break;
      case '{' : matchingChar = '}'; break;
      case '}' : matchingChar = '{'; break;
      case '[' : matchingChar = ']'; break;
      case ']' : matchingChar = '[';
   }
   return matchingChar;
}
```

7.5.2 Mathematical Notation Translation

Let us first consider various types of notations for writing mathematical expressions. In our discussion, we will consider the following set of operations.

Table 7.1: List of Operators

Symbol Used	Operation Performed	Precedence
* (asterisk)	Multiplication	Highest
/ (slash)	Division	Highest
% (percentage)	Modulus (Remainder)	Highest
+ (plus)	Addition	Lowest
– (hyphen)	Subtraction	Lowest

For simplicity, we will assume that a given expression contains no unary operation. We also assume that the operations on the same level of precedence are performed from left to right.

7.5.2.1 Infix Notation

In this notation, the operator symbol is placed between its two operands. For example

- to add A to B we can write as   A + B or B + A
- to subtract D from C we write as C – D, but we can't write D – C as this operation is not commutative

In this notation, we must distinguish between

(A + B) / C   and   A + (B / C)

7.5.2.2 Polish (Prefix) Notation

In this notation, named after the Polish mathematician ***Jan Lukasiewicz***, the operator symbol is placed before its two operands. For example,

- to add A to B we can write as +AB or +BA
- to subtract D from C we have to write as –CD not as –DC

In order to translate an arithmetic expression in infix notation to polish notation, we do step by step using brackets ([]) to indicate the partial translation.

Consider the following expression in infix notation:

(A – B / C) * (A * K – L)

partial translations may look like:

(A – [/BC]) * ([*AK] – L)

[–A/BC] * [–*AKL]

*–A/BC–*AKL

The fundamental property of polish notation is that the order in which the operations are to perform is completely determined by the positions of the operators and operands in the expression. Accordingly one never needs parentheses when writing expressions in polish notation.

This notation is also called *prefix* notation.

7.5.2.3 Reverse Polish (Postfix) Notation

In this notation the operator symbol is placed after its two operands. For example,

- to add A to B we can write as AB+ or BA+
- to subtract D from C we have to write as CD– not as DC–

In order to translate an arithmetic expression in infix notation to reverse polish notation, we do step by step using brackets ([]) to indicate the partial translation.

Consider the following expression in infix notation:

(A – B / C) * (A * K – L)

the partial translations may look like:

(A – [BC/]) * ([AK/] – L)

[ABC/–] * [AK/L–]

ABC/–AK/L–*

Like polish notation, here too one never needs the use of parentheses when writing expressions in reverse polish notation.

This notation is frequently called *postfix* (or.*suffix*) notation.

7.5.2.4 Evaluating Mathematical Expressions

Programs that perform some sort of translation often use stacks. One example of such program is one that translates an arithmetic expression from *infix* notation to *postfix* notation. Although human beings are quite used to work with mathematical expressions in infix notation, which is rather complex. Using this notation, a nontrivial set of rules must be applied to the expression in order to determine the final value. These rules, which are taken for granted, involve concepts such as operator precedence and associativity.

Using infix notation, one cannot tell the order in which the operators should be applied by looking at the expression. Therefore, whenever an expression contains more than one operator, precedence rules are applied to decide which operator and operands are evaluated first. The standard rules for precedence dictate that parentheses are evaluated first, followed by unary minus, multiplication and division, and lastly, addition and subtraction. All these operators are left associative, which means that if there is more than operator of the same precedence, the leftmost operator is applied first.

In comparison, the expression in the postfix notation is much easy to evaluate. As the operands appear before the operator, there is no need for operator precedence or for parentheses to group/order operations. In order to evaluate a postfix expression, it is scanned from left to right. As operands are encountered, they are pushed on a stack. When an operator is encountered, pop top one or two operands depending on the operator, perform the operation and place the result back on the stack. At the end of the expression, the stack contains only one element (if expression is correct) and that is the resulting value of the expression.

The problems addressed in this section are to develop procedures to translate an expression from infix notation to postfix notation and then to evaluate the resultant expression.

For simplicity, we will develop following two separate procedures:

- To translate the expression from infix notation to postfix notation.
- To evaluates the expression in postfix notation.

In each of these procedures, stack is the main tool that is used to accomplish the given task.

7.5.2.5 Infix-to Postfix Procedure

Let *q* be an arithmetic expression written in infix notation. Besides operands and operators, it may also contain left and right parentheses. We assume the given expressions contain only operators listed in Table 7.1, and operations of the same precedence are evaluated from left to right.

Algorithm 7.2:

InfixToPostfix(*q*, *p*)

Where *q* is the arithmetic expression in-infix notation. This algorithm translates this expression into its equivalent postfix expression *p*.

```
Begin
  Create Empty Stack
  while ( not end of expression q ) do
     Scan q from left and pick up the next element, say celement
     if ( celement is left parentheses ) then
        Push celement onto stack
     else if ( celement is right parentheses ) then
        while ( ( stack is not empty )&&( element at top of stack is
                  not left parentheses ) ) do
           Pop stack and append poped element to p
        endwhile
        if ( stack is empty ) then
           Print : "Error: Incorrect expression"
           Exit
        endif
        Remove the left parentheses from stack but do not add to p
     else if ( celement is operand ) then
        Append celement to P
     else if ( celement is operator ) then
        while ( ( element at top of stack is operator and its
                  precedence ≥ celement ) && ( stack is not empty ) ) do
           Pop stack and append poped element to p
        endwhile
        Push celement onto stack
     else
        Print: "Error: Incorrect element in expression"
        Exit
     endif
  endwhile
  while ( ( stack is not empty ) && ( element at top of stack is not
           left parenthesis ) do
```

```
      Pop stack and append poped element to p
   endwhile
   if ( element at top of stack is left parenthesis ) then
      Print: "Error: Incorrect expression"
   endif
End.
```

Example 7.2:

Consider the following infix expression q:

$$(7-5)*(9/2)$$

The progress of the algorithm to translate q to postfix expression p is shown:

Character Scanned	Stack	Expression *p*
(	(	
7	(	7
–	(–	7
5	(–	7 5
)	Empty	7 5 –
*	*	7 5 –
(	* (	7 5 –
9	* (	7 5 – 9
/	* (/	7 5 – 9
2	* (/	7 5 – 9 2
)	*	7 5 – 9 2 /
End of expression	Empty	7 5 – 9 2 / *

Before scanning the infix expression stack is initialized to empty status.

Listing 7.24:

```
void infixToPostfix( char *source, char *target )
{
   char *s, *t;
   LinkStack<char> charStack;
   s = source;    t = target;
   while ( *s != '\0' ) {
      if ( ( *s == ' ' ) || ( *s == '\t' ) )  // skip white spaces
      {
        s++;
        continue;
      } else if ( *s == '(' ) {
        charStack.push(*s);
        s++;
      } else if ( *s == ')' ) {
        while ((charStack.isEmpty())&&(charStack.peek()!='(')) {
           *t = charStack.pop();
           t++;
           *t = ' ';   //  add one space
           t++;
        }
        if ( charStack.isEmpty() )
        {
```

```
            cout << "\nError: Incorrect expression\n";
            exit(1);
         }
         charStack.pop(); // remove left parenthesis from stack
         s++;
      } else if ( isdigit( *s ) || isalpha( *s ) ) {
         *t = *s;
         t++;
         *t = ' ';    //  add one space
         t++;
         s++;
      } else if (*s=='+' || *s=='-' || *s=='*' || *s=='/') {
         while ((!charStack.isEmpty())&&( charStack.peek()!='(') &&
                (getPriority(charStack.peek()) >= getPriority(*s)) )
         {
            *t = charStack.pop();
            t++;
            *t = ' ';    //  add one space
            t++;
         }
         charStack.push(*s);
         s++;
      } else {
         cout << "\nError: Incorrect element in expression \n";
         exit(1);
      }
   }
   while ((!charStack.isEmpty())&&(charStack.peek()!='('))
   {
      *t = charStack.pop();
      t++;
      *t = ' ';    //  add one space
      t++;
   }
   if ( charStack.peek() == '(' )
   {
      cout << "\nError: Incorrect expression\n";
      exit(1);
   }
   *t = '\0';    //  terminate the string by null character
}
```

The *infixToPostfix()* function uses *getPriority()* function whose listing is given below.

Listing 7.25:

```
int getPriority( char op ) {
   int priority;
   if ( op == '/' || op == '*' || op == '%' )
      priority = 1;
   else if ( op == '+' || op == '(' )
      priority = 0;
   return priority;
}
```

Listing 7.26:

```
//   Program to demonstrate the use of stack in converting arithmetic
//   expression from infix notation to postfix notation
#include <iostream.h>
#include <stdlib.h>
#include <ctype.h>
// header file containing code for generic stack implemented
// using linear linked list
#include "stlnk.h"
void infixToPostfix( char *source, char *target );
int getPriority( char op );
void main()
{
   char infixExp[80], postfixExp[80];
   cout << "\nEnter arithmetic expression in infix notation\n\n";
   cin.getline(infixExp,80);
   infixToPostfix( infixExp, postfixExp );
   cout << "\nEquivalent expression in postfix notation is\n\n";
   cout << postfixExp;
} /*---- end of main function ----*/

void infixToPostfix( char *source, char *target )
{
   char *s, *t;
   LinkStack<char> charStack;
   s = source;
   t = target;
   while ( *s != '\0' ) {
      if ( ( *s == ' ' ) || ( *s == '\t' ) )  // skip white spaces
      {
        s++;
        continue;
      } else if ( *s == '(' ) {
        charStack.push(*s);
        s++;
      } else if ( *s == ')' ) {
        while ((charStack.isEmpty())&&(charStack.peek()!='(')) {
           *t = charStack.pop();
           t++;
           *t = ' ';   //  add one space
           t++;
        }
        if ( charStack.isEmpty() )
          {
           cout << "\nError: Incorrect expression\n";
           exit(1);
        }
        charStack.pop(); // remove left parenthesis from stack
        s++;
      } else if ( isdigit( *s ) || isalpha( *s ) ) {
        *t = *s;
        t++;
        *t = ' ';   //  add one space
        t++;
        s++;
```

```
      } else if (*s=='+' || *s=='-' || *s=='*' || *s=='/') {
        while ((!charStack.isEmpty())&&( charStack.peek()!='(') &&
              (getPriority(charStack.peek()) >= getPriority(*s)) )
        {
           *t = charStack.pop();
           t++;
           *t = ' ';   //  add one space
           t++;
        }
        charStack.push(*s);
        s++;
      } else {
        cout << "\nError: Incorrect element in expression \n";
        exit(1);
      }
   }
   while ((!charStack.isEmpty())&&(charStack.peek()!='('))
   {
      *t = charStack.pop();
      t++;
      *t = ' '; //  add one space
      t++;
   }
   if ( charStack.peek() == '(' )
   {
      cout << "\nError: Incorrect expression\n";
      exit(1);
   }
   *t = '\0';    //  terminate the string by null character
}
int getPriority( char op )
{
   int priority;
   if ( op == '/' || op == '*' || op == '%' )
      priority = 1;
   else if ( op == '+' || op == '(' )
      priority = 0;
   return priority;
}
```

7.5.2.6 Evaluating Expression in Postfix Notation

Algorithm 7.3:

EvaluatePostfixExpression(***p, result*** **)**

Here *p* is the arithmetic expression in postfix notation. This algorithm evaluates this expression and returns the value of the expression through variable *result*.

```
Begin
  Create Empty Stack
  while ( not end-of expression p )  do
     if ( element is operand ) then
        Push element onto stack
```

```
      else
         Pop two elements and let first one is a and the second one is b
         Evaluate b⊗a, let its value be c, where ⊗ is an operator
         Push c onto stack
      endif
   endwhile
   Pop stack and assign this value to parameter result
End.
```

Example 7.3:

Consider the following postfix expression *p*:

7 5 – 9 2 / *

The progress of the algorithm to evaluate postfix expression *p* is shown in the following table.

Character Scanned	Stack
7	7
5	7 5
–	2
9	2 9
2	2 9 2
/	2 4.5
*	9
End of expression	9

Before scanning the infix expression stack is initialized to empty status. The final number in stack, *i.e.*, 9, is the value of postfix expression *p*.

The implementation of the algorithm 7.3 is given below.

Listing 7.27:

```
float evaluatePostfixExpression( char *exp )
{
   char c;
   LinkStack<float> floatStack;
   float op1, op2, value;
   while ( *exp )
   {
      if (*exp == ' ' || *exp == '\t' || *exp == ',')
      {
         exp++;
         continue;
      }
      if ( isdigit( *exp ) )
         //  convert to numerical value
         floatStack.push((float)(*exp - '0'));
      else
      {
         op2 = floatStack.pop();  // second operand
```

```
         op1 = floatStack.pop();  // first operand
         switch ( *exp )
         {
            case '+' : value = op1 + op2;
                       break;
            case '-' : value = op1 - op2;
                       break;
            case '/' : value = (float) op1 / op2;
                       break;
            case '*' : value = op1 * op2;
                       break;
            default  : cout << "\nIllegal operation ... %x7\n";
                       exit(1);
         }
         floatStack.push(value);
      }
      exp++;
   }
   return ( floatStack.pop() );
}
```

Listing 7.28:

```
//   Program to demonstrate the use of stack in evaluating arithmetic
//   expression in postfix notation
#include<iostream.h>
#include<stdlib.h>
#include<ctype.h>
// header file containing code for generic stack implemented
// using linear linked list
#include "stlnk.h"
float evaluatePostfixExpression( char *exp );
void main()
{
   float value;
   char *postfixExp = "";
   cout << "\nEnter arithmetic expression in postfix notation\n\n" ;
   cin.getline(postfixExp,80);
   value = evaluatePostfixExpression(postfixExp);
   cout << "\nValue of expression = " << value;
} /*---- end of main function ----*/
float evaluatePostfixExpression( char *exp )
{
   char c;
   LinkStack<float> floatStack;
   float op1, op2, value;
   while ( *exp )
   {
      if (*exp == ' ' || *exp == '\t' || *exp == ',')
      {
        exp++;
        continue;
      }
      if ( isdigit( *exp ) )
```

```
                // convert to numerical value
                floatStack.push((float)(*exp - '0'));
              else
              {
                op2 = floatStack.pop();   // second operand
                op1 = floatStack.pop();   // first operand
                switch ( *exp )
                {
                  case '+' : value = op1 + op2;
                             break;
                  case '-' : value = op1 - op2;
                             break;
                  case '/' : value = (float) op1 / op2;
                             break;
                  case '*' : value = op1 * op2;
                             break;
                  default  : cout << "\nIllegal operation ... %x7\n";
                             exit(1);
                }
                floatStack.push(value);
              }
            exp++;
          }
        return ( floatStack.pop() );
    }
```

7.5.3 Quicksort Algorithm

Quicksort is an algorithm that uses *divide-and-conquer* strategy to sort an array. In the divide-and-conquer strategy, the problem to be solved is divided into two sub problems, which are then solved separately. Then the solutions of these two sub problems are combined to generate the solution of the given problem. Quicksort method reduces the problem of sorting a set of number to the problem of sorting two subsets of smaller size. This reduction step is illustrated below with the help of an example.

Consider the following list of 8 numbers.

20 22 15 10 35 12 44 38

The reduction step of the quicksort algorithm finds the final position of the first number, 20 in this case.

This is accomplished as follows.

(20) 22 15 10 35 12 44 (38)

Beginning with the rightmost (last) number, 38, scan the list from right to left, comparing each number with 20, and stopping at the first number less than 20. The number is 12. Interchange 20 and 12 to obtain the list

(12) 22 15 10 35 (20) 44 38

Now beginning with 12, scan the list from left to right, comparing each number with 20, and stopping at the first number greater than 20. The number is 22. Interchange 22 and 20 to obtain the list

12 (20) 15 10 35 (22) 44 38

Now beginning with 22, scan the list from right to left, comparing each number with 20, and stopping at the first number less than 20. The number is 10. Interchange 10 and 20 to obtain the list

12 (10) 15 (20) 35 22 44 38

Now beginning with 10, scan the list from left to right, comparing each number with 20, and stopping at the first number greater than 20. We do not meet any such number before meeting 20. This means all the numbers have been scanned and compared with 20. Further, all the numbers less than 20 now form the sub list of numbers to the left of 20, and all numbers greater than 20 now form the sub list of numbers to the right of 20 as shown below:

12 10 15 (20) 35 22 44 38

Left sub list: 12 10 15 — Right sub list: 35 22 44 38

Thus element 20 is correctly placed in its final position, and the task os sorting the entire list is now reduced to sorting two sub lists of smaller size. The above reduction step is repeated with each sub list containing two or more elements. Since we can process one list at a time, we must keep track of the other sub list for future processing. This is accomplished by using a stack with integer elements to temporarily hold these sub lists. That is, the index of the first element and the last element of each sub list are pushed onto the stack. The reduction step is applied only once these indices are removed from the stack.

Algorithm 7.4:

Reduction(***a*, *beg*, *end*, *loc*** **)**

Here *a* is an array in memory, and *beg* and *end* represents the lower bound and upper bound of the sub list in question. This algorithm places the first element of given sub list at its final position *loc*.

```
Begin
  Set left = beg, right = end, loc = beg
  Set done = false
  while ( not done ) do
    while ( a[loc] < a[right] ) and ( loc ≠ right ) ) do
      Set right = right - 1
    endwhile
    if ( loc = right ) then
      Set done = true
    else
      Interchange a[loc] and a[right]
```

```
         Set loc = right
      endif
      if ( not done ) then
         while ( a[loc] > a[left] ) and ( loc ≠ left ) ) do
            Set left = left + 1
         endwhile
         if ( loc = left ) then
            Set done = true
         else
            Interchange a[loc] and a[left]
            Set loc = left
         endif
      endif
   endwhile
End.
```

he implementation of the above algorithm is given below.

Listing 7.29:

```
void reduction( int a[], int beg, int end, int *loc )
{
   int left, right, temp;
   boolean done;
   left = *loc = beg;
   right = end;
   done = false;
   while ( !done ) {
      while ( ( a[*loc] < a[right] ) && ( *loc != right ) )
        right--;
      if ( *loc == right )
        done = true;
      else {
        temp = a[*loc];
         a[*loc] = a[right];
        a[right] = temp;
         *loc = right;
      }
      if ( !done ) {
        while ( ( a[*loc] > a[left] ) && ( *loc != left ) )
           left++;
        if ( *loc == left )
           done = true;
        else {
           temp = a[*loc];
           a[*loc] = a[left];
           a[left] = temp;
           *loc = left;
        }
      }
   }
}
```

he algorithm for iterative version of the quicksort algorithm will look likes as shown below.

Algorithm 7.5:

QuickSortIterative(*a, n*)

Here *a* is an array of size *n* (> 1) in memory. This algorithm sorts this array in ascending order using Quick sort technique.

```
Begin
  Create Empty stack
  Push array bounds (lower bound = 0, and upper bound = n-1) onto STACK.
  while ( stack is not empty ) do
     Pop stack and initialize the array bounds of the current sub list
     to variable beg and end
     Call Reduction( a, beg, end, loc)
     if ( beg < loc - 1 ) then
        Push array bounds of the left sub list onto stack
     endif
     if ( end  > loc + 1 ) then
         Push array bounds of the right sub list onto stack
     endif
  endwhile
End.
```

The implementation of the above algorithm is given below.

Listing 7.30:

```
void quickSortIterative(  int a[], int n )
{
   int loc, beg, end;
   LinkStack<int> intStack;
   intStack.push(0);
   intStack.push(n-1);
   while ( ! intStack.isEmpty() {
      end = intStack.pop();
      beg = intStack.pop();
      reduction( a, beg, end, &loc);
      if ( beg < loc - 1 ) {
           intStack.push(beg);
           intStack.push(loc-1);
      }
      if ( end > loc + 1 ) {
           intStack.push(loc+1);
           intStack.push(end);
      }
   }
}
```

The above code uses a linked stack with integer elements. This function will be called as

```
quickSortIterative( a, n );
```

However, the recursive implementation of Quicksort algorithm will look like as shown below.

Algorithm 7.6:

QuickSortRecursive(***a, lb, ub*** **)**

Here *a* is an sub list with starting index *lb* and ending index *ub*. This algorithm sorts this sub list in ascending order.

```
Begin
  if ( lb < ub )  then
     Call Reduction( a, lb, ub, loc)
     Call QuickSortRecursive( a, lb, loc - 1 )
     Call QuickSortRecursive( a, loc + 1, ub )
  endif
End.
```

The implementation of the above algorithm is shown in the following listing.

Listing 7.31:

```
void quickSortRecursive( int a[], int lb, int ub )
{
   int loc;
   if ( lb < ub )
   {
      reduction( a, lb, ub, &loc);
      quickSortRecursive( a, lb, loc - 1 );
      quickSortRecursive( a, loc + 1, ub );
   }
}
```

The original call to this function will be

```
quickSortRecursive( a, 0, n -1 );
```

Listing 7.32:

```
// Program to demonstrate the use of stack in implementing Quicksort
// algorithm to sort an array of integers in ascending order
#include<iostream.h>
#include<stdlib.h>
#include<ctype.h>
// header file containing code for generic stack implemented
// using linear linked list
#include "stlnk.h"
#define MAX 20
void reduction( int a[], int beg, int end, int *loc );
void quickSortIterative( int a[], int n );
void main()
{
   int i, n, a[MAX];
   cout << "\nEnter number of elements in array : " ;
```

```
    cin >> n;
    if ( n > MAX ) {
       cout << "\nInput size of array greater than declared size\n";
       exit(1);
    }
    cout << "\nEnter " << n << " elements\n\n";
    for ( i = 0; i < n; i++ )
        cin >> a[i];
    quickSortIterative( a, n );
    cout << "\n\nSorted list of elements\n\n";
    for ( i = 0; i < n; i++ )
        cout << a[i] << "  ";
    cout << endl;
 } /*---- end of main function ----*/
void quickSortIterative(  int a[], int n )
{
    int loc, beg, end;
    LinkStack<int> intStack;
    intStack.push(0);
    intStack.push(n-1);
    while ( ! intStack.isEmpty() ) {
       end = intStack.pop();
       beg = intStack.pop();
       reduction( a, beg, end, &loc);
       if ( beg < loc - 1 ) {
          intStack.push(beg);
       intStack.push(loc-1);
       }
       if ( end > loc + 1 ) {
          intStack.push(loc+1);
          intStack.push(end);
       }
    }
}
void reduction( int a[], int beg, int end, int *loc )
{
    int left, right, temp;
    int done = 0;
    left = *loc = beg;
    right = end;
    while ( !done )
    {
       while ( ( a[*loc] < a[right] ) && ( *loc != right ) )
         right--;
       if ( *loc == right )
         done = 1;
       else {
         temp = a[*loc];
       a[*loc] = a[right];
         a[right] = temp;
       *loc = right;
       }
       if ( !done ) {
         while ( ( a[*loc] > a[left] ) && ( *loc != left ) )
            left++;
```

```
            if ( *loc == left )
               done = 1;
            else {
               temp = a[*loc];
               a[*loc] = a[left];
               a[left] = temp;
               *loc = left;
            }
         }
      }
}
```

REVIEW EXERCISES

1. What is a stack? Is stack a linear or non-linear data structure?
2. Stack is a special type of list? Comment.
3. How does an array based stack compares with linked stack?
4. Why an operation to check stack overflow is not implemented on linked stacks?
5. Can we implement a stack in C whose elements can be of different type? If your answer is yes, the how?
6. How *peek()* operation differs from *pop()* operation?
7. While representing a stack using linked lists, we have implemented additional operation *dispose()* to remove the stack from memory. Why such operation is not implemented for stack represented using an array.
8. What are different notations to represent a mathematical expression? Which notation is most suitable for use in computers? Give at least one example in each case.
9. Translate following mathematical expressions into its equivalent postfix expressions:

   (*i*) (A – B) * (D / E)
   (*ii*) (A + B / D) / (E – F) + G
   (*iii*) A * B – (C + D) / (E – F) + G / H

   (*a*) by inspection
   (*a*) by using algorithm 7.2.
10. Given the following arithmetic expression in infix notation as

    12 / (7 – 3) + 2 * (3 + 8) – 7

    Translate this expression into postfix notation and then evaluate it.
11. How iterative implementation of quick sort method will process following list of numbers:

    23 12 11 45 30 8 55 22 66

PROGRAMMING EXERCISES

1. Write a menu driven program to implementing the various operations on a stac represented using an array.
2. Write a menu driven program to implementing the various operations on a stac represented using a linked list.
3. Design a data structure to represent two stacks in an array named *elements* of size n. Als write functions for *push()* and *pop()* operations to insert and delete element from stack $0 \leq i \leq 1$. Your functions should be able to add elements to the stacks as long as there ar less than n elements in both stacks together and should run in O(1) time.
4. Design a data structure to represent m stacks in an array named *elements* of size n. Als write functions for *push()* and *pop()* operations to insert and delete element from stack $0 \leq i \leq m-1$. These operations should run in O(1) time.
5. **Rat in a Maze problem**: A maze is a rectangular area, with m rows and n columns, with a entrance and an exit. The interior of the maze contains obstacles. The entrance is at th upper-left corner, and the exit is at the lower-right corner. One sample maze of size 8×8 i shown below:

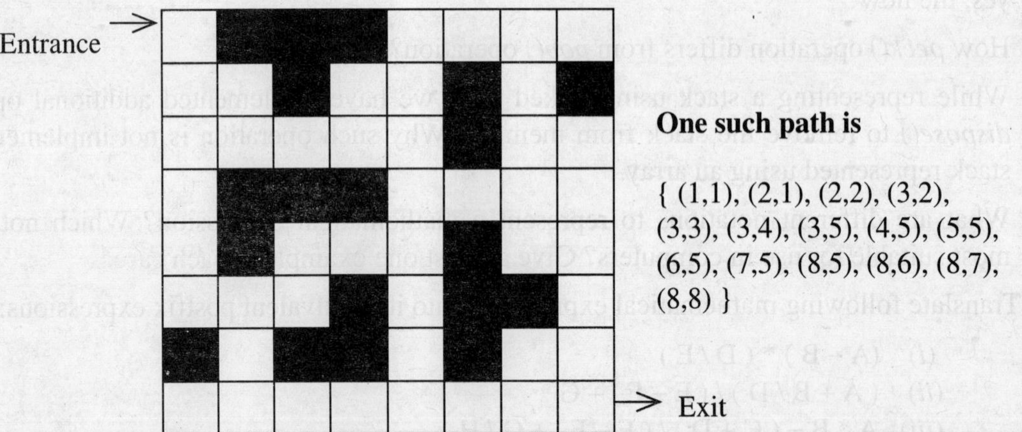

A rat in a maze problem is to find a path from the entrance to exit of a maze. A path i basically a sequence of positions, none of which is blocked, and such that each (other tha the first is the north, south, east or west neighbour of the preceding position. Write program to find such path, if exits, otherwise output message "*No solution for this maze*".

❑ ❑ ❑

Chapter 8

Queues

.1 INTRODUCTION

ll of us are familiar with queues. In simple terms, a queue is a line of persons waiting for their ırn at some service counter/window. A service counter can be a ticketing window of a cinema all, a ticketing window of a bus stand or railway station, a service counter of a bank, a service ounter of a gas agency, a fees deposit counter in a college, etc. Depending on the type of ervice provided by the service counter and the number of persons interested in this service, ıere could be queues of varying lengths. The service at the service counter is provided on the irst-Come First-Serve (FCFS) basis, *i.e.*, in order of their arrival in the queue.

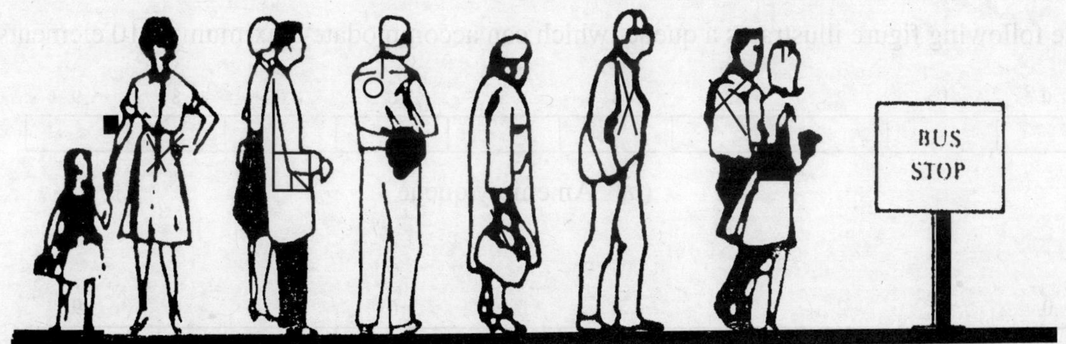

Figure 8.1: Queue of passengers waiting for a bus at a bus stop

Suppose that at service counter, t_1 units of time is needed to provide a service to a single perso and on average a new person arrives at the service counter in t_2 units of time. The followin possibilities may arise:

1. If $t_1 < t_2$, then the service counter will be free for some time before a new person arrives a the service counter. Hence, no queue in this case.
2. If $t_1 > t_2$, then service counter will be busy for some time even after the arrival of a nev person. Therefore, this person has to wait for some time. Similarly, other persons arriving a the service counter have to wait. Hence, a queue will be formed.
3. If $t_1 = t_2$, then as a person leaves the service counter, a new persons arrives at the servic counter. Hence, no queue in this cases also.

This chapter describes a queue, its representation in computer memory, and the implementatio of different operations that can be performed on them. It also describes a deque and a priorit queue in brief.

8.2 QUEUE DEFINED

In the context of data structures, a *queue* is a linear list in which insertions can take place at on end of the list, called the *rear* of the list, and deletions can take place only at other end, calle the *front* of the list. The behaviour of a queue is like a First-In-First-Out (FIFO) systen Figure 8.2 shows a queue as black box in which elements enters from one side and leaves fror other side.

In queue terminology, the insertion and deletion operations are known as *enqueue* and *dequeu* operations.

Example 8.1:

The following figure illustrates a queue, which can accommodate maximum of 10 elements.

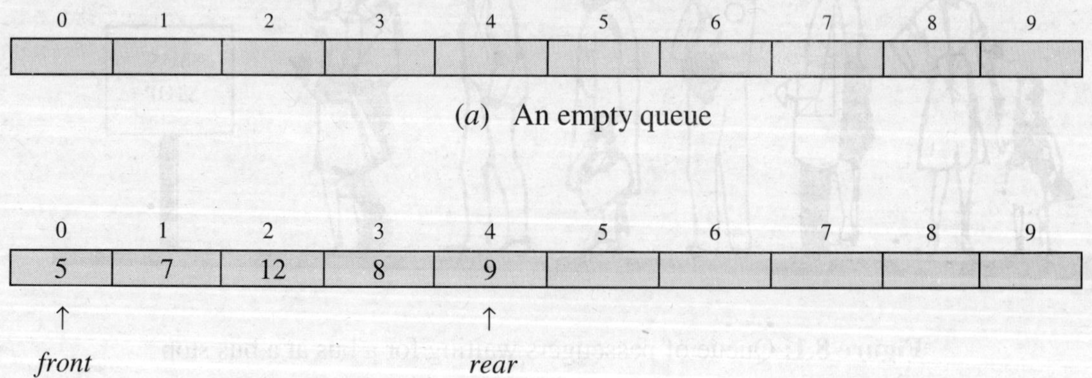

(b) Queue after enqueuing elements 5, 7, 12, 8, and 9 in order

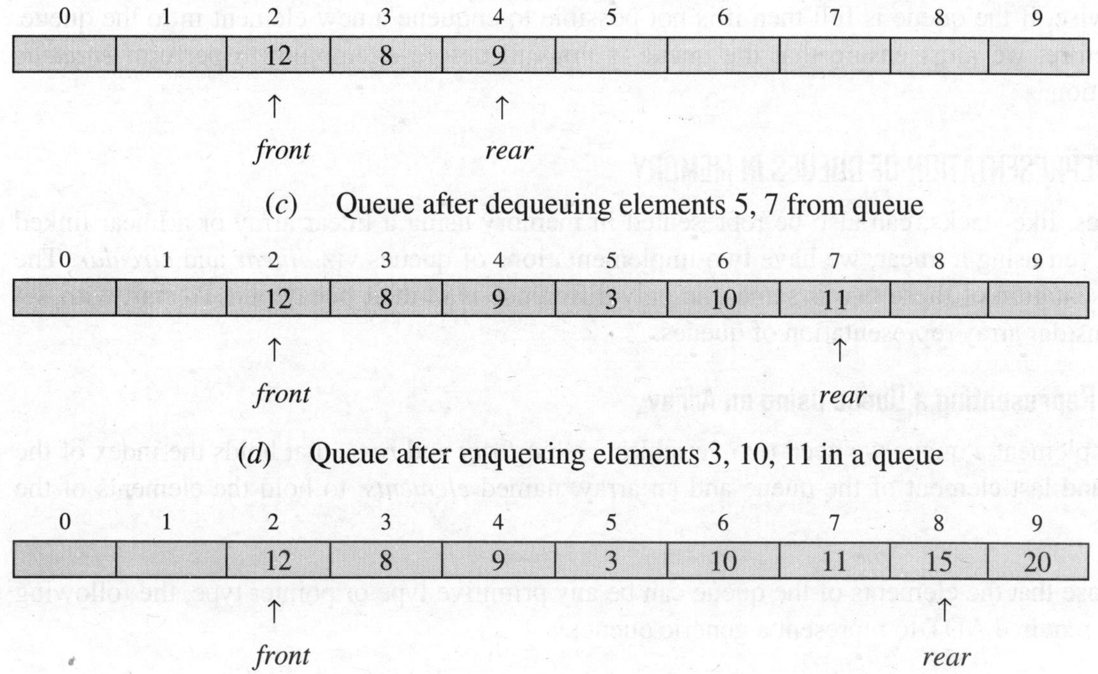

(*c*) Queue after dequeuing elements 5, 7 from queue

(*d*) Queue after enqueuing elements 3, 10, 11 in a queue

(*e*) Queue after enqueuing elements 15 and 20 in a queue

Figure 8.2: Illustration of a queue whose elements are integer values

8.3 OPERATIONS ON QUEUES

The following operations are performed on queues:

Table 8.1: Various operations performed on queues

Operation	Description
create	To create an initial queue. This task will be accomplished using a constructor.
destroy	To remove (delete) queue from memory. This task will be accomplished using a destructor.
enqueue	Insert (push) an element at the rear of the queue.
dequeue	Access and remove the front element from the queue.
peek	Access the front element of the queue without removing it from the queue.
isFull	Check whether the queue is full.
isEmpty	Check whether the queue is empty.

All of these operation runs in $O(1)$ time.

Note that if the queue is empty then it is not possible to dequeue the queue. Similarly, if there is no element in the queue, the *peek* operation is also not valid. Therefore, we must ensure that the queue is not empty before attempting to perform these operations.

Likewise, if the queue is full then it is not possible to enqueue a new element in to the queue. Therefore, we must ensure that the queue is not full before attempting to perform *enqueue* operation.

8.4 REPRESENTATION OF QUEUES IN MEMORY

Queues, like stacks, can also be represented in memory using a linear array or a linear linked list. Even using a linear, we have two implementations of queues viz. *linear* and *circular*. The representation of these two is same, the only difference is in their behaviour. To start with, let us consider array representation of queues.

8.4.1 Representing a Queue using an Array

To implement a queue we need two variables, called *front* and *rear*, that holds the index of the first and last element of the queue and an array, named *elements*, to hold the elements of the queue.

Suppose that the elements of the queue can be any primitive type or pointer type, the following is the required ADT to represent a generic queue:

The following are the necessary declarations

```
template <class T>
class LinearQueue
{
   protected:                  // data members
       int front;
       int rear;
       int size;
       T *elements;

   public:                      // member functions
       // zero argument constructor,
       // it constructs a stack with default size = 10
       LinearQueue();
       // parametrized constructor that constructs,
       // a stack with size = n
       LinearQueue(int n);
       // destructor that removes the stack from memory
       ~LinearQueue();
       // Check whether the stack is empty
       int isEmpty();
       // Check whether the stack is full
       int isFull();
       // Insert an element at the end of the queue
       void enqueue(T value);
       // Access and remove the first element of the queue
       T dequeue();
       // Access the first element of the queue
       // without removing it from the queue
       T peek();
}; // -------- End of LinearQueue class --------
```

We have defined our own data type named *LinearQueue*, which is class and whose first data member *front* will be used to hold the index of the first element of the queue, second data member *rear* will be used to hold the index of the last element of the queue, third data member *size* will be used to hold the size of the queue, and fourth data member *elements*, a dynamic array whose elements can be any primitive type or pointer type.

The implementation of the member functions is given in the subsequent sections.

With these declarations, assuming a queue whose elements are of type *int* and size is 10, a queue of Figure 8.2 will be represented in computer memory as

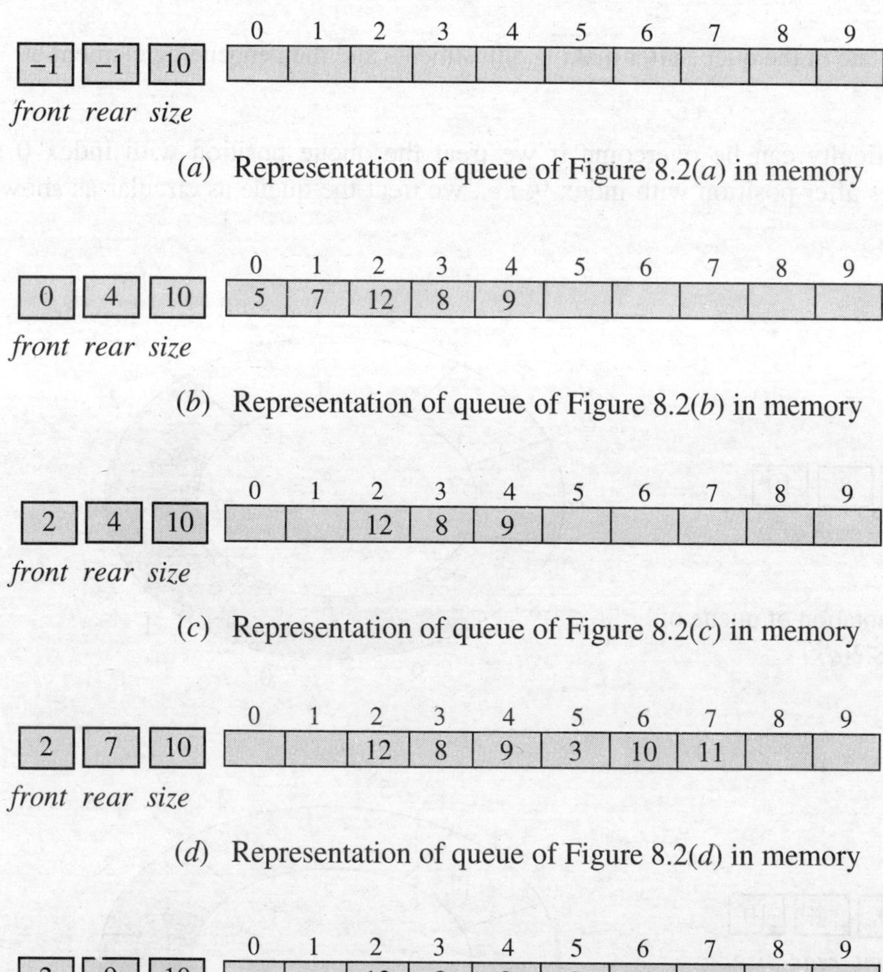

(*a*) Representation of queue of Figure 8.2(*a*) in memory

(*b*) Representation of queue of Figure 8.2(*b*) in memory

(*c*) Representation of queue of Figure 8.2(*c*) in memory

(*d*) Representation of queue of Figure 8.2(*d*) in memory

(*e*) Representation of queue of Figure 8.2(*e*) in memory

Figure 8.3: Array representation of linear queue of Figure 8.2

You must have observed, as shown in Figure 8.3(*e*), that it is not possible to enqueue more elements as such, though two positions in the linear queue are vacant. To overcome this problem, the elements of the queue are moved forward, so that the vacant positions are shifted towards the rear end of the linear queue. After shifting, *front* and *rear* are adjusted properly, and then the element is enqueued in the linear queue as usual. For example, we want to enqueue one more element, say 60, after making adjustments the queue will look as shown in Figure 8.4.

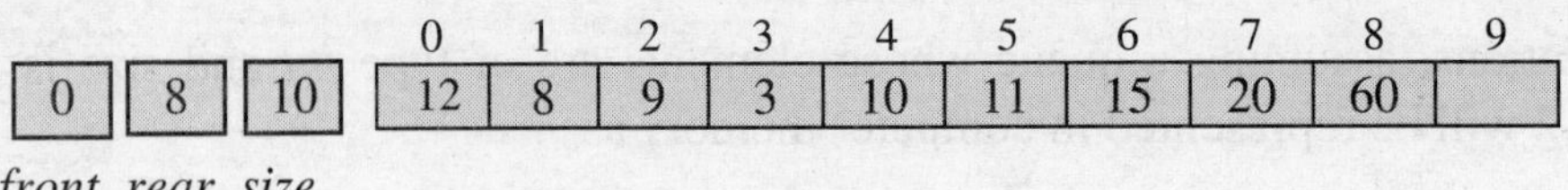

Figure 8.4: State of the queue after making adjustments and then enqeueing element 60

However, this difficulty can be overcome if we treat the queue position with index 0 as a position that comes after position with index 9, *i.e.*, we treat the queue as circular as shown in Figure 8.5.

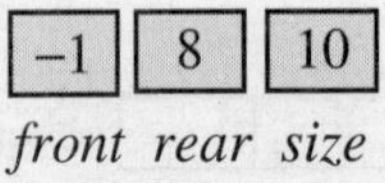

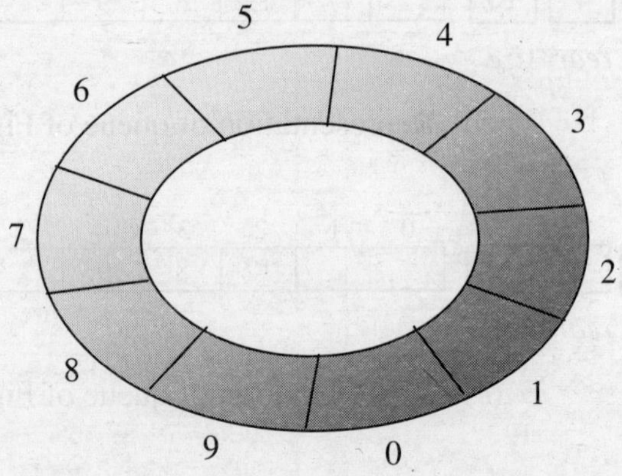

(*a*) Representation of queue of Figure 8.2(*a*)

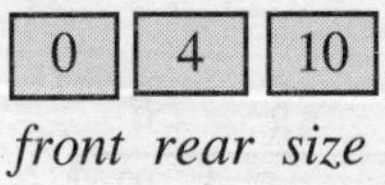

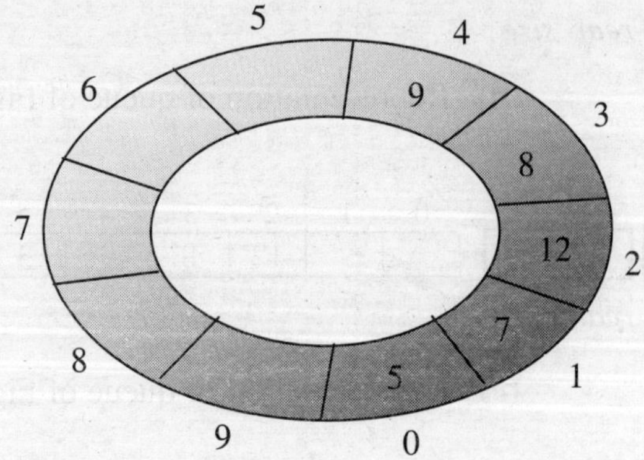

(*b*) Representation of queue of Figure 8.2(*b*)

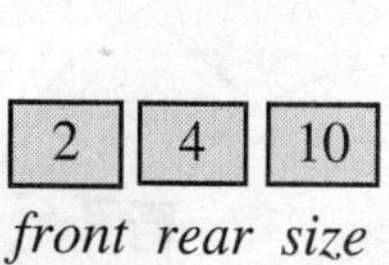

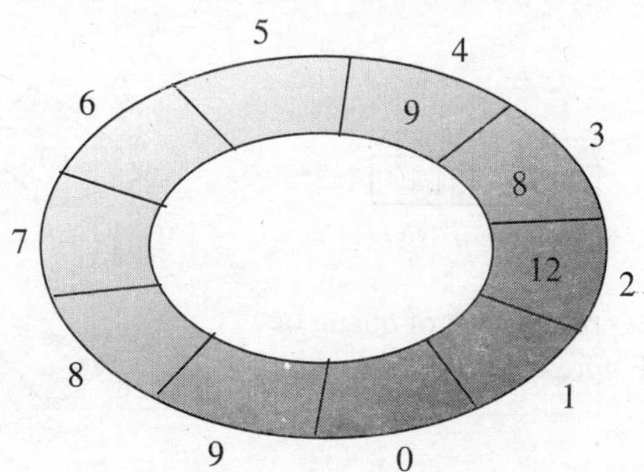

(*c*) Representation of queue of Figure 8.2(*c*)

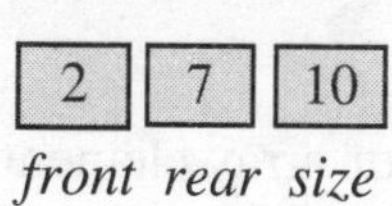

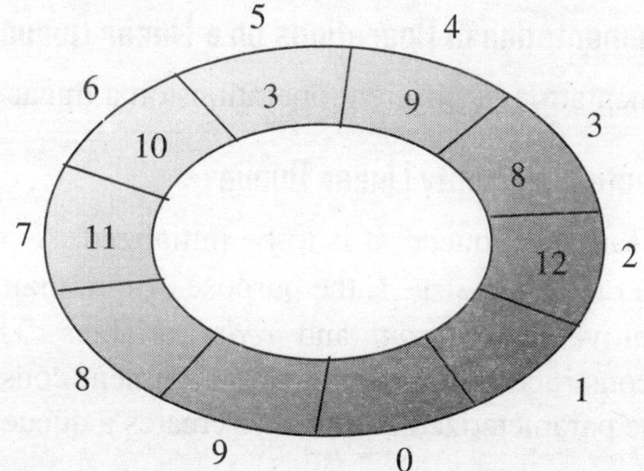

(*d*) Representation of queue of Figure 8.2(*d*)

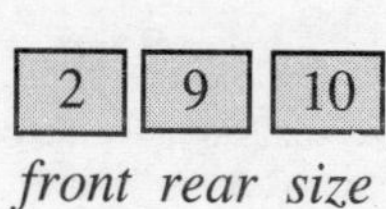

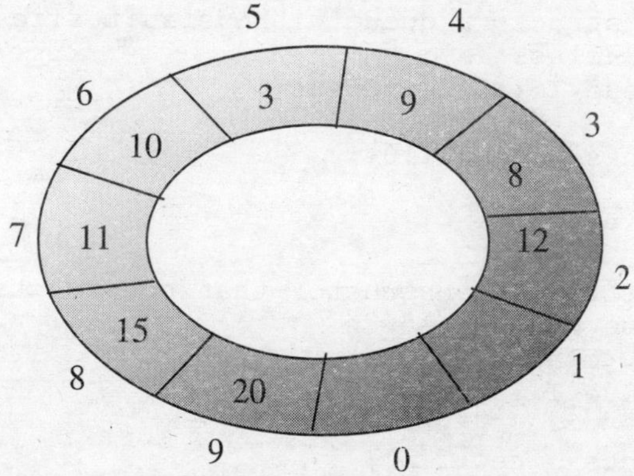

(*e*) Representation of queue of Figure 8.2(*e*)

Now to enqueue one more element, say 60, the *rear* is reset to 0, and the elements is inserted at that index as shown below.

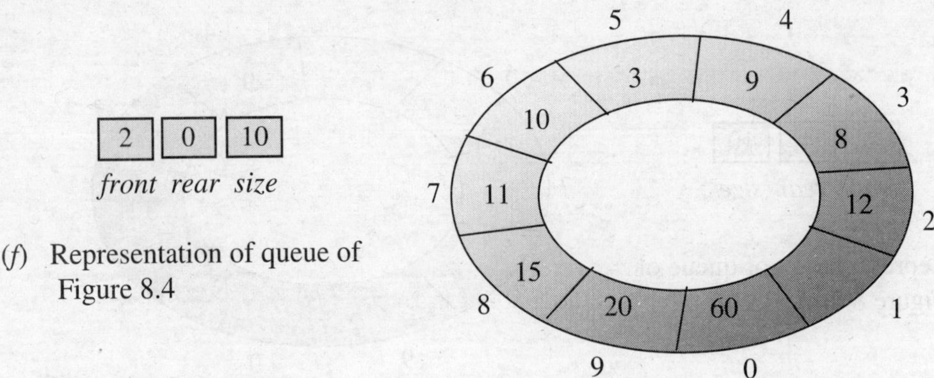

(*f*) Representation of queue of Figure 8.4

Figure 8.5: (*a*) – (*f*) Illustration of Operations on Circular Queues

8.4.1.1 Implementation of Operations on a Linear Queue

The implementation of different operations on a linear queue is described below.

8.4.1.1.1 Creating an Empty Linear Queue

Before we can use a queue, it is to be initialized. As the index of array elements can take any value in the range 0 to *size*–1, the purpose of initializing the queue is served by assigning value –1 (sentinel value) to *front* and *rear* variables. This simple task is accomplished using following constructors, where the zero argument constructors create a queue with default size 10 while the parameterized constructor creates a queue of use-defined size (*n*).

Listing 8.1:

```
// zero argument constructor,
// it constructs a queue with default size = 10
template <class T>
LinearQueue<T>::LinearQueue()
{
   elements = new T[10];
   size = 10;
   front = rear = -1;
}
// parametrized constructor that constructs,
// a queue with size = n
template <class T>
LinearQueue<T>::LinearQueue(int n)
{
   elements = new T[n];
   size = n;
   front = rear = -1;
}
```

8.4.1.1.2 Testing a Linear Queue for Underflow

Before we remove an element from a queue, it is necessary to test whether a queue still have some elements, *i.e.*, to test that whether the queue is empty or not. If it is not empty then the dequeue operation can be performed to remove the front element. This test is performed by comparing the value of *front* with sentinel value −1, as shown in the following function.

Listing 8.2:

```
// Check whether the queue is empty
template <class T>
int LinearQueue<T>::isEmpty()
{
   return ( front == -1 ? 1 : 0 );
}
```

The above function returns value 1, indicating that queue is empty, if the test condition is satisfied; otherwise it returns value 0, indicating that queue is not empty.

8.4.1.1.3 Testing a Linear Queue for Overflow

Before we insert new element in a queue, it is necessary to test whether queue still have some space to accommodate the incoming element i.e. to test that whether the queue is full or not. If it is not full then the *enqueue* operation can be performed to insert the element at rear end of the queue. This test is performed by test condition

```
( front = 0 ) and ( rear = size - 1 )
```

i.e., front element is at position with index 0 and the last element is at position with index *size*−1, which indicates that no position in linear queue is available.

This task is accomplished by the following function

Listing 8.3:

```
// Check whether the queue is full
template <class T>
int LinearQueue<T>::isFull()
{
   return ( ((front==0)&&(rear==size-1)) ? 1 : 0 );
}
```

The above function returns value 1, indicating that queue is full, if the test condition is satisfied; otherwise it returns value 0, indicating that queue is not full.

8.4.1.1.4 Enqueue Operation on Linear Queue

Even if a linear queue is not full, there is another problem that may arise during enqueue operation. That problem is that, the value of the *rear* variable is equal to *size*–1, though the value of the *front* variable is not equal to 0. This possibility implies that the incoming element cannot be enqueued unless the elements are moved forward, and variables *front* and *rear* are adjusted accordingly. Which is, of course, a time consuming process.

There are two conditions, which can occur, even if the queue is not full. These are

- If a linear queue is empty, then the value of the *front* and *rear* variables will be –1 (sentinel value), then both *front* and *rear* are set to 0.
- If a linear queue is not empty, then there are further two possibilities:
  - ◊ If the value of the *rear* variable is less than *size*–1, then the *rear* variable is incremented.
  - ◊ If the value of the *rear* variable is equal to *size*–1, then the elements of the linear queue are moved forward, and the *front* and *rear* variables are adjusted accordingly.

This task is accomplished as shown in the following function

Listing 8.4:

```
// Insert an element at the end of the queue
template <class T>
void LinearQueue<T>::enqueue(T value)
{
   int i;
   if ( LinearQueue.isEmpty() )
       front = rear = 0;
   else if ( rear == size-1 ) {
       for ( i = front, i <= rear; i++)
           elements[i - front] = elements[i];
       rear = rear - front + 1;
       front = 0;
   } else {
       rear++;
   }
   elements[rear] = value;
}
```

8.4.1.1.5 Dequeue Operation on a Linear Queue

The front element of a linear queue is assigned to a local variable, which later on will be returned via the *return* statement. After assigning the front element of a linear queue to a local variable, the value of the *front* variable is modified so that it points to the new front.

There are two possibilities:

- If there was only one element in a linear queue, then after dequeue operation queue will become empty. This state of a linear queue is reflected by setting *front* and *rear* variables to –1, the sentinel value.
- Otherwise the value of the *front* variable is incremented.

This task is accomplished as shown in the following function

Listing 8.5:

```
// Access and remove the first element of the queue
template <class T>
T LinearQueue<T>::dequeue()
{
   T temp;
   temp = elements[front];
   if ( front == rear )
       front = rear = -1;
   else
       front++;
   return temp;
}
```

8.4.1.1.6 Accessing Front Element

The element in the front of queue is accessed as shown in the following function

Listing 8.6:

```
// Access the first element of the queue
// without removing it from the queue
template <class T>
T LinearQueue<T>::peek()
{
    return elements[front];
}
```

8.4.1.1.7 Removing Queue from Memory

As soon as the *LinearQueue* goes out of scope, it needs to be removed from computer memory. This is done using following destructor:

Listing 8.7:

```
// destructor that removes the queue from memory
template <class T>
LinearQueue<T>::~LinearQueue()
{
   delete elements;
   front = rear = -1;
   size = 0;
}
```

Listing 8.8:

```
//  Program to demonstration the implementation of various operations
//  on a linear queue represented using a linear array
#include<iostream.h>
#include<iomanip.h>
template <class T>
class LinearQueue
{
   protected:             // data members
      int front;
      int rear;
      int size;
      T *elements;

   public:                // member functions
      // zero argument constructor,
      // it constructs a stack with default size = 10
      LinearQueue()
      {
         elements = new T[10];
         front = rear = -1;
         size = 10;
      }
      // parametrized constructor that constructs,
      // a stack with size = n
      LinearQueue(int n)
      {
         elements = new T[n];
         front = rear = -1;
         size = n;
      }
      // destructor that removes the stack from memory
      ~LinearQueue()
      {
         delete elements;
         front = rear = -1;
         size = 0;
      }
      // Check whether the stack is empty
      int isEmpty()
      {
         return ( front == -1 ? 1 : 0 );
      }
      // Check whether the stack is full
      int isFull()
      {
         return ( ((front==0)&&(rear==size-1)) ? 1 : 0 );
      }
      // Insert an element at the end of the queue
      void enqueue(T value);
      // Access and remove the first element of the queue
      T dequeue()
      {
         T temp;
         temp = elements[front];
         if ( front == rear )
```

```
            front = rear = -1;
         else
            front++;
         return temp;
      }
      // Access the first element of the queue
      // without removing it from the queue
      T peek()
      {
         return elements[front];
      }
}; // -------- End of LinearQueue class --------

// Insert an element at the end of the queue
template <class T>
void LinearQueue<T>::enqueue(T value)
{
   int i;
   if ( isEmpty() )
      front = rear = 0;
   else if ( rear == size-1 ) {
      for ( i = front; i <= rear; i++ )
       elements[i - front] = elements[i];
      rear= rear - front + 1;
      front = 0;
   } else {
      rear++;
   }
   elements[rear] = value;
}
void main()
{
   int choice, element, m;
   cout << "\nSize of queue you want to use : ";
   cin >> m;
   LinearQueue<int> intQueue(m);
   do
   {
      cout << "\n\nOptions available \n";
      cout << "++++++++++++++++++ \n\n";
      cout << "   1. Enqueue\n";
      cout << "   2. Dequeue\n";
      cout << "   3. Peek\n";
      cout << "   4. Exit\n\n";
      cout << "Enter your choice ( 1-4 ) : ";
      cin >> choice;
      switch ( choice )
      {
       case 1: if ( intQueue.isFull() )
                  cout << "\nQueue full...\n";
               else {
                  cout << "Enter value : " ;
                  cin >> element;
                  intQueue.enqueue(element);
               }
               break;
       case 2: if ( intQueue.isEmpty() )
                 cout << "\nQueue empty...\n";
```

```
                else
                    cout << "Value dequeued is " << intQueue.dequeue();
                break;
        case 3: if ( intQueue.isEmpty() )
                    cout << "\nQueue empty...\n";
                else
                    cout << "First Element of queue is "
                         << intQueue.peek();
        }
    }
    while ( choice != 4 );
} //---- end of main function ---
```

8.4.1.2 Limitations of a Linear Queue

The only limitation of linear queue is that —

If the last position of the queue is occupied, it is not possible to enqueue any more elements even though some positions are vacant towards the front positions of the queue.

However, this limitation can be overcome by moving the elements forward, such that the first element of the queue goes to position with index 0, and the rest of the elements move accordingly. And finally the *front* and *rear* variables are adjusted appropriately.

But this operation may be very time consuming if the length of the linear queue is very long. As mentioned earlier, this limitation can be overcome if we treat that the queue position with index 0 comes immediately after the last queue position with index *size*−1. The resulting queue is known as *circular queue*.

8.4.1.3 Implementation of Operations on a Circular Queue

The operations of initialization, testing for underflow for circular queue is similar to that of a linear queue. However, other operations are slightly different. These are described below.

8.4.1.3.1 Testing a Circular Queue for Overflow

Before we insert new element in a circular queue, it is necessary to test whether a circular queue still have some space to accommodate the incoming element i.e. to test that whether a circular queue is full or not. If it is not full then the enqueue operation can be performed to insert the element at rear of a circular queue. This test is performed by test conditions

- `( front = 0 ) and ( rear = size-1)`
- `front = rear + 1`

If any one of these two conditions is satisfied, it means circular queue is full.

This task is accomplished by the following function

Listing 8.9:

```
// Check whether the queue is full

template <class T>
int CircularQueue::isFull()
{
   if ( ((front==0)&&(rear==size-1))||(front==rear+1) )
      return 1;
   else
      return 0;
}
```

The above function returns value 1, indicating that queue is full, if the test condition is satisfied; otherwise it returns value 0, indicating that queue is not full.

8.4.1.3.2 Enqueue Operation on a Circular Queue

Before the enqueue operation, there are three conditions, which can occur, even if a circular queue is not full. These are

- If the queue is empty, then the value of the *front* and *rear* will be –1 (sentinel value), then both *front* and *rear* are set to 0.
- If the queue is not empty then the value of the *rear* will be the index of the last element of the queue, then the *rear* variable is incremented.
- If the queue is not full and the value of *rear* variable is equal to *size*–1, then *rear* variable is set to 0.

This task is accomplished as shown in the following function

Listing 8.10:

```
// Insert an element at the end of the queue

template <class T>
void CircularQueue::enqueue( T value )
{
   if ( front == -1 )
      front = rear = 0;
   else if ( rear == size-1 )
      rear = 0;
   else
      rear++;
   elements[rear] = value;
}
```

The *rear* index can also be adjusted as shown in the following code.

Listing 8.11:

```
// Insert an element at the end of the queue
template <class T>
void CircularQueue::enqueue( T value )
{
   if ( front == -1 )
      front = rear = 0;
   else
      rear = ( rear + 1 ) % size+;
   elements[rear] = value;
}
```

8.4.1.3.3 Dequeue Operation on a Circular Queue

The front element of a circular queue is assigned to a local variable, which later on will be returned via the *return* statement. After assigning the front element of a circular queue, the value of the *front* variable is modified so that it points to the new front.

There are two possibilities:

- If there was only one element in a circular queue, then after dequeue operation the circular queue will become empty. This state of a circular queue is reflected by setting *front* and *rear* variables to –1, the sentinel value.
- If value of the front variable is equal to *size*–1, then set *front* variable to 0.

If none of the above conditions hold, then the *front* variable is incremented.

This task is accomplished as shown in the following function.

Listing 8.12:

```
// Access and remove the first element of the queue
template <class T>
T LinearQueue<T>::dequeue()
{
    T temp;
    temp = elements[front];
    if ( front == rear )
       front = rear = -1;
    else if ( front == size-1 )
       front = 0;
    else
       front++;
    return temp;
}
```

The *front* index can also be adjusted as shown in the following code.

Listing 8.13:

```
// Access and remove the first element of the queue
template <class T>
T LinearQueue<T>::dequeue()
{
    T temp;
    temp = elements[front];
    if ( front == rear )
       front = rear = -1;
    else
       front = ( front + 1 ) % size;
    return temp;
}
```

Listing 8.14:

```
//  Program to demonstration the implementation of various operations
//  on a circular queue represented using a linear array
#include<iostream.h>
#include<iomanip.h>
template <class T>
class CircularQueue
{
   protected:           // data members
      int front;
      int rear;
      int size;
      T *elements;

   public:              // member functions
      // zero argument constructor,
      // it constructs a stack with default size = 10
      CircularQueue()
      {
         elements = new T[10];
         front = rear = -1;
         size = 10;
      }
      // parametrized constructor that constructs,
      // a stack with size = n
      CircularQueue(int n)
      {
         elements = new T[n];
         front = rear = -1;
         size = n;
      }
      // destructor that removes the stack from memory
      ~CircularQueue()
      {
         delete elements;
         front = rear = -1;
         size = 0;
      }
      // Check whether the stack is empty
```

```
    int isEmpty()
    {
        return ( front == -1 ? 1 : 0 );
    }
    // Check whether the stack is full
    int isFull()
    {
        if ( ((front==0)&&(rear==size-1))||(front==rear+1) )
            return 1;
        else
            return 0;
    }
    // Insert an element at the end of the queue
    void enqueue(T value)
    {
        if ( front == -1 )
            front = rear = 0;
        else
            rear = ( rear + 1 ) % size;
        elements[rear] = value;
    }
    // Access and remove the first element of the queue
    T dequeue()
    {
        T temp;
        temp = elements[front];
        if ( front == rear )
            front = rear = -1;
        else
            front = ( front + 1 ) % size;
        return temp;
    }
    // Access the first element of the queue
    // without removing it from the queue
    T peek()
    {
        return elements[front];
    }
}; // -------- End of CircularQueue class --------

void main()
{
    int choice, element, m;
    cout << "\nSize of queue you want to use : ";
    cin >> m;
    CircularQueue<int> intQueue(m);
    do
    {
        cout << "\n\nOptions available \n";
        cout << "++++++++++++++++++ \n\n";
        cout << "   1. Enqueue\n";
        cout << "   2. Dequeue\n";
        cout << "   3. Peek\n";
        cout << "   4. Exit\n\n";
        cout << "Enter your choice ( 1-4 ) : ";
        cin >> choice;
```

```
    switch ( choice )
    {
      case 1: if ( intQueue.isFull() )
                 cout << "\nQueue full...\n";
              else {
                 cout << "Enter value : " ;
                 cin >> element;
                 intQueue.enqueue(element);
              }
              break;
      case 2: if ( intQueue.isEmpty() )
                 cout << "\nQueue empty...\n";
              else
                 cout << "Value dequeued is " << intQueue.dequeue();
              break;
      case 3: if ( intQueue.isEmpty() )
                 cout << "\nQueue empty...\n";
              else
                 cout << "First Element of queue is "
                      << intQueue.peek();
    }
  }
  while ( choice != 4 );
} //---- end of main function ---
```

Note that we created *CircularQueue* from scratch, however, since the only difference in the implementation of *LinearQueue* and *CircularQueue* class is the implementation of the *isFull()*, *enqueue()*, and *dequeue()* member functions, we can create *CircularQueue* by inheriting (deriving) it from *LinearQueue* class and overriding the *isFull()*, *enqueue()*, and *dequeue()* member functions of the *LinearQueue* class, as shown below:

```
template <class T>
class CircularQueue : public LinearQueue<T>
{
  public:             // member functions
     // zero argument constructor,
     // it constructs a stack with default size = 10
     CircularQueue() : LinearQueue<T>() { }

     // parametrized constructor that constructs,
     // a stack with size = n
     CircularQueue(int n)  : LinearQueue<T>(n)  { }
     // destructor that removes the stack from memory

     ~CircularQueue() { }

     // Override method of LinearQueue class
     int isFull()
     {
      if ( ((front==0)&&(rear==size-1))||(front==rear+1) )
         return 1;
      else
         return 0;
     }
```

```
        // Override method of LinearQueue class
        // Insert an element at the end of the queue
        void enqueue(T value)
        {
         if ( front == -1 )
            front = rear = 0;
         else
            rear = ( rear + 1 ) % size;
         elements[rear] = value;
        }

        // Override method of LinearQueue class
        // Access and remove the first element of the queue
        T dequeue()
        {
         T temp;
         temp = elements[front];
         if ( front == rear )
            front = rear = -1;
         else
            front = ( front + 1 ) % size;
         return temp;
        }
}; // ------- End of CircularQueue class --------
```

8.4.2 Representing a Queue using a Linked List

A queue represented using a linked list is also known as a *linked queue*. The array-based representation of queues suffers from following limitations

- Size of the queue must be known in advance.
- We may come across situations when an attempt to enqueue an element causes overflow. However, queue, as an abstract data structure cannot be full. Hence, abstractly, it is always possible to enqueue an element in a queue. Therefore, implementing queue as an array prohibits the growth of queue beyond the finite number of elements.

The linked list representation allows a queue to grow to a limit of the computer's memory.

```
template <class T>
class node {
   public:
      T info;
      node *next;
};
template <class T>
class LinkQueue {
   protected:             // data member
      node<T> *front;
      node<T> *rear;
   public:                // member functions
      // zero argument constructor,
      // it constructs an empty queue
```

```
        LinkQueue();
        // destructor that removes queue from memory
        ~LinkQueue();
        // Check whether the stack is empty
        int isEmpty();
        // Insert an element at the end of the queue
        void enqueue(T value);
        // Access and remove the first element of the queue
        T dequeue();
        // Access the first element of the queue
        // without removing it from the queue
        T peek();
    }; // -------- End of LinkQueue class --------
```

Here we have defined two data types, classes, named *node* and *Linkqueue*. The first class *node* a self-referential class, whose first element *info* hold the element of the queue and the second element *next* holds the address of the element after it in the queue. The second class is *Linkqueue*, a class, whose first element *front* holds the address of the first element of the queue, and the second element *rear* holds the address of the last element of the queue.

With these declarations, we will write functions for various operations to be performed on a queue represented using linked list.

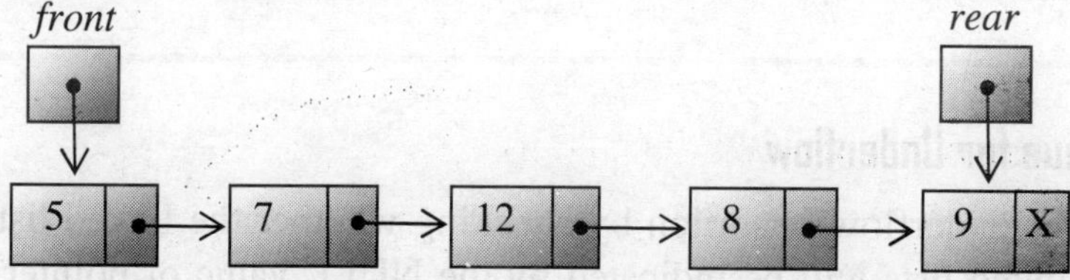

(*a*) Representation of queue of Figure 8.2(*a*) in memory

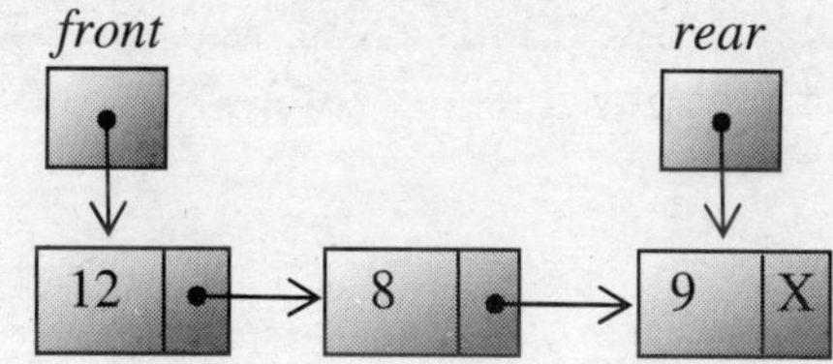

(*b*) Representation of queue of Figure 8.2(*b*) in memory

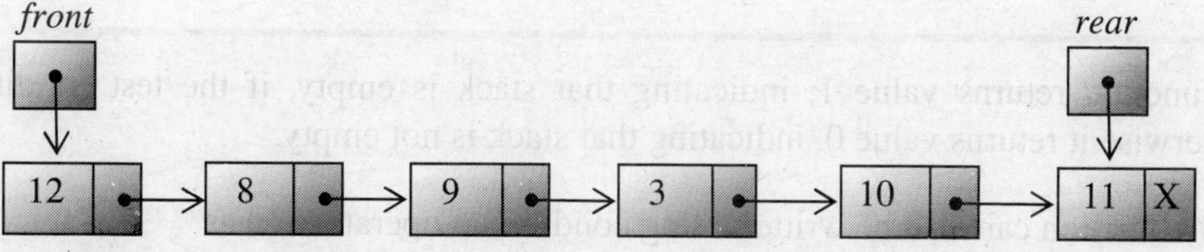

(*c*) Representation of queue of Figure 8.2(*c*) in memory

Figure 8.6: Linked representation of queue of Figure 8.2

8.4.2.1 Implementation of Operations on a Linear Queue

The implementation of different operations on a queue represented using linear linked list is described in this section.

8.4.2.1.1 Creating an Empty Queue

Before we can use a queue, it is to be created/initialized. To initialize a queue, we will create an empty linked list. Setting pointer variables *front* and *rear* to NULL value creates an empty linear linked, hence an empty queue.

This simple task can be accomplished by the following constructor.

Listing 8.15:

```
// zero argument constructor,
// it constructs an empty queue
template <class T>
LinkQueue<T>::LinkQueue()
{
    front = rear = NULL;
}
```

8.4.2.1.2 Testing Queue for Underflow

The queue is tested for underflow condition by checking whether the linked list is empty. The empty status of the linked lists will be indicated by the NULL value of pointer variable *front*. This is shown in the following member function

Listing 8.16:

```
// Check whether the stack is empty
template <class T>
int LinkQueue<T>::isEmpty()
{
   if ( front == NULL )
       return 1;
   else
       return 0;
}
```

The above function returns value 1, indicating that stack is empty, if the test condition is satisfied; otherwise it returns value 0, indicating that stack is not empty.

The *isEmpty()* function can also be written using conditional operator (?:) as

Listing 8.17:

```
// Check whether the stack is empty
template <class T>
```

```
int LinkQueue<T>::isEmpty()
{
   return ( front == NULL ? 1 : 0 );
}
```

8.4.2.1.3 Testing Queue for Overflow

Since a queue represented using a linked list can grow to a limit of a computer's memory, therefore overflow condition never occurs. Hence, this operation is not implemented for linked queues.

8.4.2.1.4 Enqueue Operation

To enqueue a new element onto the queue, the element is inserted in the end of the linked list. This task is accomplished as shown in the following function

Listing 8.18:

```
// Insert an element at the end of the queue
template <class T>
void LinkQueue<T>::enqueue(T value)
{
   node<T> *ptr;
   ptr = new node<T>;
   ptr->info = value;
   ptr->next = NULL;
   if ( rear == NULL ) //  queue initially empty
      front = rear = ptr;
   else
   {
      rear->next = ptr;
      rear = ptr;
   }
}
```

8.4.2.1.5 Dequeue Operation

To dequeue/remove an element from the queue, the element is removed from the beginning of the linked list. This task is accomplished as shown in the following function

Listing 8.19:

```
// Access and remove the first element of the queue
template <class T>
T LinkQueue<T>::dequeue()
{
   T temp;
   Node<T> *ptr;
   temp = front)->info;
   ptr = front;
   if ( front == rear )          // only one element
      front = rear = NULL;
```

```
    else
        front = front->next;
    delete ptr;
    return temp;
}
```

The element in the beginning of the linked list is assigned to a local variable *temp*, which later on will be returned via the *return* statement. And the first node from the linked list is removed.

8.4.2.1.6 Accessing Front Element

The element in the front of queue is accessed as shown in the following function

Listing 8.20:

```
// Access the first element of the queue
// without removing it from the queue
template <class T>
T LinkQueue<T>::peek()
{
    return front->info;
}
```

8.4.2.1.7 Disposing a Queue

Because queue is implemented using linked lists, therefore it is programmer's job to write the code to release the memory occupied by the queue. The following listing shows the different steps to be performed.

Listing 8.21:

```
// destructor that removes queue from memory
template <class T>
LinkQueue<T>::~LinkQueue()
{
    node<T> *ptr;
    while ( front != NULL )
    {
        ptr = front;
        front = front->next;
        delete ptr;
    }
    rear = NULL;
}
```

The complete code for *LinkQueue* class will look like

Listing 8.22:

```
//  Program to demonstration the implementation of various operations
//  on a queue represented using a linear linked list
#include <iostream.h>
#include <iomanip.h>
template <class T>
class node {
   public:
      T info;
      node *next;
};
template <class T>
class LinkQueue
{
   protected:              // data member
      node<T> *front;
      node<T> *rear;
   public:                 // member functions
      // zero argument constructor,
      // it constructs an empty queue
LinkQueue()
{
    front = rear = NULL;
}
      // destructor that removes queue from memory
      ~LinkQueue();
      // Check whether the stack is empty
int isEmpty()
{
   return ( front == NULL ? 1 : 0 );
}
// Insert an element at the end of the queue
void enqueue(T value)
{
   node<T> *ptr;
   ptr = new node<T>;
   ptr->info = value;
   ptr->next = NULL;
   if ( rear == NULL ) //  queue initially empty
      front = rear = ptr;
   else
   {
      rear->next = ptr;
      rear = ptr;
   }
}
// Access and remove the first element of the queue
T dequeue()
{
   T temp;
   node<T> *ptr;
```

```
   temp = front->info;
   ptr = front;
   if ( front == rear )          // only one element
      front = rear = NULL;
   else
      front = front->next;
   delete ptr;
   return temp;
}
// Access the first element of the queue
// without removing it from the queue
T peek()
{
   return front->info;
}
}; // -------- End of LinkQueue class --------
// destructor that removes queue from memory
template <class T>
LinkQueue<T>::~LinkQueue()
{
   node<T> *ptr;
   while ( front != NULL )
   {
      ptr = front;
      front = front->next;
      delete ptr;
   }
   rear = NULL;
}
void main()
{
   int choice, element;
   LinkQueue<int> intQueue;
   do
   {
      cout << "\n\nOptions available \n";
      cout << "++++++++++++++++++ \n\n";
      cout << "   1. Enqueue\n";
      cout << "   2. Dequeue\n";
      cout << "   3. Peek\n";
      cout << "   4. Exit\n\n";
      cout << "Enter your choice ( 1-4 ) : ";
      cin >> choice;
      switch ( choice )
      {
        case 1: cout << "Enter value : " ;
                cin >> element;
                intQueue.enqueue(element);
                break;
        case 2: if ( intQueue.isEmpty() )
                   cout << "\nQueue empty...\n";
                else
                   cout << "Value dequeued is " << intQueue.dequeue();
                break;
        case 3: if ( intQueue.isEmpty() )
                   cout << "\nQueue empty...\n";
                else
```

```
                    cout << "First Element of queue is "
                         << intQueue.peek();
        }
    }
    while ( choice != 4 );
} //---- end of main function ---
```

8.5 MULTIPLE QUEUES

We have seen that if we represent a queue using an array, we have to allocate sufficient space for the queue. If the space allocated to an array is less, it may result in frequent overflows and we may have to modify the code and reallocate more space for array. On other side, if we attempt to reduce the number of overflows by allocating large space for array, it may result in sheer wastage of space if the typical size of the queue is very small as compared to actual size of the array. In this case, we may say that there exists a trade-off between the number of overflows and the space.

One possibility to reduce this trade-off is to represent more than one queue in the same array of sufficient size. Figure 8.7 shows the possible mapping of five queues to same array. Each queue is allocated a same amount of space.

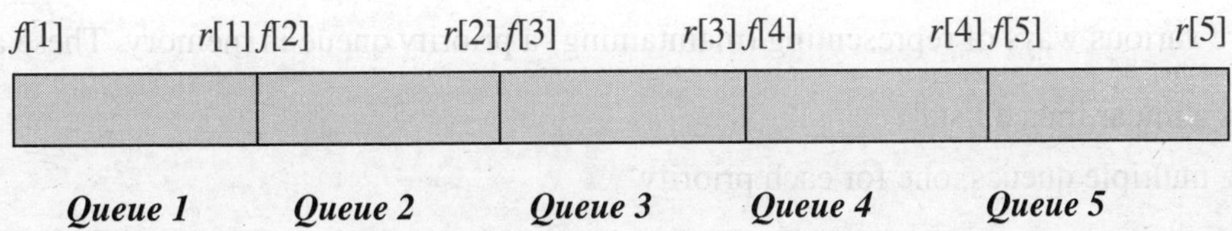

Figure 8.7: Representation of five queues by a single array

Implementations of different operations on these queues are left as an exercise for the students.

8.6 DEQUE

A *deque* is a kind of queue in which elements can be added or removed from at either end but not in the middle. The term deque is a contraction of the name *double-ended queue*.

There are two variations of a deque, which are intermediate between a deque and a queue. These are:

- ❑ ***Input-restricted deque*** – which allows insertions only at one end but allows deletions at both ends.
- ❑ ***Output-restricted deque*** – which allows insertions at both ends but allows deletions only at one end.

Deques are introduced here just for academic interest of the students their use in practical situations is almost insignificant.

8.7 PRIORITY QUEUE

A *priorities queue* is a kind of queue in which each element is assigned a priority and the order in which elements are deleted and processed comes from the following rules:

- An element with highest priority is processed first before any element of lower priority.
- Two or more elements with the same priority are processed according to the order in which they were added to the queue.

There can be different criteria's for determining the priority. Some of them are summarized below:

- A shortest job is given higher priority over the longer one.
- An important job is given the higher priority over a routine type job. For example, a transaction for on-line booking of an order is given preference over payroll processing.
- In a commercial computer center, the amount you pay for the job can determine priority for your job. Pay more to get higher priority for your job.

8.7.1 Representing a Priority Queue in Memory

There are various ways of representing (maintaining) a priority queue in memory. These are:

- Using a linear linked list
- Using multiple queues, one for each priority
- Using a heap

8.7.1.1 Linear Linked List Representation

In this representation, each node of the linked list will have three fields:

- An information field *info* that hold the element of the queue,
- A priority filed *prn* that holds the priority number of the element, and
- A next pointer filed *link* that holds the pointer to the next element of the queue.

Further, a node X precedes a node Y in the linear linked list if either node X has higher priority that Y or both nodes have same priority but X was added to the list before Y.

In a given system, we can assign higher priority to lower number or higher number. Therefore, if higher priority is for lower number, we have to maintain linear linked lists sorted on ascending order of the priority. However, if higher priority is for higher number, we have to maintain linear linked lists sorted on descending order of the priority. This way, the element to be processed next is available as the first element of the linked list.

8.7.1.2 Multiple Queue Representation

In this representation, one queue is maintained for each priority number. In order to process an element of the priority queue, element from the first non-empty highest priority number queue is accessed. In order to add a new element to the priority queue, the element is inserted in an appropriate queue for given priority number.

8.7.1.3 Heap Representation of a Priority Queue

A *heap* is a complete binary tree and with the additional property – the root element is either smallest or largest from its children. If root element of the heap is smallest from its children, it is known as *min heap*. If root element of the heap is largest from its children, it is known as *max heap*.

A priority queue having highest priority for lower number can be represented using min heap, and a priority queue having highest priority for higher number can be represented using max heap.

Hence, the element of the priority queue to be processed next is in the root node of the heap. Heaps are discussed in detail in *Chapter 10*.

If we compare the effort in adding or removing elements from the priority queue, we find that heap representation is the best.

8.8 APPLICATIONS OF QUEUES

Some of the applications of queues are listed below:

- There are several algorithms that use queues to solve problems efficiently. For example, we have used queue for performing level-order traversal of a binary tree in *Chapter 9*, and for performing breadth-first search on a graph in *Chapter 11*. Also in most of the simulation-related problems, queues are heavily used.
- When the jobs are submitted to a networked printer, they are arranged in order of arrival. Thus, essentially, jobs sent to a printer are placed on a queue.
- There is a kind of computer network where disk is attached to one computer, known as *file server*. Users on other computers are given access to files on a first-come first-served basis, so the data structure is a queue.
- Virtually every real-life line (supposed to be) a queue. For example, lines at ticket counters at cinema halls, railway stations, bus stands, etc., are queues, because the service, *i.e.*, ticket, is provided on first-come first-served basis.

REVIEW EXERCISES

1. What is a queue? Is queue a linear or non-linear data structure?
2. Queue is a special type of list? Comment.
3. How does an array based queue compares with linked queue?
4. Why an operation to check queue overflow is not implemented on linked queues?
5. Can we implement a queue in C whose elements can be of different type? If your answer is yes, then show how?
6. How *peek()* operation differs from *dequeue()* operation?
7. While representing a queue using linked lists, we have implemented additional operation *dispose()* to remove the queue from memory. Why such operation is not implemented for queue represented using an array.
8. How does a linear queue compare with circular queue?

PROGRAMMING EXERCISES

1. Write a menu driven program to implementing the various operations on a linear queue.
2. Write a menu driven program to implementing the various operations on a circular queue.
3. Write a menu driven program to implementing the various operations on a queue represented using a linked list.
4. Design a data structure to represent *m* circular queues in an array named *elements* of size *n*. Also write functions for *enqueue()* and *dequeue()* operations to insert and delete element from queue i, $0 \le i \le m-1$. These operations should run in O(1) time.
5. Using the data structure designed in question 4, write functions for *isFull()* and *isEmpty()* operations to check overflow and underflow of queue i, $0 \le i \le m-1$. These operations should also run in O(1) time.
6. **Kitty Fishing - A Simple Game of Cards:** There is a simple two-player card game called 'Kitty fishing'. When the game begins player A and B has the same number of cards. Then each gives out one card in turn. Each card given out on the table should be laid overlapped one by one. When the card newly given out finds a card which has the same value on the table, the player who gives out the card will take the cards between the two same cards following the order the cards on the table, and put them to the back of his cards. The same player continues to give out net cards. Player giving a card is called a turn.

   Note: Do not change the order of your cards.

❑ ❑ ❑

Chapter 9

Trees

9.1 INTRODUCTION

So far in the text we have discussed data structures such as arrays, linked lists, stacks and queues for representing linear and tabular data. These structures in general are not suitable for representing hierarchical data. In hierarchical data we have ancestor-descendant, superior-subordinate, whole-part, or similar relationship among data elements. The following examples will further illustrate the situations make such hierarchical data. In hierarchical data we have ancestor-descendant, superior-subordinate, whole-part, or similar relationship among data elements.

Example 9.1: *Family Structure*

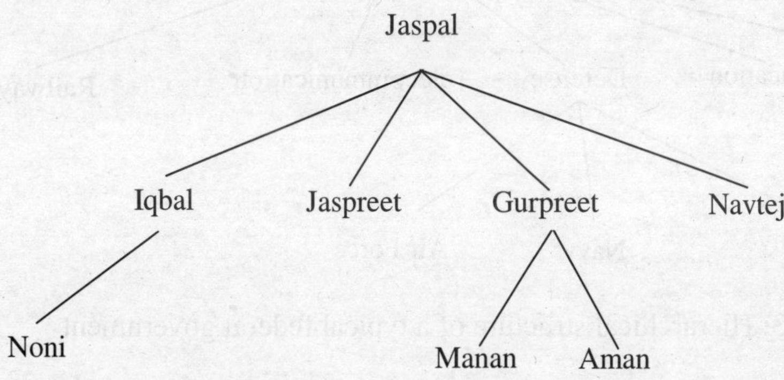

Figure 9.1: Hierarchical structure showing Jaspal's descendant

Figure 9.1 shows descendants of Jaspal arranged in hierarchical manner, beginning with Jaspal at the top of the hierarchy. Jaspal's children (Iqbal, Jaspreet, Gurpreet, and Navtej) are shown next in the hierarchy, and a line or an edge joins Jaspal and his children. Iqbal has one child,

Jaspreet has none, Gurpreet has two, and Navtej has none. Iqbal's only child is shown below him, and Gurpreet's children are shown below him. Note that there is an edge between each parent and his/her child(ren). From this hierarchical representation it is easy to identify Iqbal's siblings, Jaspal's descendants, Noni's ancestors, and so on.

Example 9.2: *Business Corporate Structure*

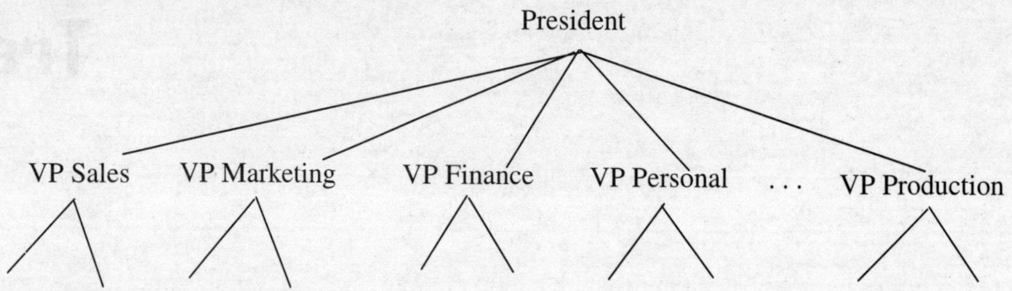

Figure 9.2: Hierarchical administrative structure of a typical business organization

Figure 9.2 shows administrative setup of a typical business organization. The person highest in the hierarchy (president in this case) appears at the top. Those who are next in the hierarchy (vice presidents (VPs) in this case) are shown next in the hierarchy below the president. The vice presidents are the president's immediate subordinates, and the present is their superior. Each vice president, in turn, has his/her subordinates who may themselves have subordinates.

Example 9.3: *Federal Government Structure*

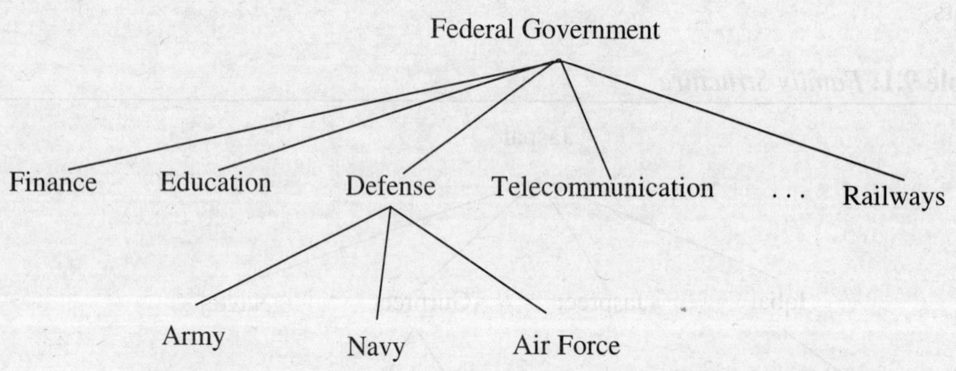

Figure 9.3: Hierarchical structure of a typical federal government

Figure 9.3 shows hierarchical subdivisions of a federal government. At the top, we have entire federal government. At the next level; we have its major subdivisions, *i.e.*, different departments. Each subdivision may have further subdivisions, which will be shown, at the next level. For example, Department of Defense has been subdivided into Army, Navy, and Air Force.

Example 9.4: *Modular Structure of a Computer Program*

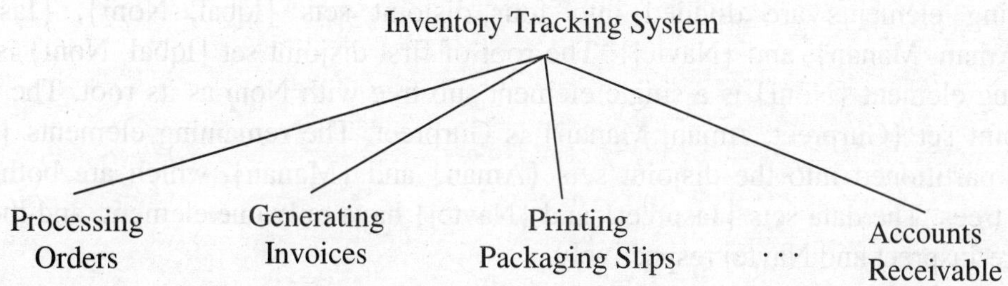

Figure 9.4: Module hierarchy for inventory tracking system

For another example of hierarchical data, consider the popular software development technique referred to as *modularization*. The objective of modularization is to divide the large and complex software system into functionally independent modules (parts) so that each can be developed independently. If necessary, each module may be further divided. It reduces the overall software develop time, as it is much easier to solve several problems than one large one. In addition, different programmers can develop different modules at the same time.

Figure 9.4 shows possible modular decomposition of computer based inventory-tracking system. The inventory tracking system is divided into several modules. Only four are shown in the figure. The first module is used to book the orders. If the orders can be met, then the second module is used to generate the invoice for the booked order. After generating the invoice, the third module is used to print the packaging slip, which will be sent to the godown for packing the goods ordered, and so on. The fourth module is used when the payments from the customers are received.

A tree is an ideal data structure for representing such kind of hierarchical data. As there are many types of trees in a forest, likewise there are many types of trees in data structures — (*general*) *trees*, *binary trees*, *expression trees*, *tournament trees*, *binary search trees*, *threaded trees*, *AVL trees* and B-*trees*.

In this chapter, we will introduce these trees while laying major stress on *binary search trees.*

9.2 TREE DEFINED

A (*general*) *tree T* is a finite nonempty set of elements. One of these elements is called the *root*, and the remaining elements, if any, are partitioned into trees, which are called the *sub trees* of *T*.

Let us see how this definition relates to our examples of hierarchical data. The element at the highest level of the hierarchy is root. The elements at the next level are the roots of the sub trees formed by partitioning of the remaining elements.

Consider Example 9.1. The data set is {Jaspal, Iqbal, Jaspreet, Navtej, Gurpreet, Noni, Aman, Manan}. Therefore, number *n* of element in the data set = 8. The root of the data set is Jaspal. The remaining elements are divided into four disjoint sets {Iqbal, Noni}, {Jaspreet}, {Gurpreet, Aman, Manan}, and {Navtej}. The root of first disjoint set {Iqbal, Noni} is Iqbal. The remaining element {Noni} is a single element sub tree with Noni as its root. The root of second disjoint set {Gurpreet, Aman, Manan} is Gurpreet. The remaining elements {Aman, Manan} are partitioned into the disjoint sets {Aman} and {Manan}, which are both single element sub trees. The data sets {Jaspreet} and {Navtej} have only one element, and therefore their roots are Jaspreet and Navtej respectively.

9.3 TREE TERMINOLOGY

Level of an Element – Very commonly used tree term is level. By definition, the root of the tree is at level 1; its children, if any, are at level 2; their children, if any, are at level 3; and so on. In Figure 9.1, Jaspal is at level 1; Iqbal, Jaspreet, Gurpreet, and Navtej are at level 2; Noni, Aman, and Manan are at level 3.

Degree of an Element – The degree of an element is the number of children it has. The degree of a leaf is zero. In Figure 9.1, Jaspal has degree 4.

Degree of a Tree – The degree of a tree is the maximum of its element degrees. The degree of tree in Figure 9.1 is 4.

Height/Depth of a Tree – If level of the root is denoted by 1, then the maximum level number of the tree is known as its *height* or *depth*.

9.4 BINARY TREES

A *binary tree T* is either empty or has a finite collections of elements. When the binary tree is not empty, one of its elements is called the *root* and the remaining elements, if any, are partitioned into two binary trees, which are called the left & right sub trees of *T*.

The essential differences between a binary tree and a tree are

- A binary tree can be empty whereas a tree cannot.
- Each element in binary tree has at most two sub trees (one or both of these sub trees may be empty). Each element in a tree can have any number of sub trees.
- The sub trees of each element in a binary tree are ordered. That is, we distinguish between the left and right sub trees. The sub trees in a tree are unordered.

Like a tree, a binary tree is drawn with its root at the top. The elements in the left (right) sub tree of the root are drawn below and to the left (right) of the root. Between each element and its children is a line or edge.

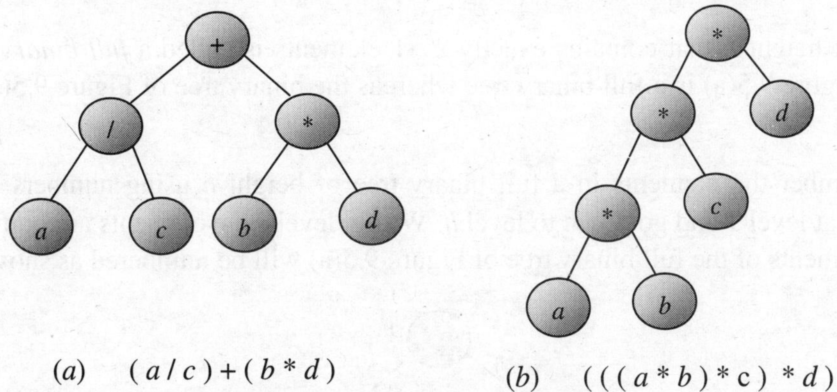

(*a*) $(a/c)+(b*d)$ (*b*) $(((a*b)*c)*d)$

Figure 9.5: Expression trees

Figure 9.5 shows some binary trees that represent arithmetic expressions. Each operator (+, –, *, /) may have one or two operands. The left operand, if any, is the left sub tree of the operator and the right operand is the right sub tree. The leaf elements in an expression tree are either constants or variables. Note that an expression tree contains no parentheses.

9.4.1 Some Properties of Binary Trees

Property 1:

A binary tree with n elements, $n > 0$, has exactly n–1 edges.

Proof: Every element in a binary tree, except the root, has exactly one parent. There is exactly one edge between each child and its parent. So the number of edges is n–1.

Property 2:

A binary tree of height h, $h > 0$, has at least h and at most 2^h-1 elements in it.

Proof: Since there must be at least one element at each level, the number of elements is at least h. As each element can have at most two children, the number of elements at level k is at most 2^{k-1} for $k > 0$. For $h = 0$, the total number of elements is 0, which equals 2^0-1. For $h > 0$, the total number of elements cannot exceed $\sum_{k=1}^{h} 2^{k-1} = 2^h - 1$.

Property 3:

The height of the binary tree that contains n elements, $n \geq 0$, is at most n and at least $\lceil \log_2(n+1) \rceil$.

Proof: Since there must be at least one element at each level, the height cannot exceed n. From property 2, we know that a binary tree of height h can have no more than 2^h-1 elements. So $n \leq 2^h-1$. Hence $h \geq \log_2(n+1)$. Since h is an integer, we get $h \geq \lceil \log_2(n+1) \rceil$.

A binary tree of height h that contains exactly 2^h-1 elements is called a *full binary tree*. The binary tree of Figure 9.5(a) is a full binary tree whereas the binary tree of Figure 9.5(b) is not a full binary tree.

Suppose we number the elements in a full binary tree of height h using numbers 1 through 2^h-1. We begin at level 1 and go down to level h. Within levels, the elements are numbered left to right. The elements of the full binary tree of Figure 9.5(a) will be numbered as shown below:

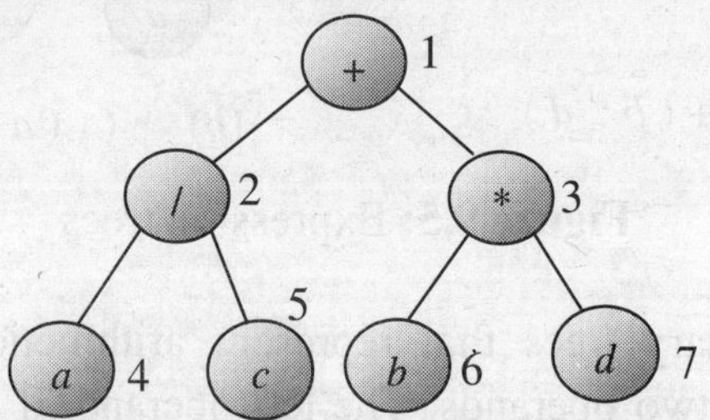

Figure 9.6: Full binary tree of height 3

Now suppose we delete the k, $k \geq 0$, elements numbered 2^h-i, $1 \leq i \leq k$ for any k. The resulting binary tree is called a *complete binary tree*. Figure 9.7 shows some examples of complete trees.

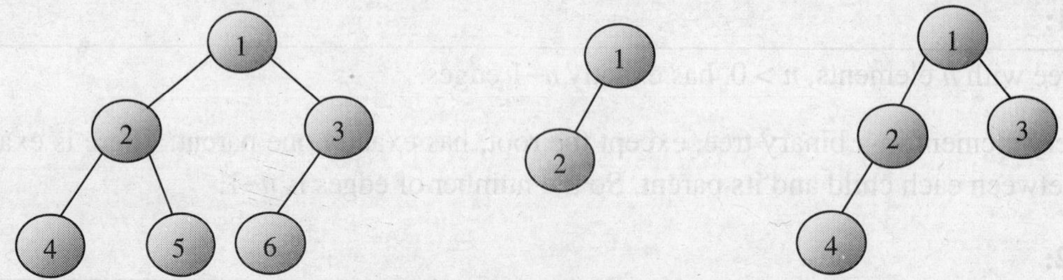

Figure 9.7: Complete Binary trees

Property 4:

Let i, $1 \leq i \leq n$, be the number assigned to an element of a complete binary tree. The following statements are true.

1. If $i = 1$, then this element is the root of the binary tree. If $i > 1$, then the parent of this element has been assigned the number $\lfloor i/2 \rfloor$.

2. If $2i > n$, then this element has no left child. Otherwise, its left child has been assigned the number $2i$.

3. If $2i + 1 > n$, then this element has no right child. Otherwise, its right child has been assigned the number $2i + 1$.

Its proof can be established by induction on i. This is left as an exercise for the readers.

9.5 TOURNAMENT TREES

Suppose *n* players enter in a chess tournament and further suppose that the tournament is played on knock-out basis. By knock-out basis means a player is eliminated from the tournament upon losing a match. Pairs of players play each other until only one remains undefeated. The undefeated player is declared winner of the tournament. Figure 9.8 shows a possible tournament involving eight players named *a* through *h*. The tournament is described by a binary tree in which each external node (leaf node) represents a player and each internal node represents a match played between players designated by the children of the node.

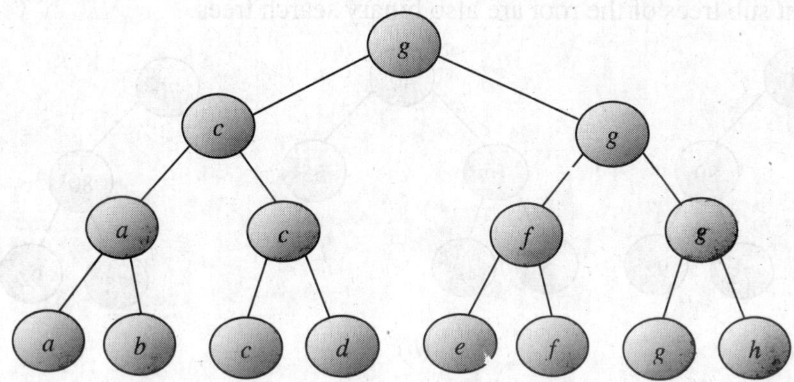

Figure 9.8: Eight Player Tournament tree

Each level of internal nodes defines a *round* of matches that can be played in parallel. In the first round player *a* and *b*, *c* and *d*, *e* and *f*, *g* and *h* play. The winner of each match is recorded at the internal node that represents the match. In our example, the four winners are *a*, *c*, *f* and *g*. In the next round of matches, players *a* and *c*, *f* and *g* play against each other. The winners are *c* and *g*. Now in the final round, players *c* and *g* play each other, and player *g* emerges winner of the final match. Hence player *g* is the winner of the tournament.

Figure 9.9 show a possible tournament that is played between 5 players. Players *c*, *d* and *e* and given byes in the first round. The winner in this case is player *e*.

The tournament trees of Figure 9.8 and 9.9 are called *winner trees* because at each internal node, we record the winner of the match played at that node. In contrast, if we record the loser of the match played at that node, the tournament tree is called a *loser tree*. Tournament trees are also called *selection trees*. Winner trees can be adapted for computer use.

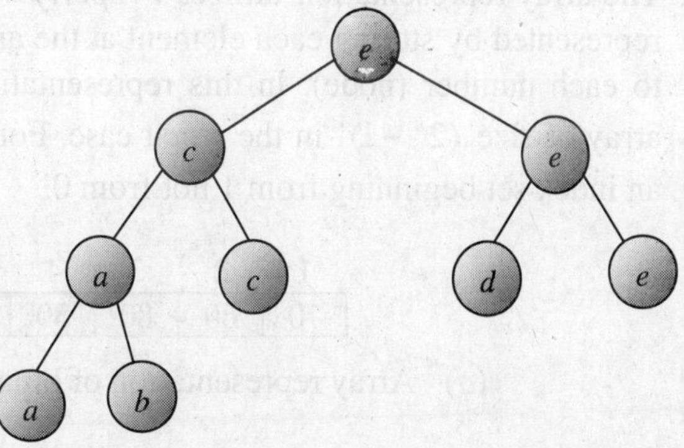

Figure 9.9: 5 Player Tournament tree

9.6 BINARY SEARCH TREES

A *binary search tree T* is a binary tree that may be empty. A non-empty binary search tree satisfies the following properties:

1. Every element has a key (or value) and no two elements have the same key i.e. all keys are unique.
2. The keys, if any, in the left sub tree of the root are smaller than the key in the node.
3. The keys, if any, in the right sub tree of the root are larger than the key in the node.
4. The left and right sub trees of the root are also binary search trees.

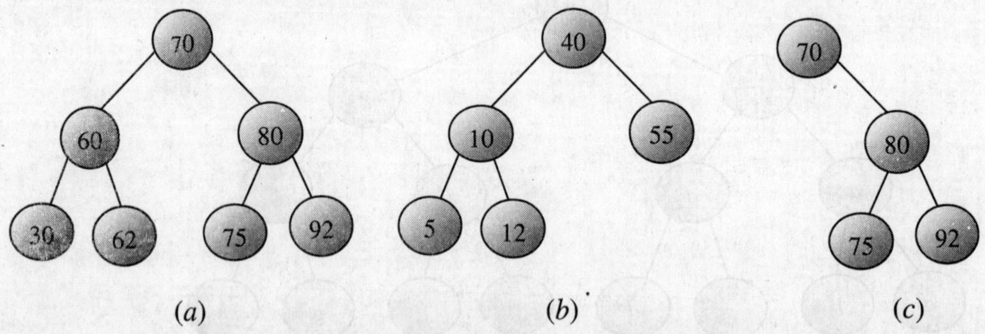

Figure 9.10: Binary Search trees

9.6.1 Representation of a Binary and Binary Search Tree

A binary tree and a binary search tree is represented in an identical manner. These can be represented using a linear array (array representation) or linked lists (linked representation). We will discuss these representations one by one and their merits and demerits.

9.6.1.1 Array Representation

The array representation utilizes *Property 4*. In this representation, the binary (search) tree is represented by storing each element at the array position corresponding to the number assigned to each number (node). In this representation, a binary (search) tree of height h requires an array of size $(2^h - 1)$, in the worst case. For simplicity, we consider that array is indexed with an index set beginning from 1 not from 0.

1	2	3	4	5	6	7
70	60	80	30	62	75	92

(*a*) Array representation of binary search trees of Figure 9.10(*a*)

1	2	3	4	5	6	7
40	10	55	5	12		

(*b*) Array representation of binary search trees of Figure 9.10(*b*)

1	2	3	4	5	6	7
70		80			75	92

(*c*) Array representation of binary search trees of Figure 9.10(*c*)

Figure 9.11: Array representation of binary search trees of Figure 9.10

Can you imagine how the following binary search tree will stored in array representation?

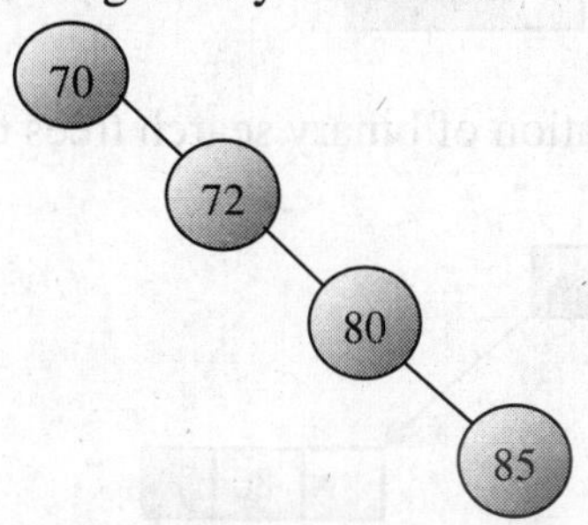

Figure 9.12: A right-skewed binary search tree

The array representation of binary search tree of Figure 9.12 will be as shown in Figure 9.13.

1	2	3	4	5	6	7	8	9	10	11	12	13	14	15
70		72				80								85

Figure 9.13: Array representation of binary search tree of Figure 9.12

This scheme of representation is quite wasteful of space when the binary (search) tree is skewed or number of elements is small as compared to its height.

Hence, array representation is useful only when the binary (search) tree is full or complete.

9.6.1.2 Linked Representation

The most popular and practical way of representing a binary (search) tree is using links (pointers).

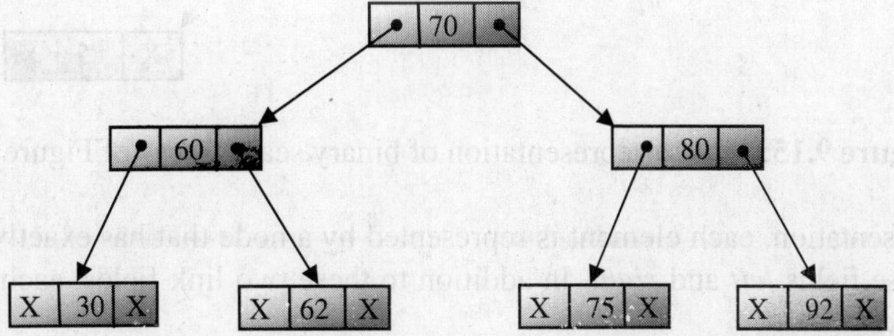

(*a*) Linked representation of binary search trees of Figure 9.10(*a*)

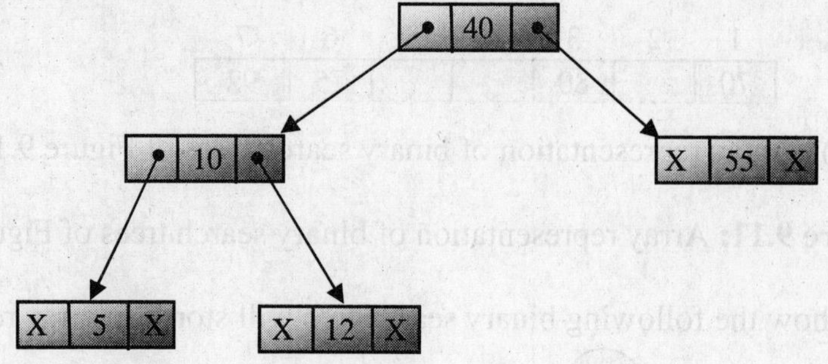

(*b*) Linked representation of binary search trees of Figure 9.10(*b*)

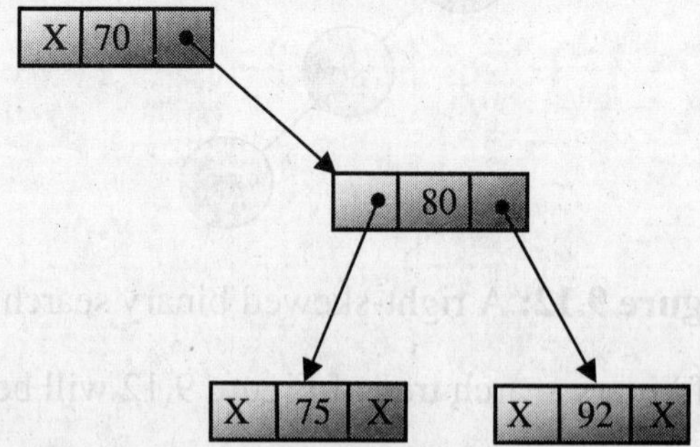

(*c*) Linked representation of binary search trees of Figure 9.10(*c*)

Figure 9.14: Linked representation of binary search trees of Figure 9.10

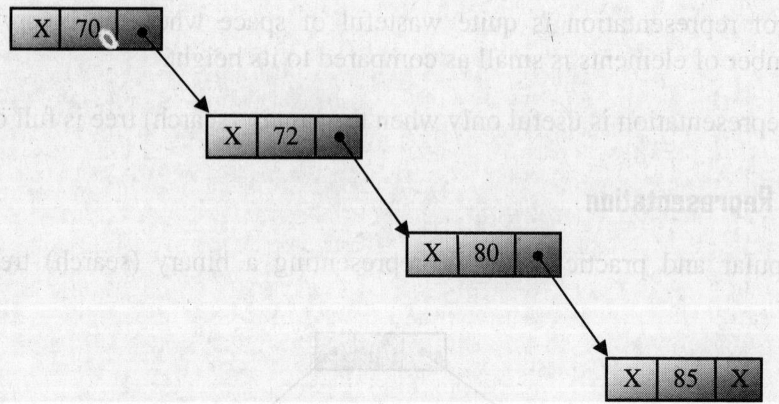

Figure 9.15: Linked representation of binary search trees of Figure 9.12

In linked representation, each element is represented by a node that has exactly two link fields. Let us call these fields *left* and *right*. In addition to these two link fields, each node has a data field called *info*.

An arrow represents each edge in the drawing of a binary tree from the parent node to the child node. This pointer is placed in the appropriate link field of the parent node. Since an *n*-element binary tree has exactly $n-1$ edges, there will be $2n-(n-1) = n+1$ link fields that have NULL values (pictured as X).

Suppose that the elements of the binary can be any primitive type or pointer type, the following is the required ADT to represent a binary tree:

```
// class definition to represent a node of a binary search tree
template <class T>
class BSTNode
{
  public:
    BSTNode *left;
    T info;
    BSTNode *right;
};
// class definition for binary search tree
template <class T>
class BSTree
{
  private:
    BSTNode<T> *root;
  public:
    // constructor to initialize binary search tree
    // to empty state
    BSTree() {
       root = NULL;
    }

    // destructor, that calles recursive function deleteTree()
    // to remove binary search tree from memory
    ~BSTree() {
       deleteTree(&root);
    }

    // member function to insert an element in binary search
    // tree, it calls recursive function insert() to
    // actually perform the insertion
    void insertElement(T);
    // member function to perform preorder traversal of binary
    // search tree, it calls recursive function
    // traversePreorder() to perform the actual traversal
    void traversePre();
    // member function to perform inorder traversal of binary
    // search tree, it calls recursive function
    // traverseInorder() to perform the actual traversal
    void traverseIn();
    // member function to perform postorder traversal of binary
    // search tree, it calls recursive function
    // traversePostorder() to perform the actual traversal
    void traversePost();
    // member function to perform the levelorder traversal of
    // binary search tree, it use linked queue
    void levelorderTraversal();
```

```
// member function to search a given element, it calls
// recursive function search() to actually perform the
// search
BSTNode<T> *searchElement(T);
// member function to delete a given element from binary
// search tree, it calls recursive function deleteNode()
// to actually delete the element from binary search tree
void deleteElement(int);
// member function that returns the location of the largest
// element of the binary search tree, it calls recursive
// function findMaximum() to find the largest element
BSTNode<T> *findLargest();
// member function that returns the location of the smallest
// element of the binary search tree, it calls recursive
// function findMinimum() to find the smallest element
BSTNode<T> *findSmallest();
// member function that returns the internal (non-leaf)
// nodes of the binary search tree, it calls recursive
// function internalNodes() to actually count the
// internal nodes
int countInternalNodes();
// member function that returns the external (leaf) nodes
// of the binary search tree, it calls recursive
// function externalNodes() to actually count the
// external nodes
int countExternalNodes();
// member function that returns the total number of nodes
// of the binary search tree, it calls recursive function
// totalNodes() to actually count the total nodes
int countTotalNodes();
// member function that returns the height of the binary
// search tree, it calls recursive function findHeight()
// to actually find the height of the binary search tree
int heightTree();
// member function to find the mirror image of the binary
// search tree, it calls recursive function reflect()
// to actually find the image
void mirrorImage();

// ------ RECURSIVE MEMBER FUNCTIONS -------

// recursive member function to insert an element into
// binary search tree
static void insert(BSTNode<T> **, T);
// recursive member to perform preorder traversal of
// binary search tree
static void traversePreorder(BSTNode<T> *);
// recursive member to perform inorder traversal of
// binary search tree
static void traverseInorder(BSTNode<T> *);
// recursive member to perform postorder traversal of
// binary search tree
static void traversePostorder(BSTNode<T> *);
// recursive member function to search a given element,
// it return the location of the element if present,
// else returns NULL indicating that the element is
// not present in binary search tree
static BSTNode<T> *search(BSTNode<T> *, T);
```

```
        // recursive member function that returns the location of
        // the largest element of the binary search tree.
        // It returns NULL if tree is empty a given element or
        // it has no right child
        static BSTNode<T> *findMaximum(BSTNode<T> *);
        // recursive member function that returns the location
        // of the smallest element of the binary search tree.
        // It returns NULL if tree is empty a given element or
        // it has no left child
        static BSTNode<T> *findMinimum(BSTNode<T> *);
        // recursive member function that delete an element from
        // binary search tree. It calls recursive member function to
        // search the element to be deleted
        static void deleteEle (BSTNode<T> **, T) {
        // recursive member function to remove the binary search
        // tree from memory
        static void deleteTree(BSTNode<T> **);
        // recursive member function that returns the number of
        // internal (non-leaf) nodes of the binary search tree
        static int internalNodes(BSTNode<T> *);
        // recursive member function that returns the number of
        // external (leaf) nodes in a binary search tree
        static int externalNodes(BSTNode<T> *);
        // recursive member function that returns the total
        // number of nodes in a binary search tree
        static int totalNodes(BSTNode<T> *);
        // recursive member function that returns the height of the
        // binary search tree
        static void findHeight(BSTNode<T> *, int *);
        // recursive member function that reflects (mirror image)
        // a binary search tree about an axis passing through
        // its root
        static void reflect(BSTNode<T> *);
    }; // -------- End of BSTree class --------
```

We have defined our own data type named *BSTree*, which is class and whose first data member is a pointer variable *left* will be used to hold the address of the left child (left subtree), second data member is *info* that can be any primitive type, will be used to hold the data of the node, and third data member is a pointer variable *right* will be used to hold the address of the right child (right subtree).

9.6.2 Common Operations on Binary and Binary Search Trees

Some of the operations that are commonly performed on binary as well as binary search trees are:

1. Create an empty tree.
2. Traverse it.
3. Determine its height.
4. Determine the number of elements in it.
5. Determine the number of internal nodes i.e. non-leaf nodes.
6. Determine the number of external nodes i.e. leaf nodes.
7. Determine its mirror image.
8. Remove it from memory.

The following are some of the operations having relevance to only binary search trees

1. Insert a new node/element.
2. Search an element.
3. Find the smallest element.
4. Find the largest element.
5. Delete a node.

9.6.2.1 Creating an Empty Binary (Search) Tree

Since the binary (search) tree will be empty in the beginning, the variable *root* is assigned a sentinel value to indicate that binary (search) tree is empty. The following listing shows the implementation of this function.

Listing 9.1:

```
// constructor to initialize binary search tree to empty state
template <class T>
class BSTree<T>::BSTree()
{
   root = NULL;
}
```

9.6.2.2 Traversing a Binary (Search) Tree

Recall that to traverse a linear linked list, we set a temporary pointer variable to *head* of the list, and then follow the links from one node to the other until we reach a node whose next pointer filed contains NULL value i.e. is the last node. Similarly, we can set a pointer variable to the root of the tree. But where do we go from there – to the left child or the right child? Do we process the root first or the leaves first? Therefore, based on the way the nodes in the tree are traversed, the traversal is classified in one of the following categories for a binary tree T with root R as shown in Figure 9.16.

- ***Pre-order traversal*** — the traversal order is
  - Process the root R
  - Traverse the left sub tree of R in pre-order
  - Traverse the right sub tree of R in pre-order
- ***In-order traversal*** — the traversal order is
  - Traverse the left sub tree of R in pre-order
  - Process the root R
  - Traverse the right sub tree of R in pre-order
- ***Post-order traversal*** — the traversal order is
  - Traverse the left sub tree of R in pre-order
  - Traverse the right sub tree of R in pre-order
  - Process the root R

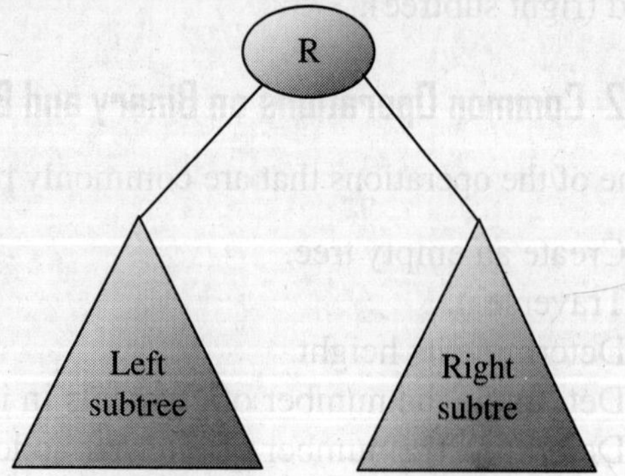

Figure 9.16: Binary tree T

In addition to above standard traversal schemes, there is another possible traversal scheme known as *Level-order traversal*. As its name suggests, in this scheme first node at level 1, *i.e.*, root is traversed, then nodes at level 2 followed by nodes at level 3, ..., and so on.

Example 9.5:

Consider the following binary tree T. Observe that A is the root, and left sub tree L_T consists of nodes B, D, and E and the right sub tree R_T consists of nodes C, F, and G.

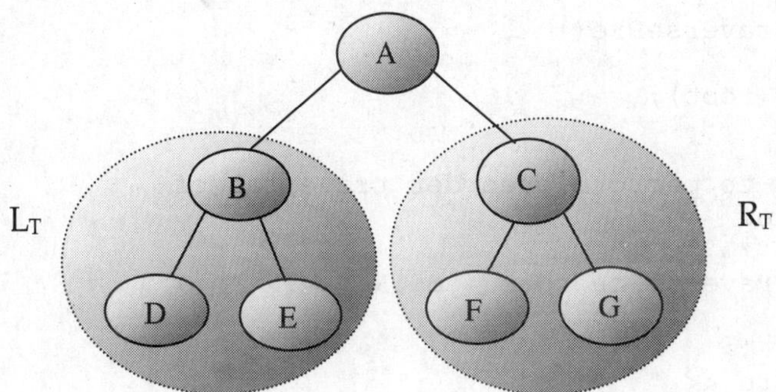

Figure 9.17: An example tree

a) The pre-order traversal of T processes A, then traverses left sub tree L_T and finally traverses right sub tree R_T. The pre-order of L_T processes its root B and then D and E. The pre-order of R_T processes its root C and then F and G.

Thus, the pre-order traversal of tree T is A B D E C F G.

b) The in-order traversal of T first traverses left sub tree L_T, then processes A and finally traverses right sub tree R_T. The in-order of L_T processes D and then B and E. The in-order of R_T processes first F then C and G.

Thus, the in-order traversal of tree T is D B E A F C G.

c) The post-order traversal of T first traverses left sub tree L_T, then traverses right sub tree R_T and finally processes A. The post-order of L_T processes D and then E and B. The post-order of R_T processes first F then G and C.

Thus, the post-order traversal of tree T is D E B F G C A.

d) The level-order traversal of T is A B C D E F G.

9.6.2.2.1 Pre-Order Traversal of a Binary (Search) Tree

The listing on the next page shows the recursive implementation of pre-order traversal algorithm.

Listing 9.2:

```
// member function to perform preorder traversal of binary
// search tree, it calls recursive function
// traversePreorder() to perform the actual traversal
template <class T>
void BSTree<T> :: traversePre()
{
   traversePreorder(root);
}

// recursive member to perform preorder traversal of
// binary search tree
template <class T>
void BSTree<T> :: traversePreorder ( BSTNode<T> *h )
{
   if ( h != NULL ) {
      cout << h->info << "  ";
      traversePreorder( h->left );
      traversePreorder( h->right );
   }
}
```

As you can see, the recursive implementation is more elegant and preferred one. However, we can also perform pre-order traversal using iterative procedure. The iterative implementation requires the explicit use of stack whose elements will be pointers of type *BSTNode*.

The following algorithm lists the various steps to be performed.

Algorithm 9.1:

PreorderTraversalIterative(***root*** **)**

Here root is a pointer variable that holds the address of the root node of the given tree. It uses a stack *s* whose elements are pointers to type *BST*. It uses a temporary pointer variable *ptr* to hold the address of current node.

```
Begin
   CreateEmptyStack(s)           // call procedure to create an empty stack
   Push( s, NULL )               // push NULL value as sentinel value
   Set ptr = root
   while ( ptr ≠ NULL ) do
      Print: ptr->info
      if ( ptr->right ≠ NULL ) then
         Push( s, ptr->right )
      endif
      if ( ptr->left ≠ NULL ) then
```

```
        Set ptr = ptr->left
    else
        Set ptr = Pop(s)      // pop value from stack and assign to ptr
    endif
  endwhile
End.
```

The implementation of the algorithm 9.1 is left as an exercise for the readers.

9.6.2.2.2 In-Order Traversal of a Binary (Search) Tree

The following listings show the recursive implementation of in-order traversal algorithm.

Listing 9.3:

```
// member function to perform inorder traversal of binary
// search tree, it calls recursive function
// traverseInorder() to perform the actual traversal
template <class T>
void BSTree<T> :: traverseIn()
{
   traverseInorder(root);
}

// recursive member to perform inorder traversal of
// binary search tree
template <class T>
void BSTree<T> :: traverseInorder  ( BSTNode<T> *h )
{
   if ( h != NULL ) {
      traverseInorder( h->left );
      cout << h->info << "  ";
      traverseInorder( h->right );
   }
}
```

Various steps required for iterative implementation of in-order traversal are shown in the following algorithm.

Algorithm 9.2:

InorderTraversalIterative(root)

Here root is a pointer variable that holds the address of the root node of the given tree. It uses a stack *s* whose elements are pointers to type *BST*. It uses a temporary pointer variable *ptr* to hold the address of current node. It also uses a flag variable *done* to control the iteration.

```
Begin
  CreateEmptyStack(s)          // call procedure to create an empty stack
  Push( s, NULL )              // push NULL value as sentinel value
  Set ptr = root
```

```
  Set done = false
  while ( not done ) do
     while ( ptr ≠ NULL ) do
        Push( s, ptr )
        Set ptr = ptr->left
     endwhile
     Set ptr = Pop(s)    // pop up value from stack and assign to ptr
     Set flag = true
     while ( ( ptr ≠ NULL ) and ( flag = true ) ) do
        Print: ptr->info
        if ( ptr->right ≠ NULL ) then
           Set ptr = ptr->right
           Set flag = false
        else
           Set ptr = Pop(s)
        endif
     endwhile
     if ( ptr  = NULL ) then
        Set done = true
     endif
  endwhile
End.
```

The implementation of the above algorithm is also left as an exercise for the readers.

9.6.2.2.3 Post-Order Traversal of a Binary (Search) Tree

The following listing shows the recursive implementation of post-order traversal algorithm.

Listing 9.4:

```
// member function to perform postorder traversal of binary
// search tree, it calls recursive function
// traversePostorder() to perform the actual traversal
template <class T>
void BSTree<T> :: traversePost()
{
   traversePostorder(root);
}
// recursive member to perform postorder traversal of
// binary search tree
template <class T>
void BSTree<T> :: traversePostorder ( BSTNode<T> *h )
{
   if ( h != NULL ) {
      traversePostorder( h->left );
      traversePostorder( h->right );
      cout << h->info << "  ";
   }
}
```

The iterative implementation of post-order traversal is bit complex as compared to pre-order and in-order traversals.

9.6.2.2.4 Level-Order Traversal of a Binary (Search) Tree

The following listing shows the implementation of level-order traversal algorithm.

Listing 9.5:

```
// member function to perform the levelorder traversal of binary
// search tree, it use linked queue
template <class T>
void BSTree<T>::levelorderTraversal()
{
   LinkQueue<BSTNode<T>*> q;
   BSTNode<T> *ptr;
   q.enqueue(root);
   while( ! q.isEmpty()  ) {
      ptr = q.dequeue();
      if ( ptr->left != NULL )
           q.enqueue(ptr->left);
      if ( ptr->right != NULL )
           q.enqueue(ptr->right);
      cout << ptr->item << "  ";
   }
}
```

In the above listing we have considered a queue named *q* represented using linked list whose implementation is given in *Chapter 7*. The elements of the queue *q* will be pointers to type *BSTNode<T>*.

Binary tree has one very interesting property – *property is that if we are given in-order traversal and either of pre-order or post-order traversals, we can construct the binary tree from these traversals.*

Example 9.6:

Consider that a binary tree T has 8 nodes. The pre-order and in-order traversals of binary tree T yield the following sequence of nodes:

Pre-order : A B D E G H C F

In-order : D B G E H A C F

Draw the binary tree T.

Solution: The binary tree T is drawn as follows:

The first node in the pre-order traversal is always a root node of the binary tree. Thus the root node of the binary tree T is node A.

After determining the root node of the binary tree, our aim is to find the nodes that comprise the left sub tree and right sub tree of node A. We know from the in-order traversal that first left sub tree is traversed, then root node, and finally the right sub tree. Thus all the nodes to the left of node A in in-order traversal comprise its left sub tree. Similarly, all the nodes to the right of node A in in-order traversal comprise its right sub tree.

The above procedure partitions the pre-order and in-order traversal sequences as shown below:

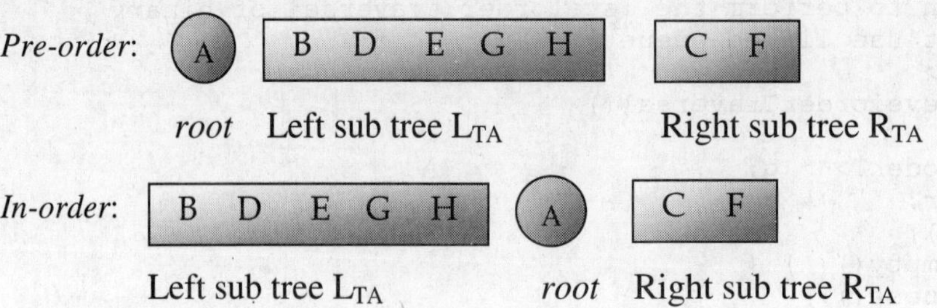

Figure 9.18 shows the partial binary tree constructed so far.

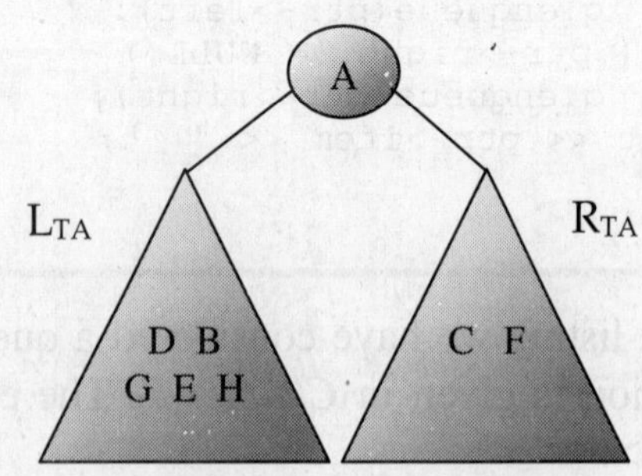

Figure 9.18

In the same way, we can construct the left sub tree L_{TA} and right sub tree R_{TB}. Let us first consider the left sub tree L_{TA}. The pre-order and in-order traversal sequences of the left sub tree L_{TA} are

Pre-order: B D E G H

In-order: D B G E H

From these traversal sequences we find that the root of the sub tree is node B, and its left sub tree consists of a single node D and the right sub tree consists of nodes G, E, and H.

The above procedure partitions the pre-order and in-order sequences as shown below:

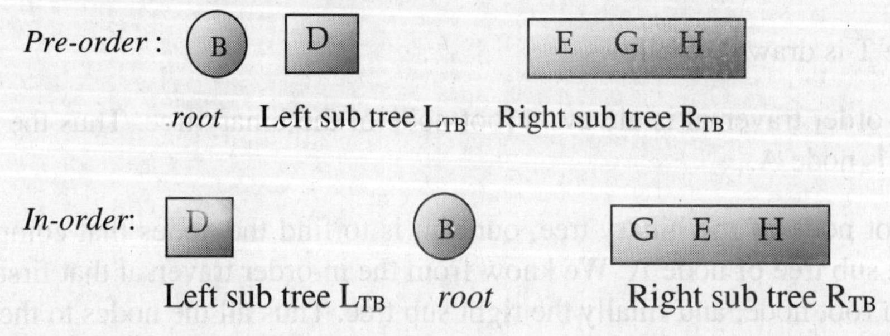

Figure 9.19 shows the partial binary tree constructed so far.

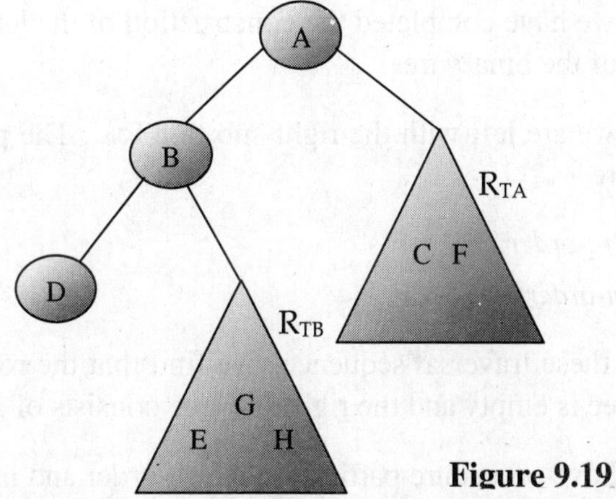

Figure 9.19

Now consider the right sub tree R_{TB}. The pre-order and in-order traversal sequences of R_{TB} are

Pre-order: E G H

In-order: G E H

From these traversal sequences we find that the root of the sub tree R_{TB} is node E, and its left sub tree consists of a single node G and the right sub tree also consists of a single node G.

The above procedure partitions the pre-order and in-order traversal sequences of R_{TB} as shown below:

Pre-order: (E) [G] [H]

root Left sub tree L_{TE} Right sub tree R_{TE}

In-order: [G] (E) [H]

Left sub tree L_{TE} *root* Right sub tree R_{TE}

Figure 9.20 shows the partial binary tree constructed so far.

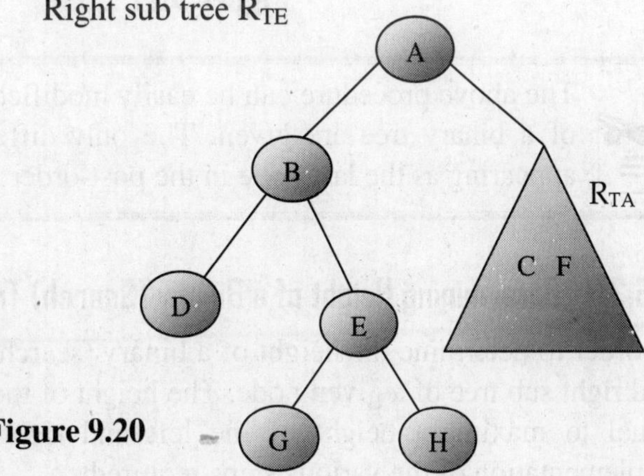

Figure 9.20

Thus we have completed the construction of the left sub tree L_{TA} of node A, which was the root node of the binary tree.

Now we are left with the right sub tree R_{TA}. The pre-order and in-order traversal sequences of R_{TA} are

Pre-order: C F

In-order: C F

From these traversal sequences we find that the root of the sub tree R_{TA} is node C, and its left sub tree is empty and the right sub tree consists of a single node F.

The above procedure partitions the pre-order and in-order traversal sequences of R_{TA} as shown:

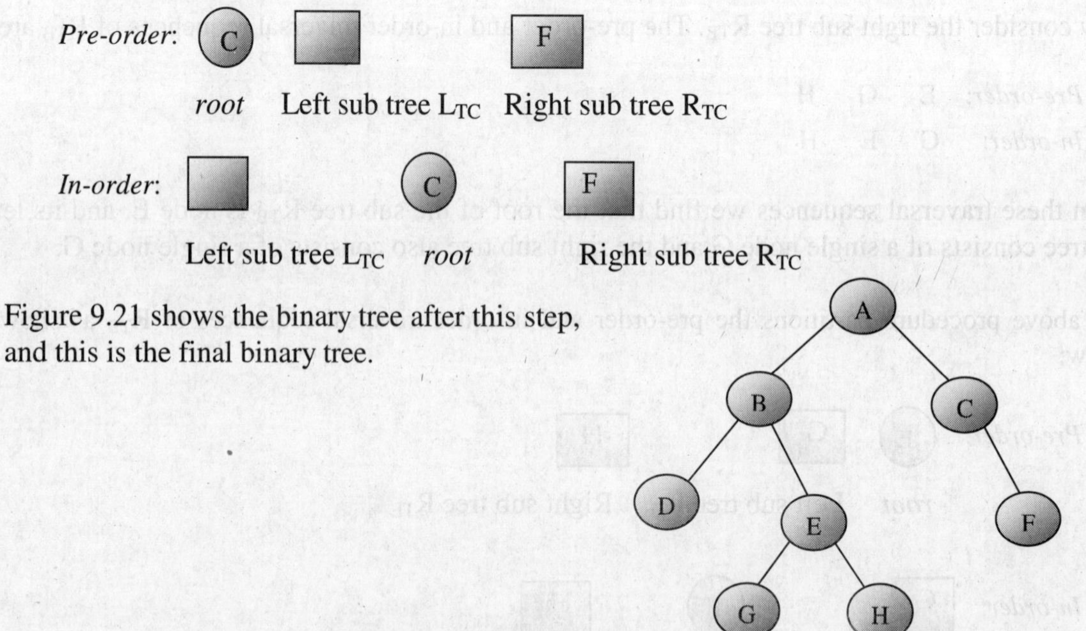

Figure 9.21 shows the binary tree after this step, and this is the final binary tree.

Figure 9.21

The above procedure can be easily modified if the in-order and the post-order traversals of a binary tree are given. The only difference is that the root of the tree will be appearing as the last node in the post-order traversal.

9.6.2.3 Determining Height of a Binary (Search) Tree

In order to determine the height of a binary (search) tree, we find the height of the left sub tree and right sub tree of a given node. The height of the binary (search) tree at a given node will be equal to maximum height of the left and right sub trees plus 1. Listing 9.6 shows the implementation of the various steps required.

Listing 9.6:

```
// member function that returns the height of the binary
// search tree, it calls recursive function findHeight()
// to actually find the height of the binary search tree
template <class T>
int BSTree<T>:: heightTree()
{
    int h;
    findHeight(root, &h);
    return h;
}
// recursive member function that returns the height of the
// binary search tree
template <class T>
void BSTree<T>:: findHeight ( BSTNode<T> *tree, int *h )
{
    int hl, hr;
    if ( tree == NULL ) {
        *h = 0;
    } else {
        findHeight ( tree->left, &hl );
        findHeight ( tree->right, &hr );
        if ( hl > hr )
        *h = hl + 1;
        else
        *h = hr + 1;
    }
}
```

In the *findHeight()* function, the height of the binary (search) tree is returned via the formal argument *h* which is a pointer to *int* type. The following listing shows another implementation to find the height of the tree.

Listing 9.7:

```
// member function that returns the height of the binary
// search tree, it calls recursive function findHeight()
// to actually find the height of the binary search tree
template <class T>
int BSTree<T>:: heightTree()
{
    return findHeight(root);
}
// recursive member function that returns the height of the
// binary search tree
template <class T>
int BSTree<T>:: findHeight ( BSTNode<T> *tree)
{
    int leftHeight, rightHeight;
    if ( tree == NULL )
        return 0;
    else
    {
        leftHeight = findHeight( tree->left );
```

```
        rightHeight = findHeight( tree->right );
        if ( leftHeight > rightHeight )
            return ++leftHeight;
        else
             return ++rightHeight;
    }
}
```

9.6.2.4 Determining Number of Nodes/Elements

Any of the traversal schemes can be used to determine the number of elements in a binary (search) tree. However, we will use a different approach. Note that the number of elements/nodes in a binary (search) tree is equal to the number of nodes in the left sub tree plus number of nodes in the right sub tree of a given node plus 1. Note that if the binary (search) tree is empty, then the number of nodes is equal to 0.

Listing 9.8 shows the implementation of the various steps required for this approach.

Listing 9.8:

```
// member function that returns the total number of nodes
// of the binary search tree, it calls recursive function
// totalNodes() to actually count the total nodes
template <class T>
int BSTree<T> :: countTotalNodes()
{
   return totalNodes(root);
}

// recursive member function that returns the total
// number of nodes in a binary search tree
template <class T>
int BSTree<T> :: totalNodes( BSTNode<T> *tree )
{
   if ( tree == NULL )
      return 0;
   else
      return (totalNodes(tree->left)+totalNodes(tree->right)+1);
}
```

9.6.2.5 Determining Number of Internal/Non-leaf Nodes

The number of internal/non-leaf nodes in a binary (search) tree is equal to the number of internal/non-leaf nodes in the left sub tree plus number of non-leaf nodes in the right sub tree of a given node plus 1. Note that if the binary (search) tree is empty or there is only one node then the number of internal/non-leaf nodes is equal to 0.

Listing 9.9 shows the implementation of the various steps required.

Listing 9.9:

```
// member function that returns the internal (non-leaf)
// nodes of the binary search tree, it calls recursive
// function internalNodes() to actually count the internal nodes
template <class T>
int BSTree<T> :: countInternalNodes() {
   return internalNodes(root);
}
// recursive member function that returns the number of
// internal (non-leaf) nodes of the binary search tree
template <class T>
int BSTree<T> :: internalNodes( BSTNode<T> *tree ) {
   if ( (tree == NULL) || ((tree->left == NULL) &&
            (tree->right == NULL) ) )
      return 0;
   else
      return ( internalNodes( tree->left ) +
               internalNodes( tree->right ) + 1);
}
```

9.6.2.6 Determining Number of External/Leaf Nodes

The number of external/leaf nodes in a tree is equal to the sum of the external/leaf nodes in the left sub tree and the external/leaf nodes in the right sub tree of a given node. Note that if the binary (search) tree is empty then the number of external/non-leaf nodes is 0 and if there is only one node in the binary (search) tree empty then the number of external/leaf nodes is equal to 1.

Listing 9.10 shows the implementation of the various steps required.

Listing 9.10:

```
// member function that returns the external (leaf) nodes
// of the binary search tree, it calls recursive
// function externalNodes() to actually count the
//external nodes
template <class T>
int BSTree<T> :: countExternalNodes() {
   return externalNodes(root);
}
// recursive member function that returns the number of
// external (leaf) nodes in a binary search tree
template <class T>
int BSTree<T> :: externalNodes( BSTNode<T> *tree ) {
   if ( tree == NULL )
      return 0;
   else if ( (tree->left == NULL )&&(tree->right == NULL ) )
      return 1;
   else
     return ( externalNodes(tree->left) + externalNodes(tree->right));
}
```

9.6.2.7 Determining Mirror Image

The mirror image of a binary (search) tree is obtained by interchanging left and right child recursively. Listing 9.11 shows the implementation of the various steps required.

Listing 9.11:

```
// member function to find the mirror image of the binary
// search tree, it calls recursive function reflect()
// to actually find the image
template <class T>
void BSTree<T>:: mirrorImage()
{
   reflect(root);
}
// recursive member function that reflects (mirror image)
// a binary search tree about an axis passing through
// its root
template <class T>
void BSTree<T>:: reflect( BSTNode<T> *tree )
{
   BSTNode<T>*  temp;
   if ( tree != NULL )
   {
      reflect( tree->left );
      reflect( tree->right );
      temp = tree->left;
      tree->left = tree->right;
      tree->right = temp;
   }
}
```

9.6.2.8 Removing Binary (Search) Tree from Memory

Before a program using binary (search) tree represented using linked representation terminates, the binary (search) tree must be removed from memory. To accomplish this task, first we delete the left sub tree and then right sub tree and then node, recursively. The following listing shows the implementation of the various steps required.

Listing 9.12:

```
// destructor, that calls recursive function deleteTree()
// to remove binary search tree from memory
~BSTree()
{
   deleteTree(&root);
}

// recursive member function to remove the binary search
// tree from memory
template <class T>
void BSTree<T>::deleteTree ( BSTNode<T> **tree )
{
```

```
    if ( *tree != NULL ) {
        deleteTree( &((*tree)->left) );
        deleteTree( &((*tree)->right) );
        delete tree;
    }
}
```

The operations discussed next are relevant to binary search trees only.

9.6.2.9 Inserting a New Element

If the binary search tree is initially empty, then the element is inserted as root node; otherwise the new element is inserted as a terminal node. If the element is less than the element in the root node, then the new element is inserted in the left sub tree else right sub tree. Listing 9.13 shows the iterative implementation of the various steps required.

Listing 9.13:

```
// iterative member function that inserts a new element into
// binary search tree
template <class T>
void BSTree<T> :: insert( BSTNode<T> **tree, T element )
{
    BSTNode<T> *ptr, *nodePtr, *parentPtr;
    ptr = new BSTNode<T>;
    ptr->info = element;
    ptr->left = ptr->right = NULL;
    if ( *tree == NULL )
        *tree = ptr;
    else
    {
        parentPtr = NULL;
        nodePtr = *tree;
         while ( nodePtr != NULL ) {
             parentPtr = nodePtr;
           if ( element < nodePtr->info )
                 nodePtr = nodePtr->left;
             else
                 nodePtr = nodePtr->right;
        }
         if ( element < parentPtr->info )
             parentPtr->left = ptr;
         else
             parentPtr->right = ptr;
    }
}
```

The recursive implementation of insert operation will look like

Listing 9.14:

```
// member function to insert an element in binary search
// tree, it calls recursive function insert() to
// actually perform the insertion
template <class T>
void BSTree<T> :: insertElement( T element )
{
    insert (&root, element);
}

// recursive member function to insert an element into
// binary search tree
template <class T>
void BSTree<T> :: insert( BSTNode<T> **h, T element )
{
    if ( *h == NULL ) {
        *h = new BSTNode<T>;
        (*h)->info = element;
        (*h)->left = (*h)->right = NULL;
    } else if ( element < (*h)->info )
        insert( &((*h)->left), element);
    else
        insert( &((*h)->right), element);
}
```

9.6.2.10 Searching an Element

The element in a binary search tree can be searched very quickly. The search operation on binary search tree is similar to applying binary search technique to a sorted linear array. The element to be searched is compared with the root node. If it matches with the root node, then search terminates here; otherwise the search is continued in the left sub tree of the node if the element is less than the root node or in the right sub tree if the element is greater than the root node. Listings 9.15 show the recursive implementation of the various steps required.

Listing 9.15:

```
// member function to search a given element, it calls
// recursive function search() to actually perform the
// search
BSTNode<T> *searchElement(T value)
{
    return searchRecursive(root, value);
}

// recursive member function to search a given element,
// it return the location of the element if present,
// else returns NULL indicating that the element is
// not present in binary search tree
BSTNode<T> *searchRecursive( BSTNode<T> *tree, T value )
{
    if ( ( tree->info == value ) || ( tree == NULL ) )
```

```
      return tree;
   else if ( value < tree->info )
      return searchRecursive( tree->left, value );
   else
      return searchRecursive( tree->right, value );
}
```

The iterative implementation of search operations is left as an exercise for the readers.

9.6.2.11 Finding Smallest Node

Because of the order property of binary search tree, we know that the smallest node in the tree will be one of the nodes in the left sub tree, if it exists; otherwise the node itself will be the smallest node. The following listings show the recursive implementation of the various steps required. Its iterative implementation is left as an exercise for the readers.

Listing 9.16:

```
// member function that returns the location of the smallest
// element of the binary search tree, it calls recursive
// function findMinimum() to find the snallest element
template <class T>
BSTNode<T>* BSTree<T> :: findSmallest()
{
   return findMinimum(root);
}
// recursive member function that returns the location of
// the smallest element of the binary search tree.
// It returns NULL if tree is empty a given element or
// it has no left child
template <class T>
BSTNode<T>* BSTree<T> :: findMinimum  ( BSTNode<T> *t )
{
   if ( ( t == NULL ) || ( t->left == NULL ) )
      return t;
   else
      return findMinimum (t->left);
}
```

9.6.2.12 Finding Largest Node

Because of the order property of BST, we know that the largest node in the tree will be one of the nodes in the right sub tree if it exists otherwise the node itself will be the largest node. The following listings show the recursive implementation of the various steps required. Its iterative implementation is left as an exercise for the readers.

Listing 9.17:

```
// member function that returns the location of the largest
// element of the binary search tree, it calls recursive
// function findMaximum() to find the largest element
template <class T>
```

```
BSTNode<T>* BSTree<T> :: findLargest()
{
   return findMaximum(root);
}

// recursive member function that returns the location
// of the largest element of the binary search tree.
// It returns NULL if tree is empty a given element or
// it has no right child
template <class T>
BSTNode<T>* BSTree<T>::findMaximum(BSTNode<T> *t)
{
   if ( ( t == NULL ) || ( t->right == NULL ) )
      return t;
   else
      return findMaximum(t->right);
}
```

9.6.2.13 Deleting a Node

To delete a node, the following possibilities may arise:

- ***node is terminal node*** — in this case, if the node is left child of its parent, then the left pointer of its parent is set to NULL otherwise it will be right child of its parent and accordingly the pointer of its parent is set to NULL.
- ***node having only one child*** — in this case, the appropriate pointer of its parent is set to its child, thus by passing it.
- ***node having two children*** — there are variety of ways in which this case can be handled. We will consider the way where its predecessor replaces the node value, and then the predecessor of the node is deleted.

Combining these three cases, the entire procedure for deleting a node can be implemented recursively as shown in the following listing.

Listing 9.18:

```
// member function to delete a given element from binary
// search tree, it calls recursive function deleteNode()
// to actually delete the element from binary search tree
template <class T>
void BSTree<T>::deleteElement(T element)
{
   deleteEle(&root,element);
}

// recursive member function that delete an element from
// binary search tree. It calls recursive member function to
// search the element to be deleted
template <class T>
void BSTree<T>::deleteNode(BSTNode<T> **tree, T element)
{
   BSTNode<T> *temp;
```

```
   if ( *tree == NULL )
   {
      cout << endl
           << "Element " << element << " not found in BST"
           << endl;
   } else if ( element < (*tree)->info )
      deleteNode( &((*tree)->left), element );
   else if ( element > (*tree)->info )
      deleteNode( &((*tree)->right), element );
   else if ( (*tree)->left && (*tree)->right ) {
      temp = findMaximum ( (*tree)->left );
      (*tree)->info = temp->info;
      deleteNode( &((*tree)->left), temp->info );
   } else {
      temp = *tree;
      if (((*tree)->left==NULL)&&((*tree)->right==NULL))
    *tree = NULL;
      else if ( (*tree)->right == NULL )
    *tree = (*tree)->left;
      else
    *tree = (*tree)->right;
      delete temp;
   }
}
```

From this onward, we will assume that the entire code of the class for implementing a binary search tree is stored in disk file named *btree.h*.

Listing 9.19:

```
// Program to illustrate the implementation of Binary Search Tree

#include <iostream.h>
#include <iomanip.h>
#include <stdlib.h>
#include "btree.h"

void main()
{
   int choice, element;
   BSTNode<int> *loc;
   BSTree<int> tree;
   while ( 1 )
   {
      cout <<  "\n\n     Options available \n" ;
      cout <<  "++++++++++++++++++++++++++++++++ \n\n" ;
      cout <<  "    1. Insert node\n" ;
      cout <<  "    2. Pre-order traversal\n" ;
      cout <<  "    3. In-order traversal\n" ;
      cout <<  "    4. Post-order traversal\n" ;
      cout <<  "    5. Level-order traversal\n" ;
      cout <<  "    6. Delete node\n" ;
      cout <<  "    7. Total nodes\n" ;
      cout <<  "    8. Total external nodes\n" ;
      cout <<  "    9. Total internal nodes\n" ;
      cout <<  "   10. Find height\n" ;
      cout <<  "   11. Smallest node\n" ;
```

```
    cout <<  "  12. Largest node\n" ;
    cout <<  "  13. Mirror Image\n" ;
    cout <<  "  14. Exit\n\n";
    cout << "Enter your choice ( 1-14 ) : " ;
    cin >> choice;

    switch ( choice )
    {
       case 1 : cout << "\nElement to be inserted into tree : ";
                cin >> element;
                tree.insertElement(element);
                break;
       case 2 : cout << "\nPre-order Traversal of BST is\n" ;
                tree.traversePre();
                break;
       case 3 : cout << "\nIn-order Traversal of BST is\n" ;
                tree.traverseIn();
                break;
       case 4 : cout << "\nPost-order Traversal of BST is\n";
                tree.traversePost();
                break;
       case 5 : cout << "\nLevel-order Traversal of BST is\n";
                tree.levelorderTraverse();
                break;
       case 6 : cout << "\nElement to delete from tree : ";
                cin >> element;
                tree.deleteElement(element);
                break;
       case 7 : cout << "\nNumber of nodes in BST = "
                     << tree.countTotalNodes();
                break;
       case 8 : cout << "\nNumber of leaf nodes in BST = "
                     << tree.countExternalNodes();
                break;
       case 9 : cout << "\nNumber of non-leaf nodes in BST = "
                     << tree.countInternalNodes();
                break;
       case 10: cout <<  "\nHeight of BST = " <<
                tree.heightTree();
                break;
       case 11: loc = tree.findSmallest();
                cout <<  "\nSmallest node in tree = " << loc->info ;
                break;
       case 12: loc = tree.findLargest();
                cout <<  "\nLargest node in tree = " << loc->info ;
                break;
       case 13: tree.mirrorImage();
                break;
       case 14: return;
    }
  }
}
```

9.7 AVL TREES

We can guarantee $O(\log_2 n)$ performance for each search tree operation by ensuring that the search tree height is always $O(\log_2 n)$. Trees with a worst-case height of $O(\log_2 n)$ are called *balanced trees*. One of the popular balanced trees is *AVL tree*, which was introduced by *Adelson-Velskii* and *Landis*.

If T is a nonempty binary tree with T_L and T_R as its left and right sub tree, then T is an AVL tree if and only if

1. $|h_L - h_R| \le 1$, where h_L and h_R are the heights of T_L and T_R, respectively, and
2. T_L and T_R are AVL trees.

An AVL search tree is a binary search tree that is also an AVL tree. The height of an empty (null) AVL tree is taken as -1.

9.7.1 Representation of an AVL Tree

The node in an AVL tree will have an additional field *bf* (for balance factor) in addition to the structure of a node in a binary search tree.

Suppose that the elements of the AVL tree can be any primitive type or pointer type, the following is the required ADT to represent an AVL tree:

```
// class definition to represent a node of AVL tree
template <class T>
class AVLNode {
   public:
      AVLNode *left;
      T info;
      int bf;
      AVLNode *right;
};

// class definition for AVL tree
template <class T>
class AVLTree {
   private:
      AVLNode<T> *root;

   public:
      // member functions
}; // -------- End of AVLTree class --------
```

The value for field *bf* will be chosen as

$$bf = \begin{cases} -1 & \text{if } h_L < h_R \\ 0 & \text{if } h_L = h_R \\ +1 & \text{if } h_L > h_R \end{cases}$$

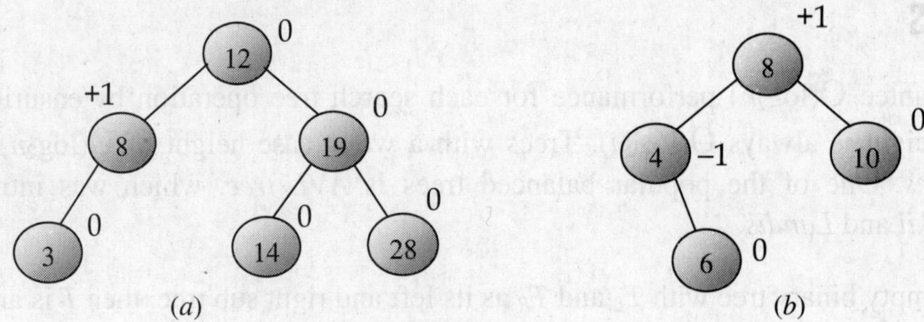

Figure 9.22: AVL trees

9.7.2 Height of an AVL Tree

Let N_h be the minimum number of nodes in an AVL tree of height h. In the worst case, the height of one of the sub trees is $h-1$, and the height of the other is $h-2$. Both these sub trees are also AVL trees. Hence

$$N_h = N_{h-1} + N_{h-2} + 1, \quad N_0 = 0, \text{ and } N_1 = 1$$

Notice the similarity between the definition for N_h and the definition of the Fibbonacci numbers

$$F_n = F_{n-1} + F_{n-2}, \quad F_0 = 0, \text{ and } F_1 = 1$$

It can be shown that $N_h = F_{h+2} - 1$ for $h \geq 0$. Fibbonacci number theory, we know that $F_h \approx \phi^h / \sqrt{5}$, where $\phi = (1+\sqrt{5})/2$. Hence, $N_h \approx \phi^{h+2} / \sqrt{5} - 1$. If there are n nodes in the tree, then its height h is at most $\log_\phi(\sqrt{5}(n+1) - 2 \approx 1.44\log_2(n+2) = O(\log_2 n)$.

If an insertion and deletion causes an AVL tree to become unbalanced, then the tree must be restructured to return it to a balanced state.

9.7.3 Operations on an AVL Tree

The operations on AVL tree that differ from a binary search tree are insertion and deletion only. These operations can disturb the balance property of an AVL tree. These operations are considered next.

9.7.3.1 Insertion of a Node

The new node is inserted using the usual binary search tree insert procedure i.e. comparing the key of the new node with that in the root, and inserting the new node into the left or right sub tree as appropriate. In some cases this insertion may not change the height of the sub tree, in which case neither the height nor the balance factor at the root will be changed. Even if it increases the height of the sub tree, there may be the case that this sub tree was shorter earlier, thus only the balance factor at the root will change where as the height of the tree remains unchanged. The only case that causes problems occurs when the node is inserted in a sub tree that is taller than the other sub tree. This would cause one sub tree to have height more by a factor of 2 than the other sub tree whereas the AVL condition does not permit a difference of more than 1.

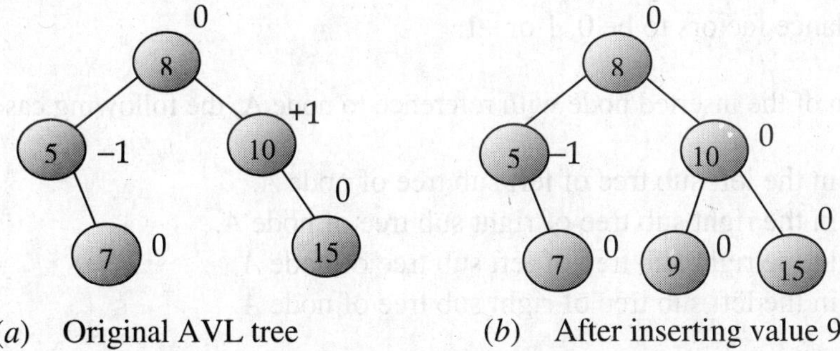

(*a*) Original AVL tree (*b*) After inserting value 9

Figure 9.23: Neither the balance factor of the root nor the height of the AVL tree is affected.

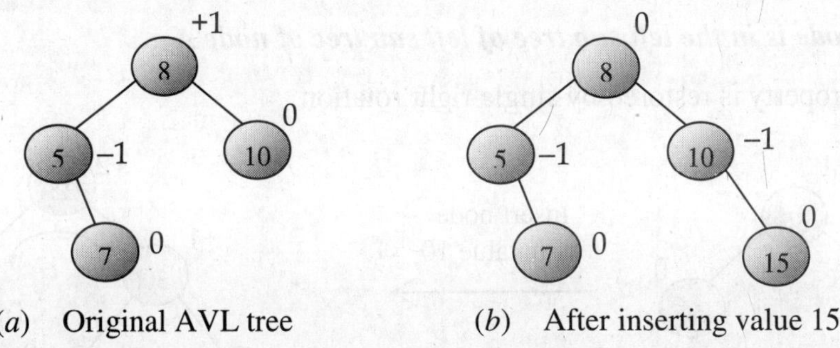

(*a*) Original AVL tree (*b*) After inserting value 15

Figure 9.24: Height remains unchanged but the balance factor of the root gets changed.

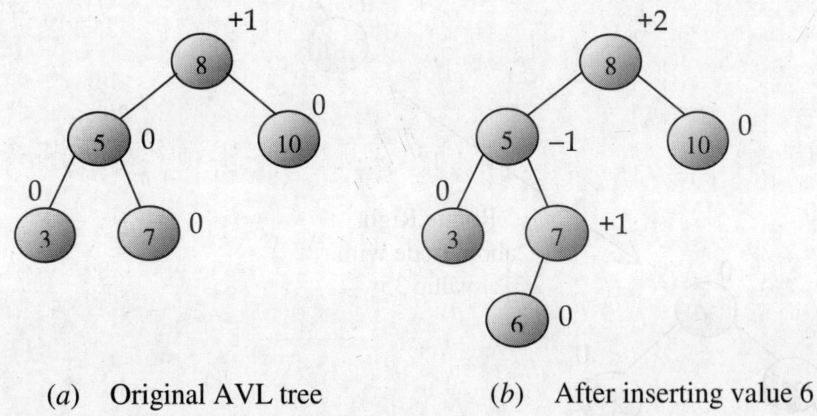

(*a*) Original AVL tree (*b*) After inserting value 6

Figure 9.25: Height as well as balance factor gets changed. It needs re-balancing about root node.

In order to restore the balance property, we use the tree rotations, which are described, in the next section.

To perform rotation it is necessary to identify a specific node, say node *A*, whose balance factor is neither 0, 1 or −1, and is the nearest ancestor to the inserted node on the path from the inserted node to the root. This implies that all nodes on the path from the inserted node to node *A* will have their balance factors to be 0, 1 or −1.

Based on the position of the inserted node with reference to node A, the following cases will arise:

- Inserted node is in the left sub tree of left sub tree of node *A*.
- Inserted node is in the right sub tree of right sub tree of node *A*.
- Inserted node is in the right sub tree of left sub tree of node *A*.
- Inserted node is in the left sub tree of right sub tree of node *A*.

These cases are demonstrated below through examples.

Case I: *Inserted node is in the left sub tree of left sub tree of node A*

Here the balance property is restored by single right rotation.

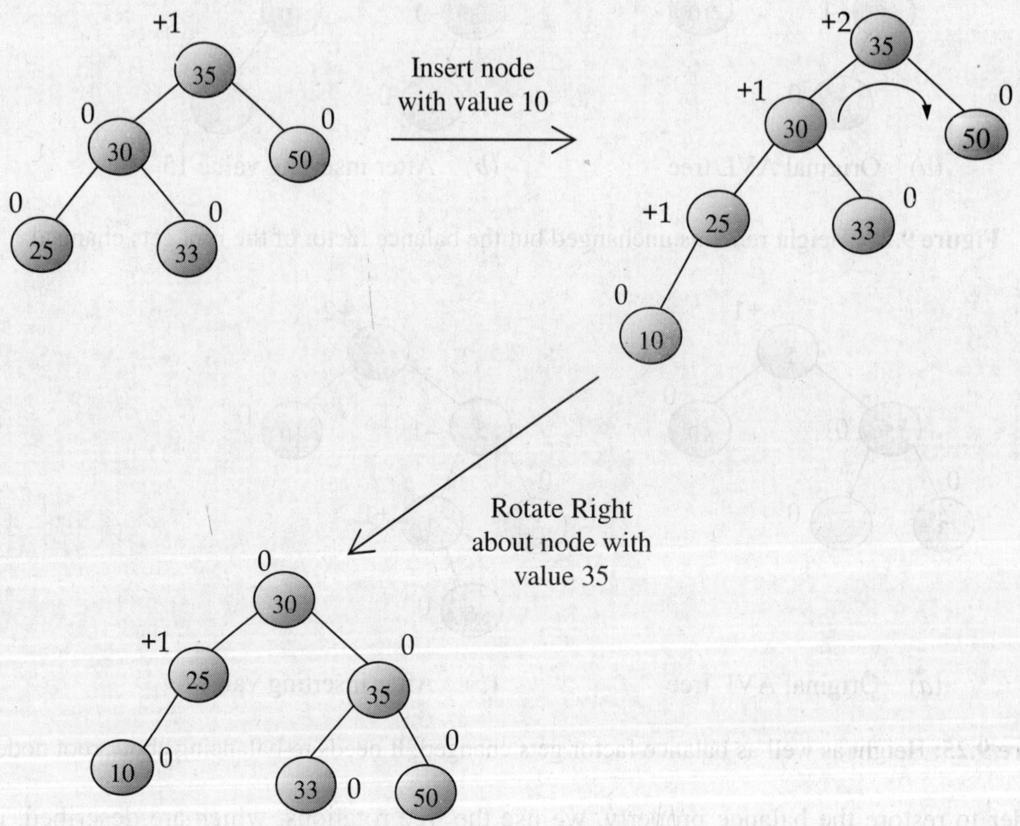

Figure 9.26: Restoring balance by right rotation

Case II: ***Inserted node is in the right sub tree of right sub tree of node A***

Here the balance property is restored by single left rotation.

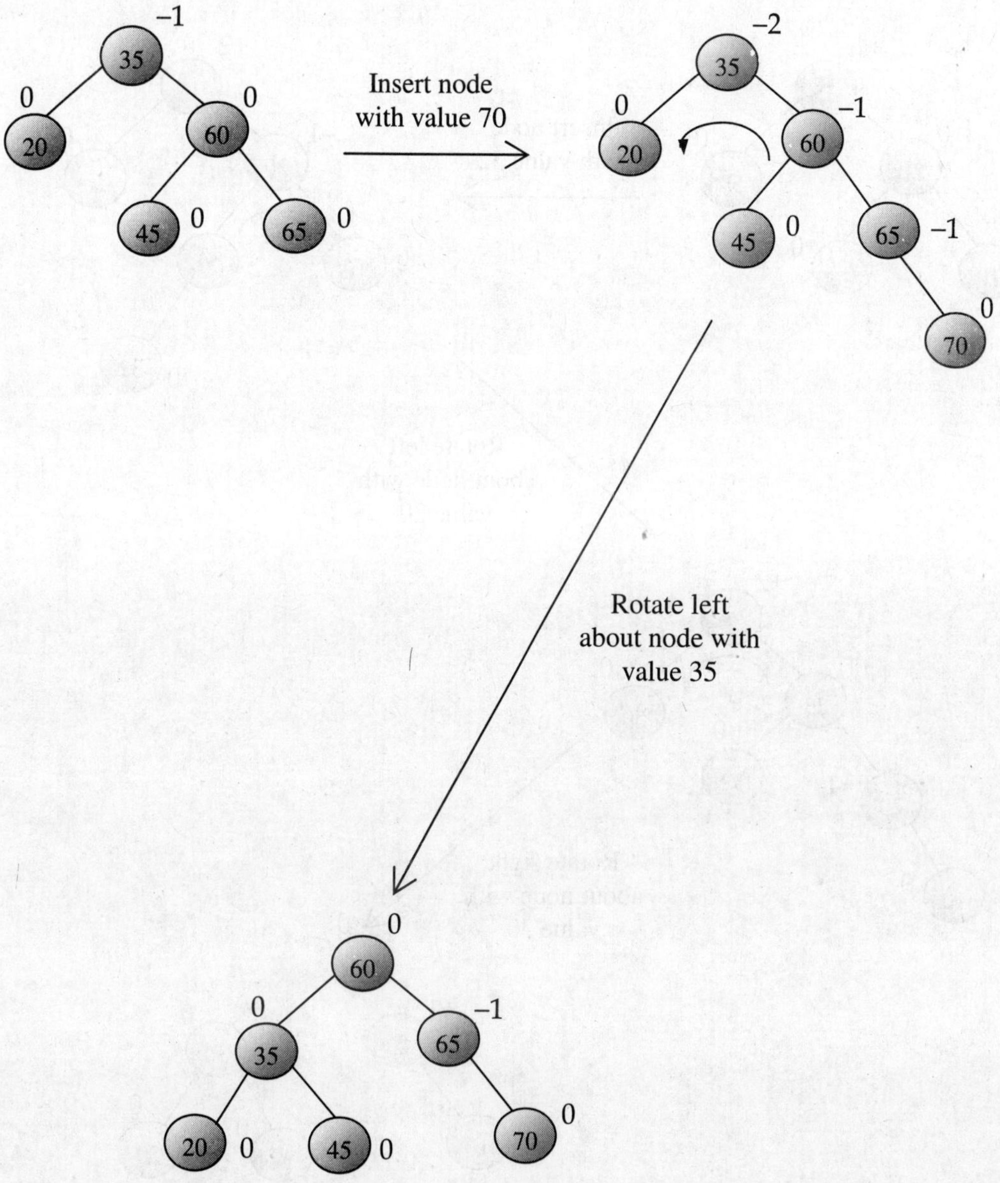

Figure 9.27: Restoring balance by left rotation

Case III: ***Inserted node is in the right sub tree of left sub tree of node A***

Here the balance property is restored by double rotation - left rotation followed by the right rotation.

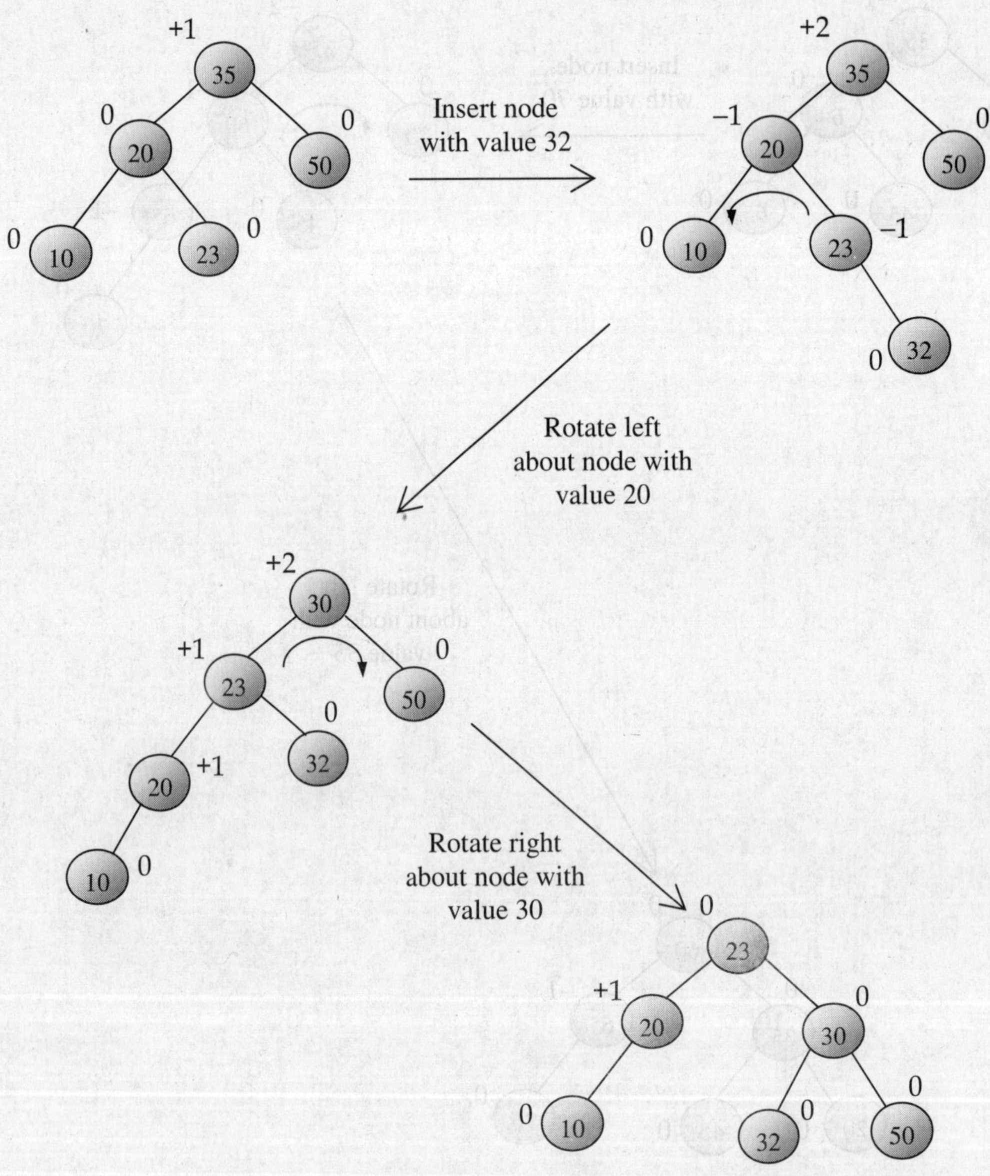

Figure 9.28: Restoring balance by double rotation (left rotation followed by right rotation)

Case IV: ***Inserted node is in the left sub tree of right sub tree of node A***

Here the balance property is restored by double rotation - right rotation followed by the left rotation.

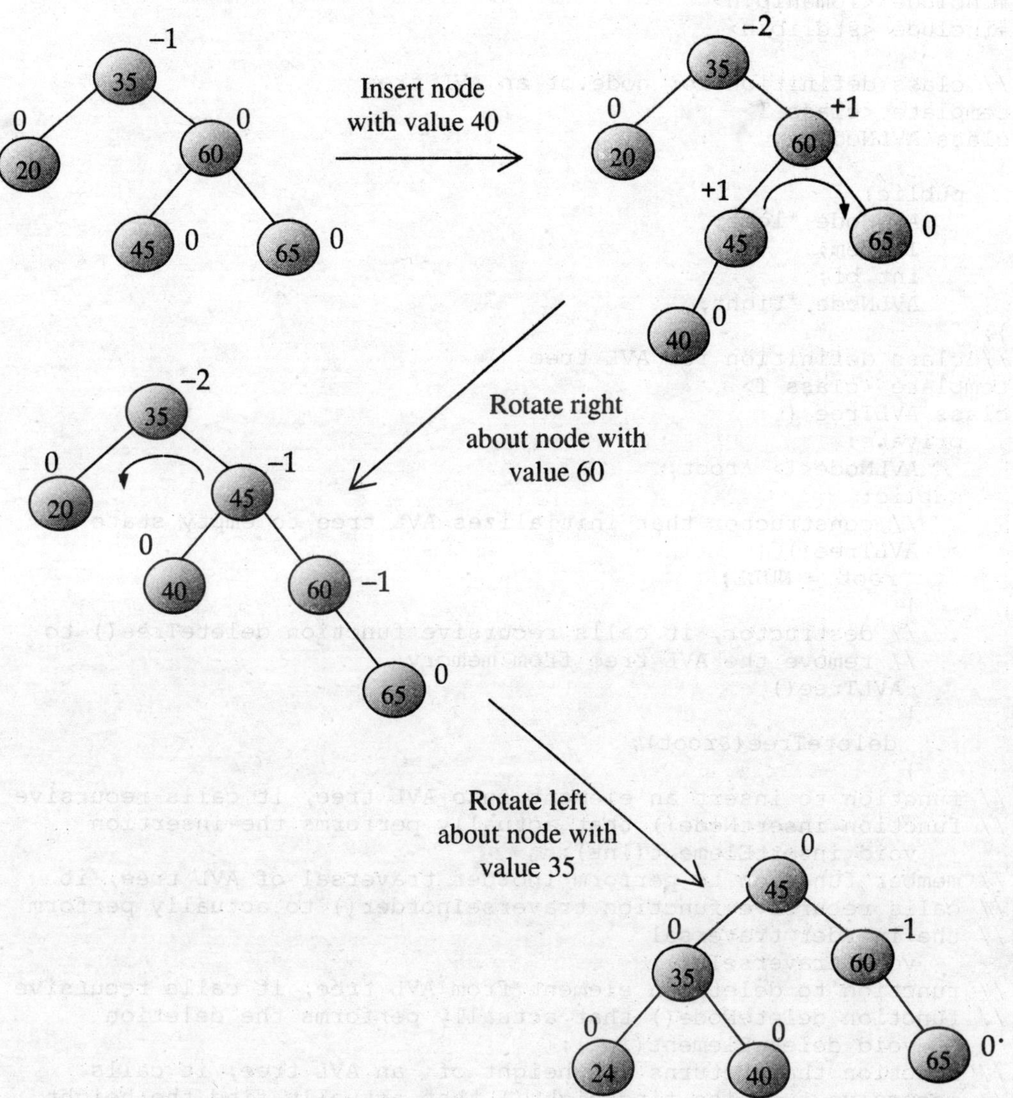

Figure 9.29: Restoring balance by double rotation (right rotation followed by left rotation)

9.7.3.2 Deletion of a Node

Deletion of a node from an *AVL* tree requires the same basic ideas including single and double rotations, which are used for insertion.

Listing 9.20

```
// Program to illustrate the implementation of AVL Tree
#include <iostream.h>
#include <iomanip.h>
#include <stdlib.h>

// class definition for node of an AVL tree
template <class T>
class AVLNode
{
   public:
      AVLNode *left;
      T item;
      int bf;
      AVLNode *right;
};
// class definition for AVL tree
template <class T>
class AVLTree {
   private:
      AVLNode<T> *root;
   public:
      // constructor that initializes AVL tree to empty state
      AVLTree() {
       root = NULL;
      }
      // destructor, it calls recursive function deleteTree() to
      // remove the AVL tree from memory
      ~AVLTree()
      {
       deleteTree(&root);
      }
// function to insert an element into AVL tree, it calls recursive
// function insertNode() that actually performs the insertion
      void insertElement(int);
// member function to perform inorder traversal of AVL tree, it
// calls recursive function traverseInorder() to actually perform
// the inorder traversal
      void traverseIn();
// function to delete an element from AVL tree, it calls recursive
// function deleteNode() that actually performs the deletion
      void deleteElement(int);
// function that returns the height of  an AVL tree, it calls
// recursive function findheight() that actually find the height
// of the AVL tree
      int heightTree();

      // ------ RECURSIVE MEMBER FUNCTIONS -------

// recursive function that inserts a new element into AVL tree,
// and readjusts it with suitable rotations so that it remains
// AVL tree after insertion
      static void insertNode(AVLNode<T> **, int);
// recursive function that performs inorder traversal
// of AVL tree
      static void traverseInorder(AVLNode<T> *);
```

```
// recursive function that return the largest element in AVL tree
     static AVLNode<T> *findMaximum(AVLNode<T> *);
// recursive function that deletes given element from AVL tree
     static void deleteNode(AVLNode<T> **, int);
// recursive function that removes AVL tree from memory
     static void deleteTree(AVLNode<T> **);
// recursive function that find the height of the AVL tree
     static void findHeight(AVLNode<T> *, int *);
};

// function to insert an element into AVL tree, it calls recursive
// function insertNode() that actually performs the insertion
template <class T>
void AVLTree<T> :: insertElement( T element ) {
   insertNode (&root, element);
}
// recursive function that inserts a new element into AVL tree, and
// readjusts it with suitable rotations so that it remains
// AVL tree after insertion
template <class T>
void AVLTree<T> :: insertNode( AVLNode<T> **h, int element ) {
   AVLNode<T> *ptr1, *ptr2;
   if ( *h == NULL ) {
      *h = new AVLNode<T>;
      (*h)->item = element;
      (*h)->left = (*h)->right = NULL;
      (*h)->bf = 0;

   } else if ( element < (*h)->item ) {
      insertNode( &((*h)->left), element);
      switch ( (*h)->bf )
      {
        case 1: ptr1 = (*h)->left;
                if ( ptr1->bf == 1 ) {
                   (*h)->left = ptr1->right;     // right rotation
                   ptr1->right = *h;
                   (*h)->bf = 0;
                   *h = ptr1;
                } else {
                   ptr2 = ptr1->right;  // double rotation, left-right
                   ptr1->right = ptr2->left;
                   ptr2->left = ptr1;
                   (*h)->left = ptr2->right;
                   ptr2->right = *h;

                   (*h)->bf = ptr2->bf == 1 ? -1 : 0;
                   ptr1->bf = ptr2->bf == -1 ? 1 : 0;

                   *h = ptr2;
                }
                break;
        case 0: (*h)->bf = 1;
                break;
        case -1: (*h)->bf = 0;
      }
   } else {
```

```
      insertNode( &((*h)->right), element);
      switch ( (*h)->bf )
      {
         case 1: (*h)->bf = 0;
               break;
         case 0: (*h)->bf = -1;
               break;
         case -1: ptr1 = (*h)->right;
                if ( ptr1->bf == -1 ) {
                   (*h)->right = ptr1->left;      // left rotation
                   ptr1->left = *h;
                   (*h)->bf = 0;
                   *h = ptr1;
                } else {
                   ptr2 = ptr1->left; // double rotation, right-left
                   ptr1->left = ptr2->right;
                   ptr2->right = ptr1;
                   (*h)->right = ptr2->left;
                   ptr2->left = *h;

                   (*h)->bf = ptr2->bf == -1 ? 1 : 0;
                   ptr1->bf = ptr2->bf == 1 ? -1 : 0;

                   *h = ptr2;
                }
                break;
      }
   }
}
// member function to perform inorder traversal of AVL tree, it calls
// recursive function traverseInorder() to actually perform the
// inorder traversal
template <class T>
void AVLTree<T> :: traverseIn()
{
   traverseInorder(root);
}
// recursive function that performs inorder traversal of AVL tree
template <class T>
void AVLTree<T> :: traverseInorder ( AVLNode<T> *h ) {
   if ( h != NULL ) {
      traverseInorder( h->left );
      cout << h->item << "  ";
      traverseInorder( h->right );
   }
}
// recursive function that return the largest element in AVL tree
template <class T>
AVLNode<T>* AVLTree<T>::findMaximum(AVLNode<T> *t) {
   if ( ( t == NULL ) || ( t->right == NULL ) )
      return t;
   else
      return findMaximum(t->right);
}
// function to delete an element from AVL tree, it calls recursive
// function deleteNode() that actually performs the deletion
template <class T>
```

```
void AVLTree<T>::deleteElement(T element) {
   deleteNode(&root,element);
}
// recursive function that deletes given element from AVL tree
template <class T>
void AVLTree<T>::deleteNode (AVLNode<T> **h, T element) {
   AVLNode<T> *temp, *ptr1, *ptr2;
   if ( *h == NULL ) {
      cout << endl
         << "Element " << element << " not found in AVL Tree";
      cout << endl
         << "Press any key to continue ...";
      getch();
   } else if ( element < (*h)->item ) {
      deleteNode( &((*h)->left), element );
      switch ( (*h)->bf )
      {
        case 1: (*h)->bf = 0;
                break;
        case 0: (*h)->bf = -1;
                break;
        case -1: ptr1 = (*h)->right;
                 if ( ptr1->bf == -1 ) {
                    (*h)->right = ptr1->left;      // left rotation
                    ptr1->left = *h;
                    (*h)->bf = 0;
                    *h = ptr1;
                 } else {
                    ptr2 = ptr1->left; // double rotation, right-left
                    ptr1->left = ptr2->right;
                    ptr2->right = ptr1;
                    (*h)->right = ptr2->left;
                    ptr2->left = *h;

                    (*h)->bf = ptr2->bf == -1 ? 1 : 0;
                    ptr1->bf = ptr2->bf == 1 ? -1 : 0;

                    *h = ptr2;
                 }
      }
   } else if ( element > (*h)->item ) {
      deleteNode( &((*h)->right), element );
      switch ( (*h)->bf )
      {
        case 1: ptr1 = (*h)->left;
                if ( ptr1->bf == 1 ) {
                   (*h)->left = ptr1->right;      // right rotation
                   ptr1->right = *h;
                   (*h)->bf = 0;
                   *h = ptr1;
                } else {
                   ptr2 = ptr1->right;  // double rotation, left-right
                   ptr1->right = ptr2->left;
                   ptr2->left = ptr1;
                   (*h)->left = ptr2->right;
                   ptr2->right = *h;
                   (*h)->bf = ptr2->bf == 1 ? -1 : 0;
```

```
                ptr1->bf = ptr2->bf == -1 ? 1 : 0;

                *h = ptr2;
              }
              break;
       case 0: (*h)->bf = 1;
              break;
       case -1: (*h)->bf = 0;
     }
   } else if ( (*h)->left && (*h)->right ) {
     temp = findMaximum ( (*h)->left );            // find predecessor
     (*h)->item = temp->item;    // replace node by predecessor
     deleteNode( &((*h)->left), temp->item );  // delete predecessor
   } else {
     temp = *h;
     if (((*h)->left==NULL)&&((*h)->right==NULL)) // terminal node
       *h = NULL;
     else if ( (*h)->right == NULL ) // left child only
       *h = (*h)->left;
     else                                    // right child only
       *h = (*h)->right;
     delete temp;
   }
}
// function that returns the height of  an AVL tree, it calls
// recursive function findheight() that actually find the height
// of the AVL tree
template <class T>
int AVLTree<T>:: heightTree() {
   int h;
   findHeight(root, &h);
   return h;
}
// recursive function to find the height of the AVL tree
template <class T>
void AVLTree<T>:: findHeight ( AVLNode<T> *tree, int *h ) {
   int hl, hr;
   if ( tree == NULL ) {
      *h = 0;
   } else {
      findHeight ( tree->left, &hl );
      findHeight ( tree->right, &hr );
      if ( hl > hr )
       *h = hl + 1;
      else
       *h = hr + 1;
   }
}
// recursive function that removes AVL tree from memory
template <class T>
void AVLTree<T>::deleteTree ( AVLNode<T> **tree ) {
   if ( *tree != NULL ) {
      deleteTree( &((*tree)->left) );
      deleteTree( &((*tree)->right) );
      delete tree;
   }
}
```

```
void main()        // ------- main function -------
{
   int choice, element;
   AVLNode<int> *loc;
   AVLTree<int> tree;
   while ( 1 )
   {
      cout << "\n\n    Options available \n" ;
      cout << "++++++++++++++++++++++++++++++ \n\n" ;
      cout << "    1. Insert node\n" ;
      cout << "    2. In-order traversal\n" ;
      cout << "    3. Delete node\n" ;
      cout << "    4. Find height\n" ;
      cout << "    5. Exit\n\n";
      cout << "Enter your choice ( 1-5 ) : " ;
      cin >> choice;
      switch ( choice )
      {
         case 1 : cout << "\n\nElement to be inserted into tree : ";
                  cin >> element;
                  tree.insertElement(element);
                  break;
         case 2 : cout  << "\n\nIn-order Traversal of AVLT is\n" ;
                  tree.traverseIn();
                  break;
         case 3 : cout << "Element to delete from tree : ";
                  cin >> element;
                  tree.deleteElement(element);
                  break;
         case 4 : cout <<  "\n\nHeight of AVL Tree = " <<
                  tree.heightTree() ;
                  break;
         case 5 : return;
      }
   }
}
```

9.8 THREADED BINARY TREES

On carefully examining the linked representation of a binary tree *T*, you will find that approximately half of the pointer fields (*left* and *right* pointer fields that hold the address of the left child and right child, respectively) contain NULL entries (pictured as X) in these fields. The space occupied by these NULL entries can be utilized to store some kind of valuable information.

One possible way to utilize this space is that we can store special pointer that point to nodes higher in the tree, *i.e.*, ancestors. These special pointers are called *threads*, and the binary tree having such pointers is called *a threaded binary tree*.

Threads in a binary tree must be distinguished from normal pointers. In the graphical representation of a threaded binary tree, the threads are shown by dotted lines. In computer memory, an extra field, called *tag* or *flag* is used to distinguish a thread from a normal pointer.

There are many ways to thread a binary tree. These are

- The right NULL pointer of each node can be replaced by a thread to the successor of that node under in-order traversal called a *right thread*, and the tree will be called a *right-threaded tree*.
- The left NULL pointer of each node can be replaced by a thread to the predecessor of that node under in-order traversal called a *left thread*, and the tree will be called a *left-threaded tree*.
- Both left and right NULL pointers can be used to point to predecessor and successor of that node, respectively, under in-order traversal. Such a tree is called a *fully threaded tree*.

A threaded binary tree where only one thread is used is also known as *one-way* threaded tree and where both the threads are used is also known as *two-way* threaded tree.

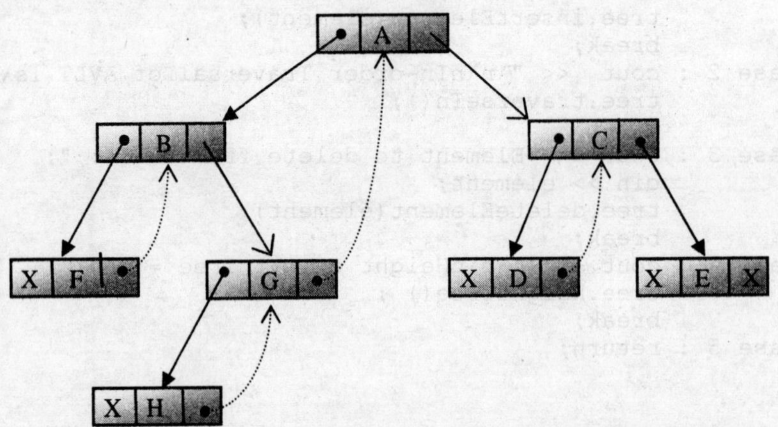

Figure 9.30: Right-threaded binary tree (*one-way threading*)

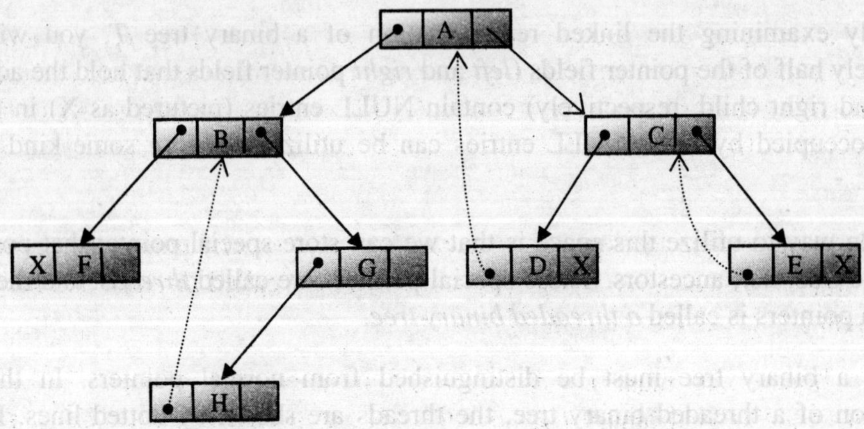

Figure 9.31: Left-threaded binary tree (*one-way threaded*)

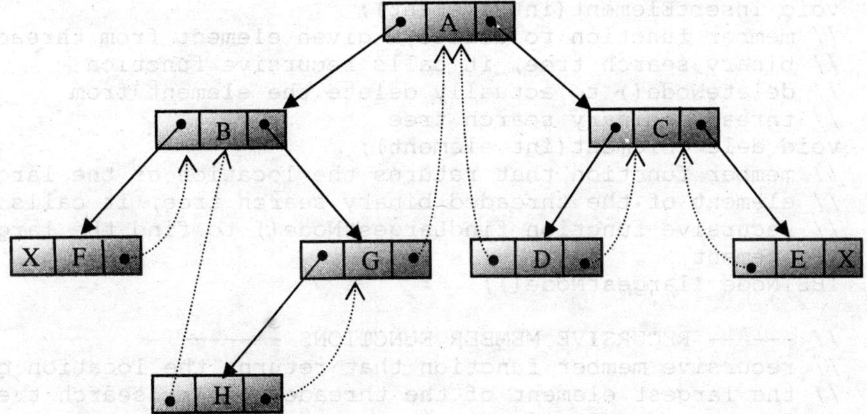

Figure 9.32: A fully threaded binary tree (*two-way threading*)

We will discuss the representation of right-threaded binary and the some operations that differ from a non-threaded binary tree (insertion, deletion, traversal, removal).

9.8.1 Representing a Threaded Binary Tree in Memory

To represent the above threaded binary tree, we need following kind of representation for the node

```
class TBSTNode
{
   public:
      int info;
      char thread;
      struct TBSTNode *left;
      struct TBSTNode *right;
};
class ThreadedBST
{
   protected:
      TBSTNode *root;
   public:
      // constructor to initialize threaded binary search tree
      // to empty state
      ThreadedBST()
      {
         root = NULL;
      }
      // destructor, that calls recursive function removeTBSTree()
      // to remove binary search tree from memory
      ~ThreadedBST()
      {
         removeTBSTree(&root);
      }
      // member function to perform inorder traversal of
      // threaded binary search tree
      void inorderTraversal();
      // member function to insert an element in threaded
      // binary search tree
```

```
        void insertElement(int element);
        // member function to delete a given element from threaded
        // binary search tree, it calls recursive function
        // deleteNode() to actually delete the element from
        // threaded binary search tree
        void deleteElement(int element);
        // member function that returns the location of the largest
        // element of the threaded binary search tree, it calls
        // recursive function findLargestNode() to find the largest
        // element
        TBSTNode *largestNode();

        // ------ RECURSIVE MEMBER FUNCTIONS -------
        // recursive member function that returns the location of
        // the largest element of the threaded binary search tree.
        // It returns NULL if tree is empty a given element.
        static TBSTNode *findLargestNode(TBSTNode *ptr);
        // recursive member function to delete a node containing
        // the given element from threaded binary search tree
        static void deleteNode(TBSTNode **ptr, int element);
        // recursive member function to remove a threaded
        // binary search tree from memory
        static void removeTBSTree( TBSTNode **tree );
};
```

In this representation, we have used *char* field *thread* as a tag. The character '0' will used for normal right pointer and character '1' will be used for thread.

9.8.2 Operations on a Threaded Binary Tree

The only operations that differ from a binary search tree are traversal, insertion of a new element, deletion of an element and deletion of the tree itself. These operations are described in the next section.

9.8.2.1 In-order Traversal of Threaded Binary Tree

Using the above representation, the iterative version of the in-order traversal can be expressed as shown in the following code.

Listing 9.21:

```
// member function to perform inorder traversal of
// threaded binary search tree
void ThreadedBST::inorderTraversal()
{
   TBSTNode *pPtr, *qPtr;
   pPtr = root;
   do
   {
      qPtr = NULL;
      while ( pPtr != NULL )   //  traverse left branch
      {
         qPtr = pPtr;
         pPtr = pPtr->left;
      }
```

```
        if ( qPtr != NULL )        //   tree is not empty
        {
            cout << qPtr->info << "     ";
            pPtr = qPtr->right;
            while ( ( qPtr->thread == '1' )&&( pPtr != NULL ) )
            {
                cout << pPtr->info << "     ";
                qPtr = pPtr;
                pPtr = pPtr->right;
            }
        }
    }
    while ( pPtr != NULL );
}
```

If you compare this implementation with the recursive implementation or earlier iterative implementation, you will find that this implementation if more efficient. It is more efficient in the sense that it uses minimum resources of the system and runs faster as no stack is used here. Note that the recursive algorithms use stack implicitly, where as we have to maintain our own stack in the iterative implementation. This adds extra overhead on the system and reduces the efficiency.

9.8.2.2 Insertion in a Threaded Binary Search Tree

The following code shows the steps required to insert an element in a threaded binary search tree.

Listing 9.22:

```
// member function to insert an element in threaded
// binary search tree
void ThreadedBST::insertElement(int element )
{
    TBSTNode *ptr, *nodePtr, *parentPtr;
    ptr = new TBSTNode;
    ptr->info = element;
    ptr->left = NULL;
    if ( root == NULL )    // Intially tree empty
    {
        root = ptr;
        ptr->right = NULL;
        ptr->thread = '0';
    }
    else
    {
        parentPtr = NULL;
        nodePtr = root;
        while ( nodePtr != NULL )
        {
            parentPtr = nodePtr;
            if ( element < nodePtr->info )
                nodePtr = nodePtr->left;
            else
            {
                if ( nodePtr->thread == '1' )
```

```
            nodePtr = NULL;
        else
            nodePtr = nodePtr->right;
      }
    }
    if ( element < parentPtr->info )
    {
        parentPtr->left = ptr;
        ptr->right = parentPtr;
        ptr->thread = '1';
    } else {
        if ( parentPtr->thread == '1' ) {
           parentPtr->thread = '0';
           ptr->thread = '1';
           ptr->right = parentPtr->right;
           parentPtr->right = ptr;
        } else {
           ptr->thread = '0';
           ptr->right = NULL;
           parentPtr->right = ptr;
        }
    }
  }
}
```

If the inserted element becomes left terminal node, then its right pointer field is a thread and points to its parent node.

If the inserted element becomes right terminal node, then its right pointer field is a thread and points to its parent node, the there two possibilities:

1. If its parent's right pointer field is NULL i.e. right pointer field is not a thread, then the right pointer field of new node will contain value NULL.
2. If its parent's right pointer field is a thread, then the right pointer field of new node will contain thread of its parent.

9.8.2.3 Finding Largest Element a Threaded Binary Search Tree

The following code shows the steps required finding the location of the largest element of a threaded binary search tree.

Listing 9.23:

```
// member function that returns the location of the largest
// element of the threaded binary search tree, it calls
// recursive function findLargestNode() to find the largest
// element
TBSTNode * ThreadedBST::largestNode()
{
   return findLargestNode(root);
}
// recursive member function that returns the location of
// the largest element of the threaded binary search tree.
// It returns NULL if tree is empty a given element.
```

```
TBSTNode * ThreadedBST::findLargestNode(TBSTNode *ptr)
{
   if ( ptr == NULL )
      return NULL;
   else if ( ( ptr->thread == '1') || ( ptr->right == NULL ) )
      return ptr;
   else
      return findLargestNode(ptr->right);
}
```

9.8.2.4 Deleting an Element From a Threaded Binary Search Tree

The following code shows the steps required deleting an element from a threaded binary search tree.

Listing 9.24:

```
// member function to delete a given element from threaded
// binary search tree, it calls recursive function
// deleteNode() to actually delete the element from
// threaded binary search tree
void ThreadedBST::deleteElement(int element) {
   deleteNode(&root,element);
}
// recursive member function to delete a node containing
// the given element from threaded binary search tree
void ThreadedBST::deleteNode(TBSTNode **ptr, int element) {
    TBSTNode *tempPtr1, *tempPtr2;
    char tempThread;
    if ( *ptr == NULL ) {
       cout << "\nElement " << element << " not found in TBST\n";
       return;
    }
    if ( element < (*ptr)->info )
       deleteNode( &((*ptr)->left), element );
    else if ( element > (*ptr)->info )
       deleteNode( &((*ptr)->right), element );
    else if ((*ptr)->left&&(*ptr)->right&&(*ptr)->thread=='0') {
       tempPtr1 = findLargestNode( (*ptr)->left );
       (*ptr)->info = tempPtr1->info;
       deleteNode( &((*ptr)->left), tempPtr1->info );
    } else {
       tempPtr1 = *ptr;
       // terminal node
       if ( ((*ptr)->left == NULL) &&
            ( ((*ptr)->right == NULL) || ((*ptr)->thread=='1') ) )
            *ptr = NULL;   // tree contains root node only
       else if ( (*ptr)->left != NULL )  // left child only
       {
            tempThread = (*ptr)->thread;
            tempPtr2 = (*ptr)->right;
            *ptr = (*ptr)->left;
            (*ptr)->thread = tempThread;
            if ( tempThread == '1' )
                (*ptr)->right = tempPtr2;
       }
```

```
        else                            // right child only
            *ptr = (*ptr)->right;
        delete tempPtr1;
    }
}
```

9.8.2.5 Deleting a Threaded Binary Tree

The following code shows the steps required to delete a threaded binary or binary search tree.

Listing 9.25:

```
// destructor, that calls recursive function removeTBSTree()
// to remove binary search tree from memory
~ThreadedBST()
{
    removeTBSTree(&root);
}
// recursive member function to remove a threaded
// binary search tree from memory
void ThreadedBST::removeTBSTree( TBSTNode **tree )
{
    if ( *tree != NULL ) {
        removeTBSTree( &(*tree)->left );
        if ( (*tree)->thread == '0' )
            removeTBSTree( &(*tree)->right );
        delete *tree;
    }
}
```

Listing 9.26:

```
//  Program to illustrate the implementation of different operations
//  discussed above on a Threaded Binary Search Tree

# include <iostream.h>
# include <iomanip.h>
# include <stdlib.h>
class TBSTNode
{
    public:
        int info;
        char thread;
        struct TBSTNode *left;
        struct TBSTNode *right;
};
class ThreadedBST
{
    protected:
        TBSTNode *root;
    public:
        ThreadedBST()
        {
          root = NULL;
        }
        ~ThreadedBST()
```

```
    {
     removeTBSTree(&root);
    }
    void inorderTraversal();
    void insertElement(int element);
    void deleteElement(int element);
    TBSTNode *largestNode();
    static TBSTNode *findLargestNode(TBSTNode *ptr);
    static void removeTBSTree( TBSTNode **tree );
    static void deleteNode(TBSTNode **ptr, int element);
};
void ThreadedBST::inorderTraversal()
{
   TBSTNode *pPtr, *qPtr;
   pPtr = root;
   do
   {
    qPtr = NULL;
    while ( pPtr != NULL )   //  traverse left branch
    {
     qPtr = pPtr;
     pPtr = pPtr->left;
    }
    if ( qPtr != NULL )      //   tree is not empty
    {
     cout << qPtr->info << "   ";
     pPtr = qPtr->right;
     while ( ( qPtr->thread == '1' )&&( pPtr != NULL ) )
     {
        cout << pPtr->info << "   ";
        qPtr = pPtr;
        pPtr = pPtr->right;
     }
    }
   }
   while ( pPtr != NULL );
}
void ThreadedBST::insertElement(int element )
{
   TBSTNode *ptr, *nodePtr, *parentPtr;
   ptr = new TBSTNode;
   ptr->info = element;
   ptr->left = NULL;
   if ( root == NULL )  // Intially tree empty
   {
      root = ptr;
      ptr->right = NULL;
      ptr->thread = '0';
   }
   else
   {
      parentPtr = NULL;
      nodePtr = root;
      while ( nodePtr != NULL )
      {
        parentPtr = nodePtr;
        if ( element < nodePtr->info )
           nodePtr = nodePtr->left;
```

```
      else
      {
        if ( nodePtr->thread == '1' )
          nodePtr = NULL;
        else
          nodePtr = nodePtr->right;
      }
    }
    if ( element < parentPtr->info )
    {
      parentPtr->left = ptr;
      ptr->right = parentPtr;
      ptr->thread = '1';
    } else {
      if ( parentPtr->thread == '1' ) {
          parentPtr->thread = '0';
          ptr->thread = '1';
          ptr->right = parentPtr->right;
          parentPtr->right = ptr;
      } else {
          ptr->thread = '0';
          ptr->right = NULL;
          parentPtr->right = ptr;
      }
    }
  }
}
TBSTNode * ThreadedBST::largestNode()
{
  return findLargestNode(root);
}
TBSTNode * ThreadedBST::findLargestNode(TBSTNode *ptr)
{
  if ( ptr == NULL )
     return NULL;
  else if ( ( ptr->thread == '1') || ( ptr->right == NULL ) )
     return ptr;
  else
     return findLargestNode(ptr->right);
}
void ThreadedBST::deleteElement(int element)
{
  deleteNode(&root,element);
}
void ThreadedBST::deleteNode(TBSTNode **ptr, int element)
{
  TBSTNode *tempPtr1, *tempPtr2;
  char tempThread;
  if ( *ptr == NULL ) {
     cout << "\nElement " << element << " not found in TBST\n";
     return;
  }
  if ( element < (*ptr)->info )
     deleteNode( &((*ptr)->left), element );
  else if ( element > (*ptr)->info )
     deleteNode( &((*ptr)->right), element );
  else if ( (*ptr)->left && (*ptr)->right && (*ptr)->thread == '0') {
     tempPtr1 = findLargestNode( (*ptr)->left );
```

```
        (*ptr)->info = tempPtr1->info;
        deleteNode( &((*ptr)->left), tempPtr1->info );
    } else {
        tempPtr1 = *ptr;
        // terminal node
        if ( ((*ptr)->left == NULL) &&
           ( ((*ptr)->right == NULL) || ((*ptr)->thread=='1') ) )
          *ptr = NULL;    // tree contains root node only
        else if ( (*ptr)->left != NULL )  // left child only
        {
          tempThread = (*ptr)->thread;
          tempPtr2 = (*ptr)->right;
          *ptr = (*ptr)->left;
          (*ptr)->thread = tempThread;
          if ( tempThread == '1' )
             (*ptr)->right = tempPtr2;
        }
        else                            // right child only
          *ptr = (*ptr)->right;
        delete tempPtr1;
    }
}
void ThreadedBST::removeTBSTree( TBSTNode **tree )
{
   if ( *tree != NULL ) {
     removeTBSTree( &(*tree)->left );
     if ( (*tree)->thread == '0' )
       removeTBSTree( &(*tree)->right );
     delete *tree;
   }
}
void main()      //   main function
{
   int choice, element, height;
   ThreadedBST tbtree;
   while ( 1 )
   {
     cout << "\n\n    Options available \n";
     cout << "++++++++++++++++++++++++++++++++ \n\n";
     cout << "   1. Insert node\n";
     cout << "   2. In-order traversal\n";
     cout << "   3. Delete node\n";
     cout << "   4. Exit\n\n";
     cout << "Enter your choice ( 1-4 ) : ";
     cin >> choice;
     switch( choice )
     {
       case 1 : cout << "Element to be inserted into tree : ";
                cin >> element;
                tbtree.insertElement(element);
                break;
       case 2 : cout << "\nIn-order Traversal of TBST is\n";
                tbtree.inorderTraversal();
                break;
       case 3 : cout << "Element to delete from tree : ";
                cin >> element;
                tbtree.deleteElement(element);
                break;
```

```
            case 4 : exit(1);
        }
    }
}
```

9.9 M-WAY SEARCH TREES

An *m-way search tree* is a tree in which each node has out-degree $\leq m$. When *m*-way search tree is not empty, it has the following properties:

- Each node has the following structure

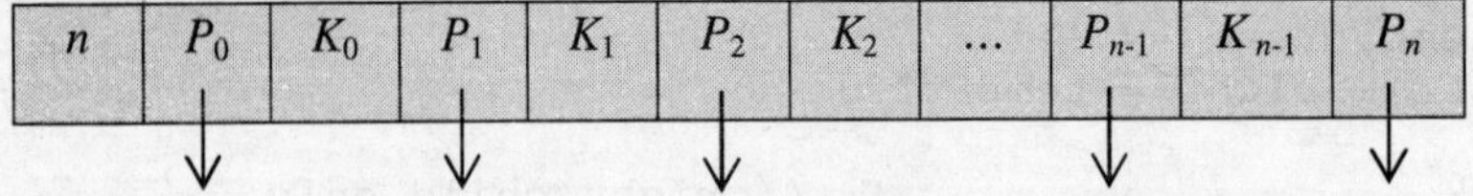

where $P_0, P_1, P_2,\ldots, P_n$ are pointers to the node's sub trees and $K_0, K_1, K_2,\ldots, K_{n-1}$ are the key values. The requirement that each node have out-degree $\leq m$ forces $n \leq m-1$.

- The key values in a node are in ascending order, *i.e.*

$$K_i < K_{i+1} \quad \text{for } i = 0, 1, 2,\ldots, n-2$$

- All key values in nodes of the sub tree pointed to by P_i are less than the key value K_i for $i = 0, 1, 2,\ldots, n-1$.
- All key values in nodes of the sub tree pointed to by P_n are greater than the key value K_{n-1}.
- The sub trees pointed to by P_i for $i = 0, 1, 2,\ldots, n$ are also *m*-way search trees.

We can define the node type for a 7-way search tree as follows:

```
class Node {
    public:
        int key[6];
        Node *nodePtr[7];
};
```

9.9.1 M-Way Search Tree as Indexes

When an *m*-way search tree is used an index, each key-pointer pair (K_i, P_i) becomes a triplet (K_i, P_i, A_i), where A_i is the address of record associated with key value K_i. Thus, each node not only points to its child nodes in the tree, but also to associated records. We can define the node type for a 7-way search tree index as follows:

```
class Node {
    public:
        int key[6];
        recordPtr *recPtr[6];
        Node *nodePtr[7];
};
```

where *recordPtr* is assumed to be a type that holds an address of the associated record with a given key.

9.9.2 Searching an M-Way Search Tree

Searching for a key in an *m*-way search tree is an extension of searching a key in a binary search tree. The procedure is as follows:

- If the key is less than K_0, then the search is continued in *m*-way search tree pointed to by P_0.
- If the key lies between K_0 and K_1, then the search is continued in *m*-way search tree pointed to by P_1.
- If the key lies between K_1 and K_2, then the search is continued in *m*-way search tree pointed to by P_2.

  ⋮

  ⋮
- If the key is greater than K_{n-1}, then the search is continued in *m*-way search tree pointed to by P_n.

9.10 B-TREE

The B-tree structure was discovered by *R. Bayer* and *E. McCreight* of Boeing Scientific Research Labs and has become one of the most popular techniques for organizing an index structure. A *B-tree of order m* is an *m*-way search tree with the following properties:

- Each node of the tree, except the root node and leaves, has at least *m*/2 sub trees and no more than *m* sub trees.
- Root of the tree has at least two sub trees unless it is a leaf node.
- All leaves of the tree are on the same level.

The first condition ensures that each node of the tree is at least half full, the second one forces the tree to branch early while the third one keeps the tree balanced.

Several variations of the basic B-tree have been developed, two of them, that have become popular are:

- ***B⁺-Tree*** — it is a B-tree in which the leave nodes are linked to each other from left to right to form a linked list of the keys in sequential order.
- ***B*-Tree*** — it is a B-tree in which each interior node is at least two-third full rather than just half full.

9.10.1 Searching a B-tree

The procedure for searching a key in a B-tree is same as searching a key in an *m*-way search tree. Then what is performance of search in B-tree? To find the answer, let us first find the minimum number of keys in a B-tree of order *m* with height *h*. By definition, the root of B-tree has at least two children. The internal nodes, that are upto level *h*-2, has at least *m*/2 children.

Therefore, the B-tree must contain at least $\left\lceil 1+2+\sum_{i=3}^{h-2} 2\lceil m/2\rceil^{i-2} \right\rceil$ internal nodes and at least $\lfloor 2\lceil m/2\rceil^{h-2} \rfloor$ leaves.

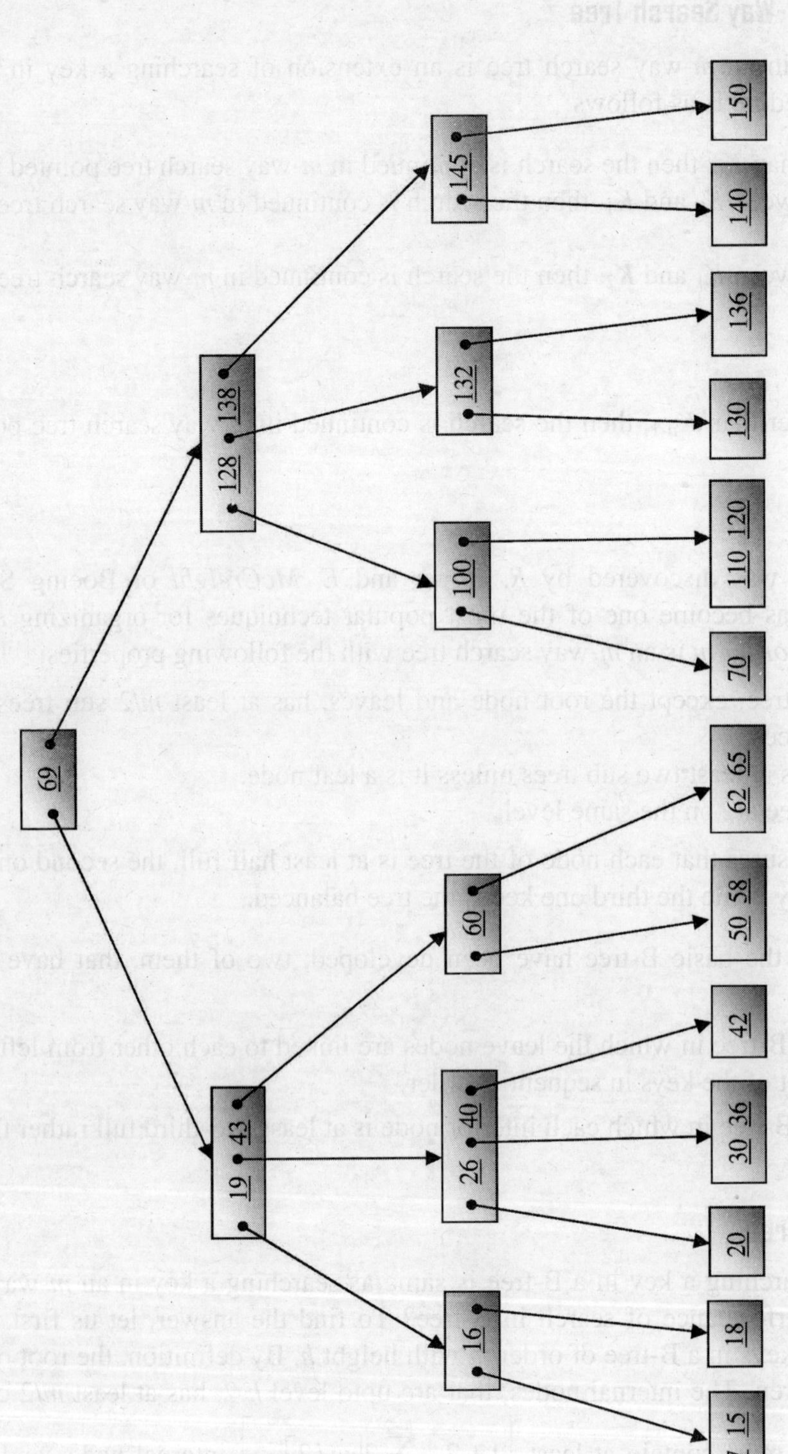

Figure 9.33 B-tree of order 3

Further, each internal node, except the root, must contain at least $[\lceil m/2 \rceil - 1]$ keys, and the root an each leaf must contain 1 element. Thus, the minimum number of keys in a B-tree is

$$n \geq 1 + \left(2 + \sum_{i=3}^{h-2} 2\lceil m/2 \rceil^{i-2}\right)(\lceil m/2 \rceil - 1) + 2\lceil m/2 \rceil^{h-2} \quad \text{which reduces to} \quad n+1 \geq 2\lceil m/2 \rceil^{h-2}$$

That is, the maximum height of the tree is

$$h \leq 2 + \log\lceil m/2 \rceil((n+1)/2) \qquad \text{for } m > 2$$

Recall that the leaves will appear at level *h*-1. Since the B-tree's height determines the maximum search length, we now know that the B-tree very well for direct searches.

9.10.2 Inserting into a B-tree

In order to insert a key into a B-tree, first a B-tree search is performed to find the correct location for the key. Then the key is inserted. Note that a node usually may have a space available for another key and pointer. However, the node may be already full and cannot accommodate another key. In that case, the node is split into two nodes, with half the key values and pointer going into one node while the other half going into another node.

These twin nodes have the same parent, which is modified for the additional key value and pointer. In the worst case, the splitting procedure may need to be carried all the way up the root of the tree. In that case, the height of the tree increases by one level. This insertion procedure is implemented as a recursion since the splitting procedure is the same, irrespective of the level.

Note that the probability of node splitting decreases as the order of the B-tree increases.

9.10.3 Deleting from a B-tree

Deletion of a key from a B-tree is slightly complicated than insertion. In order to keep the B-tree and B-tree, two nodes may need to be merged when one node contains less number of keys and pointers than the required keys and pointers.

As with insertion, first a B-tree search is performed to find the node containing the key to be deleted. If the key to be deleted is in the interior node, the tree is transformed to move this key into a leaf node because it is easier to delete a key from a leaf node. Once the deletion is made, the other keys may need to be shifted or leaves need to be merged to meet the minimum key and minimum pointer requirement for a B-tree. This shifting and merging may be needed for several levels.

If the merge percolates (bubbles) all the way to the root (highest level), a new root is formed and the height of the B-tree decreases by a factor of 1.

As with splitting, the probability, the probability of node merging decreases as the order of the B-tree increases.

9.11 B⁺-TREE

The B^+-tree data structure is another variation on the basic B-tree. It is one of the popular techniques for implementing indexed file organization.

As you can see in Figure 9.33, the leaves have been connected to form a linked list of keys in sequential order. The B^+-tree has two parts — the first part is the *index set* that constitutes interior nodes and the second part is the *sequence set* that constitutes leaves. The linked leaves are an excellent aspect of a B^+-tree since using it keys can be accessed sequentially in addition to accessing them directly.

9.11.1 Inserting into a B^+-tree

The procedure to insert a new key value into a B^+-tree is almost same as for B-tree. When a leaf node is split into two nodes, a copy of the low-order key from the rightmost node is promoted to the separator key value in the parent node. The new node also must be inserted in the linked list of the sequence set.

9.11.2 Deleting from a B^+-tree

Deletion of a key from a B^+-tree is easier than B-tree. When a key value is deleted from a leaf, there is no need to delete that key from the index set of the key. That key value still can direct searches to the proper leaves.

9.11.3 Searching a B^+-tree

Note that a direct search must terminate in a node in the sequence set. If there is a key in the index set that match the sought key, the preceding pointer is followed until the correct leaf is reached. It is not necessary that every key in the index set must also appear in the sequence set, since a key may have been deleted from the sequence set. A deleted key is retained in the index set for purposes of guiding access to the sequence set.

A B^+-tree provides as good as performance for direct searching as does a B-tree of same order. The maximum height of a B^+-tree of order m with n key values is $\left(\log_{\lceil 1/2m \rceil} \frac{n+1}{2}\right)$.

Sequential access to the data indexed by a B^+-tree is provided by scanning the sequence set. Typically, as an indexed sequential file, the sequence set may contain data records in addition to keys. However, if data records are of variable length or relatively large, then the file is can only be structured so that sequence set contains pairs of key values and pointers (address) to the data records stored in secondary storage.

9.12 B*-TREE

The B^*-tree data structure was identified by *Knuth* as one of the several possible variations on the basic B-tree. The main motivation behind the B^*-tree was to reduce the overhead involved in insertions and deletions. And the other primary motive was to improve the search performance. The B^*-tree is a B-tree in which each node is at least two-thirds full instead of at least half full. The basic idea of B*-tree is to reduce the node splitting. When a node becomes full, rather than being split, a redistribution scheme takes place and pointers from the full node and places them into a sibling node. The operations on B*-tree are performed in a manner similar to that of B-tree.

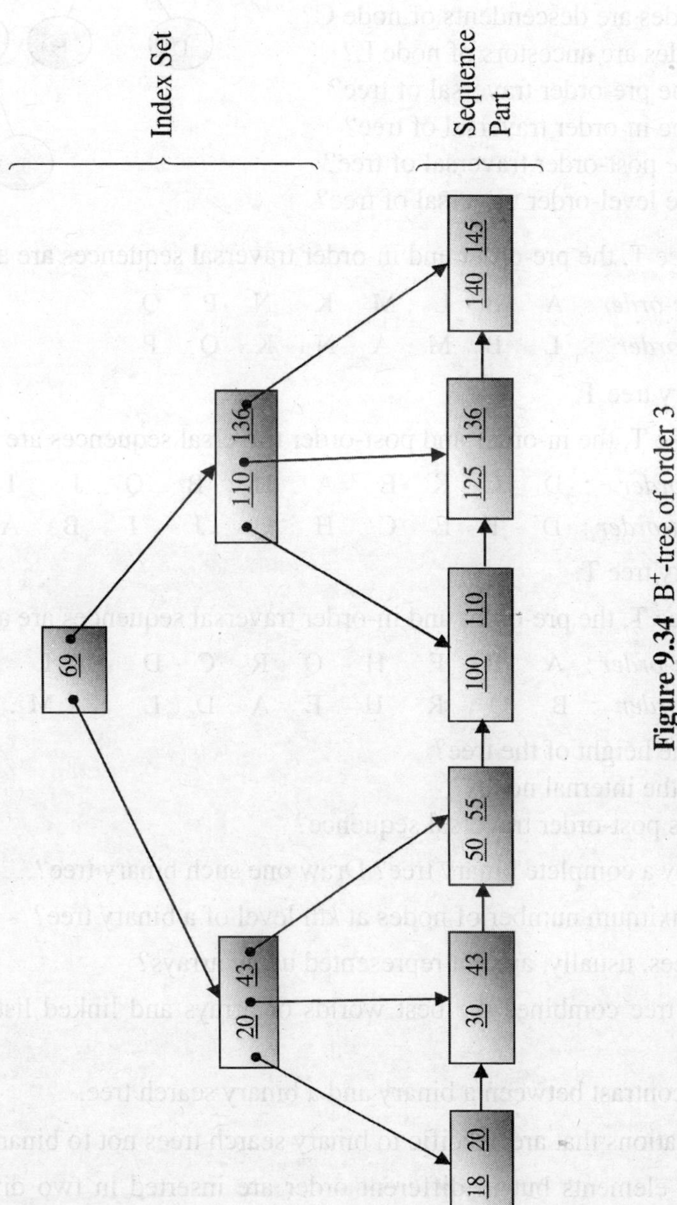

Figure 9.34 B$^+$-tree of order 3

REVIEW EXERCISES

1. Answer the following questions in the context of given binary tree.

   (*a*) Which nodes are leave nodes?
   (*b*) Which is the root node?
   (*c*) What is the height of the tree?
   (*d*) Which nodes are non-leave nodes?
   (*e*) Which nodes are descendents of node C?
   (*f*) Which nodes are ancestors of node L?
   (*g*) What is the pre-order traversal of tree?
   (*h*) What is the in-order traversal of tree?
   (*i*) What is the post-order traversal of tree?
   (*j*) What is the level-order traversal of tree?

2. For a binary tree T, the pre-order and in-order traversal sequences are as follows:

   Pre-order : A B L M K N P Q
   In-order : L B M A N K Q P

   Draw the binary tree T.

3. For a binary tree T, the in-order and post-order traversal sequences are as follows:

   In-order : D C K E A H B Q J I
   Post-order : D K E C H Q J I B A

   Draw the binary tree T.

4. For a binary tree T, the pre-order and in-order traversal sequences are as follows:

   Pre-order : A B E H Q R C D K L M
   In-order : B Q R H E A D L K M C

   (*a*) What is the height of the tree?
   (*b*) What are the internal nodes?
   (*c*) What is its post-order traversal sequence?

5. What do you by a complete binary tree? Draw one such binary tree?
6. What is the maximum number of nodes at *k*th level of a binary tree?
7. Why binary trees, usually, are not represented using arrays?
8. Binary search tree combines the best worlds of arrays and linked lists into one structure. Comment.
9. Compare and contrast between a binary and a binary search tree.
10. Name the operations that are specific to binary search trees not to binary trees.
11. If same set of elements but in different order are inserted in two different empty binary search trees, will you get identical binary search trees?
12. When we insert a new node in a binary search tree, will it become an internal node or terminal node?

13. Can we insert a new node as an internal node?
14. How the height of a binary search tree effects its performance?
15. If there are 27 nodes in a complete binary tree, what will be its height? Also tell how many nodes will be in the last level.
16. What are the different operations that modify a tree?
17. Which of the operations on binary search tree is more complex and why?
18. How an AVL tree differs from a binary search tree? How AVL trees are represented in computer memory?
19. What is a thread? How is it useful?
20. What are the advantages of threading a binary (search) tree?
21. What is an *M-way* search tree?
22. What is the difference between a B-tree and a B^*-tree? How that difference matters?
23. What is the difference between a B-tree and a B^+-tree? When you might prefer to use B^+-tree instead of a B-tree?

PROGRAMMING EXERCISES

1. Write an iterative version of a function to search an element in a binary search tree.
2. We want to have only unique elements in a binary search tree. Give the modified version of *insert()* function.
3. Give the modified version of *search()* function so that it not only returns the location of the element but also return location of its parent.
4. Write a function to perform the level order traversal of a binary search tree.
5. Write a function to find the predecessor of a given element.
6. Write a function to find the successor of a given element.
7. Write iterative versions of functions to find the smallest and largest element in a binary search tree.
8. If the node structure of a binary search tree is modified to include an additional, say *father*, pointer to hold the address of a parent node as given below:

   ```
   class Node {
       public:
           int info;
           Node *father, *left, *right;
   };
   ```

   What are the operations that are required to be modified? Also show the modified version of these operations.
9. Write functions to implement the iterative versions of pre-order, in-order, and post-order traversals of a binary tree.

❑ ❑ ❑

Chapter 10

Heaps

10.1 INTRODUCTION

A *heap* is a binary tree that satisfies the following properties:

- Shape property
- Order property

By the *shape property* we mean that heap must be a complete binary tree, whereas by *order property* we mean that for every node in the heap, the value stored in that node is greater than or equal to the value in each of its children.

A heap that satisfies these properties is known as *max heap*.

However, if the order property is such that for every node in the heap, the value stored in that node is less than or equal to the value in each of its children, that heap is known as *min heap*.

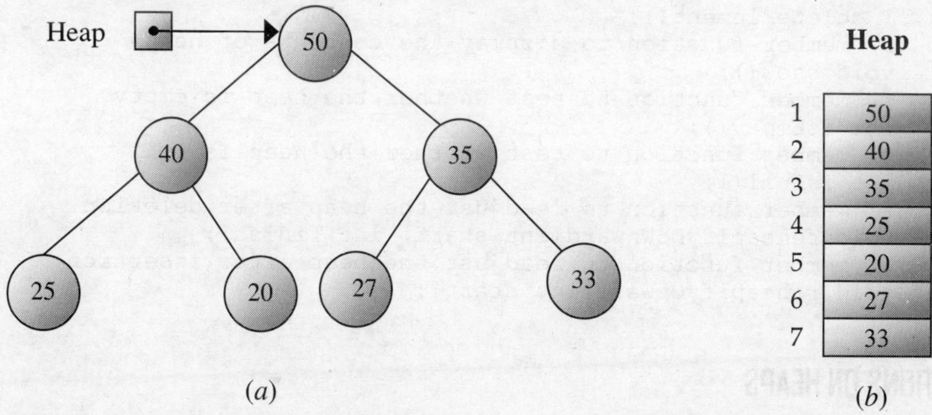

Figure 10.1: (*a*) Max heap of with 7 elements, (*b*) Sequential representation of Max heap

A heap is represented in memory using linear arrays, *i.e.*, by *sequential representation*. This chapter describes various operations on heaps, and its application in implementing priority queues and sorting a linear array. In our discussion, we will be considering max heaps.

10.2 REPRESENTING A HEAP IN MEMORY

Since a heap is a complete or nearly complete binary tree, therefore a heap of size *n* is represented in memory using a linear array of size *n*. This array representation is described in *Chapter 9*.

Following are required declarations

```
template <class T>
class MaxHeap
{
   private:
      T *heap;
      int n;
      int size;
   public:
      // constructor
      MaxHeap(int m)
      {
         heap = new T[m+1];
         n = 0;
         size = m;
      }
      // destructor
      ~MaxHeap()
      {
         delete heap;
      }
      // member function to build initial heap
      void heapify();
      // member function to insert an element into heap
      void insertElement(T item);
      // member function to delete element from root of heap
      T deleteElement();
      // member function to display the contents of heap
      void show();
      // member function to test whether the heap is empty
      int isEmpty();
      // member function to test whether the heap is full
      int isFull();
      // member function to readjust the heap after deletion
      void reheapifyDownward(int start, int finish);
      // member function to readjust the heap after insertion
      void reheapifyUpward(int start);
};
```

10.3 OPERATIONS ON HEAPS

On heaps, only two operations are performed. These are — *deleting an element from the heap* and *inserting a new element into the heap*. These are described below.

10.3.1 Deleting an Element From Heap

Element is always deleted from the root of the heap. If we delete the element from the root node, it creates a hole, *i.e.*, vacant space, in the root position. Because the heap must be complete, we fill the hole with the last (bottom) element of the heap.

Although the heap becomes complete, *i.e.*, satisfies shape property, the order property of the heaps is violated, as the values that come from the bottom are small. This situation suggests one of the basic operations:

"Given a complete binary tree whose elements satisfy the heap order property except in the root position, re-adjust the structure so that again it will be heap".

This operation involves moving the elements down from the root position until either it ends up in a position where the root property is satisfied or it hits the leaf node.

This operation in the text will be referred to as *reheapify downward* operation and works as follows:

> *Interchange the value of the root node with the value of the child, which is the largest among its children. For example, if the value of the left child is the largest, the root node is interchanged with its left child, and then the down heap property is repeated from its left child onward. Similar is the case if the right child is largest, start reheapify downward operation from that child with which the value of the root node was interchanged. This operation is recursive.*

The various steps required for the reheapify downward operation are summarized in algorithm 10.1.

Algorithm 10.1:

ReheapifyDownward(heap, start, finish)

Here *heap* is a linear array, *start* is the index of the element from where reheapify downward operation is to start, and *finish* is index of the last (bottom) element of the heap. The variable *index* is used to keep track of the index of the largest child.

```
Begin
   if heap[start] is not a leaf node then
      Set index = index of the child with largest value
      if ( heap[start] < heap[index] ) then
         Swap heap[start] and heap[index]
         Call ReheapifyDownward( heap, index, finish )
      endif
   endif
End.
```

The implementation of the above algorithm is given in the following listing.

Listing 10.1:

```
// member function to readjust the heap after deletion
template <class T>
void MaxHeap<T>::reheapifyDownward(int start, int finish) {
  int  index, lchild, rchild;
  T maximum, temp;
  lchild = 2*start;          //  index of left child
  rchild = lchild + 1;              //  index of right child
  if ( lchild <= finish ) {
     maximum = heap[lchild];
     index = lchild;
     if ( rchild <= finish ) {
        if ( heap[rchild] > maximum ) {
           maximum = heap[rchild];
           index = rchild;
        }
     }
     if ( heap[start] < heap[index] ) {
        temp = heap[start];
        heap[start] = heap[index];
        heap[index] = temp;
        reheapifyDownward(index, finish);
     }
  }
}
```

Thus, deletion of an element from heap is done using the following steps:

- Assign the value of the root node to the temporary variable, which may be required for further processing,
- Bring the last element of the heap to the root node position,
- Reduce the size of the heap by a factor of one, and
- Apply reheapify downward operation from root node.

Algorithm 10.2:

DeleteElement(***heap*****,** ***n*****,** ***item*** **)**

Here *heap* is the linear array with size *n*. This algorithm deletes the element from the root of *heap* and assign to *item* through which it is returned to the calling program. It also decreases its size by a factor of one, *i.e.*, size becomes *n*–1.

```
Begin
  Set item =  heap[1]
  Set heap[1] = heap[n]
  Set n = n-1
  Call ReheapifyDownward( heap, 1, n )
End.
```

The implementation of the above algorithm is given in the following listing.

Listing 10.2:

```
// member function to delete element from root of heap
template <class T>
int MaxHeap<T>::deleteElement()
{
    T temp;
    temp = heap[1];
    heap[1] = heap[n];
    n--;
    reheapifyDownward(1,n);
    return temp;
}
```

Example 10.1:

Following figure illustrates the deletion operation.

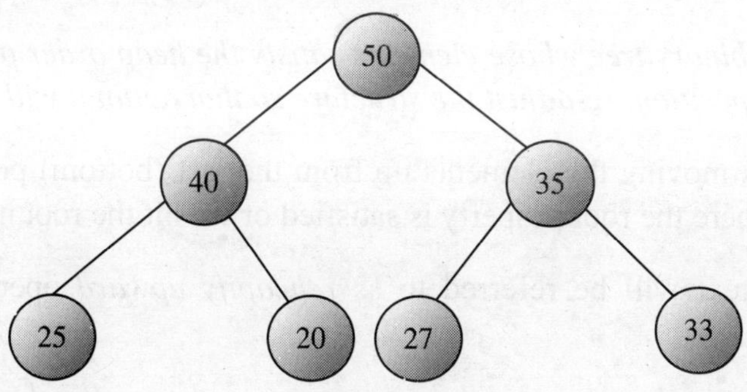

(*a*) Starting heap

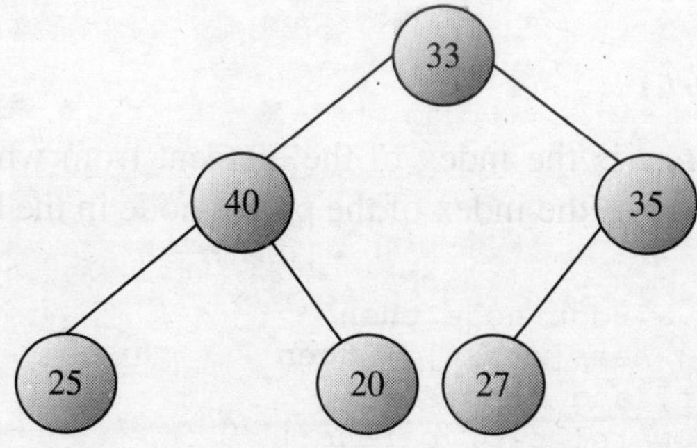

(*b*) After Removing 50 and replacing with 33

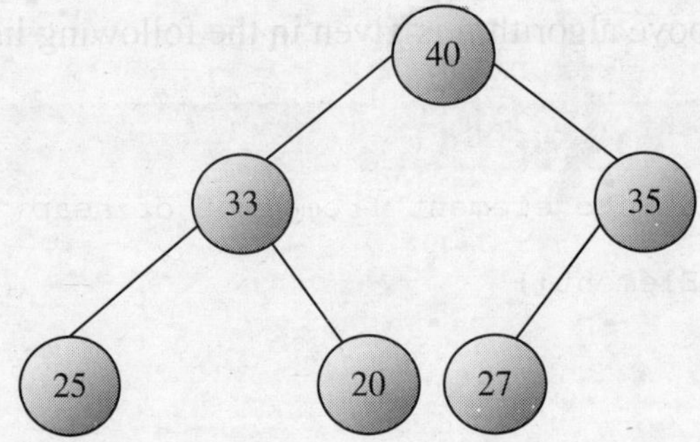

(*c*) Reheapify downward from root node (swap 33 with 40)

Figure 10.2: Illustration of deletion and reheapify downward operation

10.3.2 Inserting an Element into Heap

Element is always inserted as last (bottom) child of the original heap. Although, with this insertion, the heap remains complete, but the order property may be violated if a larger element is inserted. This situation suggests another basic operation:

"Given a complete binary tree whose elements satisfy the heap order property except in the last (bottom) position, re-adjust the structure so that again it will be heap".

This operation involves moving the elements up from the last (bottom) position until either it ends up in a position where the root property is satisfied or we hit the root node.

This operation in the text will be referred to as *reheapify upward* operation and works as follows:

If the value of the last node is greater than its parent, exchange it value with its parent, and then repeat the same process from the parent node, and so on until the order property is satisfied or we hit the root node. This operation is also recursive.

The various steps required for *reheapify upward* operation are summarized in algorithm 10.3.

Algorithm 10.3:

ReheapifyUpward(***heap, start*** **)**

Here *heap* is a linear array, *start* is the index of the element from where reheapify upward operation is to start. It use *parent* as the index of the parent node in the heap.

```
Begin
   if heap[start] is not a root node then
      if ( heap[parent] < heap[start] ) then
         Swap heap[parent] and heap[start]
         Call ReheapifyUpward(heap, parent )
      endif
   endif
End.
```

The implementation of the above algorithm is given in the following listing.

Listing 10.3:

```
// member function to readjust the heap after insertion
template <class T>
void MaxHeap<T>::reheapifyUpward(int start)
{
   T temp, parent;
   if ( start > 1 ) {
       parent = start / 2;
       if ( heap[parent] < heap[start] ) {
          temp = heap[start];
          heap[start] = heap[parent];
          heap[parent] = temp;
          reheapifyUpward(parent);
       }
   }
}
```

Thus, insertion of an element into heap is done using the following steps:

- Increase the size of the heap by a factor of one,
- Insert the element as the last (bottom) element of the heap, and
- Apply *reheapify upward* operation from last node.

These steps summarized in algorithm 10.4.

Algorithm 10.4:

InsertElement(*heap*, n, *item*)

Here *heap* is a linear array with size *n*. This algorithm inserts an element *item* into the *heap* and also increases its size by a factor of one, *i.e.*, size becomes *n*+1.

```
Begin
  Set n = n + 1
  Set heap[n] = item
  Call ReheapifyUpward(heap, n )
End.
```

The implementation of the above algorithm is given in the following listing.

Listing 10.4:

```
// member function to insert an element into heap
template <class T>
void MaxHeap<T>::insertElement(T item)
{
   n++;
   heap[n] = item;
   reheapifyUpward(n);
}
```

Example 10.2:

Following figure illustrates the insertion operation.

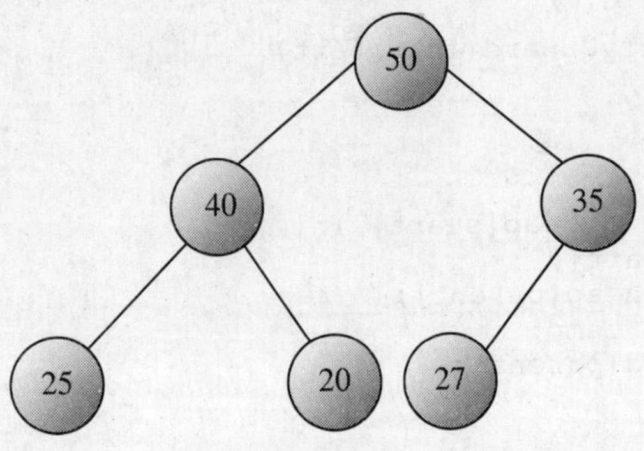

(*a*) Starting heap

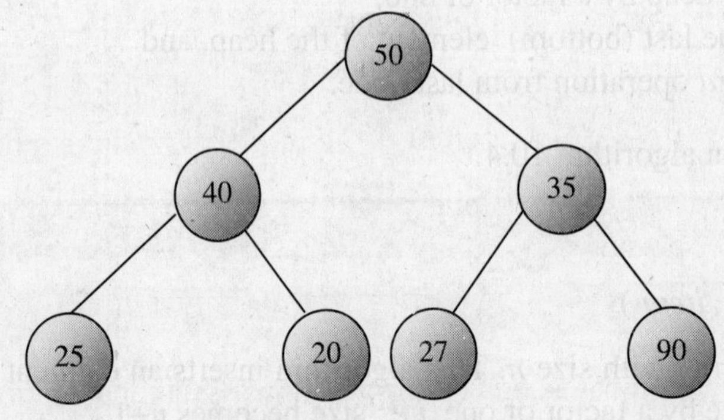

(*b*) Add value 90

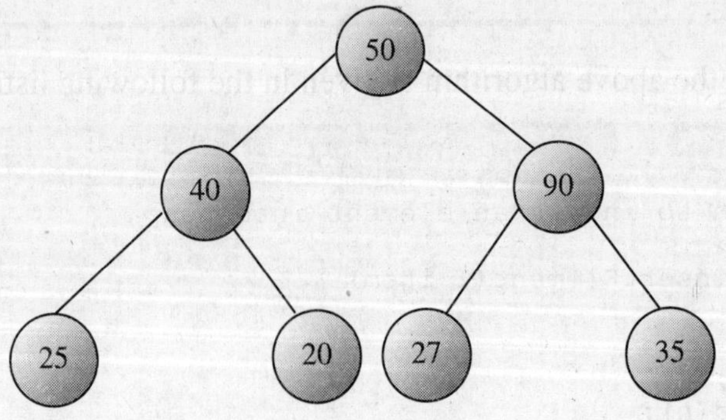

(*c*) Reheapify upward from last node with value 90

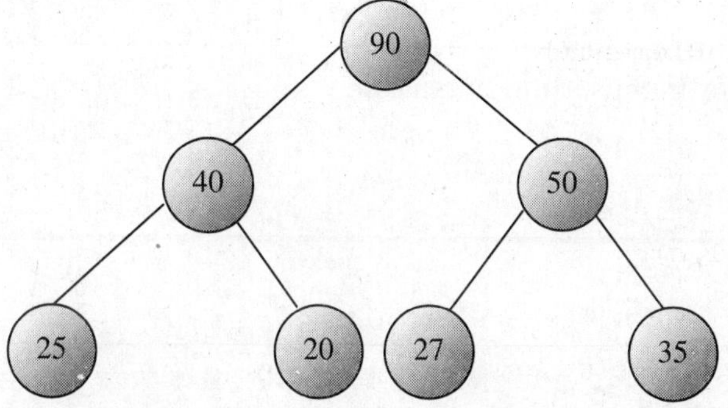

(*d*) Further reheapify upward from node with value 90

Figure 10.3: Illustration of insertion and reheapify upward operation

Listing 10.5:

```
//  Program to demonstrate the implementation of operations on a
//  Max Heap with element of type 'int'
#include <iostream.h>
#include <iomanip.h>
template <class T>
class MaxHeap
{
   private:
      T *heap;
      int n;
      int size;
   public:
      MaxHeap(int m) {
        heap = new T[m+1];
        n = 0;
        size = m;
      }
      ~MaxHeap() {
        delete heap;
      }
      void heapify();
      void insertElement(T item);
      T deleteElement();
      void show();
      int isEmpty();
      int isFull();
      void reheapifyDownward(int start, int finish);
      void reheapifyUpward(int start);
};
template <class T>
void MaxHeap<T>::insertElement(T item)
{
   n++;
   heap[n] = item;
   reheapifyUpward(n);
}
```

```
template <class T>
int MaxHeap<T>::deleteElement()
{
   T temp;
   temp = heap[1];
   heap[1] = heap[n];
   n--;
   reheapifyDownward(1,n);
   return temp;
}

template <class T>
T MaxHeap<T>::deleteElementFrom(int pos)
{
   T temp;
   temp = heap[pos];
   heap[pos] = heap[n];
   n--;
   reheapifyDownward(pos,n);
   return temp;
}

template <class T>
void MaxHeap<T>::show()
{
  int i;
  cout << "\n\nElements of Max Heap are \n\n";
  for ( i = 1; i <= n; i++ )
     cout << heap[i] << "   ";
  cout << endl;
}

template <class T>
int MaxHeap<T>::isEmpty()
{
  return ( ( n==0 ) ? 1 : 0 );
}

template <class T>
int MaxHeap<T>::isFull()
{
  return ( ( n == size ) ? 1 : 0 );
}

template <class T>
void MaxHeap<T>::reheapifyDownward(int start, int finish) {
  int  index, lchild, rchild;
  T maximum, temp;
  lchild = 2*start;              // index of left child
  rchild = lchild + 1;                // index of right child
  if ( lchild <= finish ) {
    maximum = heap[lchild];
    index = lchild;
    if ( rchild <= finish ) {
     if ( heap[rchild] > maximum ) {
       maximum = heap[rchild];
       index = rchild;
     }
```

```
    }
    if ( heap[start] < heap[index] ) {
      temp = heap[start];
      heap[start] = heap[index];
      heap[index] = temp;
      reheapifyDownward(index, finish);
    }
  }
}

template <class T>
void MaxHeap<T>::reheapifyUpward(int start)
{
  T temp, parent;
  if ( start > 1 ) {
    parent = start / 2;
    if ( heap[parent] < heap[start] ) {
      temp = heap[start];
      heap[start] = heap[parent];
      heap[parent] = temp;
      reheapifyUpward(parent);
    }
  }
}

template <class T>
void MaxHeap<T>::heapify()
{
  int i, index;
  index = n / 2;
  for ( i = index; i >= 1; i-- )
    reheapifyUpward(i);
}

void main()
{
  int choice, element, m;
  cout << "\nEnter size of the heap : ";
  cin >> m;

  MaxHeap<int> maxHeap(m);

  do
  {
    cout << "\n\n      Options available \n";
    cout << "    ++++++++++++++++++ \n\n";
    cout << "      1. Add Element  \n";
    cout << "      2. Delete Element from root \n";
    cout << "      3. Delete Element from given position \n";
    cout << "      4. Show heap  \n";
    cout << "      5. Exit\n\n";
    cout << "Enter your choice ( 1-5 ) : ";
    cin >> choice;
    switch ( choice )
    {
      case 1 : if ( maxHeap.isFull() )
            cout << "\nMax Heap already full ..";
```

```
            else {
                cout << "\nEnter Element : ";
                cin >> element;
                maxHeap.insertElement(element);
            }
            break;
    case 2 : if ( maxHeap.isEmpty() )
                cout << "\nMax Heap already empty ..";
            else {
                cout << "Element removed is "
                     << maxHeap.deleteElement();
            }
            break;
    case 3 : cout << "\nEnter position from where to delete : ";
            cin >> m;
            if ( maxHeap.isEmpty() )
                cout << "\nMax Heap already empty ..";
            else {
                cout << "Element removed is "
                     << maxHeap.deleteElementFrom(m);
            }
            break;
    case 4 : maxHeap.show();
    }
  }
  while ( choice != 5 );
} //----  end of main function ----
```

10.4 APPLICATIONS OF HEAPS

The main applications of heaps are:

- Implementing a priority queue.
- Sorting an array using efficient technique known as *heapsort*.

The *heapsort* technique is described in *Chapter* 13.

10.4.1 Priority Queues

A priority queue is a structure with an interesting accessing function: Only the *highest-priority* element can be accessed. By highest priority we mean different things depending on the application. To illustrate this consider the following situations:

- A small company has only one secretary. When other employees leave work on the secretary's desk, which get job done first? The jobs are processed in order of the employee's importance in the company. Suppose, secretary has on his table work given by president and vice president, secretary completes president's work first. This example shows that the priority of each job relates to the level of the employee who initiated it.
- In a telephone answering system, calls are answered in the order that they are received. That is, the highest-priority call is the one that has been waiting the longest. Thus a FIFO queue can be considered a priority queue whose highest-priority element is the one that has been queued the longest time.

In this section, we will describe a priority queue whose *highest-priority* element is the one with the largest key value. We will assume that as the jobs enter the system, they are assigned a value according to its importance. The more important jobs are assigned larger values.

The operations defined for the priority queue are very much similar to the operation specified for FIFO queue.

Suppose priority queue *pq* with storage capacity *MAX* is defined, the various operations are implemented as described below.

Algorithm 10.5:

CreateEmptyPQ(***pq, n*** **)**

Here *pq* is a linear array with size *n* representing a priority queue. This algorithm sets size equal to zero to indicate that there is no element in it.

```
Begin
  Set n = 0
End.
```

Algorithm 10.6:

IsEmptyPQ(***pq, n, status*** **)**

Here *pq* is a linear array with size *n* representing a priority queue. This algorithm sets the variable *status* to value *true* if the size of the *pq* is zero, *i.e.*, it is empty; otherwise it sets *status* to value *false*.

```
Begin
  if ( n = 0 ) then
     Set status = true
  else
     Set status = false
  endif
End.
```

Algorithm 10.7:

IsFullPQ(***pq, n, status*** **)**

Here *pq* is a linear array with size *n* representing a priority queue. This algorithm sets the variable *status* to value *true* if the size of the *pq* is MAX, *i.e.*, it is full; otherwise it sets *status* to value *false*.

```
Begin
```

```
    if ( n = MAX ) then
        Set status = true
    else
        Set status = false
    endif
End.
```

Algorithm 10.8:

EnqueuePQ(***pq, n, element*** **)**

Here *pq* is a linear array with size *n* representing a priority queue. This algorithm inserts *element* into it if it is not full.

```
Begin
    Call IsFullPQ( pq, n, status )
    if ( status = true ) then
        Print: "Overflow"
    else
        Call InsertElement( pq, n, element )
    endif
End.
```

Algorithm 10.9:

DequeuePQ(***pq, n, element*** **)**

Here *pq* is a linear array with size *n* representing a priority queue. This algorithm deletes the front element and stores in variable *element* into it if it is not empty.

```
Begin
    Call IsEmptyPQ( pq, n, status )
    if ( status = true ) then
        Print: "Underflow"
    else
        Call DeleteElement( pq, n, element )
    endif
End.
```

The following declarations, that use the *MaxHeap* class, can be used to implement a priority queue:

```
template <class T>
class PriorityQueue : MaxHeap<T>
{
    public:
        // constructor
        PriorityQueue(int m) : MaxHeap<T>(m) { }
        // destructor
```

```
    ~PriorityQueue() { }
    // member function that inserts a new element into priority
    // queue
     void enqueue(T item);
    // member function that removes an element from a queue
    T dequeue();
    // member function to test whether the priority
    // queue is empty
    int isEmpty();
    // member function to test whether the priority
    // queue is full
    int isFull();
    // member function to show the contents of the priority
    // queue
    void show();
};
// member function that inserts a new element into priority queue
template <class T>
void PriorityQueue<T>::enqueue(T item) {
   if ( isFull() )
      cout << "\nPriority Queue is full. . .\n";
   else
      insertElement(item);
}
// member function that removes an element from a queue
template <class T>
T PriorityQueue<T>::dequeue() {
   T temp;
   if ( isEmpty() )
      cout << "\nPriority Queue is empty. . .\n";
   else
      temp = MaxHeap<T>::deleteElement();
   return temp;
}
// member function to test whether the priority
// queue is empty
template <class T>
int PriorityQueue<T>::isEmpty() {
   return MaxHeap<T>::isEmpty();
}
// member function to test whether the priority
// queue is full
template <class T>
int PriorityQueue<T>::isFull()
{
   return MaxHeap<T>::isFull();
}
// member function to show the contents of priority queue
template <class T>
void PriorityQueue<T>::show()
{
   if ( isEmpty() )
      cout << "\nPriority Queue is empty ...";
   else {
      cout << "\nElements of Priority Queue are : ";
      MaxHeap<T>::show();
   }
}
```

Listing 10.6:

```
//  Program to demonstrate the implementation of priority queue
#include <iostream.h>
#include <iomanip.h>
template <class T>
class MaxHeap {
   private:
      T *heap;
      int n;
      int size;
   public:
      MaxHeap(int m) {
        heap = new T[m+1];
        n = 0;
        size = m;
      }
      ~MaxHeap() {
        delete heap;
      }
      void heapify();
      void insertElement(T item);
      T deleteElement();
      void show();
      int isEmpty();
      int isFull();
      void reheapifyDownward(int start, int finish);
      void reheapifyUpward(int start);
};
template <class T>
void MaxHeap<T>::insertElement(T item) {
   n++;
   heap[n] = item;
   reheapifyUpward(n);
}
template <class T>
int MaxHeap<T>::deleteElement() {
   T temp;
   temp = heap[1];
   heap[1] = heap[n];
   n--;
   reheapifyDownward(1,n);
   return temp;
}
template <class T>
void MaxHeap<T>::show() {
   int i;
   for ( i = 1; i <= n; i++ )
      cout << heap[i] << "    ";
   cout << endl;
}
template <class T>
int MaxHeap<T>::isEmpty() {
   return ( ( n==0 ) ? 1 : 0 );
}
template <class T>
int MaxHeap<T>::isFull() {
```

```
   return ( ( n == size ) ? 1 : 0 );
}
template <class T>
void MaxHeap<T>::reheapifyDownward(int start, int finish) {
   int  index, lchild, rchild;
   T maximum, temp;
   lchild = 2*start;           // index of left child
   rchild = lchild + 1;              //  index of right child
   if ( lchild <= finish ) {
      maximum = heap[lchild];
      index = lchild;
      if ( rchild <= finish ) {
         if ( heap[rchild] > maximum ) {
            maximum = heap[rchild];
            index = rchild;
         }
      }
      if ( heap[start] < heap[index] ) {
         temp = heap[start];
         heap[start] = heap[index];
         heap[index] = temp;
         reheapifyDownward(index, finish);
      }
   }
}
template <class T>
void MaxHeap<T>::reheapifyUpward(int start)
{
   T temp, parent;
   if ( start > 1 ) {
      parent = start / 2;
      if ( heap[parent] < heap[start] ) {
         temp = heap[start];
         heap[start] = heap[parent];
         heap[parent] = temp;
         reheapifyUpward(parent);
      }
   }
}
template <class T>
void MaxHeap<T>::heapify() {
   int i, index;
   index = n / 2;
   for ( i = index; i >= 1; i-- )
      reheapifyUpward(i);
}
template <class T>
class PriorityQueue : MaxHeap<T>
{
    public:
       // constructor
       PriorityQueue(int m) : MaxHeap<T>(m) { }
      // destructor
       ~PriorityQueue() { }
     // member function that inserts a new element into priority queue
       void enqueue(T item);
     // member function that removes an element from a queue
      T dequeue();
```

```
   // member function to test whether the priority
    // queue is empty
    int isEmpty();
   // member function to test whether the priority
    // queue is full
    int isFull();
    // member function to show the contents of the priority queue
    void show();
};
// member function that inserts a new element into priority
// queue
template <class T>
void PriorityQueue<T>::enqueue(T item) {
   if ( isFull() )
      cout << "\nPriority Queue is full. . .\n";
   else
      insertElement(item);
}
// member function that removes an element from a queue
template <class T>
T PriorityQueue<T>::dequeue() {
   T temp;
   if ( isEmpty() )
      cout << "\nPriority Queue is empty. . .\n";
   else
      temp = MaxHeap<T>::deleteElement();
   return temp;
}
// member function to test whether the priority
// queue is empty
template <class T>
int PriorityQueue<T>::isEmpty()
{
   return MaxHeap<T>::isEmpty();
}
// member function to test whether the priority
// queue is full
template <class T>
int PriorityQueue<T>::isFull() {
   return MaxHeap<T>::isFull();
}
// member function to show the contents of priority queue
template <class T>
void PriorityQueue<T>::show() {
   if ( isEmpty() )
     cout << "\nPriority Queue is empty ...";
   else {
     cout << "\nElements of Priority Queue are : ";
     MaxHeap<T>::show();
   }
}
void main()
{
   int choice, element, m;
   cout << "\nEnter size of the Priority Queue : ";
   cin >> m;
   PriorityQueue<int> pq(m);
   do
```

```
  {
     cout << "\n\n      Options available \n";
     cout << "   ++++++++++++++++++++ \n\n";
     cout << "        1. Insert Element   \n";
     cout << "        2. Remove Element \n";
     cout << "        3. Show Priority Queue \n";
     cout << "        4. Exit\n\n";
     cout << "Enter your choice ( 1-4 ) : ";
     cin >> choice;
     switch ( choice )
     {
        case 1 : if ( pq.isFull() )
                    cout << "\nPriority Queue is already full ..";
                 else {
                    cout << "\nEnter Element : ";
                    cin >> element;
                    pq.enqueue(element);
                 }
                 break;
        case 2 : if ( pq.isEmpty() )
                    cout << "\nPriority Queue is already empty ..";
                 else {
                    cout << "Element removed is "
                         << pq.dequeue();
                 }
                 break;
        case 3 : pq.show();
     }
  }
  while ( choice != 4 );
} //----  end of main function ----
```

10.4.2 Sorting an Array Using Heapsort

Because of the order property, the maximum value of a *max heap* is in the root node. We can take advantage of this situation by using a heap to help us to sort the given array *a* having *n* elements.

The general approach of heap sort is as follows:

1. From the given array, build the initial max heap.
2. Interchange the root (maximum) element with the last element.
3. Use *reheapifydownward* operation from root node to rebuild the heap of size one less than the starting size.
4. Repeat steps 1 and 2 until there are no more elements.

Step 1 looks very much similar to selection sort, but the step that makes the heap sort fast is step 2 – *finding the next largest element*. As the shape property of a heap guarantees a binary tree of minimum height, therefore step 2 makes only $O(\log_2 n)$ comparisons in each iteration.

10.4.2.1 Building a Heap

To have a look at how the heap relates to array of unsorted elements. The Figure 10.4 shows unsorted array and its equivalent binary tree.

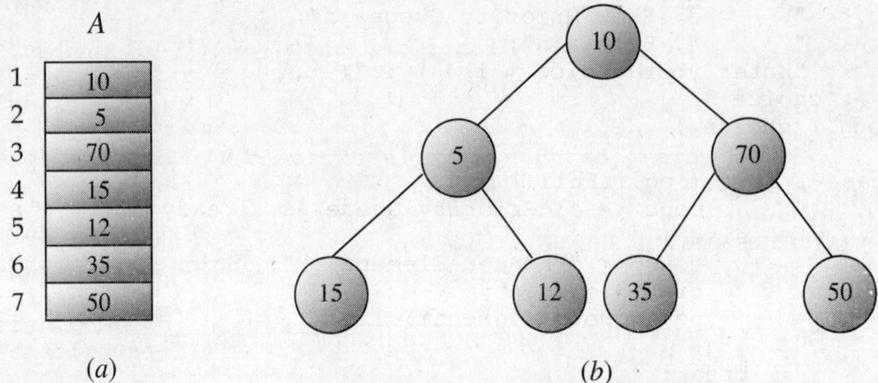

Figure 10.4: (*a*) Unsorted array *A*, (*b*) Equivalent binary tree

We want that the elements of the unsorted array must satisfy the order property of max heap. Let us first have a look at the binary tree to see that is there any part of the binary tree that already satisfies the order property. Observe that all the leaf nodes (subtrees with only single node) are heaps. In Figure 10.4(*b*), the subtrees whose roots contain values 15, 12, 35, and 50 are heaps because they are root nodes.

Now let us look at the first leftmost non-leaf node, the one containing value 5. The subtree rooted at this node is not a heap, and it is the root of the subtree that is heap. And we have already seen how to fix this problem using reheapify upward operation from this node. We apply reheapify upward operation to all the subtrees on this level, then we move up a level in the tree and continue until we reach the root node. After the reheapify upward operation is applied to the root node, the whole tree will satisfy the order property.

The heap building process, also popularly known as *heapify*, is illustrated for the given unsorted array *A* in Figure 10.4 is illustrated below:

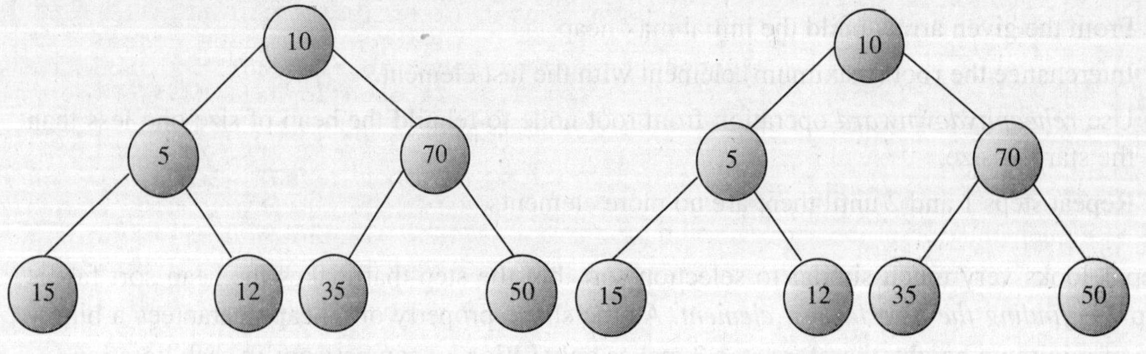

(*a*) Starting binary tree

(*b*) After reheapify upward operation at index 3

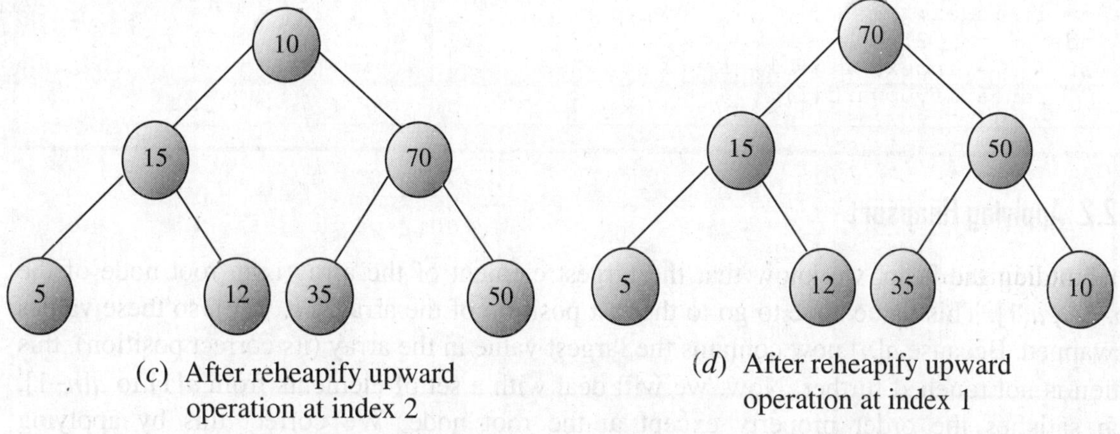

(*c*) After reheapify upward operation at index 2

(*d*) After reheapify upward operation at index 1

Figure 10.5: Illustration of heap building process

The binary tree of Figure 10.5(*d*) represents a *max* heap.

	a[1]	*a*[2]	*a*[3]	*a*[4]	*a*[5]	*a*[6]	*a*[7]
Original array A	10	5	70	15	12	35	50
After reheapify upward							
From index 3	10	5	70	15	12	35	50
From index 2	10	15	70	5	12	35	50
From index 1	70	15	50	5	12	35	10

Figure 10.6: Illustration of changing contents of array *A*

The various steps required are summarized in the following algorithm shown below.

Algorithm 10.10:

Heapify(***a*, *n*** **)**

Here *a* is the linear array with size *n*. This algorithm builds the max heap using the procedure described above.

```
Begin
  Set index = Parent of node with index n
  for i = index  to 1 by -1 do
     Call ReheapifyUpward( a, i, n )
  endfor
End.
```

The implementation of the above algorithm is given in the following listing.

Listing 10.7:

```
template <class T>
void MaxHeap<T>::heapify()
{
```

```
    int i, index;
    index = n / 2;
    for ( i = index; i >= 1; i-- )
        reheapifyUpward(i);
}
```

10.4.2.2 Applying Heapsort

After building the heap, we know that the largest element of the array is in root node of the heap, *i.e.*, *a*[1]. This value have to go to the last position of the array, *i.e.*, *a*[*n*], so these values are swapped. Because *a*[*n*] now contains the largest value in the array (its correct position), this position is not touched further. Now, we will deal with a set of elements from *a*[1] to *a*[*n*–1], which satisfies the order property except at the root node. We correct this by applying *reheapifydownward* operation.

At this point, we know that the next largest element in the array is in the root node of the heap. To put this element in the correct position in the array, we swap it with the element *a*[*n*–1]. Now two largest elements are in their final position in the array, and we are left dealing with elements from *a*[1] to *a*[*n*–2]. This process is repeated until all the elements are in their correct positions, *i.e.*, until heap contains only single element, which is the smallest element in the array.

The steps required to sort an array *a* of unsorted element in ascending order are summarized in the following algorithm.

Algorithm 10.11:

HeapSort(*a*, *n*)

Here *a* is a linear array of size *n* in memory. This algorithm sorts this array in ascending order using Heap sort method.

```
Begin
  Call Heapify( a, n )
  for i = n to 2 by -1 do
      Interchange elements a[1] and a[i]
      Call Reheapifydownward( a, 1, i-1  )
  endfor
End.
```

Implementation of the above algorithm is given below:

Listing 10.8:

```
template <class T>
void Array<T>:;heapSort()
{
   int i, temp;
   heapify();
```

```
for ( i = n; i > 1; i-- ) {
    temp = a[1];
    a[1] = a[i];
    a[i] = temp;
    reheapifydownward( a, 1, i-1 );
  }
}
```

Example 10.3:

Let us consider a working example to illustrate the working of heapsort algorithm. For this purpose consider the following array

10, 5, 70, 15, 12, 35, 50

Solution:

	a[1]	*a*[2]	*a*[3]	*a*[4]	*a*[5]	*a*[6]	*a*[7]
After heapify operation	70	15	50	5	12	35	10
Swap	10	15	50	5	12	35	70
Reheapifydownward	50	15	35	5	12	10	70
Swap	10	15	35	5	12	50	70
Reheapifydownward	35	15	10	5	12	50	70
Swap	12	15	10	5	35	50	70
Reheapifydownward	15	12	10	5	35	50	70
Swap	5	12	10	15	35	50	70
Reheapifydownward	12	5	10	15	35	50	70
Swap	10	5	12	15	35	50	70
Reheapifydownward	10	5	12	15	35	50	70
Swap	5	10	12	15	35	50	70
Final sorted array	5	10	12	15	35	50	70

Figure 10.7: Illustration of effect of heapsort on array *a*

Analysis of Heap Sort

In the heapsort algorithm, we call function *heapify()* to build the initial heap, which is $O(\log_2 n)$ operation, and inside the loop we call utility function *reheapifydownward()*. The loop is executed $(n-1)$ times, and in each iteration, the element in the root node of the heap is swapped with the last element of the reduced size heap and heap is rebuild. Swapping two elements take constant time. A complete binary tree with n nodes has $O(\log_2(n+1))$ levels. In the worst case, if the root element is bumped down to a leaf position, the *reheapifydownward* operation would perform $O(\log_2 n)$ swaps. So the swap plus *reheapifydownward* is $O(\log_2 n)$. Multiplying this activity by $(n-1)$ iteration shows that the sorting loop is $O(n\log_2 n)$.

Combining the heap build, which is $O(n)$, and the sorting loop, we can see that complexity of *heapSort* is $O(n\log_2 n)$.

Listing 10.8:

```
//  Program to sort an array of integers in ascending
//  order using heap sort method
#include<iostream.h>
#include<iomanip.h>
template <class T>
class Array
{
   private:
      T *a;
      int size;
   public:
      Array(int n) {
         size = n;
         a = new T[n+1];
      }
      ~Array() {
         delete a;
      }
      void inputArray();
      void heapify();
      void reheapifydownward(int, int);
      void heapSort();
      void outputArray();
};
template <class T>
void Array<T>::inputArray()
{
   int i;
   cout << "\nEnter " << size << " elements of array\n\n";
   for ( i = 1; i <= size; i++ ) {
      cin >> a[i];
   }
}
template <class T>
void Array<T>::heapify()
{
   int i, index;
   index = size / 2;
   for ( i = index; i >= 1; i-- )
      reheapifydownward(i, size );
}
```

```
template <class T>
void Array<T>::reheapifydownward(int start, int finish)
{
   int  index, lchild, rchild, maximum, temp;
   lchild = 2*start;
   rchild = lchild + 1;
   if ( lchild <= finish ) {
      maximum = a[lchild];
      index = lchild;
      if ( rchild <= finish ) {
          if( a[rchild] > maximum ) {
             maximum = a[rchild];
             index = rchild;
          }
      }
      if ( a[start] < a[index] ) {
          temp = a[start];
          a[start] = a[index];
          a[index] = temp;
          reheapifydownward(index, finish);
      }
   }
}
template <class T>
void Array<T>::heapSort()
{
   int i, temp;
   heapify();
   for ( i = size; i > 1; i-- ) {
      temp = a[1];
      a[1] = a[i];
      a[i] = temp;
      reheapifydownward(1, i-1);
   }
}
template <class T>
void Array<T>::outputArray()
{
   int i;
   for ( i = 1; i <= size; i++ ) {
      cout << a[i] << "\t";
   }
   cout << endl;
}
void main()
{
   int n;
   cout << "Enter size of array : ";
   cin >> n;
   Array<int> a(n);
   a.inputArray();
   cout << "\n\nInput array is : ";
   a.outputArray();
   a.heapSort();
   cout << "\n\nSorted array is : ";
   a.outputArray();
}
```

REVIEW EXERCISES

1. What is heap? What is the difference between a min heap and max heap?
2. Show the implementation of *heapify()* operation for a *min heap*.
3. Show the implementation of delete operation that can delete an element from a heap from an arbitrary index, not necessarily from root of the heap.
4. Does the sequence <23, 17, 14, 6, 13, 10, 1, 5, 7, 12> represents a max heap?
5. Does the sequence <3, 7, 4, 6, 13, 10, 1, 5, 7, 1> represents a min heap?
6. The sequence <70, 15, 50, 5, 12, 35, 10> represents a max heap. Show the heap after the following operations:

   (*a*) Insertion of element 25
   (*b*) Deletion from root
   (*c*) Insertion of element 75

   Also give the number of exchanges performed in each case.
7. Illustrate the operation *heapify()* on the sequence <13, 10, 5, 7, 22, 11, 9, 18> in order to build a *min heap*.
8. How a heap differs from a binary tree?
9. How a heap can be used to implement a priority queue?

PROGRAMMING EXERCISES

1. Write functions for implementing *reheapify upward()* and *reheapify upward()* operations on a *min* heap.
2. Write a function to delete an item at index *i* from a heap.

❑ ❑ ❑

Chapter 11

Graphs

11.1 INTRODUCTION

Graph is another important non-linear data structure. This data structure is used to represent relationship between pairs of elements, which are not necessarily hierarchical in nature. A *graph* is defines as

"Graph G is a ordered set (V, E), where V(G) represent the set of elements, called vertices, and E(G) represents the edges between these vertices".

Figure 11.1 shows a sample graph, for which $V(G) = \{ v_1, v_2, v_3, v_4, v_5\}$, and $E(G) = \{e_1, e_2, e_2, e_4, e_5\}$ i.e. there are five vertices and five edges in the graph.

A graph can be either *directed* or *undirected*. In an undirected graph, there is no specific direction associated with the edges. In general, in an undirected graph, an edges is represented by an *unordered* pair $[u, v]$ (i.e. $e = [u, v]$) , and that can be traversed from u toward v or vice versa. Figure 11.1 depicts an undirected graph. Whereas in a directed graph, an edge is represented by an *ordered* pair (u, v) (i.e. $e = (u, v)$), and that can be traversed only from u toward v. Figure 11.2 depicts a directed graph.

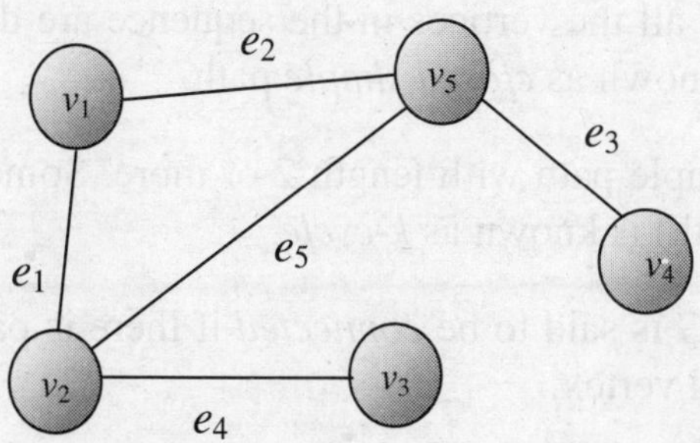

Figure 11.1: Undirected graph

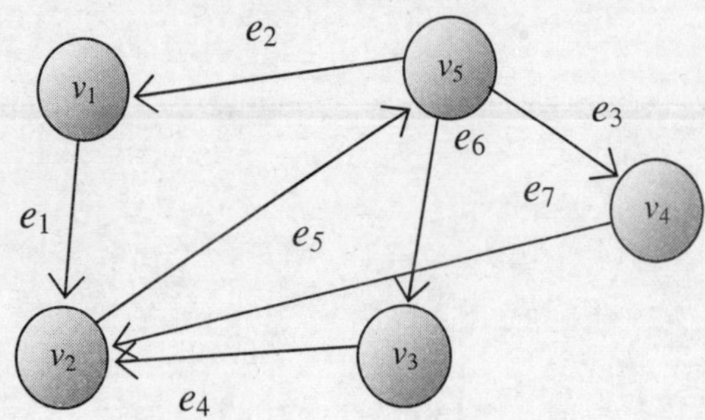

Figure 11.2: Directed graph

Before we move on to describe the storage of graphs in computer memory, and subsequent operation on these graphs, let us first review important terms in the graph terminology, which will be used, in remaining text.

11.2 GRAPH TERMINOLOGY

First we will review the terminology applicable to undirected graphs.

Adjacent Vertices – As an edge e is represented by pair of vertices denoted by $[u, v]$. The vertices u and v are called endpoints of e. These vertices are also called adjacent vertices or neighbors.

Degree of a Vertex – The degree of vertex u, written as $deg(u)$, is the number of edges containing u. If $deg(u)=0$, this means that vertex u does not belong to any edge, then vertex u is called an *isolated* vertex.

Path – A *path* P of length n from a vertex u to vertex v is defined as sequence of $(n+1)$ vertices, *i.e.*

$$P = (v_1, v_2, v_3, \ldots v_{n+1})$$

such that $u = v_1$, $v = v_{n+1}$, and v_{i-1} is adjacent to v_i for $i = 2, 3, \ldots, (n+1)$.

The path is said to be *closed* if the endpoints of the path are same i.e. $v_1 = v_{n+1}$.

The path is said to be *simple* if all the vertices in the sequence are distinct, with the exception that $v_1 = v_{n+1}$. In that case it is known as *closed simple* path.

Cycle – A *cycle* is a closed simple path with length 2 or more. Sometimes, a cycle of length k (i.e. k distinct vertices in the path) is known as *k-cycle*.

Connected Graph – A graph G is said to be *connected* if there is path between any two of its vertices, *i.e.*, there is no isolated vertex.

A connected graph without any cycles is called a *tree*. Thus we can say that tree is a special graph.

Complete Graph – A graph G is said to *complete* or *fully connected* if there is path from every vertex to every other vertex. A complete graph with n vertices will have $n(n-1)/2$ edges.

Weighted Graph – A graph is said to *weighted* graph if every edge in the graph is assigned some data. The weight of the, denoted by $w(e)$, is a non-negative value that may be representing the cost of moving along that edge or distance between the vertices.

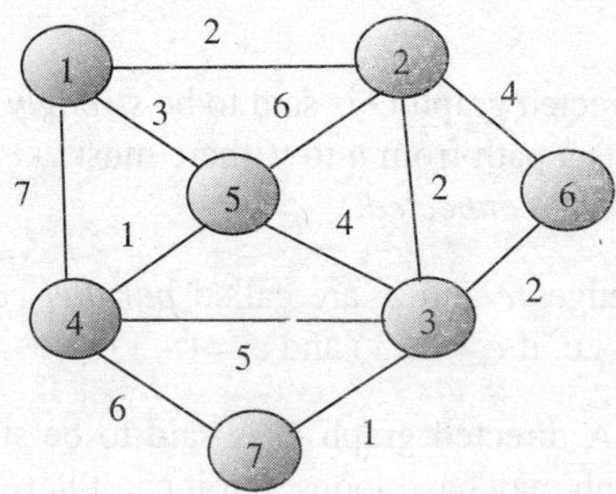

Figure 11.3: Weighted undirected graph

Multiple Edges – Distinct edges e and e' are called *multiple edges* if they connect the same endpoints, *i.e.*, if $e = [u, v]$ and $e' = [u, v]$.

Multigraph – A graph containing multiple edges.

Loop – An edge is a *loop* if it has identical endpoints, *i.e.*, if $e = [u, u]$.

Standard definition of graph usually does not permit either multiple edges or loops.

The following terms have relevance to directed graphs only.

A *directed graph* G is a graph in which each edge is assigned a certain direction, *i.e.*, each edge is an ordered pair of (u,v) of vertices rather than an unordered pair $[u, v]$.

Suppose G is a directed graph with $e = (u, v)$ as one of the edges, then

- *e begins* at u and *ends* at v,
- u is the *origin* (also known as *initial point*) of e, and v is the *destination* (also known as *terminal point*) of e,
- u is the *predecessor* of v, and v is the *successor* of u,

Outdegree and Indegree of a Vertex – The *outdegree* of a vertex *u*, denoted by *outdeg*(*u*), is the number of edges originating at *u*. Similarly, The *indegree* of a vertex *u*, denoted by *indeg*(*u*), is the number of edges terminating at *u*.

Source and Sink – A Vertex *u* is called a *source* if it has a outdegree greater than zero, but zero indegree. Similarly, a vertex *u* is called *sink* if it has indegree greater than zero, but zero outdegree.

Reachability – A vertex *v* is said to be reachable from *u* if there exists a path from vertex *u* to vertex *v*.

Strongly Connected – A directed graph *G* is said to be *strongly connected*, if for each pair *u*, *v* of vertices in *G*, if there exists a path from *u* to *v*, there must exist a path from *v* to *u;* otherwise the directed graph is *unilaterally connected*.

Parallel Edges – Distinct edges *e* and e' are called *parallel edges* if they connect the same source and terminal vertices, i.e. if $e = (u, v)$ and $e' = (u, v)$.

Simple Directed Graph – A directed graph *G* is said to be simple, if there are no parallel edges. A simple directed graph may have loops, but it can't have more than one loop at a given vertex.

Directed Acyclic Graph – A directed acyclic graph (DAG) *G* is a directed graph without cycle(s).

11.3 REPRESENTATION OF GRAPHS

There are two ways to represent a graph $G = (V, E)$:

- using an adjacency matrix
- using an adjacency list

The adjacency list representation is usually preferred because it provides a compact way to represent *sparse* graphs. A sparse graph is that for which $|E|$ is much less than $|V|^2$. When the graph is *dense* graph, we may prefer adjacency matrix representation. A dense graph is that for which $|E|$ is close to $|V|^2$ and we need to tell very quickly if there is an edge connecting given two vertices.

11.3.1 Adjacency Matrix Representation

Consider a directed graph $G = (V, E)$. We will assume that the vertices are numbered 1, 2, 3, . . ., $|V|$, in some arbitrary manner. The *adjacency matrix* representation of a graph *G* then consists of $|V| \times |V|$ matrix $A = (a_{ij})$, such that

$$a_{ij} = \begin{cases} 1 & \text{if } (i, j) \in E \\ 0 & \text{otherwise} \end{cases}$$

For undirected graph $G = (V, E)$, the adjacency matrix representation is also consists of $|V| \times |V|$ matrix $A = (a_{ij})$, but its elements are as follows:

$$a_{ij} = \begin{cases} 1 & \text{if either } [i, j] \in E \text{ or } [j, i] \in E \\ 0 & \text{otherwise} \end{cases}$$

	1	2	3	4	5
1	0	1	0	0	1
2	1	0	1	0	1
3	0	1	0	0	0
4	0	0	0	0	1
5	1	1	0	1	0

(*a*) Adjacency matrix for undirected graph of Figure 11.1

	1	2	3	4	5
1	0	1	0	0	0
2	0	0	0	0	1
3	0	1	0	0	0
4	0	1	0	0	0
5	1	0	1	1	0

(*b*) Adjacency matrix for directed graph of Figure 11.2

	1	2	3	4	5	6	7
1	0	2	0	7	3	0	0
2	2	0	2	0	6	4	0
3	0	2	0	5	4	2	1
4	7	0	5	0	1	0	6
5	3	6	4	1	0	0	0
6	0	4	2	0	0	0	0
7	0	0	1	6	0	0	0

(*c*) Adjacency matrix for weighted graph of Figure 11.3

Figure 11.4: Adjacency matrix representation of graphs

A matrix, like adjacency matrix for non-weighted graphs that contains entries of only 0 and 1 is called *bit matrix* or a *boolean matrix*.

The adjacency matrix representation of a graph requires $O(V^2)$ memory locations irrespective of the number of edges in the graph.

Observe the symmetry of the adjacency matrix of directed graph in figure 11.4(*a*), so if we store only the entries on or above of the diagonal of the adjacency matrix, we can reduce the memory requirements to store the graph to almost half.

To represent weighted graphs using adjacency matrix, the weight of edge (u, v) is simply stored as the entry in row u and column v of the adjacency matrix. In case, zero can also be the possible weight of the edge, then we have to store some sentinel value for non-existent edge, which can be a negative value since the weight of the edge is always a positive number.

11.3.2 Adjacency List Representation

The adjacency-list representation of a graph $G = (V, E)$ consists of an array *Adj* of $|V|$ lists, one for each vertex in V. For each $u \in V$, the adjacency list $Adj[u]$ contains all the vertices v such that there is an edge $(u,v) \in E$ *i.e.* $Adj[u]$ consists of all the vertices adjacent to u in G. The vertices in each adjacency list are stored in an arbitrary order.

If G is an undirected graph, the sum of the lengths of all the adjacency lists is $2|E|$, since for every $[u, v]$, u appears in v's adjacency list (i.e. $u \in Adj[v]$), and v appears in u's adjacency list (i.e. $v \in Adj[u]$). If G is a directed graph, the sum of the lengths of all the adjacency lists is $|E|$, since edges of the form (u, v) is represented by having v appearing in u's adjacency list (i.e. $v \in Adj[u]$).

Adjacency lists can be easily modified to represent weighted graphs. The weight of edge $e = (u, v)$, denoted by $w(e)$ or $w(u, v)$, is simply stored with the vertex v in $Adj[u]$ i.e. the information part of the vertex will have two fields – *one to store vertex and the second to store the weight of the edge.*

Although the adjacency list representation requires very less memory as compared to the adjacency matrix, the simplicity of adjacency matrix makes it preferable when graphs are reasonably small. Moreover, if the graph is not weighted one, there is additional advantage for the adjacency matrix representation. Rather than using one byte/word (in case of PC, to store an integer value in the range of 1–127 we need one byte, in range 1–65535, we need two bytes, etc.) for each entry of the matrix, the adjacency matrix uses only one bit per entry.

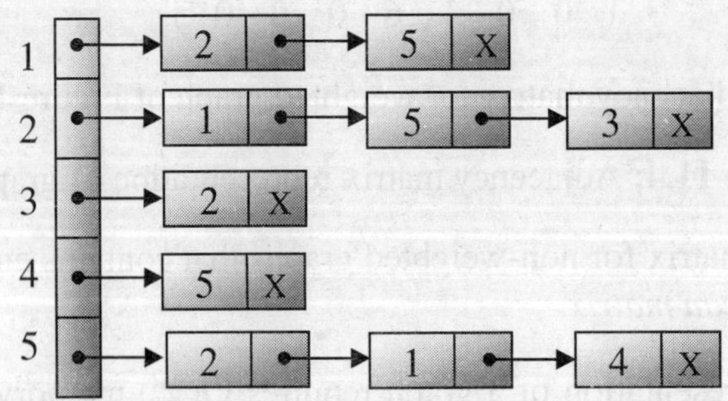

(*a*) Adjacency-list for undirected graph of Figure 11.1

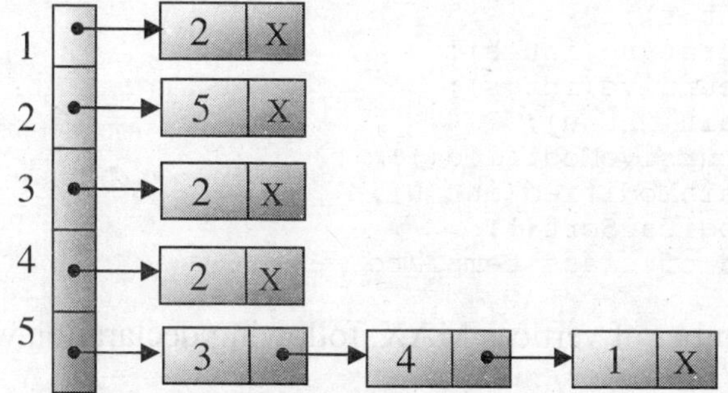

(*b*) Adjacency-list for undirected graph of Figure 11.2

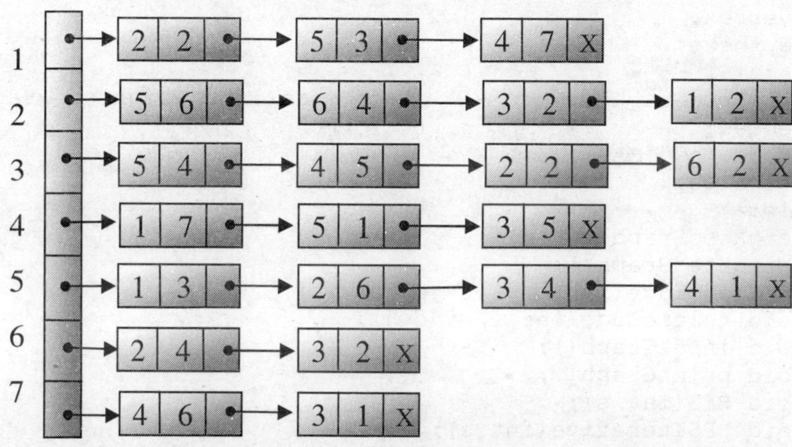

(*c*) Adjacency-list for weighted graph of Figure 11.3

Figure 11.5: Adjacency-list representation of graphs

11.3.2.1 Implementation of Adjacency List in C++ Language

Let us first consider non-weighted graph with number of vertices MAX, where MAX is defined equal to 50, say, then the following declaration will be required

```
#define MAX  20
struct NWNode {              // --- node declaration ---
   int vertex;
   NWNode *next;
};
class NonWeightedGraph      // class modelling weighted graph
{
   protected:
      NWNode *adj[MAX];
      int size;
   public:
      NonWeightedGraph(int n);
      ~NonWeightedGraph();
      void addEdge(int i, int j, int w);
      void deleteEdge(int i, int j);
      void inputGraph();
      void printGraph();
```

```
        void BFS(int s);
        void DFSIterative(int s);
        void DFSRecursive(int s);
        void DFSVisit(int u);
        void DFSRecursiveModified();
        void DFSVisitModified(int u);
        void topologicalSort();
};  //   ---- end of class template ----
```

For weighted graph with number of vertices MAX, following declaration will be required:

```
#define  MAX   20
struct Wnode {              // --- node declaration ---
   int vertex;
   int vertex;
   WNode *next;
};
class WeightedGraph {   // --- class modelling weighted graph
   protected:
      WNode *adj[MAX];
      int size;
   public:
      WeightedGraph(int n);
      ~WeightedGraph();
      void addEdge(int i, int j, int w);
      void deleteEdge(int i, int j);
      void inputGraph();
      void printGraph();
      void BFS(int s);
      void DFSIterative(int s);
      void DFSRecursive(int s);
      void DFSVisit(int u);
      void DFSRecursiveModified();
      void DFSVisitModified(int u);
      void topologicalSort();
      void MinimumSpanningTreePrim();
      void shortestPathDijkstra(int s, int d);
};  //   ---- end of class template ----
```

11.4 OPERATIONS ON GRAPHS

Unless or otherwise stated, most of the algorithms developed assumes that the input graph is represented in adjacency-list form.

11.4.1 Creating an Empty Graph

To create an empty graph, the entire adjacency list is set to NULL. This task is accomplished by the constructor of the appropriate class as shown below:

Listing 11.1:

```
//  parameterized constructor to create non-weighted graph
NonWeightedGraph::NonWeightedGraph(int n)
{
   int i;
   for ( i = 1; i <= n; i++ )
```

```
      adj[i] = NULL;
   size = n;
}
```

Listing 11.2 :

```
//  parameterized constructor to create weighted graph
WeightedGraph::WeightedGraph(int n) {
   int i;
   for ( i = 1; i <= n; i++ )
      adj[i] = NULL;
   size = n;
}
```

11.4.2 Entering Graph Information

The graph information is entered as shown in the following listing.

Listing 11.3:

```
// member function to input a non-weighted graph
void NonWeightedGraph::inputGraph()
{
   NWNode *ptr, *last;
   int i, j, m, val;
   for ( i = 1; i <= size; i++ ) {
       last = NULL;
       cout << "\nNumber of nodes in the adjacency"
          << " list of node #" << i << " : ";
       cin >> m;
       for ( j = 1; j <= m; j++ ) {
          cout << "Enter node #" << j << " : ";
          cin >> val;
          ptr = new NWNode;
          ptr->vertex = val;
          ptr->next = NULL;
          if ( adj[i] == NULL )
             adj[i] = last = ptr;
          else {
             last->next = ptr;
             last = ptr;
          }
       }
   }
}
```

Listing 11.4:

```
// member function to input a weighted graph
void WeightedGraph::inputGraph()
{
   WNode *ptr, *last;
   int i, j, m, val, wt;
   for ( i = 1; i <= size; i++ ) {
```

```
      last = NULL;
      cout << "\nNumber of nodes in the adjacency"
         << " list of node #" << i << " : ";
      cin >> m;
      for ( j = 1; j <= m; j++ ) {
         cout << "Enter node #" << j << " : ";
         cin >> val;
         cout << "Enter weight for edge ("
              << i << "," << val << ") : ";
         cin >> wt;
         ptr = new WNode;
         ptr->vertex = val;
         ptr->weight = wt;
         ptr->next = NULL;
         if ( adj[i] == NULL )
              adj[i] = last = ptr;
         else {
              last->next = ptr;
              last = ptr;
         }
      }
   }
}
```

11.4.3 Outputting a Graph

The following listing shows the way graph information can be outputted.

Listing 11.5:

```
// member function to output a non-weighted graph
void NonWeightedGraph::printGraph() {
  NWNode *ptr;
  int i;
  for ( i = 1; i <= size; i++ ) {
     ptr = adj[i];
     cout << "\n " << i;
     while ( ptr != NULL ) {
       cout << "->" << ptr->vertex
       ptr = ptr->next;
     }
     cout << endl;
  }
}
```

Listing 11.6:

```
// member function to output a weighted graph
void WeightedGraph::printGraph() {
  WNode *ptr;
  int i;
  for ( i = 1; i <= size; i++ ) {
     ptr = adj[i];
     cout << "\n " << i;
```

```
    while ( ptr != NULL ) {
      cout << "->(" << ptr->vertex
           << "," << ptr->weight << ")";
      ptr = ptr->next;
    }
    cout << endl;
  }
}
```

11.4.4 Deleting a Graph

This task is accomplished by the destructor of the respective classes as shown below:

Listing 11.7:

```
// destructor to remove non-weighted graph from memory
NonWeightedGraph::~NonWeightedGraph()
{
   int i;
   NWNode *temp, *ptr;
   for ( i = 1; i <= size; i++ )
   {
       ptr = adj[i];
       while ( ptr != NULL )
       {
          temp = ptr;
          ptr  = ptr->next;
          delete temp;
       }
       adj[i] = NULL;
   }
}
```

Listing 11.8:

```
// destructor to remove weighted graph from memory
WeightedGraph::~WeightedGraph()
{
   int i;
   WNode *temp, *ptr;
   for ( i = 1; i <= size; i++ )
   {
       ptr = adj[i];
       while ( ptr != NULL )
       {
          temp = ptr;
          ptr  = ptr->next;
          delete temp;
       }
       adj[i] = NULL;
   }
}
```

Listing 11.9:

```
//  Program to illustrate the input and output of a non-weighted graph
#include <iostream.h>
#include <iomanip.h>
#define   MAX   20
struct NWNode {         // --- node declaration ---
   int vertex;
   NWNode *next;
};
class NonWeightedGraph  // class modelling weighted graph
{
   protected:
      NWNode *adj[MAX];
      int size;
   public:
      NonWeightedGraph(int n);
      ~NonWeightedGraph();
      void addEdge(int i, int j, int w);
      void deleteEdge(int i, int j);
      void inputGraph();
      void printGraph();
      void BFS(int s);
      void DFSIterative(int s);
      void DFSRecursive(int s);
      void DFSVisit(int u);
      void DFSRecursiveModified();
      void DFSVisitModified(int u);
      void topologicalSort();
};  //   ---- end of class template ----
//  parameterized constructor
NonWeightedGraph::NonWeightedGraph(int n) {
   int i;
   for ( i = 1; i <= n; i++ )
      adj[i] = NULL;
   size = n;
}
// member function to input a weighted graph
void NonWeightedGraph::inputGraph()
{
   NWNode *ptr, *last;
   int i, j, m, val;
   for ( i = 1; i <= size; i++ ) {
      last = NULL;
      cout << "\nNumber of nodes in the adjacency"
         << " list of node #" << i << " : ";
      cin >> m;
      for ( j = 1; j <= m; j++ ) {
         cout << "Enter node #" << j << " : ";
         cin >> val;
         ptr = new NWNode;
         ptr->vertex = val;
         ptr->next = NULL;
         if ( adj[i] == NULL )
           adj[i] = last = ptr;
         else {
           last->next = ptr;
```

```
            last = ptr;
         }
      }
   }
}
// member function to input a weighted graph
void NonWeightedGraph::printGraph()
{
  NWNode *ptr;
  int i;
  for ( i = 1; i <= size; i++ ) {
     ptr = adj[i];
     cout << "\n " << i;
     while ( ptr != NULL ) {
        cout << "->" << ptr->vertex;
        ptr = ptr->next;
     }
     cout << endl;
  }
}
// destructor
NonWeightedGraph::~NonWeightedGraph()
{
   int i;
   NWNode *temp, *ptr;
   for ( i = 1; i <= size; i++ ) {
      ptr = adj[i];
      while ( ptr != NULL ) {
         temp = ptr;
         ptr  = ptr->next;
         delete temp;
      }
      adj[i] = NULL;
   }
}
void main()
{
   int n;
   cout << "\nEnter number of nodes[<=20] in the graph : ";
   cin >> n;
   NonWeightedGraph nwgraph(n);
   nwgraph.inputGraph();
   cout << "\nADJACENCY LIST FOR INPUT GRAPH \n\n";
   nwgraph.printGraph();
}
```

Listing 11.10:

```
//  Program to illustrate the input and output of a weighted graph
#include <iostream.h>
#include <iomanip.h>
#define  MAX   20
struct WNode               // --- node declaration ---
{
   int vertex;
   int weight;
```

```
   WNode *next;
};
class WeightedGraph {  // --- class modelling weighted graph
   protected:
      WNode *adj[MAX];
      int size;
   public:
      WeightedGraph(int n);
      ~WeightedGraph();
      void addEdge(int i, int j, int w);
      void deleteEdge(int i, int j);
      void inputGraph();
      void printGraph();
      void BFS(int s);
      void DFSIterative(int s);
      void DFSRecursive(int s);
      void DFSVisit(int u);
      void DFSRecursiveModified();
      void DFSVisitModified(int u);
      void topologicalSort();
      void MinimumSpanningTreePrim();
      void shortestPathDijkstra(int s, int d);
};  //   ---- end of class template ----
//  parameterized constructor
WeightedGraph::WeightedGraph(int n) {
   int i;
   for ( i = 1; i <= n; i++ )
      adj[i] = NULL;
   size = n;
}
// member function to input a weighted graph
void WeightedGraph::inputGraph()
{
   WNode *ptr, *last;
   int i, j, m, val, wt;
   for ( i = 1; i <= size; i++ ) {
      last = NULL;
      cout << "\nNumber of nodes in the adjacency"
         << " list of node #" << i << " : ";
      cin >> m;
      for ( j = 1; j <= m; j++ ) {
         cout << "Enter node #" << j << " : ";
         cin >> val;
         cout << "Enter weight for edge ("
            << i << "," << val << ") : ";
         cin >> wt;
         ptr = new WNode;
         ptr->vertex = val;
         ptr->weight = wt;
         ptr->next = NULL;
         if ( adj[i] == NULL )
            adj[i] = last = ptr;
         else {
            last->next = ptr;
            last = ptr;
         }
      }
   }
```

```
}
// member function to input a weighted graph
void WeightedGraph::printGraph()
{
  WNode *ptr;
  int i;
  for ( i = 1; i <= size; i++ )
  {
     ptr = adj[i];
     cout << "\n " << i;
     while ( ptr != NULL )
     {
        cout << "->(" << ptr->vertex
             << "," << ptr->weight << ")";
        ptr = ptr->next;
     }
     cout << endl;
  }
}
// destructor
WeightedGraph::~WeightedGraph()
{
   int i;
   WNode *temp, *ptr;
   for ( i = 1; i <= size; i++ )
   {
      ptr = adj[i];
      while ( ptr != NULL )
      {
         temp = ptr;
         ptr  = ptr->next;
         delete temp;
      }
      adj[i] = NULL;
   }
}
void main()
{
   int n;
   cout << "\nEnter number of nodes[<=20] in the graph : ";
   cin >> n;
   WeightedGraph wgraph(n);
   wgraph.inputGraph();
   cout<< "\nADJACENCY LIST FOR INPUT GRAPH \n\n";
   wgraph.printGraph();
}
```

11.4.5 Traversal

Many applications of graphs require examining the vertices and edges of a graph *G*. There are two standard ways for graph traversal:

- Breadth-first search
- Depth-first search

11.4.5.1 Breadth-First Search

Given an input graph $G = (V, E)$ and a source vertex s, from where to begin. The breadth first search (BFS) systematically explores the edges of G to discover every vertex that is reachable from s. It produces a breadth-first tree with root s that contains all such vertices that are reachable form s. For every vertex v reachable from s, the path in the breadth-first tree from s to v corresponds to a shortest path. The algorithm works on both directed as well as on undirected graphs.

To keep track of the progress, BFS colors each vertex WHITE, GRAY, or BLACK, where vertex with WHITE color indicates that the vertex is still undiscovered, vertex with GRAY color indicates that the vertex is discovered but not yet processed, and the vertex with BLACK color indicates that the vertex has been processed. These three states can also be represented by using some integer variable, say *status*. The above mentioned three states during the progress of the BFS can be indicated by assigning value 1, 2, and 3 to *status*. In our discussion, we will consider coloring scheme.

All the vertices are initially WHITE (non-discovered), and later on become GRAY (discovered) and then BLACK (finished). As soon as the vertex is discovered for the first time, it becomes non-WHITE. Therefore, GRAY and BLACK vertices are have been discovered, but the breadth-first search distinguishes between them to ensure that the search proceeds in a breadth-first manner. If $(u, v) \in E$ and vertex u is BLACK, then vertex v is either GRAY or BLACK; that is, all vertices adjacent to BLACK vertices have been discovered. GRAY vertices may have some adjacent WHITE vertices; they represent the frontier between discovered and undiscovered vertices.

The algorithm uses a FIFO queue structure to maintain the order in which the vertices are to be processed.

Algorithm 11.1:

BreadthFirstSearch(*adj*, *n*, *s*)

Here *adj* is the adjacency-list of the graph with *n* vertices, and vertex *s* is the source vertex. This algorithm uses a FIFO queue *q*, and linear array *color* of size *n*, to keep track of the progress of BFS. It also uses a local variable *u*.

```
Begin
   for i = 1 to n by 1 do
      Set color[i] = WHITE
   endfor
   Set color[s] = GRAY
   Call CreateQueue( q );
   Call Enqueue(q, s)
   while ( q is not empty ) do
```

```
        Set u = Peek( q )
        Set ptr = adj[u]
        while ( ptr ≠ NULL ) do
            if ( color[ptr->info] = WHITE ) then
                Set color[s] = GRAY
                Call Enqueue( q, ptr->info)
            endif
        endwhile
        Print: u
        Set color[u] = BLACK
    endwhile
End.
```

Example 11.1:

Consider the following graph, and source vertex 2.

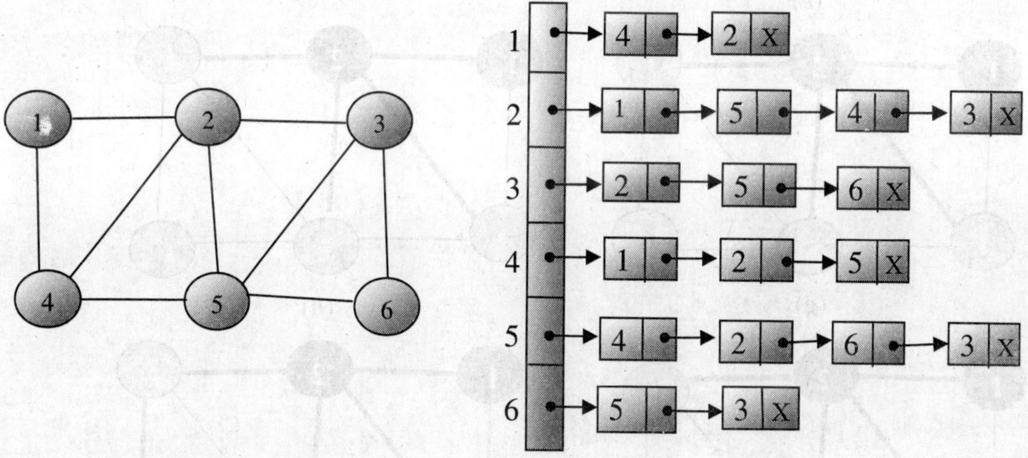

Figure 11.6: Undirected graph and its adjacency-list

Solution:

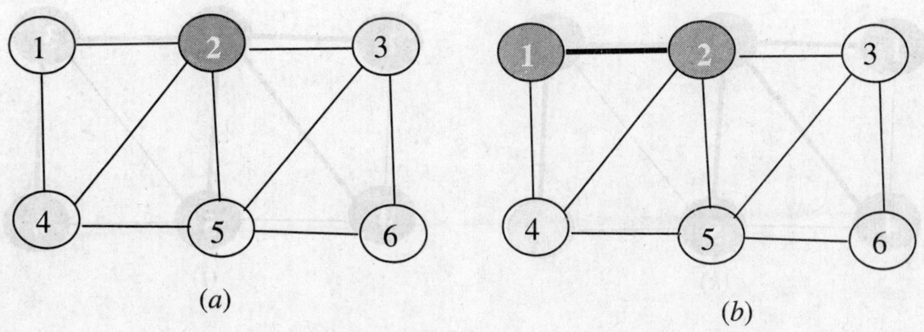

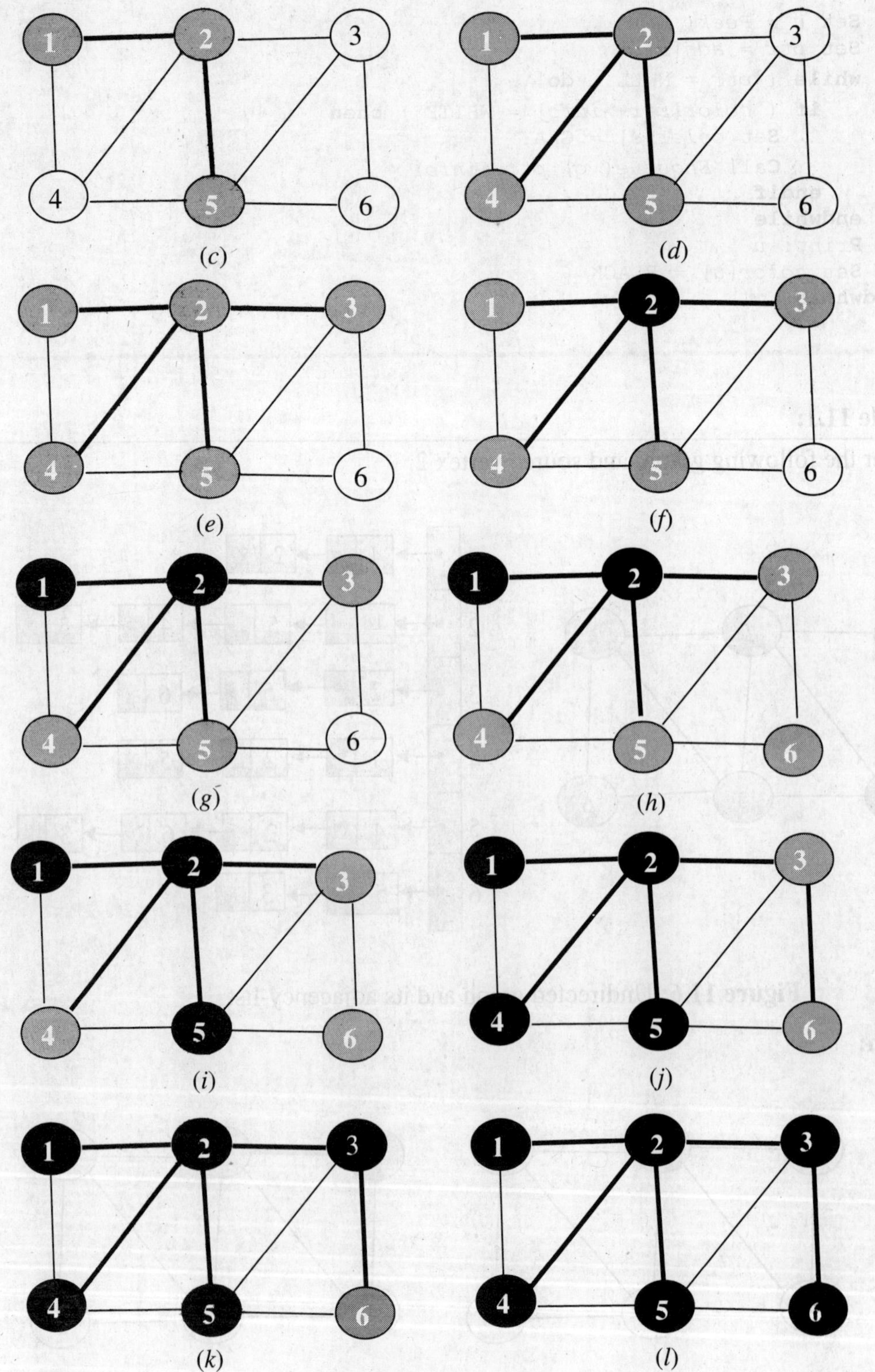

Figure 11.7: (*a*) – (*l*) illustrates BFS on undirected graph.

The vertices are traversed in following order

2 1 5 4 3 6

The following algorithm summarizes various steps required to implement the BFS.

Listing 11.11:

```
//  Program to illustrate the BFS on a non-weighted graph
//
#include <iostream.h>
#include <iomanip.h>
#include "graph.h"
#include "linkq.h"
#define WHITE 0
#define GRAY  1
#define BLACK 2
void NonWeightedGraph::BFS(int s)
{
   NWNode *ptr;
   LinkQueue<int> q;
   int i, u, v, color[MAX];
   for ( i = 1; i<= size; i++ )
      color[i] = WHITE;
   color[s] = GRAY;
   q.enqueue(s);
   while ( !q.isEmpty() )
   {
      u = q.peek();
      ptr = adj[u];
      while ( ptr != NULL )
      {
         v = ptr->vertex;
         if ( color[v] == WHITE )
         {
            color[v] = GRAY;
            q.enqueue(v);
         }
         ptr = ptr->next;
      }
      u = q.dequeue();
      cout << u << "    ";
      color[u] = BLACK;
   }
}
void main()
{
   int n, s;
   cout << "\nEnter number of nodes in the graph : ";
   cin >> n;
   NonWeightedGraph nwgraph(n);
   nwgraph.inputGraph();
   cout << "\nEnter source vertex : ";
   cin >> s;
   cout << "\n\nBFS from vertex " << s << " is\n\n";
   nwgraph.BFS(s);
}
```

11.4.5.2 Depth-First Search

The depth-first search (DFS), as its name implies, is to search *deeper* in the graph, whenever possible. The edges are explored out of the most recently discovered vertex *v* that still has unexplored edges leaving it. When all of *v*'s edges have been explored, the search *backtracks* to explore edges leaving the vertex from which *v* was discovered. This process continues until we have discovered all the vertices that are reachable from the source vertex. This algorithm also works on both directed as well as on undirected graphs.

To keep track of the progress, the DFS also uses the same coloring scheme as described for BFS. In addition, the DFS makes uses of a stack structure to maintain the order in which the vertices are to be processed, instead of queue.

The algorithm 11.2 summarizes various steps required to implement the DFS.

Algorithm 11.2:

DepthfirstSearchIterative(*adj*, *n*, *s*)

Here *adj* is the adjacency-list of the graph with *n* vertices, and vertex *s* is the source vertex. This algorithm uses a stack STACK, and linear array *color* of size *n*, to keep track of the progress of DFS. It also uses local variables *u* and *ptr*.

```
Begin
  for i = 1 to n by 1 do
     Set color[i] = WHITE
  endfor
  Set color[s] = GRAY
  CALL createStack( stack )
  Call push( stack, s )
  while ( stack is not empty ) do
     Set u = peek(stack)
     Set ptr = adj[u]
     while (ptr  ≠ NULL ) do
        if (color[ptr->info] = WHITE ) then
           Set color[ptr->info] = GRAY
           Call push(&stack, ptr->info)
           Set u = ptr->info
           Set ptr = adj[u]
        else
           Set ptr = ptr ->next
        endif
     endwhile
     Call pop(&stack, u)
     Print: u
     Set color[u] = BLACK
  endwhile
End.
```

Example 11.2:

Consider the following graph, and source vertex 2

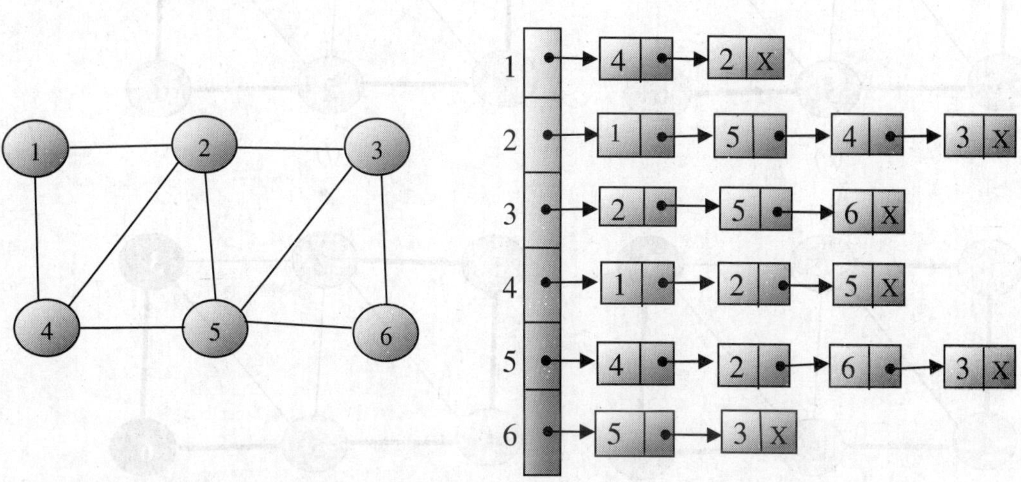

Figure 11.8: Undirected graph and its adjacency-list

Solution:

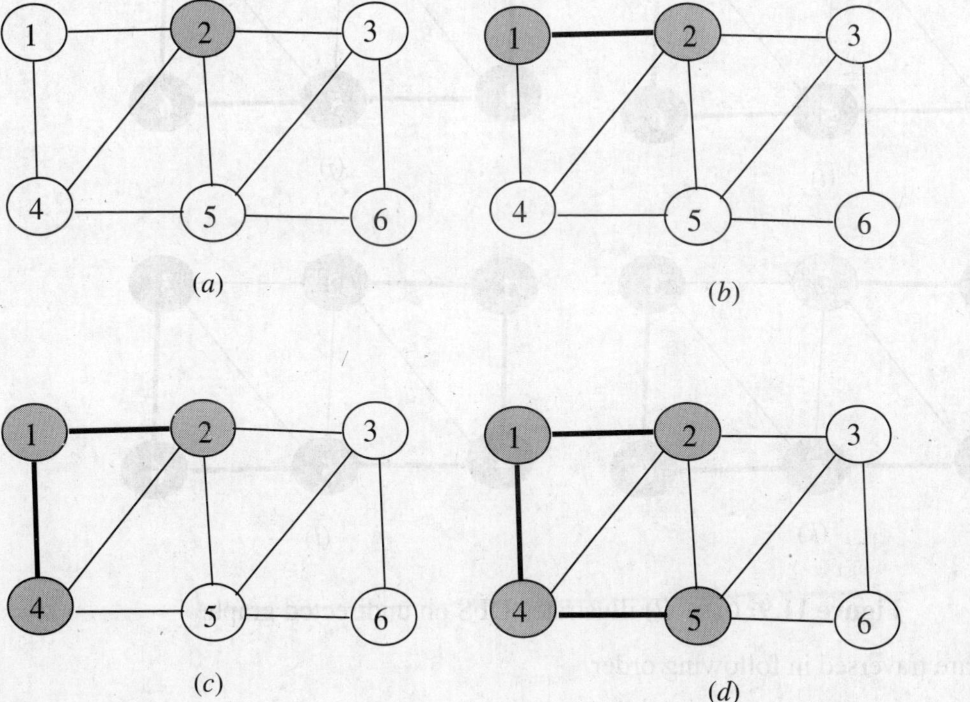

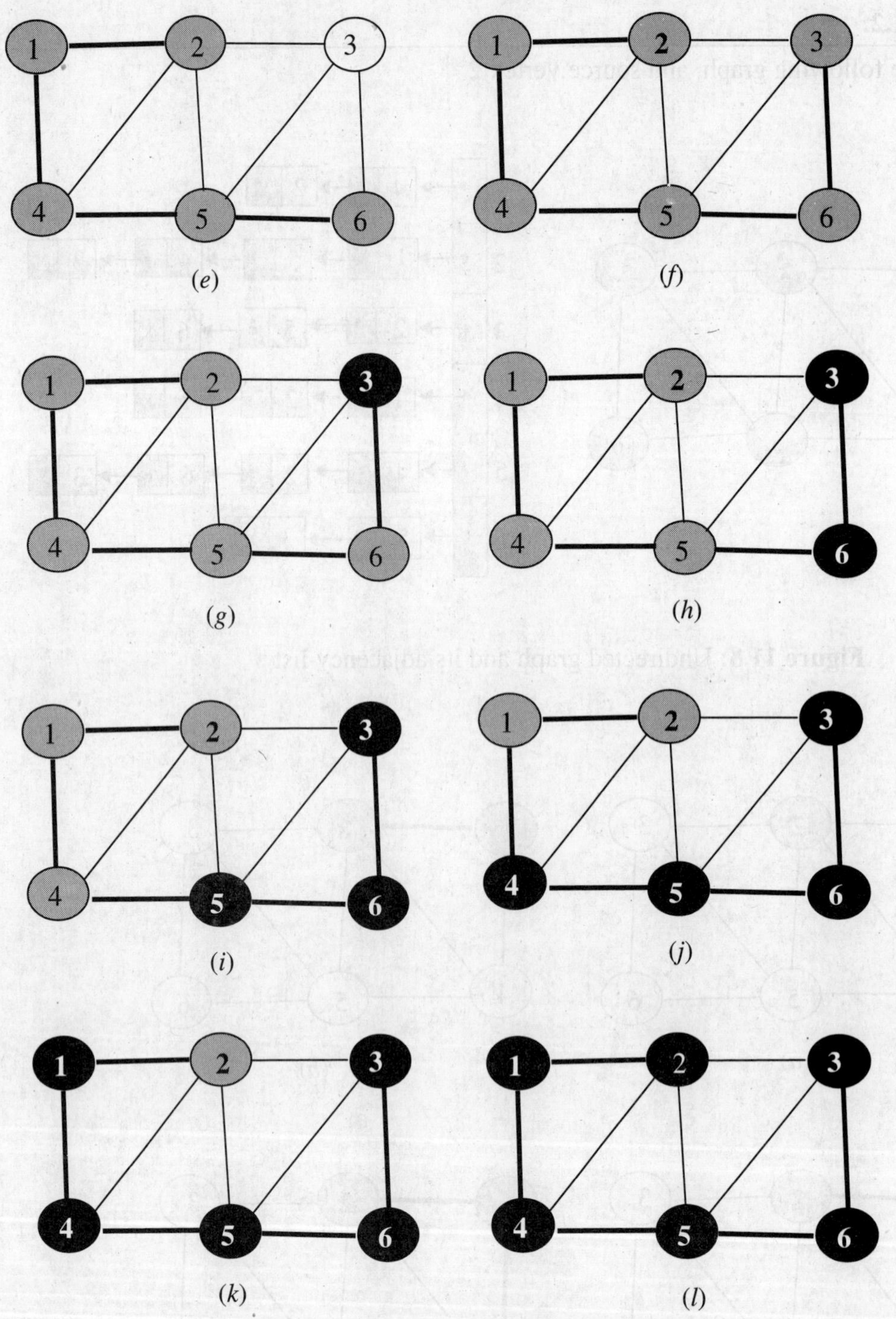

Figure 11.9: (*a*) – (*l*) illustrates DFS on undirected graph.

The vertices are traversed in following order

3 6 5 4 1 2

Listing 11.12:

```
//
//  Program to illustrate the DFS iterative on a non-weighted graph
//
#include <iostream.h>
#include <iomanip.h>
#include "graph.h"
#include "stack.h"
#define WHITE 0
#define GRAY  1
#define BLACK 2
void NonWeightedGraph::DFS(int s)
{
   NWNode *ptr;
   LinkStack<int> intStack;
   int i, u, color[MAX];
   for ( i = 1; i <= size; i++ )
      color[i] = WHITE;
   color[s] = GRAY;
   intStack.push(s);
   while ( !intStack.isEmpty() ) {
       u = intStack.peek();
       ptr = adj[u];
       while ( ptr != NULL ) {
         if (color[ptr->vertex] == WHITE ) {
             color[ptr->vertex] = GRAY;
             intStack.push(ptr->vertex);
             u = ptr->vertex;
             ptr = adj[u];
         } else {
             ptr = ptr->next;
         }
       }
       u = intStack.pop();
       cout<<u << " ";
       color[u] = BLACK;
    }
}
void main()
{
   int n, s;
   cout << "\nEnter number of nodes in the graph : ";
   cin >> n;
   NonWeightedGraph nwgraph(n);
   nwgraph.inputGraph();
   cout << "\nEnter source vertex : ";
   cin >> s;
   cout << "\n\nDFS from vertex " << s << " is\n\n";
   nwgraph.DFS(s);
}
```

In example 10.2, you must have observed that DFS is a recursive procedure. *i.e.*. traverses as deep as possible exploring each edge on the way, and backtracks once there is no further edge coming out of the recently discovered vertex.

The algorithm 11.3 summarizes the various steps to perform recursive visit to each vertex *u*.

Algorithm 11.3:

DfsVisit(***adj, n, u*** **)**

Here *adj* is the adjacency-list of the graph with *n* vertices, and vertex *u* is the vertex to be visited. This algorithm uses recursion.

```
Begin
  Set color[u] = GRAY
  Set ptr = adj[u]
  while (ptr  ≠ NULL ) do
     Set v = ptr->info
     if (color[v] = WHITE ) then
        Set color[v] = GRAY
        Call DfsVisit(adj, n, v )
     endif
  endwhile
  Print: u
  Set color[u] = BLACK
End.
```

Algorithm 11.4 summarizes the various steps to perform initialization, and call the procedure of algorithm 11.3 to perform DFS visit to undiscovered vertices.

Algorithm 11.4:

DFRecursive(***adj, n, s*** **)**

Here *adj* is the adjacency-list of the graph with *n* vertices, and vertex *s* is the source vertex. This algorithm uses linear array *color* of size *n*, to keep track of the progress of DFS. The variables *i* is used as index variable.

```
Begin
  for i = 1 to n by 1 do
     Set color[i] = WHITE
  endfor
  Call DfsVisit( adj, n, s )
End.
```

Listing 11.13:

```
//  Program to illustrate the DFS recursive on a non-weighted graph
#include <iostream.h>
#include <iomanip.h>
#include "graph.h"
#define WHITE 0
```

```
#define GRAY  1
#define BLACK 2
int color[MAX];

void NonWeightedGraph::DFSVisit(int u)
{
    int v;
    NWNode *ptr;
    color[u] = GRAY;
    ptr = adj[u];
    while ( ptr != NULL ) {
        v = ptr->vertex;
        if ( color[v] == WHITE )
         DFSVisit(v);
        ptr = ptr->next;
    }
    cout << u << "    ";
    color[u] = BLACK;
}

void NonWeightedGraph::DFSRecursive(int s)
{
    int i;
    for ( i = 1; i <= size; i++ )
       color[i] = WHITE;
    DFSVisit(s);
}

void main()
{
    int n, s;
    cout << "\nEnter number of nodes in the graph : ";
    cin >> n;
    NonWeightedGraph nwgraph(n);
    nwgraph.inputGraph();
    cout << "\nEnter source vertex : ";
    cin >> s;
    cout << "\n\nBFS from vertex " << s << " is\n\n";
    nwgraph.DFSRecursive(s);
}
```

11.5 APPLICATIONS OF GRAPHS

In this section, we will discuss some of the applications of graphs.

11.5.1 Topological Sort

A topological sort of a directed graph without cycles, also known as directed acyclic graph or simple DAG, $G = (V, E)$ is a linear ordering of all its vertices such that if G contains an edge (u, v), then u appears before v in the ordering.

If the graph is contains cycle(s), *i.e.*, graph is not DAG, then no linear ordering is possible.

A topological sort of a graph can be viewed as an ordering of its vertices along a horizontal line so that all directed edges go from left to right.

Directed acyclic graphs are used in many applications to indicate precedence among events.

To find topological sort of a DAG, the general structure of the algorithm can be described as follows:

```
Begin
    Perform DFS on G for each vertex
    As each vertex is finished, insert at front of a linked list
    Print the elements of linked list in order
End.
```

To find the topological sort of a DAG, the procedure to perform DFS visit to a vertex is slightly modified as given in the algorithm 11.5, where instead of printing the vertex, it is inserted in the beginning of the linked list.

Algorithm 11.5:

DfsVisitModified(adj, n, u)

Here *adj* is the adjacency-list of the graph with *n* vertices, and vertex *u* is the vertex to be visited. This algorithm uses recursion.

```
Begin
  Set color[u] = GRAY
  Set ptr = adj[u]
  while (ptr  ≠ NULL ) do
     Set v = ptr->info
     if ( color[v] = WHITE ) then
         Call DfsVisitModified(adj, n, v )
     endif
     Set ptr  = ptr->next
  endwhile
  Insert vertex u in beginning of linear linked list LIST
  Set color[u] = BLACK
End.
```

The algorithm 11.6 summarizes the various steps to perform the topological sort of a DAG.

Algorithm 11.6:

TopologicalSort(***adj*, *n*** **)**

Here *adj* is the adjacency-list of the graph with *n* vertices. This algorithm finds the topological sort of the graph G. It uses linear linked list LIST to store the visited by DFS-VISIT procedure in order of their traversal.

```
Begin
```

```
   Create linear linked list LIST
   for i = 1 to n by 1 do
      Set color[i] = WHITE
   Endfor
   for i = 1 to n by 1 do
      if ( color[i] = WHITE ) then
         Call DfsVisitModified(adj, n, i )
      endif
   endfor
   Set ptr = LIST
   while (ptr  ≠ NULL ) do
      Print ptr->info
      Set ptr = ptr ->next
   endwhile
End.
```

Example 11.3:

Consider the following graph

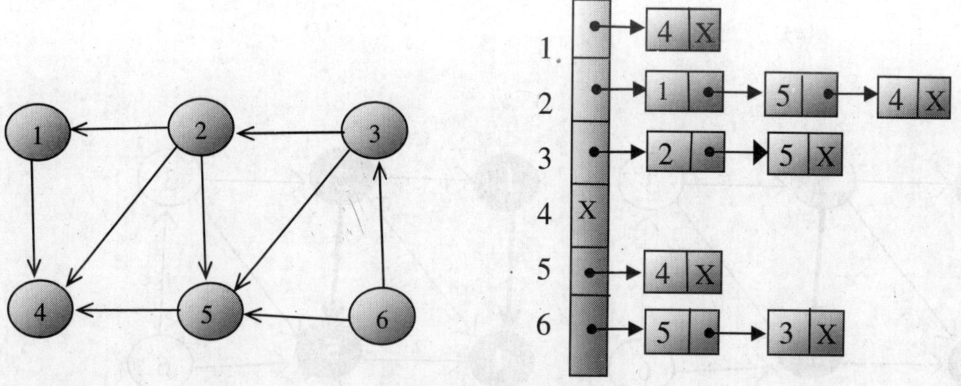

Figure 11.10: Given directed acyclic graph and its adjacency list

Solution:

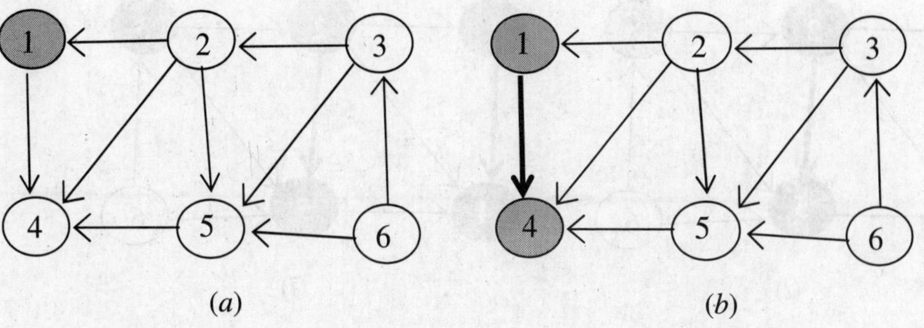

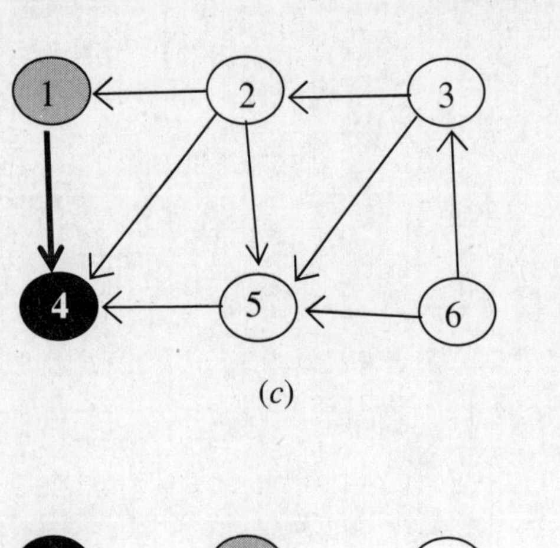

(*c*)

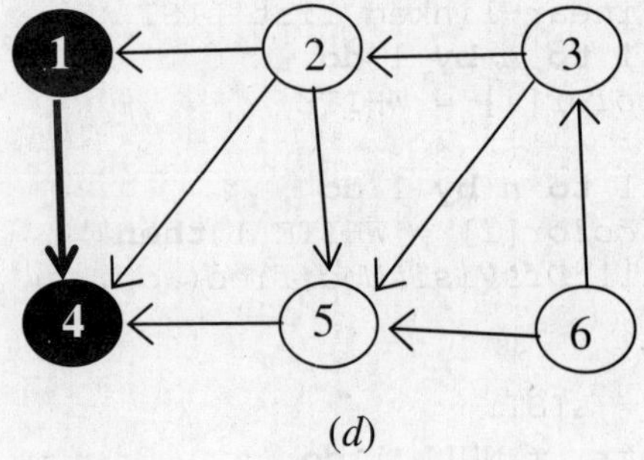

(*d*)

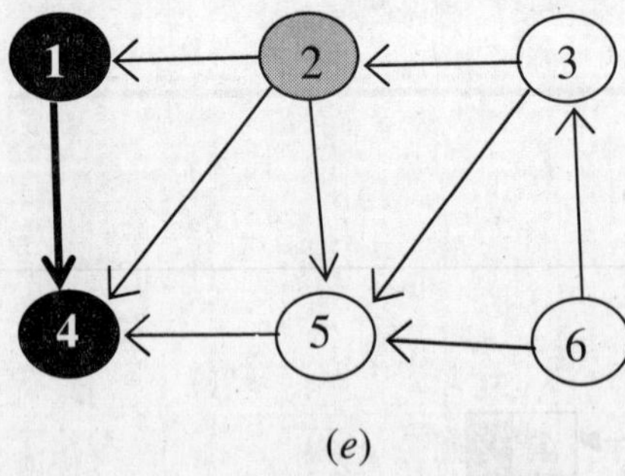

(*e*)

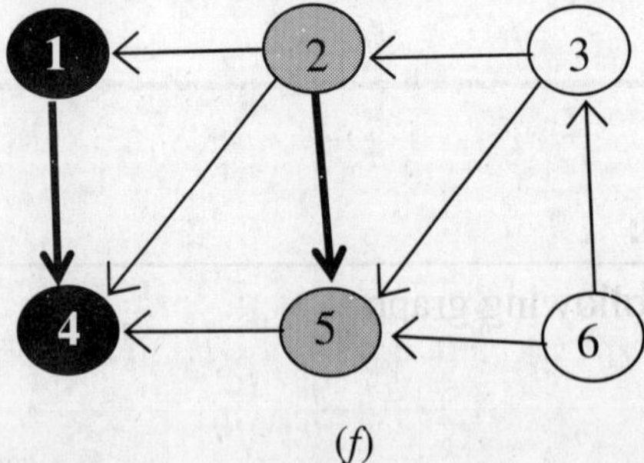

(*f*)

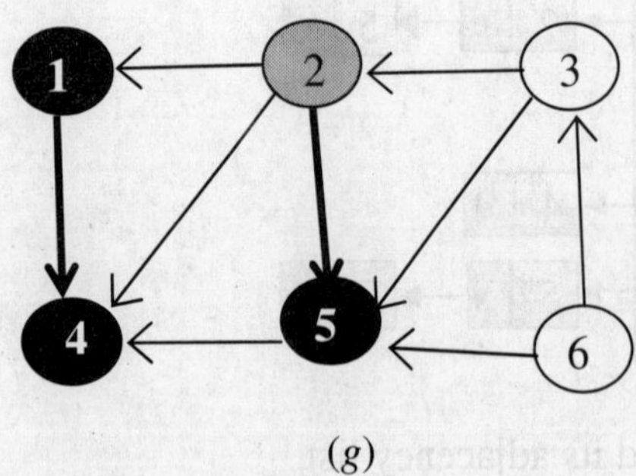

(*g*)

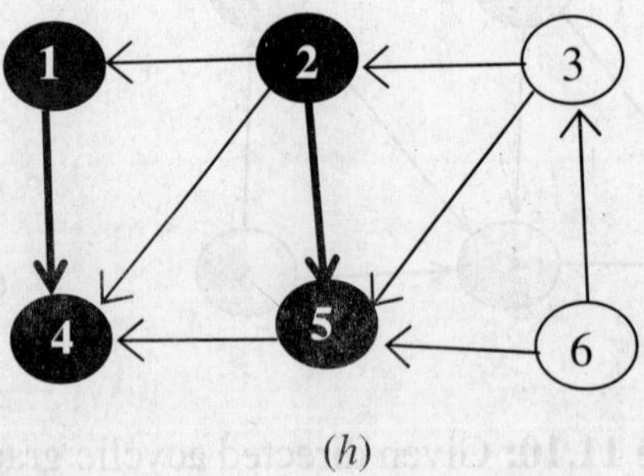

(*h*)

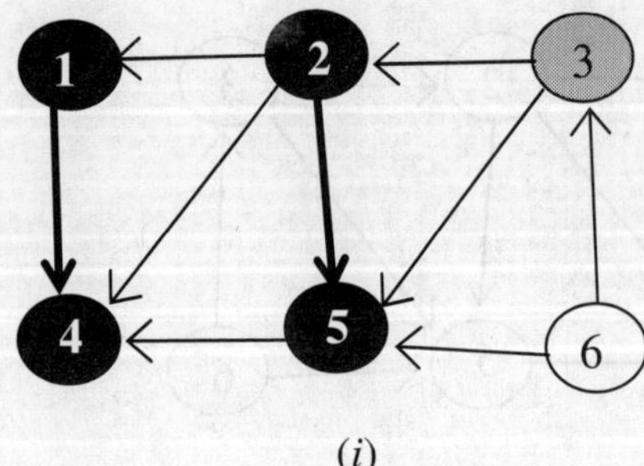

(*i*)

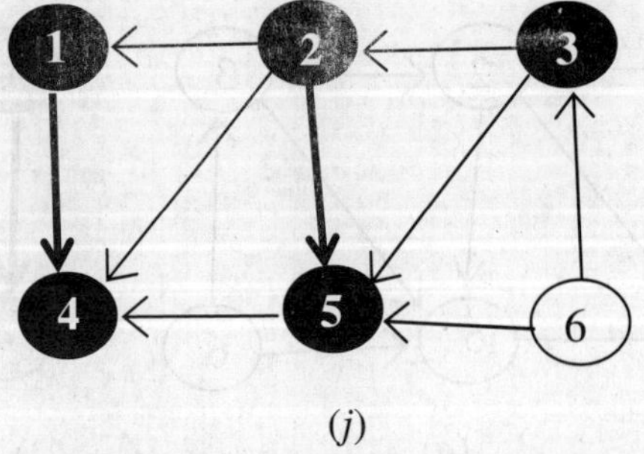

(*j*)

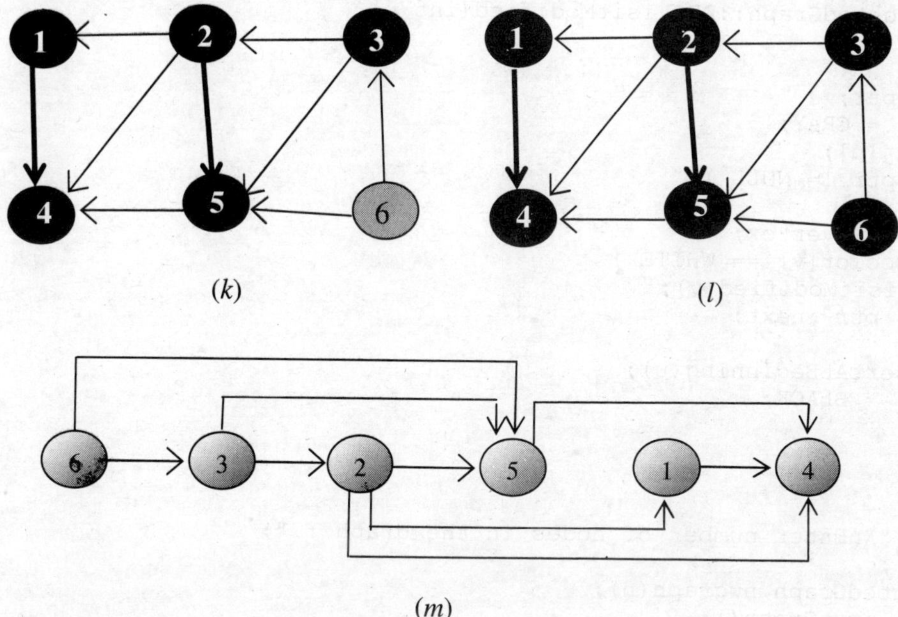

Figure 11.11: (*a*) – (*l*) illustrates DFS on undirected graph. Tree edges are shown thick as they are produced by DFS. (*m*) shows topological sort of the given graph.

Listing 11.14:

```
//  Program to illustrate the topological sort on DAG
#include <iostream.h>
#include <iomanip.h>
#include "llist.h"
#include "graph.h"
#define WHITE 0
#define GRAY  1
#define BLACK 2

int color[MAX];
LList<int> list;

void NonWeightedGraph::topologicalSort()
{
   cout << "\nTopological Sort of given graph\n";
   DFSRecursiveModified();
   list.traverseInOrder();
}
void NonWeightedGraph::DFSRecursiveModified() {
   int i;
   for ( i = 1; i <= size; i++ )
       color[i] = WHITE;
   for ( i = 1; i <= size; i++ ) {
     if ( color[i] == WHITE )
       DFSVisitModified(i);
   }
}
```

```
void NonWeightedGraph::DFSVisitModified(int u)
{
    int v;
    NWNode *ptr;
    color[u] = GRAY;
    ptr = adj[u];
    while ( ptr != NULL )
    {
      v = ptr->vertex;
      if ( color[v] == WHITE )
       DFSVisitModified(v);
      ptr = ptr->next;
    }
    list.insertAtBeginning(u);
    color[u] = BLACK;
}
void main()
{
    int n;
    cout << "\nEnter number of nodes in the graph : ";
    cin >> n;
    NonWeightedGraph nwgraph(n);
    nwgraph.inputGraph();
    nwgraph.topologicalSort();
}
```

11.5.2 Minimum Spanning Tree

A *spanning tree* for a graph, $G = (V, E)$, is a subgraph of G that is a tree and contains all the vertices of G. In a weighted graph, the weight of a graph is the sum of the weights of the edges of the graph. A *minimum spanning tree* (MST) for a weighted graph is a spanning tree with minimum weight. If graph G with n vertices, then the MST will have $(n-1)$ edges, assuming that the graph is connected. In general, a weighted graph may have more than one MST.

If G is not connected, then it cannot have any spanning tree. In this case it will have a spanning forest. For simplicity, we will assume that the given graph G is connected.

There are many situations in which MST must be found. For example;

- We want to find cheapest way to connect a set of terminals, where terminals may represent cities, electrical/electronic components of a circuit, computers or factories, by using say roads, wires, or telephone lines. The solution to this is a MST, which has an edge for each possible connection weighted by the cost of that connection.
- It is also an important sub problem in various routing algorithms. By routing means finding efficient paths through a graph that visit every vertex (or every edge).

If G is not connected, then it cannot have any spanning tree. In this case it will have a spanning forest. To simplify our discussion, we will assume that the given graph G is connected.

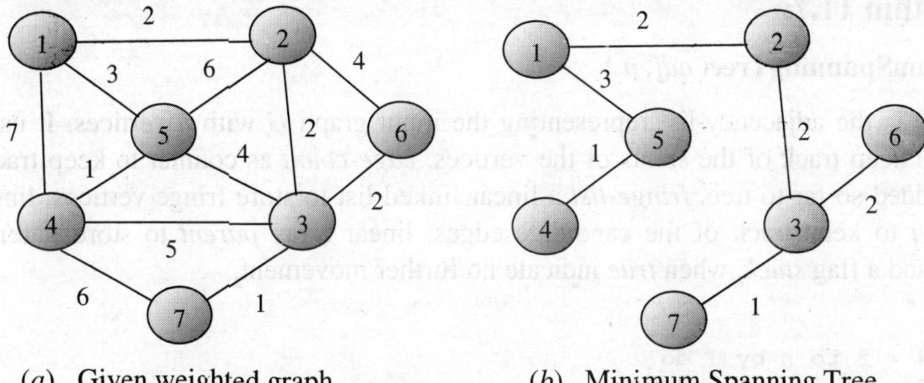

Figure 11.12: Given graph and its corresponding Minimum Spanning Tree

The Prim algorithm begins by selecting an arbitrary starting vertex, and then branches out from the part of the tree constructed so far by choosing a new vertex and edge at each iteration. During the course of the algorithm, the vertices may be thought of as divided into three disjoint categories as follows:

- **Tree vertices** – Those in the tree constructed so far.
- **Fringe vertices** – Those vertices that are not in tree, but are adjacent to some vertex in the tree.
- **Unseen vertices** – Remaining vertices of the graph.

The key step in the algorithm is the selection of a vertex from the fringe vertices and an incident edge. Actually, since the weights are on the edges, the focus of the choice is on the edge, not the vertex. The Prim's algorithm always chooses an edge from a tree vertex to a fringe vertex of minimum weight. The general structure of the algorithm can be described as follows:

```
Begin
  Select an arbitrary vertex to start the tree
  while there are fringe vertices do
     Select an edge of minimum weight between a tree and
     a fringe vertex
     Add the selected edge and the fringe vertex to the tree
  endwhile
End.
```

After each iteration of the algorithm's loop, there may be new fringe vertices, and the set of edges from which the next selection is made. For each fringe vertex, we need to keep track of only one edge to it from the tree – *the one with lowest weight*. We will call such edges candidate edges.

The various steps required are summarized in the algorithm 11.7.

Algorithm 11.7:

MinimumSpanningTree(*adj*, *n*)

Here *adj* is the adjacency-list representing the input graph *G* with *n* vertices. It uses linear *status* to keep track of the status of the vertices, *edge-count* as counter to keep track of the edges added so far to tree, *fringe-list* a linear linked list to store fringe vertices, linear array *fringe-wt* to keep track of the candidate edges, linear array *parent* to store parent of the vertex, and a flag *stuck*, when *true* indicate no further movement.

```
Begin
  for i = 2 to n by 1 do
      Set status[i] = UNSEEN
  endfor
  Set x = 1
  Set status[x] = INTREE
  Set edge-count = 0
  Set stuck = false
  Create fringe-list

  while ( ( edge-count <  n -1 ) and ( not stuck ) ) do
     Set ptr = adj[x]

     while (ptr ≠ NULL ) do
        Set y = ptr->vertex
        if ((status[y] = fringe)and(ptr->weight < fringe-wt[y])) then
           Set parent[y] = x
           Set fringe-wt[y] = ptr->weight
        else if  (status[y] = UNSEEN ) then
           Set status[y] = FRINGE
           Insert vertex y into fringe-list
           Set parent[y] = x
           Set fringe-wt[y] = ptr->weight
        endif
        Set ptr = ptr->next
     endwhile

     if ( fringe-list is empty ) then
        Set stuck = true
     else
        Traverse the fringe list to find a vertex with minimum weight
        Set x = the fringe vertex incident with the edge
        Remove x from the fringe-list
        Set status[x] = INTREE
        Set edge-count = edge-count + 1
     endif
  endwhile
  for x = 2 to n by 1 do
     Print x, parent[x]
  endfor
End.
```

Example 11.4:

Consider the following graph

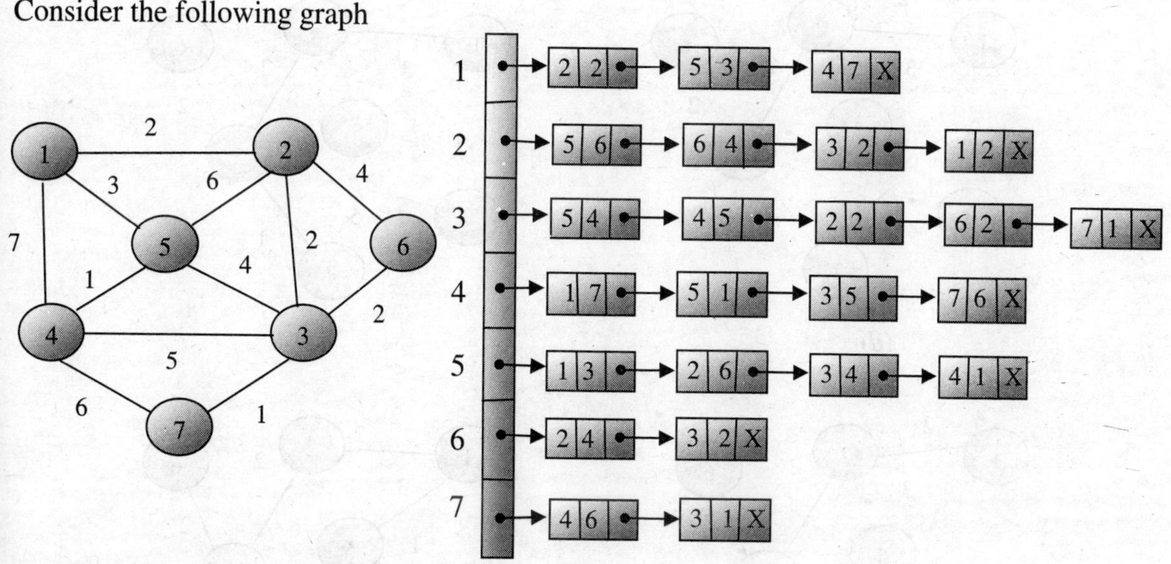

Figure 11.13: Given graph and its adjacency-list

Solution:

Following notations for tree edges and fringe edges will be used.

The procedure starts with vertex 1 as progresses as shown below.

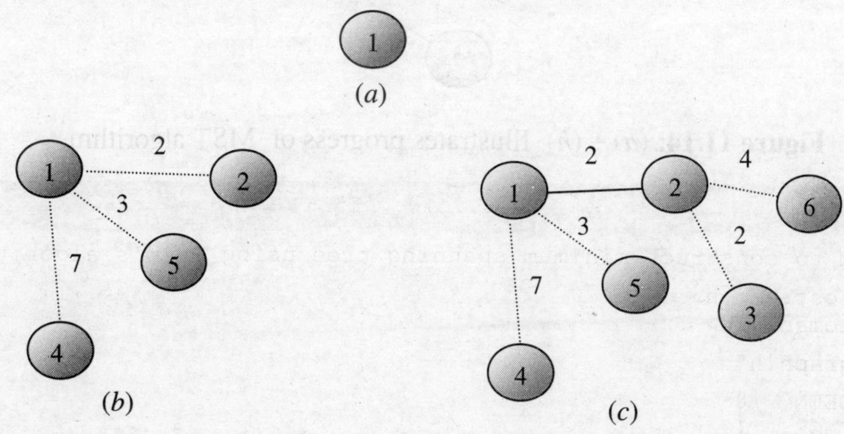

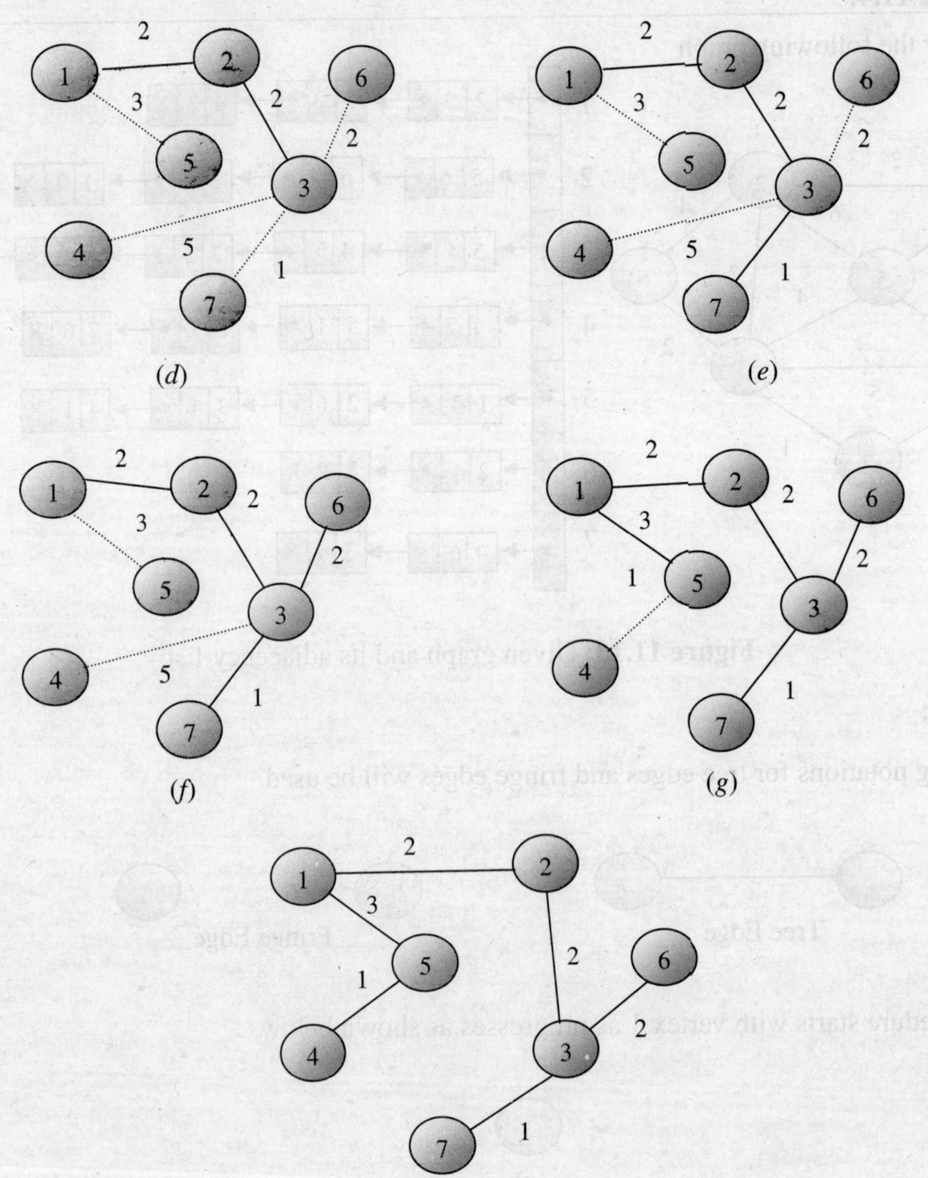

Figure 11.14: (*a*) – (*h*) Illustrates progress of MST algorithm

Listing 11.15:

```
//  Program to construct minimum spanning tree using Prim's algorithm

#include <iostream.h>
#include <iomanip.h>

#include "graph.h"

#define UNSEEN    0
#define FRINGE    1
#define INTREE    2
```

```
struct Node
{
   int vertex;
   Node *next;
};

void insertAtBeginning( Node **fringeList, int d )
{
   Node *ptr;
   ptr = new Node;
   ptr->vertex = d;
   ptr->next = *fringeList;
   *fringeList = ptr;
}
void deleteElement(Node **fringeList,  int d )
{
   Node *loc, *ploc=NULL;
   ploc = NULL;
   loc = *fringeList;
   while ( loc->vertex != d )
   {
      ploc = loc;
      loc = loc->next;
   }
   if ( ploc == NULL )
      *fringeList = (*fringeList)->next;
   else
      ploc->next = loc->next;
   delete loc;
}
int isEmpty ( Node *ptr  )
{
   return ( ptr == NULL ) ? 1 : 0;
}

void deleteList(Node **fringeList)
{
   Node *ptr;
   while ( *fringeList != NULL )
   {
      ptr = *fringeList;
      *fringeList = (*fringeList)->next;
      delete ptr;
   }
}

void WeightedGraph::MinimumSpanningTreePrim()
{
   Node *fringeList=NULL, *ptr2;
   WNode *ptr1;
   int i, x, stuck, w, edgeCount, minWt, y, weight;
   int parent[MAX], status[MAX], fringeWt[MAX];
   for ( i = 1; i <= size; i++ )
      status[i] = UNSEEN;
   x = 1;
   status[x] = INTREE;
   edgeCount = 0;
   stuck = 0;
```

```
   while ( ( edgeCount < size ) && ( !stuck ) )
   {
      ptr1 = adj[x];
      while ( ptr1 != NULL ) {
        y = ptr1->vertex;
        weight = ptr1->weight;
        if (( status[y] == FRINGE )&&( weight < fringeWt[y] ))
        {
          parent[y] = x;
          fringeWt[y] = weight;
        } else if ( status[y] == UNSEEN ) {
          status[y] = FRINGE;
          parent[y] = x;
          fringeWt[y] = weight;
          insertAtBeginning(&fringeList, y);
        }
        ptr1 = ptr1->next;
      }
      if ( isEmpty(fringeList) )
        stuck = 1;
      else
      {
        x = fringeList->vertex;
        minWt = fringeWt[x];
        ptr2 = fringeList->next;
        while ( ptr2 != NULL )
        {
           w = ptr2->vertex;
           if ( fringeWt[w] < minWt )
           {
              x = w;
              minWt = fringeWt[w];
           }
           ptr2 = ptr2->next;
        }
        deleteElement(&fringeList,x);
        status[x] = INTREE;
        edgeCount++;
      }
   }
   for ( x = 2; x <= size; x++ )
      cout << "(" << x << "," << parent[x] << ")";
   deleteList(&fringeList);
}

void main()
{
   int n;
   cout << "\nEnter number of nodes in the graph : ";
   cin >> n;
   WeightedGraph wgraph(n);
   wgraph.inputGraph();
   cout << "\n\nMinimum Spanning Tree";
   cout << " constitutes following edges\n\n";
   wgraph.MinimumSpanningTreePrim();
}
```

11.5.3 Finding Shortest Paths

A *path* from source vertex *v* to *w* is *shortest path* from *v* to *w* if there is no path from *v* to *w* with lower weights. The shortest paths are not necessarily unique.

There are many instances where we are interested in finding the most convenient paths for traveling from one place to another place. For example, suppose we have with us an airline map, which gives the cities having direct flights and the total time of flight, and air fair. We are interested to find that which route we should take so that we can reach as quickly as possible or a route for which the air fair is the minimum.

We may be interested in find a shortest path from a given city to another city, shortest paths from a given city to any other city reachable from the given city, and finally, the shortest paths from each city to the other one.

11.5.3.1 Shortest Path for Given Source and Destination

In order to find a shortest path from a given source to given destination, we discuss Dijkstra's shortest-path algorithm, which is very similar to Prim's algorithm for finding the MST.

The distance from a vertex *x* to a vertex *y*, denoted by *d*(*x*,*y*), is the weight of a shortest path from vertex *x* to vertex *y*. The Dijkstra's shortest-path algorithm finds the shortest paths in order of increasing distance from a vertex, say *v*. Like MST, it branches out by selecting certain edges that lead to new edges.

Like MST, we keep track of candidate edge (the best found so far) for each fringe vertex. For each fringe vertex *z*, there is at least one path $v(=v_0)$, v_1, v_2, . . ., v_k, *z* such that all the vertices except *z* are already in the tree. The candidate edge for *z* is the edge v_kz from a shortest path of this form. This information is stored in linear array DIST. The various steps required are summarized in the algorithm 11.8.

Algorithm 11.8:

ShortestPath(***adj*, *n*, *s*, *d*** **)**

Here *adj* is the adjacency-list representing the input graph *G* with *n* vertices, *s* is the source vertex and *d* is the destination vertex. It uses linear *status* to keep track of the status of the vertices, *fringe-list* a linear linked list to store fringe vertices, linear array *dist* to denote weight of the path to the vertex, linear array *parent* to store parent of the vertex, and a flag *stuck*, when *true* indicate no further movement.

```
Begin
  for i = 1 to n by 1 do
     Set status[i] = UNSEEN, parent[i] = 0, dist[s] = 0
  endfor
  Set status[s] = INTREE
  Create fringe-list
  Set x = s
```

```
Set stuck = false
while ( ( x ≠ d ) and ( not stuck ) ) do
   Set ptr = adj[x]
   while ( ptr ≠ NULL ) do
      Set y = ptr->vertex
      if ((status[y]=fringe)and(dist[x] + ptr->weight < dist[y])) then
         Set parent[y] = x
         Set dist[y] = dist[x] + ptr->weight
      else if  ( status[y] = UNSEEN ) then
         Set status[y] = FRINGE
         Insert vertex y into fringe-list
         Set parent[y] = x
         Set dist[y] = dist[x] + ptr->weight
      endif
      Set ptr = ptr->next
   endwhile
   if ( fringe-list is empty ) then
      Set stuck = true
   else
      Traverse the fringe-list to find a vertex with minimum distance
      Set x =  vertex with minimum distance from s
      Remove x from the fringe-list
      Set status[x] = INTREE
   endif
endwhile
if ( parent[d] = 0 ) then
   Print "No path from ", s, " to ", d, " exists"
else
   Call print-path( s, d, parent )
endif
End.
```

The steps required for outputting the path recursively are summarized in the following algorithm.

Algorithm 11.9:

PrintPath(*s*, *d*, *parent*)

Here *s* is the source vertex, *d* the destination vertex, and *parent* is a linear array with *n* elements that maintains the parent child relationship.

```
Begin
 if ( s = d ) then
    Print: s
 else
    Call PrintPath( s, parent[d], parent )
 endif
End.
```

Example 11.5:

Consider the following graph

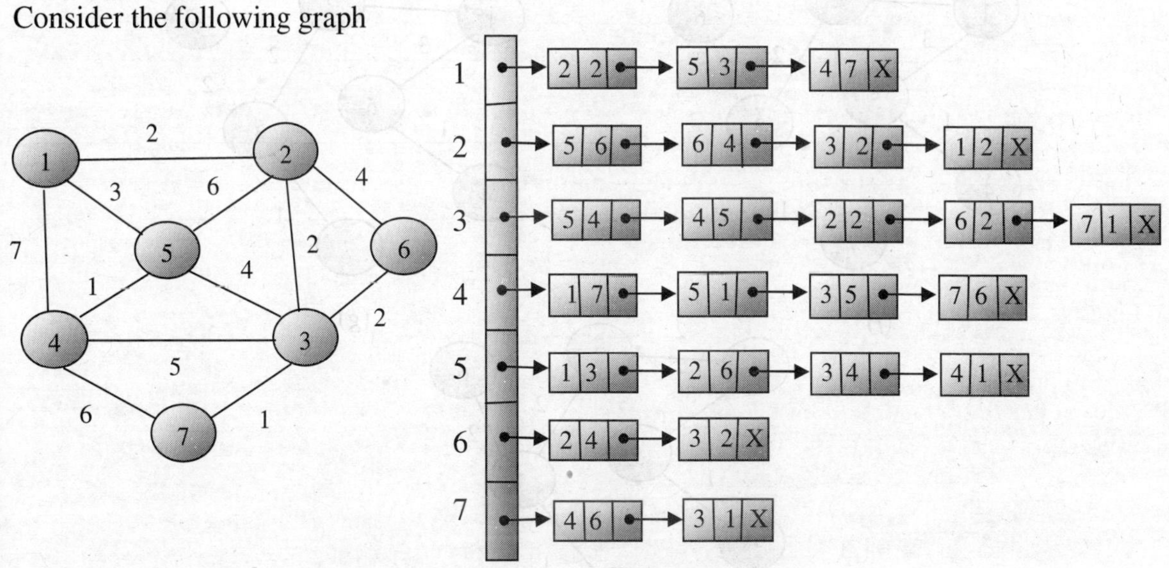

Figure 11.15: Given graph and its adjacency-list

Solution:

The following figure illustrates the working of the algorithm 11.6 by taking vertex 1 as source and vertex 6 as destination.

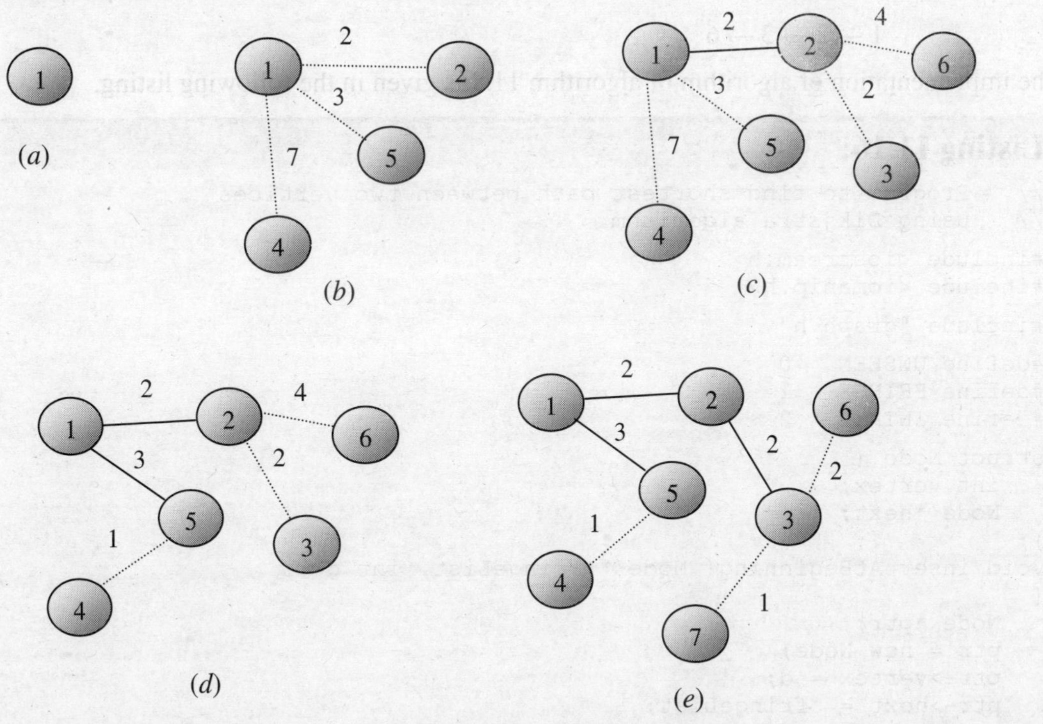

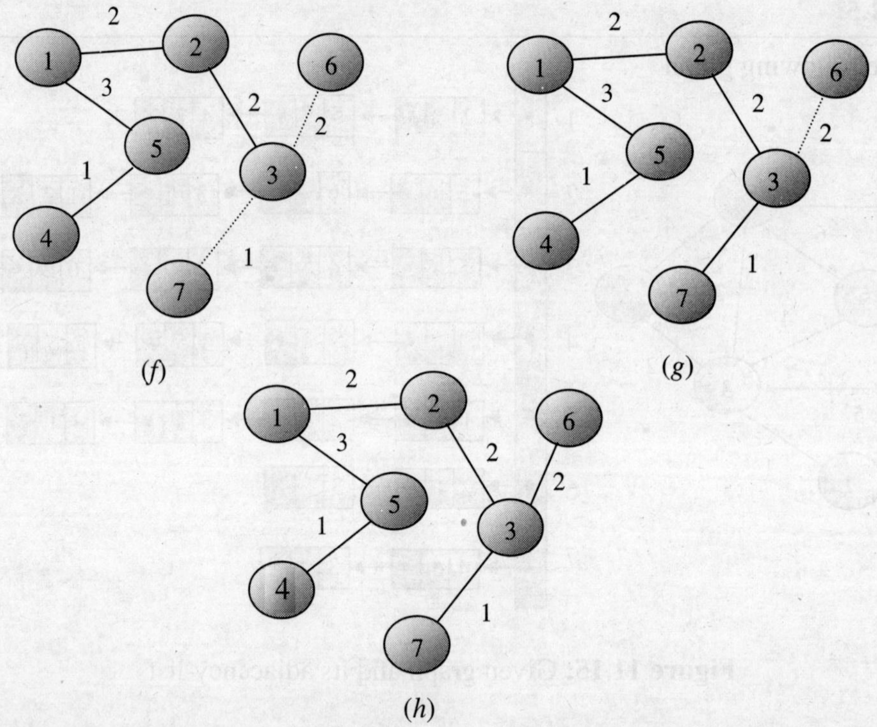

Figure 11.16: *(a) – (h)* illustrates the progress of shortest path algorithm

The algorithm terminates, as vertex just added to tree is destination vertex 6. So the shortest path from 1 to 6 is

$$1 \rightarrow 2 \rightarrow 3 \rightarrow 6$$

The implementation of algorithm of algorithm 11.8 is given in the following listing.

Listing 11.16:

```
//   Program to find shortest path between two vertices
//   using Dikjstra algorithm
#include <iostream.h>
#include <iomanip.h>
#include "graph.h"
#define UNSEEN   0
#define FRINGE   1
#define INTREE   2
struct Node {
   int vertex;
   Node *next;
};
void insertAtBeginning( Node **fringeList, int d )
{
   Node *ptr;
   ptr = new Node;
   ptr->vertex = d;
   ptr->next = *fringeList;
```

```
   *fringeList = ptr;
}
void deleteElement(Node **fringeList,  int d )
{
   Node *loc, *ploc=NULL;
   ploc = NULL;
   loc = *fringeList;
   while ( loc->vertex != d ) {
      ploc = loc;
      loc = loc->next;
   }
   if ( ploc == NULL )
      *fringeList = (*fringeList)->next;
   else
      ploc->next = loc->next;
   delete loc;
}
int isEmpty ( Node *ptr  )
{
   return ( ptr == NULL ) ? 1 : 0;
}
void deleteList(Node **fringeList)
{
   Node *ptr;
   while ( *fringeList != NULL ) {
      ptr = *fringeList;
      *fringeList = (*fringeList)->next;
      delete ptr;
   }
}
void printPath( int s, int d, int parent[] )
{
   if ( d == s )
      cout << s;
   else {
      printPath( s, parent[d], parent );
     cout << " ->" << d;
   }
}
void WeightedGraph::shortestPathDijkstra(int s, int d )
{
   Node *fringeList=NULL, *ptr2;
   WNode *ptr1;
   int i, x, stuck, w, min_dist, y, wt;
   int parent[MAX], status[MAX], dist[MAX];
   for ( i = 1; i <= size; i++ )
      status[i] = UNSEEN;
   parent[s] = 0;
   dist[s] = 0;
   status[s] = INTREE;
   x = s;
   stuck = 0;
   while ( ( x != d ) && ( !stuck ) )
   {
      ptr1 = adj[x];
      while ( ptr1 != NULL ) {
        y = ptr1->vertex;
        wt = ptr1->weight;
```

```
        if ( ( status[y] == FRINGE ) && ( dist[x] + wt < dist[y] ) ) {
            parent[y] = x;
            dist[y] = dist[x] + wt;
        }
        else
        {
            if ( status[y] == UNSEEN ) {
                status[y] = FRINGE;
                parent[y] = x;
                dist[y] = dist[x] + wt;
                insertAtBeginning( &fringeList, y );
            }
        }
      ptr1 = ptr1->next;
    }
    if ( isEmpty (fringeList) )
      stuck = 1;
    else
    {
      x = fringeList->vertex;
      min_dist = dist[x];
      ptr2 = fringeList->next;
      while ( ptr2 != NULL ) {
          w = ptr2->vertex;
          if ( dist[w] < min_dist ) {
              x = w;
              min_dist = dist[w];
          }
        ptr2 = ptr2->next;
      }
      deleteElement(&fringeList, x);
      status[x] = INTREE;
    }
  }
  if ( parent[d] == 0 )
    cout << "\nNo path from vertex "
        << s << " to vertex " << d << endl;
  else {
    cout << "\nPath from vertex "
        << s << " to vertex " << d << " is\n\n";
    printPath( s, d, parent );
  }
  deleteList(&fringeList);
}
void main()
{
  int n, s, d;
  cout << "\nEnter number of nodes in graph : " ;
  cin >> n;
  WeightedGraph wgraph(n);
  wgraph.inputGraph();
  cout << "\nEnter source vertex : ";
  cin >> s;
  cout << "\nEnter destination vertex : ";
  cin >> d;
  wgraph.shortestPathDijkstra(s, d);
}
```

11.5.3.2 Shortest Paths Among All-Pair of Vertices

We will describe the Floyd-Warshall algorithm, the runs in $O(V^3)$ time. This algorithm considers the intermediate vertices of a shortest path, where an intermediate vertex of a simple path $p = <v_1, v_2, v_3 \ldots, v_k>$ is any vertex of p other than v_1 or v_k, that is, a vertex in the set $\{v_2, v_3, v_4 \ldots, v_{k-1}\}$.

This algorithm is based on the following observation. Let the vertices of G be $V = \{1, 2, 3, \ldots, n\}$, and consider a subset $\{1, 2, 3, \ldots, k\}$ of vertices for some k. For any pair of vertices $i, j \in V$, consider all paths from i to j whose intermediate vertices are drawn from $\{1, 2, 3, \ldots, k\}$ and let p be a minimum-weight path from among them. This algorithm exploits a relationship between path p and shortest paths from i to j with all intermediate vertices in the set $\{1, 2, 3, \ldots, k-1\}$. The relationship depends on whether or not k is an intermediate vertex of path p.

- If k is not an intermediate vertex of path p, then all intermediate vertices of path p are in the set $\{1, 2, 3, \ldots, k-1\}$. Thus, a shortest path from vertex i to vertex j with all intermediate vertices in the set $\{1, 2, 3, \ldots, k-1\}$ is also a shortest path from i to j with all intermediate vertices in the set $\{1, 2, 3, \ldots, k\}$.
- If k is an intermediate vertex of path p, then we can break down p into p_1 and p_2 such that p_1 is path from i to k and p_2 is a path from k to j. Since p_1 is a shortest path from i to k with all intermediate vertices in the set $\{1, 2, 3, \ldots, k\}$. In fact, vertex k is not an intermediate vertex of path p_1, and so p_1 is a shortest path from i to k with all intermediate vertices in the set $\{1, 2, 3, \ldots, k-1\}$. Similarly, p_2 is a shortest path from vertex k to vertex j with all intermediate vertices in the set $\{1, 2, 3, \ldots, k-1\}$.

Based on the above observation, we define a recursive formulation of shortest-path estimates as follows:

Let $d_{ij}^{(k)}$ be the weight of a shortest path from vertex i to vertex j with all intermediate vertices in the set $\{1, 2, 3, \ldots, k\}$. When $k = 0$, a path from vertex i to vertex j with no intermediate vertex numbered higher than 0 has no intermediate vertices at all. It thus has at most one edge, and hence $d_{ij}^{(0)} = w_{ij}$.

A recursive definition is given by

$$d_{ij}^{(k)} = \begin{cases} w_{ij} & \text{if } k = 0 \\ \min\left(d_{ij}^{(k-1)}, d_{ik}^{(k-1)} + d_{kj}^{(k-1)}\right) & \text{if } k \geq 1 \end{cases}$$

The matrix $D^{(n)} = (d_{ij}^{(n)})$ gives the final answer.

The shortest paths, i.e., predecessor matrix P can be computed on-line as it computes the matrices $D^{(k)}$. Specifically, the sequence of matrices $P^{(0)}$, $P^{(1)}$, $P^{(2)}$, . . ., $P^{(n)}$ are computed. The element $p_{ij}^{(k)}$ is defined to be predecessor of vertex j on a shortest path from vertex i with all the intermediate vertices in the set {1, 2, 3, . . ., k}.

A recursive definition for $p_{ij}^{(k)}$ is as given below:

When $k = 0$, a shortest path from i to j has no intermediate vertices at all. Thus

$$p_{ij}^{(0)} = \begin{cases} \text{NIL} & \text{if } i = j \text{ or } w(i, j) = 0 \\ i & \text{if } i \neq j \text{ or } w(i, j) \neq 0 \end{cases}$$

For $k \geq 1$, if we take a path from i to k and from k to j, then the predecessor of j we choose is the same as the predecessor of j we choose on a shortest path from k with all intermediate vertices in the set {1, 2, 3, . . ., k–1}. Otherwise, we choose the same predecessor of j that we choose on a shortest path from i with all intermediate vertices in the set {1, 2, 3, . . ., k–1}.

Formerly, for $k \geq 1$

$$p_{ij}^{(k)} = \begin{cases} p_{ij}^{(k-1)} & \text{if } d_{ij}^{(k-1)} \leq d_{ik}^{(k-1)} + d_{kj}^{(k-1)} \\ p_{kj}^{(k-1)} & \text{if } d_{ij}^{(k-1)} > d_{ik}^{(k-1)} + d_{kj}^{(k-1)} \end{cases}$$

Based on the above recurrences, the procedure given in algorithm 11.10 can be used to compute the values $d_{ij}^{(k)}$ and $p_{ij}^{(k)}$ in order of increasing values of k.

Algorithm 11.9:

FloydWarshall(*w*, *n*)

Here w is $n \times n$ adjacency-matrix representing directed input graph G. This uses a function MIN that returns the minimum elements among the two. The constant INFINITY represents a very large value which is used as a sentinel value to indicate that there is no edge between vertex i and j.

```
Begin
  for i = 1 to n by 1 do
     for i = 1 to n by 1 do
        if ( w[i,j] = 0 ) then
           Set d[i,j] = INFINITY, p[i,j] = 0
        else
           Set d[i,j] = w[i,j], p[i,j] = i
```

```
        endif
      endfor
    endfor
    for k = 1 to n by 1 do
      for i = 1 to n by 1 do
        for j = 1 to n by 1 do
          if ( d[i,j] <= d[i,k] + d[k,j] ) then
            Set p[i,j] = p[i,j]
          else
            Set p[i,j] = p[k,j]
          endif
          Set d[i,j] = MIN(d[i,j], d[i,k] + d[k,j])
        endfor
      endfor
    endfor

    Print "Shortest path matrix is"
    for i = 1 to n by 1 do
      for j = 1 to n by 1 do
        Print d[i,j]
      endfor
    endfor

    Print "Shortest paths are"
    for i = 1 to n by 1 do
      for j = 1 to n by 1 do
        if ( i ≠ j ) then
          Call print-paths( p, i, j )
        endif
      endfor
    endfor
End.
```

The various steps required outputting all the paths are summarized in algorithm 11.10.

Algorithm 11.10:

PrintPaths(*p*, *i*, *j*)

Here *i* is the source vertex, *j* the destination vertex, and *p* is a two-dimensional array of size $n \times n$ that stores the parent child relationship.

```
Begin
  if ( i = j ) then
    Print i
  else if ( p[i,j] = NIL ) then
    Print "No path from", i, "to", j, "exists"
  else
    Call PrintPaths( p, i, p[i,j] )
    Print j
  endif
End.
```

Example 11.6:

Consider the following directed graph

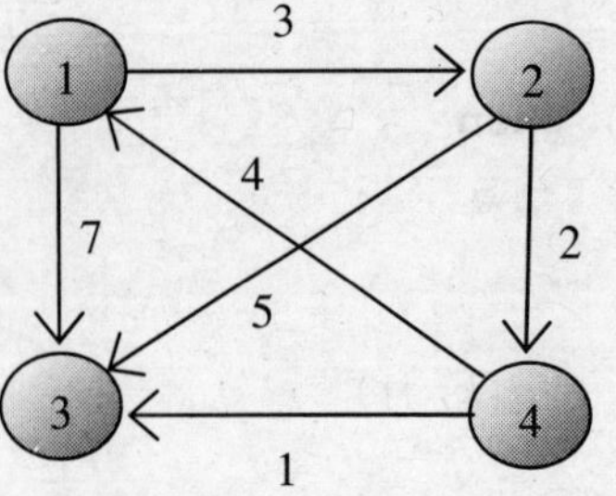

$$W = \begin{pmatrix} 0 & 3 & 7 & 0 \\ 0 & 0 & 5 & 2 \\ 0 & 0 & 0 & 0 \\ 4 & 0 & 1 & 0 \end{pmatrix}$$

Figure 11.17: Directed graph and its adjacency matrix representation

The following matrices are the sequence of matrices *D* and *P* computed by the algorithm 11.9.

$$D^{(0)} = \begin{pmatrix} \alpha & 3 & 7 & \alpha \\ \alpha & \alpha & 5 & 2 \\ \alpha & \alpha & \alpha & \alpha \\ 4 & \alpha & 1 & \alpha \end{pmatrix} \qquad P^{(0)} = \begin{pmatrix} 0 & 1 & 1 & 0 \\ 0 & 0 & 2 & 2 \\ 0 & 0 & 0 & 0 \\ 4 & 0 & 4 & 0 \end{pmatrix}$$

$$D^{(1)} = \begin{pmatrix} \alpha & 3 & 7 & \alpha \\ \alpha & \alpha & 5 & 2 \\ \alpha & \alpha & \alpha & \alpha \\ 4 & 7 & 1 & \alpha \end{pmatrix} \qquad P^{(1)} = \begin{pmatrix} 0 & 1 & 1 & 0 \\ 0 & 0 & 2 & 2 \\ 0 & 0 & 0 & 0 \\ 4 & 1 & 4 & 0 \end{pmatrix}$$

$$D^{(2)} = \begin{pmatrix} \alpha & 3 & 7 & 5 \\ \alpha & \alpha & 5 & 2 \\ \alpha & \alpha & \alpha & \alpha \\ 4 & 7 & 1 & \alpha \end{pmatrix} \qquad P^{(2)} = \begin{pmatrix} 0 & 1 & 1 & 2 \\ 0 & 0 & 2 & 2 \\ 0 & 0 & 0 & 0 \\ 4 & 1 & 4 & 0 \end{pmatrix}$$

$$D^{(3)} = \begin{pmatrix} \alpha & 3 & 7 & 5 \\ \alpha & \alpha & 5 & 2 \\ \alpha & \alpha & \alpha & \alpha \\ 4 & 7 & 1 & \alpha \end{pmatrix} \qquad P^{(3)} = \begin{pmatrix} 0 & 1 & 1 & 2 \\ 0 & 0 & 2 & 2 \\ 0 & 0 & 0 & 0 \\ 4 & 1 & 4 & 0 \end{pmatrix}$$

$$D^{(4)} = \begin{pmatrix} \alpha & 3 & 6 & 5 \\ \alpha & \alpha & 5 & 2 \\ \alpha & \alpha & \alpha & \alpha \\ 4 & 7 & 1 & \alpha \end{pmatrix} \qquad P^{(4)} = \begin{pmatrix} 0 & 1 & 4 & 2 \\ 4 & 0 & 4 & 2 \\ 0 & 0 & 0 & 0 \\ 4 & 1 & 4 & 0 \end{pmatrix}$$

Figure 11.18: Sequences of matrices computed by Algorithm 11.9

The interpretation of the above matrices is as follows:

Paths	Its weight
$1 \to 2$	3
$1 \to 2 \to 4 \to 3$	6
$1 \to 2 \to 4$	5
$2 \to 4 \to 1$	6
$2 \to 4 \to 3$	3
$2 \to 4$	2
No path from 3 to 1 exists	–
No path from 3 to 2 exists	–
No path from 3 to 4 exists	–
$4 \to 1$	4
$4 \to 1 \to 2$	7
$4 \to 3$	1

The implementation of the algorithm 11.10 and 11.9 is given in listing 11.19.

Listing 11.19:

```
#include <iostream.h>
#include <iomanip.h>
#define MAX 8
#define NIL 0
#define INFINITY  3200
void printPaths(int p[][MAX], int i, int j);
void FloydWarshall(int w[][MAX], int n);
void main()
{
   int w[MAX][MAX], i, j, n;
   cout << "\nEnter number of nodes in the graph : ";
   cin >> n;
   cout << "\nEnter weight of the edge "
        << "(0 in case there is no edge)\n\n";
   for ( i = 1; i <= n; i++ ) {
      for ( j = 1; j <= n; j++ ) {
      cout << "Enter weight for edge ("
```

```
         << i << "," << j << ") : ";
      cin >> w[i][j];
      }
   }
   FloydWarshall(w, n);
}
void FloydWarshall( int w[][MAX], int n )
{
   int d[MAX][MAX], p[MAX][MAX], i, j, k;
   for ( i = 1; i <= n; ++i ) {
      for ( j = 1; j <= n; ++j ) {
         if ( w[i][j] == 0 ) {
            d[i][j] = INFINITY;
            p[i][j] = NIL;
         } else {
            d[i][j] = w[i][j];
            p[i][j] = i;
         }
      }
   }
   for ( k = 1; k <= n; k++ ) {
      for ( i = 1; i <= n; i++ ) {
         for ( j = 1; j <= n; j++ ) {
            if ( d[i][j] <= ( d[i][k] + d[k][j] ) )
               p[i][j] = p[i][j];
            else
               p[i][j] = p[k][j];
            if ( d[i][j] <= ( d[i][k] + d[k][j] ) )
               d[i][j] = d[i][j];
            else
               d[i][j] = d[i][k] + d[k][j];
         }
      }
   }
   cout << "\n\nShortest paths are\n";
   for ( i = 1; i <= n; i++ ) {
      cout << endl;
      for ( j = 1; j <= n; j++ ) {
       if ( i != j ) {
            cout << endl;
            printPaths( p, i, j );
         }
      }
   }
}
void printPaths( int p[][MAX], int i, int j )
{
   if ( i == j )
      cout << i;
   else if ( p[i][j] == NIL )
      cout << "No path from " << i << " to " << j << " exists";
   else {
      printPaths( p, i, p[i][j] );
      cout << " -> " << j;
   }
}
```

11.5.4 Transitive Closure of a Directed Graph

Given a directed graph $G = (V, E)$ with vertex set $V = \{1, 2, 3, \ldots, n\}$, we may wish to find out whether there is a path in G from vertex i to vertex j for all pairs $i, j \in V$. The answer of the above question can be found by finding the transitive closure of given graph.

Transitivity says that if there exists a path from vertex i to vertex k and vertex k to vertex j, then there exists a path from vertex i to vertex j as shown in the following figure with a dashed line.

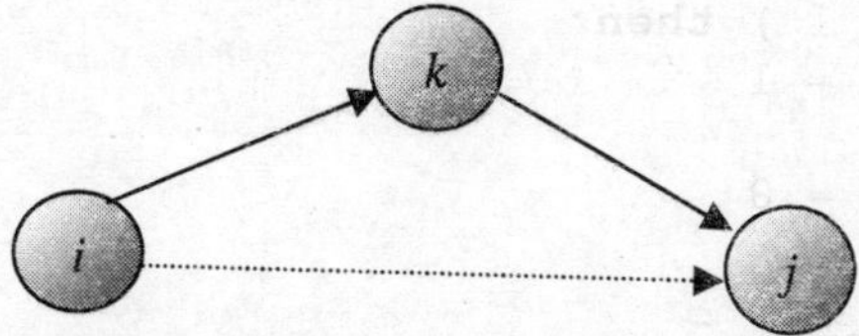

Figure 11.19: Illustration of transitivity

The *transitive closure* of a graph $G = (V, E)$ is defined as graph $G^* = (V, E^*)$, where

$$E^* = \{ (i, j) : \text{there exists a path from vertex } i \text{ to vertex } j \text{ in G} \}$$

One way to compute the transitive closure is to assign a weight of 1 to each edge of E and run the Floyd-Warshall algorithm. If there is a path from vertex i to vertex j, we get $d_{ij} < n$, otherwise, we get $d_{ij} = \infty$.

There is another way, though quite similar, that save time and space in practice. This method involves the substitution of the logical operations $\vee$ (OR) and $\wedge$ (AND) for arithmetic operations *min* and + in the Floyd-Warshall algorithm.

For $i, j, k = 1, 2, 3, \ldots, n$, we define $t_{ij}^{k} = 1$, if there exists a path in graph G from vertex i to vertex j with intermediate vertices in the set $\{1, 2, 3, \ldots, k\}$, and 0 otherwise. We construct the transitive closure $G^* = (V, E^*)$ by putting edge (i, j) into E^* iff $t_{ij}^{n} = 1$.

A recursive definition for $t_{ij}^{(k)}$ is as given below.

When $k = 0$

$$t_{ij}^{(0)} = \begin{cases} 0 & \text{if } (i,j) \notin E \\ 1 & \text{if } (i,j) \in E \end{cases}$$

and for $k \geq 1$

$$t_{ij}^{(k)} = t_{ij}^{(k-1)} \vee (t_{ik}^{(k-1)} \wedge t_{kj}^{(k-1)})$$

We compute the matrices $T^{(k)} = \left(t_{ij}^{(k)}\right)$ in the increasing order of k.

Algorithm 11.11:

TransitiveClosure(*a*, *t*, *n*)

Here *a* is *n*×*n* adjacency-matrix representing directed input graph *G*. This algorithm computes the transitive closure and stores in matrix *t* also of size *n*×*n*.

```
Begin
  for i = 1 to n by 1 do
     for i = 1 to n by 1 do
        if ( a[i,j] = 1 ) then
           Set t[i,j] = 1
        else
           Set t[i,j] = 0
        endif
     endfor
  endfor
  for k = 1 to n by 1 do
     for i = 1 to n by 1 do
        for j = 1 to n by 1 do
            Set t[i,j] = t[i,j] ∨ ( t[i,k] ∧ t[k,j]   )
        endfor
     endfor
  endfor
End.
```

Implementation of this is left as an exercise for the readers.

11.6 ARTICULATION POINTS, BRIDGES, AND BICONNECTED COMPONENTS

Let *G* = (*V*, *E*) be a connected, undirected graph. An *articulation point*, also called a *cut point*, of *G* is a vertex whose removal disconnects G. A *bridge* of G is an edge whose removal disconnects *G*. A biconnected component of *G* is a maximal set of edges such that any two edges in the set lie on a common simple cycle.

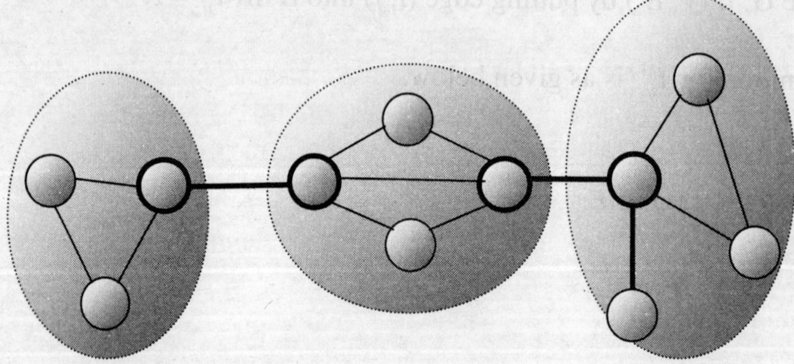

Figure 11.20 The articulation points and bridges are shown with thick lines, while biconnected components are shown inside dashed circles.

We can find articulation points, bridges, and biconnected components using depth-first search.

11.7 STRONGLY CONNECTED COMPONENTS

A directed graph $G = (V, E)$ is *strongly connected* if and only if for each pair of vertices i and j there exists a path from i to j and j to i. A *strongly connected component*, or simply *strong component*, of a directed graph is a maximal strongly connected subgraph.

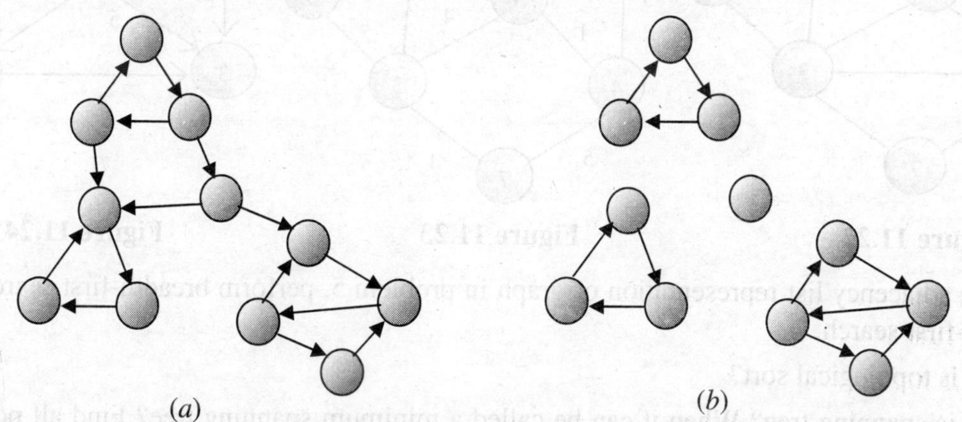

Figure 11.21: *(a)* A directed graph, *(b)* Its strong components

11.8 EULERIAN TOUR

An *Eulerian tour* through an undirected graph is a path whose edge list contains each edge of the graph exactly once. An *Eulerian graph* is a graph that possesses an Eulerian tour. It has been proved that an undirected graph is Eulerian graph if and only if it is connected and has either zero or two vertices with an odd degree.

11.9 HAMILTONIAN TOUR

A *Hamiltonian tour* through an undirected graph is a path whose vertex list contains each vertex of the graph exactly once. A *Hamiltonian graph* is a graph that possesses a Hamiltonian tour. No simple condition exists that can be used to characterize Hamiltonian graph.

REVIEW EXERCISES

1. Is graph a linear or non-linear data structure?
2. How graphs can be represented in computer memory? Give relative merits and de-merits of each representation scheme.
3. We have an application using which a railway passenger can know whether there exists a path from a given city to another city, *i.e.*, does there exists a railway link direct or indirect. Which way graph should be represented in memory?
4. How breadth-first search differs from depth-first search? Can we perform these searches on weighted graphs? Justify your answer.
5. Show the possible adjacency matrix and adjacency list representation of graph of figure 11.22.

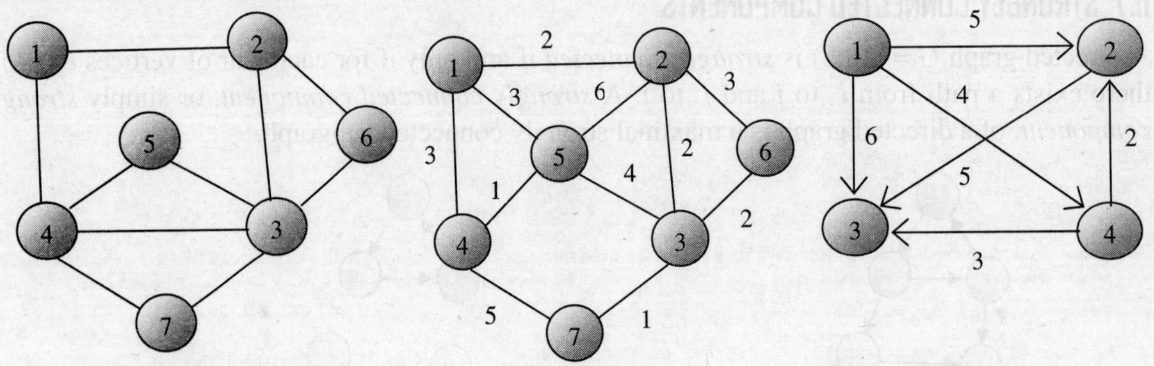

Figure 11.22 Figure 11.23 Figure 11.24

6. Using adjacency list representation of graph in problem 5, perform breadth-first search and depth-first search.
7. What is topological sort?
8. What is spanning tree? When it can be called a minimum spanning tree? Find all possible spanning trees and a minimum spanning tree of graph in figure 11.23.
9. Show the progress of Prim's algorithm to find the minimum-spanning tree for a graph shown in exercise 7.
10. Show the progress of Dijkstra's algorithm to find the shortest path from vertex 4 to vertex 6 in a graph shown in exercise 7.
11. Show the progress of Floyd-Warshall's algorithm to find the shortest paths between all pair of vertices of graph in figure 11.24.

PROGRAMMING EXERCISES

1. The *degree* of a vertex in an undirected graph is defined as the number of edges incident on it. Write a program to find the *degree* of each vertex.
2. The *indegree* of a vertex in a directed graphs is defined the number of edges in which it appears as a destination vertex. Likewise, the *outdegree* of a vertex in a directed graphs is defined the number of edges in which it appears as a source vertex. Write a program to find the *indegree* and *outdegree* of each vertex.
3. An undirected graph is said to be fully connected, if every vertex is connected to every other vertex. Write a function that takes an undirected graph as its parameter and returns value 1 if graph is fully connected else returns value 0.
4. Write a program to insert a new edge in an undirected graph.
5. Write a program to find the transitive closure of an undirected as well as directed graph.
6. Write a program to find the vertices connected by edge with maximum weight in a directed graph.

❑ ❑ ❑

Chapter 12

Hash Tables and Hashing

12.1 INTRODUCTION

In all the search algorithms considered so far, the location of the item is determined by a sequence of comparisons. In each case, a data item sought is repeatedly compared with items in certain locations of the data structure. However, the number of actual comparison depends on the data structure and the search algorithm used. For example

- In an array and linked list, the linear search requires $O(n)$ comparisons.
- In a sorted array, the binary search requires $O(\log_2 n)$ comparisons.
- In a binary search tree, search requires $O(\log_2 n)$ comparisons.

However, there are some applications that require search to be performed in constant time, *i.e.*, O(1). Ideally, it may not be possible, but still we can achieve a performance very close to it. And this is possible using a data structure known as *hash table*.

A *hash table*, in basic sense, is a generalization of the simpler notion of an ordinary array. Directly addressing into an array makes it possible to access any data element of the array in O(1) time. For example, if $a[1..100]$ is an ordinary array, then the nth data element, $1 \leq n \leq 100$, can be directly accessed as $a[n]$. However, direct addressing is applicable only when we can allocate an array that has one position for every possible key.

In addition, direct addressing suffers from following problems:

1. If the total number of possible keys is very large, it may not be possible to allocate an array of that size because of the memory available in the system or the applications software does not permit it.

2. If the actually number of keys is very small as compared to total number of possible keys, lot of space in the array will be wasted.

Therefore, in practice, when the number of keys actually stored is small relative to total number of possible keys, a hash table becomes more effective since a hash table typically uses an array of size proportional to the number of keys actually stored. Further, instead of using the key as array index directly, the array index is computed from the key.

This chapter discusses the hash tables and the different issues related to it. We begin with brief discussion on direct address tables.

12.2 DIRECT ADDRESS TABLES

Direct addressing is a simple technique that works quite well when the universe U of keys is reasonably small. As an example, consider an application that needs a dynamic set in which each element has a key drawn from the universe $U = \{0, 1, 2, 3, \ldots, m-1\}$, where m is not very large. We also assume that all elements are unique i.e. no two elements have the same key.

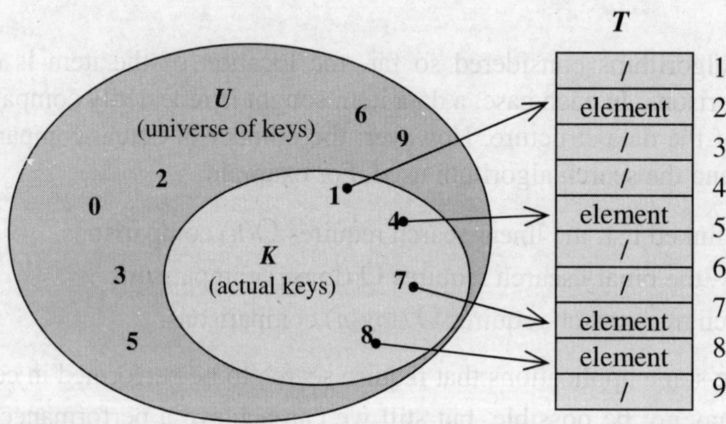

Figure 12.1: Implementing a dynamic set by a direct-address table T, where the elements are stored in the table itself.

Figure 12.1 shows the implementing a dynamic set by a direct-address table T, where the elements are stored in the table itself. Here each key in the universe $U = \{0, 1, 2, 3, \ldots, 9\}$ corresponds to an index in the table. The set $K = \{1, 4, 7, 8\}$ of actual keys determines the slots in the table that contains elements. The empty/ vacant slots are marked with slash character '/'.

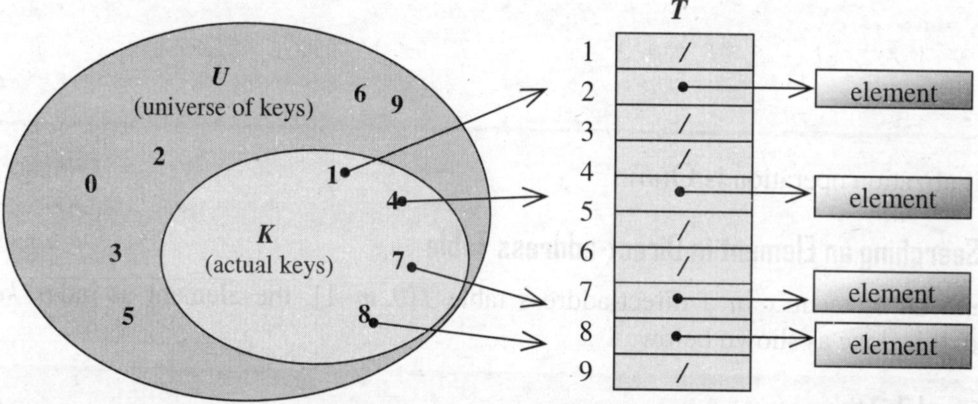

Figure 12.2: Implementing a dynamic set by a direct-address table *T*, where a pointer to the actual element is stored in the table.

The Figure 12.2 shows the implementation of a dynamic set where a pointer to an element is stored in the direct-address table *T*.

For simplification, we will consider that elements are stored in the direct-address table *T* itself and a sentinel value, −1, is stored in vacant slots.

To represent the dynamic set, we use an array *T*[0..*m*−1] in which each position or slot corresponds to a key in the universe *U*. The implementation of various operations is straightforward.

Following declarations will be used to represent a direct address table in memory:

```
class DirectAddressTable {
    private:
        int *t;
        int m;
    public:
        DirectAddressTable(int n);   // constructor
        ~DirectAddressTable(int n); // destructor
        int searchElement(int x);    // search element
        void intsertElement(int x); // insert element
        void deleteElement(int x);  // delete element
};
```

12.2.1 Initializing a Direct-address Table

In order to initialize a direct-address table *T*[0..*m*−1], sentinel value −1 is assigned to each slot. This task is accomplished by the constructor.

Listing 12.1:

```
DirectAddressTable::DirectAddressTable(int n)
{
    int i;
    t = new int[n];
```

```
    m = n;
    for ( i = 0; i < m; ++i )
        t[i] = -1;
}
```

This initialization operation is O(m).

12.2.2 Searching an Element in Direct-address Table

To search an element x in a direct-address table $T[0..m-1]$, the element at index $key[x]$ is returned. It is done as shown below.

Listing 12.2:

```
int DirectAddressTable::searchElement(int x)
{
    return t[key[x]];
}
```

12.2.3 Inserting a New Element in Direct-address Table

To insert a new element x in a direct-address table $T[0..m-1]$, the element is stored at index $key[x]$. It is done as shown below.

Listing 12.3:

```
void DirectAddressTable::insertElement(int x)
{
    t[key[x]] = x;
}
```

12.2.4 Deleting an Element from a Direct-address Table

To delete an element x from a direct-address table $T[0..m-1]$, the sentinel value −1 is stored at index $key[x]$. It is done as shown below.

Listing 12.4:

```
void DirectAddressTable::deleteElement(int x)
{
    t[key[x]] = -1;
}
```

Each of these operations (search, insert, delete) is fast: only O(1) time is required. However, the difficulties with the direct-address tables are obvious as stated below.

1. If the universe U is large, storing a table T of size $|U|$ may be impractical or even impossible given the memory available on a typical computer.
2. If the set K of actual keys is very small relative to U, most of the space allocated for T will be wasted.

12.3 HASH TABLE

A *hash table* is a data structure in which the location of a data item is determined directly as a function of the data item itself rather than by a sequence of comparisons. Under ideal conditions, the time required to locate a data item in a hash table is $O(1)$, *i.e.*, it is constant and does not depend on the number of data items stored.

When the set of *K* of keys stored is much smaller than the universe *U* of all possible keys, a hash table requires much less storage space than a direct-address table. In fact, the storage requirements can be reduced to $\Theta(|k|)$, while maintaining the search operation an $O(1)$ operation. The difference here is that this bound is for *average-case* time, whereas for direct addressing it holds for the *worst-case time*.

While in a direct-address table, an element with key *k* is stored in slot *k*, whereas this element is stored in slot $h(k)$; that is, a *hash function h* is used to compute the slot from the key *k*. Here, the *hash function h* maps the universe *U* of keys into the slots of a hash table $T[0..m-1]$. This process of mapping keys to appropriate slots in a hash table is known as *hashing*.

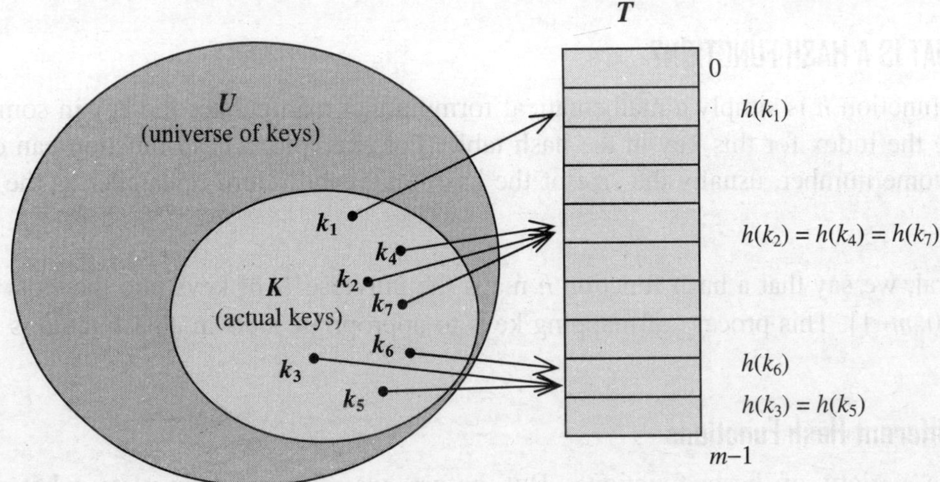

Figure 12.3: Implementing a dynamic set by a hash table $T[0..m-1]$, where the elements are stored in the table itself.

Figure 12.3 shows the implementing a dynamic set by a hash table $T[0..m-1]$, where the elements are stored in the table itself. Here each key in the dynamic set *K* of actual keys is mapped to hash table slots using hash function *h*. Note that the keys k_2, k_4 and k_7 map to the same slot. The mapping of more than one key maps to the same slot is known as *collision*. We can also say that the keys k_2, k_4 and k_7 collide. Similarly, key k_3 and k_5 also collide.

We usually say that an element with key *k* hashes to slot $h(k)$. We can also say that $h(k)$ is the hash value of key *k*.

The purpose of the hash function is to reduce the range of array indices that need to be handled. Therefore, instead of $|U|$ values, we need to handle only m values which led to the reduction in the storage requirements.

The main flaw of this beautiful idea is that two or more keys (unequal keys) may hash to the same slot, which lead to the condition called *collision*. Ideally, it would have been nice if the collision could be avoided by carefully choosing a hash function. But in practice, it is not possible to avoid collision irrespective of the nature of the hash function. Therefore, in these circumstances, the best solution is to minimise the number of collisions and device a scheme to resolve these collisions if they occur.

The following schemes for resolving collisions will be discussed in this chapter.

1. Collision resolution by separating chaining.
2. Collision resolution by open addressing.

Before describing these collision resolution schemes, let us first discuss more about hash functions.

12.4 WHAT IS A HASH FUNCTION?

A hash function h is simply a mathematical formula that manipulates the key in some form to compute the index for this key in the hash table. For example, a hash function can divide the key by some number, usually the size of the hash table, and return remainder as the index for the key.

In general, we say that a hash function h maps the universe U of keys into the slots of a hash table $T[0..m-1]$. This process of mapping keys to appropriate slots in a hash table is known as *hashing*.

12.4.1 Different Hash Functions

There is variety of hash functions. But before we discuss them, lets what are main considerations while choosing a particular hash function.

The main considerations while choosing a particular hash function h are

1. It should be possible to compute it efficiently.
2. It should distribute the keys uniformly across the hash-table i.e. it should keep the number of collisions as minimum as possible.

Some popular hash functions are described in this section.

12.4.1.1 Division Method

In division method, key k to be mapped into one of the m slots in the hash-table is divided by m and the remainder of this division is taken as index into the hash-table.

That is, the hash function is

$$h(k) = k \bmod m$$

where *mod* is the modulus operator and is supported by Pascal language as such. In C/C++ and Java, its equivalent operator is % character.

The above hash function will map the keys in the range 0 to $m-1$ and is acceptable in C/C++ and Java. But if some language supports the index from 1 onwards, then the hash function becomes

$$h(k) = k \bmod m + 1$$

Example 12.1:

Consider a hash table with 9 slots, *i.e.*, $m = 9$, then the hash function

$$h(k) = k \bmod m$$

will map the key 132 to slot 7 since

$$h(132) = 132 \bmod 9 = 7$$

Since it requires only a single division operation, hashing is quite fast.

When using the division method, certain values of m should be avoided. It has been proved in literature that good values for m are prime values not too close to exact powers of 2.

12.4.1.2 Multiplication Method

The multiplication method operates in two steps. In the first step, the key value k is multiplied by a constant A in the range $0 < A < 1$ and extract the fractional part of value kA. In the second step, the fractional value obtained above is multiplied by m and the floor of the result is taken as the hash value. That is, the hash function is

$$h(k) = \lfloor m\ (k A \bmod 1)\ \rfloor$$

where "$k A \bmod 1$" means the fractional part of $k A$ i.e. $k A - \lfloor k A \rfloor$. Note that $\lfloor x \rfloor$ read as floor of x and represents the largest integer less than or equal to x.

Although this method works with any value of A, it works better with some values than others. The best choice depends on the characteristics of the key values. Knuth has suggested in his study that the following value of A is likely to work reasonably well.

$$A \approx (\sqrt{5} - 1) / 2 = 0.6180339887 \ldots$$

Example 12.2:

Consider a hash table with 10000 slots, i.e., $m = 10000$, then the hash function

$$h(k) = \lfloor m\,(k\,A \bmod 1)\rfloor$$

will map the key 123456 to slot 41 since

$$\begin{aligned} h(123456) &= \lfloor 10000 \times (123456 \times 0.61803 \ldots \bmod 1)\rfloor \\ &= \lfloor 10000 \times (76300.0041151\ldots \bmod 1)\rfloor \\ &= \lfloor 10000 \times .0041151\ldots \rfloor \\ &= \lfloor 41.151\ldots \rfloor \\ &= 41 \end{aligned}$$

12.4.1.3 Midsquare Method

The midsquare method also operates in two steps. In the first step, the square of the key value k is taken. In the second step, the hash value is obtained by deleting digits from ends of the squared value i.e. k^2. It is important to note that same position of k^2 must be used for all keys. Thus, the hash function is

$$h(k) = s$$

where s is obtained by deleting digits from both sides of k^2.

Example 12.3:

Consider a hash table with 100 slots, *i.e.*, $m = 100$, and key values $k = 3205, 7148, 2345$

Solution:

The calculations are shown below:

k :	3205	7148	2345
k^2 :	10272025	51093904	5499025
$h(k)$:	72	93	90

The hash values are obtained by taking fourth and fifth digits counting from right.

12.4.1.4 Folding Method

The folding method also operates in two steps. In the first step, the key value k is divided into number of parts, $k_1, k_2, k_3, \ldots, k_r$, where each part has the same number of digits except the last part, which can have lesser digits. In the second step, these parts are added together and the hash value is obtained by ignoring the last carry, if any. For example, if the hash table has 1000 slots, each part will have three digits, and the sum of these parts after ignoring the last carry will also be 3-digit number in the range 0 to 999.

Example 12.4:

Consider a hash table with 100 slots, *i.e.*, $m = 100$, and key values $k = 9235, 714, 71458$

Solution:

The calculations are shown below:

k :	9235	714	71458
parts :	92, 35	71, 4	71, 45, 8
sum of parts :	127	75	124
$h(k)$:	27	75	14

In above examples, we have assumed that keys are numeric. However, if the keys are alphanumeric, then the ASCII codes of fixed number of characters can be added together to transfer the character key to its equivalent numeric key, and then any of the above hash function can be applied.

12.5 RESOLVING COLLISIONS

A Collision is a phenomenon that occurs when more than one key maps to same slot in the hash table. Though we can keep collisions to a certain minimum level, but we can not eliminate them altogether. Therefore we need some mechanism to handle them.

In this section, we will discuss different schemes used to handle/resolve collisions.

12.5.1 Collision Resolution by Synonyms Chaining

In this scheme, all the elements whose keys hash to the same hash-table slot are put in a one linked list as shown in Figure 12.4. Thus, the slot i in the hash-table contain a pointer to the head of the linked list of all the elements that hashes to value i. If there is no such element that hash to value i, the slot i contains NULL value (pictured as X).

To represent the dynamic set, we use an array $T[0..m-1]$ of pointers in which each position or slot, say i, contains a pointer to a linked lists of all the elements that hash to value i. For simplicity, assume the elements to be stored in a hash-table are of type integer.

Figure 12.4 shows the collision resolution by separating chaining, also called *synonyms chaining*. Here each hash table slot $T[i]$ contains a linked list of all the keys whose hash value is i.

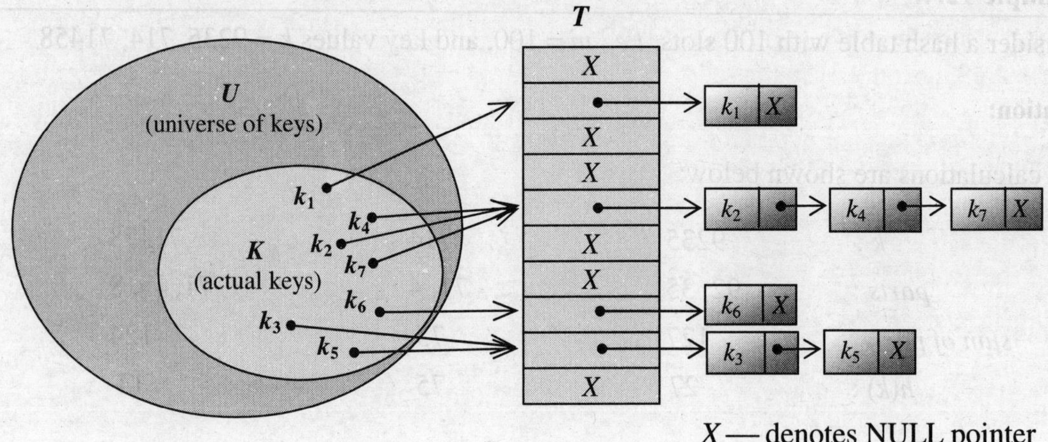

Figure 12.4: Collision resolution by separating chaining. Each hash table slot *T*[*i*] contains a linked list of all the keys whose hash value is *i*.

Following declarations will be used to represent a direct address table in memory:

```
struct Node {              // structure of the node for linked list
   int info;
   struct Node *next;
};
class HashTable {          // class for modelling hash table
    private:
        node **t;
        int m;
    public:
        HashTable(int n);              // constructor
        ~HashTable(int n);             // destructor
        int searchElement(int x);      // search element
        void intsertElement(int x);    // insert element
        void deleteElement(int x);     // delete element
};
```

The implementation of various operations is illustrated below.

12.5.1.1 Initializing a Chained-hash-table

In order to initialize a chained-hash-table *T*[[*0..m*–1], NULL pointer is assigned to each slot. It is done as shown below.

Listing 12.5:

```
HashTable::HashTable(int n)
{
    m = n;
    t= new int* [m] ;
    for ( int i = 0; i < m; i++ )
        t[i] = NULL;
}
```

This initialization operation is O(*m*).

12.5.1.2 Searching an Element in Chained-hash-table

To search an element *x* in a chained-hash-table *T*[*0..m*–1], the element is searched in the linked lists whose pointer to its head is held in slot *T*[*h*[*x*]]. The following function return the pointer to the node in the linked list where element is present if search succeeds; otherwise return value NULL to indicate failure.

Listing 12.6:

```
node* HashTable::searchElement(int x)
{
    node *ptr;
    ptr = t[h(x)];
    while ( ( ptr != NULL ) && ( ptr->info != x ) )
        ptr = ptr->next;
    if ( ptr->info == x )
        return ptr;
    else
        return NULL;
}
```

For search operation, the worst-case running time is of the order of the size of the linked list.

12.5.1.3 Inserting a New Element in Chained-hash-table

To insert a new element *x* in a chained-hash-table *T*[*0..m*–1], the element is inserted in the beginning of the linked whose pointer to its head is stored at slot *h*[*x*]. It is done as shown below.

Listing 12.7:

```
void HashTable::insertElement(int x)
{
    node *ptr;
    ptr = ( node * ) malloc( sizeof( node ) );
    ptr->info = x;
    ptr->next = t[h(x)];
    t[h(x)] = ptr;
}
```

This insertion operation is O(1) as the new element is always inserted in the beginning of the last and the operations required for that are independent of the size of the linked list and that of size of the chained-hash-table.

12.5.1.4 Deleting an Element from a Chained-hash-table

To delete an element *x* from a chained-hash-table *T*[*0..m*–1], delete element *x* from the linked list whose head is stored at slot *T*[*h*[*x*]]. In order to perform the actual deletion of element *x*, we need to know the address of its predecessor.

The entire task as performed as shown below:

Listing 12.8:

```
void HashTable::deleteElement(int x)
{
    node *nodePtr, *predecessorPtr;
    predecessorPtr = NULL;
    nodePtr = t[ h(x)];
    while ( ( nodePtr != NULL ) && ( nodePtr->info != x ) )
    {
        predecessorPtr = nodePtr;
        nodePtr = nodePtr->next;

    }
    if ( nodePtr == NULL )
    {
        printf( "\nEllement %d not found in table\n" );
        return;
    }
    Else
    {
        predecessorPtr->next = nodePtr->next;
        free ( nodePtr );
    }
}
```

Deletion operation also has the same complexity as that of search operations. Because first we have to search the location of the predecessor of the given element so that next pointer field of the predecessor can be properly set so that element can be removed without disturbing the rest of the list.

In the above functions, we have considered following code for hash function

Listing 12.9:

```
int h( int x )
{

 /*   here you add the code for selected hash function   */
}
```

Example 12.5:

Let us consider the insertion of elements 5, 28, 19, 15, 20, 33, 12, 17, 10 into a chained- hash-table. Let us suppose that hash table has 9 slots, and the hash function be $h(k)=k \bmod 9$.

Solution:

To begin with the chained-hash-table is initialized with NULL pointers as shown.

	T
0	*X*
1	*X*
2	*X*
3	*X*
4	*X*
5	*X*
6	*X*
7	*X*
8	*X*

(*a*) Initial state of the chained-hash-table

Since $h(5) = 5 \bmod 9 = 5$, create a linked list for slot *T*[5] and store value 5 in its only node.

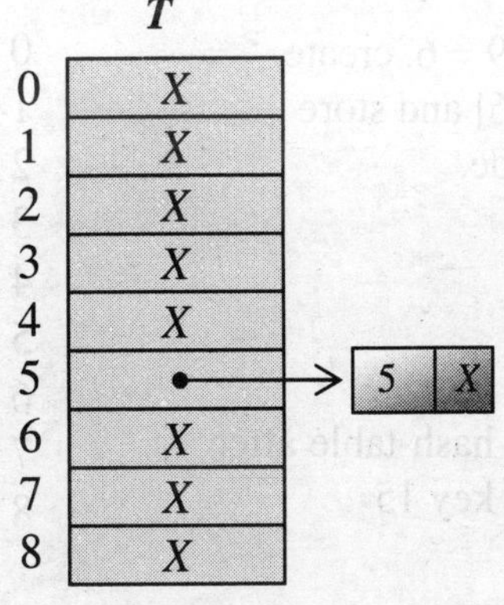

(*b*) Chained-hash-table after inserting key 5

Since $h(28) = 28 \bmod 9 = 1$, create a linked list for slot *T*[1] and store value 28 in its only node.

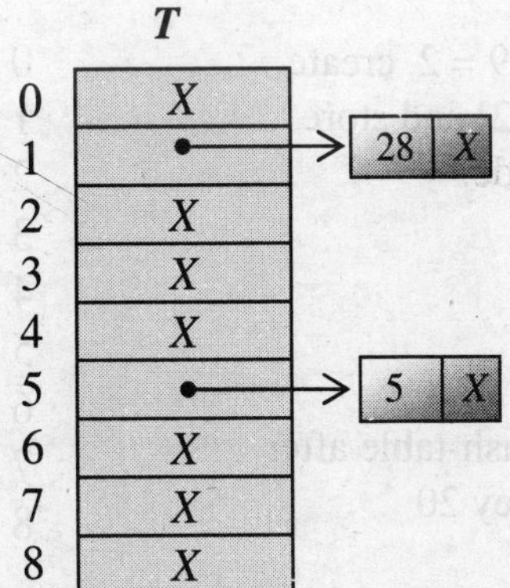

(*c*) Chained-hash-table after inserting key 28

Since $h(19) = 19 \bmod 9 = 1$, insert value 19 in the beginning of the linked list for slot $T[1]$ as shown.

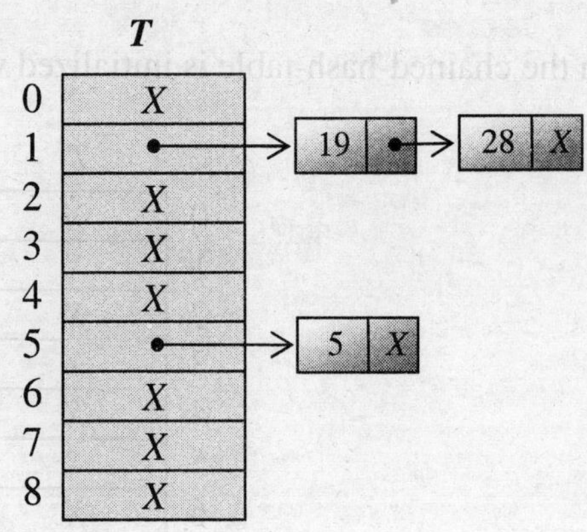

(*d*) Chained-hash-table after inserting key 19

Since $h(15) = 15 \bmod 9 = 6$, create a linked list for slot $T[6]$ and store value 15 in its only node.

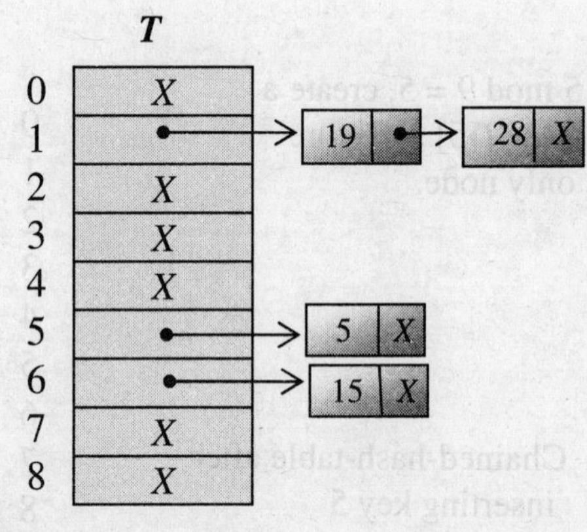

(*e*) Chained-hash-table after inserting key 15

Since $h(20) = 20 \bmod 9 = 2$, create a linked list for slot $T[2]$ and store value 20 in its only node.

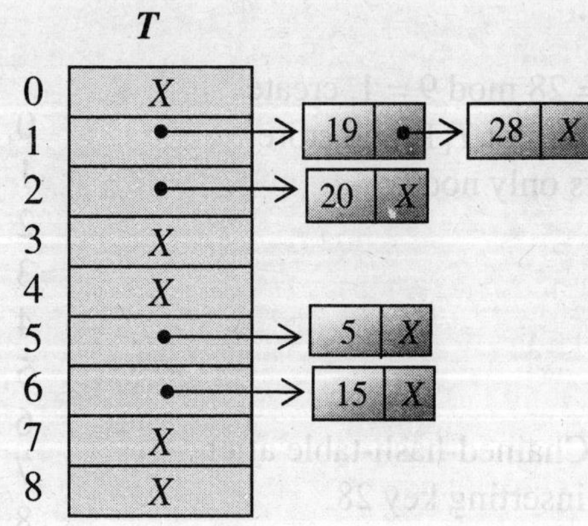

(*f*) Chained-hash-table after inserting key 20

Since $h(33) = 33 \bmod 9 = 6$, insert key 33 in the beginning of the linked list for slot $T[6]$ as shown.

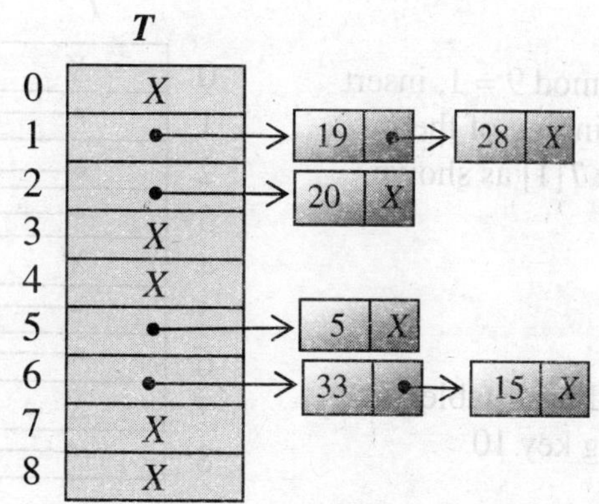

(*g*) Chained-hash-table after inserting key 33

Since $h(12) = 12 \bmod 9 = 3$, create a linked list for slot $T[3]$ and store key 12 in its only node.

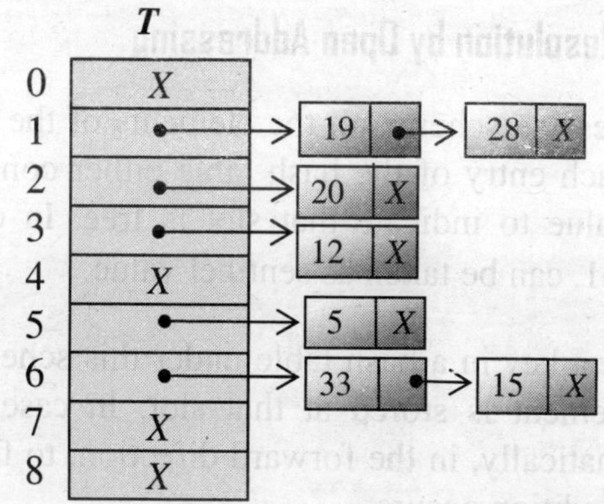

(*h*) Chained-hash-table after inserting key 12

Since $h(17) = 17 \bmod 9 = 8$, create a linked list for slot $T[8]$ and store key 17 in its only node.

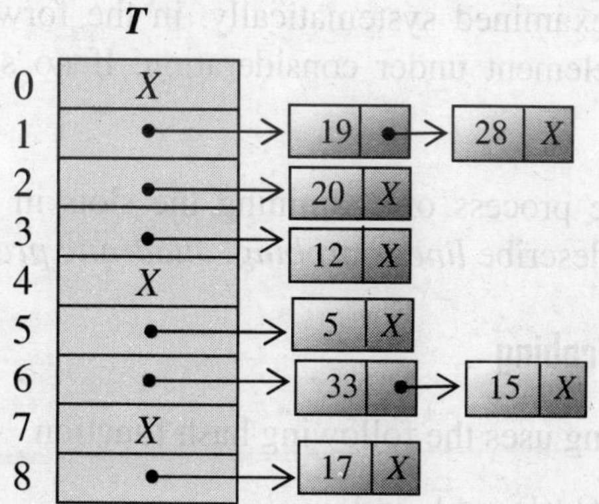

(*i*) Chained-hash-table after inserting key 17

Since $h(10) = 10 \bmod 9 = 1$, insert key 10 in the beginning of the linked list for slot $T[1]$ as shown.

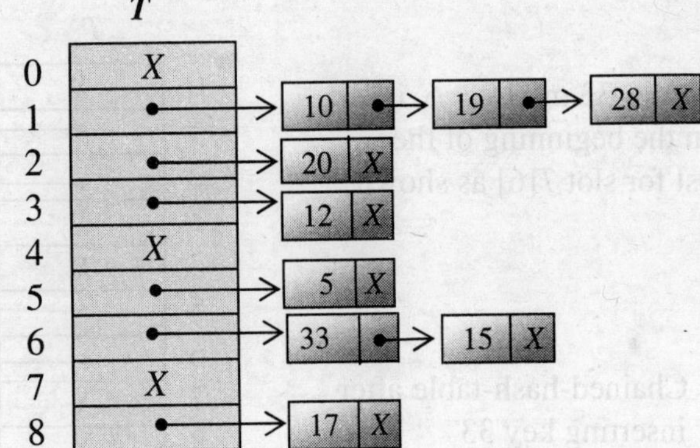

(*j*) Chained-hash-table after inserting key 10

Figure 12.5: (*a*) – (*j*) Illustrates the insertion of keys 5, 28, 19, 15, 20, 33, 12, 17, 10 in chained hash table.

12.5.2 Collision Resolution by Open Addressing

In the open addressing scheme all the elements of the dynamic set are stored in the hash-table itself. That is, each entry of the hash table either contains the element of the dynamic set or some sentinel value to indicate that slot is free. In case if it is known that no key can be negative, value –1, can be taken as sentinel value.

In order to insert a key in a hash table under this scheme, if the slot to which key is hashed is free then the element is stored at that slot. In case the slot is filled, then other slots are examined systematically, in the forward direction, to find the free slot. If no such slot is found then overflow condition occurs.

In case of searching, the element stored in the slot to which key is hashed is compared with element to be searched and if it matches search operations succeeds. If does not match, then other slots are examined systematically, in the forward direction, to find the slot contained containing the element under consideration. If no such slot is found then search ends in a failure.

In each case the process of examining the slots in the hash table is called *probing*. In this section we will describe *linear probing*, *quadratic probing* and *double hashing*.

12.5.2.1 Linear Probing

The linear probing uses the following hash function

$$h(k, i) = [h'(k) + i] \bmod m \qquad \text{for } i = 0, 1, 2, \ldots, m-1$$

where m is the size of the hash table and $h'(k) = k \bmod m$ the basic hash function (division method), and i is the probe number.

Therefore, for a given key k, the first slot probed is $T[h'(k)]$. The next slots are $T[h'(k)+1]$, $T[h'(k)+2]$, $T[h'(k)+3]$, and so on up to slot $T[m-1]$. Then we wrap around to slots $T[0]$, $T[1]$, $T[2]$, and so on until we finally probe slot $T[h'(k)-1]$. Since the initial probe position determines the entire sequence, only m distinct probe sequences are used with linear probing.

Example 12.6:

Consider inserting the keys 76, 26, 37, 59, 21, 65, 88 into a hash table of size $m = 11$ using linear probing. Further consider that the primary hash function is $h'(k) = k \bmod m$.

Solution:

	0	1	2	3	4	5	6	7	8	9	10
T	—	—	—	—	—	—	—	—	—	—	—

(*a*) Initial state of the hash table

Step 1. Consider first key $k = 76$

$$h(76, 0) = (76 \bmod 11 + 0) \bmod 11$$
$$= (10 + 0) \bmod 11 = 10 \bmod 11 = 10$$

Since slot $T[10]$ is free, insert key 76 at this place.

	0	1	2	3	4	5	6	7	8	9	10
T	—	—	—	—	—	—	—	—	—	—	76

(*b*) Hash table after inserting key 76

Step 2. Consider second key $k = 26$

$$h(26, 0) = (26 \bmod 11 + 0) \bmod 11$$
$$= (4 + 0) \bmod 11 = 4 \bmod 11 = 4$$

Since slot $T[4]$ is free, insert key 26 at this place.

	0	1	2	3	4	5	6	7	8	9	10
T	—	—	—	—	26	—	—	—	—	—	76

(*c*) Hash table after inserting key 26

Step 3. Consider third key $k = 37$

$$h(37, 0) = (37 \bmod 11 + 0) \bmod 11$$
$$= (4 + 0) \bmod 11 = 4 \bmod 11 = 4$$

Since slot $T[4]$ is occupied, the next probe sequence is computed as

$$h(37, 1) = (37 \bmod 11 + 1) \bmod 11$$
$$= (4 + 1) \bmod 11 = 5 \bmod 11 = 5$$

Since slot $T[5]$ is free. Insert key 37 at this place.

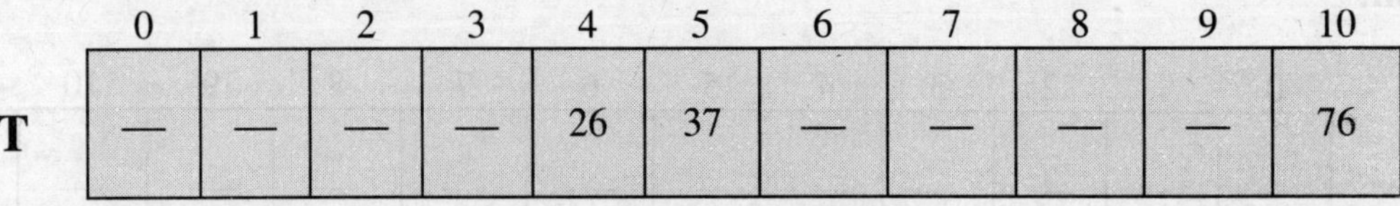

	0	1	2	3	4	5	6	7	8	9	10
T	—	—	—	—	26	37	—	—	—	—	76

(*d*) Hash table after inserting key 37

Step 4. Consider fourth key $k = 59$

$$h(59, 0) = (59 \bmod 11 + 0) \bmod 11$$
$$= (4 + 0) \bmod 11 = 4 \bmod 11 = 4$$

Since slot $T[4]$ is occupied, the next probe sequence is computed as

$$h(59, 1) = (57 \bmod 11 + 1) \bmod 11$$
$$= (4 + 1) \bmod 11 = 5 \bmod 11 = 5$$

Since slot $T[5]$ is also occupied, the next probe sequence is computed as

$$h(59, 2) = (57 \bmod 11 + 1) \bmod 11$$
$$= (4 + 2) \bmod 11 = 6 \bmod 11 = 6$$

Since slot $T[6]$ is free. Insert key 59 at this place.

	0	1	2	3	4	5	6	7	8	9	10
T	—	—	—	—	26	37	59	—	—	—	76

(*e*) Hash table after inserting key 59

Step 5. Consider fifth key $k = 21$

$$h(21, 0) = (21 \bmod 11 + 0) \bmod 11$$
$$= (10 + 0) \bmod 11 = 10 \bmod 11 = 10$$

Since slot $T[4]$ is occupied, the next probe sequence is computed as

$$h(21, 1) = (21 \bmod 11 + 1) \bmod 11$$
$$= (10 + 1) \bmod 11 = 11 \bmod 11 = 0$$

Since slot $T[0]$ is free. Insert key 21 at this place.

	0	1	2	3	4	5	6	7	8	9	10
T	21	—	—	—	26	37	59	—	—	—	76

(*f*) Hash table after inserting key 21

Step 6. Consider sixth key $k = 65$

$$h(65, 0) = (65 \bmod 11 + 0) \bmod 11$$
$$= (10 + 0) \bmod 11 = 10 \bmod 11 = 10$$

Since slot $T[10]$ is occupied, the next probe sequence is computed as

$$h(65, 1) = (65 \bmod 11 + 1) \bmod 11$$
$$= (10 + 1) \bmod 11 = 11 \bmod 11 = 0$$

Since slot $T[0]$ is also occupied, the next probe sequence is computed as

$$h(65, 2) = (65 \bmod 11 + 1) \bmod 11$$
$$= (10 + 2) \bmod 11 = 12 \bmod 11 = 1$$

Since slot $T[1]$ is free. Insert key 65 at this place.

	0	1	2	3	4	5	6	7	8	9	10
T	21	65	—	—	26	37	59	—	—	—	76

(*g*) Hash table after inserting key 65

Step 7. Consider seventh key $k = 88$

$$h(88, 0) = (88 \bmod 11 + 0) \bmod 11$$
$$= (0 + 0) \bmod 11 = 0 \bmod 11 = 0$$

Since slot $T[0]$ is occupied, the next probe sequence is computed as

$$h(88, 1) = (88 \bmod 11 + 1) \bmod 11$$
$$= (0 + 1) \bmod 11 = 1 \bmod 11 = 1$$

Since slot *T*[1] is also occupied, the next probe sequence is computed as

$$h(88, 2) = (88 \bmod 11 + 1) \bmod 11$$
$$= (0 + 2) \bmod 11 = 2 \bmod 11 = 2$$

Since slot *T*[2] is free. Insert key 88 at this place.

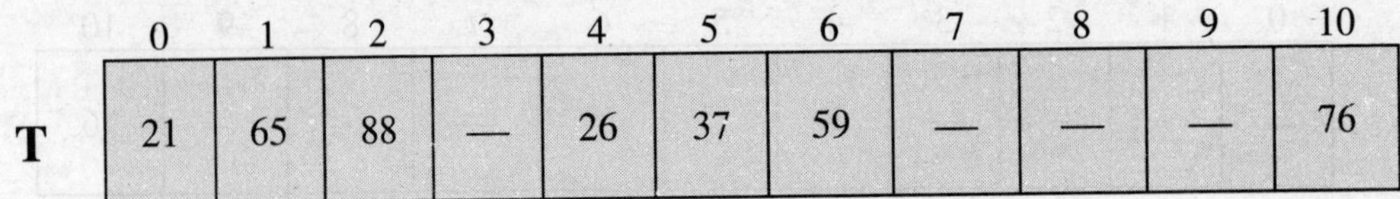

	0	1	2	3	4	5	6	7	8	9	10
T	21	65	88	—	26	37	59	—	—	—	76

(*h*) Hash table after inserting key 88

Figure 12.6: (*a*) – (*h*) Illustrates the insertion of keys 76, 26, 37, 59, 21, 65, 88 in open address hash table with linear probing.

You must have observed that if the first probe finds an occupied slot, the subsequent probes takes place in the increasing order of slots except wrap around occurs at the boundary of the hash table. This property of linear probing can be used to avoid the repetitive operations.

Linear probing is very easy to implement, but it suffers from a problem known as *primary clustering*. Here by a cluster we mean a block of occupied slots and primary clustering refers to many such blocks separated by free slots. Therefore, once clusters are formed there are more chances that subsequent insertions will also end up in one of the cluster and thereby increasing the size of cluster. Thus, increasing the number of probes required to find a free slot, and hence worsening the performance further.

To avoid problem of primary clustering, some remedies are suggested in literature. Two of them are *quadratic probing* and *double hashing*.

12.5.2.2 Quadratic Probing

The quadratic probing uses the following hash function

$$h(k, i) = [h'(k) + c_1 i + c_2 i^2] \bmod m \qquad \text{for } i = 0, 1, 2, \ldots, m-1$$

where m is the size of the hash table, $h'(k) = k \bmod m$ the basic hash function (division method), c_1 and $c_2 \neq 0$ are auxiliary constants), and i is the probe number.

The initial slot probed is $T[h'(k)]$ and the other slots probed are offset by factors that depend in a quadratic manner on the probe number i. This method works much better than linear probing, but to make full use of the hash table, the values of c_1,c_2, and m are constrained. Also, if the two keys have the same initial probe slot, the their probe sequences are same, since

$h(k_1, 0) = h(k_2, 0)$ implies $h(k_1, i) = h(k_2, i)$. This leads to a milder form of clustering called *secondary clustering*. As in linear probing, the initial probe determines the entire sequence, so only m distinct sequences are used.

Example 12.7:

Consider inserting the keys 76, 26, 37, 59, 21, 65, 88 into a hash table of size $m = 11$ using quadratic probing with $c_1 = 1$ and $c_2 = 3$. Further consider that the primary hash function is $h'(k) = k \bmod m$.

Solution: We have $h(k, i) = [k \bmod m + c_1 i + c_2 i^2] \bmod m$

$= [k \bmod m + i + 3 \times i^2] \bmod m$

	0	1	2	3	4	5	6	7	8	9	10
T	—	—	—	—	—	—	—	—	—	—	—

(*a*) Initial state of the hash table

Step 1. Consider first key $k = 76$

$h(76, 0) = (76 \bmod 11 + 0 + 3 \times 0) \bmod 11$
$= (10 + 0 + 0) \bmod 11 = 10$

The initial probe is $T[10]$, since $T[10]$ is free, insert the key 76 at this place.

	0	1	2	3	4	5	6	7	8	9	10
T	—	—	—	—	—	—	—	—	—	—	76

(*b*) Hash table after inserting key 76

Step 2. Consider first key $k = 26$

$h(26, 0) = (26 \bmod 11 + 0 + 3 \times 0) \bmod 11$
$= (4 + 0 + 0) \bmod 11 = 4 \bmod 11 = 4$

The initial probe is $T[4]$, since $T[4]$ is free, insert the key 26 at this place.

	0	1	2	3	4	5	6	7	8	9	10
T	—	—	—	—	26	—	—	—	—	—	76

(*c*) Hash table after inserting key 26

Step 3. Consider first key $k = 37$

$$h\,(37, 0) = (37 \text{ mod } 11 + 0 + 3 \times 0) \text{ mod } 11$$
$$= (4 + 0 + 0) \text{ mod } 11 = 4 \text{ mod } 11 = 4$$

Since $T[4]$ is occupied, the next probe sequence is computed as

$$h\,(37, 1) = (37 \text{ mod } 11 + 1 + 3 \times 1^2) \text{ mod } 11$$
$$= (4 + 1 + 3) \text{ mod } 11 = 8 \text{ mod } 11 = 8$$

Since $T[8]$ is free, insert the key 37 at this place.

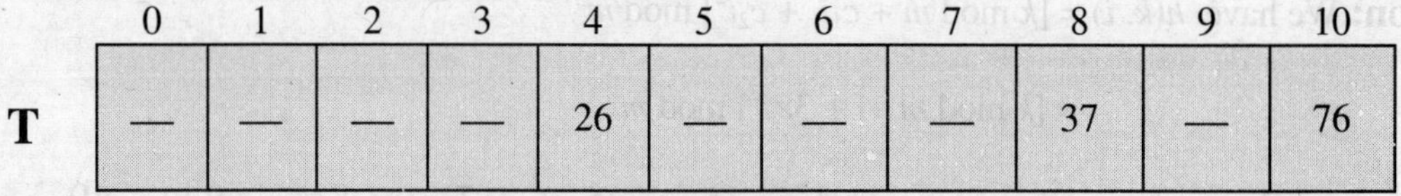

	0	1	2	3	4	5	6	7	8	9	10
T	—	—	—	—	26	—	—	—	37	—	76

(*d*) Hash table after inserting key 37

Step 4. Consider first key $k = 59$

$$h\,(59, 0) = (59 \text{ mod } 11 + 0 + 3 \times 0) \text{ mod } 11$$
$$= (4 + 0 + 0) \text{ mod } 11 = 4 \text{ mod } 11 = 4$$

Since $T[4]$ is occupied, the next probe sequence is computed as

$$h\,(59, 1) = (59 \text{ mod } 11 + 1 + 3 \times 1^2) \text{ mod } 11$$
$$= (4 + 1 + 3) \text{ mod } 11 = 8 \text{ mod } 11 = 8$$

Since $T[8]$ is also occupied, the next probe sequence is computed as

$$h\,(59, 2) = (59 \text{ mod } 11 + 2 + 3 \times 2^2) \text{ mod } 11$$
$$= (4 + 2 + 12) \text{ mod } 11 = 18 \text{ mod } 11 = 7$$

Since $T[7]$ is free, insert the key 59 at this place.

	0	1	2	3	4	5	6	7	8	9	10
T	—	—	—	—	26	—	—	59	37	—	76

(*e*) Hash table after inserting key 59

Step 5. Consider first key $k = 21$

$$h\,(21, 0) = (21 \text{ mod } 11 + 0 + 3 \times 0) \text{ mod } 11$$
$$= (10 + 0 + 0) \text{ mod } 11 = 10 \text{ mod } 11 = 10$$

Since $T[10]$ is occupied, the next probe sequence is computed as

$$h\,(21, 1) = (21 \text{ mod } 11 + 1 + 3 \times 1^2) \text{ mod } 11$$
$$= (10 + 1 + 3) \text{ mod } 11 = 14 \text{ mod } 11 = 3$$

Since $T[3]$ is free, insert the key 21 at this place.

	0	1	2	3	4	5	6	7	8	9	10
T	—	—	—	21	26	—	—	59	37	—	76

(*f*) Hash table after inserting key 21

Step 6. Consider first key $k = 65$

$$h(65, 0) = (65 \bmod 11 + 0 + 3 \times 0) \bmod 11$$
$$= (10 + 0 + 0) \bmod 11 = 10 \bmod 11 = 10$$

Since $T[10]$ is occupied, the next probe sequence is computed as

$$h(65, 1) = (65 \bmod 11 + 1 + 3 \times 1^2) \bmod 11$$
$$= (10 + 1 + 3) \bmod 11 = 14 \bmod 11 = 3$$

Since $T[3]$ is also occupied, the next probe sequence is computed as

$$h(65, 2) = (65 \bmod 11 + 2 + 3 \times 2^2) \bmod 11$$
$$= (10 + 2 + 12) \bmod 11 = 24 \bmod 11 = 2$$

Since $T[2]$ is free, insert the key 65 at this place.

	0	1	2	3	4	5	6	7	8	9	10
T	—	—	65	21	26	—	—	59	37	—	76

(*g*) Hash table after inserting key 65

Step 7. Consider first key $k = 88$

$$h(88, 0) = (88 \bmod 11 + 0 + 3 \times 0) \bmod 11$$
$$= (0 + 0 + 0) \bmod 11 = 0 \bmod 11 = 0$$

Since $T[0]$ is free, insert the key 88 at this place.

	0	1	2	3	4	5	6	7	8	9	10
T	88	—	65	21	26	—	—	59	37	—	76

(*h*) Hash table after inserting key 88

Figure 12.7 (*a*) – (*h*) Illustrates the insertion of keys 76, 26, 37, 59, 21, 65, 88 in open address hash table with quadratic probing.

12.5.2.3 Double Hashing

Double hashing is one of the best methods available for open addressing because the permutations produced have many of the characteristics of randomly chosen permutations. Double hashing uses a hash function of the form

$$h(k, i) = [h_1(k) + i\, h_2(k)\ ] \bmod m \qquad \text{for } i = 0, 1, 2, \ldots, m-1$$

where m is the size of the hash table; $h_1(k)$ [= k mod m] and$h_2(k)$ [= k mod m'] are two auxiliary hash function. Here m' is chosen to be slightly less than m (say, $m-1$ or $m-2$).

Therefore, for a given key k, the first slot probed is $T[h_1(k)]$ and the successive probes are offset from previous positions by the amount$h_2(k)$ modulo m. Thus, unlike the case of linear or quadratic probing, the probe sequence depends in two ways on the key value k, since the initial probe position and/or the offset may vary.

Double hashing represents an improvement over linear or quadratic probing as $O(m^2)$ probe sequence are used rather than $O(m)$, since each possible pair $<h_1(k), h_2(k)>$ yields a distinct probe sequence, and as we vary the key value, the initial probe position $h_1(k)$, and the offset $h_2(k)$ may vary independently. As a result, the performance of double hashing appears to be very close to the performance of the ideal scheme of uniform hashing.

Example 12.8:

Consider inserting the keys 76, 26, 37, 59, 21, 65, 88 into a hash table of size $m = 11$ using double hashing. Further, consider that the auxiliary hash functions are $h_1(k) = k$ mod 11 and $h_2(k) = k$ mod 9.

Solution:

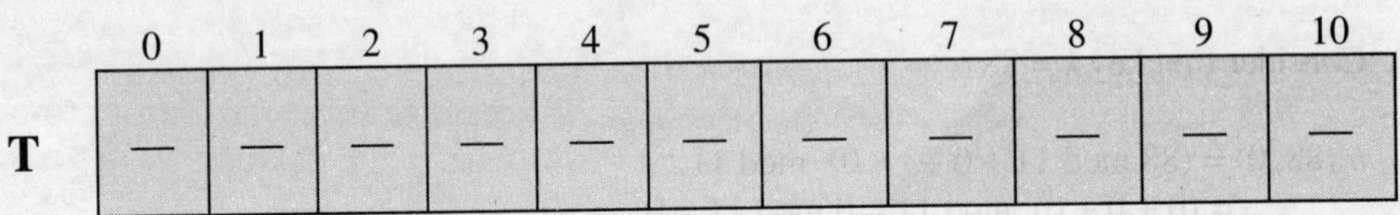

(*a*) Initial state of the hash table

Step 1. Consider first key $k = 76$

$h_1(76) = 76 \bmod 11 = 10$ $\qquad$ $h_2(76) = 76 \bmod 9 = 4$

$h(76, 0) = (10 + 0 \times 4\ ) \bmod 11 = 10 \bmod 11 = 10$

Since slot $T[10]$ is free, insert key 76 at this place.

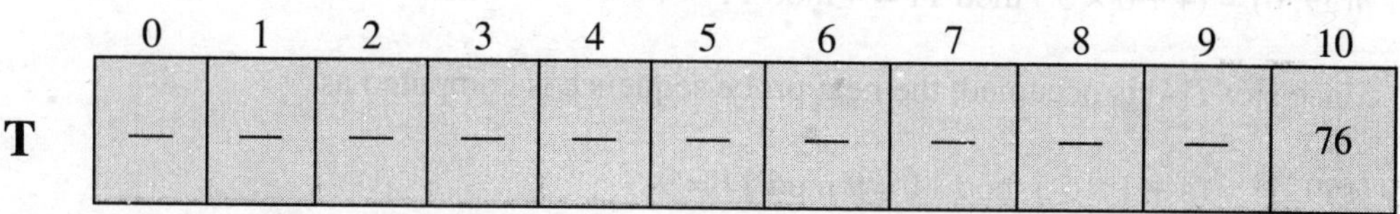

	0	1	2	3	4	5	6	7	8	9	10
T	—	—	—	—	—	—	—	—	—	—	76

(*b*) Hash table after inserting key 76

Step 2. Consider second key $k = 26$

$h_1(26) = 26 \bmod 11 = 4$ $\qquad h_2(26) = 26 \bmod 9 = 8$

$h(26, 0) = (4 + 0 \times 8) \bmod 11 = 4 \bmod 11 = 4$

Since slot $T[4]$ is free, insert key 26 at this place.

	0	1	2	3	4	5	6	7	8	9	10
T	—	—	—	—	26	—	—	—	—	—	76

(*c*) Hash table after inserting key 26

Step 3. Consider third key $k = 37$

$h_1(37) = 37 \bmod 11 = 4$ $\qquad h_2(37) = 37 \bmod 9 = 1$

$h(37, 0) = (4 + 0 \times 1) \bmod 11 = 4 \bmod 11 = 4$

Since slot $T[4]$ is occupied, the next probe sequence is computed as

$h(37, 1) = (4 + 1 \times 1) \bmod 11 = 5 \bmod 11 = 5$

Since slot $T[5]$ is free. Insert key 37 at this place.

	0	1	2	3	4	5	6	7	8	9	10
T	—	—	—	—	26	37	—	—	—	—	76

(*d*) Hash table after inserting key 37

Step 4. Consider fourth key $k = 59$

$h_1(59) = 59 \bmod 11 = 4$ $\qquad h_2(59) = 59 \bmod 9 = 5$

$h(59, 0) = (4 + 0 \times 5) \bmod 11 = 4 \bmod 11 = 4$

Since slot $T[4]$ is occupied, the next probe sequence is computed as

$h(59, 1) = (4 + 1 \times 5) \bmod 11 = 9 \bmod 11 = 9$

Since slot $T[9]$ is free. Insert key 59 at this place.

	0	1	2	3	4	5	6	7	8	9	10
T	—	—	—	—	26	37	—	—	—	59	76

(*e*) Hash table after inserting key 59

Step 5. Consider fifth key $k = 21$

$h_1(21) = 21 \bmod 11 = 10$ $\qquad h_2(21) = 21 \bmod 9 = 3$

$h(21, 0) = (10 + 0 \times 3) \bmod 11 = 10 \bmod 11 = 10$

Since slot $T[10]$ is occupied, the next probe sequence is computed as

$h(21, 1) = (10 + 1 \times 3) \bmod 11 = 13 \bmod 11 = 2$

Since slot $T[2]$ is free. Insert key 21 at this place.

	0	1	2	3	4	5	6	7	8	9	10
T	—	—	21	—	26	37	—	—	—	59	76

(*f*) Hash table after inserting key 21

Step 6. Consider sixth key $k = 65$

$h_1(65) = 65 \bmod 11 = 10$ $\qquad h_2(65) = 65 \bmod 9 = 2$

$h(65, 0) = (10 + 0 \times 2) \bmod 11 = 10 \bmod 11 = 10$

Since slot $T[10]$ is occupied, the next probe sequence is computed as

$h(65, 1) = (10 + 1 \times 2) \bmod 11 = 12 \bmod 11 = 1$

Since slot $T[1]$ is free. Insert key 65 at this place.

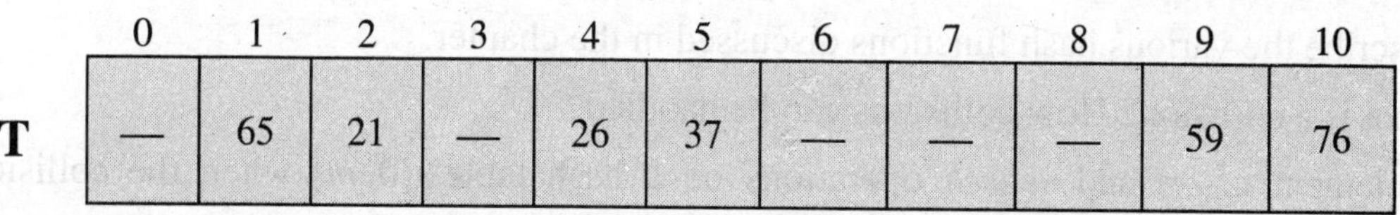

	0	1	2	3	4	5	6	7	8	9	10
T	—	65	21	—	26	37	—	—	—	59	76

(*g*) Hash table after inserting key 65

Step 7. Consider seventh key $k = 88$

$h_1(88) = 88 \bmod 11 = 0$ $\qquad$ $h_2(88) = 88 \bmod 9 = 7$

$h(88, 0) = (0 + 0 \times 7) \bmod 11 = 0 \bmod 11 = 0$

Since slot $T[0]$ is free. Insert key 88 at this place.

	0	1	2	3	4	5	6	7	8	9	10
T	88	65	21	—	26	37	—	—	—	59	76

(*h*) Hash table after inserting key 88

Figure 12.8 (*a*) – (*h*) Illustrates the insertion of keys 76, 26, 37, 59, 21, 65, 88 in open address hash table with double hashing.

12.6 REHASHING

If at any stage the hash table becomes nearly full, the running time for the operations will start taking too much time, and even the insert operation may fail for open addressing with quadratic probing. This can happen if there are too many deletions intermixed with too many insertions.

In such a situation, the best possible solution is as stated below:

1. Create a new hash table of size double than the original hash table.
2. Scan the original hash table, and for each key, compute the new hash value and insert into the new hash table.
3. Free the memory occupied by the original hash table.

REVIEW EXERCISES

1. What are the limitations of direct address tables?
2. What is a hash table? What are the advantages of hash tables over direct address tables?
3. What is hashing?
4. What is a hash function? What should be the characteristics of a good hash function?

5. Describe the various hash functions discussed in the chapter.
6. What is a collision? How collisions can be handled?
7. Implement *insert* and *search* operations on a hash table $t[0..m]$ when the collision are handled using following open addressing techniques:

   (*a*) Linear probing (*b*) Quadratic probing (*c*) Double hashing
8. Demonstrate the insertion of keys 28, 5, 19, 15, 33, 12, 17, 77, 20 into a hash table with 9 slots and collisions resolved by synonyms chaining. Let the hash function be $h(k)=k \bmod 9$.
9. Demonstrate the insertion of keys 73, 45, 37, 65, 77, 88, 100, 121 into a hash table with 11 slots using:

   (*a*) Separating chaining hash table
   (*b*) Open addressing hash table using linear probing
   (*c*) Open addressing hash table using quadratic probing with $c_1 = 0$ and $c_2 = 2$.

   Let the primary hash function be $h(k) = k \bmod 11$.
10. Consider inserting the keys 10, 22, 31, 4, 15, 28, 17, 59, 88 into a hash table with m=11 slots using open addressing with primary hash function $h_1(k) = k \bmod m$. Illustrate the result of inserting of these keys using linear probing, using quadratic probing with c_1=1 and c_2=2, and using double hashing with $h_2(k)=1+(k \bmod (m-1))$.
11. Devise a simple and easy to calculate hash function for mapping three-letter words into a hash table with *n* slots. Find the values of your hash function on the following words

    (*a*) JAN, FEB, MAR, APR, MAY, JUN, JUL, AUG, SEP, OCT, NOV, DEC
    (*b*) PAL, LAP, PAM, MAP, PAT, PET, SET, SAT, TAT, BAT, AMP, TAB

    for n = 13, 17, 19. Also show the resulting hash table when the collisions are handled with separating chaining and open addressing with linear probing.
12. Using a hash table with eleven slots indexed through 0 to 10 and the hashing function $h(k)=k \bmod 11$, show the hash table that results when the following keys are inserted in the order given: 26, 42, 5, 44, 92, 59, 40, 36, 12, 60. Assume that collisions are resolved using

    (*a*) Synonyms chaining (*b*) Linear probing
13. Suppose that the following character codes are used: 'A' = 1, 'B' = 2, 'C' = 3, . . ., 'Z' = 26. Using a hash table with eleven slots and the hashing function *h*(*identifier*) = *average* mod 11, where *average* is the average of the codes of the first and the last letters in *identifier*, show the hash table that results when following identifiers are inserted in the order given

    BETA, RATE, FREQ, ALPHA, MEAN, SUM, NUM, BAR, WAGE, PAY, KAPPA

    assuming (*a*) Synonym chaining, and (*b*) Linear probing.

❑ ❑ ❑

Chapter 13

Sorting, Searching and Merging

13.1 INTRODUCTION

Sorting is the process of arranging the elements in some logical order. This logical order may be ascending or descending in case of numeric values or dictionary order in case of alphanumeric values. We do, almost, use this process daily in our routine activities. For example, we do arrange our class notes in increasing order of date in order to refer them quickly later on. Like this there are many situations, which you can enumerate.

Searching is the process of finding the location of given element in the linear array. The search is said to be successful if the given element is found, *i.e.*, the element does exists in the array; otherwise unsuccessful.

Merging is the process of combining the elements of two similar structures, such as linear arrays, into a single structure.

In this chapter, we will discuss various sorting methods, searching methods, and merging.

We will consider the following declarations to model a generic array:

```
template <class T>
class Array {
    private:
        T *a;
```

```
      int size;
   public:
      Array(int n) {
         size = n;
         a = new T[n];
      }
      ~Array() {
         delete a;
      }
      void inputArray();
      void outputArray();
};
template <class T>
void Array<T>::inputArray() {
   int i;
   cout << "\nEnter " << size << " elements of array\n\n";
   for ( i = 0; i < size; i++ ) {
      cin >> a[i];
   }
}
template <class T>
void Array<T>::outputArray() {
   int i;
   for ( i = 0; i < size; i++ ) {
      cout << a[i] << "\t";
   }
   cout << endl;
}
```

13.2 SORTING

As mentioned earlier, sorting is the process of arranging the elements in some logical order. This logical order may be ascending or descending in case of numeric values or dictionary order in case of alphanumeric values.

Sorting is classified into following categories:

- ***Internal sorting*** — deals with sorting the data held in memory of the computer.
- ***External sorting*** — deals with sorting the data stored in data files. This method is used when the volume of the data is very large and cannot be held in computer's main memory.

In this section we will discuss internal sorting methods. External sorting will be discussed in *Chapter 14*.

We will cover the following sorting methods:

- Bubble sort
- Selection sort
- Insertion sort
- Bucket sort
- Merge Sort
- Quick sort
- Heap sort
- Tree sort
- Shell sort

For all the methods, we will consider a linear array *a* of size *n* whose elements are to be sorted in ascending order. You can modify them for the descending order just by reversing the comparison operation. To be consistent with C/C++ language conventions, the elements of the array have index in the range 0..*n*−1.

13.2.1 Bubble Sort Revisited

The Bubble sort method requires $(n-1)$ pass to sort an array. In each pass every element $a[i]$ is compared with $a[i+1]$, for $i = 0$ to $(n-k)$, where k is the pass number and if they are out of order i.e. if $a[i] > a[i+1]$, they are swapped. This will cause the largest element move or bubble up. Thus after the end of first pass the largest element in the array will be placed in nth position, and on each successive pass, the next largest element is placed at position $(n-1)$, $(n-2)$, ..., 2, respectively. For more clarity, carefully examine the following steps.

Pass 1.

Step 1. If $a[0] > a[1]$ then swap $a[0]$ and $a[1]$.
Step 2. If $a[1] > a[2]$ then swap $a[1]$ and $a[2]$.
:
Step $n-1$. If $a[n-2] > a[n-1]$ then swap $a[n-2]$ and $a[n-1]$.

Pass 2.

Step 1. If $a[0] > a[1]$ then swap $a[0]$ and $a[1]$.
Step 2. If $a[1] > a[2]$ then swap $a[1]$ and $a[2]$.
:
Step $n-2$. If $a[n-3] > a[n-2]$ then swap $a[n-3]$ and $a[n-2]$.

:

Pass k.

Step 1. If $a[0] > a[1]$ then swap $a[0]$ and $a[1]$.
Step 2. If $a[1] > a[2]$ then swap $a[1]$ and $a[2]$.
:
Step $n-k$. If $a[n-k+1] > a[n-k]$ then swap $a[n-k+1]$ and $a[n-k]$.

:

Pass $n-1$.

Step 1. If $a[0] > a[1]$ then swap $a[0]$ and $a[1]$.

Example 13.1:

To illustrate the working of bubble sort method, consider the sorting of the following array in ascending order.

12 40 3 2 15

Note that, the output of a given pass becomes the input for the next pass.

12
40
3
2
15

(*a*) Given Array

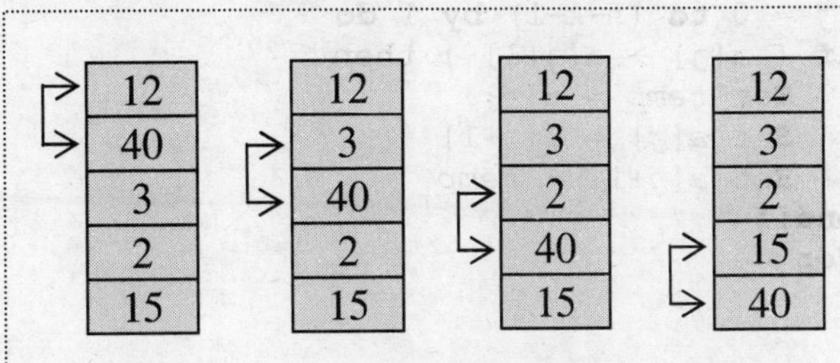

(*b*) Pass 1

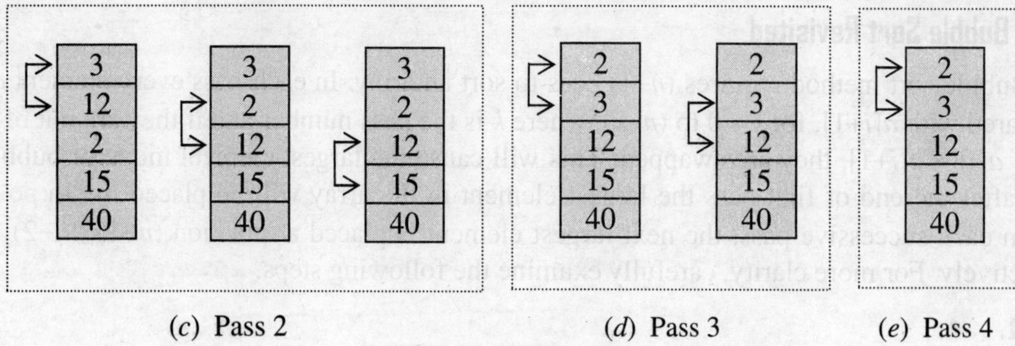

(*c*) Pass 2 (*d*) Pass 3 (*e*) Pass 4

Figure 13.1: Illustration of Bubble sort method

Analysis of Bubble Sort

As explained above, after (n–1) passes, the array will be sorted in ascending order. As you must have noticed, the first pass requires (n–1) comparisons, the second pass requires (n–2), ..., kth pass requires (n–k), and the last pass requires only one comparison.

Therefore, total comparisons are

$$f(n) = (n-1) + (n-2) + (n-3) + \ldots + (n-k) + \ldots + 3 + 2 + 1$$
$$= n(n-1)/2$$
$$= O(n^2)$$

The various steps required are for its implementation is shown in the following algorithm.

Algorithm 13.1:

bubbleSortBasic(*a*, *n*)

Here *a* is a linear array with *n* elements in memory. This algorithm sorts the elements in the ascending order. It uses a temporary variable *temp* to facilitate the exchange of two values and variable *i* to is used as loop control variable.

```
Begin
   for k = 1 to (n-1) by 1 do
      for j = 0 to (n-k-1) by 1 do
         if ( a[j] > a[j+1] ) then
            Set temp = a[j]
            Set a[j] = a[j+1]
            Set a[j+1] = temp
         endif
      endfor
   endfor
End.
```

The following code shows the implementation of above algorithm.

Listing 13.1:

```
template <class T>
void Array<T>::bubbleSortBasic()
{
    int j, k, temp;
    for ( k = 1; k < n; k++ ) {
        for ( j = 0; j < n-k; j++ ) {
            if ( a[j] > a[j+1] ) {
                temp  = a[j];
                a[j]  = a[j+1];
                a[j+1] = temp;
            }
        }
    }
}
```

Bubble sort method possess one very important property —

"*Once there is no swapping of elements in a particular pass, there will be no further swapping of elements in the subsequent passes.*"

This property can be exploited to reduce the unnecessary (redundant) passes. For this purpose, we can use a flag to determine if any interchange has taken place, if yes only then proceed with the next pass; otherwise stop.

The various steps required to implement this modified version are shown in the following algorithm.

Algorithm 13.2:

bubbleSortModified(***a, n*** **)**

Here *a* is a linear array with *n* elements in memory. This algorithm sorts the elements in the ascending order. It uses a temporary variable *temp* to facilitate the exchange of two values and variable *i* to is used as loop control variable. The variable *exchange_flag* is used as a flag to indicate whether at least one exchange took place in current iteration or not.

```
Begin
   Set k = 1
   Set exchange_flag = 1
   While ( ( k < n ) and ( exchange_flag = 1 ) ) do
      for j = 0 to (n-k-1) by 1 do
         Set exchange_flag = 0
         if ( a[j] > a[j+1] ) then
            Set exchange_flag = 1
            Set temp = a[j]
            Set a[j] = a[j+1]
            Set a[j+1] = temp
```

```
        endif
     endfor
     Set k = k + 1
  endwhile
End.
```

The following code shows the implementation of above algorithm.

Listing 13.2:

```
template <class T>
void Array<T>::bubbleSortModified()
{
   int j, k, temp, exchange_flag = 1;
   k = 1;
   while ( ( k < n)  && ( exchange_flag ) ) {
       exchange_flag = 0;
       for ( j = 0; j < n - k; j++ ) {
          if ( a[j] > a[j+1] ) {
             exchange_flag = 1;
             temp = a[j];
             a[j] = a[j+1];
             a[j+1] = temp;
          }
       }
       k++;
   }
}
```

Listing 13.3:

```
//  Program to sort an array of integers in ascending
//  order using bubble sort method
#include <iostream.h>
#include <iomanip.h>
template <class T>
class Array
{
   private:
      T*a;
      int size;
   public:
      Array(int n) {
      size = n;
      a = new T[n];
      }
      ~Array() {
      delete a;
      }
      void inputArray();
      void outputArray();
      void bubbleSortModified();
};
template <class T>
```

```
void Array<T>::inputArray() {
   int i;
   cout << "\nEnter " << size << " elements of array\n\n";
   for ( i = 0; i < size; i++ ) {
      cin >> a[i];
   }
}
template <class T>
void Array<T>::outputArray() {
   int i;
   for ( i = 0; i < size; i++ ) {
      cout << a[i] << "\t";
   }
   cout << endl;
}
template <class T>
void Array<T>::bubbleSortModified()
{
   int j, k, exchange_flag = 1;
   T temp;
   k = 1;
   while ( ( k < size )  && ( exchange_flag ) ) {
      exchange_flag = 0;
      for ( j = 0; j < size-k; j++ ) {
         if ( a[j] > a[j+1] ) {
            exchange_flag = 1;
            temp = a[j];
            a[j] = a[j+1];
            a[j+1] = temp;
         }
      }
      k++;
   }
}
void main()
{
   int n;
   cout << "Enter size of array : ";
   cin >> n;
   Array<int> a(n);
   a.inputArray();
   cout << "\n\nInput array is : ";
   a.outputArray();
   a.bubbleSortModified();
   cout << "\n\nSorted array is : ";
   a.outputArray();
}
```

13.2.2 Selection Sort

The selection sort method also requires $(n-1)$ pass to sort an array. In the first pass, find the smallest element from elements $a[0]$, $a[1]$, $a[2]$, . . ., $a[n-1]$ and swap with the first element, *i.e*, $a[0]$. In the second pass, find the smallest element from elements $a[1]$, $a[2]$, $a[3]$, . . ., $a[n-1]$ and swap with $a[1]$. And so on.

For more clarity, carefully examine the following steps.

Pass 1.

- Find the location *loc* of the smallest element in the entire array, *i.e.*, *a*[0], *a*[1], *a*[2],..., *a*[*n*−1].
- Interchange *a*[0] & *a*[*loc*]. Then *a*[0] is trivially sorted.

Pass 2.

- Find the location *loc* of the smallest element in the sub array *a*[1], *a*[2], *a*[3],. . ., *a*[*n*−1].
- Interchange *a*[1] & *a*[*loc*]. Then elements *a*[0] and *a*[1] are sorted, since $a[0] \le a[1]$.

:

:

Pass *k*.

- Find the location *loc* of the smallest element in the sub array *a*[*k*], *a*[*k*+1], *a*[*k*+2],. . ., *a*[*n*−1].
- Interchange *a*[*k*] & *a*[*loc*]. Then elements *a*[0], *a*[1], *a*[2], . . ., *a*[*k*] are sorted.

:

:

Pass *n*−1.

- Find the location *loc* of the smaller of the elements *a*[*n*−2], *a*[*n*−1].
- Interchange *a*[*n*−2] & *a*[*loc*]. Then elements *a*[0], *a*[1], *a*[2], . . ., *a*[*n*−1] are sorted.

After (*n*−1) passes, the array will be sorted in ascending order.

Example 13.2:

To illustrate the working of the selection sort method, consider the following array *a* with 7 elements as

20, 35, 40, 100, 3, 10, 15

Solution:

	a[0]	*a*[1]	*a*[2]	*a*[3]	*a*[4]	*a*[5]	*a*[6]
Given Array *a*	20	35	40	100	3	10	15

	a[0]	*a*[1]	*a*[2]	*a*[3]	*a*[4]	*a*[5]	*a*[6]	
Pass 1	20	35	40	100	3	10	15	*loc* = 4

Interchange elements *a*[0] & *a*[4], *i.e.*, 20 & 3 to obtain following array.

	a[0]	a[1]	a[2]	a[3]	a[4]	a[5]	a[6]	
Pass 2	3	35	40	100	20	10	15	*loc* = 5

Interchange elements *a*[1] & *a*[5], *i.e.*, 35 & 10 to obtain following array.

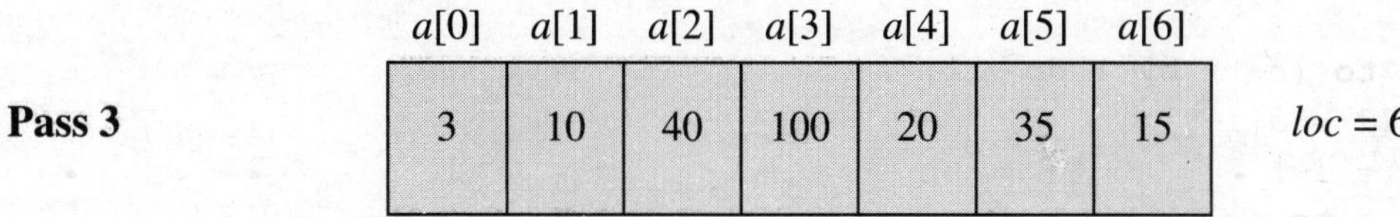

	a[0]	a[1]	a[2]	a[3]	a[4]	a[5]	a[6]	
Pass 3	3	10	40	100	20	35	15	*loc* = 6

Interchange elements *a*[2] & *a*[6] , *i.e.*, 40 & 15 to obtain following array.

	a[0]	a[1]	a[2]	a[3]	a[4]	a[5]	a[6]	
Pass 4	3	10	15	100	20	35	40	*loc* = 4

Interchange elements *a*[3] & *a*[4], *i.e.*, 100 & 20 to obtain following array.

	a[0]	a[1]	a[2]	a[3]	a[4]	a[5]	a[6]	
Pass 5	3	10	15	20	100	35	40	*loc* = 5

Interchange elements *a*[4] & *a*[5], *i.e.*, 100 & 35 to obtain following array.

	a[0]	a[1]	a[2]	a[3]	a[4]	a[5]	a[6]	
Pass 6	3	10	15	20	35	100	40	*loc* = 6

Interchange elements *a*[5] & *a*[6], *i.e.*,100 & 40 to obtain following sorted array.

a[0]	a[1]	a[2]	a[3]	a[4]	a[5]	a[6]
3	10	15	20	35	40	100

Figure 13.2: Successive passes of selection sort method

To implement the selection sort algorithm, we need a routine to find the location *loc* of the smallest element among the elements *a*[*k*−1], *a*[*k*+1], *a*[*k*+2],. . ., *a*[*n*−1], during *k*th pass.

Algorithm 13.3:

SelectionSort(*a*, *n*)

Here *a* is a linear array with *n* elements in memory. This algorithm sorts the elements in the ascending order. Temporary variable *small* is used to hold the current smallest element, temporary variable *temp* to facilitate the exchange of two values and variable *i* and *j* are used as loop control variables.

```
Begin
  for i = 1 to (n−1) by 1 do
    Set small = a[i−1]
    Set loc = i−1
    for j = i to (n−1) by 1 do
      if ( a[j] < small ) then
        Set small = a[j]
        Set loc = j
      endif
    endfor
    if ( loc ≠ (i−1) ) then
      Set temp = a[i−1]
      Set a[i−1] = a[loc]
      Set a[loc] = temp
    endif
  endfor
End.
```

The following listing shows the implementation of above algorithm.

Listing 13.4:

```
template <class T>
void Array<T>::selectionSort()
{
  int temp, small, loc, k, j;
  for ( k = 1; k <= (n-1); k++ ) {
     small = a[k-1];
     loc = k-1;
     for ( j = k; j <= (n-1); j++ ) {
        if ( a[j] < small ) {
           small = a[j];
           loc = j;
        }
     }
     if ( loc != (k-1) ) {
        temp = a[k-1];
        a[k-1] = a[loc];
        a[loc] = temp;
     }
  }
}
```

Analysis of Selection Sort

As you must have noticed, the first pass requires $(n-1)$ comparisons to find the location *loc* of smallest element, the second pass requires $(n-2)$, . . ., kth pass requires $(n-k)$, and the last pass requires only one comparison.

Therefore total comparisons are

$$f(n) = (n-1) + (n-2) + (n-3) + \ldots + (n-k) + \ldots + 3 + 2 + 1$$

$$= n(n-1)/2$$

$$f(n) = O(n^2)$$

Listing 13.5:

```
//   Program to sort an array of integers in ascending
//   order using selection sort method

#include <iostream.h>
#include <iomanip.h>

template <class T>
class Array
{
   private:
      T *a;
      int size;
   public:
      Array(int n) {
      size = n;
      a = new T[n];
      }
      ~Array() {
      delete a;
      }
      void inputArray();
      void outputArray();
      void selectionSort();
};
template <class T>
void Array<T>::inputArray() {
   int i;
   cout << "\nEnter " << size << " elements of array\n\n";
   for ( i = 0; i< size; i++ ) {
      cin >> a[i];
   }
}
template <class T>
void Array<T>::outputArray() {
   int i;
   for ( i = 0; i < size; i++ ) {
      cout << a[i] << "\t";
   }
   cout << endl;
}
template <class T>
```

```
void Array<T>::selectionSort()
{
   int temp, small, loc, k, j;
   for ( k = 1; k <= (size-1); k++ ) {
      small = a[k-1];
      loc = k-1;
      for ( j = k; j <= (size-1); j++ ) {
         if ( a[j] < small ) {
            small = a[j];
            loc = j;
         }
      }
      if ( loc != (k-1) ) {
         temp = a[k-1];
         a[k-1] = a[loc];
         a[loc] = temp;
      }
   }
}
void main()
{
   int n;
   cout << "Enter size of array : ";
   cin >> n;
   Array<int> a(n);
   a.inputArray();
   cout << "\n\nInput array is : ";
   a.outputArray();
   a.selectionSort();
   cout << "\n\nSorted array is : ";
   a.outputArray();
}
```

13.2.3 Insertion Sort

This algorithm is very popular with bridge players when they first sort their cards. In this procedure, we pick up a particular value and then insert it at the appropriate place in the sorted sub list, *i.e.*, during *k*th iteration the element $a[k]$ is inserted in its proper place in the sorted sub array $a[1]$, $a[2]$, $a[3]$,. . ., $a[k-1]$. This task is accomplished by comparing $a[k]$ with $a[k-1]$, $a[k-2]$, $a[k-3]$, and so on until the first element $a[j]$ such that $a[j] \leq a[k]$ is found. Then each of the elements $a[k-1]$, $a[k-2]$, . . ., $a[j+1]$ are moved one position up, and then element $a[k]$ is inserted in $(j+1)$st position in the array.

For more clarity, carefully examine the following steps.

Pass 1. $a[1]$ is inserted either before or after $a[0]$ so that $a[0]$ and $a[1]$ are sorted.

Pass 2. $a[2]$ is inserted either before $a[0]$ or between $a[0]$ and $a[1]$ or after $a[1]$ so that the elements $a[0]$, $a[1]$, $a[2]$ are sorted.

Pass 3. $a[3]$ is inserted either before $a[0]$ or between $a[0]$ and $a[1]$ or between $a[1]$ and $a[2]$ or after $a[2]$ so that the elements $a[0]$, $a[1]$, $a[2]$, $a[3]$ are sorted.

:
:

Pass *k*. $a[k]$ is inserted in proper place in the sorted sub array $a[0], a[1], a[2], \ldots, a[k-1]$ so that after insertion, the elements $a[0], a[1], a[2], \ldots, a[k-1], a[k]$ are sorted.

:
:

Pass *n*–1. $a[n-1]$ is inserted in proper place in the sorted sub array $a[0], a[1], a[2], \ldots, a[n-2]$, so that after insertion, the elements $a[0], a[1], a[2], \ldots, a[n-1]$ are sorted.

Thus, after $(n-1)$ passes, the array will be sorted in ascending order.

Example 13.3:

To illustrate the working of the insertion sort method, consider the following array *a* with 7 elements as

35, 20, 40, 100, 3, 10, 15

Solution :

	$a[0]$	$a[1]$	$a[2]$	$a[3]$	$a[4]$	$a[5]$	$a[6]$
Given Array *a*	35	20	40	100	3	10	15

	$a[0]$	$a[1]$	$a[2]$	$a[3]$	$a[4]$	$a[5]$	$a[6]$
Pass 1	35	20	40	100	3	10	15

Since $a[1] < a[0]$, insert element $a[1]$ before $a[0]$ giving the following array.

	$a[0]$	$a[1]$	$a[2]$	$a[3]$	$a[4]$	$a[5]$	$a[6]$
Pass 2	20	35	40	100	3	10	15

Since $a[2] > a[1]$, no action is performed.

	$a[0]$	$a[1]$	$a[2]$	$a[3]$	$a[4]$	$a[5]$	$a[6]$
Pass 3	20	35	40	100	3	10	15

Since $a[3] > a[2]$, again no action is performed.

	a[0]	a[1]	a[2]	a[3]	a[4]	a[5]	a[6]
Pass 4	20	35	40	100	3	10	15

Since $a[4]$ is less than $a[3]$, $a[2]$, $a[1]$ as well as $a[0]$, therefore insert $a[4]$ before $a[0]$, giving the following array.

	a[0]	a[1]	a[2]	a[3]	a[4]	a[5]	a[6]
Pass 5	3	20	35	40	100	10	15

Since $a[5]$ is less than $a[4]$, $a[3]$, $a[2]$, and $a[1]$, therefore insert $a[5]$ before $a[1]$, giving the following array.

	a[0]	a[1]	a[2]	a[3]	a[4]	a[5]	a[6]
Pass 6	3	10	20	35	40	100	15

Since $a[6]$ is less than $a[5]$, $a[4]$, $a[3]$, and $a[2]$, therefore insert $a[6]$ before $a[2]$, giving the following sorted array.

a[0]	a[1]	a[2]	a[3]	a[4]	a[5]	a[6]
3	10	15	20	35	40	100

Figure 13.3: Successive passes of insertion sort method

The various steps required to implement insertion sort are summarized in the algorithm given below.

Algorithm 13.4:

InsertionSort(*a*, *n*)

Here *a* is a linear array with *n* elements in memory. This algorithm sorts the elements in the ascending order. It uses a temporary variable *temp* to facilitate the exchange of two values and variable *j* and *k* are used as loop control and index variables.

```
Begin
  for k = 1 to (n-1) by 1 do
     Set temp = a[k]
     Set j = k-1
     while ( ( temp < a[j] ) and ( j ≥ 0 ) ) do
        Set a[j+1] = a[j]
```

```
            Set j = j-1
        endwhile
        Set a[j+1] = temp
    endfor
End.
```

The above algorithm moves the elements up by one position till the correct slot for the element is found and then inserts the element at that slot.

The following listing shows the implementation of above algorithm.

Listing 13.6:

```
template <class T>
void Array<T>::insertionSort()
{
    int k, temp, j;
    for ( k = 1; k <= size-1; k++ ) {
        temp = a[k];
        j = k-1;
        while ( ( temp < a[j] ) && ( j >= 0 ) ) {
            a[j+1] = a[j];
            j = j-1;
        }
        a[j+1] = temp;
    }
}
```

Analysis of Insertion Sort

The worst case performance occurs when the elements of the input array are in descending order. In that case, the first pass requires one comparison, the second pass requires two comparisons, third pass requires three comparisons, . . ., kth pass requires $(k-1)$, and the finally the last pass requires $(n-1)$ comparisons.

Therefore, total number of comparisons is

$$f(n) = 1 + 2 + 3 + \ldots + (n-k) + \ldots + (n-3) + (n-2) + (n-1)$$

$$= n(n-1)/2$$

$$f(n) = O(n^2)$$

Listing 13.7:

```
//  Program to sort an array of integers in ascending
//  order using insertion sort method
#include <iostream.h>
#include <iomanip.h>
template <class T>
class Array
{
    private:
```

```
      T *a;
      int size;
   public:
      Array(int n) {
         size = n;
         a = new T[n];
      }
      ~Array() {
         delete a;
      }
      void inputArray();
      void outputArray();
      void insertionSort();
};
template <class T>
void Array<T>::inputArray() {
   int i;
   cout << "\nEnter " << size << " elements of array\n\n";
   for ( i = 0; i < size; i++ ) {
      cin >> a[i];
   }
}
template <class T>
void Array<T>::outputArray() {
   int i;
   for ( i = 0; i < size; i++ ) {
      cout << a[i] << "\t";
   }
   cout << endl;
}
template <class T>
void Array<T>::insertionSort()
{
   int k, temp, j;
   for ( k = 1; k <= size-1; k++ ) {
      temp = a[k];
      j = k-1;
      while ( ( temp < a[j] ) && ( j >= 0 ) ) {
         a[j+1] = a[j];
         j = j-1;
      }
      a[j+1] = temp;
   }
}
void main()
{
   int n;
   cout << "Enter size of array : ";
   cin >> n;
   Array<int> a(n);
   a.inputArray();
   cout << "\n\nInput array is : ";
   a.outputArray();
   a.insertionSort();
   cout << "\n\nSorted array is : ";
   a.outputArray();
}
```

13.2.4 Bucket/Radix Sort

Bucket/radix method is used by most of the people when sorting a list of names in alphabetic order. The procedure we follow is:

- First, the names are grouped according to the first letter, thus the names are arranged in 26 classes, one for each letter of the alphabet. First class consists of those names that begin with letter *A*, the second class consists of those names that begin with letter *B*, and so on.
- Next, the names are grouped according to the second letter. After this step, the list of names will be sorted on first two letters.
- This process is continued for the number of times depending on the length of the names with maximum letters. If shorter names, we assume those names padded with blanks.

Since, there are 26 letters of the alphabet, we make use of 26 buckets, one for each letter of the alphabet. After grouping these names according to their specific letter, we collect them in order of buckets, *i.e.*, first we pick up names from first bucket (for letter *A*), then from second bucket (for letter *B*), and so on. This new list becomes input for the next pass, *i.e.*, to separate them on the next letter from left.

To sort decimal numbers, where *radix* or *base* is 10, we need ten buckets. These buckets are numbered 0, 1, 2, 3, 4, 5, 6, 7, 8, 9. Unlike, sorting names, decimal numbers are sorted from right to left, *i.e.*, first on unit digit, then on tens digit, then on hundredth digit, and so on.

Example 13.4:

To illustrate the bucket sort method, consider following list of numbers:

321, 150, 235, 65, 573, 789, 928, 542

Solution:

Pass 1

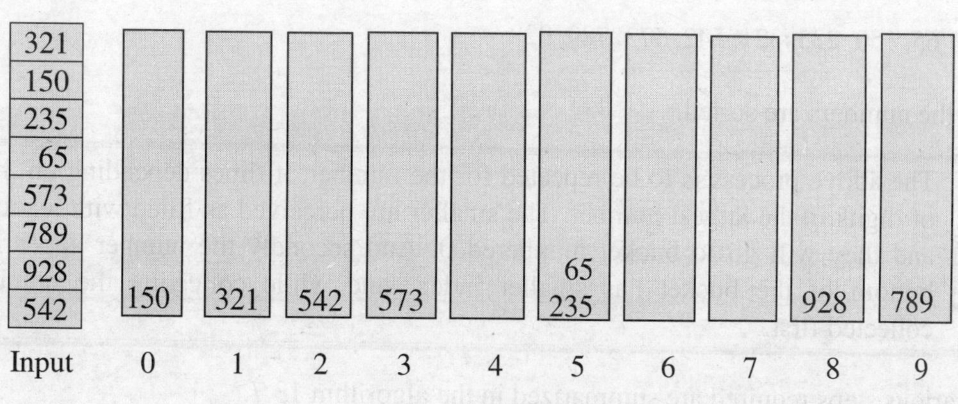

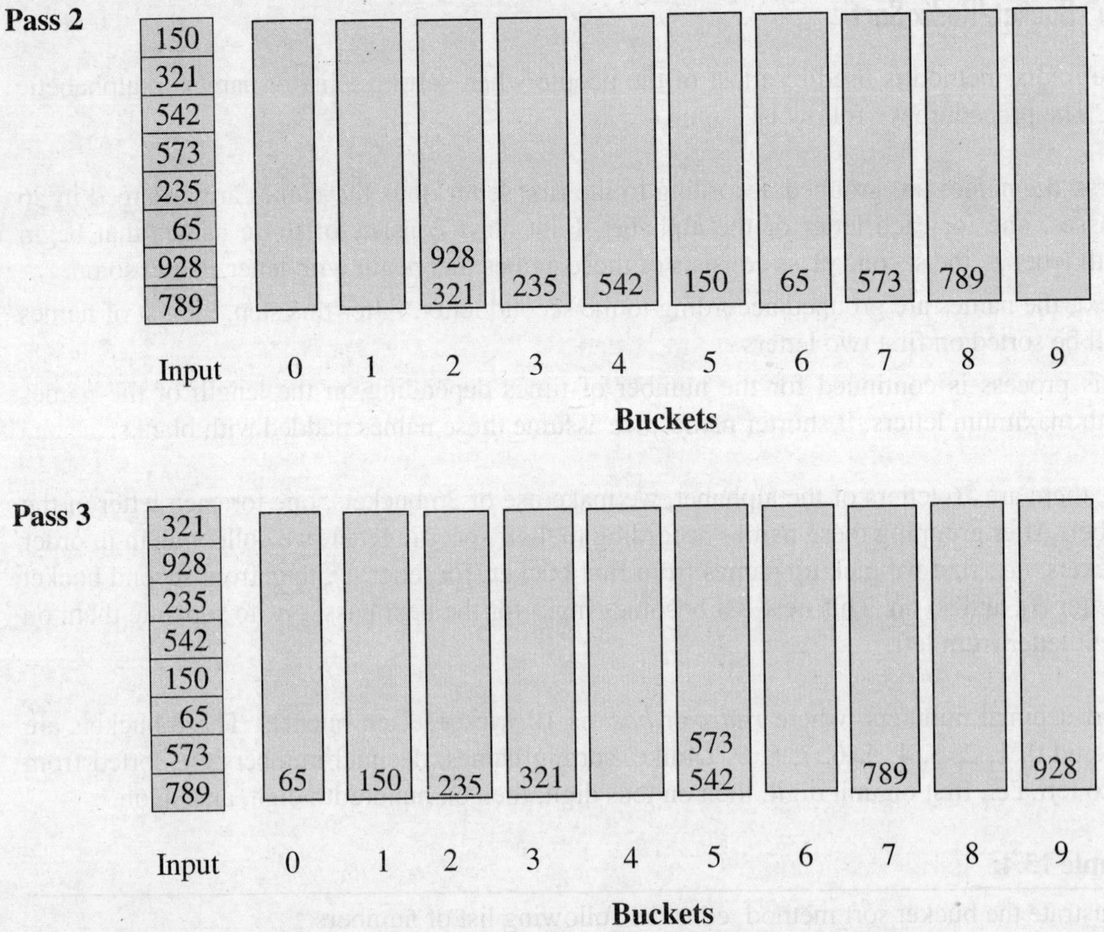

Pass 2

Input: 150, 321, 542, 573, 235, 65, 928, 789

Buckets:
0:
1:
2: 928, 321
3: 235
4: 542
5: 150
6: 65
7: 573
8: 789
9:

Pass 3

Input: 321, 928, 235, 542, 150, 65, 573, 789

Buckets:
0: 65
1: 150
2: 235
3: 321
4:
5: 573, 542
6:
7: 789
8:
9: 928

Figure 13.4: Successive passes of bucket sort method

After pass 3, when the numbers are collected, they are in the following order

65, 150, 235, 321, 542, 573, 789, 928

Thus, the numbers are sorted.

The above process is to be repeated for the number of times depending on the number of digits in the largest number. The smaller are perceived as filled with leading zeroes, and they will go to bucket numbered 0. And secondly the number appearing in the bottom of the bucket has smaller index, and while collecting the numbers, it is collected first.

The various steps required are summarized in the algorithm 13.7.

Algorithm 13.5:

BucketSort(a, n)

Here *a* is a linear array of decimal integers with *n* elements in memory. The variable *digitCount* is used to store the number of digits in the largest number in order to control the number of passes to be performed.

```
Begin
   Find the largest number of the array
   Set digitCount=Number of digits of the largest number in given array
   for pass = 1 to digitCount by 1 do
      Initialize buckets
      for i = 1 to (n-1) by 1 do
         Set digit = Obtain digit number pass of a[i]
         Put a[i] in bucket number digit
         Increment bucket count for bucket numbered digit
      endfor
      Collect all the numbers from buckets in order
   endfor
End.
```

The following listing shows the implementation of above algorithm.

Listing 13.8:

```
void Array:bucketSort()
{
   int bucket[10][20], buckCount[10];
   int i, j, k, r, digitCount = 0, divisor = 1, largest, passNo;
   largest = a[0];
   for ( i = 1; i < size; i++ ) {  // find the largest number
      if ( a[i] > largest ) largest = a[i];
   }
   // find number of digits in largest number
   while ( largest > 0 ) {
      digitCount++;
      largest /= 10;
   }
   for ( passNo = 0; passNo < digitCount; passNo++ ) {
      for ( k = 0; k < 10 ; k++ )
         buckCount[k] = 0;    // initialize bucket count
      for ( i = 0; i < size; i++ ) {
         r = ( a[i] / divisor ) % 10;
         bucket[r][buckCount[r]++] = a[i];
      }
      i = 0;     //    collect elements from bucket
      for ( k = 0; k < 10 ; k++ ) {
         for ( j = 0; j < buckCount[k]; j++ )
            a[i++] = bucket[k][j];
      }
      divisor *= 10;
   }
}
```

Analysis of Bucket Sort

Let us suppose the number of digits in the largest element of the given array is *S*. The number of passes to be performed is *S*. Then, the number of comparisons, $f(n)$, needed to sort the given array are

$$f(n) \le n*s*10$$

Here, factor 10 is because of the radix of decimal number system.

Though, *s* (the number of passes) is independent of *n* (the number of elements), but if $s = n$, then in worst case

$$f(n) = O(n^2)$$

But on other hand, if $s = \log_{10} n$, then

$$f(n) = O(n\log_{10} n)$$

Thus, from above discussion, we conclude that bucket sort performs well only when the number of digits in the elements are very small.

Listing 13.9:

```
//  Program to sort an array of integers in ascending
//  order using bucket/radix sort method
#include <iostream.h>
#include <iomanip.h>
class Array {
   private:
      int *a;
      int size;
   public:
      Array(int n) {
         size = n;
         a = new int[n];
      }
      ~Array() {
         delete a;
      }
      void inputArray();
      void outputArray();
      void bucketSort();
};
void Array::inputArray() {
   int i;
   cout << "\nEnter " << size << " elements of array\n\n";
   for ( i = 0; i < size; i++ ) {
      cin >> a[i];
   }
}
void Array::outputArray() {
   int i;
   for ( i = 0; i < size; i++ ) {
      cout << a[i] << "\t";
   }
```

```
    cout << endl;
}

void Array::bucketSort()
{
    int bucket[10][20], buckCount[10];
    int i, j, k, r, digitCount = 0, divisor = 1, largest, passNo;
    largest = a[0];
    for ( i = 1; i < size; i++ )    // find the largest number
    {
        if ( a[i] > largest ) largest = a[i];
    }
    // find number of digits in largest number
    while ( largest > 0 )
    {
        digitCount++;
        largest /= 10;
    }
    for ( passNo = 0; passNo < digitCount; passNo++ )
    {
        for ( k = 0; k < 10 ; k++ )
            buckCount[k] = 0;    // initialize bucket count
        for ( i = 0; i < size; i++ )
        {
            r = ( a[i] / divisor ) % 10;
            bucket[r][buckCount[r]++] = a[i];
        }
        i = 0;      //     collect elements from bucket
        for ( k = 0; k < 10 ; k++ )
        {
            for ( j = 0; j < buckCount[k]; j++ )
                a[i++] = bucket[k][j];
        }
        divisor *= 10;
    }
}

void main()
{
    int n;
    cout << "Enter size of array : ";
    cin >> n;
    Array a(n);
    a.inputArray();
    cout << "\n\nInput array is : ";
    a.outputArray();
    a.bucketSort();
    cout << "\n\nSorted array is : ";
    a.outputArray();
}
```

13.2.5 Merge Sort

Merge sort is a sorting algorithm that uses the idea of *divide and conquer*. This algorithm divides the array into two halves, sorts them separately, and then merges them. This procedure is recursive, with the base criteria — the number of elements in the array are not more than 1.

Suppose variable *beg* and *end* represents the index of the first and last element of the array respectively, the merge sort can be defined recursively as

```
if ( beg < end ) then
   Divide the list into two halves
   Mergesort the left half
   Mergesort the right half
   Merge the two-sorted halves into one sorted list
endif
```

Example 13.5:

To illustrate the working of the merge sort method, consider the following array *a* with 7 elements as

33, 26, 35, 29, 18, 10, 24

Solution:

The first step of mergesort is to divide the array into two sub arrays. Thus we divide the array into

33, 26, 35, 29 and 18, 10, 24

and first consider the left sub array.

It is again divided into two sub arrays as

33, 26 and 35, 29

For each of these sub arrays, we again apply the same method, dividing each of these into sub arrays of one element each. Sub arrays of size one, of course, require no sorting. Finally, we start merging the sub arrays to obtain a sorted array. The sub arrays 33 and 26 merge to give the sorted array 26, 33 and the sub arrays 35 and 29 merge to give sorted array 29, 35.

At the next step, we merge these two-sorted sub arrays of size two to obtain a sorted array of size four as

26,29, 33, 35

Now the left half of the given array is sorted, we do the same steps on the right half. First, we divide it into two sub arrays as

18, 10 and 24

The first of these is divided into two sub arrays of size one, which are merged to give 10, 18. The second sub array, 24, has size one, so needs no sorting.

Now these are merged to give the sorted array

10, 18, 24

Finally, the sorted sub arrays of size four and three are merged to give

10, 18, 24, 26, 29, 33, 35

In *Chapter 5*, we have developed an algorithm to merge two sorted arrays, we will also be discussing again in the later section. We modify the same algorithm to merge the two-sorted sub arrays of the same array as shown below.

Algorithm 13.6:

MergingSortedSubArrays(*a*, *lb*, *lr*, *rb*, *rr*)

Here *a* is a linear array, variables *lb*, *lr* represents beginning and ending index of the left sub array, and variables *rb*, *rr* represents beginning and ending index of the right sub array. The algorithm merges these two sub arrays. It uses local variables *na*, *nb* as counters to keep track of the elements of left and right sub array respectively, which are candidates to go to temporary array *c*, and *nc* as counter to keep track of the position in *c*, where the incoming elements will be stored.

```
Begin
  Set na = lb, nb = rb, and nc = lb
  while ( ( na ≤ lr ) and ( nb ≤ rr ) ) do
     if ( a[na] < b[nb] ) then
        Set c[nc] = a[na]
        Set na = na + 1
     else
        Set c[nc] = a[nb]
        Set nb = nb + 1
     endif
     Set nc = nc + 1
  endwhile
  if ( na > lr ) then
     while ( nb <= rr ) then
        Set c[nc] = b[nb]
        Set nb = nb + 1
        Set nc = nc + 1
     endwhile
  else
     while ( na <= lr ) then
        Set c[nc] = b[na]
        Set na = na + 1
        Set nc = nc + 1
     endwhile
  endif
  for k = lb to rr  by 1 do
     Set a[k] = c[k]
  endfor
End.
```

The code on next page shows the implementation of above algorithm.

Listing 13.10:

```
template <class T>
void Array<T>::mergingSortedSubArrays(int lb,int lr,int rb,int rr)
{
   int na, nb, nc, k;
   na = lb;
   nb = rb;
   nc = lb;
   while ( ( na <= lr ) && ( nb <= rr ) )
   {
      if ( a[na] < a[nb] )
        c[nc] = a[na++];
     else
        c[nc] = a[nb++];
     nc++;
   }
   if ( na > lr )
   {
      while ( nb <= rr )
      c[nc++] = a[nb++];
   } else {
      while ( na <= lr )
         c[nc++] = a[na++];
   }
   for ( k = lb; k <= rr; k++ )
      a[k] = c[k];
}
```

After the procedure for merging to halves is defined, the various steps required for Mergesort are summarized in the following algorithm.

Algorithm 13.7:

MergeSort(***a*****,** ***beg*****,** ***end*** **)**

Here *a* is a linear array with lower bound *beg* and upper bound *end*. The algorithm sorts the array using merge sort method. It uses variable *mid* to represent the index of the element at which array will be divided into two halves.

```
Begin
  if ( beg < end ) then
     Set mid = ( beg + end ) / 2
     Call MergeSort( a, beg, mid )
     Call MergeSort( a, mid + 1, end )
     Call MergingSortedSubArrays(a, beg, mid, mid+1, end)
  endif
End.
```

The following listing shows the implementation of above algorithm.

Listing 13.11:

```
template <class T>
void Array<T>::Array<T>::mergeSort(int beg, int end)
{
    int mid;
    if ( beg < end )
    {
        mid = ( beg + end ) / 2;
       mergeSortMethod(beg, mid );
       mergeSortMethod(mid + 1, end );
       mergingSortedSubArrays(beg, mid, mid + 1, end );
    }
}
```

The recursive procedure *mergeSortMethod()* will be called from the calling function by the call statement as *mergeSortMethod*(0, *n*–1), where *a* in an array of size *n*.

Analysis of Merge Sort

The major work is done in the merge procedure, which is an O(*n*) operation. The merge procedure is called from merge-sort procedure after the array is divided into two halves, and each half has been sorted. In each of the recursive calls, one for left half and one for right half, the array is divided into halves, thus dividing the array into four segments. At each level, the number of segments doubles. Therefore, the total divisions are $\log_2 n$.
Hence, total number of comparisons

$$f(n) = n \times \log_2 n$$

$$= O(n \log_2 n)$$

The only disadvantage of merge sort is that it uses an extra temporary array, of the same size as that of input array, to merge the two halves. The elements of the temporary array are copied back to the original array before the next merging.

Listing 13.12:

```
//  Program to sort an array of integers in ascending
//  order using merge sort method
#include <iostream.h>
#include <iomanip.h>
template <class T>
class Array
{
   private:
      T *a;
      T *c;
```

```
    int size;
  public:
    Array(int n) {
      size = n;
      a = new T[n];
      c = new T[n];
    }
    ~Array() {
      delete a;
      delete c;
    }
    void inputArray();
    void outputArray();
    void mergingSortedSubArrays(int, int, int, int);
    void mergeSortRecursive(int, int);
    void mergeSort();
};
template <class T>
void Array<T>::inputArray() {
  int i;
  cout << "\nEnter " << size << " elements of array\n\n";
  for ( i = 0; i < size; i++ ) {
    cin >> a[i];
  }
}
template <class T>
void Array<T>::outputArray() {
  int i;
  for ( i = 0; i < size; i++ ) {
    cout << a[i] << "\t";
  }
  cout << endl;
}
template <class T>
void Array<T>::mergingSortedSubArrays(int lb, int lr, int  rb, int rr)
{
  int na, nb, nc, k;
  na = lb;
  nb = rb;
  nc = lb;
  while ( ( na <= lr ) && ( nb <= rr ) ) {
    if ( a[na] < a[nb] )
      c[nc] = a[na++];
    else
      c[nc] = a[nb++];
    nc++;
  }
  if ( na > lr ) {
    while ( nb <= rr )
    c[nc++] = a[nb++];
  } else {
    while ( na <= lr )
      c[nc++] = a[na++];
  }
  for ( k = lb; k <= rr; k++ )
    a[k] = c[k];
}
template <class T>
```

```
void Array<T>::mergeSortRecursive(int beg, int end)
{
   int mid;
   if ( beg < end )
   {
      mid = ( beg + end ) / 2;
      mergeSortRecursive(beg, mid );
      mergeSortRecursive(mid + 1, end);
      mergingSortedSubArrays(beg, mid, mid + 1, end );
   }
}
template <class T>
void Array<T>::mergeSort()
{
   mergeSortRecursive(0,size-1);
}

void main()
{
   int n;
   cout << "Enter size of array : ";
   cin >> n;
   Array<int> a(n);
   a.inputArray();
   cout << "\n\nInput array is : ";
   a.outputArray();
   a.mergeSort();
   cout << "\n\nSorted array is : ";
   a.outputArray();
}
```

13.2.6 Quick Sort

Quicksort is a sorting algorithm that also, like merge sort, uses the idea of *divide and conquer*. This algorithm finds the element, called *pivot*, that partitions the array into two halves in such a way that the elements in the left sub array are less than and the elements in the right sub array are greater than the partitioning element. Then these two subarrays are sorted separately. This procedure is recursive in nature with the base criteria – the number of elements in the array are not more than 1.

Suppose variable *beg* and *end* represents the index of the first and last element of the array respectively, the quick sort can be defined recursively as

```
If ( beg < end ) then
    Find element that partition the array into two halves
    Quicksort the left half
    Quicksort the right half
[End of If structure]
```

The main task in quick sort is to find the element that partitions the array into two halves and to place it at its proper location in the array. Usually, the procedure places the first element in the array at its final location.

This task is performed as stated below.

To begin with, set the index of the first element of the array to *loc* and *left* variables, and index of the last element of the array to *right* variable. Then proceed as follows:

1. Beginning with the element pointed to by *right*, the array is scanned from right to left, comparing each element on the way with the element pointed to by *loc*, till either
   a) Element smaller than the element pointed to by *loc* is found. In this case, the elements are interchanged and procedure continues with step 2.
   b) If the value of the *right* variable becomes equal to the value of *loc*, the procedure terminates here. This condition indicates that the element is placed in its final position *loc*.
2. Beginning with the element pointed to by *left*, the array is scanned from left to right, comparing each element on the way with the element pointed to by *loc*, till either
   a) Element greater than the element pointed to by *loc* is found. In this case, the elements are interchanged and procedure continues with step 1.
   b) If the value of the *left* variable becomes equal to the value of *loc*, the procedure terminates here. This condition indicates that the element is placed in its final position *loc*.

As this procedure terminates, the first element, pivot, of original the array will be placed at *loc*, its final location in the sorted array. The elements to left of it will be less than this element and elements to its right will be greater than this element.

Example 13.6:

To illustrate the above procedure, consider the array

25 10 30 15 20 28

Solution:

Here the pivot element is 25. To begin with set *loc* = 0, *left* = 0, *right* = 5 as

a[0]	*a*[1]	*a*[2]	*a*[3]	*a*[4]	*a*[5]
25	10	30	15	20	28
↑					↑
loc *left*					*right*

Start scanning elements from right. Since *a*[*loc*] < *a*[*right*], we decrease the value of variable *right* to get

$a[0]$	$a[1]$	$a[2]$	$a[3]$	$a[4]$	$a[5]$
25	10	30	15	20	28
↑				↑	
loc *left*				*right*	

Now, $a[loc] > a[right]$, interchange these elements to get

$a[0]$	$a[1]$	$a[2]$	$a[3]$	$a[4]$	$a[5]$
20	10	30	15	25	28
↑				↑	
left				*loc* *right*	

Now start scanning elements from left. Since $a[loc] > a[left]$, we increase the value of variable *left* to get

$a[0]$	$a[1]$	$a[2]$	$a[3]$	$a[4]$	$a[5]$
20	10	30	15	25	28
	↑			↑	
	left			*loc* *right*	

Since again $a[loc] > a[left]$, we increase the value of variable *left* to get

$a[0]$	$a[1]$	$a[2]$	$a[3]$	$a[4]$	$a[5]$
20	10	30	15	25	28
		↑		↑	
		left		*loc* *right*	

Now $a[loc] < a[left]$, interchange these elements to get

$a[0]$	$a[1]$	$a[2]$	$a[3]$	$a[4]$	$a[5]$
20	10	25	15	30	28
		↑		↑	
		loc *left*		*right*	

Now again start scanning elements from right. Since $a[loc] < a[right]$, we decrease the value of variable *right* to get

a[0]	a[1]	a[2]	a[3]	a[4]	a[5]
20	10	25	15	30	28
		↑	↑		
		loc *left*	*right*		

Now, *a*[*loc*] > *a*[*right*], interchange these elements to get

a[0]	a[1]	a[2]	a[3]	a[4]	a[5]
20	10	15	25	30	28
		↑	↑		
		left	*loc* *right*		

Now again start scanning elements from left. Since *a*[*loc*] > *a*[*left*], we increase the value of variable *left* to get

a[0]	a[1]	a[2]	a[3]	a[4]	a[5]
20	10	15	25	30	28
			↑		
			loc *left* *right*		

Since *left* becomes equal to *loc*, thus indicating the termination of the procedure. The element 25 is placed in its final position and it divides the array into two sub arrays as

20 10 15 (Left sub array) and 30 28 (Right sub array)

As you can see, the elements in the left sub array are smaller than 25, and elements in the right sub array are greater than 25.

Algorithm 13.8:

PartitionArray(***a, beg, end, loc*** **)**

Here *a* is a linear array in memory, and *beg* and *end* represents the lower bound and upper bound of the sub array in question.

```
Begin
  Set left = beg, right = end, loc = beg
  Set done = false
  while ( not done ) do
    while ( a[loc] ≤ a[right] ) and ( loc ≠ right ) ) do
        Set right = right - 1
    endwhile
```

```
    if ( loc = right ) then
       Set done = true
    else if ( a[loc] > a[right] ) then
       Interchange a[loc] and a[right]
       Set loc = right
    endif
    if ( not done ) then
       while ( a[loc] ≥ a[left] ) and ( loc ≠ left ) ) do
          Set left = left + 1
       Endwhile
       if ( loc = left ) then
          Set done = true
       else if ( a[loc] < a[left] ) then
          Interchange a[loc] and a[left]
          Set loc = left
       Endif
    endif
  endwhile
End.
```

The following listing shows the implementation of above algorithm.

Listing 13.13:

```
template <class T>
void Array<T>::partitionArray(int beg, int end, int &loc) {
   int left, right, temp;
   loc = left = beg;
   right = end;
   done = 0;
   while ( !done ) {
     while ( ( a[*loc] <= a[right] ) && ( *loc != right ) )
        right--;
     if ( *loc == right )
        done = 1;
     else if ( a[*loc] > a[right] ) {
        temp = a[*loc];
        a[*loc] = a[right];
        a[right] = temp;
        *loc = right;
     }
     if ( !done ) {
        while ( ( a[*loc] >= a[left] ) && ( *loc != left ) )
           left++;
        if ( *loc == left )
           done = 1;
        else if  ( a[*loc] < a[left] ) {
           temp = a[*loc];
           a[*loc] = a[left];
           a[left] = temp;
           *loc = left;
        }
     }
   }
}
```

Now the QuickSort algorithm takes the following form

Algorithm 13.9:

QuickSortRecursive(*a*, *lb*, *ub*)

Here *a* is a linear array of size *n* (>1) in memory. This algorithm sorts this array in ascending order using quick sort method. The variable *loc* is used to hold the index of splitting element.

```
Begin
  if ( lb < ub )  then
     Call PartitionArray( a, lb, ub, loc )
     Call QuickSortRecursive( a, lb, loc - 1 )
     Call QuickSortRecursive( a, loc + 1, ub )
  endif
End.
```

The following listing shows the implementation of above algorithm.

Listing 13.14:

```
template <class T>
void Array<T>::quickSortRecursive(int lb, int ub) {
   int loc;
   if ( lb < ub ) {
       partitionArray(lb, ub, loc);
       quickSortRecursive(lb, loc-1 );
       quickSortRecursive(loc+1, ub );
   }
}
```

The recursive procedure *quickSortRecursive()* can be called from the calling function by the call statement as *quickSortRecursive(0, n* –1), where *a* in an array of size *n*.

Analysis of Quick Sort

To find the location of the element that splits the array into two sections is an $O(n)$ operation, because every element in the array is compared to the dividing element. After the division, each section is examined separately. If the array is split approximately in half (which is not usually), then there will be $\log_2 n$ splits.

Therefore, the total comparisons are

$$f(n) = n \times \log_2 n = O(n \log_2 n)$$

Quick sort is sensitive to the order of the input data. And it gives the worst case performance when the elements are already in the ascending order. Then it divides the array into sections of 1 and $(n-1)$ elements in each call. Thus, there will be $(n-1)$ partitions in all.

Therefore, in this case, the total number of comparisons

$$f(n) = n \times (n - 1)$$
$$= O(n^2)$$

The efficiency of quick Sort is affected by the initial order of elements.

Listing 13.15:

```
//  Program to sort an array of integers in ascending
//    order using Quick sort method
#include<iostream.h>
#include<iomanip.h>
template <class T>
class Array
{
   private:
      T *a;
      int size;
   public:
      Array(int n) {
         size = n;
         a = new T[n];
      }
      ~Array() {
         delete[] a;
      }
      void inputArray();
      void partitionArray(int, int, int &);
      void quickSortRecursive(int, int);
      void quickSort();
      void outputArray();
};
template <class T>
void Array<T>::inputArray()
{
   int i;
   cout << "\nEnter " << size << " elements of array\n\n";
   for ( i = 0; i < size; i++ ) {
      cin >> a[i];
   }
}
template <class T>
void Array<T>::outputArray()
{
   int i;
   for ( i = 0; i < size; i++ ) {
      cout << a[i] << "\t";
   }
   cout << endl;
```

```
}
template <class T>
void Array<T>::partitionArray(int beg, int end, int &loc)
{
   int left, right, temp;
   boolean done;
   loc = left = beg;
   right = end;
   done = 0;
   while ( !done ) {
     while ( ( a[*loc] <= a[right] ) && ( *loc != right ) )
        right--;
     if ( *loc == right )
        done = 1;
     else if ( a[*loc] > a[right] ) {
        temp = a[*loc];
        a[*loc] = a[right];
        a[right] = temp;
        *loc = right;
     }
     if ( !done ) {
        while ( ( a[*loc] >= a[left] ) && ( *loc != left ) )
           left++;
        if ( *loc == left )
           done = 1;
        else if  ( a[*loc] < a[left] ) {
           temp = a[*loc];
           a[*loc] = a[left];
           a[left] = temp;
           *loc = left;
        }
     }
   }
}
template <class T>
void Array<T>::quickSortRecursive(int lb, int ub)
{
   int loc;
   if ( lb < ub ) {
      splittArray(lb, ub, loc);
      quickSortRecursive(lb, loc-1 );
      quickSortRecursive(loc+1, ub );
   }
}
template <class T>
void Array<T>::quickSort()
{
   quickSortRecursive(0, size-1 );
}
void main()
{
   int n;
   cout << "Enter size of array : ";
   cin >> n;
   Array<int> a(n);
   a.inputArray();
   cout << "\n\nInput array is : ";
```

```
    a.outputArray();
    a.quickSort();
    cout << "\n\nSorted array is : ";
    a.outputArray();
}
```

13.2.7 Heap Sort Revisited

As we have seen, in *Chapter 10*, that because of the order property, the maximum value of a *max heap* is in the root node. We can take advantage of this situation by using a heap to help us sort the given array *a* having *n* elements. The general approach of heap sort is as follows:

1. From the given array, build the initial max heap.
2. Interchange the root (maximum) element with the last element.
3. Use *reheapifydownward* operation from root node to rebuild the heap of size one less than the starting.
4. Repeat steps 1 and 2 until there are no more elements.

Step 1 looks very much similar to selection sort, but the step that makes the heap sort fast is step 2 – *finding the next largest element*. As the shape property of a heap guarantees a binary tree of minimum height, therefore step 2 makes only $O(\log_2 n)$ comparisons in each iteration, as compared with $O(n)$ comparisons in each iteration of the selection sort. The heap building operation is discussed in *Chapter 10*, so here we will assume that we have with us initial heap, and we can start from there onward.

After building the heap, we know that the largest element of the array is in root node of the heap, *i.e.*, *a*[1]. This value has to go to the last position of the array, *i.e.*, *a*[*n*], so these values are swapped. Because *a*[*n*] now contains the largest value in the array (its correct position), this position is not touched further. Now, we will deal with a set of elements from *a*[1] to *a*[*n*–1], which satisfies the order property except at the root node. We correct this by applying *reheapifydownward* operation.

At this point, we know that the next largest element in the array is in the root node of the heap. To put this element in the correct position in the array, we swap it with the element *a*[*n*–1]. Now two largest elements are in their final position in the array, and we are left dealing with elements from *a*[1] to *a*[*n*–2]. This process is repeated until all the elements are in their correct positions, *i.e.*, until heap contains only single element, which is the smallest element in the array.

You must have observed in the above description, heapsort algorithm sounds like a recursive process. Each time we swap and reheap a smaller portion of the total array. This repetition can also be coded using a simple *for* loop.

Example 13.7:

Let us consider a working example to illustrate the working of heapsort algorithm. For this purpose consider the following array

10, 5, 70, 15, 12, 35, 50

Solution:

	a[1]	*a*[2]	*a*[3]	*a*[4]	*a*[5]	*a*[6]	*a*[7]
After heapify operation	70	15	50	5	12	35	10

Swap	10	15	50	5	12	35	70
Reheapifydownward	50	15	35	5	12	10	70
Swap	10	15	35	5	12	50	70
Reheapifydownward	35	15	10	5	12	50	70
Swap	12	15	10	5	35	50	70
Reheapifydownward	15	12	10	5	35	50	70
Swap	5	12	10	15	35	50	70
Reheapifydownward	12	5	10	15	35	50	70
Swap	10	5	12 .	15	35	50	70
Reheapifydownward	10	5	12	15	35	50	70
Swap	5	10	12	15	35	50	70
Final sorted array	5	10	12	15	35	50	70

Figure 10.7: Illustration of effect of heapsort on array *a*

In the discussion of heapsort algorithm, we are considering that the array is indexed from 1 to *n* not from 0 to *n*–1.

The steps required to sort an array *a* of unsorted elements in ascending order are summarized in the following algorithm.

Algorithm 13.10:

HeapSort(***a*****,** ***n*** **)**

Here *a* is a linear array of size *n* in memory. This algorithm sorts this array in ascending order using Heap sort method.

```
Begin
  Call Heapify( a, n )
  for i = n to 2 by -1 do
       Interchange elements a[1] and a[i]
       Call Reheapifydownward( a, 1, i-1  )
  endfor
End.
```

The algorithms and their implementation for building heap (*Heapify*) and for *Reheapifydownward* operation are described in *Chapter 10*.

Listing 13.16:

```
template <class T>
void Array<T>:;heapSort()
{
    int i, temp;
    heapify();
    for ( i = n; i > 1; i-- )  {
         temp = a[1];
         a[1] = a[i];
         a[i] = temp;
         reheapifydownward( a, 1, i-1 );
    }
}
```

Analysis of Heap Sort

In the heapsort algorithm, we call function *heapify()* to build the initial heap, which is $O(\log_2 n)$ operation, and inside the loop we call utility function *reheapifydownward()*. The loop is executed $(n-1)$ times, and in each iteration, the element in the root node of the heap is swapped with the last element of the reduced size heap and heap is rebuild. Swapping two elements take constant time.

A complete binary tree with n nodes has $O(\log_2(n+1))$ levels. In the worst case, if the root element is bumped down to a leaf position, the *reheapifydownward* operation would perform $O(\log_2 n)$ swaps. So the swap plus *reheapifydownward* is $O(\log_2 n)$. Multiplying this activity by $(n-1)$ iteration shows that the sorting loop is $O(n\log_2 n)$.

Combining the heap build, which is $O(n)$, and the sorting loop, we can see that complexity of *heapSortMethod()* is $O(n\log_2 n)$.

Unlike QuickSort, the efficiency of HeapSort is not affected by the initial order of elements.

Listing 13.17:

```
//  Program to sort an array of integers in ascending
//  order using heap sort method
#include<iostream.h>
#include<iomanip.h>
template <class T>
class Array
{
  private:
     T *a;
     int size;
  public:
     Array(int n) {
        size = n;
        a = new T[n+1];
     }
     ~Array() {
        delete a;
     }
     void inputArray();
     void heapify();
     void reheapifydownward(int, int);
     void heapSort();
     void outputArray();
};
template <class T>
void Array<T>::inputArray() {
   int i;
   cout << "\nEnter " << size << " elements of array\n\n";
   for ( i = 1; i <= size; i++ ) {
      cin >> a[i];
   }
}
template <class T>
void Array<T>::heapify() {
   int i, index;
   index = size / 2;
   for ( i = index; i >= 1; i-- )
      reheapifydownward(i, size );
}
template <class T>
void Array<T>::reheapifydownward(int start, int finish) {
   int  index, lchild, rchild, maximum, temp;
   lchild = 2*start;
   rchild = lchild + 1;
   if ( lchild <= finish ) {
     maximum = a[lchild];
      index = lchild;
      if ( rchild <= finish ) {
          if ( a[rchild] > maximum ) {
             maximum = a[rchild];
             index = rchild;
          }
      }
```

```
        if ( a[start] < a[index] ) {
            temp = a[start];
            a[start] = a[index];
            a[index] = temp;
            reheapifydownward(index, finish);
        }
    }
}
template <class T>
void Array<T>::heapSort() {
    int i, temp;
    heapify();
    for ( i = size; i > 1; i-- ) {
        temp = a[1];
        a[1] = a[i];
        a[i] = temp;
        reheapifydownward(1, i-1);
    }
}
template <class T>
void Array<T>::outputArray() {
    int i;
    for ( i = 1; i <= size; i++ ) {
        cout << a[i] << "\t";
    }
    cout << endl;
}

void main()
{
    int n;
    cout << "Enter size of array : ";
    cin >> n;
    Array<int> a(n);
    a.inputArray();
    cout << "\n\nInput array is : ";
    a.outputArray();
    a.heapSort();
    cout << "\n\nSorted array is : ";
    a.outputArray();
}
```

13.2.8 Shell Sort

Invented by Donald Shell in 1959, the shell sort is the most efficient of the $O(n^2)$ class of sorting algorithms. Of course, the shell sort is also the most complex of the $O(n^2)$ algorithms. The shell sort is a *diminishing increment sort*, better known as a *comb sort* to the unwashed programming masses. The algorithm makes multiple passes through the array, and each time sorts numbers that are equally distanced.

This algorithm is similar to bubble sort in the sense that it also moves elements by exchanges. However, it begins by comparing elements that are at a distance *d*. With this the elements that are quite away from their place will move more rapidly than the simple bubble sort.

Further, in each pass, the value of d is reduced to half, *i.e.*

$$d_{i+1} = \frac{d_i + 1}{2}$$

In each pass, each element is compared with element that is located d position away from it, and exchange is made if required. The next iteration starts with a new value of d. The algorithm terminates when $d = 1$.

Example 13.9:

To illustrate the working of shell sort method, consider the sorting of the following array in ascending order.

12 9 −10 22 2 35 40

Solution: Note that, the output of a given pass becomes the input for the next pass.

Starting value of $d = \frac{n}{2} = \frac{7}{2} = 3$

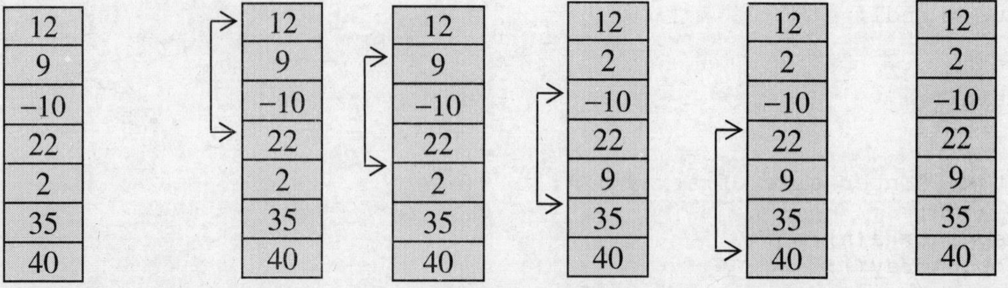

(*a*) Given Array (*b*) Pass 1

Next iteration starts with $d = 2$

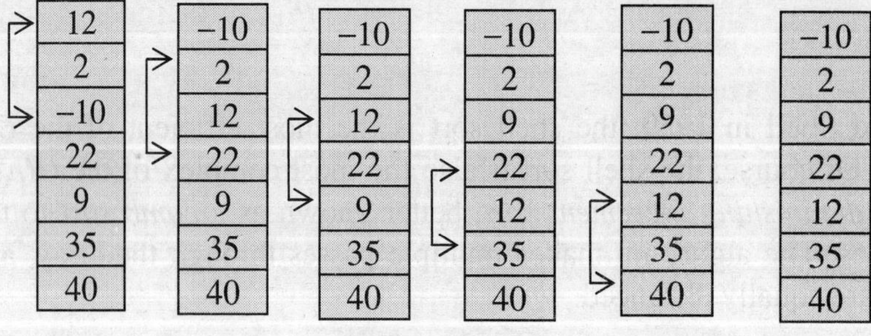

(*c*) Pass 2

Next iteration starts with $d = 1$

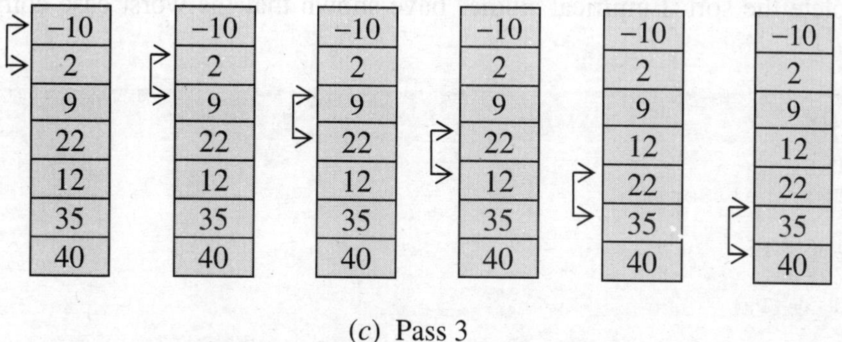

(c) Pass 3

Figure 13.7: Illustration of Shell sort method

After pass 3, the last iteration, the array will appear as

–10 2 9 12 22 35 40

which is sorted as desired.

Algorithm 12.11:

shellSort(***a***, ***n*** **)**

Here *a* is a linear array with *n* elements in memory. This algorithm sorts the elements in the ascending order. It uses a temporary variable *temp* to facilitate the exchange of two values, variable *d* for distance between element to be compared, and variable *i* to is used as loop control variable.

```
Begin
   Set d = n/2
   while ( d ≥ 1 ) do
      for i = 0 to (n–d–1) by 1 do
         if ( a[i] > a[i+d] ) then
            Set temp = a[i]
            Set a[i] = a[i+d]
            Set a[j+1] = temp
         endif
      endfor
      if ( d = 1 ) then
         Exit
      endif
      Set d = d/2
   endwhile
End.
```

Analysis of Shell Sort

It is difficult to predict the complexity of Shell sort, as it is very difficult (hard) to show the effect of one pass on another pass. One thing that is very clear that if the new distance *d* is computed using above formula, then the number of passes will approximately be $\log_2 d$ since

$d = 1$ will complete the sort. Empirical studies have shown that the worst case complexity of Shell sort is $O(n^2)$.

Listing 13.18:

```
template <class T>
void Array<T>::shellSort()
{
   int d, temp, i;
   d = size/2;
   while ( d >= 1 )
   {
      for ( i = 0; i < size - d; i++ )
      {
        if ( a[i] > a[i+d] ) {
           temp = a[i];
           a[i] = a[i+d];
           a[i+d] = temp;
        }
      }
      if ( d == 1 )
         return;
      d = d/2.0+0.5;
   }
}
```

Listing 13.19:

```
//  Program to sort an array of integers in ascending
//  order using Shell sort method

#include<iostream.h>
#include<iomanip.h>

template <class T>
class Array
{
   private:
      T *a;
      int size;
   public:
      Array(int n) {
         size = n;
         a = new T[n+1];
      }
      ~Array() {
         delete a;
      }
      void inputArray();
      void shellSort();
      void outputArray();
};
template <class T>
void Array<T>::inputArray() {
   int i;
   cout << "\nEnter " << size << " elements of array\n\n";
   for ( i = 1; i <= size; i++ ) {
```

```
        cin >> a[i];
    }
}
template <class T>
void Array<T>::shellSort()
{
    int d, temp, i;
    d = size/2;
    while ( d >= 1 )
    {
        for ( i = 0; i < size - d; i++ )
        {
            if ( a[i] > a[i+d] ) {
                temp = a[i];
                a[i] = a[i+d];
                a[i+d] = temp;
            }
        }
        if ( d == 1 )
            return;
        d = d/2.0+0.5;
    }
}
template <class T>
void Array<T>::outputArray() {
    int i;
    for ( i = 1; i <= size; i++ ) {
        cout << a[i] << "\t";
    }
    cout << endl;
}
void main()
{
    int n;
    cout << "Enter size of array : ";
    cin >> n;
    Array<int> a(n);
    a.inputArray();
    cout << "\n\nInput array is : ";
    a.outputArray();
    a.shellSort();
    cout << "\n\nSorted array is : ";
    a.outputArray();
}
```

13.3 SEARCHING

Searching is the process of finding the location of given element in the linear array. The search is said to be successful if the given element is found, *i.e.*, the element does exists in the array; otherwise unsuccessful.

There are two approaches to search operation:

- Linear search
- Binary search

The algorithm that one chooses generally depends on organization of the array elements. If the elements are in random order, then one have to use linear search technique, and if the array elements are sorted, then it is preferable to use binary search technique. These two search techniques are described in the next sections.

13.3.1 Linear Search Revisited

Given no information about the array *a*, the only way to search for given element *item* is to compare *item* with each element of *a* one by one. This method, which traverses *a* sequentially to locate *item* is called *linear search* or *sequential search.*

Algorithm 13.12:

LinearSearch(***a*, *n*, *item*, *loc*** **)**

Here *a* is an linear array of size *n*. This algorithms finds the location of the element *item* in linear array *a*. If search ends in success it sets *loc* to the index of the element; otherwise it sets *loc* to –1.

```
Begin
   for i = 0 to (n-1) by 1 do
      if ( a[i] = item ) then
         Set loc = i
         Exit
      endif
   endfor
   Set loc = -1
End.
```

The following code shows the implementation of above algorithm.

Listing 13.19:

```
template <class T>
int Array<T>::linearSearch(T item )
{
   int i;
   for ( i = 0; i < n; i++ ) {
      if ( a[i] == item )
          return i;
   }
   return -1;
}
```

Analysis of Linear Search

In the best possible case, the *item* may occur at first position. In this case, the search operation terminates in success with just one comparison. However, the worst case occurs when either the item is present at last position or missing from the array. In the former case, the search terminates in success with *n* comparisons. In the later case, the search terminates in failure with *n* comparisons. Thus, we find that in worst case the linear search is O(*n*) operations.

13.3.2 Binary Search Revisited

Suppose the elements of the array *A* are sorted in ascending order (if the elements are numbers) or dictionary order (if the elements are strings). The best searching algorithm, called *binary search,* is used to find the location of the given element. We do use this approach in our daily life. For example, suppose we want to find the meaning of the term *modem* in a computer dictionary. Obviously, we don't search page by page. We open the dictionary in the middle (roughly) to determine which half contains the term being sought. Then for the subsequent search one half is discarded, and we search in the other half. This process is continued till other we have located the required term or that term is missing from the dictionary, which will be indicated by the fact that at the end we will be left with only one page.

Example 13.10:

To illustrate the working of the binary search technique, consider the following sorted array *A* with 7 elements

3, 10, 15, 20, 35, 40, 60

and we want to search element 15.

Solution:

	a[0]	*a*[1]	*a*[2]	*a*[3]	*a*[4]	*a*[5]	*a*[6]
Given Array *a*	3	10	15	20	35	40	60

To start with, we take *beg* = 0, *end* = 6, and compute location of the middle element as

$$mid = (beg + end) / 2 = (0 + 6) / 2 = 3$$

Since *a*[*mid*], *i.e.*, *a*[3] ≠ 15, and *beg* < *end.* We start next iteration.

As *a*[*mid*] = 20 > 15, therefore, we take *end* = *mid* − 1 = 3 − 1 = 2, where as *beg* remains unchanged. Thus

$$mid = (beg + end) / 2 = (0 + 2) / 2 = 1$$

Since *a*[*mid*], *i.e.*, *a*[1] ≠ 15, and *beg* < *end.* We start next iteration.

As *a*[*mid*] = 10 < 15, therefore, we take *beg* = *mid* + 1 = 1 + 1 = 2, where as *end* remains unchanged.

Since *beg* = *end,* again compute location of the middle element as

$$mid = (beg + end) / 2 = (2 + 2) / 2 = 2$$

Since *a*[*mid*], *i.e.*, *a*[2] = 15, the search terminates on success.

The element 15 is found at index 2.

Algorithm 13.13:

BinarySearch(***a, n, item, loc*** **)**

Here *a* is an linear array of size *n*. This algorithms finds the location of the element *item* in sorted (ascending) linear array *a*. If search ends in success it sets *loc* to the index of the element; otherwise it sets loc to −1. Here variables *beg* and *end* to keep track of the first element and last element of the array to be searched, and variable *mid* is used as index of the middle element of the array under consideration.

```
Begin
  Set beg = 0
  Set end = n-1
  Set mid = ( beg + end ) / 2
  while ( ( beg ≤ end ) and ( a[mid] ≠ item ) ) do
     if ( item < a[mid] ) then
        Set end = mid-1
     else
        Set beg = mid+1
     endif
     Set mid = ( beg + end ) / 2
  endwhile
  if ( beg > end ) then
     Set loc = -1
  else
     Set loc = mid
  endif
End.
```

The following code shows the implementation of above algorithm.

Listing 13.20:

```
template <class T>
int Array<T>::binarySearchIterative(T item )
{
   int beg, end, mid;
   beg = 0;   end = n - 1;
   mid  = ( beg + end ) / 2;
   while ( ( beg <= end ) && ( a[mid] != item ) )
   {
      if ( element < a[mid] )
         end = mid - 1;
      else
         beg = mid  + 1;
```

```
      mid  = ( beg + end ) / 2;
   }
   return ( ( beg > end ) ? -1 : mid );
}
```

You must have observed that binary search is recursive procedure, with the base criteria that search will terminate either the element is located or *beg* becomes greater than *end*.

The implementation of the recursive algorithm is given below.

Listing 13.21:

```
template <class T>
int Array<T>::binarySearchRecursive(int lb, int ub, T item) {
   int mid;
   if ( lb > ub )
      return -1;
   else {
      mid  = ( lb + ub ) / 2;
      if ( item == a[mid] )
         return mid;
      else if  ( item < a[mid] )
         return binarySearchRecursive(lb, mid-1, item );
      else
         return binarySearchRecursive(mid+1, ub, item );
   }
}
```

Analysis of Binary Search

In each iteration or in each recursive call, the search is reduced to one half of the array. Therefore, for *n* elements in the array, there will be $\log_2 n$ iterations or recursive calls. Thus, the complexity of binary search is $O(\log_2 n)$. This complexity will be same irrespective of the position of the element, even if it is not present in the array.

Listing 13.22:

```
//  Program to search an element from an array of integers
//  sorted in ascending order using binary search technique

#include<iostream.h>
#include<iomanip.h>

template <class T>
class Array
{
   private:
      T *a;
      int size;
   public:
      Array(int n) {
         size = n;
         a = new T[n+1];
      }
```

```
    ~Array() {
       delete a;
    }
    void inputArray();
    void bubbleSort();
    int  binarySearchRecursive(int, int, T);
    int  binarySearch(T);
    void outputArray();
};
template <class T>
void Array<T>::inputArray() {
  int i;
  cout << "\nEnter " << size << " elements of array\n\n";
  for ( i = 1; i <= size; i++ ) {
     cin >> a[i];
  }
}
template <class T>
void Array<T>::bubbleSort()
{
   int j, k, exchange_flag = 1;
   T temp;
   k = 1;
   while ( ( k < size )  && ( exchange_flag ) ) {
      exchange_flag = 0;
      for ( j = 0; j < size-k; j++ ) {
      if ( a[j] > a[j+1] ) {
         exchange_flag = 1;
         temp = a[j];
         a[j] = a[j+1];
         a[j+1] = temp;
      }
      }
      k++;
   }
template <class T>
int Array<T>::binarySearch(T item)
{
   int loc;
   loc = binarySearchRecursive(1, size, item);
   return loc;
}
template <class T>
int Array<T>::binarySearchRecursive(int lb, int ub, T item)
{
   int mid;
   if ( lb > ub )
      return -1;
   else {
      mid  = ( lb + ub ) / 2;
      if ( item == a[mid] )
      return mid;
      else if  ( item < a[mid] )
      return binarySearchRecursive(lb, mid-1, item );
      else
      return binarySearchRecursive(mid+1, ub, item );
```

```
    }
}
template <class T>
void Array<T>::outputArray() {
    int i;
    for ( i = 1; i <= size; i++ ) {
        cout << a[i] << "\t";
    }
    cout << endl;
}
void main()
{
    int n, item, loc;
    cout << "Enter size of array : ";
    cin >> n;
    Array<int> a(n);
    a.inputArray();
    cout << "\n\nInput array is : ";
    a.outputArray();
    a.bubbleSort();
    cout << "\n\nAray after sorting is : ";
    a.outputArray();
    cout << "\nEnter element to search : ";
    cin >> item;
    loc = a.binarySearch(item);
    if ( loc == -1 )
        cout << "\nElement not found. . .\n";
    else
        cout << "\nElement found at index " << loc << endl;
}
```

13.4 MERGING

Merging is the process of combining the elements of two similar structures (linear arrays) into a single structure. Suppose that two arrays are unsorted, we can combine them end to end, *i.e.*, we can first put elements of array *a* into third array *c*, and then the elements of the second array *b* are placed after it in array *c* as pictured in Figure 13.8.

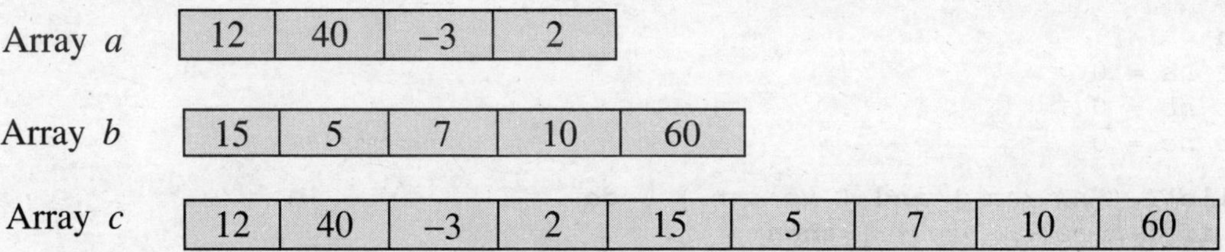

Figure 13.8: Merging end-to-end

But in most cases, we may have sorted arrays and our aim is to combine them in such a way that the combined array is also in the sorted order. One straightforward approach is to join them end to end, and then sort the combined array. But this approach in not efficient and economical. The best approach is to compare the elements of the given array, and based on this comparison, decide which element should go first to the third array.

This process is illustrated in figure 13.9, for arrays sorted in the ascending order.

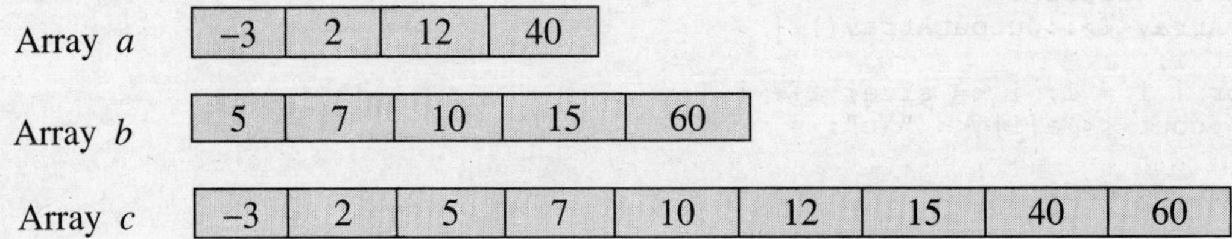

Figure 13.9: Merging of sorted arrays

In case of sorted arrays, to start with, compare first element of array *a* (element −3) with the first element of array *b* (element 5), and put the smallest of these (−3) into array *c*. Since first element of array *a* is put in array *c*, now we compare second element of array *a* (element 2) with the first element of array *b* (element 5), and since 2 is the smallest, put it into *c*. Next compare third element of *a* (element 12) with first element of *b* (element 5), since 5 is the smallest, put it into *c*. Next compare third element of *a* (element 12) with second element of *b* (element 7), since 7 is the smallest, put it into *c*, and so on. When one array is exhausted, the elements of the other array are copied one by one to *c*. to accomplish the above task, we use counters to keep track of the current element which is a candidate to go in *c*, and the position in *c* where it will be stored.

The various steps required are for its implementation is shown in the following algorithm.

Algorithm 13.14:

MergingSortedArrays(*a*, *m*, *b*, *n*, *c*)

Here *a* and *b* are sorted (ascending) linear arrays of size *m* and *n*, respectively. This algorithm merges these arrays, by comparing their elements, into array c, which will be of size *m+n*. It uses variables *na* and *nb* to keep track of the respective elements of arrays *a* and *b*, and a variable *nc* to keep track of index in array *c* where the incoming element (either from array *a* or *b*) will be stored.

```
Begin
  Set na = 0
  Set nb = 0
  Set nc = 0

  while ( ( na < m ) and ( nb < n ) ) do
     if ( a[na] < b[nb] ) then
        Set c[nc] = a[na]
        Set na = na+1
     else
        Set c[nc] = b[nb]
        Set nb = nb+1
     endif
     Set nc = nc+1
  endwhile
  if ( na = m ) then    // array a is exhausted
     while ( nb < n ) do
```

```
            Set c[nc] = b[nb]
            Set nb = nb+1
            Set nc = nc+1
        endwhile
    else                     // array b is exhausted
        while ( na < m ) do
            Set c[nc] = a[na]
            Set na = na+1
            Set nc = nc+1
        endwhile
    endif
End.
```

The following code shows the implementation of the above algorithm.

Listing 13.23:

```
template <class T>
void Array<T>::mergingSortedArrays(int *a, int m, int *b, int n, int *c)
{
   int na, nb, nc;
   na = nb = nc = 0;
   while ( (na < m) && (nb < n) ) {
       if ( a[na] < b[nb] )
          c[nc] = a[na++];
       else
          c[nc] = b[nb++];
       nc++;
   }
   if ( na == m ) {              // list 'a' is exhausted
      while ( nb < n )
        c[nc++] = b[nb++];
   } else if ( nb == n ) {   // list b is exhausted
      while ( na < m )
        c[nc++] = a[na++];
   }
}
```

Analysis of Merge Operation

The input to this algorithm consists of the total number r (= $m + n$) of elements of a and b. each comparison assigns an element to array c, which eventually has r elements. According the number $f(r)$ of comparison cannot exceed r:

$$f(r) \leq r = O(r)$$

which means, the merging algorithm can be run in linear time.

Listing 13.24:

```
// Program to demonstrate the two arrays after sorting
#include <iostream.h>
#include <iomanip.h>
template <class T>
```

```
class Array
{
   private:
      T *a;
      int size;
   public:
      Array(int n) {
        size = n;
        a = new T[size];
      }
      ~Array() {
        delete a;      // delete dynamic array
      }
      int getElements();
      void outputArray();
      void inputArray();
      void bubbleSortModified();
      void mergeSortedArrays(Array<T> &la, Array<T> &lb);
};
template <class T>
int Array<T>::getElements() {
   return size;
}
template <class T>
void Array<T>::outputArray() {
   for ( int i = 0; i < size; i++ )
      cout << a[i] << " ";
   cout << endl;
}
template <class T>
void Array<T>::inputArray() {
   for ( int i = 0; i < size; i++ ) {
      cin >> a[i];
   }
}
template <class T>
void Array<T>::bubbleSortModified()
{
   int j, i, temp, exchange_flag = 1;
   i = 0;
   while ( ( i < size-1 )  && ( exchange_flag ) ) {
      exchange_flag = 0;
      for ( j = 0; j < size-i-1; j++ ) {
      if ( a[j] > a[j+1] ) {
         exchange_flag = 1;
         temp = a[j];
         a[j] = a[j+1];
         a[j+1] = temp;
      }
      }
      i++;
   }
}
template <class T>
void Array<T>::mergeSortedArrays(Array<T> &la, Array<T> &lb)
{
   int na=0, nb=0, nc=0;
```

```
    int r, s;
    r = la.getElements();    s = lb.getElements();
    while ( (na < r) && (nb < s) ) {
      if ( la.a[na] < lb.a[nb] )
         a[nc] = la.a[na++];
      else
         a[nc] = lb.a[nb++];
      nc++;
   }
   if (na == r) {            // first array is exhausted
      while ( nb < s )
        a[nc++] = lb.a[nb++];
   }
   else if (nb == s) { // second array is exhausted
      while ( na < r )
        a[nc++] = la.a[na++];
   }
 }
 void main()              //  main function
 {
    int m, n;
    cout << "\nEnter size of array a : ";
    cin >> m;
    Array<int> a(m);
    cout << "\nEnter elements for array a\n";
    a.inputArray();
    cout << "\nEnter size of array b : ";
    cin >> n;
    Array<int> b(n);
    cout << "\nEnter elements for array b\n";
    b.inputArray();
    Array<int> c(m+n);
    a.bubbleSortModified();
    b.bubbleSortModified();
    cout << "\nArray a after sorting : ";
    a.outputArray();
    cout << "\nArray a after sorting : ";
    b.outputArray();
    c.mergeSortedArrays(a,b);
    cout << "\nElements of merged array c are\n\n";
    c.outputArray();
 }
```

REVIEW EXERCISES

1. What is sorting? What is its importance?
2. How do quick sort and heap sort methods compare as far as performance is concerned?
3. Can you implement quick sort method without recursion? If yes, show its implementation.
4. How would you implement merge sort method without recursion?
5. Sort the list 213, 145, 456, 700, 515, 295, 674, 925 using bucket sort method.
6. Sort the list 3, 1, 4, 7, 5, 2, 6, 9 using merge sort method.

How the heap sort processes the list 142, 34, 77, 23, 18, 100, 72 in order to sort it in the descending order?

8. How the quick sort processes the list 42, 34, 75, 23, 18, 100, 10, 72 in order to sort it in the descending order?
9. Here is an array of ten integers: < 5 3 8 9 1 7 0 2 6 4 >. Rewrite this array after the FIRST iteration of the selection sort in order to sort it in ascending order.
10. Here is an array of ten integers: < 5 3 8 9 1 7 0 2 6 4 >. Rewrite this array after the TWO iterations of the insertion sort in order to sort it in ascending order.
11. Here is an array, which has just been partitioned by the first step of quick sort in order to sort it in the ascending order:

    3, 0, 2, 4, 5, 8, 7, 6, 9

    Which of these elements could be the pivot?
12. Here is an array of ten integers:

    5 3 8 9 1 7 0 2 6 4

    Suppose we partition this array using quick sort's partition function and using 5 as the pivot. Rewrite the resulting array after the partition finishes.
13. Fill in the following table for the times to sort an array of *n* items. Use only Big-O notation.

Method	Worst Case	Average Case	Method	Worst Case	Average Case
Bubble sort			Quick sort		
Insertion sort			Selection sort		
Merge sort			Heap sort		

PROGRAMMING EXERCISES

1. Modify all the sorting methods discussed to sort an array of integer value in descending order.
2. Modify all the sorting methods discussed to sort an array of real values in descending as well as ascending order.
3. You are given a list of names of students in a class. Sort these names in the dictionary order using bucket sort method.
4. You are given a list of names of students in a class. The names are stored in three different fields as *first name*, *middle name*, *last name*. Sort these names on *last name*. If *last names* are same, then sort on *middle name*, and if *middle name* is also same then sort on *first name*. Note that this is an example of sorts within sorts.

Chapter 14

Files

14.1 INTRODUCTION

In many of the programs, data is supplied at the time of execution from keyboard, the standard input device. However, scientific, engineering, and business problems often deal with large volumes of data. The main limitation of this approach is that it is very difficult to handle large volume of data.

Further, computers are used to analyze data collected by other instruments such as telescopes and tele-monitoring devices. Data such as this is input data in machine-readable form. Problems such as structural analysis of buildings, wide-body crafts, or steel bridges generates large volumes of data from basic engineering equations. This data might be output data designed for use on simulation or graphics equipment. Data may also be produced by one computer and used as input to another.

These limitations can be overcome by storing the data into a disk file called a *file*. In this chapter, we will discuss about various aspects of files, but before that we will discuss briefly about the terms used in the context of files.

14.2 BASIC TERMINOLOGY

This section introduces the basic terminology related to the files. Every student must understand these terms.

Field – It is an elementary item that is characterized by its type and size. For example, *name*, which is of type character with some maximum number of characters; *age* which is of type integer with size two bytes, etc.

Record – It is a collection of related data fields and is treated as a unit from the application point of view. For example, university typically uses a student record with the fields such as *registration number (enrollment number), class roll number, name, father's name, name of subjects taken, etc.*

e – It is a collection of related (similar) records. For example, a file containing records of students in class, a file containing records of employees of an organization.

File Organization – It refers to the way records are physically arranged on a storage device.

Key – It is a field in a record that takes unique values and can be used to distinguish a record from other records in a file. It may happen that more than one field has unique values. In that case, there exist multiple keys. But at a time, we may be using only one filed as a key, called *primary key*, that too depending on the problem in hand. The other key(s) are then known as *alternate key(s)*.

In some cases, there is no field that has unique values. Then a combination of some fields can be used to form a key. Such a key is known as *composite key*.

In worst case, if there is no possibility of forming a key from within the record, then an extra field can be added to the record that can be used as a key. For example, universities add field *enrollment number* to distinguish students.

Index – It is a pointer to a record in a file. Basically, index is a pair of elements comprising *key* and a *file pointer* or record number. And an *index file* is a file that contains these pairs that sorted on keys. These indices facilitate the fast retrieval of records from a file.

14.3 ATTRIBUTES OF A FILE

Any file has associated with it some essential properties, known as *attributes*. These are:

- file name
- file position
- file structure
- file access method

Let us understand these attributes briefly.

File name - A file name is a character string identical to the name by which the file is known to the operating system. File naming conventions are determined by the operating system.

File position - A position in a file is a place where I/O will be performed and is usually set by the previous I/O operation. A file has an initial point, terminal point, current record, preceding record and next record.

File Structure – File structure refers to the way that whether the file is text file or binary file. In a text file, numbers are stored as sequence of characters, whereas in a binary file, numbers are stored in a way as they are stored in main memory. However, strings (sequence of characters) are stored in identical way in both.

File access method - In general, records in a file can be accessed sequentially as well as randomly. In sequential access mode, records can only be accessed in sequence. For example, if you want to access 100th record, you have to go through first 99 records. However, records in a sequential access file can be of different size.

On the other hand, in random access mode records can be accessed in any order. Records in a random access file are numbered sequentially beginning with number 0. All records in a random access file must be of same size.

14.4 CLASSIFICATION OF FILES

In general, the various files can be classified on the following criteria:

- Based on the functions they perform.
- Based on the way records in a file can be accessed.
- Based on the way data is stored.
- Based on the mode of use.

14.4.1 Classification of Files Based on Functions they Perform

Based on the functions they perform, files can be classified as

- ***Master files*** — A master file represents a static view of some aspect of an organization's business, *i.e.*, it contains relatively permanent data. For example, a manufacturing organization will have a payroll master file, a customer master file, a personal master file, an inventory master file, a material requirement master file, etc.

  A record on a master file keeps track of the status of something, for example, an employee, a customer, a product, an account, etc. Depending upon how recently the contents of a master file were brought up to date and how much the pertinent status has changed since that time, the master file is a more or less accurate snapshot of some aspect of the real world.

- ***Transaction files*** — Changes that are going to be applied to a master file are collected on a transaction file. A transaction may contain data to add a new record, to modify a record or to remove a record from a master file. Each record on a transaction file represents an event or change in something whose status is tracked on a master file.

- ***Report files*** — A report file contains data that are formatted for presentation to a user. The file may be spooled to a printer to produce a hard copy report or may be displayed on a terminal screen. A report file may be produced by a report-write package or by an application program.

- ***Work files*** — A work file is a temporary file. This type of file is created temporarily by an application for some purpose and the removed automatically when it is no more required.

4.2 Classification of Files Based on the way Records can be Accessed

Based on the way records can be accessed, files can be classified as:

- ***Sequential access files*** — In these files records are arranged in the sequence in which they are written to the file, *i.e.*, the first record written is the first record in the file, the second record written is the second record in the file, and so on. As a result, records can be added only at the end of the file. These records can only be accessed by reading all the previous records. These files can be stored on tapes as well as discs. These files are preferable if you need to need to process every (or nearly every) record in a file, for example, payroll processing, electricity bills, etc.

- ***Random access files*** — These files are stored in such a manner that it is possible to move the pointer directly to any record in the file and read it without passing through any intervening records. These files can only be stored on discs. These files are preferable if you need to access only a few records in a file, for example, bank account details at customer's on-line request.

14.4.3 Classification of Files Based on the way Data is Stored

Based on the way data is stored, files can be classified as

- ***Text files*** — In these files, data is stored in the form of ASCII codes irrespective of the data type, *i.e.*, for character data, their ASCII codes of the individual characters are stored and for numeric data, the ASCII code of individual digits (as well as point) of a number are stored.

  Text files can be manipulated by any text editor. Text files does not provide an efficient storage. These files are mostly used as program files and report files.

- ***Binary files*** — In these files, data is stored in the same as it is stored in memory irrespective of the data type, .*i.e.*, for character data, their ASCII codes of the individual characters are stored and for numeric data, numbers are stored in binary format.

  Binary files provide more efficient way of storage of data in terms of memory, but can be read only through programs. If you open with a text editor, you will not be able to infer anything from it.

14.4.4 Classification of Files Based on the Mode of Use

Based on the mode of use, files can be classified as

- ***Input files*** — these files are only read by the program. For example, a transaction file is generally an input file to an update program. Another example of an input file is a program file of source code to a compiler.

- ***Output files*** — these files are written to by the program, *i.e.*, created by the program. For example, a report file may be the output of a program that updates a master file. Another example of output file is a program file of object code from a compiler.
- ***Input/Output files*** — these files are both read and written by the program. A master file is usually an input/output file that is updated based on transaction file. For each record, in a transaction file, a master file record is read, update and then written back.

14.6 FILE OPERATIONS

The way the file is going to be used is an important factor in determining how the file should be organized. Two major aspects of a file's use are its mode of use and the nature of the operations on the file.

A file can be accessed by a program that executes in *batch* mode or by a program that executes interactively. In the batch mode, the transactions are generally arranged (sorted) to improve master file access, whereas in interactive mode, the transactions are processed as they arrive. Further, in the batch mode, the performance is typically measured by *throughput*, which is the number of transactions processed in a time period. In interactive mode, the performance is measured by response time to individual transactions. Some file organizations are more suited to support interactive access than others.

The fundamental operations that are performed on the files are:

- Creation
- Updation, which includes
  - Insertion of a new record
  - Modification of an existing record
  - Deletion of an existing record
- Retrieval, which includes
  - Inquiry
  - Report generation
- Maintenance, which includes
  - Restructuring
  - Reorganization

Each of these operations is described below in brief.

14.6.1 Creating a File

Before creating a file, its *name*, *mode*, and *organization* need to be decided. Then the file is opened in the writing. Then records are read from some input device (such as keyboard), validated, and then written into the file one by one using a data entry program. Once all records have been written into a file, the file is closed. This file is now available for use by any program designed to use it in some way. The initial creation of file is also referred to as *loading* of the file.

14.6.2 Updating a File

Updating a file involves changing the contents of a (master) file to reflect a recent snap shot of the real world. These changes include

- Inserting new record, *e.g.*, adding a new record for the newly selected employee.
- Modifying an existing record, *e.g.*, changing the address of an employee who has shifted his residence.
- Deleting an existing record, *e.g.*, removing the record of an employee who has left the organization.

The updated file represents a more current picture of reality.

Some file organizations permit the modifications in place, insertion of new records in available free space, and deletion to make space available for reuse. If this happens, then the file is an input/output file for that program. However, some file organizations don't permit modifications in place. For such files, an old file is input to an update program that modifies some of the records and then writes the modified record to a new file, an output file for that program. The new file is essentially created with current information.

14.6.3 Retrieving from a File

Retrieval is the process of extracting desired information from a file. There are two basic classes of file retrieval — *inquiry* and *report generation*. The volume of data they produce can distinguish these two classes. An inquiry results in a relatively low-volume response, whereas a report may create many pages of output.

A file retrieval request can be *comprehensive* or *selective*. Comprehensive retrieval reports information from all the records in a file, whereas selective retrieval applies some qualification criteria to choose which records will supply information for output.

14.6.4 Maintaining a File

Maintenance of a file includes all changes that are made to a file to improve the performance of the program that access them. There are two basic classes of maintenance operations — *restructuring* and *reorganization*.

Restructuring a file implies that some structural changes are made to the file within the context of the same file organization technique. For example, field width could be changed, new fields could be added to records, etc., but the file organization method would remain the same. Reorganizing a file implies a change from one file organization to another.

Different file organizations differ in their maintenance requirements. Further, these maintenance requirements are also dependent on the nature of activity on the file contents and how quickly that activity changes.

In general, master files and program files are created, updated, retrieved from, and maintained. Work files are created, updated, and retrieved from, but are not maintained. Report files are generally created but not updated, retrieved from, or maintained. The transaction files are generally created and used for one-time processing.

14.7 FILE SYSTEMS

It is important to note that accessing files require a great deal of activity that is transparent to a programmer. Most of the programming languages provide features that enable programmers to define rather complex file organization techniques with quite simple statements. A *file system* provides support to enable programmers to access files without being concerned about details of storage characteristics and device timings. The file system converts simple file access statements to low-level I/O instructions. For example, the simple request to read or write a record on a file typically involves a complex sequence of operations supported by device management operations. Programmer's job would have been considerably difficult if he/she has to deal with these detailed I/O operations.

The responsibilities of a file system are many and varied. These responsibilities include

- Maintaining a directory of files that include file identification and location information.
- Establishing communications paths for data flow between main memory and secondary storage devices.
- Coordinating the communication between CPU and secondary storage devices, which include
  - Handling the speed tradeoff between CPU and secondary storage devices in such a way that CPU does not spend an inordinate amount of time waiting idly for I/O operations to be completed.
  - Handling data in such a way that they can be held if the sender or receiver is not ready at the same time.
- Preparing files for input or output use.
- Handling files when the program has finished with their use.

14.7.1 File Directories

All file systems use some sort of directory structure to manage the identification and location information about files. Therefore, before a program can access a file, the file system must know where the file is located. Figure 14.1 illustrates a typical directory structure.

The label includes identifying information, access control information, and a pointer to a table of contents. The table of contents contains a control block for each file. A control block contains information about the name of a file, its attributes, and a pointer that points to the start of the file. When a file is requested, the table of contents is consulted for information required to locate the file.

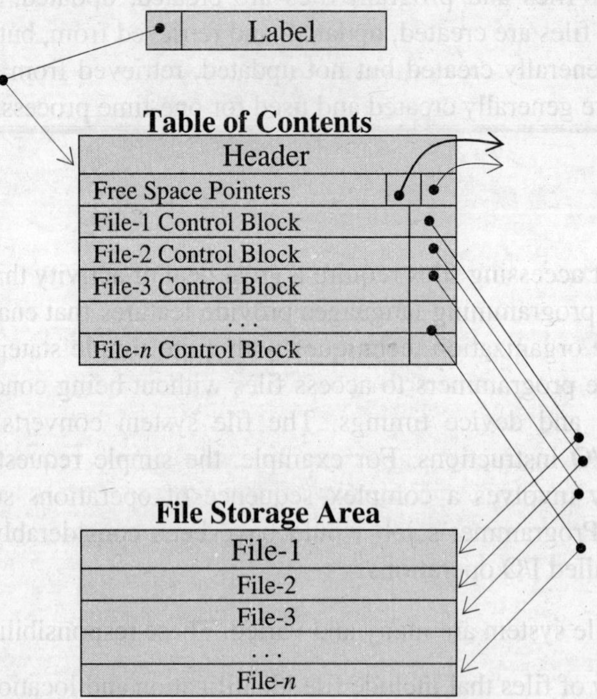

Figure 14.1: A typical directory structure

14.7.2 Device Control

I/O activities basically involve the transfer of data between main memory and secondary storage devices or devices such as printers and terminals. While these activities may appear to be simple to programmers, actually require detailed device support. For example, assume that the file directory has already been consulted and the requested file's location on a secondary storage device has been determined.

In order to be able to write to that device or read from that device, the following tasks must be accomplished: A communication path between main memory and device must be established, and it must be determined that the necessary components of the communication path are available and are ready for use. The I/O operation itself requires that appropriate signals be transmitted to the device so that it can respond properly: disk arms may be moved and read/write heads activated; a cursor on the terminal screen may be positioned; a page eject command may be sent to the printer. If errors occur during I/O activity, they must be handled.

At the end of the I/O operation, the sender must be notified that activities have terminated successfully or unsuccessfully, as the case may be.

14.7.2.1 Types of Devices

The different devices can be classified as

- ***Dedicated devices*** – devices that can be accessed only by one user at a time. Terminal is an example of dedicated device.
- ***Shared devices*** – devices that allow concurrent access by multiple users. Disk is an example of shared device. The control activities for shared devices are more complex as compared to dedicated devices. Two of the important control functions required for shared devices are space allocation and the granting of access rights.
- ***Virtual devices*** – there are devices which users would like to share but are not suitable for concurrent use such as printer. Multiple programs may want to address a printer concurrently, but the resultant output of interleaved lines from these programs will be quite useless. Virtual devices address this problem. A program that is using a virtual printer has the impression that it is writing to a printer, but in reality it is writing to disk. When the output file is completely written by the program, it is then queued and written in its entirety to the printer. Support of virtual devices is called *spooling*, after Simultaneous Peripheral Operation On-Line. The purpose of a spooling system is to permit the apparent concurrent sharing of devices that are only sequentially sharable. Almost all multi-user computer systems support spooling.

14.7.3 I/O Channels

In large systems, the CPU is not burdened with handling I/O related tasks. Instead, responsibility for device control is delegated to I/O processors, also known as *I/O channels*. An I/O channel is a programmable processor; the programs that it executes are called *channel programs*. These programs specify the operations required for device accesses and control the communication paths. The file system has routines that are used to drive the I/O channels.

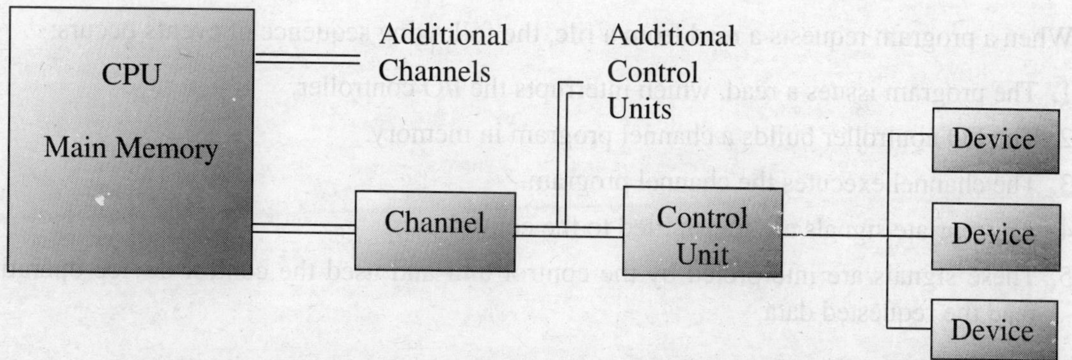

Figure 14.2: Block diagram of a computer system with I/O channels

14.7.3.1 Types of I/O Channels

The different I/O channels can be classified as

- ***Selector channel*** – it can manage data transfer between main memory and only one device at a time. Since channels are fast processors, selector channels are usually used only with high-speed devices such as disks. Putting a relatively slow device such as terminal on a selector channel will waste the channel's processing power.
- ***Multiplexer channel*** – it can manage data transfer between main memory and several devices. Multiplexer channels are more effective with slow devices. With multiplexer channel, several devices can be active simultaneously, but the channel must complete the channel program before it starts the program for other.
- ***Block multiplexer channel*** – it can interleave the data transfer to multiple devices. A block multiplexer channel can execute one instruction of the channel program for one device then it switches to execute an instruction of the channel program for another device.

14.7.3.2 Channel Activities

Now we know that a channel is an intermediary between *CPU-main memory-secondary storage devices*. The CPU communicates with a channel via some simple commands. A representative channel would respond to instructions such as

- ***Test I/O*** – to determine whether or not the communication path to the addressed device is busy.
- ***Start I/O*** – to start I/O activity.
- ***Halt I/O*** – to terminate I/O activity.

A channel commonly communicates with CPU through interrupts. An interrupt would be used when an error is detected, *e.g.*, invalid CPU command, or when an I/O activity is completed. When an interrupt occurs, control branches to an interrupt handler routine, which determines what caused the interrupt, perform appropriate actions, then returns control to the caller.

14.7.4 Processing a Read Operation

When a program requests a read from a file, the following sequence of events occurs:

1. The program issues a read, which interrupts the I/O controller.
2. The I/O controller builds a channel program in memory.
3. The channel executes the channel program.
4. Appropriate signals are transmitted to the control unit.
5. These signals are interpreted by the control unit and used the control device operations to read the requested data.

6. The requested data flows from the device along the communication path to the file's buffer area in the program's memory space.
7. The channel issues an interrupt to signal continuation of the program's execution.
8. Control returns to the program.

Note that the data is read into the buffer, which is an area of main memory reserved to hold data for this file. When the buffer is full, the program can begin to use the data.

14.7.5 Processing a Write Operation

When a program requests a write to a file, the following sequence of events occurs:

1. The program issues a write, which interrupts the I/O controller.
2. The I/O controller builds a channel program in memory.
3. The channel executes the channel program.
4. Appropriate signals are transmitted to the control unit.
5. These signals are interpreted by the control unit and used the control device operations to write the requested data.
6. The requested data flows from the file's buffer area in the program's memory space to the device along the communication path.
7. The channel issues an interrupt to signal continuation of the program's execution.
8. Control returns to the program.

14.7.6 Blocking Records

The most commonly used technique to reduce a program's device access is to block records such that multiple records are read/written in a single device access. If there are *n* records per block, then only every *n*th read by the program causes a device access.

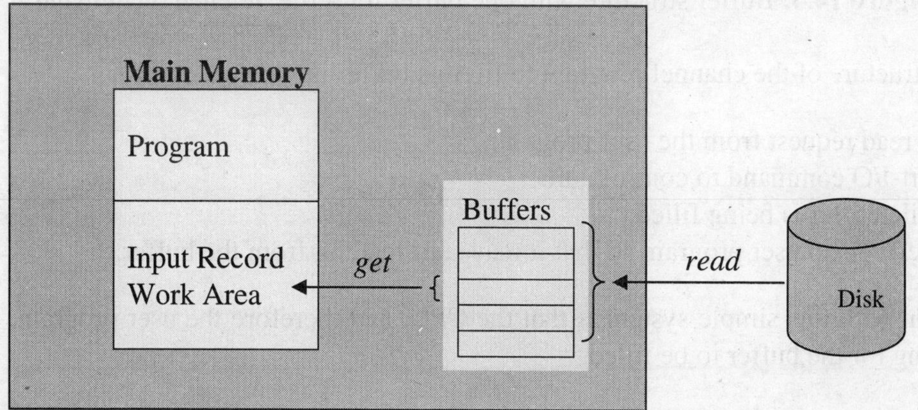

Figure 14.3: Device access with blocked records

Commonly, a program's read command is translated to a *get* instruction by the file system. The channel program then converts the *get* instruction to a device read if the buffer is empty, causing the buffer to be filled. The program's *get* instruction procures the next record from the buffer.

The buffer provides the holding area required to interface relatively slow storage devices with much faster CPU. It also provides the holding area that makes blocking of records feasible. Large blocking factors can be important to the performance of files that are accessed sequentially. Every record on the file will be accessed; so as many records as possible should be procured at once. However, the cost of a large block size is the cost of additional main memory required.

14.7.7 Managing Buffers

We will now consider several approaches to management of buffers.

14.7.7.1 Single Buffering

The structure of a buffer in a simple system in which there is one record per block and one buffer per file, and where the buffer is filled on demand from a program. The buffer structure includes a pointer to the starting address of the channel program for file's current operation.

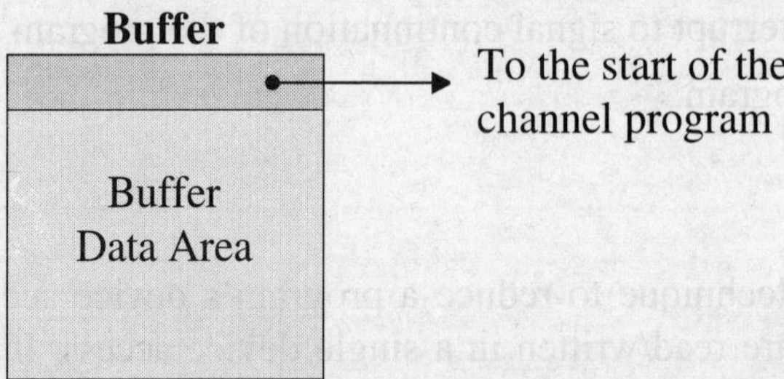

Figure 14.4: Buffer structure with one buffer for a file, fetched on demand.

The basic structure of the channel program to fill this buffer is

- Wait for read request from the user program.
- Issue start-I/O command to control unit.
- Wait while buffer is being filled.
- Issue interrupts to user program so that it may start reading from the buffer.

The problem with this simple system is that the CPU, and therefore the user program, sits idle while waiting for the buffer to be filled.

14.7.7.2 Anticipatory Buffering

Anticipatory buffering, also known as *prefetching*, removes the problem of potential wait of CPU where the file system attempts to anticipate the program's need for data. It tries to keep the buffer always full, so that the data is already there when the user program issues a read instruction. The objective of anticipatory approach is to keep the CPU from having to wait.

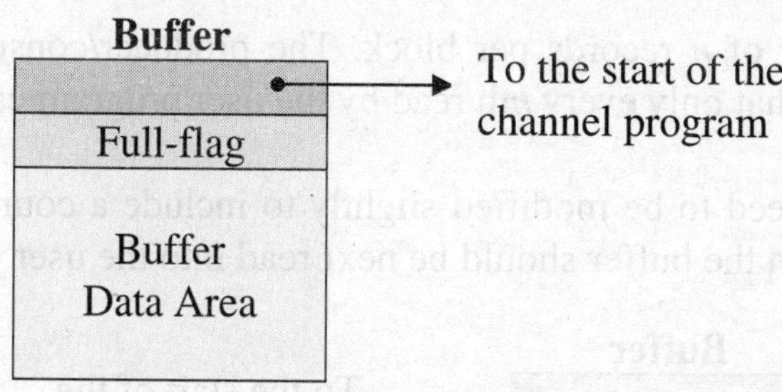

Figure 14.5: Buffer structure with one buffer for the file and prefetching.

where *Full-Flag* = 0 if the buffer is empty,
= 1 if the buffer is full.

Anticipatory buffering requires slight modification of the buffer's structure to include a flag that indicates whether or not the buffer is full. The channel program keeps testing this flag. If the buffer becomes empty because the user program has read its contents, the flag is reset and the channel program initiates refill of the buffer.

For anticipatory buffering, two routines are required – one for filling the buffer called a *producer*, and the second for emptying the buffer called *consumer*. For an input file, the producer is the channel program and the consumer is the user program. For an output file, the producer is the user program and the consumer is the channel program.

The basic structure of the producer routine for input file is

```
Loop: if Full-flag = 1 then
         goto Loop
      else
         Issue start-I/O command to control unit
         Wait while buffer is being filled
         Set Full-flag = 1
         goto Loop
      endif
```

The basic structure of the consumer routine for input file is

```
Wait: if Full-flag = 0 then
         goto Wait
      else
         Read the buffer contents into the record work area
```

```
        Set Full-flag = 0
        goto Wait
    endif
```

Initially, *Full-flag* = 0,causing the channel program to fill the buffer.

14.7.7.3 Buffering with Blocks

Consider a blocking factor of *n* records per block. The producer/consumer routines must be changed to reflect the fact that only every *n*th read by the user program causes a device access.

The buffer structure also need to be modified slightly to include a counter that keeps track of which record of *n* records in the buffer should be next read into the user program's record work area.

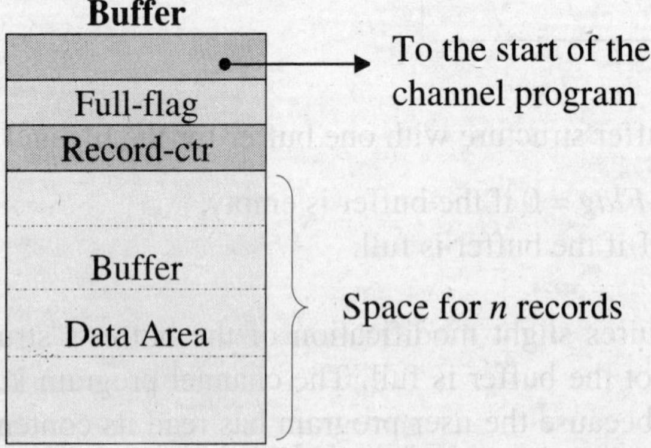

Figure 14.6: Buffer structure with *n* records per block

where *Full-Flag* = 0 if the buffer is empty,
= 1 if the buffer is full.

Record-ctr = 1, 2, 3, …, *n*

The producer routine for input file modified slightly as

```
Loop: if Full-flag = 1 then
        goto Loop
    else
        Issue start-I/O command to control unit
        Wait while buffer is being filled
        Set Record-ctr = 1
        Set Full-flag = 1
        goto Loop
    endif
```

The consumer routine for input file is changed bit more

```
Wait: if Full-flag = 0 then
        goto Wait
    else
        Read record (Record-ctr) into the record work area
```

```
        Set Record-ctr = Record-ctr + 1
        if Record-ctr > n then
            Set Full-flag = 0
        endif
        goto Wait
    endif
```

Initially, *Full-flag* = 0. The programmer's consumer routine is in the wait state between read operations, but the program itself can be executing other instructions. Does the program ever have to wait because the buffer is empty? Yes, it waits for every *n*th record. While the buffer is in the state of being emptied by a consumer, a producer also cannot be filling it.

14.7.7.4 Double Buffering

In order to reduce the probability of user program waiting, double buffering is commonly used. Two buffers instead of one are assigned for each file. The basic idea of double buffering is that while consumer is emptying one of the buffers, the producer can be filling the other one. By the time first buffer is emptied, the second should be full. The consumer can then empty the second while the producer fills the first, and so forth. The buffer structure for double buffering now includes a pointer to the other buffer.

Two auxiliary pointers are used for following purposes:

- *Pfill* pointer, which points to the next buffer to be filled or being filled.
- *Pempty* pointer, which points to the next buffer to be emptied or being emptied.

The producer fills the buffer that is pointed to by pointer *Pfill*, which initially should point to buffer 1. Initially, *Full-flags* of both buffers should be 0, since they are both empty.

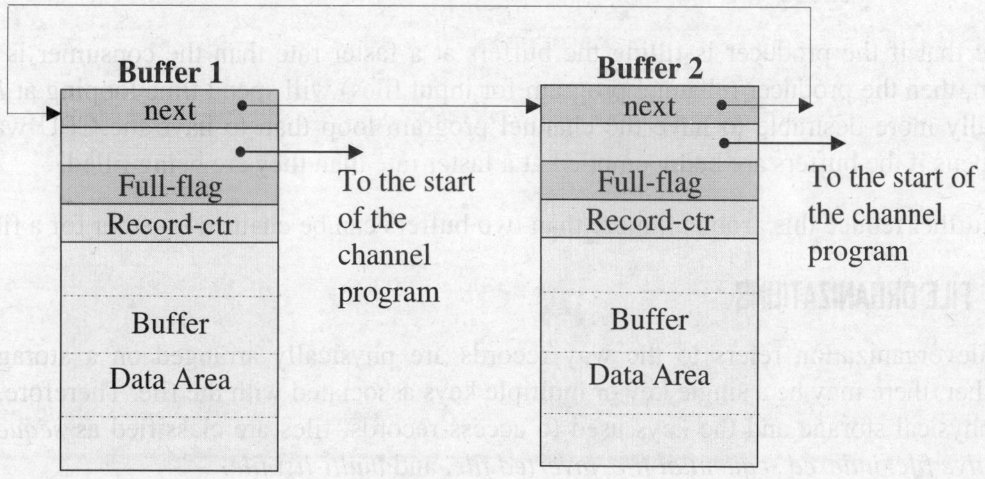

Figure 14.7: Buffer structure for double buffering

where *Full-Flag* = 0 if the buffer is empty or is being filled,
= 1 if the buffer is full or is being emptied;

Record-ctr = 1, 2, 3, …, *n*

The producer routine for input file is

```
Loop: if Pfill->Full-flag = 1 then
        goto Loop
      else
        Issue start-I/O command to control unit
        Wait while Pfill->buffer is being filled
        Set Pfill->Record-ctr = 1
        Set Pfill->Full-flag = 1
        Set Pfill = Pfill->next
        goto Loop
      endif
```

The consumer empties the buffer that is pointed to by pointer *Pempty*, which initially should point to buffer 1.

The consumer routine for input file is changed bit more

```
Wait: if Pempty->Full-flag = 0 then
        goto Wait
      else
        Read record (Pempty->Record-ctr) into
             the record work area
        Set Pempty->Record-ctr = Pempty->Record-ctr + 1
        if Pempty->Record-ctr > n then
           Set Pempty->Full-flag = 0
           Set Pempty = Pempty->next
        endif
        goto Wait
      endif
```

Note that if the producer is filling the buffers at a faster rate than the consumer is emptying them, then the producer (channel program for input files) will spend time looping at *Loop*. It is usually more desirable to have the channel program loop than to have the CPU wait, which happens if the buffers are being emptied at a faster rate than they are being filled.

To further reduce this problem, more than two buffers can be chained together for a file.

14.8 FILE ORGANIZATIONS

A file organization refers to the way records are physically arranged on a storage device. Further, there may be a single key or multiple keys associated with the file. Therefore, based on its physical storage and the keys used to access records, files are classified as *sequential file*, *relative file*, *indexed sequential file*, *inverted file*, and *multi-list file*.

Figure 14.8 shows the distinction between different files organizations based on the number of access keys.

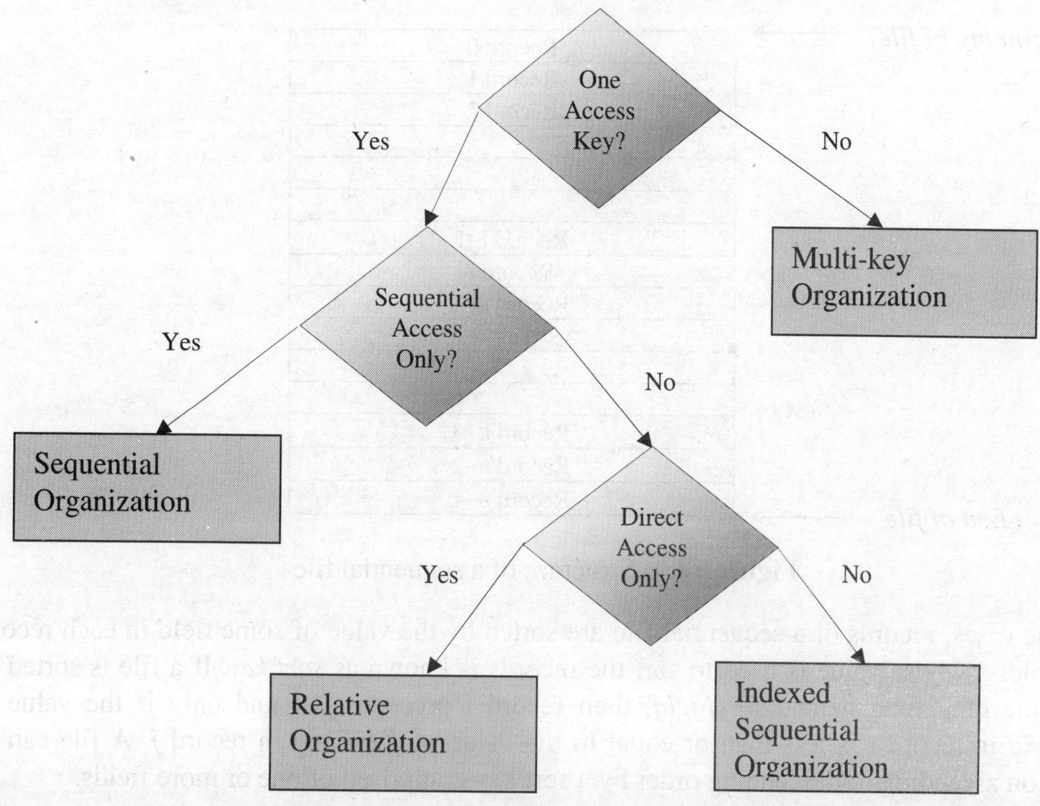

Figure 14.8: Distinguishing different file organizations

Factors that influence the choice of particular file organization for given applications are as follows:

- Economy of storage
- Convenience of updates
- Ease of retrieval
- Reliability
- Security
- Integrity

14.8.1 Sequential File Organization

The most basic way to organize a collection of records in a file is to use sequential organization. In sequential organized files, the records are written one after the other in order when the file is created and can be accessed only in that order in which they are written when the file is used for input. Figure 14.9 shows the structure of a sequential file. Note that records are numbered from 0 onwards. Therefore, if there are *n* records in a file, the first record will be numbered 0 and the last record will be numbered $n-1$.

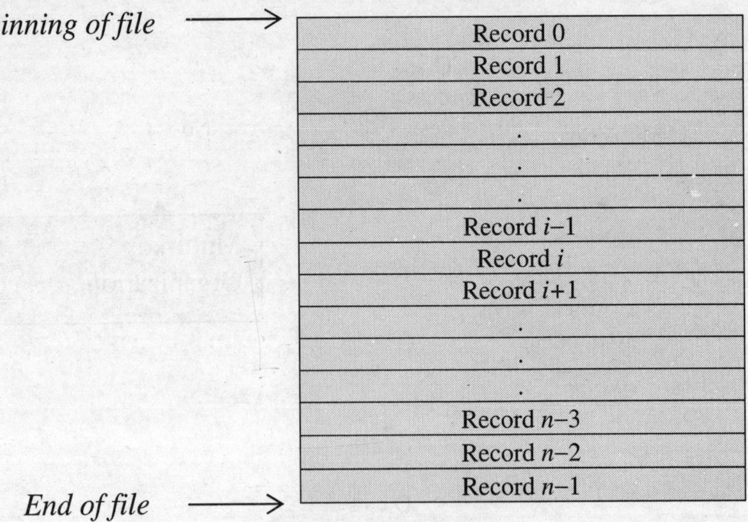

Figure 14.9: Structure of a sequential file

In some cases, records of a sequential file are sorted by the value of some field in each record. The field(s) whose value is used to sort the records is known as *sort key*. If a file is sorted by the value of a field named *KeyField*, then record *i* precedes *j* if and only if the value of *KeyField* in record *i* is less than or equal to the value of *KeyField* in record *j*. A file can be sorted on ascending or descending order by a sort key comprised of one or more fields.

Processing requirements determine the appropriate order for sorting the records of a sequential file. For example, the records of a sequential file used to generate the white pages of a telephone directory would be sorted by subscriber's last name (surname), because this is the required ordering for the report.

Information systems that are built around sequential files tend to replicate records across files that are in different sort orders. Usually not all of the files are retained; many are considered to be temporary and are deleted after a program has used them. For example, a payroll system generate a variety of reports; some would order the same pay data by employee social security number, some by source account number, some by cheque number, some by bank account number, and so on.

Because the records of a sequential file can only be accessed sequentially (serially), sequential files are used more commonly in batch processing than in interactive processing.

14.8.1.1 Advantages

- Easy to handle.
- Involve no overhead.
- Can be stored on tapes as well as disks.
- Well suited for batch-oriented applications.
- Records in a sequential file can be of varying lengths.

14.8.1.2 Disadvantages

- Records can only be accessed in sequence.
- Does not support updation operation in place.
- Does not support interactive applications.

14.8.2 Relative File Organization

Relative file organization provides an effective way to access individual records directly. In a relative file organization there is a predictable relationship between the key and the record's location in the file. However, it is important to note that the logical ordering of records bears no relationship to their physical sequencing. The records do not necessarily appear physically in sorted order by their keys. Then how a given record is found? The answer is that when a relative file is established, the relationship that will be used to translate between key value and the physical address is designated.

This relationship, say *R*, is a mapping function

R(key value) → address

from key values to addresses in a file.

Key value		Physical Position
Key_1	....	1
Key_2	....	2
Key_3	....	3
Key_4	....	4
Key_4	....	5
Key_6	....	6
.	.	.
.	.	.
.	.	.
Key_n	....	*n*

Figure 14.10: Basic relative file organization

When a record is to be written into a relative file, the mapping function *R* is used to translate the record's key to an address, which indicates where the record is to be stored. When the record for a particular key is to be retrieved, the mapping functions *R* is applied to that key value, translating it to the address where the record can be found. Thus, the predictable relationship between record's key values and record's storage locations is used both when a record is stored and when it is retrieved.

A relative file can also be accessed sequentially, but in that case the keys may not be in logical sequence. The relative file might be accessed serially when input to a sort/merge utility. A program while generating mailing labels for each customer might also access a relative file serially. Here it must be noted that the order in which mailing labels are generated is immaterial.

The fundamental techniques used for mapping function *R* are – directory lookup and address calculation (Hashing).

14.8.2.1 Directory Lookup Techniques

The simplest technique for implementing a mapping function *R* is directory lookup. The basic idea of directory lookup technique is to keep a directory of *key value*:*address* pairs. In order to find a record in a relative file, one locates its key value in the directory and then the indicated address is used to find the record on storage device.

In the simplest form, the directory is implemented as an array of *key value*:*address* pairs. Here the directory entries are sorted by key value so that a binary search can be applied to search a key value rapidly.

Alternatively, the directory can be organized as binary search tree.

14.8.2.2 Address Calculation Techniques

Another common technique for implementing a mapping function *R* is to perform a calculation (hashing) on the key value such that the result is a relative address. The basic idea of address calculation is to apply a function that translates a relatively large domain of possible key values to a relatively small range of relative address values. One potential problem with this technique is that a mapping function may not be one-to-one, *i.e.*, the calculated address may not be unique. This situation, where

$$R(key_1) = R(key_2) \quad \text{for} \quad key_1 \neq key_2$$

is called a *collision*, .*i.e.*, two unequal keys have been calculated to have the same address. These keys are called *synonyms*.

Just as there are many address calculation techniques (hashing functions), there are variety of collision resolution techniques. All these techniques have been discussed in *Chapter 12*.

14.8.2.3 Advantages

- Records can be accessed out-of-sequence, randomly.
- Well suited for interactive (on-line) applications.
- Support updation operation in place.

14.8.2.4 Disadvantages

- Can only be stored on disks.
- Involve more overhead in the form of maintenance of indexes.
- Handling bit complex as compared to sequential files.
- Records can only be of fixed length.

14.8.3 Indexed Sequential File Organization

Indexed sequential file organization is an effective way of organizing the records when there is need both to access sequentially by some key value and also to access the records individually by the same key. An indexed sequential file provides the combination of access types that are supported by a sequential file and a relative file.

One way to think of a structure as indexed sequential file is an index with pointers in a sequential file as shown in Figure 14.11.

Index has been structured as a binary search tree. This index is used to service a request for access to a particular record and the sequential data file alone is used to support sequential access to the entire collection of records.

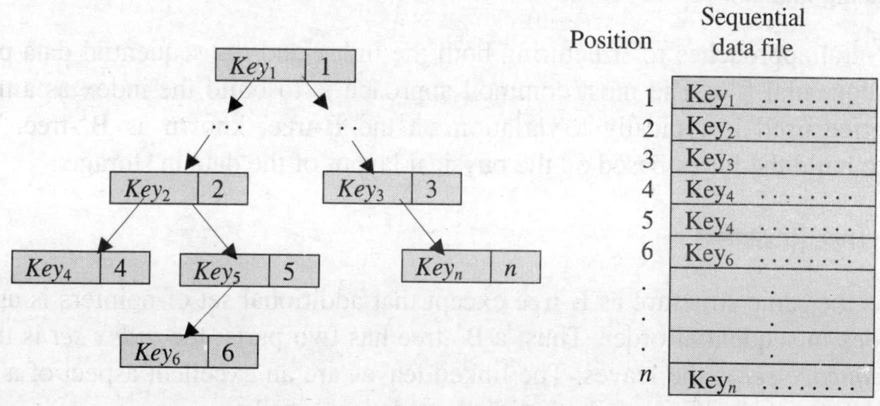

Figure 14.11: Use of a binary search tree and a sequential file to provide indexed sequential access

Because of its capability to support both sequential and direct access, indexed sequential file organization is used frequently to support applications that require both batch and interactive processing.

For example, consider a credit card billing system with an indexed master file of customer account information. An appropriate key for the file would be would be the account number. The file could be accessed in batch mode to generate customer invoices and to build summary reports of accounts activity on monthly basis. Each record will be accessed once in this processing. The bills and the details on the summary report will appear in account number sequence. On the other hand, the credit card management agency wants to use the master file of account information to support interactive inquiry of the current credit status of any account. When a customer makes a purchase, the master file will be consulted to determine the credit limit and then update the credit amount. This kind of processing cannot be supported by sequential access to master file instead the need to access an individual account dictates the use of the index of the index sequential file organization.

14.8.3.1 Advantages

- Records can be accessed sequentially and randomly.
- Supports interactive as well as batch-oriented applications.
- Support updation operation in place.

14.8.3.2 Disadvantages

- Can only be stored on disks.
- Involve more overhead in the form of maintenance of indexes.
- Handling bit complex as compared to sequential files.
- Records can only be of fixed length.

14.8.3.3 Handling Indexes

There are several approaches to structuring both the index and the sequential data portions of an indexed sequential file. The most common approach is to build the index as a tree of key values. The tree used is typically a variation on the B-tree, known as B^+-tree. The other approach is to build the index based on the physical layout of the data in storage.

14.8.3.3.1 B^+-Tree Revisited

A B^+-tree has the same structure as B-tree except that additional set of pointers is used to link the leave nodes in sequential order. Thus, a B^+-tree has two parts: the *index set* is the interior nodes; the *sequence set* is the leaves. The linked leaves are an excellent aspect of a B^+-tree as the keys can be accessed efficiently both directly and sequentially.

14.8.3.3.1.1 Inserting a New Key into a B^+-tree

Inserting a new key into a B^+-tree is done in almost the same way as insertion of a new key into a B-tree. When a leaf node is split into two nodes, a copy of low-order key value from the rightmost node is promoted to be the separator key value in the parent node. The new node also must be inserted in the linked list of the sequence set.

14.8.3.3.1.2 Deleting a Key from a B^+-tree

Deleting a key from a B^+-tree is somewhat easier as compared to B-tree. When a key value is deleted from a leaf, there is not need to delete that key from the index of the tree. The key value still can direct searches to the proper leaves.

14.8.3.3.1.3 Searching a B^+-tree

A search in a B^+-tree terminates in a node in the sequence set. If there is a key in the index that matches the sought key, the preceding pointer is followed until the correct leaf is reached. Note that not every key in the index set need to appear in the sequence set, since the deleted keys are retained in the index set.

A B^+-tree provides as good performance as B-tree of same order. The maximum height of B^+-tree of order m with n keys is $[\log_{1/2m}((n+1)/2)]$.

Sequential access to the records indexed by a B^+-tree is provided by scanning the keys in the sequence set. Typically, in an indexed sequential file, the sequence set contains not only keys, but also the corresponding data records.

14.8.4 Multi-key File Organizations

There may be some applications that require support for multi-key files. As an example, consider a banking system in which there are several types of users – *tellers*, *loan officers*, *branch managers*, *bank officers*, *account holders*, and so forth. All these users need to access the same data in different ways. Consider the following record format:

ACCOUNT

ID	NAME		GROUP-CODE		SOCNO	BALANCE	OVERDRAFT LIMIT
	LAST	FIRST	BRANCH	TYPE			
...	...	...	...	...	...	...	...

Figure 14.13: Example record format

A teller might identify an account record by its ID value. A loan officer may need to access all records with a given value of OVERDRAFT LIMIT or all records for a given value of SOCNO. A branch manager might access records by the GROUP-CODE. An account holder might want to access his/her own account by giving ID number or a combination of NAME, SOCNO and TYPE.

One possible approach to support all these types of access is to use several files, each one organized to serve one type of request. This approach will lead to duplication of lot of data that is not desirable as it will not only lead to wastage of secondary storage but also may cause inconsistencies. A multi-key file that uses indexes provides an efficient solution to this multi-path retrieval problem. A multi-key file organization has only one data file and set of indexes to provide different access paths to data records of the file. We have already seen that an index can be structured in several ways, for exampie as a table, a binary search tree, a B-tree, B^*-tree or B^+-tree.

In this section, we will discuss following multi-key file organizations:

- Inverted file organization
- Multi-list organization

14.8.4.1 Inverted File Organization

One fundamental approach to providing a linkage between an index and a file is called *inversion*. A key's *inversion index* contains all the values that the key presently has in the records of the file. Each key-value entry in the inversion index points to all data records that have the corresponding value. The file is said to be inverted on that key.

The inversion approach to providing multi-key access has been used as the basis for physical data structures in commercially available relational DBMS, such as IBM's DB2, Oracle Inc.'s ORACLE and Relational Technology's INGRES. These systems were designed to provide rapid access to records via as many inversion keys as the designer cares to identify. They have user-friendly, natural-language-like query languages to assist the user in formulating enquiries.

A *completely inverted file* has an inversion index for every data field. If a file is not completely inverted but has at least one inversion index, it is said to be a *partially inverted file*.

14.8.4.2 Multi-List Organization

The other approach to providing a linkage between an index and a file is called *multi-list organization*. Like an inverted file, a multi-list file maintains an index or each secondary key. There is one entry in the secondary key's index for each value that the secondary key presently has in the file. However, the multi-list organization differs from inversion in that sense that entry in the inversion index for a key value has a pointer to each data record with that key value, the entry in the multi-list index for a key has just one pointer to the first record with that key value, which in turn points to the next record with that key value, and so forth. Thus, there is a linked list of records for each value of the secondary key. Multi-list chains usually are bi-directional and occasionally are circular to improve update performance.

The multi-list organization approach to providing multi-key access has been used as the basis for physical data structures in many commercially available hierarchical and network DBMS, such as CODASYL family of systems, Cincom's TOTAL, and IBM's IMS.

There are two variations to basic multi-list structure. These are

- ***Controlled-length multi-list*** – a maximum length is imposed upon the linked list of the data records. If more data records than length allows possess the secondary-key value, then the key value would appear more than once in the index and there would be more than one linked list of data records with that value.
- ***Cellular multi-list*** – the list structures are determined in part by the characteristics of storage. For example, a cell could be defined as a cylinder, as a track, or as a page. A linked list is not allowed to cross cell- boundaries. If there are records in three cylinders that have the same secondary-key value, then there would be three index entries and three linked lists for that value. This multi-list variation can be useful in reducing disk arm movement requirements and I/O accesses.

14.9 EXTERNAL SORTING

External sort also called *file sort*, deals with sorting the data stored in data files. This technique is used when the volume of the data is very large and cannot be held in computer's main memory. For example, consider a file of 4000 records that must be sorted, and further consider that only 2000 such records can be held in main memory at once. One approach to sort this file is to sort, using an internal sort algorithm, separately two subsets of the file — records 1-2000 and records 2001-4000.

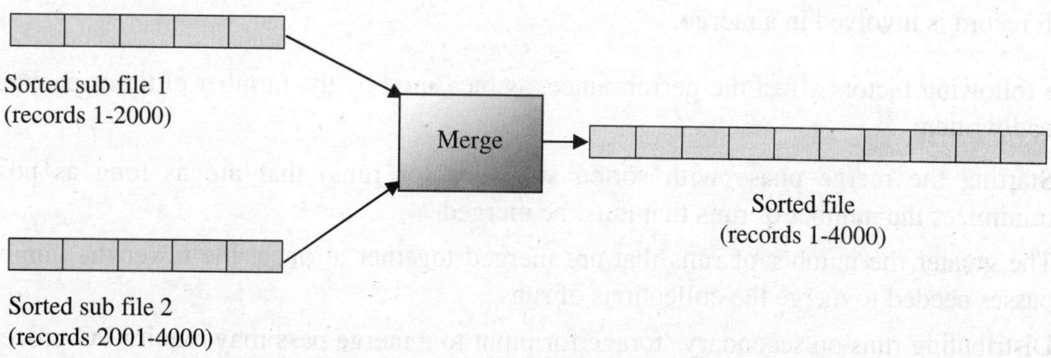

Figure 14.14: Natural merge of two sorted lists

The output from each internal sort is a file containing a sorted sub file. Then these sorted sub files can be merged. The merge involves pair-wise comparison of the next record's key in each of the two sorted sub files. Whichever record has the lower key value (if sort is for ascending order) is the next record to be written to the merged file.

14.9.1 Phases of External Sorting

An external sort has following three phases:

1. ***Internal sort phase*** – which sorts the records into several runs distributed on two or more storage devices.
2. ***Merge phase*** – which combines the sorted runs in to a single file.
3. ***Output phase*** – which copies the sorted file onto its final storage device.

The different external sort techniques differ from each other in the following ways:

1. The internal sort technique used.
2. The amount of main memory space allocated to the internal sort.
3. The distribution of sorted sub files on secondary storage.
4. The number of sorted sub files that are merged together in one merge pass.

Given a file to be sorted, these parameters then determine the number of sorted sub files generated by the internal sort phase and the number of merge phases.

14.9.2 Performance of External Sort

While evaluating the performance of internal sort techniques, we considered the number of comparisons performed to sort *n* items. But this measure to evaluate the performance of external sort techniques is inappropriate, because the CPU time required for comparison is negligible as compared to the I/O time required to access the secondary storage in reading and writing files. Thus, the external sort techniques are compared by their relative frequencies of references to secondary storage. One good measure of this frequency is the number of times each record is involved in a merge.

The following factors affect the performance, as measured by the number of times each record is read/written:

1. Starting the merge phase with sorted sub files (or runs) that are as long as possible minimizes the number of runs that must be merged.
2. The greater the number of runs that are merged together at once, the fewer the number of passes needed to merge the collections of runs.
3. Distributing runs on secondary storage for input to a merge pass may require I/O processing in addition to that actually required in performing the merge.

14.9.3 Types of Merges

As for as internal sorting of sub files is concerned, any of the internal sort techniques, discussed in *Chapter 13*, can be used. In this section, we will look at the ways the sorted sub files can be handled in the merge phase. Following are different ways to handle merge phase:

- Natural merge
- Balanced merge
- Polyphase merge
- Cascade merge

14.9.3.1 Natural Merge

A merge that handles two input files at once is called a *two-way* merge; a merge that handles three input files at once is called a *three-way* merge; and so on. In general, a merge that handles *M* input files at once is called *M-way* merge, where *M* is referred to as the *degree* of merge.

Thus, an *M-way natural merge* is defined as a merge with *M* input files and just one output file.

14.9.3.2 Balanced Merge

Nearly half the I/O activity of a natural merge is devoted to redistributing newly merged runs output from one pass onto multiple files in preparation for input to the next pass. The I/O requirements of a natural merge can be reduced by using a *balanced merge*.

A balanced merge avoids much of this copying of records back and forth by distributing the results of a merge pass directly onto the appropriate number of files for input to the next merge pass. By contrast, a natural merge distributes all its output merge runs onto a single file. An *M*-way natural merge uses *M*+1 files, while an *M*-way balanced merge uses 2*M* files. In a balanced merge, the data are moved back and forth between equal number of input and output files.

14.9.3.3 Polyphase Merge

We have seen that an *M*-way balanced merge uses 2*M* files. At any given time, runs are being read from *M* files and being written on one file. Thus, *M*-1 files are always idle. Thus unbalancing this merge can result in better file use. These unbalanced merges attempt to achieve a merge power greater than M by reading from more than M files at a time, using upto 2*M*-1 input files and a single output file.

One type of unbalanced merge is *polyphase merge*, in which a constant number of input files are used. An *M-way polyphase merge* used 2*M*-1 input files.

14.9.3.4 Cascade Merge

Another type of unbalanced merge that attempts to reduce the copying of records is called the *cascade merge*. A cascade merge of degree *M* uses 2*M*-1, then 2*M*-2, then 2*M*-3, . . ., the two input files during the various phases of a merge pass. Like a polyphase merge, a cascade merge relies on a clever initial distribution of the runs by the internal phase.

Each merge pass begins with a merge from 2*M*-1 input files to one output files. When the first input file is emptied, it becomes the output file, and the prior output file is set aside. Now 2*M*-2 input files are merged onto the new output file. As an input file is emptied, it becomes the output file and the prior output file is retired temporarily. Eventually, all input files will be emptied. At the end of the merge pass, each record has been processed once.

Then the next merge pass starts. The 2*M*-1 input are merged, then 2*M*-2, and so on until the cycles of merge phases have been completed.

14.10 DATABASE SYSTEMS

Just as a file system relieves the application programmer from dealing with directories, devices, channels and buffers, a *Data Base Management System* (DBMS) further raises the level of interface provided for the application programmer.

A typical file-oriented information system is depicted in Figure 14.15. Each application program owns its own set of files and uses file-system services to access these files.

In many situations, the data that are required to support one application is also required by another application. Sometimes both application programs expect the same format and organization but sometimes they do not. The result is replication (duplication) of data across multiple files, for use with different application programs. Data duplication is not attractive as it causes inconsistency problems and wastage of storage space. In addition, it will be difficult to correlate and integrate data across application programs. As an example to illustrate these problems, consider a sales manager's request for a graph that correlates sales person's salaries versus their revenue-generate-to-date figures. It is most likely that sales person's salaries are stored in a payroll master file, and the revenue related data is stored in accounts-receivable master file. Although the required data exist, it will be quite difficult task to overcome data formats, coding, and organization incompatibilities to be able to respond to the request.

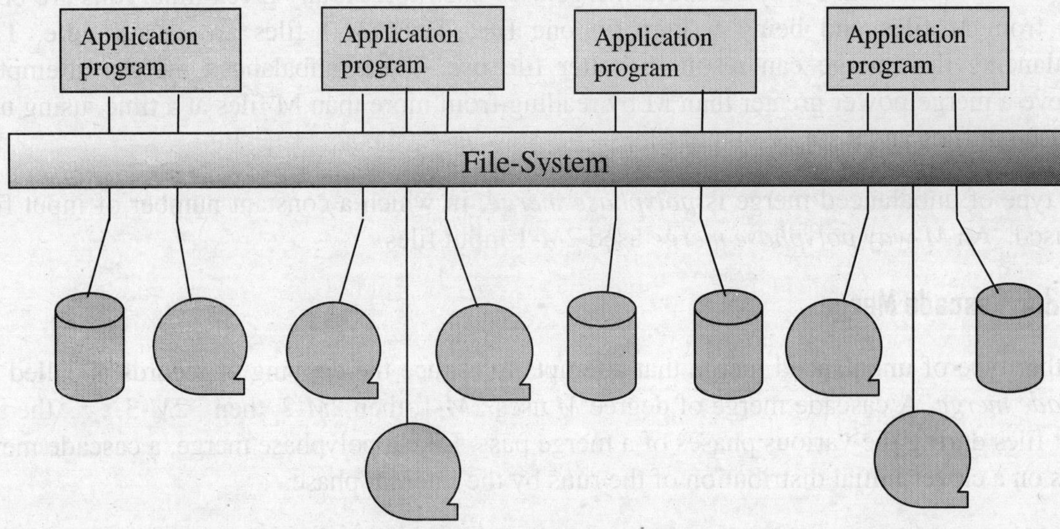

Figure 14.15: Application programs using file system directly

A *database* is a collection of logically related data that supports shared access by multiple end users and application programs. In contrast to a file that contains data about one type of entity (such as personnel, orders, customers, sales, etc.), a database contains data about multiple entities and the information about how these entities are logically related to each other. Further, the data is integrated and there are multiple access paths provided through the data. A typical database-oriented information system is depicted in Figure 14.16.

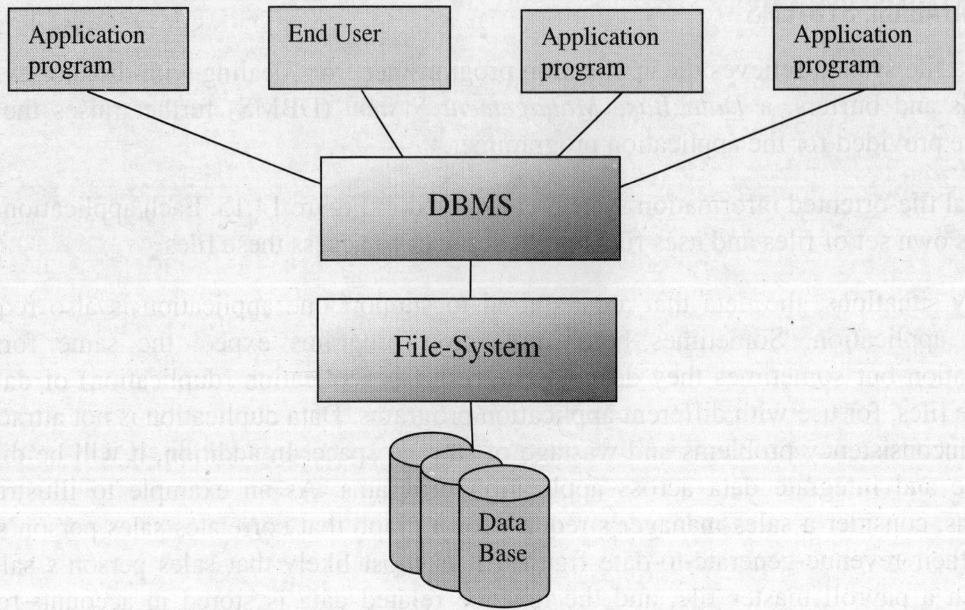

Figure 14.16: Application programs using DBMS services

A DBMS provides services necessary for controlling shared access to the files that comprise the database. Application programs use DBMS services while the DBMS uses the file-system services. A database typically is structured physically using the file organization techniques.

A DBMS also provides services for

- Defining, representing, and storing data so that it can be accessed later.
- Organizing data so that it can be accessed selectively and efficiently.
- Interfacing with users in a way that effectively support the user's decision-making environments.
- Protecting the data including security, integrity, recovery, shared access control.

The DBMS maintains a stored description of the database structure and its contents. An application program need not recode these descriptions. The DBMS manages the internal implementation of the data and the application program need not maintain indexes and access paths. The DBMS provides appropriate interface facilities for users that are natural, easy-to-learn in the form of query languages and report writers for non-computer users and procedural languages for application programmers. The DBMS also provides access control, backup, concurrency and integrity protection. Therefore, an application programmer need not build this functionality in each new program developed.

The market for DBMS products is well established, especially for supporting Decision Support Systems (DSS) and On-Line Transaction Processing (OLTP) (like banking, airline and railway reservations, super markets, etc.). Whereas a file system is always provided as part of the operating system, the DBMS may be provided by the same vendor or may be acquired from third party.

REVIEW EXERCISES

1. Explain with the help of example the usefulness of files.
2. Describe the terms — *field*, *record*, *file organization*, *key*, and *index*.
3. What are the different attributes of a file?
4. Describe are the files classified?
5. How are multi-key files different from other files?
6. What are the different operations performed on files?
7. Discuss the different single-key file organizations, and also give their relative merits and demerits.
8. What is a blocking? How is it useful?
9. What is a buffer? How is it useful? Describe various buffer management techniques.
10. What is the purpose served by a file system?
11. What is a channel? What are various types of channels?
12. Draw a block diagram of computer system with an I/O channel.
13. Describe the different multi-key file organizations.

14. What is an external sort? What are the factors on which the performance of an external sort depends?
15. What are the different phases of an external sort?
16. What is a buffer? How is it useful? Describe various buffer management techniques.
17. Describe the various types of merges.
18. Compare and contrast between a file-oriented system and database-oriented system?
19. Consider an application that maintains a class records system in an academic institute. The requirements for this system include the following:
    - Print the mailing address of all students.
    - Compute the average age of students.
    - Compute the mean and standard deviation for student's grade point averages.
    - Display the grade record for a particular system.
    - Insert a record for a new system.
    - Update the record of a particular student.
    - Delete the record for a particular student who has withdrawn from the institute.

    What type of file organization will be most suitable to support the above application? Justify your answer.

❑ ❑ ❑

Glossary

Absolute Addressing - A technique for mapping records to storage where the key value is the record's actual address. See ***relative addressing***.

Access Mechanism - The means for reading and/or writing data from and/or to a storage device.

Access Time - Time a computer takes to locate and transfer data to or from storage. It includes seek time and transfer time.

Activity Graph - A graph representing the precedence required and parallelism possible among set of activities or task; often the nodes of the graph represent the activities and the edges represent precedence requirements.

Acyclic Graph - A graph that has no cycles.

Adjacency List - The adjacency-list is used to represent of a graph $G = (V, E)$, where V is the set of vertices and E is the set of edges of the graph. It consists of an array oflinked lists, one for each vertex in V. For each vertex, the adjacency list contains all the vertices that are adjacent to it. The vertices in each adjacency list are stored in an arbitrary order.

Adjacency Matrix - A matrix A used to represent the structure of a graph $G = (V, E)$, where V is the set of vertices and E is the set of edges of the graph. The element $a_{ij} = 1$ if and only if edge (v_i, v_j) ε E, and 0 otherwise.

Algorithm - A step-by-step procedure, written in a human-oriented language, to solve a particular problem.

American Standard Code for Information Interchange (ASCII) - Acronym for, a 7-bit character-encoding scheme developed as a standard for data transmission and now widely used for data representation.

Anticipatory Buffering - A buffer management technique where data is read into a buffer before it is requested by a program. Compare with ***demand buffering***.

Array - A collection of homogeneous data elements referred to by a common name where individual elements are accessed using a subscript.

AVL Tree - A height-balanced binary tree where for each node *R* of the tree, the height of the left subtree of *R* and height of the right subtree *R* differ by at most 1.

B-Tree - A B-tree of order *m* is an *m*-way such that each node, except the root and leaves, has at least $\lceil 1/(2m) \rceil$ subtrees and no more that *m* subtrees; the root has at least two subtrees, unless it is itself a leaf; and all leaves are on the same level.

B*-Tree - A special case of B-tree in which each node is at least two-thirds full instead of at least one-half full.

B$^+$-Tree - A tree resembling a B-tree in which there is linked list connecting leaf nodes. When used as an index, indexed key values appear in the leaf nodes; the interior nodes provide relatively direct access to the leaf nodes.

Balanced Merge - A merge technique that uses an equal number of input devices and output devices.

Base Address - The starting address of a data structure.

Batch Processing - Batch processing, as the name implies, involves the collection of transactions into groups (batches), which are subsequently processed at some specific type. The time of processing is predetermined and depends mainly on the operational role of the batch of transactions within the organization, which can be hourly, daily, weekly or monthly, etc.

Binary Search - A search technique that is applied to a list of ordered keys. At each step of the search, the list is partitioned into two equal parts, with the selection of the appropriate partition to probe in the next iteration made on the basis of relative key values.

Binary Search Tree - A binary tree where for each node *R* of the tree, all keys in the left subtree of *R* are less than the key value of node *R* and all keys in the right subtree of *R* are greater than the key value of node *R*. A binary search tree is a special case of *m*-way search tree where $m = 2$. Also see *m*-way search tree.

Binary Tree - A tree where each node can have maximum out-degree of 2.

Bit - An acronym for a binary digit. A unit of information equals to one binary decision or one of the two possible states (on or off), true or false, (1 or 0) and represents the smallest piece of information in a binary system.

Bit String - A sequence of symbols derived from the alphabet {0,1}.

Block - A collection of contiguous records recorded as a unit; some times called a ***physical record***.

Block Multiplexer Channel - A channel that can execute one instruction of the channel program for one device, then switch to perform an instruction for another device's channel program.

Blocking Factor - Number of records per block.

Boolean - A primitive data structure with values taken from the set {*false*, *true*} and with fundamental operators: *not*, *and*, and *or*. Also called *logical*. Note that C language does not support Boolean data.

Breadth-first - A method of graph traversal in which one node is selected as the starting point, it is visited, the all nodes adjacent to that node are visited, then nodes adjacent to those nodes are visited, and so until the entire graph has been traversed.

B-Tree of Order *m* - A Special case of *m*-way search tree in which each non-root and non-leaf node have between $\lceil 1/(2m) \rceil$ and *m* subtrees, the root has either zero or at least two subtrees, and all leaf nodes are on the same level.

Bubble Sort - An internal sort in which each key floats up to its proper position through a series of pairwise comparisons and exchanges with adjacent key values, require $O(n^2)$ comparisons to sort *n* key values. Also known as *exchange sort*.

Bucket Addressing - A technique for managing records on storage where record's key value is mapped to an area of space (bucket) that can hold multiple records.

Buffer - An area of storage reserved for use in performing I/O operations, into which data is read and from which data are written; used to compensate for a difference in the rate of flow of data between devices, for example, between a CPU and a peripheral.

Bug - A mistake in a computer program/software or a malfunction in a computer hardware component. To debug means to remove mistakes and correct malfunctions.

Cache Memory - An ultra-high speed, directly accessible, relatively small semiconductor memory used to store data/instructions that the processor may need in the immediate future. It increases system bandwidth by reducing the number of external memory fetches required by the processor.

Cascade Merge - A merge technique that uses a decreasing number of input devices at each phase of a pass, temporarily retiring intermediate output files to be input at the start of the next phase.

Cellular Multi-list File - A multi-list file in which no linked list crosses a boundary between physical cell areas.

Channel - A device that connects the CPU and the main memory with the I/O control units.

Channel Program - A set of instructions that are executed by a channel to access devices and control communication paths.

Circular Linked List - A linked list in which the last node points to the first node.

Code - A system of symbols or a set of rules for the representation of data in a digital computer. Some examples include binary, BCD, ASCII, EBCDIC, etc.

Collision - A situation occurring when two unequal key values map to the same address.

Collision Resolution Technique - A technique applied to determine an alternative address for a key value when a collision occurs.

Column-Major Order - An array linearization technique that stores all the elements from one column, before storing any elements from the next column. Subscripts are varied left-to-right, *i.e.*, the left-most subscript is varied fastest. Compare with ***row-major order***.

Compiler - A program that translates the program written in a high level programming language into machine language that is understandable to the processor.

Complete Binary Tree - A binary tree that contains the maximum number of nodes possible for its height.

Completely Inverted File - A file structure, which includes an inversion index for every field of the records.

Connected Graph - A graph that cannot be partitioned to two graphs without removing at least one edge. Also called a graph where each node is reachable node from any other node.

Controlled-length Multi-list File - A multi-list file in which no linked list exceeds a specified length.

Controller - A device that controls I/O operations of one or more devices.

Coprocessor - A specialized microprocessor that performs specific functions independent from the main processor (CPU) to speed up the overall operations.

Critical Path - The longest path in the activity graph.

Cycle - A path in a graph where no edge appears more than once in the sequence of edges and the initial node of the path is the same as the terminal node of the path.

Cylinder - In a disk pack, the set of all tracks with the same distance from the axis about which the disk pack rotates; the tracks of a cylinder can be accessed without repositioning the access mechanism.

Cylinder Addressing - A technique for addressing the records on a disk, where record's address is its cylinder number, surface number, and record number.

Cylinder Index - In an indexed sequential file, an index to the key values stored on each cylinder allocated to the file

Dangling Pointer – It is a pointer that is not initialized with a valid address. Such a pointer can end up pointing anywhere in memory that may include the program code itself or to the code of the operating system. The use of such pointer can lead to undesirable results. Therefore, care must be taken to initialize pointers with valid address before use.

Data - Basic elements of information that can be processed or produced by a computer. Data represents any group of operands made up of numerals, letters, or symbols denoting any condition, value, or state. Current typical computer operand sizes include a word that contains 2 bytes, double word that contains 4 bytes, and a quad word that contains 8 bytes.

Data Structure - A class of data characterized by its logical organization and the operations that are defined on it. Also known as *data type*.

Data Type - See ***data structure***.

Database - A collection of logically related data that supports controlled shared access to multiple users and programs.

DataBase Management System (DBMS) - A software that provides an interface between programs and file systems, with responsibility of defining, representing, storing, organizing, and protecting data, as well as for interfacing users and programs with the database.

Debugger - A program that executes and debugs the object program generated by the assembler or compiler. The debugger provides a single stepping, breakpoint, and program tracing facilities.

Debugging - The process of locating and correcting the bugs of a computer program or computer hardware component.

Dedicated Device - A device that is suitable for access by only one user at a time.

Degree – A characteristics of a graph node; the number of edges incident at that node; the sum of the node's in-degree and out-degree.

Demand Buffering - A buffer management technique whereby data are read into a buffer only when they are actually requested by a program. Compare with ***anticipatory buffering***.

Dense Index - An index that contains all the key values of the data collection being indexed.

Depth-First - A method of graph traversal in which one node is selected as the starting point, it is visited, then all the nodes on one path leading from that node are visited, then all nodes on another path leading from the start node are visited, and so on until the entire graph has been traversed.

Direct Access - The ability to access any of the collection of records without necessitating access to physically preceding records.

Direct Addressing - Addressing or indexing that maps a record's key value directly to a corresponding relative or absolute address. Compare with ***indirect addressing***.

Direct Memory Access (DMA) - A type of I/O technique in which data can be transferred between the main memory and external devices without the CPU's involvement.

Direct-Access Storage Device (DASD) - A storage device that supports direct access. Examples are disks.

Directed Graph - A graph in which directionality is assigned to the edges; an edge has its source in one node and terminates in another node; each node than has both an in-degree and an out-degree.

Directory - A structure that is used to manage identification and location information about files and records.

Directory Lookup Addressing - A technique for managing access to records where by an index is used as an intermediary between key values and record addresses.

Distributed Processing - Distributed processing is the concept of performing operations in a computer system whose terminals and the central processing units are separated geographically but are linked together functionally in a communications network.

Division-Remainder Hashing - An address resolution-calculation technique whereby an appropriate number divides the key value and the remainder is used as the record's relative address.

Double Buffering - Buffer management techniques whereby two buffers are allocated in accommodate the I/O activity for a file.

Double Hashing - A collision resolution technique whereby a second hash function is applied to the key value.

Doubly Linked List - A linked list in which each node points to both the next node and the prior node in the list.

Dynamic Hashing - A virtual hashing technique that uses a binary tree index structure to keep track of buckets and to guide access to records.

Elementary Item - A field that is not decomposable to component fields.

Equivalence class – A set of unequal keys that map to same home address.

Equivalent Trees - Trees that have the same structure and node contents. Compare with ***similar trees***.

Even Parity - A technique in which an extra bit is appended to the representation of each character and is set such that the number of 1-bits for the character is even. Compare with ***odd parity***.

Exchange Sort - One of a family of internal sort algorithms in which pairs of key values are compared and exchanged if they are not in proper relative positions.

Extended Binary Coded Decimal Interchange Code (EBCDIC) - An 8-bit character-encoding scheme widely used for both data storage and data transmission purposes.

External Sort - A method for arranging a collection of key values into a specified order, where the collection resides on a secondary storage device. Read/write time is a significant factor in determining sort performance. Also called a ***file sort***. Compare with ***internal sort***.

Field - A specified area of a record used to represent a particular kind of information.

File - A collection of logically related records occurrences that are treated as a unit and are persistent, *i.e.*, independent of the execution of a particular run-unit.

File Activity Ratio - The ratio of the number of records with activity during the period to the total number of records on the file.

File Organization - The technique used to represent, structure, and store the records on a file.

File System - A set of routines that manage directories, device accesses, and buffers, enabling programs to access files without being concerned with details of physical storage characteristics and device timings.

First-In-First-Out (FIFO) - A method of linear management in which the first element into the list will be the first element taken out of the list; defines the mode of operation of a queue. Compare with ***Last-In-First-Out (LIFO)***. See also ***queue***.

Fixed Head Disk - A disk in which there is one read/write head per track; the access mechanism never has to be moved. Compare with ***moveable-head disk***.

Flowchart - A pictorial/graphical representation of the various processes performed to solve a particular problem on computer, where each pictorial symbol represents a distinct operation to be performed, and flow lines show the sequence of operations.

Forest - A collection of rooted trees.

Free Space - Memory allocated to a file but not containing meaningful records. See also ***padding***.

Front - The element that has been in the queue longest. Also, the next element to be removed from a queue.

Generation File - One of the multiple versions of a file created during successive cycles of processing.

Generic Key - The leading portion of a key field.

Graph - A collection of nodes and edges, where each edge connects a pair of nodes.

Graph Order - The number of nodes in a graph.

Group Item - A field that is decomposable into component elementary and/or group items.

Hash Function - A calculation applied to a key value to obtain a relative address.

Hashing - An address calculation technique. Also known as ***hash table method, direct addressing technique, key-to-address transformation method, randomizing technique,*** **and** ***scatter storage technique***.

Head Node - The distinguishable first node of a list. It may or may not contain meaningful data.

Height Balanced Tree - See ***AVL tree***.

High Level Language - A type of computer programming language that uses a more understandable human-oriented language, for example FORTRAN, BASIC, COBOL, PASCAL, C/C++, Java, etc.).

Hit Ratio - The percentage of records read or written by a given request or set of requests.
Home Address - The address to which key value hashes.

In-degree - The number of edges directed into a node in a directed graph. Compare with ***out-degree***.

Index - A collection of a key value, address pairs, used to facilitate access to a collection of records. Also see ***subscript***.

Indexed Sequential File Organization - A file organization technique that supports both sequential and direct access to records by a key field.

Indirect Addressing - Addressing or indexing that maps a key value to an intermediary value, which is then mapped to a record's relative or absolute address. Compare with ***direct addressing***.

Infix Notation - A method of representing an arithmetic expression whereby a binary operator appears between its operands. Compare with ***postfix*** and ***prefix*** notations.

In-order Traversal - A method of visiting all the nodes of a binary tree, recursively defined by first traversing the left subtree in in-order, then visiting the root, then traversing the right subtree in in-order. Compare with ***pre-order*** and ***post-order*** traversals.

Input File - A file that is read, but not written, by a program. Compare with ***output file*** and ***input/output file***.

Input/Output File - A file that is both read from and written to by a program. Compare with ***input file*** and ***output file***.

Insertion Sort – An internal sort in which the next entry in the unsorted list is inserted into its proper relative position in a growing sorted list.

Instruction Cycle - The sequence of operations that a central processor has to carry out while executing an instruction.

Inter Block Gap (IBG) - The space between two consecutive blocks on a storage device.

Interactive Mode - The processing of transactions as they occur. Compare with ***batch mode***.

Internal Sort - A method for arranging a collection of key values into a specified order, where the collection resides in main memory. Read/write time is not a significant factor in determining sort performance. Compare with ***external sort***.

Internal Sort Phase - In an external sort, the phase in which an internal sort technique is used to sort records into several runs and to distribute those runs into two or more storage devices.

Interrupt - A temporary halt in the execution of a process, with a switch to the execution of another. When the second has terminated, control may or may not return to the first to resume its execution.

Inversion Index - An index containing all the values that a primary or secondary key has in the data file and pointers to all of the data records that have the corresponding values.

Inverted File Organization - A multi-key file organization technique that uses inversion indices.

Iterative Procedure - A procedure that repeatedly executes a series of steps but that does not invoke itself. Compare with ***recursive procedure***.

Key - The identifying field of a record. Also called a field whose value is used to place a collection of records into a sorted ordering.

Key-sequenced Data Set - The data records in an indexed sequential file; a control interval containing records in ascending order by a given key.

Latency - See ***rotational delay***.

Leaf Node - A node of a tree or a graph with out-degree zero.

Left Thread - A link from a node in a binary tree to its predecessor node in the in-order traversal. Compare with ***right thread***.

Level - A characteristic of a node in a tree; a node's level is the length of the path from the root to that node.

Linear List - A general data structure comprised of an ordered set of nodes; for each node there is a single next node. Compare with ***tree***.

Linear Probing - A collision resolution technique in which a search for an empty location proceeds serially from the record's home address. Compare with ***double hashing***.

Linear Search - A technique applied to find the record of a collection with a particular key value; views the collection as a linear list and starts at the beginning of the linear list, sequentially comparing each record's key value with the sought key value until the target record is found or the end of the list is reached; requires O(*n*) comparisons to search a collection of *n* key values.

Linked List - A data structure in which the ordering of nodes is indicated by the use of direct or indirect pointers rather than by physically sequentially.

Linker - A program that links other object program(s)/ object modules with system library into one executable program.

Lirst-In-First-Out (LIFO) - A method of linear management in which the element most recently added to the list will be the next element taken out of the list; defines the mode of operation of a stack. Compare with ***Fast-In-First-Out (FIFO)***. See also ***stack***.

Load Factor - The percentage of the space allocated to a file that is actually in use holding records.

Load Point - The beginning of the permissible recording area on a reel of magnetic tape.

Loader - A Program or service routine designed to read executable programs into internal storage and prepare them for execution.

Logical - See ***boolean***.

Logical Error - Programming mistake that causes the wrong processing to take place even though there is no syntax error, *i.e.*, the program is syntactically correct.

Loop - An edge that connects a node in a graph to itself.

Lower Bound - The minimum value that a subscript may validly have. Compare with ***upper bound***.

Lower Triangular Array - An array in which all elements above diagonal are zero. If the diagonal is also zero, the array is strictly lower triangular. Compare with ***upper triangular***.

Mass Storage - A Very large capacity storage device.

Master File - A file that contains relatively permanent data; each record represents the status of some aspect of an organization's business at a point in time.

Master Index - In an indexed sequential file, an index to the key values indexed by each cylinder index.

Max Heap - An almost complete binary tree, in which the key values are arranged such that for each node i, $key(i) \le key(j)$, where j is the father of node i.

Merge - The combination of records in two or more sorted files to form one sorted file.

Memory Leak – It Memory leak is a situation where the programmer fails to release the memory allocated at run time in a module. Note that when memory is allocated, a pointer variable is used to hold the address of the allocated block, however, when the module completes its execution, the pointer variable goes out of scope and there will be no way to reach that memory block. Therefore, care must be taken to release the allocated memory block in a module where memory was allocated.

Merge Degree - The number of files input to a merge.

Min Heap - An almost complete binary tree, in which the key values are arranged such that for each node *i*, $key(i) \geq key(j)$, where *j* is the father of node *i*.

Minimal Spanning Tree - A minimum cost spanning tree for a graph. See ***spanning tree***.

Mode of Processing - The way in which transactions are collected and processed is referred as modes of processing.

Modular Programming - Programming technique that produces relatively small,, easily understandable,, computer modules. A complex or large program is broken into number of logically self-contained modules. These modules may be written and tested separately by number of programmers. Finally the modules can be then put together to form the complete program/system.

Movable Hard Disk - A disk in which there is one read/write head per recording surface; the access mechanism must be moved from cylinder to cylinder. Compare with ***fixed head disk***.

Multi-key File Organization - A file organization technique that supports direct access to records by two or more key fields.

Multi-list File Organization - A multi-key file organization is a technique that maintains an index for every key. The index contains all values that the key has in the data file and a pointer to a linked list of data records with that key value.

Multi Graph - A graph that is not simple. The graph has at least one loop or there is at least one pair of nodes such that there are two or more edges connecting them.

Multiplexer Channel - A channel on which several devices can be active simultaneously, but which must complete execution of the channel program for one device before starting another device's channel program. Compare with ***selector channel*** and ***block multiplexer channel***.

M-Way Search Tree - A tree in which each node has out-degree $\leq m$, each node is composed of a set of pointers and key values, and the key values are arranged in a specific manner that facilitates search through the pointer structures. See ***binary search tree*** for a special case.

Natural Merge - A merge technique that uses one output device and a constant number of input devices.

Node - An elementary component of a list, tree, or graph.

NULL - The value given to a pointer variable that is empty, *i.e.*, that points nowhere.

Null Graph - A graph with no node.

Object Code - The binary (machine) code into which a compiler or an assembler translates a source program.

Odd Parity - A technique in which an extra bit is appended to the representation of each character and is set such that the number of 1-bits for the character is odd. Compare with ***even parity***.

Online Processing - On-line processing can be defined as the processing mode under which a user can interact with the computer at any time through I/O devices that are under the control of CPU.

Open Addressing - An approach to collision resolution whereby synonyms are all stored in the file's (table's) primary address space. Compare with ***separate-overflow addressing***.

Out-degree - The number of edges coming out of a node in a directed graph. Compare with ***in-degree***.

Output File - A file that is written, but not read, by a program. Compare with ***input file*** and ***input/output file***.

Overflow Data Area - An auxiliary file that contains records that do not fit in the area originally allocated to a file. Compare with ***prime data area***.

Padding – (1) Space inserted into a record for purposes of ensuring the correct alignment of fields on appropriate word boundaries. (2) Allocated space intentionally left empty when a file is created, for purposes of accommodating future additions to the file. Also called ***free space***.

Parity - An error-control technique by which one redundant bit is appended to the representation of each character. See also ***even parity*** and ***odd parity***.

Partition-exchange Sort - An exchange sort. At each step of the sort, the list is partitioned into two parts such that the key values in one partition are less than a particular key value and key values in the other partition are greater than particular key value; the partitions are then treated independently in following steps of the sort. See ***quicksort***.

Path - A sequence of one or more edges that connects two nodes in a graph.

Path Length - The number of edges in a path; a measure of the number of comparisons required to use the tree.

Peripheral - An I/O device capable of operating under the control of a CPU through communication channels. Examples include disk drives, keyboard, VDU, printer, etc.

Physical Record - See ***block***.

Pointer Variable - A variable whose value must be an address or NULL.

Poly-phase Merge - A merge technique that uses a constant number of input devices and recycles each output device as an input device in the next phase of a pass.

Postfix Notation - A method of representing an arithmetic expression whereby a binary operator appears after its operands. Compare with ***infix*** and ***prefix*** notations. Also known a ***reverse-polish*** notation.

Post-order Traversal - A method of visiting all the nodes of a binary tree, recursively defined by first traversing the left subtree in post-order, then traversing the right subtree in post-order, then visiting the root. Compare with ***pre-order*** and ***in-order*** traversals.

Pre-fetching - See ***anticipatory buffering***.

Prefix Notation - A method of representing an arithmetic expression whereby a binary operator appears before its operands. Compare with ***infix*** and ***postfix*** notations.

Pre-order Traversal - A method of visiting all the nodes of a binary tree, recursively defined by first visiting the root, then traversing the left subtree in pre-order, then traversing the right subtree in pre-order. Compare with ***in-order*** and ***post-order*** traversals.

Primary Key - The main key field of a multi-key file. In an alternate-key indexed sequential file, the field for which direct and sequential access are supported.

Prime Data Area - The main space allocated to a file. Compare with ***overflow data area***.

Primitive - A data structure that cannot be decomposed to other data structure. Also known as data structure or data type for which there is a built-in support.

Program File - A file that contains instructions for processing.

Protocol - A list of procedures or rule or conventions that encompass the timing, control, formatting, and data representation by which two devices are to communicate.

Query Language - An end-user-oriented language for retrieving selected data from a file or database.

Query Processor - Software that translates a user's request (phrased in a query language) into instructions that can be used directly for file or a database access.

Queue - A linear list in which elements are added only to the rear of the list and are removed only from the front of the list. See ***first-in-first-out (FIFO)***.

Queuing Theory - A formal analytic body of knowledge about the behaviour of systems that involve queues.

Quick Sort - See ***partition-exchange sort***.

Radix - The base of a system of numbers. For example, the radix of the decimal number system is 10; the radix of binary number system is 2.

Reachability Matrix - A matrix ***R*** used to represent the paths that exist between each pair of nodes in a graph; $r_{ij} = 1$ if and only if there is a path between nodes v_i and v_j in the graph. See also ***transitive closure***.

Real Time Processing - Real time processing is a special case of on-line processing, where the computer accepts transaction from the user, processes these transaction and returns the results to the user within such a time period so as to affect the user's activities or environment. The length of time between entering transactions and receiving back the results, which is of critical importance, varies from one application to other.

Record - A collection of logically related fields treated as a unit.

Record Key - A primary or secondary key.

Recursive Procedure - A procedure in which each step makes use of the results of the earlier steps, generally by invoking execution of some part of itself. Compare with ***iterative procedure***.

Relative Addressing - A technique for mapping records to storage whereby a key value is mapped to the record's ordinal position in the file. Compare with ***absolute addressing***.

Relative File Organization - A file organization technique that supports access directly to records by a key field.

Report File - A file containing data that are formatted for presentation to an end-user.

Report Writer Package - A software product that translates a user-oriented request for a report into instructions that are used to create that report from accesses to a master file or a database.

Response Time - CPU time or elapsed time required to process a transaction.

Reverse-polish Notation - See ***postfix notation***.

Right Thread - A link from a node in a binary tree to its successor node in the in-order traversal. Compare with ***left thread***.

Rooted Tree - A tree in which one node, called the root, is distinguished from other nodes.

Rotation - A type of restructuring applied to a tree to return it to a state of balance.

Rotational Delay - The time required for an addressed block to appear under the read/write head of a rotating disk.

Row-Major Order - An array linearization technique that stores all the elements from one row, before storing any elements from the next row. Subscripts are varied right-to-left, *i.e.*, the right-most subscript is varied fastest. Compare with ***column-major order***.

Run - A sorted sequence.

Searching - The process of trying to find the record or records that meets a given criterion.

Secondary Key - In a multi-key file, any field except the primary key.

Secondary Storage - A storage device with the property that the time required to access the contents of one location may be different from the time required to access the contents of another location on the same device; generally slower and cheaper per bit than a primary storage device. Also called ***auxiliary storage***.

Sector - That part of a track on a disk that can be accessed by the read/write heads in the course of a pre-determined rotational displacement of the particular device.

Sector Addressing - A technique for addressing the data records on a disk, whereby a record's address is the sector number, record number. Compare with ***cylinder addressing***.

Seek Time - Time required to position the access mechanism of a direct access storage device at a specified position, such as the time needed to position the read/write head in a drive over the specified track of the disk.

Selection Sort - One of the family of internal sort algorithm in which the next logically sequential key in the unsorted list is selected and placed in the next position in a growing sorted list.

Selector Channel - A channel that can manage data flow between main memory and only one device at a time.

Separate Overflow Addressing - An approach to collision resolution whereby all records that cannot be stored at their home addresses are stored in a separate file from the file's primary address space. Compare with ***open addressing***.

Sequence Set - The leaves of a B$^+$-tree.

Sequential File Organization - A file organization technique that supports serial access to records.

Sequential Search - See ***linear search***.

Serial Access - Access in physically consecutive order. Compare with ***direct access***.

Serial Access Device - A storage device that supports only serial access. Example is magnetic tape. Compare with ***direct access device***.

Shared Device - A device that supports concurrent access by multiple users. Compare with ***dedicated device, virtual device***.

Similar Trees - Trees that have the same structure but not necessarily the same node contents. Compare with *equivalent trees*.

Simple Graph - A graph that has no loops and in which no pair of nodes is connected by more than one edge. See ***multigraph***.

Slack Bytes - See ***padding***.

Software - Software is the generic name for any kind of program. The programs may be written by a programmer to solve particular problem, referred to as application software or for systems use to perform certain tasks, referred to as system software, for example, operating system, compiler, editor, linker, loader, etc.

Sort Key - A field (elementary or group item) whose value is used to order records of a collection.

Sorted File - A file in which the records are ordered logically by the value of a sort key.

Sorting - The process of arranging a collection of keys (and records) into a specified order.

Source Code - The original program written in a high level language or assembly language to solve a particular problem by the programmer, which must be translated into machine code.

Spanning Tree - A tree that contains all the nodes of a graph and no other nodes; its branches are a subset of the graph's edges.

Sparse Array - An array with relatively high density of elements with value zero.

Sparse Index - An index that contains a proper subset of the key values of the data collection being indexed. Compare with ***dense index***.

Spooling - The use of buffers on auxiliary memory to reduce the effects of speed mismatch between the CPU and peripheral equipment, commonly printers.

Stack - A linear list in which the elements are added to and removed from only the top of the list. Also see ***last-in-first-out (LIFO)***.

Strictly Triangular Array - An upper-triangular array or a lower triangular array in which the elements on the diagonal all have value zero.

String - A finite sequence of characters taken from an alphabet, *i.e.*, character set.

String Length - The number of characters in a string.

Structured Programming - Programming technique that assumes the disciplined use of a few coding structures and the use of top-down concepts to decompose main functions into lower-level components for modular programming. The main aim of this technique is to improve the programming process through better organization and with better programming notations to facilitate correct and clear description of data and control structures.

Subprogram - A program carrying out a particular function and which can be called by another program known as the calling program. A subprogram needs to be placed only once in memory and can be called by the main program or other subprogram as many times as the programmer wants. Also known by various names as *function*, *subroutine* or *procedure*.

Subscript - A value that designates the ordinal position of an element in an array, also called an index.

Synonym Chaining - An approach to collision resolution in which access to synonyms is facilitated by maintaining a linked list of the records in equivalence class.

Synonyms - Two or more unequal key values that hash to the same home address. See also ***equivalence class***.

Syntax - Grammar rules for the formation of the allowable strings of a vocabulary.

Syntax Error - An error caused by the violation of the rules governing the structure of the programming language being used.

Table - A two-dimensional array. See also an ***array***.

Tape Drive - A mechanism for moving a magnetic tape, controlling the tape's motion, and reading/writing on the tape.

Text File - A file of alphanumeric information created and edited using a text editor.

Threaded Tree - A tree that includes a linked list of the nodes according to a tree traversal ordering.

Throughput - The number of transactions or volume of work that a system can process in a given period of time.

Time Sharing – Time sharing, also called as *multiprocessing*, and is defined as the processing mode in which the processor time is shared between various users. The access to the system is via terminal, which are connected on-line to the computer.

Track - An area on a single surface of a rotating disk that can be read or written without repositioning the read/write head.

Transaction - A transaction may be defined as an entry that describes a particular activity carried out by an organization. For example, when a manufacturer company deals with customer's orders, a number of transaction may be generated based on the activities such as sale of items, the billing of the customer, and corresponding payment, etc.

Transaction File - A file of transactions to be processed against a master file or database.

Transitive Closure - The sum of all powers of a graph's adjacency matrix. See also ***reachability matrix***.

Transpose - Transpose of a matrix is another matrix whose elements are obtained by reversing the subscript positions.

Tree - An acyclic, simple, and connected graph.

Tree Height - One plus the number of the highest level on which the tree has non-null nodes, where the root is on level zero.

Tree Weight - The number of leaf nodes in a tree.

Triangular Array - An array in which all elements either above or below the diagonal have value zero. See also ***lower-triangular array, upper triangular array, strictly-triangular array***.

Undirected Graph - A graph in which edges do not have directionality. Compare with ***directed graph***.

Upper Bound - The maximum value that a subscript may validly have. Compare with ***lower bound***.

Upper Triangular Array - An array in which all elements below diagonal are zero. If the diagonal is also zero, the array is strictly upper triangular. Compare with ***lower triangular***.

Vector - A one-dimensional array. See ***array***.

Vertex - See ***node***.

Virtual Device - A device that does not physically exist, used to make a dedicated device appear to be shared.

Virtual Hashing - Any hashing technique that may dynamically change its hash function.

Virtual Memory - A memory management technique that allows programs or data to exceed the physical size of the internal memory. Program or data segments/pages are swapped from external storage as needed. Therefore the programmer need not be concerned with the actual size of the internal memory while writing the programs.

Vocabulary - The set of all possible strings that can be obtained from an alphabet. The vocabulary that is derived from alphabet A is denoted by A^* (contains the null string) or A^+ (contains the non-null strings only).

Winchester Disk - A form of magnetic disk storage in which the recording surfaces, access mechanism, and read/write heads are manufactured together and packaged in a sealed cartridge.

Word Processor - Word processor is the generic name for the software that provides facilities for manipulation of text. It can be used for writing documents,, inserting or changing words,, sentences,, paragraphs,, and printing documents. Examples are WordStar, WordPerfect, MicroSoft Word, Ventura, PageMaker, etc.

Work File - A temporary file, typically used to store large volumes of data during the execution of a program.

Index

A

B

C

D

E

F

G

H

I

J

K

L

M

N

O

P

Q

R

S

T

U

V

W

❑ ❑ ❑

OTHER USEFUL BOOKS BY THE AUTHOR

DATA STRUCTURES & ALGORITHMS USING C

Theory, Design and Implementation

Salient Features

- Provides a comprehensive coverage of the subject.
- Includes numerous illustrative example.
- Demonstrates the development of algorithms in a lucid manner.
- Demonstrates the implementation of algorithms in a good programming style.
- Provides challenging programming exercise to test your knowledge gained about the subject.
- Glossary of terms for ready reference.

Edition : Fifth **ISBN : 9789381068588** **Pages (Approx.) : 560**

COMPUTER ORIENTED NUMERICAL METHODS

Salient Features

- Provides a comprehensive coverage of the subject.
- Emphasis is laid to ensure the conceptual understanding of different numerical methods.
- Formulae for different numerical methods have been derived in the simplest manner.
- Algorithms for these methods are developed using pseudo language.
- Large number of programming exercises to test your programming skills acquired.
- Majority of the algorithms are implemented in C, C++ and FORTRAN languages.

Edition : Fifth **ISBN : 9789381068489** **Pages (Approx.) : 480**

APPLICATION PROGRAMMING IN C

Concepts, Problems and Applications

Salient Features

- Provides a comprehensive coverage of the subject.
- Demonstrates the development of programs in a good programming style.
- Large number of ready to run programs for reference.
- Large number of multiple choice, true/false type and short answer questions to test your knowledge about the subject learned.
- Large number of programming exercises to test your programming skills acquired.

Edition : Fourth **ISBN : 9789381068427** **Pages (Approx.) : 600**

A Modern Approach to

PROGRAMMING IN FORTRAN

Theory, Problems and Applications to Science & Engineering

Salient Features

- Introduces Computers in a very simple and attractive style.
- Illustrates the importance of problem solving and program design.
- Illustrates the usage of various program design tools.
- Provides comprehensive coverage of the language.
- Provides numerous programming examples.
- Explains graphic capabilities of the language at a greater length.
- Introduces FORTRAN 90.

Edition : Fourth **ISBN : 9788190698887** **Pages (Approx.) : 400**

Advanced Object-Oriented Programming Using C++

A Textbook Specially Designed for Readers Who Know C Language

R. S. Salaria

Most Indispensable Book for Fast Track to Learning Object-Oriented Programming Using C++

ADVANCED OBJECT-ORIENTED PROGRAMMING USING C++

A Textbook Specially Designed for Readers Who Know C Language

Salient Features

- Provides a comprehensive coverage of the subject.
- Demonstrates the development of programs in a good programming style.
- Large number of ready to run programs for reference.
- Large number of multiple choice questions, true/false questions and review exercises to test your knowledge about the subject learned.
- Large number of programming exercise to test your programming skills acquired.

Edition : Latest **ISBN : 9788190744485** **Pages (Approx.) : 524**

A Practical Approach to

Programming in C

A Textbook Customized for BCA, BSc(IT), PGDCA, and Three Years Diploma in Computer Engineering/Information Technology

R. S. Salaria

- Meticulously explains every concept of the C Language
- Written in a lucid manner using simple and easy language
- Hundreds of multiple choice questions and review exercises
- Hundreds of ready to run programs
- Hundreds of challenging programming exercises

The Most Indispensable Book on Programming in C

A Practical Approach to

PROGRAMMING IN C

Salient Features

- Provides a comprehensive coverage of the subject.
- Demonstrates the development of programs in a good programming style.
- Large number of ready to run programs for reference.
- Large number of multiple choice questions and review exercises to test your knowledge about the subject learned.
- Large number of programming exercises to test your programming skills acquired.

Edition : Latest **ISBN : 9788190744867** **Pages (Approx.) : 328**

OBJECT-ORIENTED PROGRAMMING USING C++

Concept, Problems & Applications

Salient Features

- Provides a comprehensive coverage of the subject.
- Demonstrates the development of programs in a good programming style.
- Large number of ready to run programs for reference.
- Large number of multiple choice questions and review exercises to test your knowledge about the subject learned.
- Large number of programming exercises to test your programming skills acquired.

Edition : Fifth **ISBN : 9789381068557** **Pages (Approx.) : 760**

C PROGRAMMING AND DATA STRUCTURES

Concepts, Problems and Applications

Salient Features

- Provides a comprehensive coverage of the subject.
- Demonstrates the development of programs in a good programming style.
- Large number of ready to run programs for reference.
- Large number of multiple choice questions and review exercises to test your knowledge about the subject learned.
- Large number of programming exercises to test your programming skills acquired.

Edition : Latest **ISBN : 9788190698863** **Pages (Approx.) : 698**

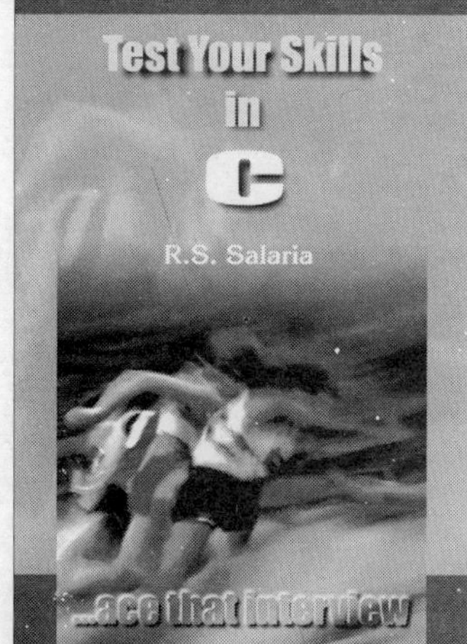

Test Your Skills in C

Salient Features

- Some Useful tips • Multiple
- Choice Type questions • True-false type
- questions • Short answer type questions

Edition : Latest **ISBN : 8187325496** **Pages (Approx.) : 281**

Computer Concepts and Programming in C

The subject on *Computer Concepts and Programming in C* (or with the name *Fundamentals of Computers and Programming in C)* is one of the core courses in various undergraduate and postgraduate programmes of various institutions and universities of India. This book is designed to serve as textbook for those programmes of study.

While writing the book, special emphasis is given to keep the language very simple and lucid; level of presentation is kept simple and illustrative so that even an average reader can grasp the subject matter with quite ease.

Salient Features

- ❖ **Provides a comprehensive coverage of the subject**
- ❖ **Demonstrates the development of programs in a good programming style**
- ❖ **Large number of ready to run programs for reference**
- ❖ **Large number of multiple choice questions and review exercises to test your knowledge about the subject learned**
- ❖ **Large number of programming exercises to test your programming skills acquired**

Edition : Latest **ISBN : 9789381068540** **Pages (Approx.) : 635**

SOME OTHER USEFUL BOOKS

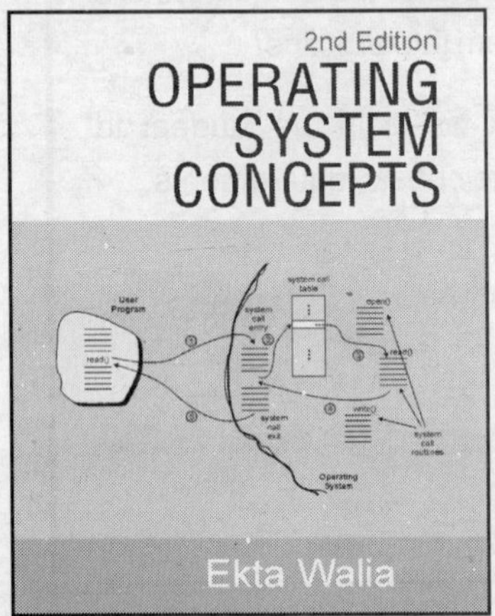

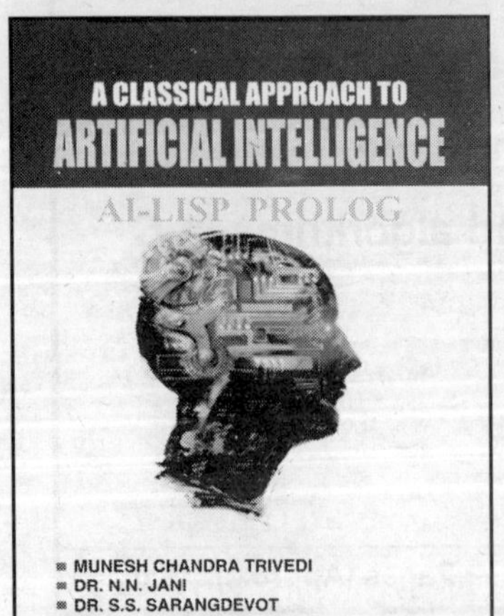

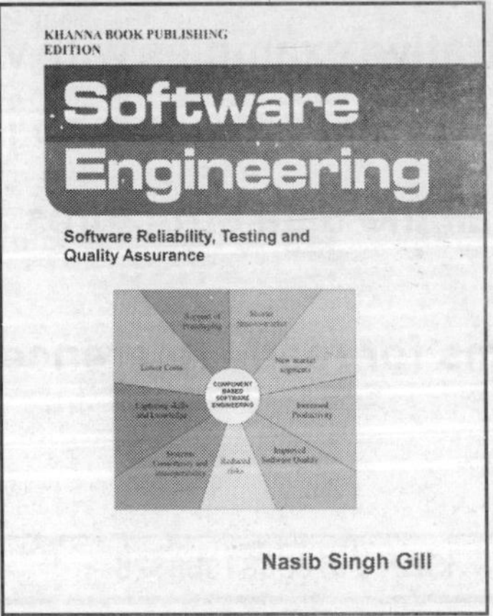